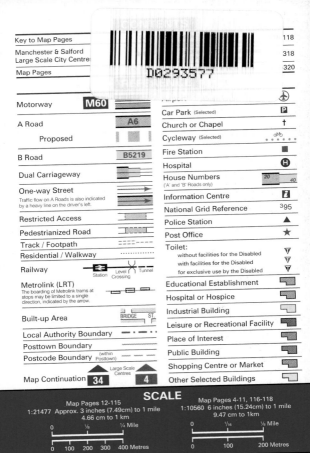

Key to Map Pages	118
Manchester & Salford Large Scale City Centre	318
Map Pages	320

D0293577

Motorway	**M60**	Airport	✈
A Road	A6	Car Park (Selected)	🅿
Proposed		Church or Chapel	†
B Road	B5219	Cycleway (Selected)	🚲
Dual Carriageway		Fire Station	■
One-way Street		Hospital	🅗
Traffic flow on A Roads is also indicated by a heavy line on the driver's left.		House Numbers ('A' and 'B' Roads only)	20 40
Restricted Access		Information Centre	🆔
Pedestrianized Road		National Grid Reference	395
Track / Footpath		Police Station	▲
Residential / Walkway		Post Office	★
Railway	Station Level Crossing Tunnel	Toilet: without facilities for the Disabled with facilities for the Disabled for exclusive use by the Disabled	▽ ▽ ▽
Metrolink (LRT) The boarding of Metrolink trams at stops may be limited to a single direction, indicated by the arrow.		Educational Establishment	
		Hospital or Hospice	
Built-up Area	BRIDGE ST.	Industrial Building	
Local Authority Boundary		Leisure or Recreational Facility	
Posttown Boundary		Place of Interest	
Postcode Boundary (within Posttown)		Public Building	
Map Continuation 34	Large Scale Centres 4	Shopping Centre or Market	
		Other Selected Buildings	

SCALE

Map Pages 12-115
1:21477 Approx. 3 inches (7.49cm) to 1 mile
4.66 cm to 1 km

0 ⅛ ¼ Mile
0 100 200 300 400 Metres

Map Pages 4-11, 116-118
1:10560 6 inches (15.24cm) to 1 mile
9.47 cm to 1km

0 ¹⁄₁₆ ⅛ Mile
0 100 200 Metres

Copyright of Geographers' A-Z Map Company Limited

Fairfield Road, Borough Green, Sevenoaks, Kent TN15 8PP
Telephone: 01732 781000 (Enquiries & Trade Sales)
01732 783422 (Retail Sales)

OS Ordnance Survey®

This product includes mapping data licensed from Ordnance Survey® with the permission of the Controller of Her Majesty's Stationery Office.

www.a-zmaps.co.uk

Copyright © Geographers' A-Z Map Co. Ltd.
Edition 3   2008

© Crown Copyright 2007. All Rights Reserved.
Licence number 100017302

KEY TO MAP PAGES

2

BURY

BOLTON

Radcliffe

Redvales

Little Lever

12 **13** **14**

Farnworth

Kearsley

Whitefield

18 **19** **20** **21** **22** **23** **24**

Prestwich

Walkden

Clifton

Rainsough

Crumpsall

32 **33** **34** **35** **36** **37** **38**

Swinton

Pendlebury

Kersal

Worsley

Charlestown

Cheetham Hill

Monton

Ellesmere Park

46 **47** **48** **49** **50** **51** **52**

SALFORD

Tyldesley

Peel Green

Eccles

60 **61** **62** **63** **64** **65** **66**

Trafford Park

Old Trafford

Hulme

Urmston

Moss Side

74 **75** **76** **77** **78** **79** **80**

Stretford

Chorlton-cum-Hardy

Irlam

Carrington

88 **89** **90** **91** **92**

Sale

Albert Park

Brooklands

Kenworthy

LARGE SCALE
MANCHESTER
CITY CENTRE

4 5 6 7
8 9 10 11

98 **99** **100** **101** **102**

Timperley

Altrincham

Newhall Green

Gatley

108 **109** **110**

Wythenshawe

Hale

112 **113** **114**

*MANCHESTER
INTERNATIONAL AIRPORT*

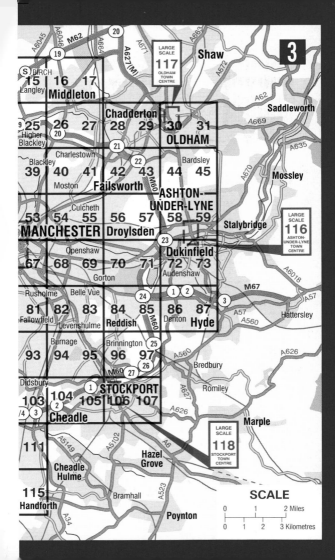

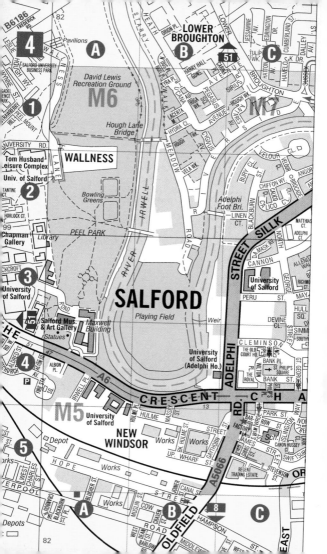

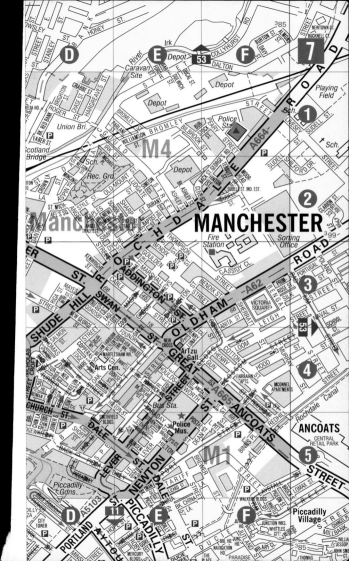

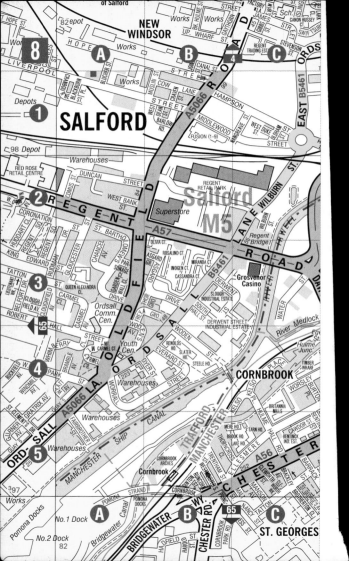

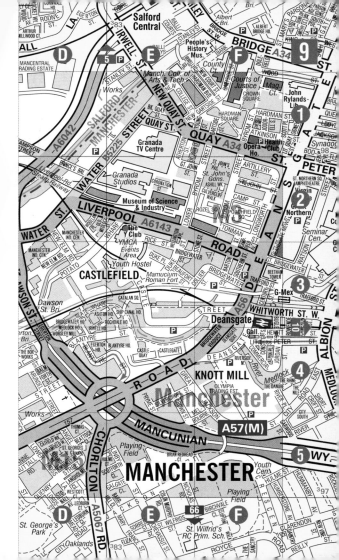

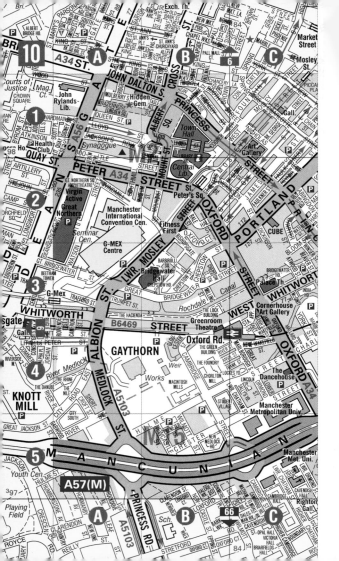

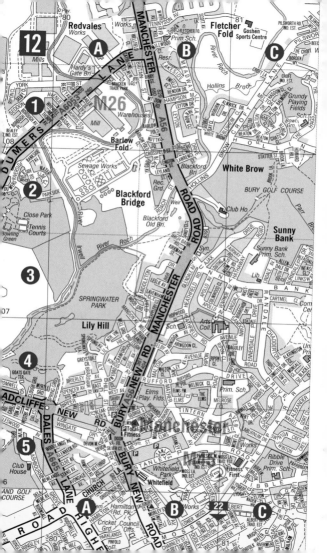

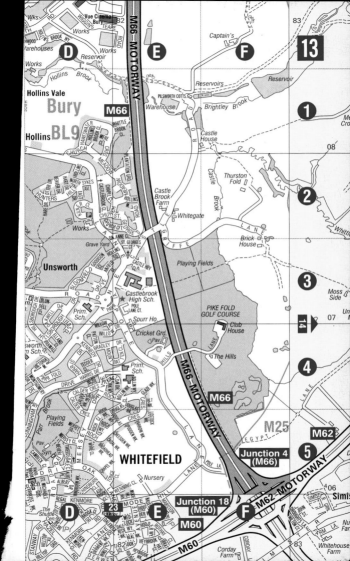

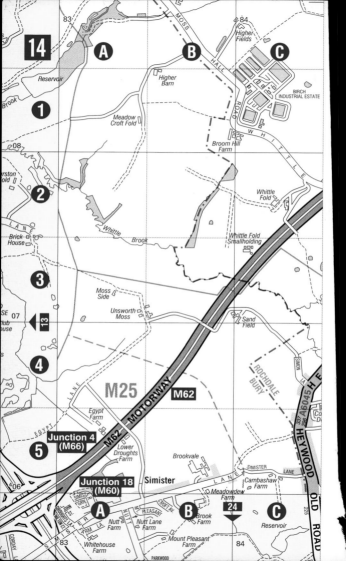

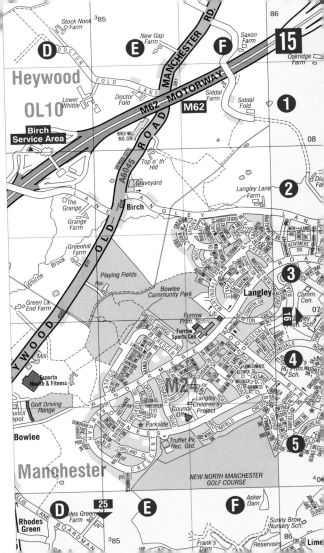

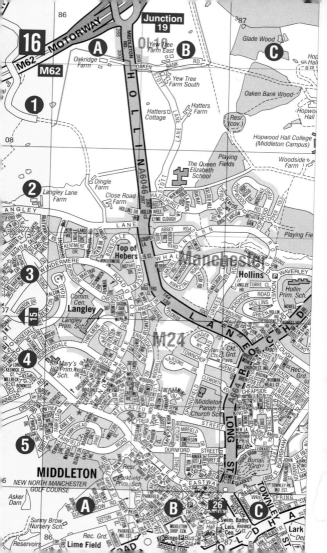

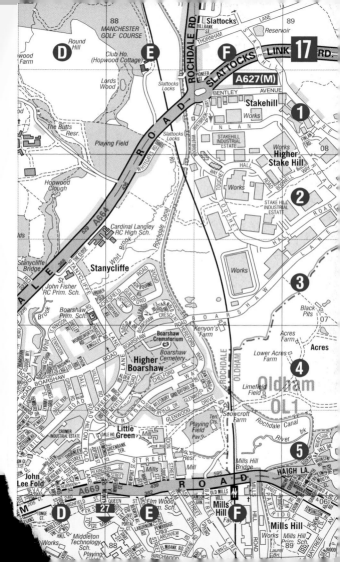

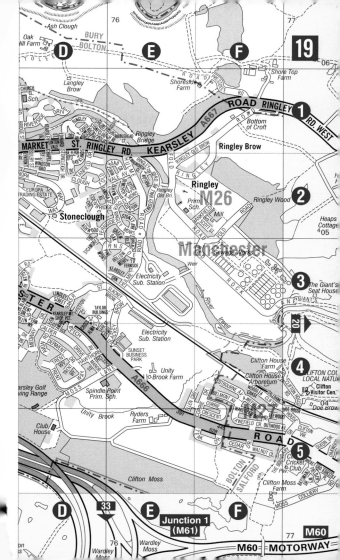

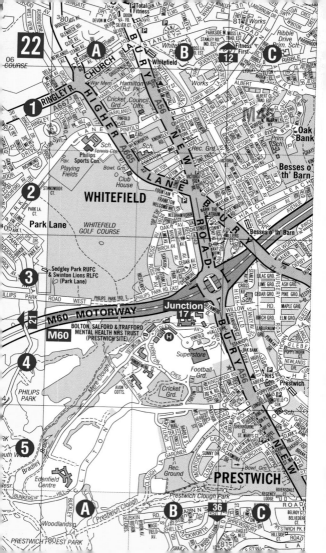

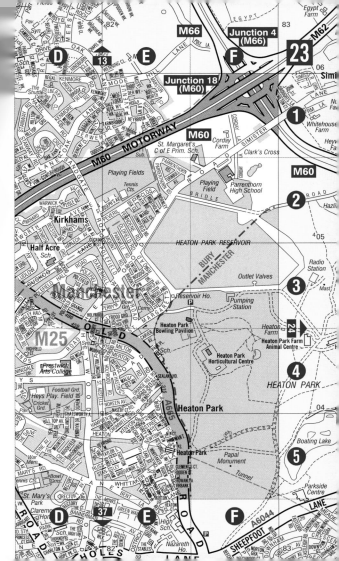

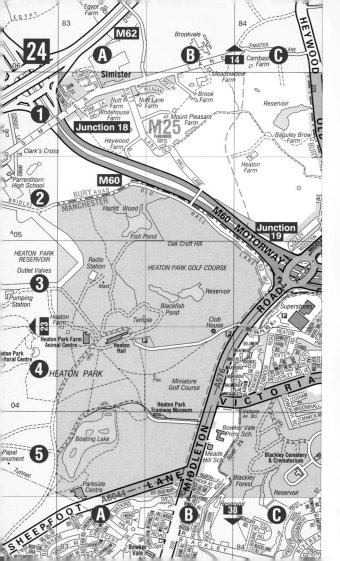

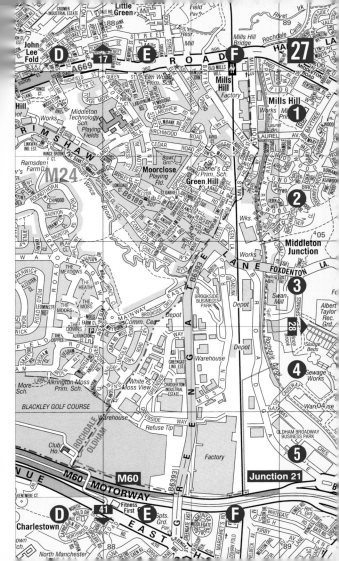

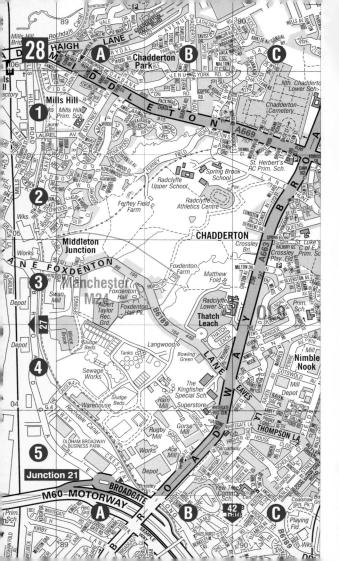

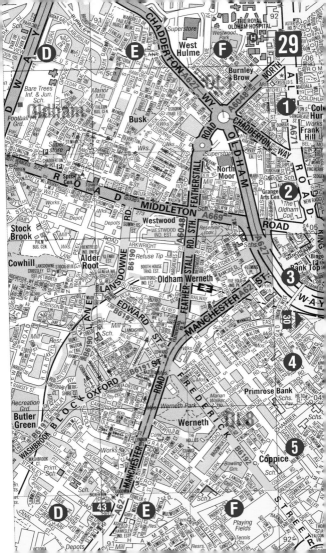

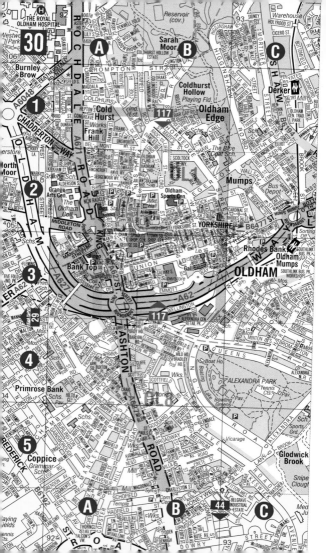

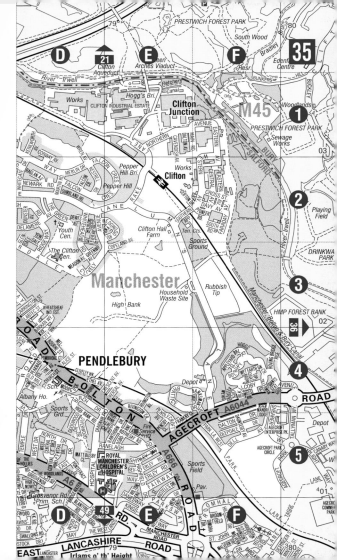

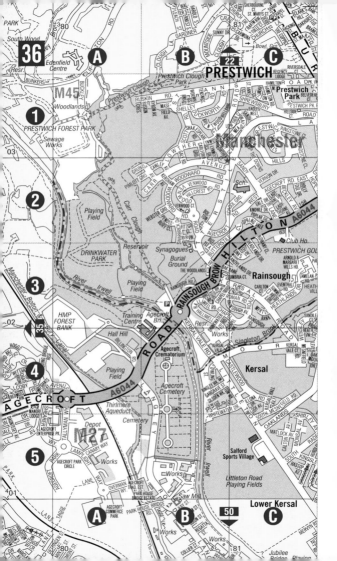

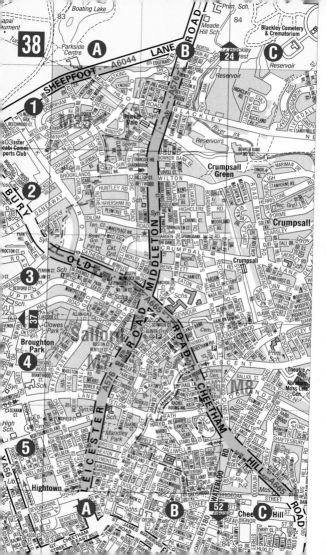

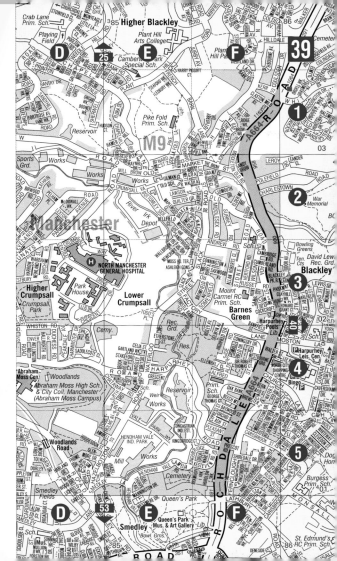

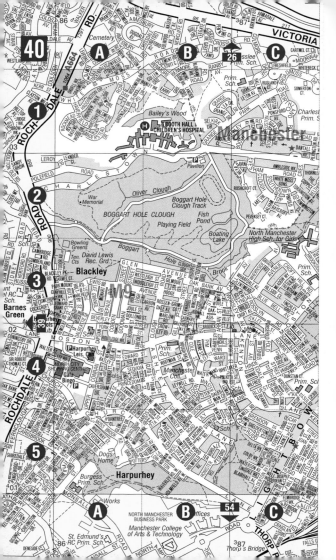

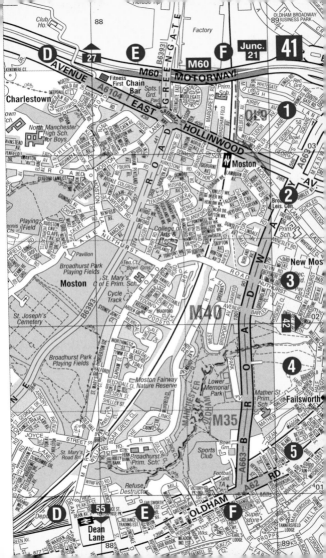

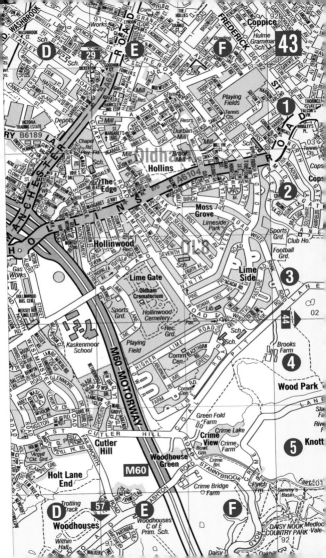

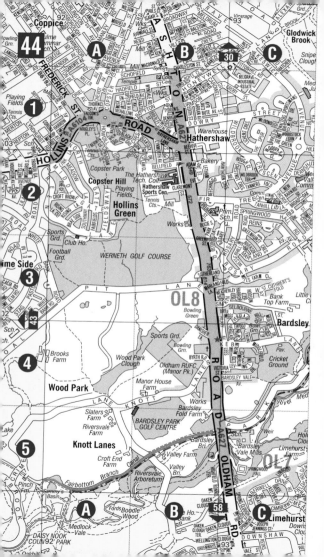

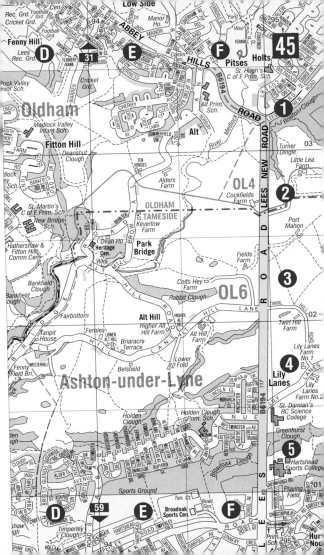

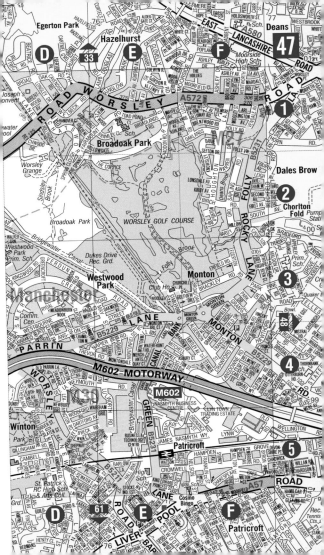

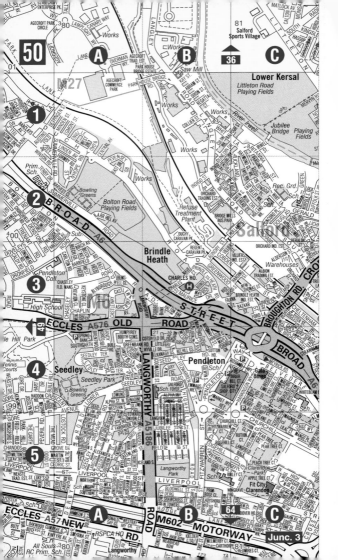

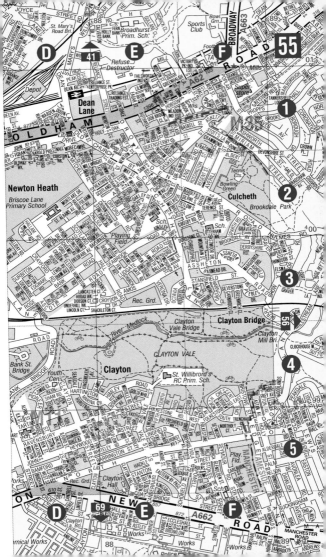

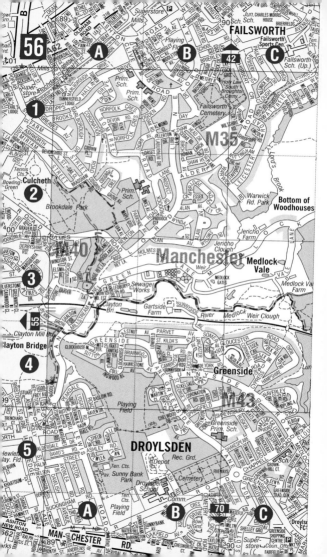

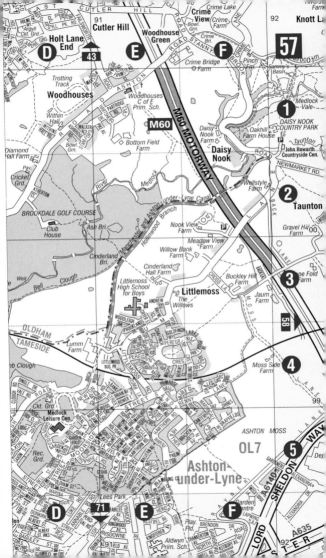

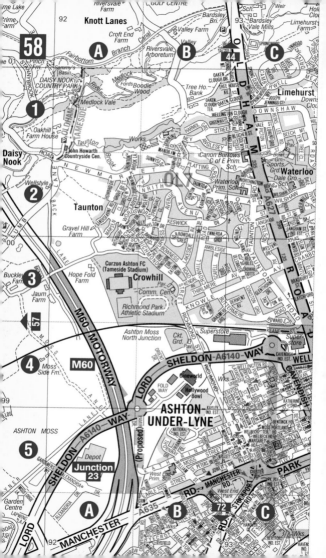

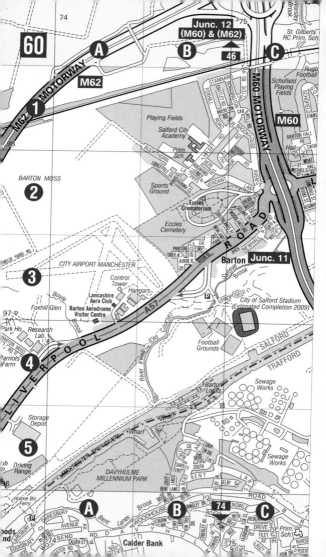

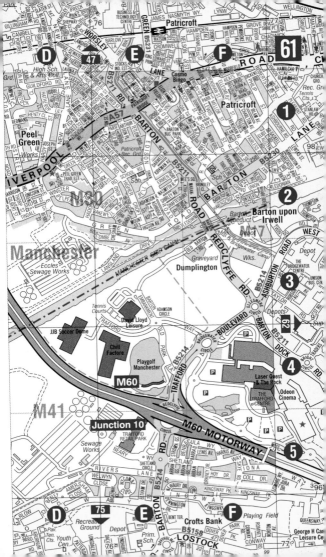

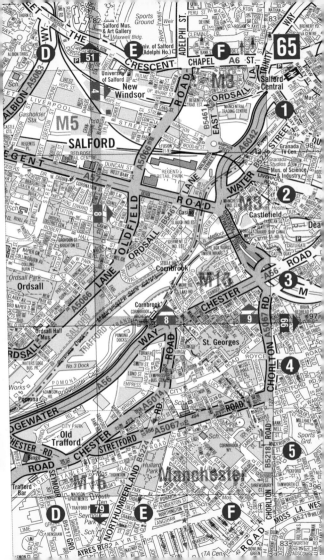

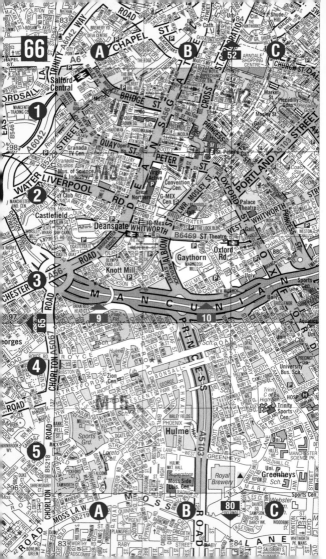

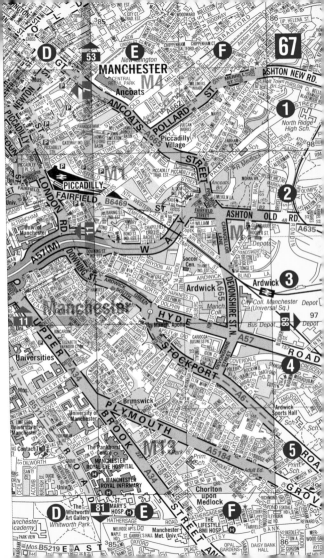

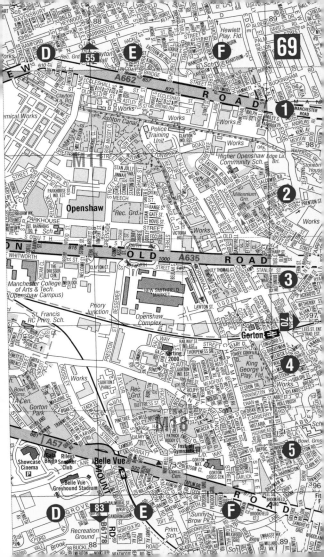

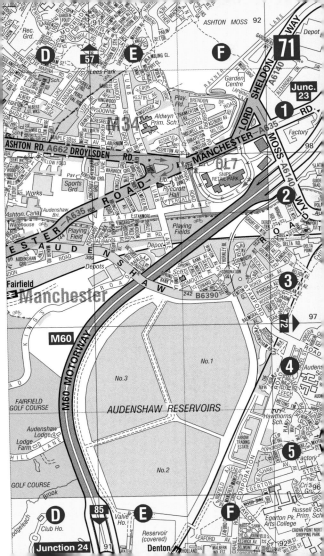

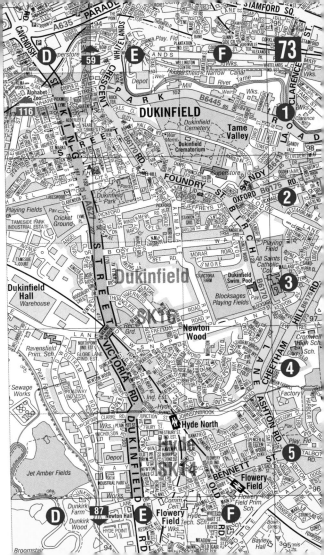

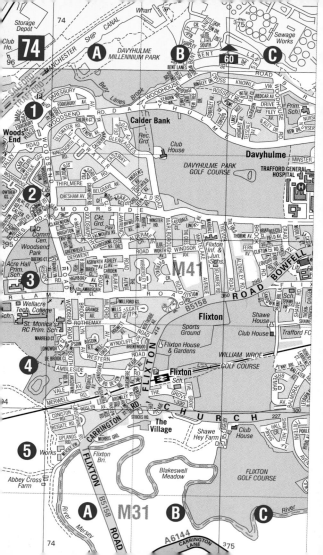

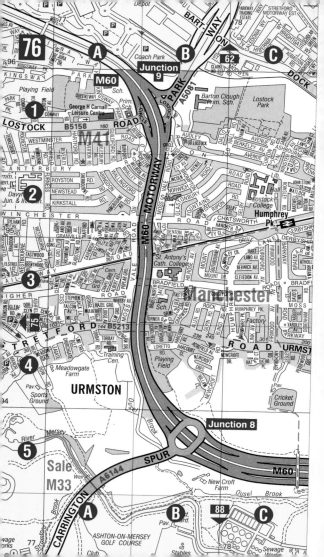

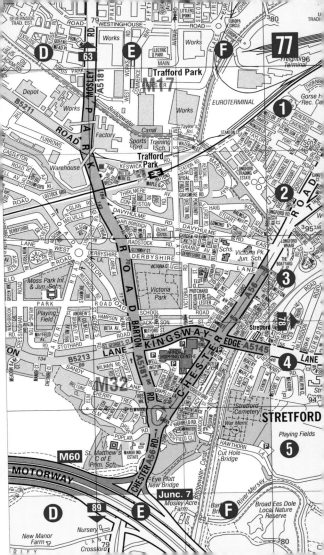

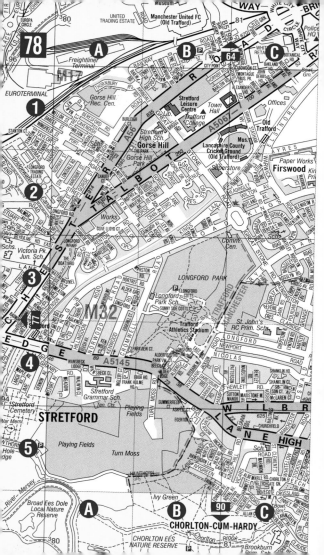

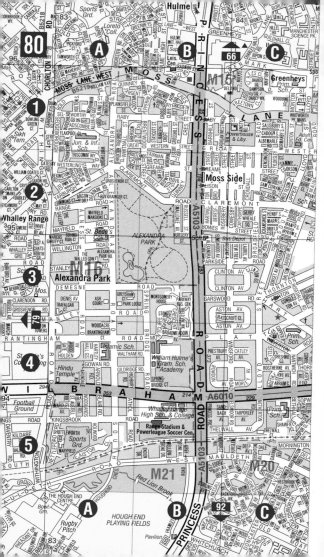

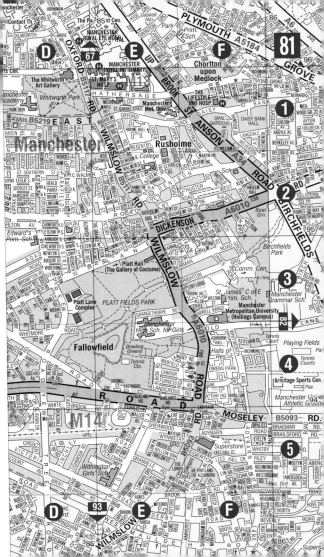

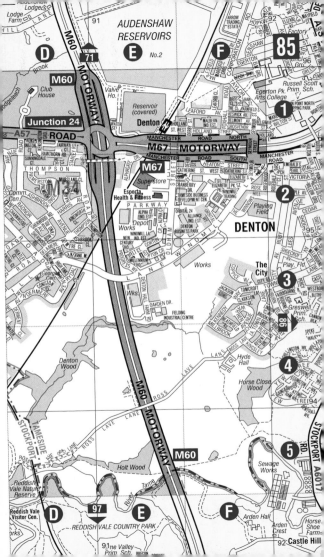

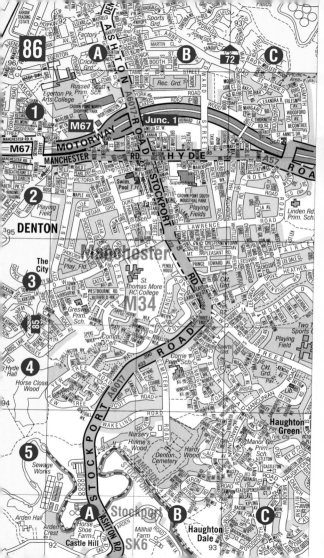

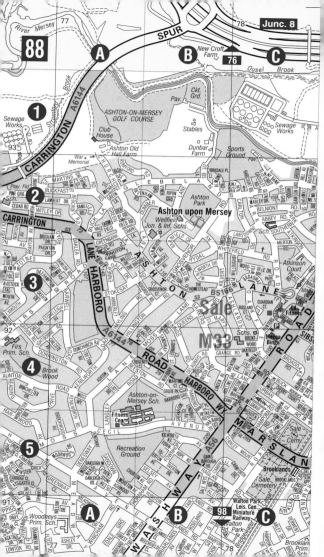

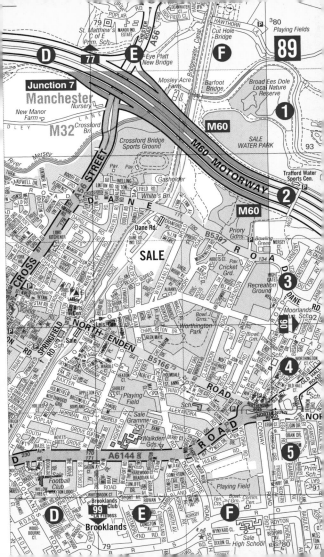

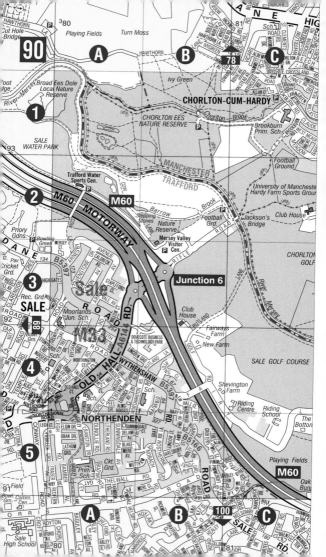

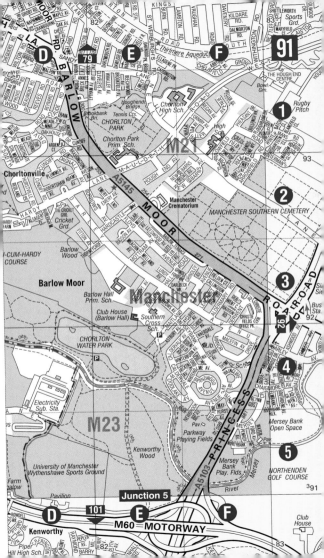

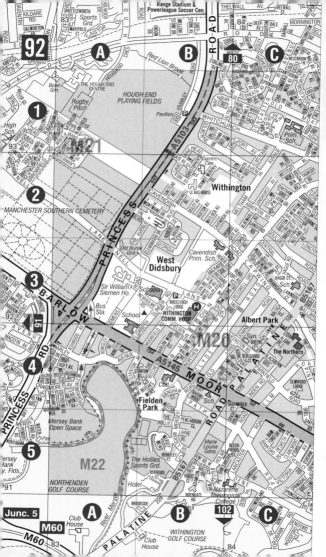

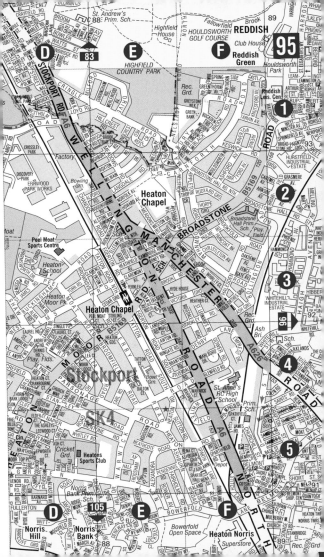

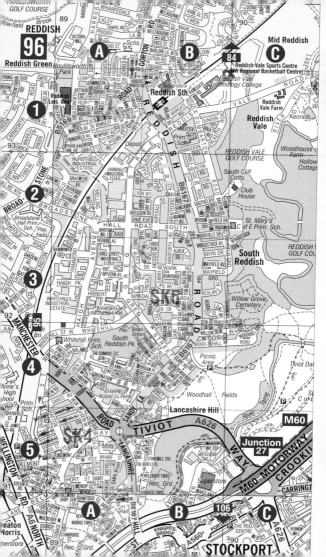

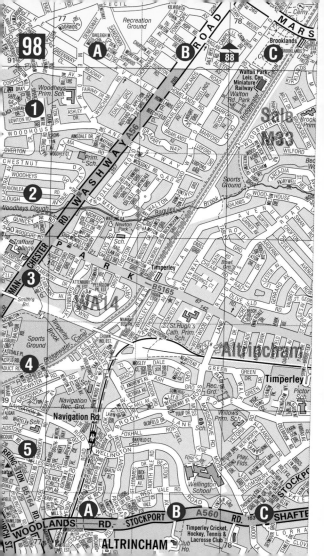

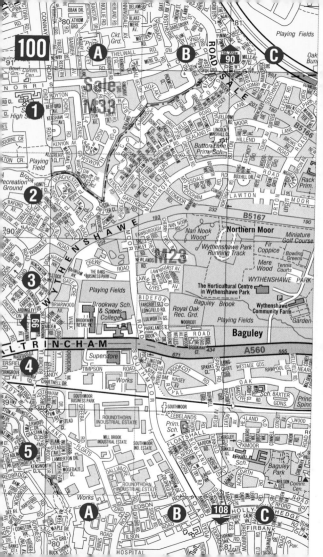

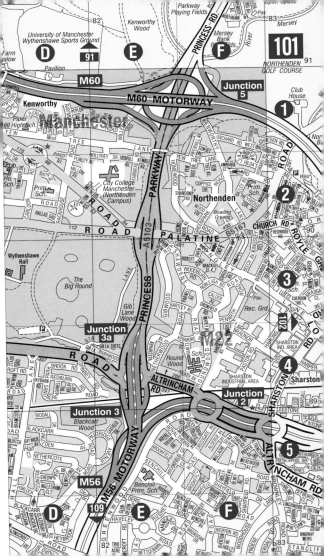

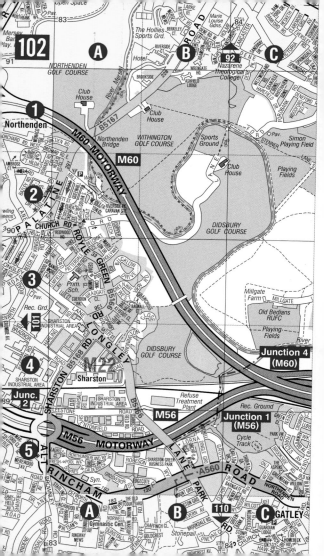

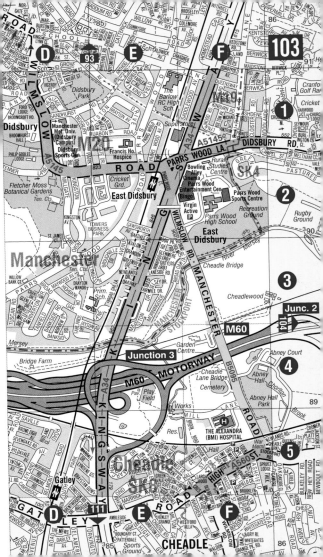

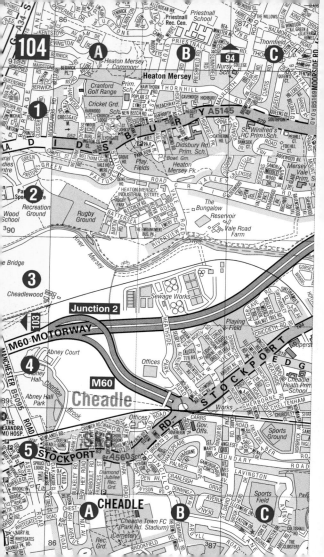

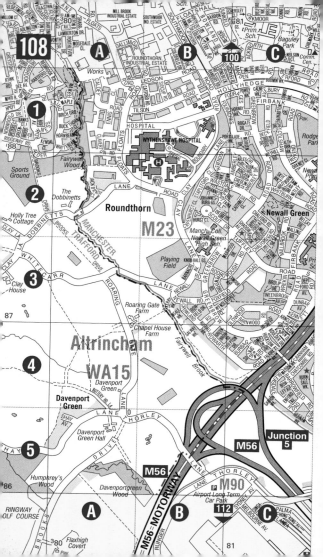

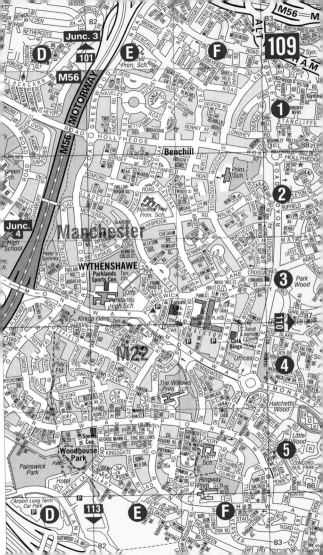

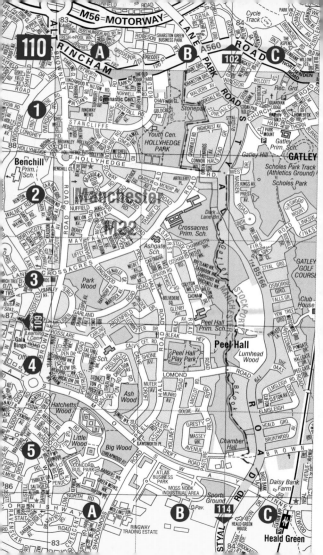

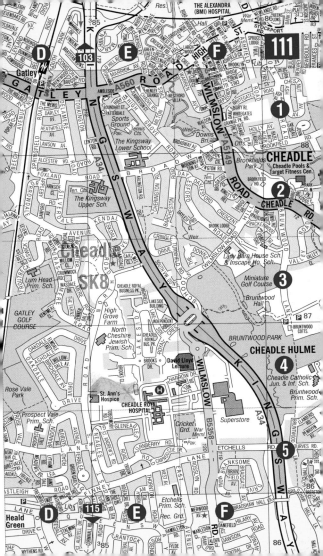

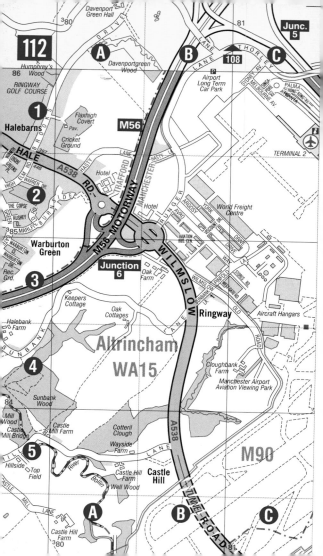

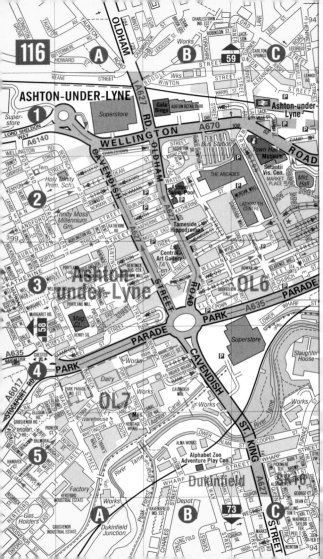

INDEX

Including Streets, Places & Areas, Industrial Estates,
Selected Flats & Walkways, Junction Names,
Stations and Selected Places of Interest.

HOW TO USE THIS INDEX

1. Each street name is followed by its Postcode District, then by its Locality abbreviation(s) and then by its map reference; e.g. **Abbey Hey La.** M11: Man . . . .3A **70** is in the M11 Postcode District and the Manchester Locality and is to be found in square 3A on page **70**. The page number is shown in bold type.

2. A strict alphabetical order is followed in which Av., Rd., St., etc. (though abbreviated) are read in full and as part of the street name; e.g. **Ashtead Rd.** appears after **Ash Sq.** but before **Ash St.**

3. Streets and a selection of flats and walkways too small to be shown on the maps, appear in the index with the thoroughfare to which it is connected shown in brackets; e.g. **Abbey Ct.** *M30: Ecc* . . . .5A **48** *(off Abbey Gro.)*

4. Addresses that are in more than one part are referred to as not continuous.

5. Places and areas are shown in the index in **BLUE TYPE** and the map reference is to the actual map square in which the town centre or area is located and not to the place name shown on the map; e.g. **ADSWOOD** 5F **105**

6. An example of a selected place of interest is **Heaton Pk. Tramway Mus.** 4B **24**

7. An example of a station is **Ardwick Station (Rail)** . . . .3A **68**. Included are Rail **(Rail)** and Metro **(Metro)**.

8. Junction names and Service Areas are shown in the index in **BOLD CAPITAL TYPE**; e.g. **CROWN POINT** . . . .2B **86** *(Junc. of A57 with A6017)*

9. Map references for entries that appear on large scale pages **4-11** & **116-118** are shown first, with small scale map references shown in brackets; e.g. **Abingdon St.** M1: Man 2C **10** (2C **66**)

GENERAL ABBREVIATIONS

All. : Alley
App. : Approach
Arc. : Arcade
Av. : Avenue
Bk. : Back
Blvd. : Boulevard
Bri. : Bridge
B'way. : Broadway
Bldg. : Building
Bldgs. : Buildings
Bungs. : Bungalows
Bus. : Business
Cvn. : Caravan
Cen. : Centre
Chyd. : Churchyard
Circ. : Circle
Cl. : Close
Cnr. : Corner
Cott. : Cottage
Cotts. : Cottages
Ct. : Court
Cres. : Crescent
Cft. : Croft
Dr. : Drive
E. : East
Emb. : Embankment
Ent. : Enterprise

Est. : Estate
Fld. : Field
Flds. : Fields
Gdn. : Garden
Gdns. : Gardens
Ga. : Gate
Gt. : Great
Grn. : Green
Gro. : Grove
Hgts. : Heights
Ho. : House
Ho's. : Houses
Ind. : Industrial
Info. : Information
Intl. : International
La. : Lane
Lit. : Little
Lwr. : Lower
Mnr. : Manor
Mans. : Mansions
Mkt. : Market
Mdw. : Meadow
Mdws. : Meadows
M. : Mews
Mt. : Mount
Mus. : Museum
Nth. : North

General Abbreviations

No. : Number
Pde. : Parade
Pk. : Park
Pas. : Passage
Pl. : Place
Pct. : Precinct
Ri. : Rise
Rd. : Road
Rdbt. : Roundabout
Shop. : Shopping
Sth. : South
Sq. : Square
Sta. : Station

St. : Street
Ter. : Terrace
Twr. : Tower
Trad. : Trading
Up. : Upper
Va. : Vale
Vw. : View
Vs. : Villas
Vis. : Visitors
Wlk. : Walk
W. : West
Yd. : Yard

LOCALITY ABBREVIATIONS

Alt : Altrincham
A Lyme : Ashton-under-Lyme
Aud : Audenshaw
Bred : Bredbury
B'ath : Broadheath
Bury : Bury
C'ton : Carrington
Chad : Chadderton
Chea : Cheadle
Chea H : Cheadle Hulme
Chor : Chorlton-cum-Hardy
Clif : Clifton
Dent : Denton
Droy : Droylsden
Duk : Dukinfield
Ecc : Eccles
Fail : Failsworth
Farn : Farnworth
Gat : Gatley
Hale : Hale
Haleb : Halebarns
Hand : Handforth
H Grn : Heald Green
H'ood : Heywood
Hyde : Hyde
Kea : Kearsley
Lees : Lees
Man : Manchester

Man A : Manchester Airport
Mid : Middleton
Nor : Northenden
O'ham : Oldham
Old T : Old Trafford
Pen : Pendlebury
Pres : Prestwich
Rad : Radcliffe
Ring : Ringway
Sale : Sale
Sal : Salford
Shar : Sharston
Stal : Stalybridge
Stoc : Stockport
Stre : Stretford
Sty : Styal
Swin : Swinton
Tim : Timperley
T Pk : Trafford Park
Urm : Urmston
Walk : Walkden
Ward : Wardley
W Tim : West Timperley
W Ran : Whalley Range
White : Whitefield
Wors : Worsley
Wyth : Wythenshawe

A

Abberley Dr. M40: Man 2F **41**
Abberton Rd. M20: Man 2C **92**
Abbey Cl. M32: Stre 2B **76**
Abbey Ct. M18: Man 4A **70**
    M30: Ecc 5A **48**
                   (off Abbey Gro.)
    SK1: Stoc 3D **107**
                   (off Abbey Gro.)
Abbeydale Rd. M40: Man 4E **41**
Abbey Dr. M27: Swin 4A **34**
Abbeyfield Cl. SK3: Stoc 5A **106**
Abbeyfield Sq. M11: Man 2D **69**
                   (off Herne St.)
Abbey Gro. M30: Ecc 5A **48**
    OL9: Chad 5C **28**
    SK1: Stoc 3D **107**
ABBEY HEY 4B **70**
Abbey Hey La. M11: Man 3A **70**
    M18: Man 5A **70**
Abbey Hills Rd. OL4: O'ham 4D **31**
    OL8: O'ham 4D **31**

Abbey Lawn M16: Old T 2D **79**
Abbey Rd. M24: Mid 2B **16**
    M33: Sale 2C **88**
    M35: Fail 4D **43**
    M43: Droy 4B **56**
    SK8: Chea 5C **104**
Abbeystead Av. M21: Chor 5F **79**
Abbeyville Wlk. M15: Man 5A **66**
            (off Wilberforce Cl.)
Abbeywood Av. M18: Man 1A **84**
Abbotsbury Cl. M12: Man 4C **68**
Abbots Cl. M33: Sale 3F **89**
Abbots Ct. M33: Sale 3F **89**
Abbotsfield Ct. M8: Man 5C **38**
Abbotsford Dr. M24: Mid 2F **15**
Abbotsford Gro. WA14: Tim 3A **98**
Abbotsford Pk. Miniature Railway
    . . . . .3D **75**
Abbotsford Rd. M21: Chor 3D **79**
    OL1: O'ham 1D **31**
    OL9: Chad 1A **28**
Abbotside Cl. M16: W Ran 2F **79**
Abbotsleigh Av. M23: Wyth 3B **100**
Abercarn Cl. M8: Man 5C **38**

Abercorn St. OL4: O'ham 3F **31**
Abercrombie St. M33: Sale 3F **89**
Aberdare Wlk. M9: Man 4A **26**
(off Crossmead Dr.)
Aberdaron Wlk. M13: Man 5F **11**
Aberdeen M30: Ecc 5A **48**
(off Monton La.)
Aberdeen Cres. SK3: Stoc 3F **105**
Aberdeen Gro. SK3: Stoc 3F **105**
Aberdeen Ho. M15: Man 5D **67**
Aberdeen St. M15: Man 5D **67**
Aberford Rd. M23: Wyth 1C **108**
Abergele Rd. M14: Man 5A **82**
Abergele St. SK2: Stoc 5C **106**
Abernant Cl. M11: Man 1B **68**
Aber Pk. SK8: Chea 5C **104**
Abersoch Av. M14: Man 5A **82**
Abingdon Av. M45: White 4B **12**
Abingdon Cl. M45: White 4B **12**
OL9: Chad 5D **29**
Abingdon Rd. M41: Urm 2A **76**
SK5: Stoc 1B **96**
Abingdon St. M1: Man 2C **10** (2C **66**)
OL2: A Lyme 5F **59**
Abinger Wlk. M40: Man 3F **55**
(off Eastmoor Dr.)
Abington Rd. M33: Sale 5E **89**
Abito M3: Sal 3A **6** (5B **52**)
Abney Rd. SK4: Stoc 3E **95**
Abraham Moss Cen. 4D **39**
Abraham Moss Leisure Cen. 4C **38**
Abraham Moss Theatre 4C **38**
Abram Cl. M14: Man 4C **80**
Abram St. M6: Sal 1B **50**
Absalom Dr. M8: Man 4B **38**
Acacia Av. M27: Swin 1A **48**
M34: Dent 2C **86**
Acacia Dr. M6: Sal 4D **49**
Acacia Gro. SK5: Stoc 4B **96**
Acacia Rd. OL8: O'ham 3F **43**
Acacias M41: Urm 2A **76**
(off Granville Rd.)
Academy Wlk. M15: Man 5A **66**
(off Wilberforce Cl.)
Acer Gro. M7: Sal 5F **37**
(off Wellington St. W.)
Acheson St. M18: Man 5F **69**
Acheson Way M17: T Pk 3E **63**
Ackers St. M13: Man 5D **67**
Ackroyd Av. M18: Man 4B **70**
Ackroyd St. M11: Man 3A **70**
Ackworth Dr. M23: Wyth 5C **100**
Ackworth Rd. M27: Swin 3A **34**
Acme Dr. M27: Pen 4D **35**
Acomb Ho. M15: Man 5D **67**
(off Dilworth St.)
Acomb St. M14: Man 2D **81**
M15: Man 5D **67**
Acorn Av. SK8: Chea 1F **111**
Acorn Bus. Pk. SK4: Stoc 2F **105**
Acorn Cen., The OL1: O'ham 1D **31**
Acorn Cl. M19: Man 5B **82**
M45: White 3B **22**
Acorn Ho. M22: Shar 5A **102**
(off Altrincham Rd.)
Acorn M. SK2: Stoc 5E **107**
Acorn St. OL4: Lees 3F **31**
Acorn Way OL1: O'ham 2D **117** (2A **30**)
ACRE 1D **31**
Acrefield M33: Sale 5C **88**

Acrefield Av. M41: Urm 4B **76**
SK4: Stoc 4D **95**
Acregate M41: Urm 3C **74**
(off Penny Bri. La.)
Acre La. OL1: O'ham 1C **30**
ACRES 4F **17**
Acres Ct. M22: Wyth 2F **109**
Acresfield Av. M34: Aud 1E **71**
Acresfield Cl. M27: Swin 1C **48**
Acresfield Rd. M6: Sal 2F **49**
M24: Mid 3D **17**
WA15: Tim 3C **98**
Acres Fold Av. M22: Wyth 3A **110**
Acres Pass M21: Chor 5C **78**
Acres Rd. M21: Chor 5C **78**
SK8: Gat 1C **110**
Acre St. M34: Dent 2A **86**
OL9: Chad 2D **43**
Acre Top Rd. M9: Man 4D **25**
Acton Av. M40: Man 3D **55**
Acton Sq. M5: Sal 4A **4** (5D **51**)
Acton St. OL1: O'ham 1C **30**
Actonville Av. M22: Wyth 3F **109**
Adair St. M1: Man 2E **67**
Adams Av. M21: Chor 2D **91**
Adamson Circ. M30: Urm 3E **61**
Adamson Gdns. M20: Man 5B **92**
Adamson Ho. M5: Sal 4C **64**
(off Elmira Way)
M16: Old T 4D **65**
Adamson Rd. M30: Ecc 2E **61**
Adamson St. SK16: Duk 4E **73**
Adamson Wlk. M14: Man 2D **81**
(off Walmer St.)
Adam St. OL6: A Lyme 4E **59**
OL8: O'ham 2B **44**
Adastral Ho. M21: Chor 5E **79**
Ada St. M9: Man 3F **39**
Adbaston Rd. M32: Stre 5C **62**
Adcroft St. SK1: Stoc 4B **106**
Addenbrook Rd. M8: Man 2A **52**
Addingham Cl. M9: Man 5D **25**
Addington St. M4: Man 3E **7** (5D **53**)
Addison Av. OL6: A Lyme 4F **59**
Addison Cl. M13: Man 4E **67**
Addison Cres. M16: Old T 1D **79**
Addison Dr. M24: Mid 4E **17**
Addison Grange M33: Sale 5E **89**
(off Princes Rd.)
Addison Rd. M32: Stre 3D **77**
M41: Urm 4F **75**
Adelaide Rd. SK3: Stoc 3E **105**
Adelaide St. M8: Man 2B **52**
M24: Mid 1C **26**
M27: Swin 5F **33**
M30: Ecc 1F **61**
Adelphi Ct. M3: Sal 2C **4** (4F **51**)
Adelphi St. M3: Sal 4C **4** (5F **51**)
Aden Cl. M12: Man 2F **67**
Aden St. OL4: O'ham 4F **31**
Adlington Cl. WA15: Tim 5F **99**
Adlington Dr. M32: Stre 1B **78**
Adlington St. M12: Man 2F **67**
OL4: O'ham 1F **31**
Adlington Wlk.
SK1: Stoc 1A **118** (2A **106**)
Adlington Way M34: Dent 4C **86**
(off Two Trees La.)
Admel Sq. M15: Man 4B **66**
(off Eden Cl.)

Adolph & Pauline Cassel Ho.
  M25: Pres 3D 37
Adrian St. M40: Man 5C 40
Adria Rd. M20: Man 5E 93
Adscombe St. M16: W Ran 1A 80
Adshall Rd. SK8: Chea 5C 104
Adshead Cl. M22: Wyth 3D 109
Adstock Wlk. M40: Man 4E 53
(off Bothwell Rd.)
Adstone Cl. M4: Man 1F 67
ADSWOOD .5F 105
Adswood Cl. OL4: O'ham 1F 31
Adswood Gro. SK3: Stoc 5F 105
Adswood Ind. Est. SK3: Stoc 5F 105
Adswood La. E. SK2: Stoc 5B 106
Adswood La. W. SK3: Stoc 5B 106
Adswood Old Rd. SK3: Stoc 5A 106
Adswood Rd. SK3: Stoc 5F 105
Adswood St. M40: Man 5A 54
Adswood Ter. SK3: Stoc 5A 106
Advent Ho. M4: Man 1F 67
(off Blantyre St.)
Aegean Gdns. M7: Sal 2E 51
Affleck Av. M26: Rad 1C 18
Afghan St. OL1: O'ham 1D 31
Age Cft. OL8: O'ham 1E 45
Agecroft Commerce Pk. M27: Pen 1A 50
Agecroft Crematorium M27: Pen 4B 36
Agecroft Ent. Pk. M27: Pen 5F 35
Agecroft Pk. Circ. M27: Pen 5F 35
Agecroft Rd. M27: Pen 5E 35
Agecroft Rd. E. M25: Pres 2C 36
Agecroft Rd. W. M25: Pres 2B 36
Agecroft Trad. Est. M6: Sal 5A 36
Agnes Cl. OL9: O'ham 5E 29
Agnes St. M14: Man 1E 93
Agnes St. M7: Man 5B 38
  M19: Man 3C 82
  OL9: Chad 4D 29
Agnew Pl. M6: Sal 3C 50
Agnew Rd. M18: Man 5E 69
Aigburth Gro. SK5: Stoc 3A 84
Ailsa Cl. M40: Man 2F 53
Ailsa Ho. M6: Sal 1B 64
(off Langworthy Rd.)
Aimson Pl. WA15: Tim 5E 99
Aimson Rd. E. WA15: Tim 5E 99
Aimson Rd. W. WA15: Tim 4E 99
Aines St. M12: Man 3C 68
Ainley Rd. M22: Wyth 3F 109
Ainley Wood SK16: Duk 3F 73
Ainsbrook Av. M9: Man 1D 41
Ainsdale Av. M7: Man 3F 37
Ainsdale Cl. OL8: O'ham 5F 29
Ainsdale Dr. M33: Sale 1A 98
  SK8: H Grn 5D 111
Ainsdale Gro. SK5: Stoc 5B 84
Ainsdale St. M12: Man 4B 68
Ainsford Rd. M20: Man 3F 93
Ainsley St. M40: Man 2E 55
Ainsty Rd. M14: Man 1C 80
Ainsworth Cl. M34: Dent 2D 85
Ainsworth Ct. M28: Walk 2A 32
Ainthorpe Wlk. M40: Man 2F 55
(off Droyden Rd.)
Aintree Gro. SK3: Stoc 5A 106
Aintree St. M11: Man 1D 69
Aintree Wlk. OL9: Chad 2E 29
(off Bentley St.)
Airedale Cl. SK8: Chea 5E 103

Airedale Ct. WA14: Alt 5A 98
(off Mill St.)
Airton Cl. M40: Man 4E 53
Aitken St. M19: Man 4E 83
Ajax Dr. BL9: Bury 3B 12
Aked Cl. M12: Man 4F 67
Akesmoor Dr. SK2: Stoc 5E 107
Alan Av. M35: Fail 2B 56
Alanbrooke Wlk. M15: Man 5A 66
(off Rankin Cl.)
Alandale Av. M34: Aud 3A 72
Alandale Rd. SK3: Stoc 4E 105
Alan Rd. M20: Man 2E 93
  SK4: Stoc 5C 94
Alan Turing Way M11: Man 4B 54
Alasdair Cl. OL9: Chad 1B 28
Alba Cl. M30: Ecc 1E 61
Alban Ct. OL6: A Lyme 5F 45
Alban St. M7: Man 2F 51
Albany Av. M11: Man 3B 70
Albany Ct. M20: Man 2D 93
(off Redcar Av.)
  M33: Sale 3E 89
  M41: Urm 2D 75
Albany Rd. M21: Chor 4D 79
  M30: Ecc 4D 47
Albany St. M24: Mid 2D 27
Albany Trad. Est. M21: Chor 4D 79
Albany Way M6: Sal 4C 50
(off Salford Shop. City)
Alba Way M32: Stre 5C 62
Albemarle Av. M20: Man 2C 92
Albemarle Rd. M21: Chor 5C 78
  M27: Swin 5A 34
Albemarle St. M14: Man 1C 80
Albemarle Ter. OL6: A Lyme 4E 59
Alberbury Av. WA15: Tim 4F 99
Albermarle St. OL6: A Lyme 4E 59
(not continuous)
Alberta St. SK1: Stoc 4C 118 (3B 106)
Albert Av. M18: Man 1B 84
  M25: Pres 3E 37
  M41: Urm 3A 76
  SK16: Duk 4E 73
Albert Bri. Ho. M3: Sal 5F 5 (1A 66)
Albert Cl. M45: White 1C 22
Albert Cl. Trad. Est. M45: White 1C 22
Albert Dr. M45: White 5D 13
Albert Fildes Wlk. M8: Man 5B 38
(off Greenland St.)
Albert Gdns. M40: Man 2F 55
Albert Gro. M12: Man 1C 82
(not continuous)
Albert Hill St. M20: Man 5D 93
ALBERT PARK 3C 92
Albert Pk. Rd. M7: Sal 2E 51
Albert Pl. M13: Man 2B 82
  M45: White 5D 13
Albert Rd. M19: Man 4B 82
  M30: Ecc 5B 48
  M33: Sale 4E 89
  M45: White 1C 22
  SK4: Stoc 5C 94
  SK14: Hyde 3F 87
Albert Sq. M2: Man 1D 10 (1B 66)
Albert St. BL4: Kea 1A 18
  M11: Man 1B 68
  M24: Mid 1C 26
  M25: Pres 5E 23

Albert St. M30: Ecc 5B **48**
    M34: Dent 2B **86**
    M43: Droy 1D **71**
    OL8: O'ham 3D **43**
    OL9: Chad 1D **43**
    SK3: Stoc 2F **105**
Albert St. W. M35: Fail 1F **55**
Albert St. Works M43: Droy 1D **71**
Albert Ter. SK1: Stoc 2B **118**
Albert Wlk.
    OL7: A Lyme 5A **116** (1C **72**)
Albine St. M40: Man 4B **40**
Albion Cl. SK4: Stoc 5A **96**
Albion Dr. M43: Droy 5C **56**
Albion Fold M43: Droy 5C **56**
Albion Gro. M33: Sale 3B **88**
Albion Pl. M5: Sal 4A **4** (5E **51**)
    M7: Sal 2E **51**
    M25: Pres 5C **22**
Albion Rd. M14: Man 4E **81**
Albion St. BL4: Kea 2C **18**
    M1: Man 4A **10** (3B **66**)
    M16: Old T 1F **79**
    M26: Rad 1D **21**
    M27: Pen 4C **34**
    M33: Sale 4D **89**
    M35: Fail 5A **42**
    OL1: O'ham 3D **117** (2B **30**)
                (not continuous)
    OL6: A Lyme 4E **59**
                (not continuous)
    OL9: Chad 2C **28**
Albion Towers M5: Sal 5D **51**
Albion Trad. Est. M6: Sal 3C **50**
    OL6: A Lyme 4F **59**
Albion Way M5: Sal 1D **65**
Albury Dr. M19: Man 1F **103**
Albyns Av. M8: Man 5C **38**
Alcester Av. SK3: Stoc 4B **104**
Alcester Cl. M24: Mid 3D **27**
Alcester Rd. M33: Sale 1D **99**
    SK8: Gat 2D **111**
Alcester St. OL9: Chad 1C **42**
Alcester Wlk. M9: Man 4E **25**
Alconbury Ct. *M43: Droy* *2D 71*
             (off Florence St.)
Alconbury Wlk. M9: Man 3D **25**
Aldborough Cl. M20: Man 2D **93**
Aldbourne Cl. M40: Man 3F **53**
Aldcroft St. M18: Man 4B **70**
Alden Cl. M45: White 1C **22**
Alden Wlk. SK4: Stoc 1F **95**
Alderbank Cl. BL4: Kea 3B **18**
Alder Cl. OL6: A Lyme 5D **45**
    SK8: H Grn 1F **115**
Alder Ct. M8: Man 3B **38**
Aldercroft Av. M22: Wyth 4E **109**
Alderdale Cl. SK4: Stoc 4C **94**
Alderdale Dr. M43: Droy 5F **55**
    SK4: Stoc 3C **94**
Alder Dr. M27: Ward 3E **33**
    WA15: Tim 2A **108**
Alder Edge M21: Chor 4B **78**
Alderfield Ho. M21: Chor 4B **78**
Alderfield Rd. M21: Chor 4B **78**
Alderford Pde. M8: Man 1B **52**
ALDER FOREST 3C **46**
Alder Forest Av. M30: Ecc 3C **46**
Aldergate Ct. M27: Swin 5E **33**
Alderglen Rd. M8: Man 1B **52**

Alder Gro. M32: Stre 3A **78**
    M34: Dent 2C **86**
    SK3: Stoc 3E **105**
Alder Hgts. SK1: Stoc 1D **107**
Alder La. OL8: O'ham 2F **43**
Alderley Dr. SK6: Bred 5F **97**
Alderley Rd. M33: Sale 1A **100**
    M41: Urm 3C **74**
    SK5: Stoc 3B **96**
Alderley St. OL6: A Lyme 2F **59**
Alderley Ter.
    SK16: Duk 5C **116** (1D **73**)
Alderman Sq. M12: Man 2A **68**
Aldermary Rd. M21: Chor 3F **91**
Aldermaston Gro. M9: Man 3D **25**
Aldermere Cres. M41: Urm 2B **74**
Aldermoor Cl. M11: Man 2E **69**
Alder Rd. M24: Mid 4E **17**
    M35: Fail 2B **56**
    SK8: Chea 1F **111**
ALDER ROOT 3D **29**
Alders Ct. OL8: O'ham 4C **44**
Aldersgate Rd. SK2: Stoc 5D **107**
Aldershot Wlk. *M11: Man* *1B 68*
            (off Newcombe Cl.)
Alderside Rd. M9: Man 4F **39**
Aldersley Av. M9: Man 4D **25**
Alderson St. M6: Sal 3C **50**
    OL9: O'ham 2A **30**
Alders Rd. M22: Wyth 1E **109**
Alder St. M6: Sal 5B **50**
    M30: Ecc 3C **46**
Alderue Av. M22: Wyth 5F **101**
Alderwood Av. SK4: Stoc 2C **104**
Alderwood Wlk. *M8: Man* *1B 52*
            (off Ermington Dr.)
Aldfield Rd. M23: Wyth 2B **100**
Aldford Cl. M20: Man 5E **93**
Aldham Av. M40: Man 3E **55**
Aldow Ind. Pk. M12: Man 2E **67**
Aldred Cl. M8: Man 1D **53**
Aldred St. M5: Sal 4A **4** (5D **51**)
    M30: Ecc 1E **61**
    M35: Fail 5A **42**
Aldridge Wlk. *M11: Man* *2B 68*
             (off Bell Cres.)
Aldwick Av. M20: Man 5E **93**
Aldwinians Cl. M34: Aud 5A **72**
Aldworth Dr. M40: Man 1A **54**
Aldwych Av. M14: Man 2D **81**
Aldwyn Cl. M34: Aud 5A **72**
Aldwyn Pk. Rd. M34: Aud 2E **71**
Alexander Av. M35: Fail 4C **42**
Alexander Ct. *M5: Sal* *2C 64*
             (off Rowland St.)
Alexander Dr. BL9: Bury 5C **12**
    WA15: Tim 5C **98**
Alexander Gdns. M7: Sal . . .1D **5** (3F **51**)
Alexander Pk. OL6: A Lyme 5F **59**
Alexander St. M6: Sal 5A **50**
Alexandra, The M14: Man 5F **81**
    M50: Sal 3B **64**
Alexandra Av. M14: Man 3B **80**
    M45: White 1C **22**
    SK14: Hyde 3E **87**
Alexandra Cen. Retail Pk.
    OL4: O'ham 5F **117** (3B **30**)
Alexandra Cl. SK3: Stoc 5E **105**
Alexandra Ct. M41: Urm 4A **74**

Alexandra Cres. OL1: O'ham 1D 31
Alexandra Dr. M19: Man 1B 94
Alexandra Ho. M30: Ecc 1E 61
(off Liverpool Rd.)
  OL1: O'ham 1D 31
Alexandra M. OL8: O'ham 4C 30
ALEXANDRA PARK 3A 80
Alexandra Pk.
  Alexandra Rd. Sth. 2B 80
  Queens Rd. 4C 30
Alexandra Pk. Ho.
  M16: W Ran 3A 80
Alexandra Rd. BL4: Kea 3C 18
  M16: W Ran 2A 80
  M26: Rad .1C 18
  M30: Ecc .1D 61
  M33: Sale .5E 89
  M34: Dent 1C 86
  OL6: A Lyme 1C 116 (4D 59)
  OL8: O'ham 5C 30
  SK4: Stoc .5E 95
Alexandra Rd. Sth.
  M16: W Ran 2A 80
  M21: Chor .2A 80
Alexandra St. M7: Sal 1D 5 (4F 51)
  OL6: A Lyme 3F 59
  OL8: O'ham 4C 30
  SK14: Hyde 4E 87
Alexandra Ter. M19: Man 4C 82
Alexandria Dr. OL7: A Lyme 5A 58
Alford Av. M20: Man 5C 80
Alford Rd. SK4: Stoc 2D 95
Alford St. OL9: O'ham 2D 43
Alfred Av. M28: Wors 5C 32
Alfred James Cl. M40: Man 4E 53
Alfred Morris Cl. M23: Wyth 1C 100
(off Fellpark Rd.)
Alfred St. BL4: Kea 1B 18
  M9: Man 4F 39
  M28: Walk 1A 32
  M30: Ecc .4F 47
  M35: Fail .4B 42
  OL6: A Lyme 3F 59
  OL9: O'ham 3E 29
(not continuous)
  SK14: Hyde 2E 87
Alfreton Av. M34: Dent 5C 86
Alfreton Rd. SK2: Stoc 5F 107
Alfreton Wlk. M40: Man 1C 54
(off Halliford Rd.)
Alfriston Dr. M23: Wyth 1C 100
Alger M. OL6: A Lyme 3F 59
Algernon St. M27: Swin 4F 33
  M30: Ecc .4F 47
Alger St. OL6: A Lyme 3F 59
Algreave Rd. SK3: Stoc 3C 104
Alice St. M27: Pen 4D 35
  M33: Sale .4F 89
  SK14: Hyde 5F 87
Alison Ct. SK4: Stoc 4D 95
Alison Kelly Cl. M9: Man 4B 40
Alison St. M14: Man 2B 80
Alker Rd. M40: Man 4F 53
Alkrington Cl. BL9: Bury 4C 12
Alkrington Dr. M24: Mid 4D 27
ALKRINGTON GARDEN VILLAGE 4C 26
Alkrington Grn. M24: Mid 3B 26
Alkrington Hall M24: Mid 2B 26
Alkrington Hall Rd. Nth. M24: Mid 2B 26
Alkrington Hall Rd. Sth. M24: Mid 3A 26

Alkrington Pk. Rd. M24: Mid 1A 26
Allama Iqbal Rd. OL4: O'ham 4E 31
Allanadale Ct. M7: Sal 3A 38
Allan Ct. M21: Chor 1C 90
Allandale Rd. M19: Man 4B 82
Allan Roberts Cl. M9: Man 3F 39
Alldis Cl. M12: Man 5A 68
Allenby Rd. M27: Swin 1E 47
Allenby Wlk. M40: Man 2E 53
(off Dalbury Dr.)
Allendale Dr. BL9: Bury 3D 12
Allendale Wlk. M3: Sal 3C 4 (5F 51)
Allen Hall M14: Man 3F 81
Allen St. OL8: O'ham 4F 29
Allerdean Wlk. SK4: Stoc 5B 94
Allerford St. M16: W Ran 1A 80
Allerton Wlk. M13: Man 4D 67
(off Glenbarry Cl.)
Allesley Dr. M7: Sal 2A 52
Allgreave Cl. M33: Sale 2A 100
Alliance Ind. Est. M34: Dent 2F 85
Alligin Cl. OL9: Chad 1C 28
Allingham St. M13: Man 1A 82
Allington Dr. M30: Ecc 3A 48
Alliott Wlk. M15: Man 5A 66
(off Elverdon Cl.)
Allison Gro. M30: Ecc 1D 61
Allison St. M8: Man 2B 52
Allonby Wlk. M24: Mid 4E 15
Alloway Wlk. M40: Man 1C 54
(off Halliford Rd.)
All Saints Ct. M32: Stre 3D 77
(off Manor Rd.)
All Saints' Rd. SK4: Stoc 4F 95
All Saints St. M40: Man 2E 55
Alma Ct. M15: Man 1A 80
(off Moss La. W.)
ALMA PARK 5D 83
Alma Rd. M19: Man 5C 82
  M33: Sale .1A 98
  SK4: Stoc .3D 95
Alma St. BL4: Kea 4D 19
  M30: Ecc .1B 62
Alma Works SK16: Duk 5B 116 (1D 73)
Alminstone Cl. M40: Man 3F 55
Almond Cl. M6: Sal 5C 50
  M35: Fail .1B 56
  SK3: Stoc 3E 105
Almond Ct. SK16: Duk 1E 73
(off Combermere St.)
Almond Dr. M33: Sale 2B 88
Almond St. M40: Man 1F 7 (3D 53)
Alms Hill Rd. M8: Man 5C 38
Almshouses M33: Sale 4A 90
Alness Rd. M16: W Ran 2A 80
Alnwick Dr. BL9: Bury 1B 12
Alnwick Rd. M9: Man 4F 25
Alperton Wlk. M40: Man 3F 55
(off Thaxmead Dr.)
Alphabet Zoo Adventure Play Cen.
. . . . .5B 116 (1D 73)
Alpha Ct. M34: Dent 2E 85
Alpha Ct. Ind. Est. M34: Dent 2E 85
Alphagate Dr. M34: Dent 2E 85
Alpha Pl. M15: Man 4F 9
Alpha Rd. M32: Stre 3E 77
Alpha St. M6: Sal 4B 50
  M11: Man 3A 70

Alpha St. W. M6: Sal 4A 50
Alphonsus St. M16: Old T 1E 79
Alpine Rd. SK1: Stoc 1C 106
(not continuous)
Alpine St. M11: Man 4D 55
Alpington Wlk. M40: Man 2E 41
(off Ogmore Wlk.)
Alport Av. M16: W Ran 3E 79
Alresford Rd. M6: Sal 2F 49
M24: Mid 4B 26
Alric Wlk. M22: Wyth 1A 114
Alsager Cl. M21: Chor 2D 91
Alsham Wlk. M8: Man 1C 52
(off Heatherdale Dr.)
Alsop Av. M7: Sal 5D 37
Alston Av. M32: Stre 2D 77
M33: Sale 5B 88
Alstone Rd. SK4: Stoc 2E 95
Alston Gdns. M19: Man 3B 94
Alston Rd. M18: Man 1E 83
Alston Wlk. M24: Mid 4E 15
ALT 1F 45
Altair Av. M22: Wyth 5F 109
Altair Pl. M7: Sal 3E 51
Altcar Gro. SK5: Stoc 3A 84
Altcar Wlk. M22: Wyth 4E 109
Alt Gro. OL6: A Lyme 1D 59
Altham Wlk. M40: Man 1C 54
(off Craiglands Av.)
ALT HILL 3E 45
Alt Hill La. OL6: A Lyme 4D 45
Alt Hill Rd. OL6: A Lyme 3E 45
Althorn Wlk. M23: Wyth 1C 108
Althorpe Wlk. M40: Man 3F 55
(off Eastmoor Dr.)
Alt La. OL6: O'ham 2E 45
OL8: O'ham 2E 45
Alton Cl. BL9: Bury 1C 12
OL6: A Lyme 5E 45
Alton Sq. M11: Man 3A 70
Alton St. OL8: O'ham 1B 44
Alton Towers M16: W Ran 4F 79
ALTRINCHAM 5A 98
Altrincham Garrick Playhouse 5A 98
Altrincham Rd. M22: Shar 4E 101
(not continuous)
M23: Wyth 4F 99
SK8: Gat 4E 101
SK9: Sty 5A 114
Altrincham St. M1: Man 3E 11 (2D 67)
Alt Rd. OL6: A Lyme 1D 59
Alt Wlk. M45: White 4E 13
Alum Cres. BL9: Bury 3C 12
Alvanley Cl. M33: Sale 2D 99
Alvanley Cres. SK3: Stoc 5E 105
Alvan Sq. M11: Man 3A 70
Alvaston Av. SK4: Stoc 5D 95
Alvaston Rd. M18: Man 1A 84
Alveley Av. M20: Man 3E 93
Alverstone Rd. M20: Man 2E 93
Alwinton Av. SK4: Stoc 5A 94
Alworth Rd. M9: Man 4F 25
Alwyn Dr. M13: Man 1A 82
Ambassador Pl. WA15: Alt 5A 98
Amber Gdns. SK16: Duk 2D 73
(off Railway La.)
Amberley Dr. M23: Wyth 2C 108
Amberley Rd. M33: Sale 3A 88
Amberley Wlk. OL9: Chad 2E 29

Amberwood OL9: Chad 1A 28
Amberwood Dr. M23: Wyth 5F 99
Ambleside Av. OL7: A Lyme 3B 58
WA15: Tim 5E 99
Ambleside Cl. M24: Mid 5A 16
Ambleside Ct. SK8: Chea 1E 111
Ambleside Rd. M41: Urm 4A 74
SK5: Stoc 2B 96
Ambleside Wlk. M9: Man 2C 40
Ambrose Ct. M22: Nor 2F 101
(off Kenworthy La.)
Ambrose Dr. M20: Man 4A 92
Ambrose Gdns. M20: Man 4F 91
Ambrose St. M12: Man 3C 68
SK14: Hyde 5F 87
Ambuscade Ct. M41: Urm 3A 74
Ambush St. M11: Man 3B 70
Amelan Rd. M25: Pres 3C 36
Amelia St. W. M34: Dent 1B 86
Amersham Cl. M41: Urm 5D 61
Amersham Pl. M19: Man 2C 94
Amersham St. M5: Sal 1B 64
Amesbury Gro. SK5: Stoc 3B 96
Amesbury Rd. M9: Man 5A 26
Amherst Rd. M14: Man 1E 93
M20: Man 1E 93
Amlwch Av. SK2: Stoc 5F 107
Ammon Wrigley Cl.
OL1: O'ham 2E 117 (2B 30)
Amory St. M12: Man 2E 67
Amos Av. M40: Man 3E 55
Amos St. M6: Sal 5A 50
M9: Man 5B 40
Ampney Cl. M30: Ecc 1D 61
Amport Wlk. M40: Man 2E 41
Amwell St. M8: Man 5D 39
Amy St. M24: Mid 5D 17
Anaconda Dr. M3: Sal 2E 5 (4A 52)
Ancaster Wlk. M40: Man 2E 41
Anchorage Quay M50: Sal 2C 64
Anchorage Rd. M41: Urm 4C 76
Anchorage Station (Metro) 2C 64
Anchorage Wlk. M18: Man 4E 69
(off Briercliffe Cl.)
Anchor Cl. M19: Man 4E 83
Anchor Ct. M8: Man 3B 38
Anchorside Cl. M21: Chor 1D 91
Anchor St. OL1: O'ham 1E 117
ANCOATS 5E 7 (1D 67)
Ancoats Gro. M4: Man 2F 67
Ancoats Gro. Nth. M4: Man 1F 67
Ancroft St. M15: Man 4A 66
Anderton Gro. OL6: A Lyme 2F 59
Andoc Av. M30: Ecc 1C 62
Andover Av. M24: Mid 4D 27
Andover St. M30: Ecc 1E 61
Andover Wlk. M8: Man 4C 38
Andre St. M11: Man 5E 55
Andrew Cl. M20: Man 2D 93
(off Aldborough Cl.)
Andrew Gro. SK16: Duk 2F 73
Andrew Ho. SK4: Stoc 4D 95
Andrew Rd. M9: Man 3F 39
Andrews Av. M41: Urm 2A 74
Andrews Bldgs. OL6: A Lyme 4E 59
(off Newton St.)
Andrews Cl. M34: Dent 4D 87
Andrew St. M24: Mid 2E 27
M35: Fail 4A 42
M43: Droy 3E 57

Andrew St. OL6: A Lyme 2F 59
  OL9: Chad 1D 29
  SK4: Stoc 1F 105
Andy Nicholson Wlk. M9: Man 4B 40
  (off Amos St.)
Anerley Rd. M20: Man 4D 93
Anfield Cl. BL9: Bury 3D 13
Anfield Rd. M33: Sale 3E 89
  M40: Man 3F 41
Angela St. M15: Man 5D 9 (3F 65)
Angel Cl. SK16: Duk 2D 73
Angel St. M4: Man 2D 7 (4C 52)
  M34: Dent 1C 86
Angel Trad. Est. M4: Man 2D 7
Angier Gro. M34: Dent 2B 86
Anglesea Av. SK2: Stoc 5B 106
Anglesey Cl. OL7: A Lyme 1C 58
Anglesey Gro. SK8: Chea 5C 104
Anglesey Rd. OL7: A Lyme 1B 58
Angleside Av. M19: Man 4A 94
Angora Dr. M3: Sal 2C 4 (4F 51)
Aniline St. M11: Man 1D 69
Anita St. M4: Man 3F 7 (5D 53)
Annable Rd. M18: Man 4A 70
  M43: Droy 1D 71
  SK6: Bred 5F 97
Annald Sq. M43: Droy 2C 70
Annan St. M34: Dent 1B 86
Anne Cl. OL7: A Lyme 1C 58
Anne Nuttall Rd. M15: Man 5D 9 (3F 65)
Annesley Ct. M30: Ecc 5A 48
Annesley Gdns. M18: Man 4F 69
  (off Keary Cl.)
Annesley Rd. M40: Man 3A 42
Anne St. SK16: Duk 2F 73
Annie Darby Ct. M9: Man 5F 39
Annie St. M6: Sal 5A 50
Annisdale St. M30: Ecc 5D 47
Annis St. M9: Man 5A 40
Ann Sq. OL4: O'ham 1F 31
Ann St. BL4: Kea 2A 18
  M34: Dent 2A 86
  OL7: A Lyme 2B 72
  SK5: Stoc 4A 96
  SK14: Hyde 2E 87
Anscombe Cl. M40: Man 4F 53
Ansdell Av. M21: Chor 5E 79
Ansdell Dr. M43: Droy 5A 56
Ansdell Rd. SK5: Stoc 4C 84
Ansdell St. M8: Man 5C 38
Ansell Cl. M18: Man 4F 69
Anselms Ct. OL8: O'ham 5E 29
Ansford Wlk. M9: Man 1E 53
  (off Hendham Va.)
Ansleigh Av. M8: Man 3C 38
Ansley Gro. SK4: Stoc 5D 95
Anslow Cl. M40: Man 2F 53
Anson Av. M27: Swin 1A 48
Anson Rd. M14: Man 1F 81
  M27: Swin 1A 48
  M34: Dent 3C 84
Anson St. M30: Ecc 4D 47
Answell Av. M8: Man 2C 38
Antares Av. M7: Sal 1C 4 (4F 51)
Anthistle Ct. M5: Sal 5F 49
  (off Sheader Dr.)
Anthony Cl. M12: Man 3A 68
Antilles Cl. M12: Man 1C 82
Anton Wlk. M9: Man 5F 39
  (off Shiredale Dr.)

Antrim Cl. M19: Man 1F 103
Anvil St. M1: Man 4B 10
Anvil Way OL1: O'ham 2D 117 (2A 30)
Apethorn La. SK14: Hyde 5E 87
Apfel La. OL9: Chad 2D 29
Apollo Av. BL9: Bury 3B 12
Apollo Wlk. M12: Man 4C 68
  (off Bridgend Cl.)
Apperley Grange M30: Ecc 3A 48
Appian Way M7: Sal 3A 48
Appleby Av. M12: Man 2C 82
  SK14: Hyde 5E 73
  WA15: Tim 5E 99
Appleby Cl. SK3: Stoc 5F 105
Appleby Gdns. BL9: Bury 3B 12
Appleby Lodge M14: Man 3F 81
Appleby Rd. SK8: Gat 2D 111
Applecross Wlk. M11: Man 2E 69
  (off Bill Williams Cl.)
Appledore Dr. M23: Wyth 4F 99
Appledore Wlk. OL9: Chad 3D 29
Appleford Av. M23: Wyth 2C 108
Appleford Dr. M8: Man 1D 53
Appleton Av. St. M8: Man 5D 39
Appleton Ct. M33: Sale 4D 89
Appleton Gro. M33: Sale 1A 98
Appleton Rd. SK4: Stoc 2F 95
Apple Tree Ct. M5: Sal 5C 50
Apple Way M42: Mid 3D 27
Applewood OL9: Chad 2F 27
Appleyard Cl. M27: Pen 4F 35
Apprentice Cl. M9: Man 4A 40
  (off Caversham Dr.)
Apprentice La. SK9: Sty 5B 114
April Cl. M13: Man 5F 67
  (off Markfield Av.)
  OL8: O'ham 5E 31
Apsley Gro. M12: Man 4E 67
Apsley Pl. OL6: A Lyme 5C 58
Apsley Rd. M34: Dent 1B 86
Apsley St. SK1: Stoc 2C 118 (2B 106)
Aquarius La. M6: Sal 3E 51
  (off Gemini Rd.)
Aquarius St. M15: Man 5C 66
Arbor Av. M19: Man 1B 94
Arbor Dr. M19: Man 1B 94
Arbor St. M43: Droy 4B 56
Arbory Av. M40: Man 4D 41
Arbour Cl. M6: Sal 4B 50
Arbroath St. M11: Man 1A 70
Arbury Av. SK3: Stoc 4C 104
Arcade, The SK5: Stoc 3E 97
Arcades, The
  OL6: A Lyme 2B 116 (4D 59)
Arcadia Av. M33: Sale 2C 98
Arcadia Sports Cen. 4C 82
Archer Pk. M24: Mid 1A 26
Archer Pl. M32: Stre 2B 76
Archer St. M11: Man 5C 54
Archie St. M5: Sal 5B 66
Archway M17: Man 1B 64
Arcon Dr. M16: W Ran 2A 80
Arcon Pl. SK1: Stoc 5D 97
Ardale Av. M40: Man 2E 41
Ardcombe Av. M9: Man 4E 25
Ardeen Wlk. M13: Man 4E 67
  (off Bramwell Dr.)
Arden Av. M24: Mid 4D 27
Arden Bldgs. SK3: Stoc 4A 118

Arden Cl. SK8: H Grn 2E **115**
Arden Cl. M21: Chor 1D **91**
Ardenfield M34: Dent 5C **86**
Ardenfield Cl. M26: Rad 1D **21**
Ardenfield Dr. M22: Wyth 3A **110**
Arden Gro. M40: Man 3E **41**
Arden Lodge Rd. M23: Wyth 4A **100**
ARDEN PARK 5F **97**
Arden Rd. SK6: Bred 5A **86**
Ardens Cl. M27: Swin 2F **33**
Arden St. OL9: Chad 1C **42**
Ardent Way M25: Pres 3D **37**
Arderne Rd. WA15: Tim 3C **98**
Ardern Fld. St.
 SK1: Stoc 5C **118** (4B **106**)
Ardern Gro. SK1: Stoc 5C **118** (3B **106**)
Ardern Rd. M8: Man 2B **38**
Ardern Wlk. SK1: Stoc 2A **118**
Ardingley Wlk. M23: Wyth 3F **99**
Ardmore Wlk. M22: Wyth 4A **110**
ARDWICK 3E **67**
Ardwick Grn. Nth.
 M12: Man 4F **11** (3E **67**)
Ardwick Grn. Sth.
 M13: Man 4F **11** (3E **67**)
Ardwick Sports Hall 5A **68**
Ardwick Station (Rail) 3A **68**
Ardwick Ter. M12: Man 4F **67**
 (off Aked Cl.)
Argosy Dr. M30: Ecc 3B **60**
 M90: Man A 2B **112**
Argus St. OL8: O'ham 2E **43**
Argyle Av. M14: Man 1A **82**
 M45: White 1C **22**
Argyle St. M18: Man 5F **69**
 M27: Swin 5A **34**
 M43: Droy 1C **70**
 OL1: O'ham 1D **31**
Argyll Av. M32: Stre 3D **77**
Argyll Cl. M35: Fail 5D **43**
Argyll Pk. Rd. M35: Fail 5D **43**
Argyll Rd. OL9: Chad 1B **42**
 SK8: Chea 5B **104**
Argyll St. OL6: A Lyme 4F **59**
Arkendale Cl. M35: Fail 5E **43**
Arkholme Wlk. M40: Man 5D **41**
Arkle Dr. OL9: Chad 1B **28**
Arkley Wlk. M13: Man 5F **11**
Ark St. M19: Man 3C **82**
Arkwright St. OL9: O'ham 3E **29**
Arley Av. M20: Man 3B **92**
Arley Cl. SK16: Duk 4F **73**
 WA14: W Tim 3A **98**
Arley Dr. M33: Sale 1C **98**
Arley Ho. M23: Wyth 2C **108**
Arley Moss Wlk. M13: Man 5F **11**
Arley Way M34: Dent 4C **86**
 (off Two Trees La.)
Arlies St. OL6: A Lyme 3F **59**
Arlington Av. M25: Pres 2D **37**
 M27: Swin 1F **47**
 M34: Dent 3C **86**
Arlington Rd. M32: Stre 3D **77**
 SK8: Chea 5C **111**
Arlington St. M3: Sal 3D **5** (5F **51**)
 M8: Man .4B **38**
 OL6: A Lyme 4E **59**
Arliss Av. M19: Man 5C **82**
Armadale Av. M9: Man 5C **26**
Armadale Rd. SK16: Duk 2E **73**

Armitage Cl. M24: Mid 2F **25**
 OL8: O'ham 1E **43**
Armitage Ho. M6: Sal 4E **49**
 (off Edgehill Rd.)
Armitage Owen Wlk. M40: Man 5C **40**
 (off Brendon Av.)
Armitage Sports Cen. 4A **82**
Armitage St. M30: Ecc 1E **61**
Armour Pl. M9: Man 2E **39**
 (off Oakworth St.)
Armoury St. SK3: Stoc 5A **118** (3A **106**)
Arncliffe Dr. M23: Wyth 3C **99**
Arndale Shop. Cen.
 M4: Man 4C **6** (5C **52**)
 M32: Stre 4E **77**
Arnesby Av. M33: Sale 3A **90**
Arne St. OL9: Chad 4C **28**
Arnfield Rd. M20: Man 2D **93**
 SK3: Stoc 5F **105**
Arnold & Margaret Wills Ho.
 M25: Pres 3C **36**
Arnold Ct. M16: W Ran 4A **80**
 (off Wilbraham Rd.)
Arnold Dr. M24: Mid 3E **17**
 M43: Droy 1C **70**
Arnold Rd. M16: W Ran 4A **80**
Arnold St. OL1: O'ham 1C **30**
 OL6: A Lyme 3E **59**
 SK3: Stoc 4A **106**
Arnold Wlk. M34: Dent 5C **86**
 (off Wordsworth Rd.)
Arnott Cres. M15: Man 5B **66**
Arnside Av. OL9: Chad 4C **28**
 SK4: Stoc 2F **95**
Arnside Cl. SK8: Gat 2D **111**
Arnside Dr. M6: Sal 4D **49**
 SK14: Hyde 1E **87**
Arnside Gro. M33: Sale 3D **89**
Arnside St. M14: Man 3D **81**
Arosa Ct. M8: Man 1E **93**
Arran Av. M32: Stre 3C **76**
 M33: Sale 5E **89**
 OL8: O'ham 1B **44**
Arrandale Ct. M41: Urm 2F **75**
Arran Gdns. M41: Urm 5E **61**
 (not continuous)
Arran Rd. SK16: Duk 3E **73**
Arran St. M7: Sal 1F **51**
 M40: Man 4B **40**
Arras Gro. M34: Dent 2B **84**
Arreton Sq. M14: Man 2F **81**
 (off Rusholme Gro.)
Arrivals Way M90: Man A 2D **113**
Arrowfield Rd. M21: Chor 2F **91**
Arrowsmith Wlk. M11: Man 1B **68**
 (off Redfield Cl.)
Arrow St. M7: Sal 2F **51**
Arrow Trad. Est. M34: Aud 5F **71**
Arthog Rd. M20: Man 5E **93**
Arthur Millwood Ct. M3: Sal 5D **5**
Arthur Rd. M16: Old T 2E **79**
Arthur St. BL4: Farn 1A **18**
 (off Ellesmere St.)
 M25: Pres 5B **22**
 M27: Swin 5F **33**
 (not continuous)
 M28: Walk 2B **32**
 (Old Clough La.)
 M28: Walk 3A **32**
 (Walkden Rd.)

Arthur St. M30: Ecc 1E **61**
   SK5: Stoc 1A **96**
   (not continuous)
   SK14: Hyde 4E **87**
Arthur Ter. SK5: Stoc 1A **96**
   (off Arthur St.)
Artillery Ct. M13: Man 3E **67**
   (off Wadeson Rd.)
Artillery Pl. M22: Wyth 2B **110**
Artillery St. M3: Man 2F **9** (2A **66**)
ArTzu Gallery .4E **7**
Arundale Av. M16: W Ran 4A **80**
Arundale Ct. M16: W Ran 4A **80**
   (off Arundale Av.)
Arundel Av. M45: White 2D **23**
Arundel Cl. M9: Man 4C **24**
Arundel St. M15: Man 4D **9** (3F **65**)
   M27: Ward 3E **33**
   OL4: O'ham 2E **31**
   OL6: A Lyme 4F **59**
Arundel Wlk. OL9: Chad 3C **28**
Asbury Ct. M30: Ecc 4E **47**
Asby Cl. M24: Mid 4F **15**
Ascension Rd. M7: Sal 3F **51**
Ascot Av. M32: Stre 2B **78**
Ascot Cl. OL9: Chad 2E **29**
Ascot Ct. M7: Sal 1F **51**
Ascot Pde. M19: Man 2B **94**
Ascot Rd. M40: Man 3D **55**
Ascot Wlk. M6: Sal 2C **50**
Ascroft Ct. OL1: O'ham 4E **117**
Ascroft St. OL1: O'ham 4E **117** (3B **30**)
   OL9: Chad 4C **28**
Asgard Dr. M5: Sal 3B **8** (2E **65**)
Asgard Gro. M5: Sal 3B **8**
Ash Av. SK8: Chea 1F **111**
Ashbourne Av. M24: Mid 3E **17**
   M41: Urm 3A **74**
   SK8: Chea 5B **104**
Ashbourne Cres. M33: Sale 1F **99**
Ashbourne Gro. M7: Sal 5A **38**
   M28: Wors 4A **32**
   M45: White 1F **21**
Ashbourne Rd. M6: Sal 2E **49**
   M30: Ecc 1A **62**
   M32: Stre 1C **76**
   M34: Dent 3A **86**
Ashbourne Sq. OL8: O'ham 4A **30**
Ashbridge M17: T Pk 4D **63**
   (not continuous)
Ashbridge Rd. M35: Fail 1D **57**
Ashbrook Av. M34: Dent 2D **85**
Ashbrook Cl. M34: Dent 2D **85**
   M45: White 5D **13**
   SK8: H Grn 5D **111**
Ashbrook Farm Cl. SK5: Stoc 3B **84**
Ashbrook La. SK5: Stoc 3B **84**
Ashbrook St. M11: Man 3C **70**
Ashburn Av. M19: Man 3B **94**
Ashburne Hall M14: Man 4F **81**
Ashburne Ho. M14: Man 1F **81**
   (off Conyngham Rd.)
Ashburn Gro. SK4: Stoc 5F **95**
Ashburn Rd. SK4: Stoc 5E **95**
Ashburton Rd. W. M17: T Pk 3F **61**
   M41: Urm 3F **61**
Ashbury Pl. M40: Man 3A **54**
Ashburys Station (Rail) 3C **68**
Ashby Av. M19: Man 4A **94**
Ashby Gro. M45: White 2D **23**

Ash Cl. OL6: A Lyme 2F **59**
   SK2: Stoc 5E **107**
Ashcombe Wlk. M11: Man 1B **68**
   (off Newcombe Cl.)
Ashcott Av. M22: Wyth 2F **109**
Ash Ct. M16: W Ran 3A **80**
   SK4: Stoc 5D **95**
Ashcroft Av. M6: Sal 3A **50**
Ashdale Cl. SK5: Stoc 3B **96**
Ashdale Cres. M43: Droy 1B **70**
Ashdale Dr. M20: Man 4F **93**
   SK8: H Grn 4D **111**
Ashdene OL6: A Lyme 5F **59**
Ashdene Cl. OL1: Chad 1E **29**
Ashdene Rd. M20: Man 2F **93**
   SK4: Stoc 1F **103**
Ashdown Av. M9: Man 5F **25**
Ashdown Dr. M27: Swin 1C **48**
Ashdown Rd. SK4: Stoc 5E **95**
Ashdown Ter. M9: Man 5F **25**
Ash Dr. M27: Ward 2E **33**
Ashfell Ct. M21: Chor 5B **78**
Ashfield M34: Dent 5C **72**
Ashfield Cl. M6: Sal 4A **50**
Ashfield Cres. SK8: Chea 5F **103**
Ashfield Dr. M40: Man 3F **55**
Ashfield Gro. M18: Man 1B **84**
Ashfield Lodge M20: Man 1B **102**
Ashfield Rd. M13: Man 2A **82**
   M33: Sale 3D **89**
   M41: Urm 3F **75**
   SK8: Chea 5F **103**
Ashfield Sq. M43: Droy 5B **56**
Ashfield St. OL8: O'ham 1E **43**
Ashford Av. M27: Swin 1E **47**
   M30: Ecc 1E **47**
   SK5: Stoc 3B **84**
Ashford Cl. SK9: Hand 5E **115**
Ashford Ct. OL4: O'ham 1F **31**
   SK5: Stoc 3B **84**
   (off Ashford Av.)
Ashford Gro. M28: Wors 4B **32**
Ashford Rd. M20: Man 1C **92**
   SK4: Stoc 2F **95**
Ashford Wlk. OL9: Chad 3D **29**
Ashgate Av. M22: Wyth 2A **110**
Ashgill Wlk. M9: Man 5A **40**
   (off Osborne Rd.)
Ash Gro. M14: Man 1A **82**
   M25: Pres 3C **22**
   M27: Swin 2F **47**
   M28: Walk 3A **32**
   M32: Stre 5E **77**
   M43: Droy 2C **70**
   SK4: Stoc 3F **95**
   SK8: H Grn 1D **115**
   SK9: Hand 5E **115**
   (off Sagars Rd.)
   WA15: Tim 4B **98**
Ashill Wlk. M3: Man 2F **9**
Ashkirk St. M18: Man 5F **69**
Ashlands M33: Sale 3C **88**
Ashlands Av.
   M27: Swin 1E **47**
   M40: Man 3E **41**
Ashlands Dr. M34: Aud 4A **72**
Ashlands Rd. WA15: Tim 2C **98**
Ashlar Dr. M12: Man 2F **67**
Ash-Lea Ct. M25: Pres 5C **22**
   (off Greengate La.)

Ash Lea Grange M30: Ecc 4B 48
Ashleigh Gdns. M9: Man 3E 39
Ashleigh Rd. WA15: Tim 3D 99
Ashley Av. M16: Old T 1F 79
  M27: Swin 1F 47
  M41: Urm 3A 74
Ashley Ct. M27: Pen 2B 34
              (off Hall St.)
  M40: Man 3B 42
  SK4: Stoc 4D 95
        (off Heaton Moor Rd.)
Ashley Ct. Dr. M40: Man 3B 42
Ashley Cres. M27: Swin 5F 33
Ashley Dr. M27: Swin 5F 33
  M33: Sale 1A 98
Ashley La. M9: Man 4B 40
Ashley M. M45: White 2D 23
Ashley Rd. M43: Droy 5A 56
  SK2: Stoc 3E 107
Ashleys, The SK4: Stoc 1D 95
Ashley St. M4: Man 2E 7 (4D 53)
  M6: Sal .5A 50
  OL9: O'ham 1E 29
Ashlyn Gro. M40: Man 5F 41
Ashlynne OL6: A Lyme 4E 59
Ashmill Wlk. M9: Man 1E 53
Ashmoor M22: Wyth 5A 110
Ashmoor Wlk. M22: Wyth 5A 110
Ashmore Av. SK3: Stoc 4B 104
Ashmount Ct. SK4: Stoc 1B 104
Ashness Dr. M24: Mid 3F 15
Ashover Av. M12: Man 4B 68
Ashover St. M32: Stre 2A 78
Ashridge Dr. M30: Ecc 2E 61
  SK16: Duk 3D 73
Ash Rd. BL4: Kea 4B 18
  M34: Dent 2B 84
  M43: Droy 5B 56
Ash Sq. OL4: O'ham 1F 31
Ashstead Rd. M33: Sale 2E 99
Ash St. M6: Sal 5B 50
  M9: Man 5F 39
  M24: Mid 5E 17
  M34: Aud 3F 71
  M35: Fail 4A 42
  OL4: O'ham 3D 31
  SK3: Stoc 3D 105
Ashton Av. WA14: Alt 5A 98
Ashton Ct. M33: Sale 4A 88
  M34: Aud 4B 72
Ashton Cres. OL9: Chad 1C 42
Ashton Gro. M9: Man 5F 25
Ashton Hill La. M43: Droy 2C 70
Ashton Ho. M4: Man 2C 6
  M15: Man 3D 9
Ashton La. M24: Mid 1C 26
  M33: Sale 3B 88
Ashton New Rd. M11: Man 1A 68
  M12: Man 1A 68
Ashton Old Rd. M11: Man 2F 67
  M12: Man 2F 67
Ashton on Mersey Health & Fitness Cen.
  . . . . .5A 88
Ashton Retail Pk.
  OL6: A Lyme 1B 116 (4D 59)
Ashton Rd. M9: Man 4F 25
  M34: Dent 5A 72
  M35: Fail 1E 57
  M43: Droy 1D 71
  OL8: O'ham 5D 117 (4A 30)

Ashton Rd. SK6: Bred . . . . .3F 97 & 5A 86
  SK14: Hyde 4F 73
Ashton Rd. E. M35: Fail 4B 42
Ashton Rd. W. M35: Fail 5A 42
Ashton St. OL9: Chad 1C 42
  SK16: Duk 4C 72
Ashton Swimming Pool 2B 116 (4D 59)
ASHTON-UNDER-LYNE 1C 116 (4D 59)
Ashton-under-Lyne Station (Rail)
  . . . . .1C 116 (4D 59)
Ash Tree Av. M43: Droy 5B 56
Ash Tree Rd. M8: Man 3C 38
Ashurst Av. M11: Man 5D 55
Ashurst Dr. SK3: Stoc 5D 105
Ashurst Gdns. OL6: A Lyme 2D 59
Ashurst Gro. M26: Rad 1D 21
Ashurst Rd. M22: Wyth 2B 110
Ash Vw. OL6: A Lyme 3E 59
Ashville Ter. M40: Man 3B 40
Ash Wlk. M24: Mid 3B 26
  OL9: Chad 1D 29
Ashway OL6: A Lyme 2A 116 (4C 58)
Ashway Clough SK2: Stoc 5F 107
          (not continuous)
Ashwell Rd. M23: Wyth 4D 101
Ashwin Wlk. M8: Man 1B 52
        (off Ermington Dr.)
Ashwood M26: Rad 2D 19
  OL9: Chad 2A 28
Ashwood Av. M20: Man 4A 92
  M33: Sale 5A 88
  M34: Dent 2C 84
  M41: Urm 3A 74
Ashworth Cl. OL9: Chad 5D 29
Ashworth St. M34: Dent 1A 86
  M35: Fail 1F 55
  OL1: O'ham 4F 117 (3B 30)
        (not continuous)
Asia Ho. M1: Man 3D 11 (2C 66)
Askern Av. M22: Wyth 3F 109
Askett Cl. M40: Man 1F 55
Askrigg Wlk. M13: Man 1B 82
        (off Bates St.)
Aspell Cl. M24: Mid 1B 26
Aspen Cl. SK4: Stoc 2C 104
  WA15: Tim 1A 108
Aspen Grn. M34: Dent 3C 86
Aspens, The SK8: Gat 5C 102
Aspenwood Dr. M9: Man 2F 39
  OL9: Chad 2A 28
Aspinall Gdns. M24: Mid 2F 27
Aspinall St. M24: Mid 2E 27
  M14: Man 2E 81
Aspin La. M4: Man 2C 6 (4C 52)
Aspull St. OL4: O'ham 4E 31
Aspull Wlk. M13: Man 4E 67
Asquith Av. SK16: Duk 4E 73
Asquith Rd. M19: Man 2B 94
Asquith St. SK5: Stoc 4B 84
Assheton Av. M34: Aud 1E 71
Assheton Cl. OL6: A Lyme . . .1B 116 (4D 59)
Assheton Cres. M40: Man 3F 55
Assheton Ho. OL6: A Lyme 1B 116
Assheton Rd. M40: Man 3F 55
Assheton St. M24: Mid 4C 16
Assheton Way M24: Mid 1C 26
Assisi Gdns. M12: Man 4D 69
Assumption Rd. M24: Mid 3F 15
Astan Av. M43: Droy 4F 55

Astbury Av. M21: Chor 4E **91**
    M34: Aud 1F **71**
Astbury Cl. WA15: Alt 5A **98**
Astbury Cres. SK3: Stoc 5F **105**
Aster Ho. OL1: O'ham 1A **30**
Aster St. OL1: O'ham 1A **30**
Astley Gdns. SK16: Duk 2D **73**
Astley St. M11: Man 1A **68**
    SK4: Stoc 2A **118** (2A **106**)
    SK16: Duk 3C **72**
Astley Ter. *SK16: Duk* 1E **73**
    (off Peel St.)
Aston Av. M14: Man 3B **80**
Aston Cl. SK3: Stoc 5E **105**
Aston Cl. OL1: O'ham 1D **117**
Aston Way *SK9: Hand* 4F **115**
    (off Spath La.)
Astor Rd. M19: Man 1A **94**
    M50: Sal 1E **63**
Astra Bus. Pk. M17: T Pk 2B **62**
Astral M. M14: Man 3F **81**
Atcham Gro. M9: Man 3D **25**
Athenian Gdns. M7: Sal 2E **51**
Athens St. SK1: Stoc 2C **106**
Athens Way OL4: Lees 3F **31**
Atherfield Cl. M18: Man 4B **70**
Atherley Gro. M40: Man 2B **42**
    OL9: Chad 2B **42**
Atherstone Av. M8: Man 2C **38**
Atherton Cl. M35: Fail 2D **57**
Atherton St. M3: Man 1E **9** (1A **66**)
    M30: Ecc 1D **61**
    OL4: Lees 4F **31**
    SK3: Stoc 3F **105**
Atherton Way M30: Ecc 1D **61**
Athlone Av. M40: Man 4C **40**
Athole Av. M5: Sal 1B **64**
Atholl Av. M32: Stre 3C **76**
Athol Rd. M16: W Par 4A **80**
Athol St. M18: Man 2A **84**
    M30: Ecc 1D **61**
    OL6: A Lyme 4E **59**
    SK4: Stoc 5F **95**
Athos Wlk. M40: Man 2E **41**
Atkinson Ho. *M33: Sale* 3D **89**
    (off Atkinson Rd.)
Atkinson Rd. M33: Sale 2C **88**
    M41: Urm 3F **75**
Atkinson St. M3: Man 1F **9** (1A **66**)
    OL9: O'ham 1F **29**
    SK1: Stoc 4C **106**
Atkin St. M28: Walk 2A **32**
Atlanta Av. M90: Man A 1C **112**
Atlantic Wlk. *M11: Man* 1B **68**
    (off Yeoman Wlk.)
Atlas Bus. Pk. M22: Wyth 5B **110**
Atlas St. OL7: A Lyme 2C **58**
    OL8: O'ham 5D **117**
    SK16: Duk 2F **73**
Atlow Dr. M23: Wyth 1D **109**
Atrium, The M45: White 2B **22**
Attenburys La. WA14: Tim 3A **98**
Attenbury's Pk. Est. WA14: Tim 3A **98**
Attercliffe Rd. M21: Chor 1C **90**
Attewell St. M11: Man 2C **68**
Attingham Wlk. M34: Dent 4A **86**
Attleboro Rd. M40: Man 5C **40**
    (not continuous)
Attlee Way M12: Man 1A **68**
Attock Cl. OL9: Chad 4D **29**

Attwood Rd. WA15: Tim 5D **99**
Attwood St. M12: Man 2C **82**
Atwood Rd. M20: Man 5E **93**
Atwood St. M1: Man 3C **10** (2C **66**)
Auberge Ho. SK2: Stoc 5D **107**
Aubrey Rd. M14: Man 1A **94**
Aubrey St. M50: Sal 2C **64**
Auburn Av. SK14: Hyde 4F **87**
Auburn Dr. M41: Urm 4A **76**
Auburn Rd. M16: Old T 1D **79**
    M34: Dent 3A **86**
Auburn St. M1: Man 2E **11** (1D **67**)
Auckland Dr. M6: Sal 2C **50**
Auckland Rd. M19: Man 5B **82**
Audax Wlk. M40: Man 3D **55**
Auden Cl. M11: Man 1F **69**
Auden Ct. *M11: Man* 1F **69**
    (off Auden Cl.)
AUDENSHAW 4B **72**
Audenshaw Ct. M34: Aud 4A **72**
Audenshaw Hall Gro. M34: Aud 3D **71**
Audenshaw Rd. M34: Aud 3D **71**
    (not continuous)
Audlem Cl. M40: Man 5F **53**
Audley Av. M32: Stre 1B **76**
Audley Rd. M19: Man 3D **83**
Audley St. OL6: A Lyme 5F **59**
Audrey Av. M18: Man 5A **70**
Audrey St. M9: Man 5B **40**
Augustine Webster Cl. M9: Man 4A **40**
Augustus St. M3: Man 1C **6** (3C **52**)
Augustus Way M15: Man 1A **80**
Auriga Wlk. M7: Sal 1B **4**
Austell Rd. M22: Wyth 1F **113**
Austen Rd. M30: Ecc 1F **61**
Austin Cl. *M14: Man* 5C **80**
    (off Bethnall Dr.)
Austin Ct. *M20: Man* 4E **93**
    (off Milden Cl.)
Austin Dr. M20: Man 4E **93**
Austin Gro. M19: Man 5B **82**
Austins Fold M6: Sal 1F **49**
Autumn St. M13: Man 1E **81**
Avalon Dr. M20: Man 3E **103**
Avebury Cl. M7: Sal 1B **52**
Avebury Rd. M23: Wyth 1C **108**
Avenham Cl. M15: Man 5A **66**
Avening Wlk. M22: Wyth 4E **109**
Avenue, The M7: Sal 2E **51**
    M20: Man 3A **92**
    M28: Wors 5A **32**
    (Delaford Av.)
    M28: Wors 3A **46**
    (Rock Rd.)
    M30: Ecc 1F **61**
    M33: Sale 5A **88**
    M41: Urm 3A **74**
    SK6: Bred 5F **97**
    SK8: H Grn 5C **110**
Avenue St. SK1: Stoc 1C **118** (1B **106**)
Averill St. M40: Man 2F **55**
Aveson Av. M21: Chor 2D **91**
Avian Cl. M30: Ecc 3B **60**
Avian Dr. M14: Man 5D **81**
Aviary Rd. M28: Wors 1B **46**
Aviator Way M22: Wyth 1E **113**
Avonbrook Dr. M40: Man 2B **42**
Avon Cotts. M25: Pres 4A **22**
Avon Ct. *M15: Man* 4F **65**
    (off Eastnor Cl.)

Avoncourt Dr. M20: Man 4C 92
Avondale M27: Clif 2C 34
Avondale Cres. M41: Urm 2E 75
Avondale Dr. M6: Sal 2D 49
Avondale Ind. Est. SK3: Stoc 4D 105
Avondale Lodge M33: Sale 5D 89
        (off Whitehill Rd.)
Avondale Recreation Cen. 4D 105
Avondale Rd. M32: Stre 1A 78
  M45: White 5A 12
  SK3: Stoc 4D 105
Avondale St. M8: Man 5C 38
  OL8: O'ham 5A 30
Avon Gdns. M19: Man 2C 94
Avonlea Dr. M19: Man 2A 94
Avonlea Rd. M33: Sale 2A 98
  M43: Droy 5A 56
Avonleigh Gdns. OL1: O'ham 1E 31
        (off Clyde St.)
Avon Rd. BL4: Kea 4D 19
  M19: Man 2B 94
  OL9: Chad 1B 28
  SK8: H Grn 2D 115
Avon St. OL8: O'ham 5B 30
  SK3: Stoc 4A 106
Avril Cl. SK5: Stoc 5B 84
Avro Cl. M14: Man 4D 81
Avro Ct. M24: Mid 1F 27
Avroe Rd. M30: Ecc 3B 60
Avro Way M90: Man A 2B 112
Axbridge Wlk. M40: Man 5F 53
        (off Ridgway St.)
Axford Cl. M7: Sal 1B 52
Axon Sq. M16: W Ran 1B 80
Aycliffe Av. M21: Chor 3F 91
Aylcliffe Dr. M13: Man 2A 82
Aylesbury Av. M34: Dent 4B 86
  M41: Urm 1A 76
Aylesbury Cl. M5: Sal 1C 64
Aylesbury Gro. M24: Mid 4E 17
Aylesby Av. M18: Man 1D 83
Aylesby Ct. M21: Chor 4E 79
Aylesford Rd. M14: Man 2F 81
Aylestone Wlk. M40: Man 5C 40
        (off Hugo St.)
Aylsham M27: Swin 2F 47
Aylwin Dr. M33: Sale 5E 89
Ayr Av. OL8: O'ham 1B 44
Ayres Rd. M16: Old T 1C 78
Ayrshire Rd. M7: Sal 1D 51
Aysgarth Av. M18: Man 4A 70
  SK8: Chea 5E 103
Aysgarth Cl. M33: Sale 5A 88
Ayton Ct. M16: Old T 1F 79
        (off Ayres Rd.)
Ayton Gro. M14: Man 1A 82
Aytoun St. M1: Man 1D 11 (1C 66)
Azalea Av. M18: Man 4F 69

B

Babbacombe Gro. M9: Man 4D 25
Babbacombe Rd. SK2: Stoc 5E 107
Bk. Acton St. M1: Man 2E 11
Bk. Adcroft St. SK1: Stoc 5C 118
Bk. Ashley St. M4: Man 2E 7
Bk. Bridge St. M3: Man 5A 6
Bk. Cambridge St. OL7: A Lyme 1B 72
        (off Bennett St.)
Bk. Camp St. M7: Sal 2F 51
Bk. Chapel St. M19: Man 4C 82
        (off Bankley St.)
  M30: Ecc 5B 48
        (off Church St.)
Bk. China La. M1: Man 1E 11 (1D 67)
Bk. College Land M3: Man 4A 6
Bk. Deacon's Dr. M6: Sal 1F 49
Bk. Deyne Av. M25: Pres 5D 23
Bk. Duncan St. M7: Sal 5E 37
Bk. Elsworth St. M8: Man 1C 6
Bk. Fletcher St. M26: Rad 2D 19
Backford Wlk. M20: Man 1C 92
Bk. George St. M1: Man 2C 10 (2C 66)
        (not continuous)
Bk. Gladstone St. OL4: O'ham 3D 31
Bk. Greaves St. OL1: O'ham 3F 117
Bk. Hamilton St. M7: Sal 5F 37
Bk. Hampson St. M40: Man 3F 53
        (off Hampson St.)
Bk. Hilton St. M7: Sal 5F 37
Bk. Hope St. M7: Sal 5F 37
Bk. Howe St. M7: Sal 5E 37
Bk. Hulme St. M5: Sal 5B 4 (1E 65)
Bk. King St. OL1: O'ham 4D 117 (3A 30)
Back La. OL7: A Lyme 2A 58
        (not continuous)
Bk. Massie St. SK8: Chea 5F 103
Back Piccadilly M1: Man 5D 7 (1C 66)
Bk. Pool Fold M2: Man 5B 6 (1B 66)
Bk. Portland St.
  OL6: A Lyme 3A 116 (5C 58)
Bk. Quay St. M3: Man 1E 9
Bk. Red Bank M4: Man 1D 7 (4C 52)
Bk. Roman Rd. M7: Sal 1A 52
        (off Appian Way)
Bk. St George's Rd. M4: Man . . .2F 7 (4D 53)
Bk. St James St. OL1: O'ham 2D 31
Bk. St Marks' La. M8: Man 4B 38
        (off Cheetham Hill Rd.)
Bk. Scott St. OL8: O'ham 4B 30
        (off Scott St.)
Bk. South Pde. M3: Man 5A 6
Bk. Spear St. M1: Man 4E 7
Bk. Thomas St. M4: Man 4D 7
Backton Pl. M40: Man 3F 53
        (off Sawley Rd.)
Bk. Tootal Rd. M5: Sal 5F 49
        (off Tootal Rd.)
Bk. Turner St. M4: Man 4D 7 (5C 52)
Bk. Vernon St. SK14: Hyde 3F 87
        (off Vernon St.)
Bk. Water St. OL6: A Lyme 3E 59
  SK1: Stoc 1C 118
Bk. Young St. BL4: Farn 2A 18
Bacon Av. M34: Dent 5C 86
Bacup St. M40: Man 4C 40
Badby Cl. M4: Man 1F 67
Baddeley Cl. SK3: Stoc 5F 105
Badgers Wlk. M22: Wyth 5A 110
Bagnall Ct. M22: Nor 3A 102
Bagnall Wlk. M22: Nor 3A 102
Bagot St. M11: Man 5E 55
  M27: Ward 3E 33
Bagshaw St. SK14: Hyde 5F 73
BAGULEY 4B 100
Baguley Cres. M24: Mid 2C 24
  SK3: Stoc 5F 105
Baguley Dr. BL9: Bury 4C 12

Baguley La. M33: Sale 5A 90
 (not continuous)
Baguley Rd. M33: Sale 4A 90
Baguley St. M43: Droy 1D 71
Baildon St. M40: Man 3C 40
Bailey St. M90: Man A 5D 109
Bailey Rd. M17: T Pk 3C 62
Bailey St. M11: Man 1A 70
 M25: Pres 5E 23
 OL1: O'ham 3F 117 (2C 30)
Baillie St. M26: Rad 1A 12
Bails, The M7: Sal 1E 51
 M28: Walk 1A 32
Bainbridge Cl. M12: Man 4F 67
Bainbridge Rd. OL4: O'ham 1F 31
Bainburgh Clough
 OL8: O'ham 5E 31
Bain St. M27: Swin 5B 34
Bainton Wlk. M9: Man 4E 25
 (off Munn Rd.)
Baird St. M1: Man 2F 11 (2D 67)
Bakersfield Pl. M33: Sale 4E 89
Baker St. BL4: Kea 3D 19
 M24: Mid 1D 27
 SK4: Stoc 5A 96
 WA15: Tim 4E 99
Bakery Ct. OL6: A Lyme 2F 59
Bakewell Av. M34: Dent 5C 86
Bakewell Rd. M30: Ecc 2E 61
 M32: Stre 2C 76
 M43: Droy 5A 56
Bakewell St. M18: Man 1E 83
 SK3: Stoc 3F 105
Bala Cl. M5: Sal 5C 50
Baldock Rd. M20: Man 5F 93
Baldwin Rd. M19: Man 2B 94
Bale St. M2: Man 2B 10 (2B 66)
Balfour Gro. SK5: Stoc 5B 84
Balfour Rd. M41: Urm 3D 75
 WA14: B'ath 4A 98
Balfour St. M6: Sal 1C 50
 M8: Man .4C 38
 OL4: O'ham 2E 31
Balham Wlk. M12: Man 4B 68
 (off Pollitt Cl.)
Ballantine St. M40: Man 3E 55
Ballater Av. M41: Urm 4C 74
Ballater Wlk. M8: Man 5B 38
 (off Heath St.)
Ballbrook Av. M20: Man 3C 92
Ballbrook Ct. M20: Man 4D 93
Balleratt St. M19: Man 4C 82
Balliol St. M8: Man 4C 38
 M27: Swin 4A 34
Balloon La. M4: Man 3C 6
Balloon St. M4: Man 3C 6 (5C 52)
Balmain Av. M18: Man 2E 83
Balmain Rd. M41: Urm 2D 75
Balmer Dr. M23: Wyth 2D 109
Balmfield St. M8: Man 2C 52
Balmforth St. M15: Man 4D 9
Balmoral Av. M32: Stre 2F 77
 M34: Aud 3F 71
 M41: Urm 4D 75
 M45: White 2C 22
 SK14: Hyde 5F 87
Balmoral Cl. BL9: Bury 1C 12
Balmoral Ct. M9: Man 4C 24
 OL7: A Lyme 5A 116

Balmoral Dr. M34: Dent 1C 84
 WA14: Tim 3B 98
Balmoral Grange M25: Pres 1A 38
Balmoral Ho. M30: Ecc 5E 47
 (off Queen Victoria St.)
Balmoral Rd. M14: Man 5F 81
 M27: Clif .2C 34
 M41: Urm 4C 74
 SK4: Stoc 5C 94
Balmoral St. M18: Man 1E 83
Balsam Cl. M13: Man 5F 11 (3E 67)
Baltic St. M5: Sal 5A 50
Baltimore St. M40: Man 2B 54
Bamber Av. M33: Sale 5A 90
Bamburgh Dr. OL7: A Lyme 2A 58
Bamford Av. M24: Mid 4C 16
 M34: Dent 5B 86
Bamford Bus. Pk. SK4: Stoc 3A 96
Bamford Cl. SK8: H Grn 1F 115
Bamford Gdns. WA15: Tim 5F 99
Bamford Gro. M20: Man 5C 92
 M20: Man 4F 25
 M20: Man 5C 92
Bamford St. M11: Man 5D 55
 OL9: Chad 1E 29
 SK1: Stoc 4B 118 (3B 106)
Bampton Cl. SK2: Stoc 4D 107
Bampton Rd. M22: Wyth 5F 109
Bampton Wlk. M24: Mid 4A 16
Banbury Dr. WA14: Tim 3A 98
Banbury M. M27: Ward 3F 33
Banbury Rd. M23: Wyth 1B 108
 M24: Mid 4B 26
 M35: Fail .3A 56
Banbury St. SK1: Stoc 3B 118 (2B 106)
Bancroft Cl. SK6: Bred 5F 97
Bancroft Rd. M27: Swin 3A 34
Bandy Flds. Pl. M7: Sal 2F 51
Banff Rd. M14: Man 1E 81
Bangor Rd. SK8: Chea 5B 104
Bangor St. M15: Man 5F 65
 OL6: A Lyme 5F 59
 SK5: Stoc 4B 96
Bank Bri. Rd. M11: Man 4D 55
Bankfield Av. M13: Man 2A 82
 M43: Droy 5C 56
 SK4: Stoc 1E 105
Bankfield Bus. Pk. SK5: Stoc 4A 96
Bankfield Dr. OL8: O'ham 2D 45
Bankfield Rd. BL4: Farn 3A 18
 M33: Sale 2A 88
Bankfield St. M9: Man 4F 39
 M26: Rad 2F 19
 SK5: Stoc 4A 96
Bankfoot Wlk. M8: Man 2C 52
 (off Barnsdale Dr.)
Bankhall Rd. SK4: Stoc 5C 94
Bankhall Wlk. M9: Man 5A 40
 (off Craigend Dr.)
Bank Hill St. OL4: O'ham 2E 31
Bankhirst Cl. M8: Man 3C 38
Bank Ho. Rd. M9: Man 5D 25
Bank La. M6: Sal 2F 49
 M27: Pen .1F 49
Bankley St. M19: Man 4C 82
Bankmill Cl. M13: Man 5F 11
Bank Pl. M3: Sal 4C 4
Bank Rd. M8: Man 2C 38
Banks Ct. WA15: Tim 5F 99

Bankside Av. M26: Rad 2A 12
Bankside Cl. OL9: O'ham 3F 29
Bankside Ct. M12: Man 1C 82
    SK4: Stoc 1C 104
Bankside Rd. M20: Man 4D 103
Banks La. SK1: Stoc 3D 107
Banksman Way M27: Pen 4F 35
Bank St. BL4: Farn 1A 18
    M3: Sal 4C 4 (5F 51)
    M7: Sal 4B 38
    M11: Man .4C 54
    M33: Sale .3E 89
    M34: Aud .4B 72
    M34: Dent .5D 87
    M43: Droy .2B 70
    M45: White 5A 12
    OL4: O'ham 3F 31
    OL7: A Lyme 4B 116 (5D 59)
    SK8: Chea 5A 104
    SK14: Hyde 2F 87
BANK TOP
    OL4 . . . . .3F 31
    OL8 . . . . .3A 30
Bank Top M24: Mid 2C 26
    OL6: A Lyme 5E 59
Bank Top Pk. OL4: O'ham 3F 31
Bank Top Vw. BL4: Kea 2C 18
Bankwell St. M15: Man 5A 66
Bankwood Dr. M9: Man 3F 39
Bannach Dr. OL9: Chad 1C 28
Bannatyne Cl. M40: Man 3A 42
Bannatyne's Health Club
    Manchester, Quay St. 1F 9
    Manchester, Whitworth St. 2D 11
Banner Dale Cl. M13: Man *1B 82*
    (off Bowscale Cl.)
Bannerman Av. M25: Pres 1D 37
Bannerman Rd. M43: Droy 1D 71
Banner Wlk. M11: Man *1B 68*
    (off Pilgrim Dr.)
Bannister St. SK1: Stoc 4B 106
Bann St. SK3: Stoc 3A 106
Banstead Av. M22: Nor 4F 101
Bantry Dr. M9: Man 1D 39
Baptist St. M4: Man 2E 7 (4D 53)
Barbeck Cl. M40: Man 4A 54
Barber St. M11: Man 3A 70
Barbican St. M20: Man 1D 93
    (not continuous)
Barbirolli Sq. M2: Man 3B 10
Barbury Ct. BL4: Farn 2A 18
Barcheston Rd. SK8: Chea 2E 111
Barcicroft Rd. M19: Man 4A 94
    M19: Man 4A 94
Barcicroft Wlk. M19: Man 4A 94
Barclay Dr. M30: Ecc 4A 48
Barclays Av. M6: Sal 1F 49
Barcliffe Av. M40: Man 2E 41
Barcombe Cl. M32: Stre 2B 76
Barcombe Wlk. M9: Man *5F 39*
    (off Fernclough Rd., not continuous)
Bardon Rd. M23: Wyth 5B 100
Bardsea Av. M22: Wyth 5F 109
BARDSLEY 4C 44
Bardsley Av. M35: Fail 5B 42
Bardsley St. M24: Mid 5C 16
    M40: Man 2F 55
    OL4: O'ham 1F 31
    OL9: Chad 1B 42
    SK4: Stoc 5F 95

Bardsley Va. Av. OL8: O'ham 4C 44
Barff Rd. M5: Sal 5E 49
Barford Wlk. M23: Wyth 2D 109
Bar Gap Rd. OL1: O'ham 1E 117 (1B 30)
Baric Cl. M30: Ecc *1B 62*
    (off Lane End)
Baring St. M1: Man 3F 11 (2D 67)
Baring St. Ind. Est. M1: Man . .3F 11 (2E 67)
Barkan Way M27: Pen 4D 35
Barkers La. M33: Sale 3B 88
Barker St. M3: Man 1A 6 (4B 52)
    OL1: O'ham 2D 117 (2A 30)
Barking St. M40: Man 4A 54
Bark St. BL4: Kea 4D 19
Bark Wlk. M15: Man 5B 10
Barkway Rd. M32: Stre 3C 76
Barkworth Wlk. *M40: Man* *1D 55*
    (off Harold Priestnall Cl.)
Barlby Wlk. *M40: Man* *1D 55*
    (off Harold Priestnall Cl.)
Barlea Av. M40: Man 3F 41
Barleycorn Cl. M33: Sale 5C 90
Barleycroft St. M16: W Ran 1B 80
Barleyfield Wlk. M24: Mid 5B 16
Barleywood Dr. M11: Man 2B 68
Barlow Ct. M28: Walk 1A 32
BARLOW FOLD 1A 12
Barlow Fold BL9: Bury 1B 12
Barlow Fold Cl. BL9: Bury 1A 12
Barlow Fold Rd. SK5: Stoc 5B 84
Barlow Hall Rd. M21: Chor 3E 91
Barlow Ho. OL8: O'ham 5E 117 (4A 30)
Barlow La. M30: Ecc 5E 47
Barlow La. Nth. SK5: Stoc 5B 84
BARLOW MOOR 3E 91
Barlow Moor Cl. M20: Man 4B 92
Barlow Moor Rd. M21: Chor 4D 79
Barlow Rd. M5: Sal 1B 8 (1E 65)
    M19: Man 4C 82
    M32: Stre 1B 78
    SK16: Duk 2F 73
Barlow's Cft. M3: Sal . . . .*4F 5 (5A 52)*
Barlow St. M30: Ecc 1F 61
    OL4: O'ham 3C 30
Barlow Ter. M21: Chor 2E 91
Barlow Wlk. *SK5: Stoc* *5B 84*
    (off Barlow La. Nth.)
Barmouth St. M11: Man 2B 68
Barmouth Wlk. OL8: O'ham 2D 43
Barnacre Av. M23: Wyth 3B 108
Barnard Av. M45: White 2D 23
    SK4: Stoc 1D 105
Barnard Cl. OL7: A Lyme 2B 58
Barnard Rd. M18: Man 2D 83
Barnby St. M12: Man 2C 82
Barnclose Rd. M22: Wyth 5F 109
Barncroft Gdns. M22: Wyth 1E 109
Barncroft Rd. BL4: Farn 1A 18
Barnes Av. SK4: Stoc 1C 104
Barnes Cl. BL4: Farn 1A 18
BARNES GREEN 3F 39
Barnes Ho. BL4: Farn *1A 18*
    (off Hesketh Wlk.)
Barnes Ter. BL4: Kea 2C 18
Barneswell St. M40: Man 2E 55
Barnett Av. M20: Man 2D 93
Barnett Dr. M3: Sal 3D 5 (5F 51)
Barnfield M41: Urm 4D 75
Barnfield Cl. M5: Sal 1B 64
Barnfield Cres. M33: Sale 3B 88

Barnfield Ho. M3: Sal 4A **6**
Barnfield Rd. M19: Man 4A **94**
  M27: Ward 2F **33**
Barnfield St. M34: Dent 1F **85**
Barnfield Wlk. WA15: Tim 5E **99**
  (off Merefield Rd.)
Barngate Rd. SK8: Gat 5C **102**
Barn Gro. M34: Aud 3A **72**
Barnham Wlk. M23: Wyth 3A **100**
Barnhill Av. M25: Pres 2D **37**
Barnhill Dr. M25: Pres 1D **37**
Barnhill Rd. M25: Pres 1D **37**
Barnhill St. M14: Man 1B **80**
Barnsdale Dr. M8: Man 1C **52**
Barnsfold Av. M14: Man 5E **81**
Barnside Av. M28: Walk 2A **32**
Barnside Way M35: Fail 1E **57**
Barnsley St. SK1: Stoc 3D **107**
Barnstaple Dr. M40: Man 1E **53**
Barnstead Av. M20: Man 3F **93**
Barnston Av. M14: Man 3D **81**
Barn St. M45: White . . . .
  OL1: O'ham 4D **117** (3A **30**)
Barn Wlk. M11: Man 3A **70**
Barnway Wlk. M40: Man 2E **41**
Barnwell Cl. M34: Aud 5A **72**
Barnwood Rd. M23: Wyth 3C **108**
Baroness Gro. M7: Sal 3E **51**
Baron Grn. SK8: H Grn 2F **115**
Barons Ct. M35: Fail 1F **55**
Baron St. OL4: O'ham 4D **31**
Barrack St. M15: Man 5C **8** (3F **65**)
Barra Dr. M41: Urm 5F **61**
Barrass St. M11: Man 3F **69**
Barratt Gdns. M24: Mid 3F **15**
Barrett Av. BL4: Kea 2B **18**
Barrett St. OL4: O'ham 4D **31**
Barrfield Rd. M6: Sal 3A **50**
Barr Hill Av. M6: Sal 2A **50**
Barrhill Cl. M15: Man 5E **9** (4A **66**)
Barrington Av. M43: Droy 1B **70**
Barrington Cl. WA14: Alt 5A **98**
Barrington Rd. WA14: Alt 5A **98**
Barrington St. M11: Man 5E **55**
Barrowfield Rd. M22: Wyth 4C **108**
Barrowfields M24: Mid 4A **16**
Barrowfield Wlk. M24: Mid 5C **16**
Barrow Hill Rd. M8: Man 2B **52**
Barrow St. M3: Sal 5C **4** (1F **65**)
Barry Ct. M20: Man 2D **93**
Barry Lawson Cl. M8: Man 5B **38**
Barry Rd. M23: Wyth 1D **101**
  SK5: Stoc 3B **96**
Barry St. OL1: O'ham 1D **31**
Bartlam Pl. OL1: O'ham 3F **117**
Bartlemore St. OL1: O'ham 1C **30**
Bartlett St. M11: Man 3D **69**
Bartley Rd. M22: Nor 3E **101**
BARTON 2C **60**
Barton Aerodrome Vis. Cen. 3A **60**
Barton Arc. M3: Man 5B **6**
Barton Av. M41: Urm 3D **75**
Barton Bri. M30: Ecc 2F **61**
Barton Bus. Pk. M30: Ecc 1E **61**
Barton Ct. M30: Ecc 2F **61**
  (off Barton La.)
Barton Dock Rd. M32: Stre 5B **62**
  M41: Stre, Urm 4F **61**
Barton Emb. M30: Urm 3E **61**
Barton Fold SK14: Hyde 4F **87**

Barton Hall Av. M30: Ecc 1C **60**
Barton Ho. *M6: Sal* 3E **49**
  (off Moss Mdw. Rd.)
Barton La. M30: Ecc 2F **61**
Barton Moss Rd. M30: Ecc 4A **60**
Barton Pl. M4: Man 1C **6**
Barton Rd. M24: Mid 1B **26**
  M27: Swin 5C **34**
  M28: Wors 2B **46**
  M30: Ecc 1E **61**
  M32: Stre 1B **76**
  M41: Urm 1E **75**
  SK4: Stoc 2A **104**
  SK16: Duk 4E **73**
Barton Sq. M2: Man 5A **6** (1B **66**)
Barton St. BL4: Farn 2A **18**
  M3: Man 3F **9** (2A **66**)
  OL1: O'ham .1F **29**
BARTON UPON IRWELL 2F **61**
Barway Rd. M21: Chor 4B **78**
Barwell Cl. SK5: Stoc 5B **84**
Barwell Rd. M33: Sale 3A **88**
Barwick Pl. M33: Sale 4C **88**
Basechurch Wlk. *M12: Man* 4B **68**
  (off Skarratt Cl.)
Basford Rd. M16: Old T 2D **79**
Basildon Rd. M13: Man 5F **67**
Basil St. M14: Man 2E **81**
  SK4: Stoc 5A **96**
Baslow Av. M19: Man 3E **83**
Baslow Dr. SK8: H Grn 2E **115**
Baslow Gro. SK5: Stoc 3B **96**
Baslow Rd. M32: Stre 2C **76**
  M34: Dent 5B **86**
  M43: Droy 4A **56**
Baslow St. M11: Man 1A **68**
Bassenthwaite Cl.
  M24: Mid 3F **15**
Basset Av. M6: Sal 2E **51**
Bass St. SK16: Duk 2D **73**
Basten Dr. M7: Sal 1A **52**
Batchelor Cl. M21: Chor 1A **92**
Bateson St. SK1: Stoc 1C **106**
Bateson Way
  OL8: O'ham 5E **117** (4B **30**)
Bates St. M13: Man 1B **82**
  SK16: Duk 2E **73**
Bath Cres. M16: Old T 5E **65**
Bath St. OL9: Chad 2D **29**
  OL9: O'ham .4E **29**
Batley St. M9: Man 4A **40**
Batsmans Dr. M27: Clif 5A **20**
Battersby St. M11: Man 3A **70**
Battersea Rd. SK4: Stoc 2A **104**
Batty St. M8: Man 2E **53**
Baxter Gdns. M23: Wyth 4C **100**
Baxter Pk. Tennis Club 1B **110**
Baxter Rd. M33: Sale 4D **89**
Baxter St. OL8: O'ham 2D **43**
Baycliffe Wlk. *M8: Man* 1B **52**
  (off Felthorpe Dr.)
Baycroft Gro. M23: Wyth 2C **100**
Baydon Av. M7: Sal 1B **52**
Bayfield Gro. M40: Man 3C **40**
Bayley Cl. SK14: Hyde 5F **73**
Bayleyfield SK14: Hyde 1F **87**
Bayley St. SK15: Stal 5F **59**
Baynard Wlk. *M9: Man* 5D **25**
  (off Crab La.)
Baysdale Wlk. M11: Man 1B **68**

Bayston Wlk. *M12: Man* 4B **68**
 (off Kempley Cl.)
Bay St. OL9: O'ham 2F **29**
Bayswater Av. M40: Man 3E **55**
Bay Tree Av. M28: Wors 2C **46**
Baytree Av. M34: Dent 1C **86**
 OL9: Chad .1A **28**
Baytree La. M24: Mid 1F **27**
Baywood St. M9: Man 4F **39**
Bazaar St. M6: Sal 3C **50**
Bazley Rd. M22: Nor 2F **101**
BBC Broadcasting House 4D **11** (3C **66**)
Beacon Dr. M23: Wyth 4C **108**
Beaconfield Av. SK14: Hyde 3F **87**
Beacon Gro. OL8: O'ham 5E **31**
Beacon Rd. M17: T Pk 2A **78**
Beaconsfield M14: Man 1E **93**
Beaconsfield Rd. WA14: B'ath 4A **98**
Beadham Dr. M9: Man 4C **24**
Beaford Rd. M22: Wyth 1F **113**
Beagle Wlk. M22: Wyth 1A **114**
Beal Cl. SK4: Stoc 5F **93**
Beale Gro. M21: Chor 5D **79**
Bealey Av. M26: Rad 1A **12**
Bealey Cl. M18: Man 5D **69**
Bealey Ind. Est. M26: Rad 1A **12**
Beal Wlk. M45: White 1E **23**
Beaminster Rd. SK4: Stoc 5B **94**
Beaminster Cl. SK4: Stoc 5B **94**
Beaminster Rd. *SK4: Stoc* *5B 94*
 (off Priestnall Rd.)
Beaminster Rd. SK4: Stoc 5B **94**
Beaminster Wlk. *M13: Man* *5E 67*
 (off Lauderdale Cres.)
Beamish Cl. M13: Man 4E **67**
Beamsley Dr. M22: Wyth 4D **109**
Beanfields M28: Wors 2B **46**
Beanfield Ter. M28: Wors 2B **46**
Beard Rd. M18: Man 1E **83**
Beard St. M43: Droy 1B **70**
Beardwood Rd. M9: Man 5F **25**
Beatrice Av. M18: Man 1B **84**
Beatrice Rd. M28: Wors 5D **33**
Beatrice St. M27: Swin 3F **33**
 M34: Dent .2A **86**
Beatrice Wignall St. M43: Droy 2C **70**
Beattock Cl. M15: Man 5D **9** (3F **65**)
Beauchamp St. OL6: A Lyme 3E **59**
Beaufont Dr. OL4: O'ham 4E **31**
Beaufort Av. M20: Man 3C **92**
 M27: Swin .5F **33**
 M33: Sale .5E **89**
Beaufort Rd. M33: Sale 5E **89**
 OL6: A Lyme 4F **59**
Beaufort St. M3: Man 3E **9** (2A **66**)
 M25: Pres .5E **23**
 M30: Ecc 4D **47**
Beaumaris Cl. M12: Man 4B **68**
Beaumont Cl. *SK9: Hand* *4E 115*
 (off Clay La.)
Beaumont Rd. M21: Chor 1D **91**
Beaumont St. OL6: A Lyme 4E **59**
Beauvale Av. SK2: Stoc 4E **107**
Beaver Dr. BL9: Bury 2D **13**
Beaver Ho. SK1: Stoc 3D **107**
Beaver Rd. M20: Man 5D **93**
Beaver St. M1: Man 3C **10** (2C **66**)
Bebbington Cl. M33: Sale 5B **90**
Bebbington St. M11: Man 1E **69**
Beccles Rd. M33: Sale 2D **99**

Beckenham Rd. M8: Man 5C **38**
Becket Av. M7: Sal 1A **52**
Becket Mdws. OL4: O'ham 3D **31**
Becket Mdw. St. OL4: O'ham 3D **31**
Beckett St. M18: Man 1E **83**
Beckfield Rd. M23: Wyth 1C **108**
Beckfoot Dr. M13: Man 2A **82**
Beckford St. M40: Man 2A **54**
Beck Gro. M28: Walk 3A **32**
Beckhampton Cl. M13: Man 5E **67**
Beckley Av. M25: Pres 2C **36**
Beckside SK5: Stoc 4C **84**
Beck St. M11: Man 3A **70**
Beckton Gdns. M22: Wyth 3E **109**
Becontree Av. M34: Dent 1C **86**
Becontree Dr. M23: Wyth 4F **99**
Bedfont Wlk. *M9: Man* *3A 40*
 (off Hemsley St. Sth.)
Bedford Av. M16: W Ran 5A **80**
 M27: Swin .5A **34**
 M33: Sale .1F **99**
 SK14: Hyde 2F **87**
Bedford Ct. M7: Sal 3F **37**
 WA15: Tim .4B **98**
Bedford Dr. WA15: Tim 4E **99**
Bedford Rd. M16: Old T 2C **78**
 M30: Ecc 4A **48**
 M41: Urm 1E **75**
Bedfordshire Cl. OL9: Chad 4D **29**
Bedford St. M25: Pres 4E **23**
 OL6: A Lyme 5E **59**
 SK5: Stoc .5A **84**
 (not continuous)
Bedford Wlk. M34: Dent 3B **86**
Bedlington Cl. M23: Wyth 5A **100**
Bednal Av. M40: Man 3A **54**
Bedwell St. M16: W Ran 2B **80**
Beech Av. BL4: Kea 4D **19**
 M6: Sal 3A **50**
 M22: Nor 3F **101**
 M26: Rad 1B **20**
 M32: Stre 4A **78**
 M34: Dent .1F **85**
 M41: Urm 3E **75**
 M43: Droy 1B **70**
 M45: White .2B **22**
 OL4: O'ham 1F **31**
 SK3: Stoc .5B **106**
 SK8: Gat 2D **111**
 WA15: Tim .3D **99**
Beech Cl. M25: Pres 1E **37**
Beech Ct. M6: Sal 4C **50**
 M8: Man 3B **38**
 M14: Man .5E **81**
 M21: Chor .4B **78**
 M33: Sale .4B **88**
Beechcroft M25: Pres 1E **37**
Beechcroft Cl. M40: Man 4F **53**
Beechdale Cl. M40: Man 4E **41**
Beecher Wlk. *M9: Man* *1F 53*
 (off Kelvington Dr.)
Beeches, The M20: Man 4B **92**
 M30: Ecc 4B **48**
 OL6: A Lyme *5F 59*
 (off Crawford M.)
Beechfield Av. M26: Rad 1E **21**
 M41: Urm 2C **74**
Beechfield Cl. M33: Sale 1B **98**
Beechfield Rd. M27: Swin 2A **48**
Beechfield St. M8: Man 1C **52**

Beech Gro. M6: Sal 3A 50
   M14: Man 1F 93
   M33: Sale .4B 88
   OL7: A Lyme 1B 72
Beech Holme Gro. SK2: Stoc 3E 107
Beech Ho. M20: Man 4A 92
   M22: Shar 5A 102
      (off Lauriston Cl.)
   M30: Ecc 1D 61
      (off New La.)
Beech Ho. Gdns. WA15: Tim 3C 98
Beech Hurst Cl. M16: W Ran 3F 79
Beech M. M21: Chor 5C 78
Beech Mt. M9: Man 4F 39
   OL7: A Lyme 1C 58
Beechpark Av. M22: Nor 4E 101
Beech Range M19: Man 4C 82
Beech Rd. M21: Chor 5C 78
   M33: Sale .4F 89
   SK2: Stoc 5B 106
   SK3: Stoc 5A 106
Beech St. M24: Mid 1B 26
   M26: Rad .1E 21
   M27: Swin 5B 34
   M30: Ecc 1D 61
   M35: Fail 4A 42
   OL1: O'ham 2C 30
   SK14: Hyde 2F 87
      (off John St.)
Beech Tree Bank M25: Pres 5C 22
Beech Vs. M33: Sale 4F 89
      (off Carlyn La.)
Beech Wlk. M24: Mid 3B 26
   M32: Stre .4E 77
Beechwood BL9: Bury 1C 12
Beechwood Av. M21: Chor 1E 91
   M41: Urm .2A 74
   SK5: Stoc .4B 96
Beechwood Ct. M20: Man 5C 92
   M25: Pres .1F 37
Beechwood Dr. M28: Wors 1D 47
Beechwood Gdns. M14: Man 5F 81
      (off Ladybarn La.)
Beechwood Gro. M9: Man 5A 40
Beechwood Rd. M25: Pres 1F 37
   OL8: O'ham 2B 44
Beechy Sq. OL1: O'ham 2C 30
      (off Egerton St.)
Beede St. M11: Man 2D 69
Beehive St. OL8: O'ham 1B 44
Beeley St. M6: Sal 2D 51
   SK14: Hyde 3F 87
Beesley Grn. M28: Wors 4B 32
Beeston Av. M7: Sal 1D 51
   WA15: Tim 5B 98
Beeston Gro. M45: White 2D 23
Beeston Rd. M33: Sale 4A 88
   SK9: Hand 4F 115
Beeston St. M9: Man 4A 40
Beetham Twr. M3: Man 3F 9
Beeth St. M11: Man 3F 69
Beeton Gro. M13: Man 1A 82
Beever St. M16: Old T 5E 65
   OL1: O'ham 3F 117 (2C 30)
Begonia Wlk. M12: Man 4B 68
      (off Clowes St.)
Belcroft Cl. M22: Nor 3A 102
Belding Av. M40: Man 3B 42
Beldon Rd. M9: Man 5D 25
Belfairs Cl. OL7: A Lyme 5D 45

Belfield Rd. M20: Man 5D 93
   M25: Pres .1A 38
   SK5: Stoc .2B 84
Belford Av. M34: Dent 2C 84
Belford Rd. M32: Stre 2F 77
Belford Wlk. M23: Wyth 5C 100
Belgate Cl. M12: Man 1C 82
Belfort Dr. M5: Sal 3A 8 (2D 65)
Belgrave Av. M14: Man 2A 82
   M35: Fail .4D 43
   M41: Urm .2A 74
   OL8: O'ham 5C 30
Belgrave Ct. M34: Dent 1F 85
      (off Belgrave St.)
   OL8: O'ham 4B 30
Belgrave Cres. M30: Ecc 4B 48
Belgrave Ind. Est.
   OL8: O'ham 1C 44
Belgrave Rd. M33: Sale 4C 88
   M40: Man .3A 42
   OL8: O'ham 5B 30
Belgrave St. M34: Dent 1F 85
   M40: Man .1A 54
Belgrave Ter. M40: Man 1A 54
Belgravia Gdns. M21: Chor 5C 78
Belhaven Av. M8: Man 2B 38
Belhill Gdns. M6: Sal 4B 50
Bellam Ct. M27: Ward 3E 33
Bell Clough Rd. M43: Droy 4D 57
Bell Cres. M11: Man 2A 68
      (not continuous)
Belldale Cl. SK4: Stoc 1C 104
Bellerby Cl. M45: White 1A 22
Belleville Av. M22: Wyth 1A 114
BELLE VUE 1E 83
Belle Vue Av. M12: Man 5B 68
Belle Vue Greyhound Stadium 5D 69
Belle Vue Leisure Cen. 1C 82
Belle Vue Station (Rail) 5E 69
Belle Vue St. M12: Man 4C 68
Bellew St. M11: Man 2A 68
Bellfield Av. OL8: O'ham 2B 44
Bellfield Cl. M9: Man 2E 39
Bellis Cl. M12: Man 1A 68
Bellott St. M8: Man 1C 52
Bellott Wlk. OL1: O'ham 1A 30
      (off Crompton St.)
Bellscroft Av. M40: Man 5D 41
Bell St. M43: Droy 5D 57
   OL1: O'ham 2C 30
Bell Ter. M30: Ecc 2E 61
Belmont Av. M6: Sal 4C 48
   M27: Clif 4F 19
   M34: Dent .1F 85
Belmont Cl. SK4: Stoc 5A 96
Belmont Ct. SK4: Stoc 5A 96
Belmont Rd. M33: Sale 2C 88
   SK8: Gat .5D 103
Belmont Shop. Cen. SK4: Stoc 1A 106
Belmont St. M5: Sal 1F 63
      (off Foster St.)
   M16: Old T 5F 65
   M30: Ecc 4F 47
   OL1: O'ham 1D 117 (1A 30)
   OL4: Lees .4F 31
   SK4: Stoc .5F 95
Belmont Wlk. M13: Man 4E 67
      (off Bramwell Dr.)
Belmont Way OL9: Chad 1E 29
   SK4: Stoc 1F 105
Belmore Av. M8: Man 3B 38

Belper Rd. M30: Ecc 2D 61
  SK4: Stoc 2B 104
Belper St. OL6: A Lyme 3D 59
Belper Wlk. M18: Man 4E 69
  (off Peacock Cl.)
Belper Way M34: Dent 5C 86
  (off Heanor Av.)
Belroy Ct. M25: Pres 1D 37
Belsay Cl. OL7: A Lyme 2B 58
Belsay Dr. M23: Wyth 2C 108
Belstone Av. M23: Wyth 3C 108
Belsyde Wlk. M9: Man 5A 40
  (off Craigend Dr.)
Belthorne Av. M9: Man 2C 40
Beltone Cl. M32: Stre 4D 77
Belton Wlk. M8: Man 1C 52
  (off Cranlington Dr.)
  OL9: O'ham 3F 29
Belvedere Av. SK5: Stoc 3B 84
Belvedere Ct. M25: Pres 1C 36
Belvedere Dr. SK6: Bred 5E 97
  SK16: Duk 2F 73
Belvedere Gdns. SK4: Stoc 4D 95
  (off Heaton Moor Rd.)
Belvedere Rd. M6: Sal 4C 50
  M14: Man 5A 82
Belvedere Sq. M22: Wyth 3B 110
Belvoir Av. M19: Man 3C 82
Belvor Av. M34: Aud 3A 72
Belwood Rd. M21: Chor 1D 91
Bembridge Cl. M41: Man 3E 81
Bembridge Dr. M34: Dent 5D 87
Bemsley Pl. M5: Sal 2C 64
Benbecula Way M41: Urm 5E 61
Benbow Av. M12: Man 5B 68
Benbow St. M33: Sale 3D 89
Benbrierley Wharf M35: Fail 4B 42
BENCHILL 1F 109
Benchill Av. M22: Wyth 1F 109
Benchill Cl. M22: Wyth 2A 110
Benchill Ct. Rd. M22: Wyth 2A 110
Benchill Dr. M22: Wyth 1F 109
Benchill Rd. M22: Wyth 5E 101
Bendall St. M11: Man 2A 70
Bendemeer M41: Urm 2E 75
Bendix Ct. SK14: Hyde 3F 87
  (off Mottram Rd.)
Bendix St. M4: Man 3E 7 (5D 53)
  (not continuous)
Benedict Cl. M7: Sal 2E 51
  (off Cromwell Gro.)
Benedict Dr. SK16: Duk 4F 73
Benfield Av. M40: Man 2E 41
Benfleet Cl. M12: Man 4C 68
Benfold Wlk. M24: Mid 3F 15
Bengain M7: Sal 1F 51
Bengal La. OL6: A Lyme 3E 59
  (not continuous)
Bengal Sq. OL6: A Lyme 3E 59
Bengal St. M4: Man 3F 7 (5E 53)
  SK3: Stoc 5A 118 (3A 106)
Benhale Wlk. M8: Man 1C 52
  (off Tamerton Dr.)
Benham Cl. M20: Man 5E 93
Benin Wlk. M40: Man 2E 55
  (off Marlinford Dr.)
Benjamin St. OL7: A Lyme 5A 116 (1C 72)
  (not continuous)
Benjamin Wilson Ct. M7: Sal 1D 5

Benmore Rd. M9: Man 5B 26
Bennett Cl. SK3: Stoc 3E 105
Bennett Dr. M7: Sal 1A 52
Bennett M. SK14: Hyde 5F 73
  (off Harding St.)
Bennett Rd. M8: Man 3B 38
Bennett St. M12: Man 4A 68
  M32: Stre 3E 77
  OL7: A Lyme 1B 72
  (not continuous)
  SK3: Stoc 3E 105
  SK14: Hyde 5E 73
Benny La. M43: Droy 4E 57
Benson Cl. M7: Sal 2A 52
Ben St. M11: Man 5D 55
Bentcliffe Way M30: Ecc 1B 62
Bentfield Ind. Units OL9: Chad 3D 29
Bent Fold Dr. BL9: Bury 5C 12
Benthall Wlk. M34: Dent 5A 86
Bentinck Bus. Cen. OL6: A Lyme 3A 116
Bentinck Ho. OL6: A Lyme 3A 116 (5C 58)
Bentinck Ind. Est. M15: Man 5C 8
Bentinck St. M15: Man 5C 8 (3F 65)
  OL6: A Lyme 2A 116 (4C 58)
  (not continuous)
  OL7: A Lyme 4B 116 (5D 59)
  OL8: O'ham 5B 30
Bentinck Ter. OL6: A Lyme 3A 116
Bent La. M8: Man 5B 38
  M25: Pres 5E 23
Bent Lanes M41: Urm 5B 60
  (not continuous)
Bentley Av. M24: Mid 1F 17
Bentley Ct. M7: Sal 4A 38
Bentley Rd. M7: Sal 4A 38
  M21: Chor 4C 78
  M34: Dent 2B 86
Bentleys, The SK5: Stoc 5B 96
Bentley St. OL1: O'ham 1D 31
  OL9: Chad 2D 29
Benton St. M9: Man 5B 40
Bents Av. M41: Urm 4B 74
Bent Spur Rd. BL4: Kea 2A 18
Bent St. BL4: Kea 3C 52
  M8: Man 2A 18
Bent Ter. M41: Urm 1E 75
Bentworth Wlk. M9: Man 5A 40
  (off Broadwell Dr.)
Benville Wlk. M40: Man 1D 55
  (off Harold Priestnall Cl.)
Beresford Ct. M20: Man 4C 92
Beresford Cres. OL4: O'ham 1F 31
  SK5: Stoc 2A 84
Beresford Rd. M13: Man 2B 82
  M32: Stre 1A 78
Beresford St. M14: Man 2B 80
  M35: Fail 5A 42
  OL4: O'ham 1F 31
Bergman Wlk. M40: Man 1D 55
  (off Harmer Cl.)
Berigan Cl. M12: Man 5A 68
Berisford Cl. WA15: Tim 4A 98
Berkeley Av. M14: Man 1A 82
  M32: Stre 1C 76
  OL9: Chad 1B 42
Berkeley Cl. SK2: Stoc 3E 107
  SK14: Hyde 4F 87
Berkeley Ct. M7: Sal 3A 38
  M20: Man 5B 92
Berkeley Cres. SK14: Hyde 4F 87

Berkeley St. OL6: A Lyme 2A **116** (4C 58)
Berkley Av. M19: Man 4C **82**
Berkshire Cl. OL9: Chad 4D **29**
Berkshire Pl. OL9: O'ham 4E **29**
Berkshire Rd. M40: Man 4F **53**
Berlin Rd. SK3: Stoc 5F **105**
Bermondsay St. M5: Sal 2D **65**
(off St Joseph's Dr.)
Bernard St. M9: Man 4F **39**
Berne Cl. OL9: Chad 3E **29**
Bernice Av. OL9: Chad 3D **29**
Berriedale Cl. M16: W Ran 3F **79**
Berrie Gro. M19: Man 5D **83**
(off Henderson St.)
Berry Brow M40: Man 3F **55**
Berry St. M1: Man 3F **11** (2D **87**)
   M27: Pen 2B **34**
   M30: Ecc 2D **61**
Bertha St. M11: Man 3D **69**
Bertram St. M12: Man 4C **68**
   M33: Sale 4A **90**
Berwick Av. M41: Urm 3C **76**
   M45: White 2C **22**
   SK4: Stoc 5F **93**
Berwyn Av. M9: Man 4E **25**
   M24: Mid 1E **27**
Berwyn Cl. OL8: O'ham 1A **44**
Bessemer St. M11: Man 3E **69**
Bessemer Way OL1: O'ham 2D **117** (2A **30**)
BESSES O' TH' BARN 2C **22**
Besses o' th' Barn Station (Metro) . . .2C **22**
BESWICK .2B **68**
Beswick Dr. M35: Fail 1C **56**
Beswick Row M4: Man 2C **6** (4C **52**)
Beswick St. M4: Man 5F **53**
   M43: Droy 1D **71**
Beta Av. M32: Stre 4E **77**
Bethel Av. M35: Fail 5A **42**
Bethesda Ho. M7: Sal 4A **38**
Bethesda St. OL8: O'ham 5B **30**
Bethnal Dr. M14: Man 4C **80**
Betley Rd. SK5: Stoc 4B **84**
Betley St. M1: Man 2E **67**
Betnor Av. SK1: Stoc 2D **107**
Betsham St. M15: Man 5B **66**
Bettwood Dr. M8: Man 2B **38**
Betula Gro. M7: Sal 5F **37**
(off Bk. Hilton St.)
Beulah St. M11: Man 3E **69**
Bevan Cl. M12: Man 1A **68**
Bevendon Sq. M7: Sal 1A **52**
Beveridge St. M14: Man 2C **80**
Beverley Av. M34: Dent 3C **86**
   M41: Urm 1A **76**
Beverley Cl. M45: White 5D **13**
   OL6: A Lyme 1D **59**
Beverley Rd. M27: Pen 5E **35**
   SK2: Stoc 3E **107**
Beverley St. M9: Man 3A **40**
Beverley Wlk. OL8: O'ham 4A **30**
Beverly Rd. M14: Man 1F **93**
Beverston Dr. M7: Sal 1A **52**
Bevill Sq. M3: Sal 3E **5** (5A **52**)
Bewley St. OL8: O'ham 2F **43**
Bewley Wlk. M40: Man 1C **54**
Bexhill Av. WA15: Tim 5B **98**
Bexhill Dr. M13: Man 2A **82**
Bexhill Wlk. OL9: Chad 3D **29**
Bexington Dr. M16: W Ran 2A **80**
Bexley Cl. M41: Urm 1D **75**

Bexley Sq. M3: Sal 4D **5** (5F **51**)
Bexley St. OL9: O'ham 4E **29**
Bexley Wlk. M40: Man 1D **55**
(off John Foran Cl.)
Beyer Cl. M18: Man 5E **69**
Bibby La. M19: Man 2B **94**
(not continuous)
Bibby St. BL9: Bury 1B **12**
   SK14: Hyde 5F **73**
Bibury Av. M22: Wyth 3D **109**
Bickerdike Av. M12: Man 2D **83**
Bickerdyke Ct. M12: Man 2D **83**
Bickerton Ct. OL9: Chad 1D **43**
Biddall Dr. M23: Wyth 5D **101**
Biddisham Wlk. M40: Man 2F **53**
(off Thornton St. Nth.)
Biddulph Av. SK2: Stoc 4E **107**
Bideford Rd. M23: Wyth 3B **100**
   SK2: Stoc 2E **107**
Bidston Av. M14: Man 3D **81**
Bigginwood Wlk. M40: Man 5C **40**
Bilbrook St. M4: Man 1E **7** (4D **53**)
Billberry Cl. M45: White 1D **23**
Billing Av. M12: Man 3E **67**
Billington Rd. M27: Pen 4A **36**
Bill La. M45: White 1B **22**
Bill Williams Cl. M11: Man 2E **69**
Billy La. M27: Clif 2B **34**
Billy Meredith Cl. M14: Man 2C **80**
Billy Whelan Wlk. M40: Man 2E **55**
(off Tommy Taylor Cl.)
Bilsland Wlk. M40: Man 2E **55**
(off Orford Rd.)
Bilson Dr. SK3: Stoc 4D **105**
Bilton Wlk. M8: Man 4E **39**
(off Nunthorpe Dr.)
Bincombe Wlk. M13: Man 5E **67**
(off Carmoor Rd.)
Bindloss Av. M30: Ecc 4B **48**
Bindon Wlk. M9: Man 5F **39**
(off Carisbrook St.)
Bingham Dr. M23: Wyth 5B **100**
Bingham St. M27: Swin 4B **34**
Bingley Cl. M11: Man 2B **68**
Bingley Dr. M41: Urm 1B **74**
Bingley Wlk. BL4: Farn 2A **18**
   M7: Sal 4B **36**
Binns Pl. M4: Man 5F **7** (1D **67**)
Binstead Ct. M14: Man 2A **82**
BIRCH 2E **15**
Birchacre Gro. M14: Man 1F **93**
Birchall Cl. SK16: Duk 3F **73**
Birchall Way M15: Man 4B **66**
Birch Av. M6: Sal 3A **50**
   M16: Old T 1C **78**
   M24: Mid 2C **26**
   M33: Sale 5D **89**
(off Hazel Av.)
   M35: Fail 1B **56**
   M45: White 3B **22**
   OL8: O'ham 2F **43**
   SK4: Stoc 4D **95**
Birch Ct. M13: Man 2A **82**
   SK16: Duk 2F **73**
(off Birch La.)
Birchdale Av. SK8: H Grn 4D **111**
Birch Dr. M27: Pen 4D **35**
Birchenall St. M40: Man 4B **40**
Birchenlea St. OL9: Chad 1C **42**

Birches, The. M33: Sale 3A 88
Birchfield. OL7: A Lyme 2B 72
Birchfield M. SK14: Hyde 3F 87
Birchfield Rd. SK3: Stoc 4C 104
Birchfields Av. M13: Man 2A 82
Birchfields Rd. M13: Man 2A 82
    M14: Man .2A 82
Birch Gro. M14: Man 2F 81
    M25: Pres .3C 22
    M34: Aud 4B 72
    M34: Dent .2A 86
    WA15: Tim 1A 108
Birch Hall La. M13: Man 3A 82
Birch Ind. Est. OL10: H'ood 1C 14
Birchington Rd. M14: Man 5C 80
Birchin La. M4: Man 5D 7 (1C 66)
Birchin Pl. M4: Man 5D 7
Birch La. M13: Man 2A 82
    SK16: Duk .2F 73
                (not continuous)
Birchleaf Gro. M5: Sal 5E 49
Birch Mill Bus. Cen. OL10: H'ood 1E 15
Birch Polygon M14: Man 2F 81
Birch Rd. BL4: Kea 3B 18
    M8: Man 3D 39
    M24: Mid 4E 17
    M27: Swin .2F 47
    M28: Walk .3A 32
    SK8: Gat .1C 110
Birch St. M12: Man 4C 68
    M26: Rad 1A 12
    M43: Droy .2D 71
    OL7: A Lyme 1A 72
Birch Ter. SK14: Hyde 3E 87
Birch Tree Ct. M22: Wyth 3F 109
Birch Tree Dr. M22: Wyth 3F 109
Birchvale M15: Man 5F 9 (4A 66)
Birchwood M43: Droy 4D 57
    OL9: Chad .2A 28
Birchwood Cl. SK4: Stoc 2C 104
Birchwood Dr. M40: Man 1F 53
Birchwood Rd. M24: Mid 1E 27
Birchwood Way SK16: Duk 4F 73
Birdhall Gro. M19: Man 5C 82
Bird Hall La. SK3: Stoc 4D 105
Birdlip Dr. M23: Wyth 3C 108
Birkby Dr. M24: Mid 4A 16
Birkdale Av. M45: White 3F 21
Birkdale Dr. M33: Sale 1A 98
Birkdale Gro. M30: Ecc 5B 48
    SK5: Stoc .3B 96
Birkdale Pl. M33: Sale 2B 88
Birkdale Rd. SK5: Stoc 3A 96
Birkdale St. M8: Man 5C 38
Birkinbrook Cl. M45: White 5C 12
Birkworth Ct. SK2: Stoc 5F 107
Birley Cl. WA15: Tim 4B 98
Birley Ct. M5: Sal 5B 50
Birley Flds. M15: Man 5B 66
Birley Pk. M20: Man 5B 92
Birling Dr. M23: Wyth 2D 109
Birstall Wlk. M23: Wyth 5C 100
Birtles, The M22: Wyth 3F 109
Birtles Av. SK5: Stoc 2B 84
Birtles Cl. SK16: Duk 4F 115
Birtles Way SK9: Hand 4F 115
              (off Sandiway Rd.)
Birt St. M40: Man 3F 53
Birwood Rd. M8: Man 2D 39
Biscay Cl. M11: Man 1B 68

Bishop Cl. OL7: A Lyme 2C 58
Bishopgate St. OL9: Chad 3C 28
Bishop Marshall Cl. M40: Man 2F 53
Bishop Marshall Way M24: Mid 2F 15
Bishop Rd. M6: Sal 3D 49
    M41: Urm 3A 74
Bishops Cnr. M15: Man 4B 66
           (off Stretford Rd.)
Bishopscourt M7: Sal 4E 37
Bishopsgate M2: Man 2B 10 (2B 66)
Bishops Mdw. M24: Mid 3F 15
Bishops M. M33: Sale 2A 88
Bishops M. M25: Pres 1E 37
Bishop St. M24: Mid 2F 27
    SK1: Stoc 2C 106
Bishops Wlk. OL7: A Lyme 5A 116
Bishopton Cl. M19: Man 4E 83
Bisley Av. M23: Wyth 5B 100
Bisley St. OL8: O'ham 3F 29
Bismarck St. OL4: O'ham 4C 30
Bispham Av. SK5: Stoc 3B 84
Bispham Gro. M7: Sal 5A 38
Bittern Dr. M43: Droy 4E 57
Blackberry La. SK5: Stoc 1D 97
Black Brook Rd. SK4: Stoc 1F 95
Blackburn Gdns. M20: Man 4C 92
Blackburn Pl. M5: Sal 1A 8 (1E 65)
Blackburn St. M3: Sal 2C 4 (4F 51)
    M16: Old T .5E 65
    M25: Pres 5E 23
Blackcarr Rd. M23: Wyth 5D 101
Blackcroft Cl. M27: Swin 4A 34
Blackdown Gro. OL8: O'ham 1A 44
Blackett St. M12: Man 2F 67
Blackfield La. M7: Sal 4E 37
Blackfields M7: Sal 4F 37
          (off Bury New Rd.)
Blackford Av. BL9: Bury 2B 12
BLACKFORD BRIDGE 2A 12
Blackford Rd. M19: Man 1D 95
Blackford Wlk. M40: Man 4F 53
          (off Denver Av.)
Black Friar Ct. M3: Sal 1D 5
Blackfriars Rd. M3: Sal 2D 5 (4F 51)
Blackfriars St. M3: Man 5B 52
    M3: Sal 4A 6 (5B 52)
Blackhill Cl. M13: Man 5F 11 (3D 67)
Black Horse St. BL4: Farn 2A 18
Blackleach Country Pk. 4A 18
Blackleach Country Pk. Nature Reserve
          . . . . .4A 18
Blackleach Country Pk. Vis. Cen. 5A 18
BLACKLEY 3A 40
Blackley Cemetery & Crematorium
    M9: Man 5C 24
Blackley Cl. BL9: Bury 4C 12
Blackley Health Studio 2F 39
Blackley New Rd. M9: Man 1B 38
Blackley Pk. Rd. M9: Man 3F 39
Blackley St. M16: Old T 5E 65
    M24: Mid 2D 25
Black Lion Pas. SK1: Stoc 4C 118
Blacklock St. M8: Man 3B 52
Blackmore Rd. M32: Stre 5D 63
Blackpool St. M11: Man 5E 55
Blackrock St. M11: Man 1B 68
Blacksail Wlk. OL1: O'ham 1C 30
Blackshaw St. SK3: Stoc 4A 118 (3A 106)
Blackstock St. M13: Man 1E 81
Blackstone Rd. SK2: Stoc 5F 107

Blackstone Wlk. M9: Man 1F 53
(off Carisbrook St.)
Blackthorn Av. M19: Man 1C 94
Blackthorne Dr. M33: Sale 1A 98
Blackthorn Rd. OL8: O'ham 4F 43
Blackwin St. M12: Man 4C 68
Blackwood Dr. M23: Wyth 3F 99
Blair Av. M41: Urm 3A 74
Blairhall Av. M40: Man 5C 40
Blair Rd. M16: W Ran 4A 80
Blair St. BL4: Kea 3D 19
M16: Old T 5F 65
Blakedown Dr. M12: Man 5A 68
(off Cochrane Av.)
Blakefield Dr. M28: Walk 3A 32
Blakemere Av. M33: Sale 5A 90
Blakemore Wlk. M12: Man 1A 68
Blakeswell Cl. M41: Urm 2A 74
Blakey St. M12: Man 1C 82
Blanchard St. M15: Man 5A 66
Blanche Wlk. OL1: O'ham 2C 30
Bland Cl. M35: Fail 5A 42
Blandford Av. M28: Wors 4B 32
Blandford Cl. OL6: A Lyme . . .2A 116 (4C 58)
Blandford Dr. M40: Man 2F 41
Blandford Rd. M6: Sal 2D 51
M30: Ecc 5D 47
SK4: Stoc 1D 105
Blandford Cl. OL6: A Lyme . . .2A 116 (4C 58)
Bland Rd. M25: Pres 2D 37
Bland St. M16: W Ran 1A 80
Blanefield Cl. M21: Chor 1A 92
Blantyre Av. M28: Walk 2A 32
Blantyre Ho. M15: Man 4E 9
Blantyre Rd. M27: Swin 1D 49
Blantyre St. M15: Man 4D 9 (3F 65)
M27: Swin 4F 33
M30: Ecc 4C 46
Blanwood Dr. M8: Man 5D 39
Bleak Hey Rd. M22: Wyth 4B 110
Bleakley St. M45: White 5A 12
Bleasby St. OL4: O'ham 2E 31
Bleasdale Cl. BL9: Bury 3C 12
Bleasdale Rd. M22: Wyth 4C 108
Bleatarn Rd. SK1: Stoc 4D 107
Bledlow Cl. M30: Ecc 4A 48
Blencarn Wlk. M9: Man 1F 53
(off Ravelston Dr.)
Blendworth Cl. M8: Man 5B 38
(off Broomfield St.)
Blenheim Av. M16: W Ran 3F 79
Blenheim Cl. BL9: Bury 1B 12
Blenheim Cl. M9: Man 4C 24
(off Deanswood Dr.)
Blenheim Rd. M16: Old T 2C 78
Blenheim Way OL6: A Lyme 3F 59
Bletchley Cl. SK4: Stoc 2A 104
Blinco Rd. M41: Urm 4B 76
Blind La. M12: Man 3F 67
Blisworth Av. M30: Scc 2A 62
Blisworth Cl. M4: Man 1F 67
Blithfield Wlk. M34: Dent 3A 86
Block La. OL9: Chad 4D 29
Blocksage St. SK16: Duk 3F 73
Blodwell St. M6: Sal 5B 50
Bloomfield Dr. BL9: Bury 3D 13
M8: Sal 2A 52
Bloomfield Rd. BL4: Farn 3A 18
Bloomsbury Gro. WA15: Tim 5C 98
Bloomsbury La. WA15: Tim 5C 98

Bloom St. M1: Man 3C 10 (2C 66)
M3: Sal 4E 5 (5A 52)
OL9: O'ham 3A 30
SK3: Stoc 3E 105
Blossoms St. SK2: Stoc 5B 106
Blossom St. M3: Sal 3F 5
M4: Man 4F 7 (5D 53)
Bloxham Wlk. M9: Man 1B 40
Blucher St. M5: Sal 1A 8 (1E 65)
M12: Man 4A 68
OL7: A Lyme 1C 58
Blue Bell Av. M40: Man 3C 40
Bluebell Gro. SK8: Chea 2F 111
Blueberry Av. M40: Man 2E 41
Blue Ribbon Wlk. M27: Swin 3C 34
Bluestone Dr. SK4: Stoc 5A 94
Bluestone Rd. M34: Dent 3C 84
M40: Man 4C 40
Bluestone Ter. M34: Dent 3C 84
Blundell Cl. BL9: Bury 3D 13
Blunn St. OL8: O'ham 5B 30
Blyborough Cl. M6: Sal 3A 50
Blyth Av. M23: Wyth 1E 101
Blyth Cl. WA15: Tim 5F 99
Blyton Cl. M15: Man 5D 67
Blyton Way M34: Dent 5B 84
Boad St. M1: Man 2F 11 (2D 67)
Boardale Dr. M24: Mid 5A 16
Boardman Cl. SK5: Stoc 4B 96
Boardman Fold Cl. M24: Mid 4C 26
Boardman Fold Rd. M24: Mid 4B 26
Boardman La. M24: Mid 1D 25
Boardman Rd. M8: Man 2B 38
Boardman St. M30: Ecc 1A 62
Board St. OL6: A Lyme 3F 59
Boar Grn. Cl. M40: Man 5E 41
Boarshaw Clough M24: Mid 4D 17
Boarshaw Clough Way M24: Mid 4D 17
Boarshaw Crematorium
M24: Mid 4E 17
Boarshaw Cres. M24: Mid 4E 17
Boarshaw La. M24: Mid 3F 17
Boarshaw Rd. M24: Mid 5C 16
Boat La. M22: Nor 2A 102
Boat La. Ct. M22: Nor 2A 102
Boatman's Wlk.
OL7: A Lyme 5A 116 (1C 72)
Boatyard, The M32: Stre 3A 78
Bobbin Wlk. OL4: O'ham 3C 30
Bob Massey Cl. M11: Man 1E 69
Boddens Hill Rd. SK4: Stoc 2C 104
Boddington Rd. M30: Ecc 1B 60
Bodley St. M11: Man 5E 55
Bodmin Cres. SK5: Stoc 3D 97
Bodmin Dr. M33: Sale 3A 88
Bodmin Rd. M23: Wyth 1C 108
Bodney Wlk. M9: Man 1D 39
Bodyline Health & Fitness Cen 3C 68
B of the Bang 1B 68
Bogart Ct. M6: Sal 3A 50
(off Monroe St.)
Boggart Hole Clough 2A 40
Bolam Cl. M23: Wyth 2B 100
Boland Dr. M14: Man 5F 81
Bolbury Cres. M27: Pen 4F 35
Bolderod Pl. OL1: O'ham 1C 30
Bold St. M15: Man 5A 66
M16: W Ran 1A 80
Bolesworth Cl. M21: Chor 5B 78
Bolivia St. M5: Sal 5E 49

Bollin Cl. BL4: Kea 3D 19
Bollin Ct. M15: Man 4F 65
　　　　　　　　　　　　　(off Johnson St.)
M33: Sale 1D 99
　　　　　　　　　　　　　(off Bollin Dr.)
Bollin Dr. M33: Sale 1D 99
WA14: Tim .3A 98
Bollington Rd. M40: Man 5F 53
SK4: Stoc 3F 95
Bollington St.
OL7: A Lyme 5A 116 (1C 72)
Bollin Ho. M7: Sal 2F 51
　　　　　　　　　　　　　(off Victoria Lodge)
Bollin Wlk. M45: White 4E 13
SK5: Stoc 3B 96
Bollin Way M45: White 4E 13
Bolney Wlk. M40: Man 3F 53
　　　　　　　　　　　　　(off Collyhurst St.)
Bolshaw Farm La. SK8: H Grn 3E 115
Bolshaw Rd. SK8: H Grn 3D 115
Bolton Av. M19: Man 1F 103
Bolton Cl. M25: Pres 2B 36
Bolton Rd. BL4: Kea 2A 18
M6: Sal 1E 49
M27: Pen 2B 34
Bolton St. OL4: O'ham 3D 31
　　　　　　　　　　　　　(not continuous)
SK5: Stoc 1A 96
Bombay Ho. M1: Man 2C 66
　　　　　　　　　　　　　(off Whitworth St.)
Bombay Rd. SK3: Stoc 4E 105
Bombay Sq. M1: Man 2C 66
Bombay St. M1: Man 3D 11 (2C 66)
　　　　　　　　　　　　　(not continuous)
OL6: A Lyme 3F 59
Bonar Cl. SK3: Stoc 3E 105
Bonar Rd. SK3: Stoc 3E 105
Boncarn Dr. M23: Wyth 2C 108
Bonchurch Wlk. M18: Man 4D 69
Bond St. M3: Sal 3F 5 (5A 52)
M12: Man 3F 11 (2E 67)
M34: Dent 2B 86
Bond St. Ind. Est. M12: Man 2E 67
Bonhill Wlk. M11: Man 5D 55
　　　　　　　　　　　　　(off Coghlan Cl.)
Bonny Brow St. M24: Mid 2D 25
Bonsall St. M15: Man 4B 66
Bonscale Cres. M24: Mid 3A 16
Boodle St. OL6: A Lyme . . .1B 116 (3D 59)
Bookham St. M9: Man 4A 40
　　　　　　　　　　　　　(off Swainsthorpe Dr.)
Boond St. M4: Man 1F 67
Booth Av. M14: Man 1F 93
Booth Bri. Cl. M24: Mid 2E 25
Boothby Ct. M27: Swin 3F 33
　　　　　　　　　　　　　(off Boothby Rd.)
Boothby Rd. M27: Swin 3A 34
Booth Clibborn Ct. M7: Sal 4F 37
　　　　　　　　　　　　　(off Park La.)
Boothcote M34: Aud 4F 71
Booth Dr. M41: Urm 5B 60
Boothfield M30: Ecc 4C 46
Boothfield Av. M22: Wyth 5F 101
Boothfield Dr. M22: Wyth 5F 101
Boothfield Rd. M22: Wyth 5E 101
Booth Hall Rd. M9: Man 1C 40
Booth Hill La. OL1: O'ham 1A 30
Booth Ho. Trad. Est. OL9: O'ham 3E 29
Boothman Ct. M30: Ecc 4B 48

Booth Rd. M16: Old T 2E 79
M33: Sale 2D 89
M34: Aud 3C 70
Boothroyden Cl. M24: Mid 2E 25
Boothroyden Rd. M9: Man 3E 25
M24: Mid 2E 25
Boothroyden Ter. M9: Man 3E 25
Booth St. M2: Man 1B 10 (1B 66)
M3: Sal 4A 6 (5B 52)
M24: Mid 3F 27
M34: Dent 5B 72
M35: Fail 5A 42
OL4: Lees 3F 31
OL6: A Lyme 3B 116 (5D 59)
OL9: O'ham .3A 30
SK3: Stoc 5A 118 (4A 106)
Booth St. E. M13: Man 5E 11 (4D 67)
Booth St. W. M15: Man 4C 66
Boothway M30: Ecc 5B 48
Bootle St. M2: Man 1A 10 (1B 66)
Bordale Av. M9: Man 5B 40
Bordan St. M11: Man 2B 68
Borden Way BL9: Bury 1C 12
Bordley Wlk. M23: Wyth 2A 100
Bordon Rd. SK3: Stoc 4D 105
Boringdon Cl. M40: Man 1D 55
Borland Av. M40: Man 3F 41
Borough Arc. SK14: Hyde 2F 87
Borough Av. M26: Rad 1A 12
M27: Pen 3C 34
Borough Rd. M50: Sal 1F 63
Borron St. SK1: Stoc 1C 106
Borrowdale Av. SK8: Gat 2D 111
Borrowdale Cres. M20: Man 4A 92
OL7: A Lyme 2B 58
Borrowdale Dr. BL9: Bury 3C 12
Borrowdale Rd. M24: Mid 4F 15
SK2: Stoc 4D 107
Borsden St. M27: Ward 2F 33
Borth Av. SK2: Stoc 4D 107
Borth Wlk. M23: Wyth 5B 100
Borwell St. M18: Man 4F 69
Boscombe Av. M30: Ecc 2E 61
Boscombe St. M14: Man 3D 81
SK5: Stoc 3B 84
Bosden Cl. SK1: Stoc 4C 118
SK9: Hand 4F 115
Bosden Fold SK1: Stoc 4C 118 (3B 106)
Bosdin Rd. E. M41: Urm 4A 74
Bosdin Rd. W. M41: Urm 4A 74
Boslam Wlk. M4: Man 5E 53
　　　　　　　　　　　　　(off Saltford Av.)
Bosley Av. M20: Man 5C 80
Bosley Rd. SK3: Stoc 3C 104
Bossall Av. M9: Man 5A 26
Bossington Cl. SK2: Stoc 3E 107
Bostock Wlk. M13: Man 5F 11
Boston Cl. M35: Fail 3B 42
Boston Ct. M50: Sal 2A 64
Boston St. M15: Man 5B 66
OL6: O'ham .5B 30
Boston Wlk. M34: Dent 4C 86
Boswell Av. M34: Aud 1F 71
Boswell Way M24: Mid 2F 17
Bosworth Cl. M45: White 1E 23
Bosworth St. M11: Man 2C 68
Botanical Av. M16: Old T 5C 64
Botanical Ho. M16: Old T 5C 64
Botany La. OL6: A Lyme 3E 59
Botany Rd. M30: Ecc 3C 46

Botha Cl. M11: Man 3F **69**
Botham Cl. M15: Man 5B **66**
Botham Ct. *M30: Ecc* 4D **47**
          (off Worsley Rd.)
Bothwell Rd. M40: Man 4E **53**
Bottesford Av. M20: Man 3B **92**
Bottomfield Cl. OL1: O'ham 1C **30**
Bottomley Side M9: Man 2E **39**
BOTTOM OF WOODHOUSES 2C **56**
Bottom o' th' Moor OL1: O'ham 2C **30**
    OL1: O'ham .2C **30**
Boulder Dr. M23: Wyth 4C **108**
Boulevard, The M20: Man 2A **92**
          (not continuous)
Bouley Wlk. *M12: Man* 4C **68**
        (off Conquest Cl.)
Boulters Cl. M24: Mid 3B **16**
Boundary, The M27: Clif 5F **19**
Boundary Cl. SK4: Stoc 1C **94**
    SK8: Chea .1E **111**
Boundary Gdns. OL1: O'ham 1A **30**
Boundary Grn. M34: Dent 5A **72**
Boundary Gro. M33: Sale 5B **90**
Boundary La. M15: Man 4C **66**
Boundary Rd. M23: Wyth 2B **108**
    M27: Swin 3B **34**
    SK8: Chea .5B **104**
Boundary St. M12: Man 5C **68**
Boundary St. E. M13: Man 5D **11** (3C **66**)
Boundary St. W.
    M15: Man 5C **10** (4C **66**)
Bourdon St. M40: Man 4F **53**
Bourget St. M7: Sal 4B **38**
Bourne Av. M27: Swin 5B **34**
Bourne Dr. M40: Man 3D **41**
Bourne Ho. *M5: Sal* 5B **50**
        (off Amersham St.)
Bournelea Av. M19: Man 2B **94**
Bourne St. OL9: Chad 2D **43**
    SK4: Stoc 4A **96**
Bournville Av. SK4: Stoc 4A **96**
Bournville Gro. M19: Man 4E **83**
Bourton Dr. M18: Man 1D **83**
Bowden Rd. M27: Swin 5C **34**
Bowden St. M34: Dent 2A **86**
Bowdon Av. M14: Man 4B **80**
Bowdon Ct. M16: Old T 5C **64**
Bowdon Ho. SK3: Stoc 3A **106**
Bowdon St. SK3: Stoc 5A **118** (3A **106**)
          (not continuous)
Bower Av. SK4: Stoc 5E **95**
Bowerfold La. SK4: Stoc 1E **105**
          (not continuous)
Bowers Av. M41: Urm 1D **75**
Bowers St. M14: Man 1A **94**
Bower St. M7: Sal 5A **38**
    M40: Man 2B **54**
    OL1: O'ham .2D **31**
    SK5: Stoc 3B **84**
Bower Ter. M43: Droy 4E **57**
Bowes St. M14: Man 2B **80**
Bowfell Circ. M41: Urm 2D **75**
Bowfell Gro. M9: Man 5D **25**
Bowfell Rd. M41: Urm 3C **74**
Bowfell Wlk. *M40: Man* 2E **55**
        (off Langcroft Dr.)
Bowgreen Wlk. *M15: Man* 4F **65**
        (off Shawheath Cl.)
Bowker Av. M34: Dent 5C **87**
Bowker Bank Av. M8: Man 2B **38**

Bowker Bank Ind. Est. M8: Man 1C **38**
Bowker Ct. M7: Sal 1F **51**
Bowker St. M7: Sal 1F **51**
Bowker Va. Gdns. M9: Man 1B **38**
Bowker Vale Stop (Metro) 1B **38**
Bowlacre Rd. SK14: Hyde 5F **87**
Bowland Av. M18: Man 1C **84**
Bowland Cl. OL6: A Lyme 5E **45**
Bowland Rd. M33: Sale 4D **89**
Bowland Rd. M23: Wyth 5B **100**
    M34: Dent 2D **85**
Bow La. M2: Man 1B **10** (1B **66**)
BOWLEE 5E **15**
Bowlee Cl. BL9: Bury 5C **12**
Bowlers Leisure Cen. 4C **62**
Bowler St. M19: Man 5D **83**
Bowling Grn. Cl. OL9: Chad 5C **28**
Bowling Grn. Ct. M16: W Ran 1F **79**
Bowling Grn. St. SK14: Hyde 3F **87**
Bowling Rd. M18: Man 2A **84**
Bowling St. OL9: Chad 2D **43**
Bowman Cres. OL6: A Lyme 4F **59**
Bowmeadow Grange M12: Man 1B **82**
Bowmead Wlk. *M8: Man* 1B **52**
        (off Ermington Dr.)
Bowness Av. SK4: Stoc 2A **96**
Bowness Ct. M24: Mid 4F **15**
Bowness Dr. M33: Sale 3B **88**
Bowness Rd. M24: Mid 5E **15**
    OL7: A Lyme .3B **58**
    WA15: Tim 5F **99**
Bowness St. M11: Man 3B **70**
    M32: Stre 2F **77**
Bowring St. *M7: Sal* 2E **51**
        (off Croft St.)
Bowscale Cl. M13: Man 1B **82**
Bow St. M2: Man 5A **6** (1B **66**)
    OL1: O'ham 3F **117** (2B **30**)
    OL6: A Lyme 2C **116** (4D **59**)
    SK3: Stoc 3E **105**
    SK16: Duk 5E **59**
Boxgrove Rd. M33: Sale 3B **88**
Boxgrove Wlk. *M8: Man* 1C **52**
        (off Brentfield Av.)
Boxhill Dr. M23: Wyth 2C **100**
Boxtree Av. M18: Man 1F **83**
Box Works, The M15: Man 4D **9** (1F **65**)
Boyd St. M12: Man 3C **68**
Boyd's Wlk. SK16: Duk 3E **73**
Boyer St. M16: Old T 5D **65**
Boyle St. M8: Man 1D **53**
Brabham Cl. M21: Chor 5D **79**
Brabham M. M27: Swin 5E **33**
Brabyns Rd. SK14: Hyde 5F **87**
Bracadale Dr. SK3: Stoc 5A **106**
Bracewell Cl. M12: Man 5C **68**
Bracken Av. M28: Walk 1A **32**
Bracken Cl. M43: Droy 5E **57**
Bracken Dr. M23: Wyth 1D **109**
Brackenfield Wlk. *WA15: Tim* 5F **99**
        (off Aimson Rd. E.)
Brackenhill Ter. *M34: Dent* 5C **86**
        (off Wordsworth Rd.)
Brackenlea Pl. SK3: Stoc 5F **105**
Brackenside SK5: Stoc 4C **84**
Bracken Trade Pk. BL9: Bury 1A **12**
Brackenwood Dr. SK8: Chea 2F **111**
Brackley Av. M15: Man 5C **8** (3F **65**)
Brackley Ct. M22: Nor 3F **101**

Brackley Dr. M24: Mid 4C 26
Brackley Lodge M30: Ecc 4B 48
Brackley Rd. M30: Ecc 3F 47
   SK4: Stoc .4F 95
Brackley Sq. OL1: O'ham 1C 30
                (off St Stephens St.)
Brackley St. BL4: Farn 1A 18
                (not continuous)
   OL1: O'ham 1F 117 (1C 30)
Bradburn Av. M30: Ecc 1F 61
Bradburn Cl. M30: Ecc 1F 61
Bradburn Gro. M30: Ecc 1F 61
Bradburn St. M30: Ecc 1F 61
Bradburn Wlk. M8: Man 1D 53
                (off Moordown Cl.)
Bradbury St. OL7: A Lyme 3C 58
   SK14: Hyde 4F 87
Braddan Av. M33: Sale 5E 89
Bradden Cl. M5: Sal 1C 64
Braddon Av. M41: Urm 3F 75
Braddon St. M11: Man 1E 69
Brade Cl. M11: Man 2E 69
Bradfield Av. M6: Sal 5E 49
Bradfield Cl. SK5: Stoc 3A 84
Bradfield Rd. M32: Stre 3C 76
   M41: Urm .3B 76
BRADFORD .5C 54
Bradford Cl. M40: Man 3E 41
Bradford Rd. M30: Ecc 2A 48
   M40: Man .5F 53
Bradford St. BL4: Farn 2A 18
                (not continuous)
   OL1: O'ham 1A 30
Bradgate Av. SK8: H Grn 5F 111
Bradgate Cl. M22: Nor 3A 102
Bradgate Rd. M33: Sale 1D 99
Bradgate St. OL7: A Lyme 4A 116
                (off Park St.)
   OL7: A Lyme 5A 116 (1C 72)
                (Victoria St.)
Bradgreen Rd. M30: Ecc 4E 47
Brading Wlk. M22: Wyth 1A 114
Bradley Av. M7: Man 5D 37
Bradley Cl. M34: Aud 3A 72
   WA15: Tim .4A 98
Bradley Dr. BL9: Bury 4D 13
Bradley Ho. OL8: O'ham 4B 30
Bradley La. M32: Stre 1C 88
Bradley's Ct. M1: Man 5E 7
Bradley St. M1: Man 4E 7
Bradney Cl. M9: Man 5D 25
Bradnor Rd. M22: Shar 4F 101
Bradshaw Av. M20: Man 1D 93
   M35: Fail 2A 56
   M45: White 4A 12
Bradshaw Fold Av. M40: Man 1F 41
Bradshaw Hall La. SK8: H Grn 5F 111
                (not continuous)
Bradshaw La. M32: Stre 5F 77
Bradshaw St. M7: Sal 1A 52
   M24: Mid 2E 27
                (off Shawbury St.)
   OL1: O'ham 3F 117 (2B 30)
Bradstock Rd. M16: W Ran 2A 80
Bradstone Rd. M8: Man 2B 52
Bradwell Av. M20: Man 2B 92
   M32: Stre .2C 76
Bradwell Dr. SK8: H Grn 2E 115
Bradwell Wlk. M41: Urm 2A 74
                (off Padbury Cl.)

Bradwen Av. M8: Man 3C 38
Bradwen St. M34: Dent 4C 86
Braemar Av. M32: Stre 3C 76
   M41: Urm .4C 74
Braemar Ct. M9: Man 4C 24
Braemar Rd. M14: Man 5A 82
Brae Side OL8: O'ham 2A 44
Braeside M32: Stre 4C 76
                (off Urmston La.)
Bragenham St. M18: Man 5E 69
Brailsford Rd. M14: Man 5A 82
Braintree Rd. M22: Wyth 1F 113
Braithwaite Rd. M24: Mid 2F 15
Brakenhurst Dr. M7: Sal 1B 52
Brakenlea Dr. M9: Man 2E 39
Braley St. M12: Man 4F 11 (3D 67)
Bramall Cl. BL9: Bury 4D 13
Bramall Ct. M3: Sal 2D 5 (4F 51)
Bramall St. SK14: Hyde 1F 87
Bramber Way OL9: Chad 3D 29
                (off Petworth Rd.)
Bramble Av. M5: Sal 4A 8 (3E 65)
   OL4: O'ham 1F 31
Bramble Wlk. M22: Wyth 4E 109
Bramblewood OL9: Chad 1A 28
Brambling Cl. M34: Aud 5E 57
Bramcote Av. M23: Wyth 5D 101
Bramfield Wlk. M15: Man 5D 9
Bramhall Cl. M33: Sale 5A 90
   SK16: Duk .4F 73
   WA15: Tim .5F 99
Bramhall La. SK2: Stoc 5B 106
   SK3: Stoc .5B 106
Bramhall Mt. SK2: Stoc 5B 106
Bramhall Rd. M18: Man 5A 70
Bramhall Wlk. M34: Dent 4B 86
Bramhope Wlk. M9: Man 5F 39
Bramley Av. M19: Man 5C 82
   M32: Stre .3D 77
Bramley Cl. M27: Swin 1E 47
Bramley Cres. SK4: Stoc 2D 105
Bramley Meade M7: Sal 5A 38
Bramley St. M7: Sal 3A 52
Brampton Wlk. M40: Man 1D 55
             (off Harold Priestnall Cl.)
Bramwell Dr. M13: Man 4E 67
Bramwell St. SK1: Stoc 3D 107
Brancaster Rd. M1: Man 4D 11 (3C 66)
Brandforth Rd. M8: Man 4E 39
Brandish Cl. M13: Man 5F 67
Brandlehow Dr. M24: Mid 4E 15
Brandon Av. M22: Nor 3E 101
   M30: Ecc 2C 48
   M34: Dent .2B 84
   SK8: H Grn 5D 111
Brandon Brow OL1: O'ham 1A 30
                (off Sunfield Rd.)
Brandon Rd. M6: Sal 3D 49
Brandram Rd. M25: Pres 5E 23
Brandsby Gdns. M5: Sal 2C 64
Brandwood OL1: Chad 1A 28
Brandwood Av. M21: Chor 4F 91
Branfield Av. SK8: H Grn 5F 111
Brankgate Ct. M20: Man 3C 92
Branksome Av. M25: Pres 5C 22
Branksome Dr. M6: Sal 2C 48
   M9: Man 4D 25
   SK8: H Grn 5F 111
Branksome Rd. SK4: Stoc 2D 105
Bransby Av. M9: Man 5A 26

Bransford Rd. M11: Man 2A **70**
  M41: Urm 1E **75**
Branson St. M40: Man 5F **53**
Branson Wlk. WA15: Tim 5F **99**
Branston Rd. M40: Man 2F **41**
Brantingham Ct. M16: W Ran 4A **80**
Brantingham Rd. M21: Chor 4D **79**
Brantwood Ct. M7: Sal 4F **37**
Brantwood Rd. M7: Sal 4F **37**
  SK4: Stoc 4E **95**
Brantwood Ter. M9: Man 5B **40**
Brassey St. M24: Mid 5C **16**
  OL6: A Lyme 3D **59**
Brassica Cl. M30: Ecc 3C **46**
Brassington Av. M5: Sal 2D **65**
  M21: Chor 1D **91**
Brassington Rd. SK4: Stoc 4A **94**
Brathay Cl. M45: White 1E **23**
Brattice Dr. M27: Pen 4E **35**
Brattray Dr. M24: Mid 3A **16**
Braunston Cl. M30: Ecc 2A **62**
Braxton Wlk. *M9: Man* *4A 40*
                  (off Hillier St.)
Bray Av. M30: Ecc 4D **47**
Brayford Rd. M22: Wyth 5F **109**
Brayside Rd. M19: Man 4F **93**
  M20: Man 4F **93**
Braystan Gdns. SK8: Gat 5D **103**
Braystones Cl. WA15: Tim 5F **99**
Brayston Fold M24: Mid 1E **25**
Brayton Av. M20: Man 1E **103**
  M33: Sale 2A **88**
Brazennose St. M2: Man 1A **10** (1B **66**)
Brazil St. M1: Man 2D **11** (2C **66**)
Bread St. M18: Man 4A **70**
Brean Wlk. M22: Wyth 5E **109**
Brechin Wlk. *M11: Man* *1E 69*
          (off Bob Massey Cl.)
Breck Rd. M30: Ecc 5D **47**
Brecon Av. M19: Man 1B **94**
  M34: Dent 4B **86**
Brecon Cres. OL6: A Lyme 1D **59**
Brecon Towers SK5: Stoc 1E **97**
BREDBURY 5F **97**
Bredbury Dr. BL4: Farn 1A **18**
Bredbury Pk. Ind. Est. SK6: Bred . . .2F **97**
                   (Ashton Rd.)
  SK6: Bred 2F **97**
                   (Stuart Rd.)
Bredbury Pk. Way SK6: Bred 3F **97**
Bredbury Rd. M14: Man 3D **81**
Bredbury St. OL9: Chad 3D **29**
  SK14: Hyde 5F **73**
Brede Wlk. M23: Wyth 2F **99**
Bredon Way OL8: O'ham 1A **44**
Breeze Hill Rd. OL4: O'ham 4F **31**
Breeze Mt. M25: Pres 2D **37**
Brenchley Dr. M23: Wyth 1C **100**
Brencon Av. M23: Wyth 2E **99**
Brendon Av. M40: Man 5C **40**
  SK5: Stoc 2B **96**
Brendon Dr. M34: Aud 1F **71**
Brenley Wlk. *M9: Man* *4F 39*
              (off Alfred St.)
Brennan Cl. M15: Man 5C **66**
Brennan Ct. OL8: O'ham 2E **43**
Brennock Cl. M11: Man 2B **68**
Brentbridge Rd. M14: Man 5D **81**
Brentfield Av. M8: Man 1B **52**
Brentford Rd. SK5: Stoc 2B **96**

Brentford St. M9: Man 5A **40**
Brentnall St. SK1: Stoc 5B **118** (3B **106**)
Brentnor Rd. M40: Man 2E **41**
Brenton Av. M33: Sale 4C **88**
Brent Rd. M23: Wyth 1C **100**
  SK4: Stoc 2E **105**
Brentwood M6: Sal 4A **50**
  M33: Sale 4C **88**
  M41: Urm 4B **74**
Brentwood Av. M28: Wors 1D **47**
  M41: Urm 3F **75**
  WA14: Tim 4A **98**
Brentwood Cl. SK5: Stoc 3E **97**
Brentwood Ct. M25: Pres 1B **36**
  M30: Ecc 4B **48**
Brentwood Cres. WA14: Alt 5A **98**
Brentwood Dr. M30: Ecc 3F **47**
  SK8: Gat 1D **111**
Brentwood Rd. M27: Swin 1F **47**
Brentwood St. M16: W Ran 1B **80**
Brereton Ct. SK8: Chea H 5F **111**
Brereton Dr. M28: Wors 5B **32**
Brereton Rd. M30: Ecc 1B **60**
  SK9: Hand 5F **115**
Breslyn St. M3: Man 2B **6**
Brethren St. M43: Droy 2C **70**
Bretland Wlk. M22: Wyth 3B **110**
Breston Ho. *SK2: Stoc* *5C 106*
             (off Canada St.)
Brettargh St. M6: Sal 3C **50**
Bretton Ct. BL4: Kea 3D **19**
Bretton Wlk. M22: Wyth 1F **113**
Brett St. M22: Nor 2A **102**
             (not continuous)
Brewer St. M1: Man 5E **7** (1D **67**)
Brewerton Rd. OL4: O'ham 4E **31**
Brewery Cl. SK1: Stoc 1C **118** (1B **106**)
             (not continuous)
Brewery Yd. M3: Sal 4F **5** (5A **52**)
Brewster St. M9: Man 4F **39**
  M24: Mid 4C **16**
Brian Av. M43: Droy 4E **57**
Brian Farrell Dr. SK16: Duk 4F **73**
Brian Redhead Ct. M15: Man . . .5E **9** (3A **66**)
Brian Statham Way M16: Old T 1C **78**
Briar Cl. M41: Urm 2C **74**
Briar Cres. M22: Shar 1A **110**
Briardene M34: Dent 1C **86**
Briardene Gdns. M22: Wyth 2A **110**
Briarfield Rd. M20: Man 2F **93**
  M28: Wors 5B **32**
  SK4: Stoc 2A **96**
  WA15: Tim 5E **99**
Briarfields Hall M15: Man 5C **10**
Briarlands Av. M33: Sale 1B **98**
Briarlea Gdns. M19: Man 3A **94**
Briarmere Wlk. OL9: Chad 2E **29**
Briars Mt. SK4: Stoc 1C **104**
Briarwood Av. M23: Wyth 3A **100**
  M43: Droy 4A **56**
Brice St. SK16: Duk 2D **73**
Brickley St. M3: Man 1C **6** (4C **52**)
Bricknell Wlk. M22: Wyth 3B **110**
Brick St. M4: Man 4D **7**
Bridcam St. M8: Man 2C **52**

Briddon St. M3: Man 1A **6** (4B 52)
Brideoak St. M8: Man 1C **52**
   OL4: O'ham 1F **31**
Bridge Apartments, The
   M3: Sal 4F **5** (1A 66)
Bridge Dr. SK8: Chea 2F **111**
   SK9: Hand 5F **115**
Bridgefield St. SK1: Stoc 2A **118** (2A 106)
Bridgeford Ct. M32: Stre 5F **77**
                 (off Highfield Rd.)
Bridgeford St. M15: Man 4C **66**
Bridge Gro. WA15: Tim 4B **98**
Bridge Ho. M1: Man 1F **11**
Bridgelea Rd. M20: Man 2D **93**
Bridgeman Ho. BL4: Farn 2A **18**
Bridgeman St. BL4: Farn 1A **18**
Bridge Mills Bus. Pk. M6: Sal 2B **50**
Bridgend Cl. M12: Man 4C **68**
Bridgenorth Av. M41: Urm 3B **76**
Bridge Rd. M23: Wyth 4E **99**
Bridgeside Bus. Cen. SK6: Bred 2F **97**
Bridge St. BL4: Farn 1A **18**
   M3: Man, Sal 5F **5** (1A 66)
   M24: Mid 1C **26**
   M26: Rad 1D **19**
   M27: Pen 4C **34**
   M34: Aud 3B **72**
   M43: Droy 2A **70**
   OL1: O'ham 4F **117** (3C **30**)
   SK1: Stoc 1B **118** (1B 106)
   SK16: Duk 4C **72**
Bridge St. Brow SK1: Stoc 1B **118** (1B 106)
Bridge St. W. M3: Sal 5F **5** (1A 66)
Bridges Way M34: Dent 5B **86**
Bridgewater Cen., The M41: Urm 3A **62**
Bridgewater Circ. M41: Urm 4F **61**
Bridgewater Ct. SK8: H Grn 2E **115**
Bridgewater St. M32: Stre 2A **78**
Bridgewater Hall 3B **10** (2B 66)
Bridgewater Ho. M1: Man 3C **10**
   M15: Man 3D **9**
Bridgewater Pl. M4: Man 5C **6** (1C 66)
Bridgewater Rd. M27: Swin 5D **35**
   WA14: Alt 4A **98**
Bridgewater St. BL4: Farn 1A **18**
   M3: Man 3E **9** (2A 66)
                 (not continuous)
   M3: Sal 1E **5** (4A 52)
   M30: Ecc 5D **47**
   M32: Stre 3A **78**
   M33: Sale 3D **89**
   OL1: O'ham 1C **30**
Bridgewater Viaduct M3: Man 4F **9** (3A 66)
Bridgewater Vw. M30: Ecc 3E **47**
                 (off Anson St.)
Bridgewater Way M16: Old T 5A **8** (5C 64)
Bridgnorth Av. M9: Man 1C **38**
Bridle Cl. M41: Urm 3A **74**
   M43: Droy 4E **57**
Bridle Rd. M25: Pres 2F **23**
Bridlington Av. M6: Sal 4E **49**
Bridlington Cl. M40: Man 1E **55**
Bridport Av. M40: Man 4F **41**
Bridson St. M5: Sal 1A **64**
   OL4: O'ham 2E **31**
Brien Av. WA14: Alt 4A **98**
Briercliffe Cl. M18: Man 4E **69**
Brierfields M35: Fail 5C **42**
Brierley Av. M35: Fail 5B **42**
   M45: White 4A **12**

Brierley Cl. M34: Dent 4A **86**
Brierley Dr. M24: Mid 2C **26**
Brierley Rd. E. M27: Swin 3A **34**
Brierley Rd. W. M27: Swin 3A **34**
Brierley St. OL8: O'ham 1B **44**
   OL9: Chad 1E **29**
   SK16: Duk 1F **73**
Brierley Wlk. OL9: Chad 1E **29**
Brierton Dr. M22: Wyth 5D **109**
Brigade Dr. M32: Stre 2E **77**
Brigadier Cl. M20: Man 2D **93**
Brigantine Cl. M5: Sal 2C **64**
                 (off Jennings Av.)
Briggs Rd. M32: Stre 1B **78**
Briggs St. M3: Sal 2D **5** (4F 51)
Brigham St. M11: Man 2E **69**
Bright Circ. M41: Urm 4A **62**
Brightgate Way M32: Stre 5C **62**
Brightman St. M18: Man 4A **70**
Brighton Av. M7: Sal 1A **52**
   M19: Man 1B **94**
   M41: Urm 3A **74**
   SK5: Stoc 3B **84**
Brighton Ct. M5: Sal 3D **65**
Brighton Gro. M14: Man 3F **81**
   M33: Sale 3C **88**
   M41: Urm 3A **74**
   SK14: Hyde 4F **87**
Brighton Pl. M13: Man 5D **67**
Brighton Range M18: Man 1B **84**
Brighton Rd. SK4: Stoc 2E **105**
Brighton Rd. Ind. Est. SK4: Stoc 2E **105**
Brighton St. M4: Man 1D **7** (4C 52)
Bright Rd. M30: Ecc 5A **48**
Brightstone Wlk. M13: Man 1A **82**
               (off Clarence Rd.)
Bright St. M43: Droy 1D **71**
   OL6: A Lyme 5F **59**
   OL8: O'ham 4F **29**
   OL9: Chad 5C **28**
Brightwater Cl. M45: White 1C **22**
Brightwell Wlk. M4: Man 4E **7**
                 (off Oak St.)
Brigsteer Wlk. M40: Man 2F **53**
            (off Bishop Marshall Cl.)
Brigstock Av. M18: Man 5E **69**
Brimelow St. SK6: Bred 5E **97**
Brimfield Wlk. M11: Man 1E **55**
             (off Bridlington Cl.)
Brimpton Wlk. M8: Man 1B **52**
            (off Kilmington Dr.)
Brimscombe Av. M22: Wyth 4E **109**
Brindale Ho. SK5: Stoc 4E **97**
Brindale Rd. SK5: Stoc 4E **97**
Brindle Cl. M6: Sale 3B **50**
BRINDLE HEATH 3B **50**
Brindle Heath Ind. Est. M6: Sal 3C **50**
Brindle Heath Rd. M6: Sal 3B **50**
Brindle Pl. M15: Man 4B **66**
Brindley Av. M9: Man 4D **25**
   M33: Sale 2E **89**
Brindley Cl. M30: Ecc 2F **61**
Brindley Lodge M27: Swin 1A **48**
               (off Worsley Rd.)
Brindley Rd. M16: Old T 5D **65**
Brindley St. M27: Pen 2B **34**
                 (not continuous)
   M28: Walk 2A **32**
   M30: Ecc 4D **47**
Brinklow Cl. M11: Man 3A **70**

Brinkshaw Av. M22: Wyth 3A 110
Brinksway St3: Stoc 3E 105
Brinksway Trad. Est. SK4: Stoc 2E 105
BRINNINGTON 2E 97
Brinnington Cres. SK5: Stoc 4D 97
Brinnington Ri. SK5: Stoc 4D 97
Brinnington Rd. SK1: Stoc 5C 96
   SK5: Stoc .5C 96
Brinnington Station (Rail) 2E 97
Brinsop Sq. M12: Man 4D 69
Brinston Wlk. M40: Man 5C 40
(off Whitehill Dr.)
Brinsworth Dr. M8: Man 1C 52
Brisbane St. M15: Man 5D 67
Briscoe La. M40: Man 4B 54
Briscoe St. OL1: O'ham 1E 117 (1B 30)
Briscoe Wlk. M24: Mid 4E 15
Bristol Av. M19: Man 5D 83
   OL6: A Lyme 1D 59
Bristol Cl. SK8: H Grn 2E 115
Bristol St. M7: Sal 3A 38
Bristol St. M7: Sal 5A 38
Bristowe St. M11: Man 4F 55
Britain St. BL9: Bury 1A 12
Britannia Mills M15: Man 4C 8 (3F 65)
Britannia Rd. M33: Sale 3D 89
Britannia St. M6: Sal 1C 50
   OL1: O'ham 2C 30
Britnall Av. M12: Man 5A 68
Britton Ho. M4: Man 1C 6
Britwell Wlk. M8: Man 4E 39
(off Mawdsley Dr.)
Brixham Dr. M33: Sale 2A 88
Brixham Rd. M16: Old T 1D 79
Brixton Av. M20: Man 2C 92
Brixworth Wlk. M9: Man 1A 40
(off Greendale Dr.)
Broadacre M18: Man 2A 84
Broadbent Av. OL6: A Lyme 1E 59
   SK16: Duk .2F 73
Broadbent St. M27: Swin 5F 33
   SK14: Hyde .1F 87
Broad Ees Dole Nature Reserve 1F 89
Broadfield Cl. M34: Dent 3C 86
Broadfield Gro. SK5: Stoc 2A 84
Broadfield Rd. M14: Man 3C 80
   SK5: Stoc .2A 84
Broadgate M24: Mid 3F 27
   OL9: Chad .5A 28
(not continuous)
Broadgate Mdw. M27: Swin 1B 48
Broadgate Wlk. M9: Man 4A 40
(off Augustine Webster Cl.)
Broadhaven Rd. M40: Man 4F 53
(off Farnborough Rd.)
Broadhead Wlk. M45: White 5D 13
Broadhill Rd. M19: Man 2A 94
Broadhurst M34: Dent 5C 72
Broadhurst Av. M27: Clif 1B 34
   OL1: Chad .1D 29
Broadhurst Gro. OL6: A Lyme 1E 59
Broadhurst St. SK3: Stoc 4A 106
Broadlands Rd. M28: Wors 1E 47
Broadlands Wlk. M40: Man 1C 54
(off Halliford Rd.)
Broadlea M41: Urm 2E 75
Broadlea Rd. M19: Man 3A 94
Broadley Av. M22: Wyth 2F 109
Broadlink M24: Mid 3F 27
Broadmeadow Av. M16: W Ran 4B 80

Broadmoss Dr. M9: Man 1C 40
Broadmount Ter. OL9: O'ham 5D 29
(off Devon St.)
BROAD OAK 1D 47
Broadoak Av. M22: Wyth 1E 109
Broadoak Ct. M8: Man 1D 53
Broad Oak Cres. OL8: O'ham 2C 44
Broadoak Cres. OL6: A Lyme 2D 59
Broadoak Dr. M22: Wyth 1F 109
Broad Oak Ind. Pk. M17: T Pk 3B 62
Broad Oak La. M20: Man 3E 103
(Morningside Dr.)
   M20: Man .3D 103
(Parrs Wood Rd.)
BROADOAK PARK 1E 47
Broad Oak Pk. M30: Ecc 3F 47
Broad Oak La. M28: Wors 1D 47
Broadoak Rd. M22: Wyth 2E 109
   OL6: A Lyme 2D 59
Broadoak Sports Cen.
   Ashton-under-Lyne 1E 59
Broadoaks Rd. M33: Sale 4C 88
   M41: Urm .4D 75
Broad Rd. M33: Sale 3E 89
Broadstone Cl. M25: Pres 1C 36
Broadstone Hall Rd. Nth. SK4: Stoc 2F 95
Broadstone Hall Rd. Sth. SK4: Stoc 2F 95
   SK5: Stoc .2A 96
Broadstone Ho. SK5: Stoc 1A 96
Broadstone Rd. SK4: Stoc 2F 95
   SK5: Stoc .2F 95
Broad St. M6: Sal 1F 49
(not continuous)
   M24: Mid .2E 25
Broadwalk M6: Sal 4C 50
Broadway M28: Walk, Wors 4A 32
   M33: Sale .3C 88
   M35: Fail 5F 41
   M40: Man .5F 41
   M41: Urm .1C 74
   M43: Droy .3C 70
   M50: Sal 2F 63
   OL9: Chad .1A 42
   SK2: Stoc .4E 107
   SK8: Chea .2E 111
   SK14: Hyde .5D 73
   SK16: Duk, Hyde 4D 73
Broadway, The SK6: Bred 4F 97
Broadway Av. SK8: Chea 1F 111
Broadway Ind. Est. M50: Sal 2C 64
   SK14: Hyde .4D 73
Broadway Leisure Cen. 2A 42
Broadway Nth. M43: Droy 2C 70
Broadway Station (Metro) 2B 64
Broadway St. OL8: O'ham 5B 30
Brocade Cl. M3: Sal 2C 4 (4F 51)
Brock Cl. M11: Man 3F 69
Brockford Dr. M9: Man 4A 26
Brocklebank Rd. M14: Man 5E 81
Brocklehurst St. M9: Man 4C 40
Brockley Av. M14: Man 3D 81
Brock St. M1: Man 5F 7 (1D 67)
Brockton Wlk. M8: Man 4C 38
Brocton Ct. M7: Sal 3F 37
Brodick St. M40: Man 4B 40
Brodie Cl. M30: Ecc 5D 47
Brogan St. M18: Man 5F 69
Brogden Dr. SK8: Gat 1D 111

Brogden Gro. M33: Sale 5C **88**
Brogden Ter. M33: Sale 4C **88**
Bromborough Av. M20: Man 5C **80**
Bromfield Av. M9: Man 3F **39**
Bromleigh Av. SK8: Gat 5D **103**
Bromley Av. M41: Urm 4A **74**
Bromley Cres. OL6: A Lyme 1D **59**
Bromley Rd. M33: Sale 1E **99**
Bromley St. M4: Man 1E **7** (4D **53**)
  M34: Dent 1B **86**
  OL9: Chad 1C **42**
Bromlow St. M11: Man 1E **69**
Brompton Av. M35: Fail 4D **43**
Brompton Rd. M14: Man 3D **81**
  M32: Stre 2B **76**
  SK4: Stoc 1C **104**
Brompton St. OL4: O'ham 4C **30**
Brompton Ter. SK16: Duk 5C **73**
Brompton Way SK9: Hand 4F **115**
Bromsgrove Av. M30: Ecc 5E **47**
Bromshill Dr. M7: Sal 1A **52**
Bromwich Dr. M9: Man 5F **39**
Bronington Cl. M22: Nor 4A **102**
Bronte St. M15: Man 5C **66**
Brookash Rd. M22: Wyth 1C **114**
Brook Av. M19: Man 3D **83**
  M27: Swin 5B **34**
  M43: Droy 1B **70**
  SK4: Stoc 3F **95**
  WA15: Tim 5A **98**
Brookbank Cl. M24: Mid 2D **27**
Brookburn Rd. M21: Chor 1C **90**
Brook Bus. Complex M12: Man . . .3B **68**
Brook Cl. M45: White 1D **23**
  WA15: Tim 5A **98**
Brookcot Rd. M23: Wyth 4B **100**
Brook Ct. M7: Sal 3E **37**
Brookcroft Av. M22: Wyth 1F **109**
Brookcroft Rd. M22: Wyth 1F **109**
Brookdale Av. M34: Aud 3F **71**
  M34: Dent 3D **87**
  M40: Man 3F **55**
Brookdale Ct. M33: Sale 2E **99**
Brookdale Rd. SK8: Gat 1B **110**
Brookdale St. M35: Fail 5A **42**
Brookdene Rd. BL9: Bury 5C **12**
  M19: Man 2A **94**
Brook Dr. M45: White 1D **23**
Brooke Av. SK9: Hand 5F **115**
Brooke Ct. SK9: Hand 5F **115**
Brooke Dr. SK9: Hand 5F **115**
Brooke Pk. SK9: Hand 5F **115**
Brookes St. M24: Mid 4D **17**
Brooke Way SK9: Hand 5F **115**
Brookfield M25: Pres 5D **23**
Brookfield Av. M6: Sal 4E **49**
  M21: Chor 1E **91**
  M41: Urm 3C **74**
  SK1: Stoc 4C **106**
  WA15: Tim 3B **98**
Brookfield Cl. M25: Pres 5D **23**
  SK1: Stoc 4C **106**
Brookfield Ct. M18: Man 1F **83**
  M19: Man 5B **82**
Brookfield Cres. SK8: Chea 2F **111**
Brookfield Dr. M27: Swin 3A **34**
  WA15: Tim 4C **98**
Brookfield Gdns. M22: Wyth 5E **101**
Brookfield Gro. M18: Man 1F **83**
  OL6: A Lyme 5F **59**

Brookfield Ho. SK8: Chea 2F **111**
Brookfield Rd. M8: Man 3C **38**
  M30: Ecc 3D **47**
  SK8: Chea . . . . . . .1F **111** & 5B **104**
Brookfield St. OL8: O'ham 5E **117** (4B **30**)
Brookfold M35: Fail 4A **42**
Brookfold Rd. SK4: Stoc 2F **95**
BROOK GREEN 1A **84**
Brook Grn. La. M18: Man 2B **84**
Brookhead Av. M20: Man 1B **92**
Brookhead Dr. SK8: Chea 5C **104**
Brook Hey SK14: Hyde 2D **87**
Brookhill St. M40: Man 4A **54**
Brook Ho. M15: Man 5C **8**
  M23: Wyth 4E **99**
  (off Bridge Rd.)
Brookhouse Av. M30: Ecc 1C **60**
Brookhurst Rd. M18: Man 1F **83**
BROOKLANDS 1D **99**
Brooklands Av. M20: Man 2C **92**
  M34: Dent 3F **85**
  OL9: Chad 4D **29**
Brooklands Cl. M34: Dent 1F **85**
  SK4: Stoc 3F **95**
Brooklands Ct. M8: Man 2B **38**
  M33: Sale 1D **99**
Brooklands Cres. M33: Sale 5D **89**
Brooklands Dr. M43: Droy 4E **57**
Brooklands Ho. M33: Sale 5D **89**
  (off Brooklands Rd.)
Brooklands Pl. M33: Sale 5C **88**
Brooklands Rd. M8: Man 2A **38**
  M25: Pres 2A **38**
  M27: Swin 1F **47**
  M33: Sale 5D **89**
  SK5: Stoc 3A **84**
Brooklands Sports Club 1D **99**
Brooklands Station (Metro) 5C **88**
Brooklands Sta. App. M33: Sale . . .5C **88**
Brooklands St. M24: Mid 5C **16**
Brook La. BL9: Bury 2C **12**
  OL4: Lees 3F **31**
  OL8: O'ham 5C **30**
  (not continuous)
  WA15: Tim 5A **98**
Brooklawn Dr. M20: Man 4D **93**
  M25: Pres 3E **23**
Brookleigh Rd. M20: Man 2F **93**
Brook Lodge SK8: Chea 2F **111**
Brooklyn Av. M16: W Ran 3E **79**
  M41: Urm 3A **74**
Brooklyn Ct. M20: Man 1E **93**
Brooklyn Cres. SK8: Chea 1F **111**
Brooklyn Pl. SK8: Chea 5F **103**
Brooklyn Rd. SK2: Stoc 5E **107**
  SK8: Chea 1F **111**
Brook Rd. M14: Man 1E **93**
  M41: Urm 2C **74**
  SK4: Stoc 3E **95**
  SK8: Chea 5F **103**
Brooks Av. SK14: Hyde 4F **87**
Brooks Dr. M35: Fail 1A **56**
  SK8: Chea 4E **111**
  WA15: Hale, Tim 2A **108**
  WA15: Haleb 1A **112**
  WA15: Tim 4F **99**
Brookshaw St. M11: Man 1C **68**
Brook Side OL4: O'ham 3F **31**
Brookside M20: Man 1B **102**
Brookside Av. M43: Droy 4E **57**

Brookside Bus. Pk. M24: Mid 3F 27
Brookside Cl. SK8: Chea 2F 111
Brookside Ct. M19: Man 3C 82
Brookside Cres. M24: Mid 3E 27
   M28: Walk 1A 32
Brookside Dr. M7: Sal 3F 37
Brookside Rd. M33: Sale 1C 98
   M40: Man 3C 40
   SK8: Gat 5C 102
Brookside Vs. *SK8: Gat* *5C 102*
   (off Pendlebury Rd.)
Brook's Rd. M16: Old T 2E 79
Brooks St. SK1: Stoc 5C 118 (4B 106)
Brookstone Cl. M21: Chor 2F 91
Brook St. BL4: Farn 1A 18
   M1: Man 4D 11 (3D 67)
   M26: Rad 2C 18
   M27: Swin 4F 33
   M33: Sale 3E 89
   M35: Fail 1F 55
   OL1: O'ham 2C 30
   OL9: Chad 1D 29
   SK8: Chea 5B 104
Brook St. E. OL6: A Lyme 3A 116 (5C 58)
Brook St. Ind. Est. SK1: Stoc 5C 118
Brook St. W.
   OL6: A Lyme 3A 116 (5C 58)
Brook Ter. M12: Man 2B 82
   M41: Urm 1E 75
Brookthorpe Av. M19: Man 2A 94
Brook Wlk. M34: Dent 5B 86
Brookway OL4: Lees 4F 31
   WA15: Tim 4B 98
Brookway Cl. M19: Man 4A 94
Brookway Cl. M23: Wyth 4B 100
Brookway Retail Pk. M23: Wyth 3A 100
Brookwood Av. M8: Man 4E 39
   M33: Sale 5A 88
Brookwood Cl. M34: Dent 5C 86
Broom Av. M7: Sal 4A 38
   M19: Man 5D 83
   SK5: Stoc 2B 96
Broom Cres. M6: Sal 4E 49
Broomcroft Ho. M20: Man 1D 103
Broomedge M7: Sal 4F 37
Broome Gro. M35: Fail 1B 56
Broome St. OL9: O'ham 3F 29
Broomfield M27: Pen 1F 49
Broomfield Cl. SK5: Stoc 2B 96
Broomfield Cl. M20: Man 4C 92
Broomfield Cres. M24: Mid 5F 15
Broomfield Dr. M8: Man 5B 38
   SK5: Stoc 2B 96
Broomfield Rd. SK4: Stoc 4E 95
Broomfields M34: Dent 5C 72
Broomgrove La. M34: Dent 1C 86
Broomhall Rd. M9: Man 4C 24
   M27: Pen 1F 49
Broomhurst Av. OL8: O'ham 5F 29
Broomhurst Hall M20: Man 1D 103
Broom La. M7: Sal 5F 37
   M19: Man 5D 83
Broomstair Rd. M34: Aud 4B 72
Broom St. M27: Swin 5B 34
Broomville Av. M33: Sale 4D 89
Broomwood Gdns. WA15: Tim 5E 99
Broomwood Rd. WA15: Tim 5E 99
Broomwood Wlk. *M15: Man* *5C 10*
   (off Chevril Cl.)
Broseley Av. M20: Man 5F 93

Broseley Rd. M16: Old T 3C 78
Brotherton Cl. M15: Man 5C 8 (4F 65)
Brotherton Ct. *M14: Man* *1F 81*
   (off Hope Rd.)
Brotherton Dr. M3: Sal 3D 5 (5F 51)
Brough St. M11: Man 3A 70
Broughton Bri. M7: Sal 4F 51
Broughton Cl. M24: Mid 4F 15
Broughton Grn. Sq. M7: Sal 5F 37
Broughton La. M7: Sal 2F 51
   (not continuous)
   M8: Man 2F 51
Broughton M. M33: Sale 5E 89
BROUGHTON PARK 4F 37
Broughton Rd. M6: Sal 3C 50
   SK5: Stoc 4B 96
Broughton Rd. E. M6: Sal 3D 51
Broughton St. M8: Man 2B 52
Broughton Trade Cen. M7: Sal 3F 51
Broughton Vw. M6: Sal 4D 51
Broughville Dr. M20: Man 3E 103
Brow, The M9: Man 2F 39
Brow Av. M24: Mid 3D 27
Browbeck OL1: O'ham 2D 117 (2A 30)
Browfield Av. M5: Sal 3D 65
Browmere Dr. M20: Man 4B 92
Brownacre St. M20: Man 2D 93
Brownbank Wlk. *M15: Man* *5B 66*
   (off Arnott Cres.)
Browncross St. M3: Sal 5F 5 (1A 66)
Brown Edge Rd. OL4: O'ham 5F 31
Browning Av. M43: Droy 1C 70
Browning Rd. M24: Mid 4D 17
   M27: Swin 4A 34
   OL1: O'ham 1D 31
   SK5: Stoc 4F 83
Browning St. M3: Sal 4D 5 (5F 51)
   M15: Man 4F 65
Brownlea Av. SK16: Duk 3E 73
Brownley Ct. M22: Wyth 1A 110
Brownley Ct. Rd. M22: Wyth 1F 109
Brownley Rd. M22: Shar 5A 102
Brownrigg Cl. M24: Mid 5E 15
Brownslow Wlk. M13: Man 5F 11
Brownson Wlk. *M9: Man* *4A 40*
   (off Sequoia St.)
Brown St. M2: Man 1B 10 (1B 66)
   M6: Sal 1B 64
   M24: Mid 4C 16
   M34: Aud *5A 72*
   (off Denton Rd.)
   M35: Fail 5A 42
   OL1: O'ham 2C 30
   OL9: Chad 1C 28
   SK1: Stoc 1A 118 (2A 106)
Brownsville Rd. SK4: Stoc 3D 95
Brownville Gro. SK16: Duk 3F 73
Brownwood Cl. SK1: Stoc 2D 107
Brownwood Cl. M33: Sale 2E 99
Brows Av. M23: Wyth 1C 100
Brow Wlk. M9: Man 1F 39
Broxton St. M40: Man 4B 54
Broxwood Cl. *M18: Man* *5F 69*
   (off Kirk St.)
Broyne Cl. M11: Man 2B 68
Bruce Wlk. *M11: Man* *3F 69*
   (off Brock Cl.)
Brundage Rd. M22: Wyth 4F 109
Brundrett Pl. M33: Sale 4B 88

Brundrett's Rd. M21: Chor 5D 79
Brundrett St. SK1: Stoc 3C 106
Brunel Av. M5: Sal 1D 65
Brunel Cl. M32: Stre 3A 78
Brunet Wlk. M12: Man 4B 68
(off Skarratt Cl.)
Bruno St. M9: Man 5D 25
Brunstead Cl. M23: Wyth 5F 99
BRUNSWICK 4E 67
Brunswick Rd. M20: Man 2E 93
WA14: Alt 4A 98
Brunswick Sq. OL1: O'ham 4E 117
Brunswick St. M13: Man 5F 11 (4D 67)
M32: Stre 5F 77
OL1: O'ham 4D 117 (3A 30)
SK16: Duk 1E 73
Brunton Rd. SK5: Stoc 2B 96
Brunt St. M14: Man 2D 81
Bruntwood Av. SK8: H Grn 5C 110
Bruntwood Cotts. SK8: Chea 4F 111
Bruntwood La. SK8: Chea 2F 111
SK8: H Grn .5F 111
Bruntwood Pk. 4F 111
Brussels Rd. SK3: Stoc 5F 105
Bruton Av. M32: Stre 4D 77
Brutus Wlk. M7: Sal 1A 52
(off Bradshaw St.)
Bryan Av. M21: Chor 3D 79
Bryan St. OL4: O'ham 1E 31
Bryant Cl. M13: Man 5E 67
Bryceland Cl. M12: Man 2A 68
Bryce St. SK14: Hyde 1F 87
Brydon Av. M12: Man 3E 67
Brydon Cl. M6: Sal 5B 50
Bryndale Gro. M33: Sale 2B 98
Brynden Av. M20: Man 3E 93
Bryn Dr. SK5: Stoc 3B 96
Brynford Av. M9: Man 4C 24
Brynorme Rd. M8: Man 2C 38
Brynton Rd. M13: Man 2A 82
(not continuous)
Bryone Dr. SK2: Stoc 5D 107
Bryony Cl. M22: Wyth 5E 109
Bryson Wlk. M18: Man 5E 69
Buccleuch Lodge M20: Man 3B 92
Buchanan St. M27: Pen 3B 34
Buchan St. M11: Man 5D 55
Buckden Rd. SK4: Stoc 1F 95
Buckden Wlk. M23: Wyth 1B 100
Buckfast Av. OL8: O'ham 5E 31
Buckfast Cl. M21: Chor 4D 79
Buckfast Rd. M24: Mid 3B 16
M33: Sale 2A 88
Buckfast Wlk. M7: Sal 1A 52
Buckfield Av. M5: Sal 4A 8 (3D 65)
Buckhurst Rd. M19: Man 4C 82
Buckingham Av. M6: Sal 5F 49
M34: Dent 3D 87
M45: White 2C 22
Buckingham Bingo
Manchester 2F 103
Middleton .1B 26
Old Trafford 5D 65
Buckingham Gro.
WA14: Tim .2B 98
Buckingham Rd. M21: Chor 3D 79
M25: Pres 2D 37
M27: Clif 2C 34
M32: Stre 1B 78
M43: Droy 1A 70

Buckingham Rd. SK4: Stoc 3D 95
(not continuous)
Buckingham Rd. W. SK4: Stoc 4C 94
Buckingham St. M5: Sal 1B 64
SK2: Stoc 5C 106
Buckingham Way SK2: Stoc 5B 106
(off Windsor St.)
WA15: Tim .4C 98
Buckland Av. M9: Man 1C 38
Buckland Rd. M6: Sal 3F 49
Buck La. M33: Sale 2A 88
Buckle Ho. M30: Ecc 5A 48
Buckley Av. M18: Man 1E 83
Buckley La. M45: White 1A 36
Buckley Rd. M18: Man 1D 83
OL4: O'ham .1F 31
Buckley St. M11: Man 2F 69
M34: Aud 3F 71
M43: Droy 2C 70
OL4: Lees 4F 31
OL9: Chad 2C 28
SK5: Stoc 3A 84
Bucklow Av. M14: Man 3D 81
Bucklow Dr. M22: Nor 3A 102
Bucknell Ct. M40: Man 1F 7 (3E 53)
Buckthorn Ct. M21: Chor 2F 91
WA15: Tim .1A 108
Buckthorn La. M30: Ecc 1B 60
Budding Vw. M4: Man 1C 6
Buddleia Gro. M7: Sal 1F 51
(off Bk. Hilton St.)
Bude Av. M41: Urm 5D 75
SK5: Stoc 3D 97
Bude Ter. SK16: Duk 5C 116 (1D 73)
Bude Wlk. M23: Wyth 1D 109
Budsworth Av. M20: Man 1D 93
Budworth Gdns. M43: Droy 1D 71
Budworth Rd. M33: Sale 5A 90
Buerton Av. M9: Man 4C 24
Buffalo Ct. M50: Sal 2A 64
Buffoline Trad. Est. M19: Man 4D 83
Bugle St. M1: Man 3F 9 (2A 66)
Buildbase Way SK3: Stoc 5D 105
Buile Dr. M9: Man 5B 26
Buile Hill Dr. M5: Sal 4F 49
Buile Ho. M6: Sal 4A 50
Buile St. M7: Sal .5A 38
Bulford Av. M22: Wyth 4D 109
Bulkeley Rd. SK8: Chea 5A 104
SK9: Hand 5E 115
Bulkeley St. SK3: Stoc 3F 105
Buller Rd. M13: Man 3B 82
Buller St. M43: Droy 2D 71
OL4: O'ham .1F 31
Bullfinch Wlk. M21: Chor 1F 91
Bull Hill Cres. M26: Rad 1D 21
Bullock St. SK1: Stoc 4B 106
Bulteel St. M30: Ecc 4D 47
Bunkers Hill M45: White 1F 35
Bunsen St. M1: Man 5E 7 (1D 67)
Bunyard St. M8: Man 1D 53
Burbage Rd. M23: Wyth 4C 108
Burbridge Cl. M11: Man 1A 68
Burdale Dr. M6: Sal 3D 49
Burdale Wlk. M23: Wyth 2B 100
Burder St. OL8: O'ham 2E 43
Burdett Way M12: Man 5A 68
(off Chipstead Av.)
Burdith Av. M14: Man 3C 80
Burdon Av. M22: Wyth 3A 110

Burford Av. M16: W Ran 3F 79
   M41: Urm .1A 76
Burford Dr. M16: W Ran 3F 79
   M27: Swin .2A 34
Burford Gro. M33: Sale 2A 98
Burford Rd. M16: W Ran 3F 79
Burford Wlk. *M16: W Ran* *3F 79*
   (off Burford Rd.)
Burgess Av. OL6: A Lyme 2E 59
Burgess Dr. M35: Fail 5B 42
Burghley Av. OL4: O'ham 3F 31
Burgin Wlk. M40: Man 2E 53
Burkitt St. SK14: Hyde 3F 87
Burland Cl. M7: Sal 2A 52
Burleigh Ho. *M15: Man* *5D 67*
   (off Dilworth St.)
Burleigh M. M21: Chor 2D 91
Burleigh Rd. M32: Stre 2A 78
Burleigh St. M15: Man 5D 67
Burley Ct. SK4: Stoc 1E 105
Burlin Ct. M16: W Ran 2F 79
Burlington Av. OL8: O'ham 5A 30
Burlington Cl. SK4: Stoc 1A 104
Burlington Ct. WA14: Alt 5A 98
Burlington Ho. OL6: A Lyme 2A 116
Burlington Rd. M20: Man 1E 93
   M30: Ecc .3A 48
   WA14: Alt .5A 98
Burlington St. M15: Man 5C 66
   OL6: A Lyme 3A 116 (5C 58)
   OL7: A Lyme 5B 58
Burlington St. E. M15: Man 5C 66
Burman St. M11: Man 3B 70
   M43: Droy 2B 70
Burnaby St. OL8: O'ham 4E 29
BURNAGE 3A 94
Burnage Av. M19: Man 5B 82
Burnage Hall Rd. M19: Man 1A 94
Burnage La. M19: Man 1F 103
Burnage Range M19: Man 4C 82
Burnage Station (Rail) 4F 93
Burnbray Av. M19: Man 2A 94
Burnby Wlk. M23: Wyth 2B 100
Burndale Dr. BL9: Bury 3C 12
Burnell Cl. M40: Man 4F 53
Burnett Av. M5: Sal 2D 65
Burnett Cl. M40: Man 2F 53
Burnfield Rd. M18: Man 2F 83
   SK5: Stoc 2B 84
Burnham Av. SK5: Stoc 4B 84
Burnham Dr. M19: Man 5B 82
   M41: Urm 2E 75
Burnham Rd. M34: Dent 2C 84
BURNLEY BROW 1A 30
Burnley La. OL1: Chad 1D 29
   OL9: Chad 1D 29
   (not continuous)
Burnley St. M35: Fail 4C 42
   OL9: Chad 2D 29
Burnsall Av. M45: White 1F 21
Burnsall Wlk. M22: Wyth 4C 108
Burns Av. M27: Swin 3F 33
   SK8: Chea 5B 104
Burns Cl. M11: Man 1B 68
Burns Gdns. M25: Pres 1B 36
Burns Gro. M43: Droy 5C 56
Burnside WA15: Haleb 2A 112
Burnside Av. M6: Sal 2D 49
   SK4: Stoc 2A 96

Burnside Cres. M24: Mid 3A 16
Burnside Dr. M19: Man 2A 94
Burnside Rd. SK8: Gat 1C 110
Burns Rd. M34: Dent 5C 86
Burnthorp Av. M9: Man 1D 39
Burntwood Wlk. *M9: Man* *4A 40*
   (off Princedom St.)
Burran Rd. M22: Wyth 1F 113
Burrows Av. M21: Chor 2D 91
Burrwood Dr. SK3: Stoc 5F 105
Burslem Av. M20: Man 5C 80
Burstead St. M18: Man 3A 70
Burstock St. M4: Man 1E 7 (4D 53)
Burston St. M18: Man 4E 69
Burtinshaw St. M18: Man 5F 69
Burton Av. M20: Man 2D 93
   WA15: Tim 2C 98
Burton Gro. M28: Wors 5E 33
Burton M. M20: Man 3B 92
Burton Pl. M15: Man 4C 8 (3F 65)
Burton Rd. M20: Man 4B 92
Burton St. M24: Mid 1B 26
   (not continuous)
   M40: Man 1F 7 (3D 53)
   OL4: Lees 4F 31
   SK4: Stoc 5A 96
Burton Wlk. M3: Sal 3D 5 (5F 51)
   SK4: Stoc *5A 96*
   (off Heskith St.)
Burtonwood Ct. M24: Mid 5B 16
Burtree St. M12: Man 4C 68
Burwell Gro. M23: Wyth 4B 100
Bury Av. M16: W Ran 3E 79
Bury New Rd. M7: Sal 5F 37
   M8: Man 1A 6 (2A 52)
   M25: Pres 4C 22
   M45: White 5A 12
Bury Old Rd. M7: Sal 2F 37
   M8: Man .2F 37
   M25: Pres 2F 37
   M45: Pres, White 2B 22
Bury Pl. M11: Man 5E 55
Bury St. M3: Sal 3F 5 (5A 52)
   SK5: Stoc 5B 96
Bushey Dr. M23: Wyth 1C 108
Busheyfield Cl.
   SK14: Hyde 5F 73
Bushfield Wlk. *M23: Wyth* *4A 100*
   (off Sandy La.)
Bushgrove Wlk. *M9: Man* *4F 25*
   (off Claygate Dr.)
Bushmoor Wlk. M13: Man 5F 67
Bushnell Wlk. *M9: Man* *4A 26*
   (off Claygate Dr.)
Bush St. M40: Man 2A 54
Bushton Wlk. *M40: Man* *2E 53*
   (off Ribblesdale Dr.)
Bushway Wlk. *M8: Man* *1D 53*
   (off Appleford Dr.)
Business & Technology Cen.
   M30: Ecc .5E 47
BUSK 1E 29
Busk Rd. OL9: Chad 1E 29
   (not continuous)
Busk Wlk. OL9: Chad 1E 29
Butcher La. M23: Wyth 4F 99
   (not continuous)
Bute Av. OL8: O'ham 1B 44
Bute St. M40: Man 4B 40
   M50: Sal .1F 63

Butler Ct. M32: Stre 4F 77
   M40: Man 4E 53
      (off Gunson St.)
BUTLER GREEN 5C 28
Butler Grn. OL9: Chad 5C 28
Butler St. M4: Man 4E 53
Butler St. M4: Man 4B 70
Butman St. M18: Man 1E 91
Butler La. M3: Man 5A 6 (1B 66)
   M27: Swin 1B 48
Buttermere Av. M22: Wyth 4D 109
Buttermere Cl. M32: Stre 2E 77
Buttermere Dr. M24: Mid 4A 16
Buttermere Rd. OL4: O'ham 1F 31
   OL7: A Lyme 1A 116 (3B 58)
   SK8: Gat 3D 111
Butterstile Av. M25: Pres 2B 36
Butterstile Cl. M25: Pres 3B 36
Butterstile La. M25: Pres 2B 36
Butterwick Cl. M12: Man 2D 83
Butterworth La. OL9: Chad 1A 42
Butterworth St. M11: Man 2C 68
   M24: Mid 2E 27
   OL4: O'ham 2E 31
   OL9: Chad 1D 29
Buttery Ho. La. WA15: Haleb 4A 108
Butt Hill Av. M25: Pres 1D 37
Butt Hill Ct. M25: Pres 1D 37
Butt Hill Dr. M25: Pres 1D 37
Butt Hill Rd. M25: Pres 1D 37
Button La. M23: Wyth 4E 69
Buttress St. M18: Man 1D 31
Buxted Rd. OL1: O'ham 2B 92
Buxton Av. M20: Man 4E 83
Buxton Ct. SK2: Stoc 5C 106
Buxton Cres. M33: Sale 2F 99
Buxton La. M43: Droy 2A 30
Buxton Pl. OL8: O'ham 2C 76
Buxton Rd. M32: Stre 5C 106
   SK2: Stoc 5C 106
Buxton St. M1: Man 3F 11 (2D 67)
   SK8: Gat 1C 110
Buxton Way M34: Dent 5B 86
      (off Eastmoor Dr.)
Bycroft Wlk. *M40: Man* 3F 55
      (off Eastmoor Dr.)
Bye St. M34: Aud 3B 72
Byfield Rd. M22: Wyth 2E 109
Byland Av. OL4: O'ham 5F 31
Bylands Fold SK16: Duk 4F 73
Byland Wlk. M22: Wyth 5F 109
Byng St. BL4: Farn 1A 18
Byre Cl. M33: Sale 5C 90
Byroe Ct. WA14: Alt 5A 98
Byrom Av. M19: Man 4E 83
Byrom Ct. M43: Droy 1B 70
Byrom Pde. M19: Man 4E 83
Byrom Pl. M3: Man 1F 9
Byrom St. M3: Man 2F 9 (2A 66)
   M5: Sal 2C 64
   M16: Old T 1F 79
Byron Av. M25: Pres 1B 36
   M27: Swin 4A 34
   M43: Droy 5C 56
Byron Dr. SK8: Chea 5B 104
Byron Gro. SK5: Stoc 4A 84
Byron Ho. *OL8: O'ham* 2D 43
      (off Grammar School Rd.)
Byron Rd. M24: Mid 4D 17
   M32: Stre 2A 78
   M34: Dent 5B 86

Byrons Dr. WA15: Tim 5C 98
Byron St. M30: Ecc 5F 47
   OL8: O'ham 2D 43
Byrth Rd. OL8: O'ham 4B 44
Bywell Wlk. *M8: Man* 5B 38
      (off Levenhurst Rd.)

C

Cablestead Wlk. *M11: Man* 2C 68
      (off Dapple Gro.)
Cable St. M3: Sal 3F 5 (5A 52)
   M4: Man 3E 7 (5D 53)
Cabot Pl. SK5: Stoc 4B 96
Cabot St. M13: Man 4D 67
Caddington Rd. M21: Chor 1E 91
Cadleigh Wlk. *M40: Man* 5C 40
      (off Shelderton Cl.)
Cadmium Wlk. M18: Man 1E 83
Cadnam Dr. M22: Wyth 3B 110
Cadogan Pl. M7: Sal 3A 38
Cadogan St. M14: Man 1C 80
Cadum Wlk. *M13: Man* 4E 67
      (off Bramwell Dr.)
Caen Av. M40: Man 1E 41
Caernarvon Way M34: Dent 4B 86
Cairn Dr. M6: Sal 2E 51
Cairns Pl. OL6: A Lyme 2F 59
Cairnwell Rd. OL9: Chad 1B 28
Caister Av. M45: White 2C 22
Caister Cl. M16: W Ran 5A 80
Caistor St. SK1: Stoc 5D 97
Caistor Wlk. OL1: O'ham 2E 117
Caithness Cl. M23: Wyth 2C 108
Cajetan Ho. M24: Mid 4B 26
Cakebread St. M12: Man 4F 11 (3E 67)
Calbourne Cres. M12: Man 2D 83
Calcot Wlk. M23: Wyth 5B 100
Calcutta Rd. SK3: Stoc 4E 105
Caldbeck Av. M33: Sale 3A 90
Caldbeck Dr. M24: Mid 5A 16
Caldecott Rd. M9: Man 4C 24
Calder Av. M22: Nor 3F 101
CALDER BANK 1B 74
Calderbank Av. M41: Urm 1A 74
Calderbeck Way M22: Shar 5A 102
Calderbrook Wlk. *M9: Man* 5F 39
      (off Grangewood Dr.)
Calderbrook Way OL4: O'ham 4D 31
Calder Cl. SK5: Stoc 3C 96
Calder Cl. M41: Urm 1A 74
Calder Cres. M45: White 4D 13
Calder Dr. BL4: Kea 4D 19
   M27: Swin 3A 34
Calder Ho. M7: Sal 2E 51
Caldervale Av. M21: Chor 4E 91
Calder Wlk. M24: Mid 4E 15
   M45: White 4D 13
Calder Way M45: White 4D 13
Caldey Rd. M23: Wyth 1A 108
Caldon Cl. M30: Ecc 2F 61
Caldwell St. SK5: Stoc 4B 84
Caldy Rd. M6: Sal 3F 49
   SK9: Hand 5F 115
Caledon Av. M40: Man 4C 40
Caledonian Dr. M30: Ecc 2A 62
Caledonia Way M32: Stre 5C 62
CALE GREEN 5B 106
Cale Grn. SK2: Stoc 5B 106

Cale Grn. Ct. SK2: Stoc 5B 106
Cale St. SK2: Stoc 4B 106
Caley St. M1: Man 3C 10
Calgarth Dr. M24: Mid 3F 15
Calgary St. M18: Man 5E 69
Calico Cl. M3: Sal 2C 4 (4F 51)
Callingdon Rd. M21: Chor 3F 91
Callum Wlk. M13: Man 4E 67
                                  (off Watkin Cl.)
Calluna M. M20: Man 4C 92
Calne Wlk. M23: Wyth 1C 108
Calthorpe Av. M9: Man 5E 39
Calton Av. M7: Sal 5C 36
Calvary Ct. SK3: Stoc 3F 105
Calve Cft. Rd. M22: Wyth 4A 110
Calver Av. M30: Ecc 2E 61
Calver Cl. M41: Urm 2A 74
Calverley Av. M19: Man 1B 94
Calverton Dr. M40: Man 5E 41
Calvert St. M5: Sal 5F 49
Calver Wlk. M34: Dent 5C 86
    SK8: Chea H 5F 111
Calvine Wlk. M40: Man 4E 53
                                (off Bothwell Rd.)
Cambeck Cl. M45: White 5D 13
Cambeck Wlk. M45: White 5C 12
Cambell Rd. M30: Ecc 5D 47
Cambert La. M18: Man 5E 69
                                    (Garratt Way)
    M18: Man .5F 69
                                   (Wellington St.)
Camberwell Dr. OL7: A Lyme 1C 58
Camberwell St. M8: Man 3C 52
    OL8: O'ham 5A 30
Camborne St. M14: Man 3D 81
Cambo Wlk. SK4: Stoc 5B 94
Cambrai Cres. M30: Ecc 3C 46
Cambrian Rd. SK3: Stoc 3E 105
Cambrian St. M40: Man 5E 54
Cambria St. OL4: O'ham 2F 31
Cambridge Av.
    M16: W Ran 3E 79
Cambridge Cl. M33: Sale 5A 88
Cambridge Dr. M34: Dent 2C 84
Cambridge Gro. M30: Ecc 5B 48
    M45: White 1C 22
Cambridge Hall M13: Man 4D 67
                                 (off Rudcroft Cl.)
    M15: Man .5C 10
Cambridge Ho. M15: Man 5C 10
Cambridge Ind. Est. M7: Sal 1E 5 (3A 52)
Cambridge Rd. M9: Man 3F 39
    M35: Fail 2B 56
    M41: Urm .4D 75
    M43: Droy .4B 56
    SK4: Stoc .3E 95
    SK8: Gat .5D 103
Cambridge St. M1: Man 4B 10 (3B 66)
                                 (not continuous)
    M7: Sal 1E 5 (3A 52)
    M15: Man 5C 10 (3C 66)
    OL7: A Lyme 1B 72
    OL9: O'ham 4D 29
    SK2: Stoc 5C 106
    SK16: Duk .1E 73
Cambridge Ter. SK2: Stoc 5C 106
                                 (off Russell St.)
Camdale Wlk. M8: Man 1B 52
                                (off Felthorpe Dr.)
Camden Av. M40: Man 3E 55

Camelford Cl. M15: Man 4C 66
Camelia Rd. M9: Man 5E 39
Cameron St. M1: Man 3A 10 (2B 66)
Caminada Ho. M15: Man 4F 65
                            (off St Lawrence St.)
Camley Wlk. M8: Man 1D 53
                               (off Appleford Dr.)
Campanula Wlk. M8: Man 1C 52
                                (off Magnolia Dr.)
Campbell Rd. M13: Man 3B 82
    M27: Swin .1A 48
    M33: Sale .5B 88
Campbell St. SK5: Stoc 4B 84
Campden Way SK9: Hand 5F 115
Campfield Av. M3: Man 3F 9
Campion Rd. M11: Man 2B 68
Campion Way M34: Dent 5C 86
Camponia Gdns. M7: Sal 2F 51
Camp St. M3: Man 2F 9 (2A 66)
    M7: Sal 3E 51
    OL6: A Lyme 1C 116 (4D 59)
Camrose Wlk. M13: Man 5F 67
                             (off Winterford Av.)
Canada St. M40: Man 3A 54
    SK2: Stoc .5C 106
Canal Bank M30: Ecc 4E 47
Canal Circ. M30: Ecc 4E 47
Canal Rd. WA14: Tim 1C 62
Canal Side M30: Ecc 4A 98
Canalside Nth. M17: T Pk 5A 64
Canal Side Wlk.
    OL7: A Lyme 4B 116 (1D 73)
Canal St. M1: Man 2D 11 (2C 66)
    M5: Sal 5B 4 (1E 65)
    M43: Droy .1C 70
    OL9: Chad .1D 43
    SK1: Stoc 3C 118 (2B 106)
    SK14: Hyde 2E 87
Canal Wharf SK4: Stoc 5A 96
Canary Way M27: Pen 5A 36
Canberra St. M11: Man 1E 69
Candleford Rd. M20: Man 2D 93
Canisp Cl. OL9: Chad 1B 28
Canley Cl. SK1: Stoc 5C 118 (3B 106)
Canning St.
    SK4: Stoc 1A 118 (1A 106)
Cannock Dr. SK4: Stoc 1C 104
Cannon Ct. M3: Man 4B 6
                                 (off Cateaton St.)
Cannon St. M3: Sal 3C 4 (5F 51)
    M30: Ecc 5A 48
    OL9: O'ham .3A 30
                             (off Middleton Rd.)
Cannon Wlk. M34: Dent 3A 86
Canon Grn. Ct. M3: Man 3E 5
Canon Grn. Dr. M3: Sal 2E 5 (4A 52)
Canon Hussey Ct. M3: Sal 5C 4
Canons Gro. M40: Man 2A 54
Canonsleigh Cl. M8: Man 2A 52
Canonsway M27: Swin 4A 34
Canon Tighe Ct. OL9: Chad 2C 28
Cansfield Ct. BL4: Kea 3C 18
Canterbury Cl. SK16: Duk 4F 73
Canterbury Cres. M24: Mid 4F 17
Canterbury Dr. M25: Pres 2E 37
Canterbury Gdns. M5: Sal 5C 48
Canterbury Pk. M20: Man 5B 92
Canterbury Rd. M41: Urm 2D 75
    SK1: Stoc .2D 107
Canterbury St. OL6: A Lyme 3E 59

Canterfield Cl. M43: Droy 5F 57
Cantley Wlk. M8: Man 1C 52
                (off Dinnington Dr.)
Cantrell St. M11: Man 1D 69
Canute Ct. M32: Stre 2A 78
Canute Rd. M32: Stre 2A 78
Capella Dr. M11: Man 2B 68
Capella Wlk. M7: Sal 3E 51
Capenhurst Cl. M23: Wyth 2B 108
Capesthorne Rd. SK16: Duk 4F 73
    WA15: Tim 5F 99
Capesthorne Wlk. M34: Dent 3A 86
Cape St. M20: Man 1E 93
Capital Ho. M50: Sal 3C 64
Capital Quay M50: Sal 3C 64
Capital Rd. M11: Man 3B 70
Capricorn Rd. M9: Man 1D 41
Capricorn Way M6: Sal 3E 51
                (off Gemini Rd.)
Capstan St. M9: Man 4A 40
Captain Clarke Rd. SK14: Hyde 5D 73
Captain Wlk. M5: Sal 2D 65
             (off Robert Hall St.)
Caradoc Av. M8: Man 1D 53
Carberry Rd. M18: Man 5F 69
Cardale Wlk. M9: Man 5F 39
              (off Conran St.)
Carden Av. M27: Swin 5F 33
    M41: Urm 3A 74
Carder Cl. M27: Swin 5B 34
Cardew Av. M22: Wyth 2B 110
Cardiff Cl. OL8: O'ham 2D 43
Cardiff St. M7: Sal 5A 38
Cardiff Wlk. M34: Dent 4B 86
Cardigan Rd. OL8: O'ham 2D 43
Cardigan St. M6: Sal 1A 64
Cardigan Ter. M14: Man 1B 80
Cardinal M. M24: Mid 4F 15
Cardinal St. M8: Man 1D 53
    OL1: O'ham 3F 117 (2C 30)
Carding Gro. M3: Sal 2E 5 (4A 52)
Cardus St. M19: Man 1C 60
Cardwell Rd. M30: Ecc 4C 82
Cardwell St. OL8: O'ham 1B 44
Caremine Av. M19: Man 3D 83
Carey Cl. M7: Sal 1D 5 (3F 51)
Carey Wlk. M15: Man 5B 66
             (off Wellhead Cl.)
Carfax St. M18: Man 5F 69
Cargate Wlk. M8: Man 1B 52
Carib St. M15: Man 5B 66
Carill Av. M9: Man 3B 40
    M40: Man 3C 40
Carill Dr. M14: Man 5F 81
Carina Pl. M7: Sal 1B 4 (3E 51)
Cariocca Bus. Pk. M12: Man 4F 67
    M40: Man 4F 53
Carisbrook Av. M41: Urm 4E 75
    M45: White .1C 48
Carisbrook Dr. M27: Swin 1C 48
Carisbrook St. M9: Man 5F 39
Carlburn St. M11: Man 5E 25
Carley Gro. M9: Man 1B 40
Carlford Gro. M25: Pres 1B 36
Carlin Ga. WA15: Tim 4A 110
Carling Dr. M22: Wyth 3C 40
Carlingford Cl. SK3: Stoc 3A 106
Carlisle Cl. M45: White 2D 23
Carlisle Cres. OL6: A Lyme 5E 45
Carlisle Dr. WA14: Tim 3A 98

Carlisle St. M27: Pen 2B 34
    OL9: O'ham .5E 29
              (not continuous)
    SK3: Stoc 3A 106
Carlisle Way M34: Dent 4B 86
Carloon Rd. M23: Wyth 2D 101
Carlow Dr. M22: Wyth 4A 110
Carlton Av. M14: Man 2D 81
    M16: Old T .1D 79
    M25: Pres 2A 38
    M45: White .5A 12
Carlton Ct. M25: Pres 3C 36
Carlton Cres. M41: Urm 4F 75
    SK1: Stoc 1C 106
Carlton Dr. M25: Pres 2A 38
    SK8: Gat 5C 102
Carlton Ho. M16: W Ran 2E 79
Carlton Mans. M16: W Ran 2E 79
Carlton Pl. BL4: Farn 1A 18
    M45: White .2E 21
Carlton Range M18: Man 1B 84
Carlton Rd. M6: Sal 3A 50
    M16: W Ran 2F 79
    M33: Sale 2C 88
    M41: Urm 4E 75
    OL6: A Lyme 2E 59
    SK4: Stoc 1C 104
Carlton Springs OL6: A Lyme 1C 116
Carlton St. BL4: Farn 1A 18
    M16: Old T .1E 79
    M30: Ecc 4F 47
Carlyle Cl. M8: Man 1C 52
Carlyn Av. M33: Sale 4F 89
Carmel Av. M5: Sal 3A 8 (2E 65)
Carmel Cl. M5: Sal 3A 8 (2E 65)
Carmel Ct. M8: Man 2B 38
    M9: Man 3A 40
Carmichael St. SK3: Stoc 3F 105
Carmine Fold M24: Mid 4B 16
Carmona Dr. M25: Pres 5C 22
Carmona Gdns. M7: Sale 3E 37
Carmoor Rd. M13: Man 5E 67
Carnaby St. M9: Man 3B 40
Carna Rd. SK5: Stoc 3A 84
Carnarvon St. M3: Man 1B 6 (4B 52)
    M7: Sal 5A 38
    OL8: O'ham .2D 43
    SK1: Stoc 3C 106
Carnation Rd. OL4: O'ham 5F 31
Carnegie Av. M19: Man 4D 83
Carnforth Av. OL9: Chad 3C 28
Carnforth Dr. M33: Sale 5C 88
Carnforth Rd. SK4: Stoc 2F 95
Carnforth St. M14: Man 2D 81
Carnoustie Cl. M40: Man 5E 41
Carnoustie Dr. SK8: H Grn 5E 111
Carnwood Cl. M40: Man 3F 55
Carolina Way M50: Sal 1A 64
Caroline St. M7: Sal 3A 52
    OL6: A Lyme 4E 59
    SK3: Stoc 4F 105
             (not continuous)
Carpenters La. M4: Man 4D 7 (5C 52)
Carpenters Wlk. M43: Droy 1B 70
Carradale Wlk. M40: Man 1C 54
             (off Halliford Rd.)
Carr Av. M25: Pres 2B 36
Carr Bank Av. M9: Man 1B 38
Carr Cl. SK1: Stoc 3D 107
Carrfield SK14: Hyde 1F 87

Carrfield Av. WA15: Tim 5F 99
Carrgate Rd. M34: Dent 4D 87
Carrgreen Cl. M19: Man 3B 94
Carriage Dr. M40: Man 2F 53
Carriage St. M16: Old T 5F 65
Carrick Gdns. M22: Wyth 2F 109
   M24: Mid 2B 16
Carrigart M25: Pres 1D 37
Carrill Gro. M19: Man 4C 82
Carrill Gro. E. M19: Man 4C 82
Carrington Fld. St. SK1: Stoc 4B 106
Carrington Ho. M6: Sal 3E 49
                (off Moss Mdw. Rd.)
Carrington La. M31: C'ton 5B 74
   M33: Sale 2A 88
Carrington Rd. M14: Man 5E 81
   M41: Urm 5A 74
   SK1: Stoc 5C 96
Carrington Spur M33: Sale 2A 88
   M41: Urm 5A 76
Carrington St. M27: Pen 3D 35
   OL9: Chad 1D 43
Carrington Ter. M27: Pen 3D 35
                 (off Carrington St.)
Carrock Wlk. M24: Mid 5D 15
Carron Av. M9: Man 3B 40
Carrs Av. SK8: Chea 5C 104
Carrsdale Dr. M9: Man 2E 39
Carrsfield Rd. M22: Shar 5A 102
Carrs Rd. SK8: Chea 5B 104
Carr St. M27: Swin 5F 33
   OL6: A Lyme 2F 59
Carrsvale Av. M41: Urm 2D 75
Carrswood Rd. M23: Wyth 3E 99
Carruthers St. M4: Man 5F 53
Carsdale Rd. M22: Wyth 1A 114
Carslake Av. M40: Man 2F 53
Carson Rd. M19: Man 5C 82
Carstairs Cl. M8: Man 5B 38
Car St. OL1: O'ham 2C 30
Carter Cl. M34: Dent 3B 86
Carter Pl. SK14: Hyde 5F 73
Carter St. BL4: Kea 2A 18
   M7: Sal 2F 51
   SK14: Hyde 5F 73
Carthage St. OL8: O'ham 5B 30
Carthorpe Arch M5: Sal 1B 64
Cartmel Av. SK4: Stoc 2F 95
Cartmel Cl. BL9: Bury 3C 12
   OL8: O'ham .1F 43
   SK8: Gat 3E 111
Cartmel Cres. OL9: Chad 2B 42
Cartmel Dr. WA15: Tim 5F 99
Cartmel Gro. M28: Wors 5D 33
Cartmell Ct. M9: Man 5C 26
Cartmel Wlk. M9: Man 5F 39
       (off Shiredale Dr., not continuous)
   M24: Mid 4A 16
Cartridge Cl. M22: Wyth 3B 110
Cartwright Rd. M21: Chor 5B 78
Cartwright St. M34: Aud 4B 72
Carver Av. M25: Pres 4E 23
Carver Cl. M16: Old T 5D 65
Carver St. M16: Old T 5D 65
Carver Wlk. M15: Man 5B 66
              (off Wellhead Cl.)
Carville Rd. M9: Man 1D 41
Cascade Dr. M7: Sal 2A 52
Cashel Ct. M27: Ward 3E 33
Cashgate Ct. OL8: O'ham 1F 43

Cashmere Rd. SK3: Stoc 4E 105
Cashmore Wlk. M12: Man 4A 68
              (off Langport Av.)
Caspian Rd. M9: Man 1D 41
Cassandra Ct. M5: Sal 3B 8 (2E 65)
Cass Av. M5: Sal 2C 64
Cassidy Cl. M4: Man 3F 7 (5D 53)
Cassidy Ct. M50: Sal 2A 64
Cassidy Gdns. M22: Mid 2F 15
Casson St. M35: Fail 5B 42
Castle Av. M34: Dent 3A 86
Castlebrook Cl. BL9: Bury 2D 13
Castle Cl. M43: Droy 5D 57
Castle Ct. OL6: A Lyme 5D 45
Castle Courts M5: Sal 1D 65
Castledene Av. M6: Sal 4A 50
Castle Farm Dr. SK2: Stoc 5D 107
Castle Farm La. SK2: Stoc 5D 107
              (not continuous)
CASTLEFIELD 3E 9 (2A 66)
Castlefield Av. M7: Sal 4A 38
Castlefield Gallery 4A 38
Castleford St. OL1: Chad 1E 29
Castleford Wlk. M21: Chor 1F 91
             (off Arrowfield Rd.)
Castlegate M15: Man 4E 9 (3A 66)
Castle Hey Cl. BL9: Bury 3E 13
CASTLE HILL
   SK6 . . . . .1F 97
   WA15 . . . . .5B 112
Castle Hill SK6: Bred 1F 97
Castle Hill Dr. M9: Man 2E 39
            (off Marshbrook Dr.)
Castle Hill Rd. M25: Pres 2F 37
Castle Irwell Student Village
   M6: Sal 2D 51
Castlemere Rd. M9: Man 1E 39
Castle M. BL4: Farn 2A 18
              (off Castle St.)
Castle Mill La. WA15: Alt 5A 112
Castlemill St. OL1: O'ham 2D 31
Castlemoor Av. M7: Sal 4D 37
Castle Pk. Ind. Est. OL1: O'ham 2D 31
Castle Quay M15: Man 4E 9 (3A 66)
Castlerea Cl. M30: Ecc 2F 61
Castlerigg Cl. SK4: Stoc 1F 95
Castlerigg Dr. M24: Mid 3E 15
Castle Rd. BL9: Bury 3E 13
Castle Shaw Rd. SK2: Stoc 5F 107
Castle St. BL4: Farn 2A 18
   M3: Man 3E 9 (2A 66)
   M24: Mid 2F 27
   M30: Ecc 5B 48
   SK3: Stoc 4F 105
Castleton Av. M32: Stre 1D 77
Castleton Ct. M34: Dent 5C 86
Castleton Rd. M7: Sal 3A 38
Castleton St. OL9: O'ham 3E 29
Castleton Wlk. M11: Man 1B 68
              (off Burns Cl.)
Castleton Way M34: Dent 5C 86
Castle Wlk. OL6: A Lyme 5D 45
Castle Way M27: Clif 2C 34
Castleway M6: Sal 3A 50
Castlewood Gdns. SK2: Stoc 5E 107
Castlewood Rd. M7: Sal 4C 36
Castle Yd. SK1: Stoc 1B 118 (1B 106)
Catalan Sq. M3: Man 3E 9
Catchdale Cl. M9: Man 4E 25
Cateaton St. M3: Man 4B 6 (5B 52)

Caterham St. M4: Man 1F **67**
Catesby Rd. M16: W Ran 2F **79**
Catfield Wlk. M15: Man 5D **9**
Catford Rd. M23: Wyth 1B **108**
Cathedral App. M3: Sal 3B **6** (5B **52**)
Cathedral Cl. SK16: Duk 4F **73**
Cathedral Gates M3: Man 4B **6**
Cathedral Rd. OL9: Chad 1B **28**
Cathedral St. M4: Man 4B **6** (5B **52**)
Cathedral Yd. M3: Man 4B **6**
Catherine Ho. SK4: Stoc 1B **104**
Catherine Rd. M8: Man 3A **38**
   M27: Swin 5E **33**
Catherine St. BL9: Bury 1A **12**
   M11: Man 3A **70**
   M30: Ecc 4C **46**
   OL4: Lees 3F **31**
   SK14: Hyde 2F **87**
Catherine St. E. M34: Dent 2F **85**
Catherine St. W. M34: Dent 2F **85**
Catherston Rd. M16: W Ran 2A **80**
Catlow La. M4: Man 4D **7**
Catlow St. M7: Sal 1F **5** (3A **52**)
Catskowl Cl. M18: Man 2F **83**
Catterick Av. M20: Man 5E **93**
Catterick Rd. M20: Man 5E **93**
Cattlin Way OL8: O'ham 2E **43**
Cauldale Cl. M24: Mid 3F **15**
Causeway, The OL9: Chad 4F **27**
Causey Dr. M24: Mid 3F **15**
Cavalier St. M40: Man 5F **53**
Cavanagh Cl. M13: Man 4F **67**
Cavan Cl. SK3: Stoc 4B **104**
Cavell St. M1: Man 5E **7**
Cavell Way M5: Sal 1C **64**
   M6: Sal 5C **50**
Cavendish Av. M20: Man 2B **92**
   M27: Clif 1E **35**
Cavendish Cl. M7: Sal 3F **37**
   M9: Man 4C **24**
               (off Deanswood Dr.)
   M32: Stre 1A **78**
                 (off Nansen Cl.)
   M41: Urm 3A **76**
              (off Cavendish Rd.)
   SK4: Stoc 1B **104**
Cavendish Gro. M30: Ecc 4A **48**
Cavendish Hall M15: Man 5C **10**
Cavendish Ho. M30: Ecc 4A **48**
              (not continuous)
   OL6: A Lyme 4B **116**
             (off Cavendish St.)
Cavendish Ind. Est. OL6: A Lyme 4C **58**
Cavendish Mill
   OL6: A Lyme 4B **116** (5D **59**)
Cavendish Pl. M11: Man 5C **54**
   M27: Pen 4C **34**
               (off Bridge St.)
Cavendish Rd. M7: Sal 3E **37**
   M20: Man 2B **92**
   M28: Wors 1D **47**
   M30: Ecc 4A **48**
   M32: Stre 1A **78**
   M41: Urm 3A **76**
   SK4: Stoc 1B **104**
Cavendish St. M15: Man 5C **10** (4C **66**)
   OL6: A Lyme 2A **116** (4C **58**)
   OL8: O'ham 5D **117** (3A **30**)
Cavendish Ter. M21: Chor 5D **79**
             (off Wilbraham Rd.)

Cavenham Wlk. M9: Man 5E **39**
             (off Mannington Dr.)
Caversham Dr. M9: Man 4A **40**
Cawdor Ho. M30: Ecc 2F **61**
              (off Enfield Cl.)
Cawdor Pl. WA15: Tim 5E **99**
Cawdor Rd. M14: Man 4E **81**
Cawdor St. M15: Man 5C **8** (3F **65**)
   M27: Swin 4F **33**
   M28: Walk 2A **32**
   M30: Ecc 1E **61**
Cawley Av. M25: Pres 2B **36**
Cawley Ter. M9: Man 4C **24**
Cawood Ho. SK5: Stoc 2E **97**
Cawood Sq. SK5: Stoc 1E **97**
Cawston Wlk. M8: Man 1C **52**
            (off Cranlington Dr.)
Cawthorne Ct. M27: Ward 3F **33**
Caxton Rd. M14: Man 4D **81**
Caxton St. M3: Man 4F **5** (5A **52**)
Caygill St.
   M3: Sal 3F **5** (5A **52**)
Caythorpe St. M14: Man 2C **80**
Cayton St. M12: Man 2C **82**
Cecil Av. M33: Sale 5A **88**
Cecil Ct. SK3: Stoc 3D **105**
Cecil Dr. M41: Urm 3A **74**
Cecil Gro. M18: Man 5F **69**
Cecil Rd. M9: Man 4F **25**
   M30: Ecc 1A **62**
   M32: Stre 4E **77**
Cecil St. M15: Man 5D **67**
   M28: Walk 1A **32**
   OL7: A Lyme 1C **72**
   OL8: O'ham 4A **30**
   SK3: Stoc 4A **106**
              (off James St.)
   SK16: Duk 2D **73**
Cecil Wlk. OL7: A Lyme 1C **72**
              (off Cecil St.)
Cedar Av. M45: White 3B **22**
   OL6: A Lyme 2F **59**
Cedar Ct. M14: Man 4E **81**
   M25: Pres 4C **22**
            (off Longfield Rd.)
   WA15: Tim 5D **99**
            (off Edenhurst Dr.)
Cedar Cres. OL9: Chad 1D **29**
Cedar Dr. M27: Clif 5F **19**
   M41: Urm 4E **75**
   M43: Droy 5E **57**
Cedar Gro. M14: Man 5F **81**
   M25: Pres 3C **22**
   M34: Dent 2A **86**
   SK4: Stoc 3E **95**
Cedar M. OL7: A Lyme 2D **59**
Cedar Pl. M7: Sal 3E **51**
Cedar Rd. M24: Mid 1E **27**
   M33: Sale 2A **88**
   M35: Fail 1B **56**
   SK8: Gat 1C **110**
Cedars Rd. M22: Wyth 3F **109**
Cedar St. OL4: O'ham 2E **31**
             (not continuous)
   OL6: A Lyme 3F **59**
   SK14: Hyde 5F **73**
Cedar Vw. OL6: A Lyme 3F **59**
             (off Cedar St.)
Cedarwood Av. SK4: Stoc 2C **104**
Cedarwood Cl. M22: Nor 3A **102**

Cedric Rd. M8: Man 2A **38**
   OL4: O'ham 2E **31**
Cedric St. M5: Sal 5A **50**
Celia St. M8: Man 4E **39**
Celtic St. SK1: Stoc 3C **106**
Cemetery Rd. BL4: Kea 1B **18**
   M5: Sal 1A **64**
   M34: Aud 4B **72**
   M34: Dent 4B **86**
   M35: Fail 1B **56**
   M43: Droy 1B **70**
Cemetery Rd. Nth. M27: Swin 2A **34**
Cemetery Rd. Sth. M27: Swin 3A **34**
Cemetery St. M24: Mid 5C **16**
Cenacle Ho. M16: W Ran 3A **80**
   (off Alexandra Rd. Sth.)
Cennick Cl. OL4: O'ham 3F **31**
Centaur Cl. M27: Clif 2B **34**
Centaur Way M8: Man 5B **38**
   (off Narburth Dr.)
Centenary Circ. M30: Ecc 1C **62**
Centenary Way M17: T Pk 1D **63**
   M30: Ecc 1C **62**
Central Art Gallery
   Ashton-under-Lyne 3B **116**
Central Av. M6: Sal 1A **50**
   M19: Man 3C **82**
   M27: Clif 2F **35**
   M33: Sale 2A **98**
Central Cl. Apartments M3: Sal 4D **5**
Central Dr. M8: Man 3D **39**
   M27: Swin 5D **35**
   M41: Urm 3F **75**
   SK5: Stoc 3B **96**
   SK8: H Grn 1F **115**
Central Ho. M9: Man 4A **26**
Central Pk. Est. M17: T Pk 4D **63**
Central Retail Pk.
   M4: Man 5F **7** (1E **67**)
Central Rd. M20: Man 3C **92**
   M23: Wyth 2B **108**
Central St. M2: Man 1B **10** (1B **66**)
Centrepoint M17: T Pk 5C **62**
Centurion Gro. M7: Sal 1A **52**
Century St. M3: Man 3F **9** (2A **66**)
Ceylon St. M40: Man 4A **54**
   OL4: O'ham 4F **31**
CHADDERTON 2D **29**
Chadderton Dr. BL9: Bury 4C **12**
Chadderton Hall Rd. OL1: Chad 1B **28**
   OL9: Chad 1B **28**
Chadderton Ind. Est. M24: Mid 4E **17**
CHADDERTON PARK 1B **28**
Chadderton Pk. Rd. OL9: Chad 1D **29**
Chadderton Pct. OL9: Chad 2D **29**
Chadderton Sports Cen. 1B **28**
Chadderton St. M4: Man 3E **7** (5D **53**)
Chadderton Way OL1: O'ham 1E **29**
   OL9: O'ham 1F **29**
Chaddesley Wlk. M11: Man 2C **68**
   (off Windcroft Cl.)
Chadvil Rd. SK8: Chea 1E **114**
Chadwell Rd. SK2: Stoc 4F **107**
Chadwick Cl. M14: Man 2D **81**
   (off Union Pl.)
Chadwick Rd. M30: Ecc 5A **48**
   M41: Urm 3B **76**
Chadwick St. M27: Swin 4B **34**
   OL6: A Lyne 5F **59**
   SK1: Stoc 5B **118** (3B **106**)

Chadwick Wlk. M27: Swin 4B **34**
   (off Chadwick St.)
Chaffinch Cl. M22: Shar 1B **110**
   M43: Droy 4E **57**
   OL4: O'ham 5F **31**
CHAIN BAR 1E **41**
Chainhurst Wlk. M13: Man 3F **25**
Chain Rd. M9: Man 3F **25**
Chain St. M1: Man 1C **10** (1C **66**)
Chain Wlk. M9: Man 4A **26**
Chalcombe Grange M12: Man 1B **82**
Chale Cl. M40: Man 4F **53**
Chale Dr. M24: Mid 3E **27**
Chalfont Av. M41: Urm 3A **76**
   (off Gladstone Rd.)
Chalfont Cl. OL8: O'ham 5D **31**
Chalfont Dr. M8: Man 5C **38**
   M28: Walk 4A **32**
Chalfont Ho. M5: Sal 5B **50**
   (off Amersham St.)
Chalford Rd. M23: Wyth 2C **108**
Challenor Sq. M12: Man 4C **68**
   (off Polesworth Cl.)
Challum Dr. OL9: Chad 1C **28**
Chamber Hall Cl. OL8: O'ham 5F **29**
Chamber Rd. OL8: O'ham 1E **43**
Chambers, The M33: Sale 3C **88**
   (off York Rd.)
Chambersfield Ct. M5: Sal 1B **64**
Champagnole Ct. SK16: Duk 5C **116**
Champneys Wlk. M9: Man 1F **53**
   (off Penerley Dr.)
Chancel Av. M5: Sal 3A **8** (2E **65**)
Chancel Cl. SK16: Duk 4E **73**
Chancellor La. M12: Man 2F **67**
Chancel M. SK1: Stoc 2C **106**
Chancel Pl. M1: Man 1F **11**
Chancery La. M2: Man 1B **10** (1C **66**)
Chancery Pl. M2: Man 1B **10**
Chancery St. OL4: O'ham 3E **31**
   OL9: Chad 1E **29**
Chancery Wlk. OL9: Chad 1E **29**
Chandlers Point M50: Sal 2C **64**
Chandlers Row M28: Wors 2C **46**
Chandley Ct. SK1: Stoc 4C **106**
   (off Ward St.)
Chandley St. SK8: Chea 5F **103**
Chandos Gro. M5: Sal 5F **49**
Chandos Hall M1: Man 3E **11**
Chandos Rd. M21: Chor 4E **79**
   M25: Pres 2D **37**
   SK4: Stoc 2D **95**
Chandos Rd. Sth. M21: Chor 5E **79**
Change Way M3: Sal 2E **5** (4A **52**)
Chanters Cl. M9: Man 1A **96**
Chantry Cl. SK5: Stoc 1A **96**
Chantry Wlk. M8: Man 5B **38**
   (off Lanfield Dr.)
Chapel Cl. BL9: Bury 2D **13**
   SK16: Duk 2B **73**
Chapel Ct. M33: Sale 2A **88**
   (off Green La.)
   SK14: Hyde 4E **87**
Chapel Dr. OL6: A Lyme 2F **59**
CHAPEL FIELD 1E **21**
Chapelfield M26: Rad 1E **21**
Chapel Fld. Rd. M34: Dent 2B **86**
Chapelfield Rd. M12: Man 2E **67**
Chapel Gdns. M34: Aud 4B **72**
   (off Guide La.)

Chapel Grn. M34: Dent 2B 86
Chapel Gro. M26: Rad 1C 20
   M41: Urm 3A 76
Chapel Hill SK16: Duk 2E 73
Chapel Hill Dr. M9: Man 1E 39
Chapel Ho. SK5: Stoc 5A 84
Chapel La. M9: Man 5D 25
   M32: Stre 4E 77
   M33: Sale 2A 88
Chapel Pl. M41: Urm 2F 61
Chapel Rd. M22: Nor 3F 101
   M25: Pres 3B 36
   M27: Swin 5E 33
   M33: Sale 3D 89
   OL8: O'ham 1E 43
Chapel St. BL4: Farn 1A 18
   M3: Sal 4C 4 (5F 51)
   M19: Man 4C 82
   M24: Mid 2E 25
     (Manchester Old Rd.)
   M24: Mid 1B 26
     (Wood St., not continuous)
   M25: Pres 5C 22
   M26: Rad 2D 19
   M27: Pen 3C 34
   M30: Ecc 1E 61
   M34: Aud 4B 72
   M43: Droy 1D 71
   OL6: A Lyme 4E 59
   SK4: Stoc 1F 103
   SK8: Chea 1F 111
   SK14: Hyde 3F 87
   SK16: Duk 2D 73
Chapel Ter. M20: Man 1D 93
Chapeltown Rd. M26: Rad 1C 20
Chapeltown St. M1: Man 2F 11 (2D 67)
Chapel Vw. SK16: Duk 2E 73
Chapel Wlk. M24: Mid 2E 25
     (off Chapel St.)
   M25: Pres 3C 36
   M30: Ecc 5B 48
     (off Cambridge Gro.)
   M45: White 5D 13
Chapel Walks M2: Man 5B 6 (1B 66)
   M33: Sale 3D 89
Chaplin Cl. M6: Sal 3A 50
Chapman Gallery 2A 4 (5D 51)
Chapman M. M18: Man 5F 69
Chapman St. M18: Man 4F 69
Chappell Rd. M43: Droy 5C 56
Chapter St. M40: Man 3B 54
Chard Dr. M22: Wyth 5F 109
Charges St. OL7: A Lyme 1B 72
Chariot St. M11: Man 2F 69
Charlbury Av. M25: Pres 1A 38
   SK5: Stoc 2B 96
Charles Av. M34: Aud 3C 70
Charles Ct. WA15: Tim 5D 99
     (off Thorley La., not continuous)
Charles Halle Rd. M15: Man 5C 66
Charles Morris Cl. M35: Fail 4D 43
Charles Morris Ho. M35: Fail 5C 42
Charles Shaw Cl. OL4: O'ham 1F 31
Charles St. BL4: Farn 1A 18
   BL4: Kea 2A 18
   M1: Man 4C 10 (3C 66)
   M6: Sal .3B 50
     (not continuous)
   M27: Swin 3F 33
   M34: Dent 5B 72

Charles St. M43: Droy 1A 70
   M45: White 2B 22
   OL7: A Lyme 4B 116 (5D 59)
   OL9: O'ham 3E 29
   SK1: Stoc 4B 106
     (not continuous)
   SK16: Duk 5B 116 (2D 73)
Charleston Sq. M41: Urm 2D 75
Charleston St. OL8: O'ham 5B 30
CHARLESTOWN
   M6 . . . . .2D 51
   M9 . . . . .1C 40
Charlestown Ct. OL6: A Lyme 3D 59
Charlestown Ind. Est.
   OL6: A Lyme 1B 116 (3D 59)
Charlestown Rd. M9: Man 2F 39
Charlestown Way
   OL6: A Lyme 1A 116 (4C 58)
Charles Wlk. M45: White 2B 22
Charlesworth Av. M34: Dent 5B 86
Charlesworth St. M11: Man 2B 68
   SK1: Stoc 5B 118 (4B 106)
Charley Av. M7: Sal 3F 51
Charlotte St. M1: Man 1C 10 (4E 67)
   SK1: Stoc 5D 97
   SK8: Chea 1F 111
Charlton Av. M25: Pres 1D 37
   M30: Ecc 1F 61
Charlton Ct. M25: Pres 1D 37
Charlton Dr. M27: Ward 2F 33
   M33: Sale 4E 89
Charlton Pl. M12: Man 4F 11 (3D 67)
Charlton Rd. M19: Man 4D 83
Charminster Dr. M8: Man 4D 39
Charminster M. M27: Swin 1B 48
Charmouth Wlk. M22: Wyth 3B 110
Charnley Cl. M33: Sale 4C 88
   M40: Man 4A 54
Charnley St. M45: White 1B 22
Charnville Rd. SK8: Gat 1B 110
Charnwood Av. M34: Dent 2D 85
Charnwood Cl. OL6: A Lyme 5E 45
Charnwood Rd. M9: Man 4F 25
Charter Cl. M33: Sale 5A 88
Charter Ho. M30: Ecc 1B 62
Charter St. M3: Man 1B 6 (4B 52)
   OL1: O'ham 1F 117 (1C 30)
Chartist Ho. SK14: Hyde 3F 87
Chartwell Cl. M5: Sal 5B 50
Chartwell Dr. M23: Wyth 4A 100
Chase, The M28: Wors 2C 46
Chaseley Fld. Mans. M6: Sal 3A 50
Chaseley Rd. M6: Sal 3A 50
Chase St. M4: Man 1D 7 (4C 52)
Chasetown Rd. M23: Wyth 5F 99
Chasewood M19: Man 4C 82
     (off Motherwell Av.)
Chassen Av. M41: Urm 3C 74
Chassen Ct. M41: Urm 4D 75
Chassen Rd. M41: Urm 3D 75
Chassen Road Station (Rail) 4D 75
Chataway Rd. M8: Man 4E 39
Chatburn Rd. M21: Chor 5E 79
Chatcombe Rd. M22: Wyth 4C 108
Chatfield Rd. M21: Chor 5D 79
Chatford Cl. M7: Sal 1E 5 (3A 52)
Chatham Cl. M20: Man 2C 92
Chatham Gro. M20: Man 2C 92
Chatham Ho. SK3: Stoc 3A 106
     (off York St.)

Chatham Rd. M16: Old T 2E **79**
  M18: Man 2A **84**
Chatham St. M1: Man 1E **11** (1D **67**)
  SK3: Stoc 5A **118** (3F **105**)
  SK14: Hyde .5F **87**
Chatley Rd. M30: Ecc 1B **60**
Chatley St. M3: Man 1B **6** (3B **52**)
Chatswood Av. SK2: Stoc 5B **106**
Chatsworth Av. M25: Pres 5D **23**
Chatsworth Cl. BL9: Bury 1C **12**
  M41: Urm 3A **76**
  M43: Droy 4F **55**
  WA15: Tim 5E **99**
Chatsworth Ct. M9: Man 4C **24**
              (off Deanswood Dr.)
Chatsworth Cres. M32: Stre 2B **76**
             (off Chatsworth Rd.)
Chatsworth Rd. M18: Man 5E **69**
  M28: Wors .1D **47**
  M30: Ecc 3B **48**
  M32: Stre 2B **76**
  M43: Droy 5A **56**
Chatsworth St. OL4: O'ham 4E **31**
Chatterton Cl. M20: Man 2E **93**
Chattock St. M16: W Ran 2A **80**
Chatwood Rd. M40: Man 2F **41**
Chaucer Av. M43: Droy 1C **70**
  SK5: Stoc 5F **83**
Chaucer M. SK1: Stoc 2D **107**
Chaucer Rd. M24: Mid 4D **17**
Chaucer St. OL1: O'ham 4D **117** (3A **30**)
Chaumont Way
  OL6: A Lyme 2C **116** (4D **59**)
Chauncy Rd. M40: Man 4A **42**
Chaytor Av. M40: Man 5D **41**
CHEADLE 5A **104**
Cheadle Av. M7: Sal 5C **36**
Cheadle Grn. SK8: Chea 5A **104**
CHEADLE HEATH 4C **104**
CHEADLE HULME 4F **111**
Cheadle Old Rd. SK3: Stoc 5C **104**
Cheadle Pl. SK8: Chea 5B **104**
Cheadle Pools & Target Fitness Cen.
  . . . . .2F **111**
Cheadle Rd. SK8: Chea 2F **111**
Cheadle Royal Bus. Pk. SK8: Chea . . .3E **111**
Cheadle St. M11: Man 2F **69**
Cheam Cl. M11: Man 3D **69**
Cheam Rd. WA15: Tim 3B **98**
Cheapside M2: Man 5B **6** (1B **66**)
  M24: Mid 4C **16**
  OL1: O'ham 3D **117** (2A **30**)
Cheddar St. M18: Man 5F **69**
Chedlee Dr. SK8: Chea H 5F **111**
Chedlin Dr. M23: Wyth 2C **108**
Chedworth Dr. M23: Wyth 5D **101**
Cheeky Chimps Activity Cen. 3F **31**
Cheeryble St. M11: Man 3B **70**
             (not continuous)
  M43: Droy 2B **70**
Cheesden Wlk. M45: White 5E **13**
Cheetham Av. M24: Mid 5D **17**
Cheetham Fold Rd. SK14: Hyde 5F **87**
CHEETHAM HILL 5B **38**
Cheetham Hill Rd. M4: Man . . .1C **6** (4C **52**)
  M8: Man 1C **6** (4B **38**)
  SK16: Duk 4F **73**
Cheetham Pde. M8: Man 4B **38**
Cheetham Pk. Cen. M8: Man 2B **52**

Cheetham Rd. M27: Swin 5C **34**
Cheetham St. M24: Mid 1B **26**
  M35: Fail 4C **42**
              (not continuous)
  M40: Man 2A **54**
  OL1: O'ham .2D **31**
Cheetwood Rd. M8: Man 3B **52**
Cheetwood St. M8: Man 1F **5** (3A **52**)
Chelbourne Dr. OL8: O'ham 2D **43**
Chelburn Ct. SK3: Stoc 5A **106**
Cheldon Wlk. M40: Man 1E **55**
             (off Bridlington Cl.)
Chelford Cl. M13: Man 5F **67**
  M24: Mid 4E **17**
  WA15: Alt 5A **98**
Chelford Dr. M27: Swin 2A **34**
Chelford Gro. SK3: Stoc 5E **105**
Chelford Rd. M16: Old T 2E **79**
  M33: Sale .1A **100**
  SK9: Hand .4F **115**
Chell St. M12: Man 1B **82**
Chelmsford Av. M40: Man 3D **55**
Chelmsford Rd. SK3: Stoc 3E **105**
Chelmsford St. OL8: O'ham 4A **30**
Chelmsford Wlk. M34: Dent 4C **86**
             (off Kendal Av.)
Chelsea Rd. M40: Man 2E **55**
Chelsea St. BL9: Bury 1B **12**
Chelsfield Gro. M21: Chor 5F **79**
Chelston Av. M40: Man 2F **41**
Chelston Dr. SK8: H Grn 3E **115**
Cheltenham Cres. M7: Sal 4A **38**
Cheltenham Dr. M33: Sale 4E **89**
Cheltenham Grn. M24: Mid 3C **26**
Cheltenham Rd. M21: Chor 3D **79**
  M24: Mid 3C **26**
  SK3: Stoc .4C **104**
Cheltenham St. M6: Sal 3C **50**
  OL1: O'ham .1D **31**
Chelt Wlk. M22: Wyth 4D **109**
Chelwood Dr. M43: Droy 5B **56**
Chendre Cl. M27: Pen 2B **34**
Chendre Rd. M9: Man 1D **41**
Cheney Cl. M11: Man 3F **69**
Chepstow Ho. M1: Man 3B **10**
Chepstow Rd. M21: Chor 4C **78**
  M27: Clif 2C **34**
Chepstow St. M1: Man 3B **10** (2B **66**)
             (not continuous)
Chepstow St. Sth. M1: Man . . .3B **10** (2B **66**)
Chequers Rd. M21: Chor 5D **79**
Cherington Cl. M23: Wyth 1D **101**
Cherington Rd. SK8: Chea 2E **111**
Cheriton Av. M33: Sale 3E **89**
Cheriton Rd. M41: Urm 3A **76**
Cherry Av. M41: Urm 3F **69**
  OL6: A Lyme 1D **59**
  OL8: O'ham .1E **45**
Cherry Ct. M33: Sale 4C **88**
  WA15: Tim 4E **99**
             (off Whitley Pl.)
Cherry Dr. M27: Swin 4C **34**
Cherry Hinton OL1: O'ham 1F **29**
             (off Cottam St.)
Cherry Holt Av. SK4: Stoc 4B **94**
Cherry St. M25: Pres 4E **23**
Cherryton Wlk. M13: Man 4E **67**
Cherry Tree Cl. WA15: Tim 5D **99**
Cherry Tree Ct. M6: Sal 5C **50**
Cherry Tree La. SK2: Stoc 5E **107**

Cherry Tree Rd. M23: Wyth	.2B **100**
Cherry Tree Wlk. M32: Stre	.4E **77**
Cherrywood OL9: Chad	.2F **42**
Chertsey Cl. M18: Man	.5A **70**
Chervil Cl. M14: Man	.5E **81**
Cherwell Cl. M45: White	.1C **22**
OL8: O'ham	.3E **43**
Chesham Av. M22: Wyth	.2E **109**
M41: Urm	.2A **74**
Chesham Ho. *M5: Sal*	.1B **64**
(off Amersham St.)	
Chesham Rd. M30: Ecc	.2E **61**
OL4: O'ham	.3E **31**
Cheshill Ct. M7: Sal	.1B **52**
Cheshire Cl. M32: Stre	.4D **77**
Cheshire Gdns. M14: Man	.4C **80**
Chesney Av. OL9: Chad	.2A **42**
Chesshyre Av. M4: Man	.5F **53**
Chessington Ri. M27: Clif	.1C **34**
Chester Av. M41: Urm	.2A **76**
M45: White	.2C **22**
Chesterfield Gro. OL6: A Lyme	.4F **59**
Chesterfield Cl. OL4: O'ham	.3D **31**
Chesterfield Wlk. M34: Dent	.5C **86**
Chestergate SK1: Stoc	.2A **118** (2A **106**)
SK3: Stoc	.3A **118** (2F **105**)
(not continuous)	
Chester Rd. M15: Man	.5B **8** (5D **65**)
M16: Old T	.5D **65**
M32: Stre	.5E **77**
Chester Sq. OL6: A Lyme	.4A **116** (5C **58**)
Chester St. M1: Man	.5B **10** (3C **66**)
M15: Man	.5B **10** (3B **66**)
M25: Pres	.4C **22**
M27: Swin	.5A **34**
M34: Dent	.3B **86**
OL9: O'ham	.4E **29**
SK3: Stoc	.2F **105**
Chesterton Gro. M43: Droy	.5C **56**
Chesterton Rd. M23: Wyth	.3F **99**
Chestnut Av. M21: Chor	.5D **79**
M28: Walk	.2A **32**
M43: Droy	.4A **56**
M45: White	.2B **22**
SK8: Chea	.1F **111**
Chestnut Cl. OL4: O'ham	.1F **31**
Chestnut Cres. OL8: O'ham	.2C **44**
Chestnut Dr. M33: Sale	.2A **98**
Chestnut Gdns. M34: Dent	.3A **86**
Chestnut Gro. M26: Rad	.1C **20**
M35: Fail	.1B **56**
Chestnut Ho. M30: Ecc	.3C **46**
Chestnut St. OL9: Chad	.1B **42**
Chestnut Vs. SK4: Stoc	.1E **105**
Chesworth Cl. SK1: Stoc	.5B **118**
Chesworth Ct. M43: Droy	.1B **70**
Chesworth Fold	
SK1: Stoc	.5B **118** (3B **106**)
Chetwynd Av. M41: Urm	.3E **75**
Chetwynd Cl. M33: Sale	.2A **88**
Chevassut St. M15: Man	.5E **9** (4A **66**)
Chevington Dr. M9: Man	.1F **53**
SK4: Stoc	.5F **93**
Cheviot Av. OL8: O'ham	.1A **44**
Cheviot Cl. M6: Sal	.4A **50**
M24: Mid	.1F **27**
OL9: Chad	.4C **28**
SK4: Stoc	.5F **95**
Cheviot Ct. OL8: O'ham	.5A **30**
Cheviot St. M3: Man	.1B **6**

Chevril Cl. M15: Man	.5C **10** (4C **66**)
Chevron Cl. M6: Sal	.5D **51**
Chevron Pl. WA14: Alt	.4A **98**
Chicago Av. M90: Man A	.2D **113**
Chichester Cl. M33: Sale	.5A **88**
Chichester Cres. OL9: Chad	.1C **28**
Chichester Rd. M15: Man	.5A **66**
(Bold St.)	
M15: Man	.4B **66**
(Old Birley St.)	
Chichester Rd. Sth. M15: Man	.5A **66**
Chichester Way *M34: Dent*	.4C **86**
(off Trowbridge Rd.)	
Chicken La. SK5: Stoc	.3B **84**
Chidlow Av. M20: Man	.1C **92**
Chidwall Rd. M22: Wyth	.4D **109**
Chief St. OL4: O'ham	.3C **30**
Chiffon Way M3: Sal	.2C **4** (4F **51**)
Chigwell Cl. M22: Wyth	.1A **110**
Chilcombe Wlk. *M9: Man*	.4A **26**
(off Crossmead Dr.)	
Chilcote Av. M33: Sale	.4A **88**
Chilham Rd. M28: Walk	.2A **32**
M30: Ecc	.3B **48**
Chilham St. M27: Swin	.1A **48**
Chill Factore	.4E **61**
Chillington Wlk. M34: Dent	.4A **86**
Chilmark Dr. M23: Wyth	.5C **100**
Chiltern Av. M41: Urm	.2A **74**
Chiltern Cl. M28: Walk	.4A **32**
Chiltern Dr. M27: Swin	.1B **48**
Chiltern Gdns. M33: Sale	.2E **99**
Chilton Av. OL9: Chad	.3C **28**
Chilton Dr. M24: Mid	.2E **27**
Chilworth St. M14: Man	.3D **81**
Chime Bank M8: Man	.1E **53**
China La. M1: Man	.1E **11** (1D **67**)
Chinese Arts Cen.	.4D **7**
Chingford Wlk. *M13: Man*	.1B **82**
(off Bates St.)	
Chinley Av. M32: Stre	.1C **76**
M40: Man	.4C **40**
Chinley Cl. M33: Sale	.5F **89**
SK4: Stoc	.5D **95**
Chinley St. M6: Sal	.2D **51**
OL1: O'ham	.1D **31**
Chinwell Vw. *M19: Man*	.4C **82**
(off Carrill Gro. E.)	
Chippendale Av. SK2: Stoc	.4F **107**
Chippenham Av. M4: Man	.5F **53**
Chippenham Rd. M4: Man	.5E **53**
Chipping Sq. M12: Man	.1B **82**
Chipstead Av. M12: Man	.5A **68**
Chirton Wlk. *M40: Man*	.5C **40**
(off Webdale Dr.)	
Chiseldon Av. M22: Wyth	.4A **110**
Chiselhurst St. M8: Man	.5C **38**
Chisholm Ct. *M24: Mid*	.5B **16**
(off Cross St.)	
Chisholm St. M11: Man	.3F **69**
Chisledon Av. M7: Sal	.1B **52**
Chislehurst Av. M41: Urm	.2E **75**
Chiswick Rd. M20: Man	.5E **93**
Chisworth Wlk. *M34: Dent*	.5C **86**
(off Matlock Av.)	
Choir St. M7: Sal	.3A **52**
Cholmondeley Av. WA14: Tim	.2A **98**
Cholmondeley Rd. M6: Sal	.3D **49**
Chomlea Mnr. M6: Sal	.3E **49**
Choral Gro. M7: Sal	.2A **52**

Chorley Rd. M27: Ward 3F **33**
  M33: Sale 1A **100**
Chorley St. M32: Stre 1B **78**
Chorley Wood Av. M19: Man 2B **94**
Chorlton Brook M30: Ecc 2F **47**
Chorlton Brook Ho. SK8: Chea 5A **104**
  (off Stockport Rd.)
Chorlton Ct. M16: Old T 2E **79**
  (off Up. Chorlton Rd.)
CHORLTON-CUM-HARDY 5A **78**
Chorlton Dr. SK8: Chea 5A **104**
Chorlton Ees Nature Reserve 1B **90**
CHORLTON FOLD 2F **47**
Chorlton Fold M30: Ecc 2F **47**
  (not continuous)
Chorlton Grn. M21: Chor 5C **78**
Chorlton Gro. SK1: Stoc 4D **107**
Chorlton Leisure Cen. 4D **79**
Chorlton Mill M1: Man 4B **10**
Chorlton Pk. 1E **91**
Chorlton Pl. M21: Chor 4D **79**
Chorlton Point M21: Chor 5C **78**
  (off Wilbraham Rd.)
Chorlton Rd. M15: Man 1F **79**
  M16: Old T 5D **9** (1F **79**)
Chorlton St. M1: Man 2D **11** (2C **66**)
  M16: Old T 5C **65**
CHORLTON UPON MEDLOCK 1F **81**
Chorlton Vw. M21: Chor 5C **78**
  (off Whitelow Rd.)
CHORLTONVILLE 2E **91**
Chorlton Water Pk. 4D **91**
Chretien Rd. M22: Nor 1F **101**
Christchurch Av. M5: Sal 4A **4** (5D **51**)
Christchurch Ct. OL9: O'ham 4E **29**
Christie Flds. Office Pk. M21: Chor . .3F **91**
Christie Ct. M32: Stre 2A **78**
Christie St. SK1: Stoc 4C **106**
Christie St. Ind. Est. SK1: Stoc 4C **106**
Christie Way M21: Chor 3F **91**
Christleton Av. SK4: Stoc 3F **95**
Christleton Way SK9: Hand 4F **115**
  (off Spath La.)
Christopher St. M5: Sal 1C **64**
  M40: Man 3F **55**
Christy Cl. SK14: Hyde 2E **87**
Chudleigh Rd. M8: Man 2C **38**
Church Av. M6: Sal 5C **59**
  M34: Dent 5C **86**
  M40: Man 2E **55**
Church Brow M24: Mid 5C **16**
  SK14: Hyde 4F **87**
Church Cl. M26: Rad 1D **19**
  M34: Aud 3B **72**
  (off Ashworth La.)
  SK9: Hand 5F **115**
  SK16: Duk 5C **116** (1D **73**)
Church Cft. BL9: Bury 2D **13**
Churchdale Rd. M9: Man 5D **25**
Church Dr. M25: Pres 5C **22**
Churches, The OL6: A Lyme 5E **59**
Churchfield M21: Chor 5C **78**
Churchfield Cl. M26: Rad 2F **19**
Churchfield Rd. M6: Sal 3A **72**
Churchfields M34: Aud 2C **68**
Churchfield Wlk. M11: Man 4A **76**
  (off Pitman Cl.)
Churchgate M41: Urm 4A **76**
  SK1: Stoc 2C **118** (2B **106**)
Churchgate Bldgs. M1: Man 2E **67**

Church Grn. M6: Sal 4B **50**
Church Gro. M30: Ecc 1A **62**
Churchill Av. M16: W Ran 3F **79**
Churchill Cl. M6: Sal 5B **50**
Churchill Cres. SK5: Stoc 4A **84**
Churchill Pl. M30: Ecc 3E **47**
Churchill Rd. WA14: B'ath 4A **98**
Churchill St. E. OL4: O'ham . . .5F **117** (3C **30**)
  SK4: Stoc 5F **95**
Churchill St. E. OL4: O'ham 3C **30**
Churchill Way M6: Sal 5C **50**
  M17: T Pk 3E **63**
Church La. M7: Sal 3D **37**
  M9: Man 5A **40**
  (Kingscliffe St.)
  M9: Man 4F **39**
  (Water St.)
  M19: Man 2B **94**
  M25: Pres 5C **22**
  M33: Sale 2A **88**
  M45: White 1A **22**
  OL1: O'ham 3E **117** (2B **30**)
Churchley Cl. SK3: Stoc 5C **104**
Churchley Rd. SK3: Stoc 4C **104**
Church Lodge SK4: Stoc 1A **104**
Church Mnr. SK4: Stoc 4D **95**
Church Mdw. BL9: Bury 1D **13**
  SK14: Hyde 2E **87**
Church Mdw. Gdns. SK14: Hyde 2E **87**
Church M. M34: Dent 2A **86**
Church Pas. OL1: O'ham 3E **117** (2B **30**)
Church Rd. BL4: Farn, Kea 1A **18**
  M22: Nor 2F **101**
  M24: Mid 2F **27**
  M26: Rad 1C **18**
  M28: Walk 1A **32**
  M30: Ecc 5B **48**
  M33: Sale 4F **89**
  M41: Urm 4B **74**
  SK4: Stoc 1F **105**
  SK8: Gat 1C **110**
  SK9: Hand 5F **115**
Church Rd. E. M33: Sale 4F **89**
Church Rd. W. M33: Sale 4F **89**
Churchside Cl. M9: Man 2F **39**
Church Sq. SK16: Duk 5B **116** (1D **73**)
Churchstoke Wlk. M23: Wyth 4A **100**
Church St. BL4: Farn 1A **18**
  BL4: Kea 2A **18**
  M4: Man 4D **7** (5C **52**)
  M24: Mid 4C **16**
  M27: Pen 4D **35**
  M27: Swin 5A **34**
  M30: Ecc 5A **48**
  (not continuous)
  M32: Stre 4E **77**
  M34: Aud 3A **72**
  (off Ryecroft La.)
  M35: Fail 4B **42**
  M43: Droy 1C **70**
  OL1: O'ham 3E **117** (2B **30**)
  OL6: A Lyme 3C **116** (5D **59**)
  SK4: Stoc 5A **96**
  (not continuous)
  SK8: Chea 5F **103**
  SK14: Hyde 4F **87**
  SK16: Duk 5C **116** (1D **73**)
  WA14: Alt 5A **98**
Church St. E. OL4: O'ham 1F **31**
Church St. Ind. Est. M24: Mid 4C **16**

Church Ter. *M33*: Sale 2C **88**
          (off Stamford St.)
    OL1: O'ham 3E **117** (2B **30**)
    SK4: Stoc 1F **105**
    SK9: Hand 5F **115**
Church Vw. *M35*: Fail 4B **42**
    SK14: Hyde 4F **87**
Churchwood Rd. *M20*: Man 5D **93**
Churnet *M40*: Man 2F **53**
Churston Av. *M9*: Man 5A **26**
Churton Av. *M14*: Man 3D **81**
    M33: Sale 5B **88**
Churton Rd. *M18*: Man 2E **83**
Churwell Av. *SK4*: Stoc 4B **94**
Cicero St. *M9*: Man 4A **40**
    OL1: O'ham 1C **30**
Cinder St. *M4*: Man 5E **53**
Cineworld Cinema
    Ashton-under-Lyne 4B **58**
    Manchester 2F **103**
    Stockport 4A **118**
Cinnabar Dr. *M24*: Mid 4B **16**
Cinnamon Cl. *M22*: Nor 3A **102**
Cipher St. *M4*: Man 2F **7** (4E **53**)
Circle, The *M32*: Stre 1B **76**
Circle Ct. *M32*: Stre 1B **76**
Circle Sth. *M17*: T Pk 4A **64**
Circuit, The *M20*: Man 3D **93**
    SK3: Stoc 5E **105**
Circular Rd. *M20*: Man 3D **93**
    M25: Pres 2D **37**
    M34: Dent 3A **86**
Ciss La. *M41*: Urm 3A **76**
Citadel, The *SK1*: Stoc 4B **118**
Citrus Way *M6*: Sal 5C **50**
CITY, THE 3F **85**
City Airport Manchester 3A **60**
City Av. *M34*: Dent 3A **86**
City Course Trad. Est.
    M11: Man 3C **103**
        (off Whitworth St.)
City Ct. Trad. Est. *M4*: Man 5E **53**
City Gdns. *M34*: Dent 3F **85**
City Lofts Salford Quays
    M50: Sal 3B **64**
City of Manchester Stadium 1B **68**
City Pk. *M16*: Old T 5D **65**
City Point *M3*: Man 4E **5** (5A **52**)
    M32: Stre 5B **64**
City Rd. *M15*: Man 5D **9** (4E **65**)
City Rd. E. *M15*: Man 4A **10** (3B **66**)
City Rd. Sth. *M15*: Man 4A **10** (3B **66**)
City Tower *M1*: Man 1D **11** (1C **66**)
City Wlk. *M27*: Pen 4D **35**
Clack Rd. *M9*: Man 3F **39**
Clacton Wlk. *M13*: Man 4E **67**
        (off Kirkstall Sq.)
Clague St. *M11*: Man 5C **54**
Claife Av. *M40*: Man 2D **41**
CLAMMERCLOUGH 1A **18**
Clammerclough Rd. *BL4*: Kea 1A **18**
Clandon Av. *M30*: Ecc 1D **61**
Clapham St. *M40*: Man 4E **41**
Clara St. *OL9*: O'ham 5E **29**
Clare Av. *SK9*: Hand 5E **115**
Clare Ct. *SK1*: Stoc 2C **106**
Claremont Av. *M20*: Man 3C **92**
    SK4: Stoc 3E **95**
    WA14: W Tim 3A **98**

Claremont Dr. *WA14*: W Tim 3A **98**
Claremont Gdns.
    OL6: A Lyme 2F **59**
Claremont Gro. *M20*: Man 5C **92**
Claremont Range *M18*: Man 1B **84**
Claremont Rd. *M6*: Sal 2F **49**
    M16: W Ran 2A **80**
    M33: Sale 3D **89**
Claremont St. *M35*: Fail 4B **42**
    OL6: A Lyme 3F **59**
    OL8: O'ham 2B **44**
    OL9: Chad 1E **29**
Clarence Arc. *OL6*: A Lyme . . .3C **116** (5D **59**)
Clarence Av. *M17*: T Pk 3B **62**
    M45: White 2C **22**
    OL8: O'ham 5F **29**
Clarence Rd. *M13*: Man 2A **82**
    M27: Swin 5E **33**
    OL6: A Lyme 3E **59**
    SK4: Stoc 3D **95**
Clarence St. *BL4*: Farn 1A **18**
    M2: Man 1B **10** (1B **66**)
    M7: Sal 3E **51**
    SK15: Stal 1F **73**
Clarendon Av. *SK4*: Stoc 5D **95**
    WA15: Alt 5A **98**
Clarendon Cotts. *SK9*: Sty 5C **114**
Clarendon Cres. *M30*: Ecc 4B **48**
    M33: Sale 3F **89**
Clarendon Ind. Est. *SK14*: Hyde 2F **87**
Clarendon Pl. *M30*: Ecc 5B **48**
        (off Wellington St.)
    SK14: Hyde 3F **87**
Clarendon Rd. *M16*: W Ran 3E **79**
    M27: Swin 4B **34**
    M30: Ecc 4B **48**
    M33: Sale 4F **89**
    M34: Aud 3C **70**
    M34: Dent 3D **87**
    M41: Urm 2A **74**
    SK14: Hyde 2F **87**
Clarendon Rd. W. *M21*: Chor 3D **79**
Clarendon St. *M15*: Man 5A **10** (4B **66**)
        (not continuous)
    M45: White 1B **22**
    SK5: Stoc 5B **96**
    SK14: Hyde 2F **87**
        (Clarke Way, not continuous)
    SK14: Hyde 3F **87**
        (Market St.)
    SK16: Duk 2C **72**
        (not continuous)
Clarendon Wlk. *M5*: Sal 5C **50**
        (off Cavell Way)
Clare Rd. *M19*: Man 5C **82**
    SK5: Stoc 4B **96**
Clare St. *M1*: Man 4F **11** (3D **67**)
    M34: Dent 1A **86**
Claribel St. *M11*: Man 2A **68**
Claridge Rd. *M21*: Chor 3C **78**
Clarion St. *M4*: Man 2F **7** (4E **53**)
Clark Av. *M18*: Man 5A **70**
Clarke Av. *M5*: Sal 3D **65**
Clarke Brow *M24*: Mid 5C **16**
Clarke Ind. Est.
    M32: Stre 5B **62**
Clarke's Hill *M45*: White 2D **21**
Clarke St. *BL4*: Farn 2A **18**
    OL7: A Lyme 2B **72**
Clarkethorn Ter. *SK5*: Stoc 5A **96**

Clarke Way SK14: Hyde 2F 87
Clarksfield Rd. OL4: O'ham 3E 31
Clarksfield St. OL4: O'ham 3E 31
Clark's Hill M25: Pres 5C 22
Clarkson Cl. M24: Mid 2E 25
   M34: Dent 3F 85
Clarkwell Cl. OL1: O'ham 1A **30**
             (off Redvers St.)
Clatford Wlk. M9: Man 5F **39**
           (off Carisbrook St.)
Claude Av. M27: Swin 4F 33
Claude Rd. M21: Chor 1C 90
Claude St. M8: Man 3C 38
   M27: Swin 4F 33
   M30: Ecc 4D 47
Claverham Wlk. M23: Wyth 4A **100**
          (off Sandy La.)
Claverton Rd. M23: Wyth 1A 108
Claxton Av. M9: Man 1F 39
Clay Bank M43: Droy 1B 70
Claybrook Wlk. M11: Man 1C **68**
        (off Sledmere Cl.)
Clayburn St. M15: Man 4A 66
Claycourt Av. M30: Ecc 3D 47
Claygate Dr. M9: Man 4F 25
Clayhill Wlk. M9: Man 3A 40
Clay La. M23: Wyth 2B 108
   SK9: Sty 5D 115
   WA15: Hale, Tim 2A 108
Claymoor OL1: O'ham 2D 117
Claymore St. M18: Man 4A 70
Clay St. OL8: O'ham 5A 30
Claythorpe Wlk. M8: Man 1A 38
CLAYTON 1E 69
Clayton Av. M20: Man 4D 93
CLAYTON BRIDGE 3A 56
Claytonbrook Rd. M11: Man 1E 69
Clayton Cl. M15: Man 5A 66
Clayton Ct. M11: Man 3E 69
Clayton Hall Rd.
   M11: Man 5E 55
Clayton Ind. Est. M11: Man 1F 69
Clayton La. M11: Man 2D 69
Clayton La. Sth. M11: Man 3C 68
Clayton St. M11: Man 4D 55
   M34: Dent 3B 86
   M35: Fail 5B 42
   OL9: Chad 1C 42
   SK16: Duk 2F 73
Clayton Va. M11: Man 4E 55
Cleadon Av. M18: Man 1E 83
Clearwater Dr. M20: Man 3B 92
Cleavley St. M30: Ecc 5D 47
Clee Av. M13: Man 3B 82
Cleethorpes Av. M9: Man 1D 39
Cleeve Rd. M23: Wyth 1C 100
   OL4: O'ham 3E 31
Clegg Pl. OL6: A Lyme 3F 59
Clegg St. M43: Droy 1B 70
   M45: White 2B 22
   OL1: O'ham 4E 117 (3B 30)
           (not continuous)
   OL4: O'ham 5F 117 (3B 30)
Clelland St. BL4: Farn 2A 20
Clematis Wlk. M27: Ward 2A 34
Clement Ct. M11: Man 3B **70**
        (off Toxteth St.)
Clementine Cl. M6: Sal 5D **51**
       (off Coconut Gro.)
Clement Stott Cl. M9: Man 5B 26

Clement St. OL9: O'ham 1D 43
   SK4: Stoc 5A 96
Cleminson St. M3: Sal 4C 4 (5F 51)
Clerewood Av. SK8: H Grn 2D 115
Clerk's Ct. M5: Sal 3C 76
Clevedon Av. M41: Urm 1D 88
Clevedon Rd. OL9: Chad 1C 28
Clevedon St. M9: Man 5A 40
Cleveland Av. M6: Sal 4E 49
   M19: Man 3D 83
   SK14: Hyde 3E 87
Cleveland Cl. M27: Clif 2C 34
Cleveland Rd. M8: Man 3D 39
   SK4: Stoc 4C 94
Cleveleys Av. M21: Chor 1E 91
   SK8: H Grn 5D 111
Cleveleys Gro. M7: Sal 5A 38
Cleworth Rd. M24: Mid 4B 16
Cleworth St. M15: Man 5C 8 (3F 65)
Cleworth Wlk. M15: Man 5C 8
Clibran St. M8: Man 1D 53
Clifden Dr. M22: Wyth 4A 110
CLIFF, THE 5F 37
Cliff Av. M7: Sal 1E 51
Cliff Cres. M7: Sal 5F 37
Cliffdale Dr. M8: Man 3C 38
Cliff Grange M7: Sal 5F 37
Cliff Gro. SK4: Stoc 4D 95
Clifford Av. M34: Dent 5A 72
   WA15: Tim 5D 99
Clifford Ct. M15: Man 5A **66**
       (off Chorlton Rd.)
   SK2: Stoc 5D 107
Clifford Lamb Ct. M9: Man 2D 41
Clifford St. M13: Man 5E 11 (4D 67)
   M27: Pen 4D 35
   M30: Ecc 2D 61
Cliff Rd. BL9: Bury 1B 12
CLIFTON 1B 34
Clifton Av. M14: Man 5F 81
   M30: Ecc 4F 47
   OL4: O'ham 4D 31
   SK8: H Grn 4C 110
Clifton Cl. M16: Old T 5F 65
   OL4: O'ham 4D 31
Clifton Country Pk. Local Nature Reserve
                   . . . . 4A 20
Clifton Ct. M27: Clif 5A 20
   SK4: Stoc 4C 94
Clifton Dr. M27: Clif 2E 35
   M27: Ward 3F 33
   SK8: Gat 1B 110
   SK8: H Grn 4C 110
CLIFTON GREEN 1C 34
Clifton Gro. M16: Old T 5F **65**
        (off Hamilton St.)
   M27: Ward 2F 33
Clifton Ho. M30: Ecc 4F **47**
        (off Clifton Rd.)
Clifton House Arboretum 4F 19
Clifton Ho. Rd. M27: Clif 4F 19
        (not continuous)
Clifton Ind. Est. M27: Clif 1D 35
CLIFTON JUNCTION 1E 35
Clifton Lodge SK2: Stoc 5C 106
Clifton Pk. Rd. SK2: Stoc 5C 106
Clifton Pl. M25: Pres 4C 22
Clifton Rd. M21: Chor 5E 79
   M25: Pres 5A 22
   M30: Ecc 4F 47

Clifton Rd. M33: Sale 5D **89**
    M41: Urm 3C **74**
    SK4: Stoc 5C **94**
Clifton Station (Rail) 2E **35**
Clifton St. BL4: Kea 5F **65**
    M16: Old T 2B **18**
        (not continuous)
    M35: Fail 3C **42**
    M40: Man 4B **54**
    OL6: A Lyme 4C **58**
Clifton Vw. M27: Clif 5A **20**
Clifton Vs. M35: Fail 3C **42**
Cliftonville Dr. M6: Sal 1D **49**
    M27: Swin 1C **48**
Clifton Vis. Cen. **4A 20**
Clifton Wlk. M14: Man 3F **15**
Climax Works SK5: Stoc 3A **84**
Clinton Av. M14: Man 3B **80**
Clinton Gdns. M14: Man 3C **80**
Clinton Ho. M5: Sal 1B **64**
        (off Amersham St.)
Clinton St. OL6: A Lyme 3F **59**
Clinton Wlk. OL4: O'ham 3C **30**
Clippers Quay M50: Sal 4C **64**
Clitheroe Rd. M13: Man 2B **82**
Clito St. M9: Man 4B **40**
Clive Av. M45: White 5A **12**
Cliveley Wlk. M27: Pen 4D **35**
Clive Lloyd Ct. M32: Stre 2A **78**
Clively Av. M27: Clif 3D **35**
Clive Rd. M35: Fail 5A **42**
Clive St. M4: Man 2E **7** (4D **53**)
    OL7: A Lyme 2C **58**
    OL8: O'ham 2F **43**
        (not continuous)
Clivewood Wlk. M12: Man **4A 68**
        (off Bennett St.)
Clivia Gro. M7: Sal 1F **51**
        (off Bk. Hilton St.)
Cloak St. M1: Man 4D **11** (3C **66**)
Clockhouse Av. M43: Droy 4A **56**
Clockhouse M. M43: Droy 4A **56**
Clock St. OL9: Chad 2D **43**
Cloister Cl. SK16: Duk 1F **103**
Cloister Rd. SK4: Stoc 4F **89**
Cloisters, The M33: Sale 5C **104**
    SK8: Chea 4B **40**
Cloister St. M9: Man 4B **40**
Clopton Wlk. M15: Man 5F **9** (4A **66**)
        (Birchvale Cl.)
    M15: Man **4A 66**
        (off Rolls Cres.)
Close, The M24: Mid 3D **17**
    M34: Dent 1F **85**
Clothorn Rd. M20: Man 4D **93**
Clough, The OL7: A Lyme 1D **59**
    SK5: Stoc 2D **97**
Clough Av. M33: Sale 2A **98**
Clough Bank M9: Man 2F **39**
Cloughbank M26: Rad 2E **19**
Clough Ct. M24: Mid 4D **17**
Clough Dr. M25: Pres 5B **22**
Cloughfield
    M5: Sal 3A **8** (2D **65**)
Clough Fold M26: Rad 2D **19**
Clough Fold Rd. SK14: Hyde 4E **87**
Clough Ga. OL8: O'ham 2F **43**
Cloughgate Ho. OL8: O'ham 2F **43**
        (off Hollins Rd.)
Clough Gro. M45: White 4A **12**

Clough La. M25: Pres 5B **22**
Clough Rd. M9: Man 4B **40**
    M24: Mid 4C **16**
    M35: Fail 5C **42**
    M43: Droy 5C **56**
Cloughs Av. OL9: Chad 1F **27**
Clough Side M9: Man 3B **40**
Clough St. BL4: Kea 2B **18**
    M24: Mid 4D **17**
    M26: Rad 1E **21**
    M40: Man 3E **55**
Cloughton Wlk. M40: Man 2F **55**
        (off Terence St.)
Clough Top Rd. M9: Man 2C **40**
Clough Wlk. SK5: Stoc 2D **97**
Clove Av. M18: Man 4A **70**
Clovelly Av. OL8: O'ham 2E **43**
Clovelly Rd. M21: Chor 5E **79**
    M27: Swin 5E **33**
    SK2: Stoc 3E **107**
Clovelly St. M40: Man 2F **55**
Clover Av. SK3: Stoc 5F **105**
Cloverbank Av. M19: Man 4F **93**
Clover Cres. OL8: O'ham 1F **45**
Clover Cft. M33: Sale 2F **99**
Cloverfield Wlk. M28: Walk 1A **32**
        (off Malvern Gro.)
Cloverley M33: Sale 1D **99**
Clover Rd. WA15: Tim 5C **98**
Clowes St. M3: Sal 4F **5** (5A **52**)
    M12: Man 4B **68**
        (not continuous)
    OL9: Chad 2D **43**
Club St. M11: Man 3B **70**
Clumber Rd. M18: Man 1B **84**
Clwyd Av. SK3: Stoc 4F **105**
Clyde Av. M45: White 3B **22**
Clyde Rd. M20: Man 4B **92**
    SK3: Stoc 4E **105**
Clydesdale Gdns. M11: Man 1C **68**
Clydesdale St. OL8: O'ham 5A **30**
Clyde St. OL1: O'ham 1E **31**
    OL7: A Lyme 2B **72**
Clyffe M. M5: Sal 3D **65**
Clyne St. M32: Stre 1B **78**
        (off Adlington Dr.)
Clyne St. M32: Stre 5B **64**
Coalbrook Wlk. M12: Man **2A 68**
        (off Aden Cl.)
Coalburn St. M12: Man 4C **68**
Coal Pit La. OL8: O'ham 5E **43**
Coalshaw Grn. Rd. OL9: Chad 1C **42**
Coatbridge St. M11: Man 1E **69**
Cobalt Av. M41: Urm 4B **62**
Cobalt Way M24: Mid 3F **27**
Cobb Cl. M8: Man 1A **38**
Cobble Bank M9: Man 1F **39**
Cobden Cen., The M50: Sal 1B **64**
        (off Vere St.)
Cobden St. M6: Sal 3B **50**
    M9: Man 4A **40**
    OL4: O'ham 1F **31**
    OL6: A Lyme 5F **59**
    OL9: Chad 2D **29**
Coberley Av. M41: Urm 1B **74**
Cob Hall Rd. M32: Stre 4E **77**
Cobham Av. M40: Man 2E **41**
Cobourg St. M1: Man 2E **11** (2D **67**)
Coburg Av. M7: Sal 3F **51**
Cochrane Av. M12: Man 5A **68**

COCKBROOK 4E **59**
Cockcroft Rd. M5: Sal 3A **4** (5D **51**)
Cockcroft St. M9: Man 3F **39**
Coconut Gro. M6: Sal 5D **51**
Coddington Av. M11: Man 2A **70**
Cody Ct. M50: Sal 2A **64**
Coghlan Cl. M11: Man 5D **55**
Coke St. M7: Sal 4B **38**
Coke St. W. M7: Sal 4B **38**
Colborne Av. M30: Ecc 5D **47**
  SK5: Stoc 2B **84**
Colbourne Av. M8: Man 3B **38**
Colby Wlk. M40: Man 5C **40**
Colchester Av. M25: Pres 2E **37**
Colchester Cl. M23: Wyth 2A **100**
Colchester Pl. SK4: Stoc 5D **95**
Colchester Wlk. OL1: O'ham 2E **117**
Colclough Cl. M40: Man 1D **55**
Coldfield Dr. M23: Wyth 5B **100**
COLD HURST 1D **117** (1A **30**)
COLDHURST HOLLOW 1E **117** (1B **30**)
Coldhurst Hollow Est. OL1: O'ham . .1A **30**
Coldhurst St. OL1: O'ham . . .1D **117** (1A **30**)
Coldhurst St. W. OL1: O'ham 1A **30**
  (off Trafalgar St.)
Coldstream Av. M9: Man 5F **25**
Colebrook Dr. M40: Man 1C **54**
Colebrook Rd. WA15: Tim 5C **98**
Coleby Av. M16: Old T 1E **79**
  M22: Wyth 5B **110**
Coledale Dr. M24: Mid 4E **15**
Colemore Av. M20: Man 5F **93**
Colenso Gro. SK4: Stoc 5D **95**
Colenso St. OL8: O'ham 1F **43**
Colenso Way M4: Man 1C **6** (4C **52**)
Coleridge Av. M24: Mid 3E **17**
Coleridge Cl. SK5: Stoc 4A **84**
Coleridge Rd. M16: Old T 2E **79**
  SK5: Stoc 4A **84**
Coleridge St. M40: Man 3E **55**
Coleridge Way SK5: Stoc 4A **84**
Coleshill St. M40: Man 4A **54**
Colesmere Wlk. M40: Man 3F **41**
Cole St. M40: Man 4B **40**
Colgate Cres. M14: Man 5D **81**
Colgate La. M5: Sal 4C **64**
Colgrove Av. M40: Man 2E **41**
Colina Dr. M7: Sal 2A **52**
  M8: Man 2A **52**
Colindale Av. M9: Man 5A **26**
Colin Murphy Rd. M15: Man . . .5E **9** (4A **66**)
Colin Rd. SK4: Stoc 4A **96**
Colinwood Cl. BL9: Bury 3B **12**
Coll Dr. M41: Urm 5F **61**
College Av. M43: Droy 2B **70**
  OL8: O'ham 1F **43**
College Cl. SK2: Stoc 5C **106**
College Ct. SK4: Stoc 5C **94**
College Cft. M30: Ecc 5B **48**
College Dr. M16: W Ran 3E **79**
College Ho. SK4: Stoc 4D **95**
College Land M3: Man 5A **6** (1B **66**)
College Rd. M16: W Ran 2E **79**
  M30: Ecc 5C **48**
  (off St Mary's Rd.)
  OL8: O'ham 5F **29**
Collegiate Way M27: Clif 1B **34**
Collett St. OL1: O'ham 1E **31**
Colley St. M32: Stre 5B **64**
Collie Av. M6: Sal 2E **51**

Collier Hill OL8: O'ham 1F **43**
Collier Hill Av. OL8: O'ham 1E **43**
Collier St. M3: Man 3F **9** (2A **66**)
  M3: Sal 3F **5** (5A **52**)
  M6: Sal .1B **50**
  M27: Swin 5A **34**
Colliery St. M11: Man 1C **68**
  (not continuous)
Collin Av. M18: Man 1E **83**
Collingburn Av. M5: Sal 3D **65**
Collingburn Ct. M5: Sal 3D **65**
Collinge Av. M24: Mid 1E **27**
Collinge St. M24: Mid 2F **27**
Collingham St. M8: Man 3D **53**
Collington Cl. M12: Man 5C **68**
Collingwood Av. M43: Droy 4A **56**
Collingwood Dr. M27: Swin 5D **35**
Collingwood Rd. M19: Man 4B **82**
Collingwood Way
  OL1: O'ham 1E **117** (1B **30**)
Collins Way OL9: Chad 1E **43**
COLLYHURST 2F **53**
Collyhurst Av. M28: Walk 2A **32**
Collyhurst Rd. M40: Man 1F **7** (3D **53**)
Collyhurst St. M40: Man 3E **53**
Colman Gdns. M5: Sal 3D **65**
Colmore Dr. M9: Man 5C **26**
Colonial Rd. SK2: Stoc 5C **106**
Colshaw Rd. M23: Wyth 1C **108**
Colson Dr. M24: Mid 2B **26**
Coltishall Ho. SK8: Chea 5C **104**
Coltness Wlk. M40: Man 2E **55**
  (off Marlinford Dr.)
Columbia Av. M18: Man 1B **84**
Columbia St. OL8: O'ham 5B **30**
Columbine St. M11: Man 3F **69**
Columbus Way M50: Sal 2F **63**
Colville Gro. M33: Sale 2A **98**
  WA15: Tim 5C **98**
Colwell Av. M32: Stre 3D **77**
Colwell Wlk. M9: Man 4D **25**
Colwick Av. WA14: Alt 5A **98**
Colwood Wlk. M8: Man 1B **52**
  (off Kilmington Dr.)
Colwyn Av. M14: Man 5A **82**
  M24: Mid 3C **26**
Colwyn Cres. SK5: Stoc 3B **96**
Colwyn Rd. M27: Swin 1E **47**
Colwyn St. M6: Sal 4B **50**
  OL7: A Lyme 1C **58**
  OL9: O'ham 2F **29**
Colwyn Ter. OL7: A Lyme 1C **58**
  (off Colwyn St.)
Colyton Wlk. M22: Wyth 3B **110**
Combe Cl. M11: Man 4D **55**
Combermere Av. M20: Man 1C **92**
Combermere St. SK16: Duk 1E **73**
Comer Ter. M33: Sale 4C **88**
Commerce Way M17: T Pk 1E **77**
Commercial St. M15: Man 4F **9** (3A **66**)
  OL7: A Lyme 1B **72**
Community St. OL7: A Lyme 1B **72**
Como Wlk. M18: Man 4D **69**
Compass St. M11: Man 3E **69**
Compstall Av. M14: Man 3D **81**
Compstall Gro. M18: Man 4A **70**
Compton Dr. M23: Wyth 4C **108**
Compton Way M24: Mid 2E **27**
Comrie Wlk. M23: Wyth 1C **108**
Comus St. M5: Sal 2A **8** (2E **65**)
Concastrian Ind. Est. M9: Man 5E **39**

Concert La. M2: Man 1C **10** (1C 66)
Concord Bus. Pk. M22: Wyth 5A **110**
Concord Pl. M6: Sal 2C **50**
Concord Way SK16: Duk 2F **73**
Condor Cl. M43: Droy 4E **57**
Condor Pl. M6: Sal 2C **50**
Condor Wlk. M13: Man 4D **67**
⠀⠀⠀⠀⠀⠀⠀⠀⠀⠀⠀⠀⠀⠀⠀(off Glenbarry Cl.)
Conduit St. OL6: A Lyme 5E **59**
Coney Gro. M23: Wyth 4C **100**
Congham Rd. SK3: Stoc 3E **105**
Congleton Av. M14: Man 3C **80**
Congou St. M1: Man 2F **11** (2E **67**)
Congreave St. OL1: O'ham 1A **30**
Coningsby Dr. M9: Man 4F **39**
Conisborough Pl. M45: White 2D **23**
Coniston Av. M9: Man 4F **39**
⠀⠀⠀M33: Sale 1E **99**
⠀⠀⠀M45: White 1B **22**
⠀⠀⠀OL8: O'ham 1F **43**
⠀⠀⠀SK14: Hyde 1E **87**
Coniston Cl. M34: Dent 3D **85**
⠀⠀⠀OL9: Chad 2C **28**
Coniston Ct. M22: Shar 5A **102**
⠀⠀⠀⠀⠀⠀⠀⠀⠀⠀⠀⠀⠀⠀(off Downes Way)
Coniston Dr. M24: Mid 4A **15**
⠀⠀⠀SK9: Hand 5E **115**
Coniston Gro. OL7: A Lyme . . .1A **116** (3C **58**)
Coniston Hall M13: Man 1F **81**
⠀⠀⠀⠀⠀⠀⠀⠀⠀⠀⠀⠀(off Hathersage Rd.)
Coniston Ho. M28: Walk 2A **32**
⠀⠀⠀⠀⠀⠀⠀⠀⠀⠀⠀⠀⠀(off Holyoake Rd.)
Coniston Rd. M27: Swin 5B **34**
⠀⠀⠀M32: Stre 2E **73**
⠀⠀⠀M41: Urm 5A **74**
⠀⠀⠀SK5: Stoc 2B **96**
⠀⠀⠀SK8: Gat 5D **103**
Coniston St. M6: Sal 3D **51**
⠀⠀⠀M40: Man 2E **55**
Coniston Wlk. WA15: Tim 5F **99**
Conival Way OL9: Chad 1C **28**
Conmere Sq. M15: Man 5B **10** (3B **66**)
Connaught Av. M19: Man 1B **94**
⠀⠀⠀M45: White 2C **22**
Connaught St. OL8: O'ham . . .5D **117** (3A **30**)
Connell Rd. M23: Wyth 5C **100**
Connery Cres. OL6: A Lyme 1F **59**
Connie St. M11: Man 2E **69**
Connington Av. M9: Man 3F **39**
Connor Way SK8: Gat 2B **110**
Conquest Cl. M12: Man 4C **68**
Conran St. M9: Man 5F **39**
Consett Av. M23: Wyth 5C **100**
Consort Cl. SK16: Duk 4E **73**
Constable Ho. M34: Dent 2B **86**
Constable St. M18: Man 4A **70**
Constable Wlk. M34: Dent 5C **86**
Constance Gdns. M5: Sal 1B **64**
Constance St. M15: Man 4F **9** (3A **66**)
Constantine Ct. M5: Sal 2A **4** (4D **51**)
Constantine St. OL4: O'ham 3F **31**
Consul St. M22: Nor 2A **102**
Contact Theatre 5D **67**
Convent St. OL4: O'ham 5E **31**
Conway Av. M27: Clif 1D **35**
⠀⠀⠀M45: White 2B **22**
Conway Cen., The SK5: Stoc 4A **96**
Conway Cl. M16: Old T 2C **78**
⠀⠀⠀M24: Mid 2C **26**
⠀⠀⠀M45: White 2B **22**

Conway Dr. WA15: Tim 5E **99**
Conway Gro. OL9: Chad 1B **28**
Conway Rd. M33: Sale 5F **89**
⠀⠀⠀M41: Urm 1F **75**
Conway St. BL4: Farn 2A **18**
⠀⠀⠀SK5: Stoc 4A **96**
Conway Towers SK5: Stoc 1E **97**
Conyngham Rd. M14: Man 1F **81**
Cooke St. BL4: Farn 2A **18**
⠀⠀⠀M34: Dent 2A **86**
⠀⠀⠀M35: Fail 4B **42**
Cook St. M3: Sal 4F **5** (5A **52**)
⠀⠀⠀M30: Ecc 5E **47**
⠀⠀⠀M34: Aud 4B **72**
⠀⠀⠀OL4: O'ham 2E **31**
⠀⠀⠀SK3: Stoc 2A **106**
Cook Ter. SK16: Duk 5C **116**
⠀⠀⠀⠀⠀⠀⠀⠀⠀⠀⠀⠀⠀⠀⠀⠀⠀(off Hill St.)
Coomassie St. M6: Sal 4B **50**
Coombes St. SK2: Stoc 5D **107**
Co-operation St. M35: Fail 3B **42**
Co-operative St. M6: Sal 5B **50**
Cooper Fold M24: Mid 2C **16**
Cooper Ho. M15: Man 4C **66**
⠀⠀⠀⠀⠀⠀⠀⠀⠀⠀⠀⠀⠀(off Camelford Cl.)
Cooper La. M9: Man 4F **25**
⠀⠀⠀M24: Mid 3B **16**
Coopers Brow SK1: Stoc 2B **118**
Cooper St. M2: Man 1B **10** (1B **66**)
⠀⠀⠀⠀⠀⠀⠀⠀⠀⠀⠀⠀⠀⠀(not continuous)
⠀⠀⠀M32: Stre 4F **77**
⠀⠀⠀SK1: Stoc 5C **118** (4B **106**)
⠀⠀⠀SK16: Duk 5C **116** (1D **73**)
Coop St. M4: Man 3E **7** (5D **53**)
Cope Cl. M11: Man 3A **70**
Copeland Av. M27: Clif 3E **35**
Copeland Cl. M24: Mid 5E **15**
Copeland St. SK14: Hyde 5F **73**
Copeman Cl. M13: Man 4E **67**
Copenhagen St. M40: Man 1C **54**
Copgrove Rd. M21: Chor 1D **91**
Copgrove Wlk. M22: Wyth 2A **114**
Copley Rd. M21: Chor 3C **78**
Copperas La. M43: Droy 2A **70**
⠀⠀⠀⠀⠀⠀⠀⠀⠀⠀⠀⠀⠀⠀(not continuous)
Copperas St. M4: Man 4D **7** (5C **52**)
Copperbeech Cl. M22: Nor 2A **102**
Copper La. M45: White 2D **21**
Copper Pl. M14: Man 4C **80**
Copperways M20: Man 3D **93**
COPPICE .5A **30**
Coppice, The M9: Man 2C **40**
⠀⠀⠀M24: Mid 4D **27**
⠀⠀⠀M25: Pres 5C **22**
⠀⠀⠀M28: Wors 2E **47**
⠀⠀⠀⠀⠀⠀⠀⠀⠀⠀⠀⠀⠀⠀(Chatsworth Rd.)
⠀⠀⠀M28: Wors 4B **32**
⠀⠀⠀⠀⠀⠀⠀⠀⠀⠀⠀⠀⠀⠀(Old Clough La.)
Coppice Av. M33: Sale 1A **98**
Coppice Cl. SK8: H Grn 1D **115**
Coppice Dr. M22: Nor 2F **101**
Coppice Ind. Est. OL8: O'ham 4F **29**
⠀⠀⠀⠀⠀⠀⠀⠀⠀⠀⠀⠀⠀⠀(off Windsor Rd.)
Coppice St. OL8: O'ham 4F **29**
Coppice Wlk. M34: Dent 3F **85**
Copping St. M12: Man 4B **68**
Coppleridge Dr. M8: Man 3C **38**
Copplestone Ct. M27: Ward 3E **33**
Copse, The WA15: Haleb 2A **112**
Copse Av. M22: Wyth 3A **110**

Copson St. M20: Man 1D **93**
Copster Av. OL8: O'ham 1A **44**
COPSTER HILL 1A **44**
Copster Hill Rd. OL8: O'ham 1A **44**
Copster Pl. OL8: O'ham 1A **44**
Copthall La. M8: Man 4B **38**
. . . .(not continuous)
Copthorne Cres. M13: Man 3A **82**
Coptic Rd. OL9: Chad 1B **28**
Coral St. M13: Man 5F **11** (3E **67**)
Coram St. M18: Man 4B **70**
Corbar Rd. SK2: Stoc 5C **106**
Corbel Ho. M30: Ecc 4F **47**
. . . .(off Clifton Rd.)
Corbel Way M30: Ecc 4F **47**
Corbett St. M11: Man 1C **68**
Corbridge Wlk. M8: Man 1D **53**
. . . .(off Appleford Dr.)
Corbrook Rd. OL9: Chad 5F **17**
Corby St. M12: Man 4C **68**
Corda Av. M22: Nor 3F **101**
Corday La. M25: Pres 1F **23**
Cordingley Av. M43: Droy 2B **70**
Cordova Av. M34: Dent 2B **84**
Corelli St. M40: Man 3B **54**
Corinthian Av. M7: Sal 2E **51**
Corkland Cl. OL6: A Lyme 5F **59**
Corkland Rd. M21: Chor 5B **79**
Corkland St. OL6: A Lyme 5F **59**
Cork St. M12: Man 2F **67**
. . . . OL6: A Lyme 4E **59**
Corley Av. SK3: Stoc 4B **104**
Corley Wlk. M11: Man 1B **68**
Cormallen Gro. M35: Fail 5C **42**
Cormorant Wlk. M12: Man 4C **68**
. . . .(off Flamingo Cl.)
CORNBROOK 4C **8** (3F **65**)
Cornbrook Arches M15: Man . . .5B **8** (3E **65**)
Cornbrook Ct. M15: Man 4F **65**
Cornbrook Gro. M16: Old T 5F **65**
Cornbrook Pk. Rd. M15: Man . . .5B **8** (4E **65**)
Cornbrook Rd. M16: Old T 5B **8** (3E **65**)
Cornbrook Stop (Metro) 5B **8** (3E **65**)
Cornbrook St. M16: Old T 5F **65**
. . . . (not continuous)
Cornbrook Way M16: Old T 5F **65**
Corn Cl. M13: Man 5E **67**
Cornell St. M4: Man 3F **7** (5D **53**)
Cornerhouse Art Gallery 3C **10** (2C **66**)
Corner St. OL6: A Lyme 5E **59**
Cornfield Cl. M33: Sale 5B **90**
. . . .(off Pimmcroft Way)
Cornfield Dr. M22: Wyth 3E **109**
Cornford Av. M18: Man 2D **83**
Cornhill Av. M41: Urm 2D **75**
Corn Hill La. M34: Aud 5C **70**
Cornhill Rd. M41: Urm 1D **75**
Cornish Cl. M22: Wyth 1F **113**
Cornishway M22: Wyth 5E **109**
Cornishway Ind. Est.
. . . . M22: Wyth 1F **113**
. . . .(off Cornishway)
Corn Mill Dr. BL4: Farn 2A **18**
Corn St. M35: Fail 1E **55**
. . . . OL4: O'ham 2C **30**
. . . .(off Lees Rd.)
Cornwall Av. M19: Man 5D **83**
Cornwall Ct. M18: Man 4B **70**
Cornwall Cres. SK5: Stoc 2E **97**
Cornwall Ho. M3: Sal 5D **5**

Cornwall Rd. M43: Droy 4C **56**
. . . . SK8: H Grn 1D **115**
Cornwall St. M11: Man 3F **69**
. . . . M30: Ecc 1E **61**
. . . . OL9: O'ham 4D **29**
Cornwall St. Ind. Est. M11: Man 3F **69**
. . . .(off Cornwall St.)
Cornwood Cl. M8: Man 5B **38**
. . . .(off Narbuth Dr.)
Corona Av. OL8: O'ham 1F **43**
Coronation Av. SK14: Hyde 4F **87**
Coronation Rd. M35: Fail 1A **56**
. . . . M43: Droy 4B **56**
. . . . OL6: A Lyme 1E **59**
Coronation Sq. M12: Man 2E **67**
. . . . M34: Aud 3F **71**
Coronation St. M3: Man 2E **9** (2A **66**)
. . . . M5: Sal 2A **8** (2D **65**)
. . . . M11: Man 2E **69**
. . . . M27: Pen 3B **34**
. . . . M34: Dent 2F **85**
. . . . OL1: O'ham 2C **30**
. . . . SK5: Stoc 4A **96**
Coronet Way M50: Sal 1D **63**
Corporation Rd. M30: Ecc 5B **48**
. . . . M34: Aud, Dent 5F **71**
Corporation St. M3: Man 4B **6** (5B **52**)
. . . . M4: Man 4B **6** (5B **52**)
. . . . M24: Mid 1C **26**
. . . . SK1: Stoc 1C **118** (1B **106**)
. . . . SK14: Hyde 3F **87**
Corporation Yd. SK5: Stoc 5B **84**
Corran Cl. M30: Ecc 5D **47**
Corrie Cl. M34: Dent 4B **86**
Corrie Cres. BL4: Kea 4F **19**
Corrie Dr. BL4: Kea 5F **19**
Corrie Rd. M27: Clif 1C **34**
Corrigan St. M18: Man 4A **70**
Corringham Rd. M19: Man 1E **95**
Corris Av. M9: Man 4C **24**
Corston Wlk. M40: Man 2D **55**
Corwen Cl. OL8: O'ham 2D **43**
Cosgrove Cres. M35: Fail 2A **56**
Cosgrove Rd. M35: Fail 2A **56**
Cosham Rd. M22: Wyth 3B **110**
Cosmo Bingo 1E **61**
Costabeck Wlk. M40: Man 3F **55**
. . . .(off Stansfield St.)
COSTON PARK 3C **82**
Cotefield Rd. M22: Wyth 4D **109**
Cote Royd OL6: A Lyme 4F **59**

Cotham St. M3: Man 3B **52**
Cotswold Av. M41: Urm 2B **74**
. . . . OL9: Chad 4C **28**
Cotswold Cl. M25: Pres 4E **23**
Cotswold Dr. M6: Sal 4B **50**
Cotswold Rd. SK4: Stoc 5F **95**
Cottage Gdns. SK6: Bred 5F **97**
Cottage Wlk. M43: Droy 4B **56**
Cottam Gro. M27: Swin 5C **34**
Cottam St. OL1: O'ham 1F **29**
Cottenham La. M3: Sal 1F **5** (4A **52**)
. . . . M7: Sal 1E **5** (3A **52**)
Cottenham St. M13: Man 4D **67**
Cotterdale Cl. M16: W Ran 3F **79**
Cotteril Cl. M23: Wyth 2E **99**
Cotterill St. M6: Sal 5C **50**
Cotter St. M12: Man 3E **67**
Cottesmore Dr. M8: Man 4E **39**

Cottingham Dr. OL6: A Lyme 3E 59
Cottingham Rd. M12: Man 4A 68
Cottonfield Rd. M20: Man 2E 93
Cotton Hill M20: Man 3E 93
Cotton La. M20: Man 2E 93
Cotton Mill Cres. OL9: O'ham 5D 29
Cotton St. M4: Man 4F 7 (5D 53)
Cotton St. E. OL6: A Lyme . . .3A 116 (5C 58)
Cotton St. W. OL6: A Lyme . . .3A 116 (5C 58)
Cotton Tree Cl. OL4: O'ham 1F 31
Cotton Tree La. SK14: Hyde 3F 87
(off Reynold St.)
Cotton Tree Rd. SK4: Stoc 2A 118 (2A 106)
Coucill Sq. BL4: Farn 1A 18
Coulsden Dr. M9: Man 1F 39
Coulthart St. OL6: A Lyme . . .2C 116 (4D 59)
Coulton Cl. OL1: O'ham 1C 30
Coulton Wlk. M5: Sal 5B 50
Councillor La. SK8: Chea 5B 104
Councillor St. M12: Man 1A 68
Countess Gro. M7: Sal 3F 51
Countess Pl. M25: Pres 5E 23
Countess Rd. M20: Man 5D 93
Countess St. OL6: A Lyme 5F 59
SK2: Stoc 5C 106
Counthill Dr. M8: Man 2A 38
County Av. OL6: A Lyme 3F 59
County St. M2: Man 1B 10
OL8: O'ham 2E 43
Coupland St. M15: Man 5C 66
Coupland St. E. M15: Man 4C 66
Courier St. M18: Man 4A 70
Course Vw. OL4: O'ham 1F 45
Court, The M25: Pres 1D 37
Court Dr. M40: Man 3A 56
Courtfield Av. M9: Man 5F 25
Courthill St. SK1: Stoc 3C 106
Courts Vw. M33: Sale 3E 89
Courtyard, The M7: Sal 4E 37
Covall Wlk. M8: Man 1D 53
(off Hawkeshead Rd.)
Covent Gdns. SK1: Stoc 3B 118 (2B 106)
Coventry Av. SK3: Stoc 4B 104
Coverdale Cres. M12: Man 4F 67
Coverham Av. OL4: O'ham 5F 31
Covert Rd. M22: Shar 1A 110
OL4: O'ham 1F 45
Cowan St. M40: Man 5F 53
Cowburn St. M3: Man 1B 6 (4B 52)
Cowesby St. M14: Man 2C 80
COWHILL 3D 29
Cowhill La. OL6: A Lyme 4E 59
Cowhill Trad. Est. OL6: A Lyme 3E 59
(off Tramway Rd.)
Cow La. M5: Sal 1B 8 (1E 65)
M33: Sale 2A 90
M35: Fail 5A 42
OL4: O'ham 2E 31
Cowley St. M40: Man 1E 55
Cowling St. M7: Sal 4B 36
OL8: O'ham 5B 30
Cowper St. M24: Mid 1F 27
OL6: A Lyme 4E 59
Cowper Wlk. M11: Man 1B 68
(off Newcombe Cl.)
Coxton Rd. M22: Wyth 5A 110
Crabbe St. M4: Man 1D 7 (4C 52)
Crab La. M9: Man 5D 25
Crabtree La. M11: Man 2F 69
(not continuous)

Crabtree Rd. OL1: O'ham 1D 31
Craddock Rd. M33: Sale 1E 99
Cradley Av. M11: Man 2F 69
Craig Av. M41: Urm 2C 74
Craig Cl. SK4: Stoc 2D 105
Craigend Dr. M9: Man 5A 40
Craighall Av. M19: Man 5B 82
Craigie St. M8: Man 2B 52
Craiglands Av. M40: Man 1C 54
Craigmore Av. M20: Man 4F 91
Craignair Cl. M27: Pen 5D 35
Craig Rd. M18: Man 1E 83
SK4: Stoc 2B 104
Craig Wlk. OL8: O'ham 4A 30
Craigweil Av. M20: Man 5F 93
Craigwell Rd. M25: Pres 2A 38
Craigwell Wlk. M13: Man 5E 11
Cramer St. M40: Man 2B 54
Crammond Cl. M40: Man 1F 55
Cranage Cl. SK9: Hand 4F 115
(off Spath La.)
Cranage Rd. M19: Man 5D 83
Cranberry Dr. M34: Dent 2F 85
Cranberry St. OL4: O'ham 3D 31
Cranbourne Cl. OL7: A Lyme 3C 58
WA15: Tim 5C 98
Cranbourne Ct. SK4: Stoc 4D 95
Cranbourne Rd. M16: Old T 1E 79
M21: Chor 5D 79
OL6: A Lyme 3C 58
OL7: A Lyme 3C 58
SK4: Stoc 4D 95
Cranbourne St. M5: Sal 1A 8 (1D 65)
Cranbourne Ter. OL6: A Lyme 2D 59
Cranbrook Dr. M25: Pres 2E 37
Cranbrook Gdns.
OL7: A Lyme 1B 116 (3D 59)
Cranbrook Pl. OL4: O'ham 3E 31
Cranbrook Rd. M18: Man 2A 84
M30: Ecc 3C 46
Cranbrook St. OL4: O'ham 3D 31
OL7: A Lyme 1A 116 (3C 58)
Cranbrook Wlk. OL9: Chad 3C 28
Crandon Cl. M27: Pen 3C 34
Crandon Dr. M20: Man 3E 103
Cranesbill Cl. M22: Wyth 5E 109
Crane St. M12: Man 2E 67
Cranfield Cl. M40: Man 5F 53
Cranford Av. M20: Man 4F 93
M32: Stre 2B 78
M33: Sale 2E 89
M45: White 4A 12
Cranford Cl. M27: Swin 1D 49
M45: White 4A 12
Cranford Gdns. M41: Urm 2A 74
Cranford Ho. M30: Ecc 4B 48
(off Half Edge La.)
M41: Urm 2A 74
Cranham Rd. M22: Wyth 4C 108
Cranleigh Av. SK4: Stoc 4B 94
Cranleigh Cl. OL4: O'ham 1F 31
Cranleigh Dr. M28: Walk 4A 32
M33: Sale 2E 99
(Ashstead Rd.)
M33: Sale 3C 88
(Ashton La.)
SK8: Chea 5B 104
Cranlington Dr. M8: Man 1B 52
Cranmer Av. M19: Man 3E 83
Cranmere Dr. M33: Sale 1A 98

Cranmer Rd. M20: Man 4D **93**
Cranston Dr. M20: Man 3D **103**
   M33: Sale .5A **90**
Cranston Gro. SK8: Gat 1B **110**
Cranswick St. M14: Man 2C **80**
Crantock Dr. SK8: H Grn 1E **115**
Crantock St. M12: Man 2D **83**
Cranwell Ct. *M43: Droy* *2D 71*
   (off Williamson La.)
Cranwell Dr. M19: Man 4A **94**
Craston Rd. M13: Man 3A **82**
Craunton Ho. M30: Ecc 5B **48**
Craven Av. M5: Sal 2D **65**
Craven Dr. M5: Sal 4C **64**
Cravenhurst Av. M40: Man 3D **55**
Craven Pl. M11: Man 5E **55**
Craven Rd. SK5: Stoc 2B **96**
Craven St. M5: Sal 1B **8** (1E **65**)
   M43: Droy .1C **70**
   OL1: O'ham 1A **30**
   OL6: A Lyme 2F **59**
Craven Ter. M33: Sale 4E **89**
Cravenwood Rd. M8: Man 4C **38**
   SK5: Stoc 3A **84**
Crawford Av. M28: Wors 4B **32**
Crawford M. OL6: A Lyme 5F **59**
Crawford St. M30: Ecc 4F **47**
   M40: Man 2E **55**
   OL6: A Lyme 5F **59**
Crawley Av. M22: Wyth 3F **109**
   M30: Ecc 4C **48**
Crawley Gro. SK2: Stoc 5D **107**
Crawley Way OL9: Chad 3C **28**
Craydon St. M11: Man 2E **69**
Crayfield Rd. M19: Man 5D **83**
Crayford Rd. M40: Man 3D **55**
Cray Wlk. M13: Man 5E **11**
Creaton Way M24: Mid 2E **15**
Creden Av. M22: Wyth 3B **110**
Crediton Cl. M15: Man 5B **66**
Crediton Ho. M6: Sal 4C **48**
Creel Cl. M9: Man 5D **25**
Cremer Ho. M30: Ecc 5B **48**
Cresbury St. M12: Man 3F **67**
Crescent, The M5: Sal 4A **4** (5D **51**)
   M19: Man 4C **82**
   M24: Mid 1A **26**
   M25: Pres .5D **23**
   M28: Wors .2C **46**
   M41: Urm 2B **74**
   M43: Droy .1B **70**
   SK6: Bred .4F **97**
   SK8: Chea .5F **103**
   WA15: Tim .4B **98**
Crescent Av. M8: Man 4C **38**
   M25: Pres .2D **37**
   M27: Pen 4F **35**
Crescent Cl. SK16: Duk 1E **73**
Crescent Ct. *M21: Chor* *4B 78*
   (off Alderfield Rd.)
   M33: Sale .5D **89**
Crescent Dr. M8: Man 3D **39**
Crescent Gro. M19: Man 4C **82**
   M25: Pres .2D **37**
   SK8: Chea .5E **103**
Crescent Pk. SK4: Stoc 1E **105**
Crescent Range M14: Man 2E **81**
Crescent Rd. BL4: Kea 5B **18**
   M8: Man 4B **38**
   OL9: Chad .2A **42**

Crescent Rd. SK1: Stoc 5D **97**
   SK8: Chea .5E **103**
   SK16: Duk .1E **73**
Crescent St. M8: Man 4E **39**
Crescent Vw. *SK16: Duk* *1E 73*
   (off Peel St.)
Cressfield Way M21: Chor 1F **91**
Cressingham Rd. M32: Stre 4D **77**
Cressington Cl. M5: Sal 5A **50**
   (off Cedric St.)
Cresswell Gro. M20: Man 3C **92**
Crest, The M43: Droy 3C **70**
Crest St. M3: Man 2C **6** (4B **52**)
Crestwood Wlk. *M40: Man* *1E 53*
   (off Barnstaple Dr.)
Crete St. OL8: O'ham 5B **30**
Crewe Rd. M23: Wyth 3A **100**
Criccieth Rd. SK3: Stoc 4C **104**
Criccieth St. M16: W Ran 1B **80**
Cricket Gro., The M21: Chor 2D **91**
Crickets La. OL6: A Lyme 4E **59**
   (not continuous)
Crickets La. Nth. OL6: A Lyme 4E **59**
Cricket St. M34: Dent 1C **86**
Cricklewood Rd. M22: Wyth 4E **109**
Crime La. M35: O'ham 5F **43**
   OL8: O'ham 5F **43**
CRIME VIEW **5F 43**
Crimsworth Av. M16: Old T 3D **79**
Crinan Wlk. *M40: Man* *4F 53*
   (off Nuneaton Dr.)
Cringle Dr. SK8: Chea 2E **111**
Cringleford Cl. M12: Man 5B **68**
Cringle Hall Rd. M19: Man 5B **82**
Cringle Rd. M19: Man 1D **95**
Crispin Rd. M22: Wyth 1A **114**
Criterion St. SK5: Stoc 3B **84**
Croal Wlk. M45: White 5D **13**
Croasdale Av. M14: Man 5D **81**
Crocker Wlk. *M9: Man* *4A 40*
   (off Kingscliffe St.)
Crocus Wlk. *M7: Sal* *1F 51*
   (off Hilton St. Nth.)
Croft, The BL9: Bury 1C **12**
   OL8: O'ham 2A **44**
   SK2: Stoc .5D **107**
Croft Av. M25: Pres 1B **24**
Croft Bank M7: Sal 2E **51**
   M18: Man 5A **70**
Croft Brow OL8: O'ham 2A **44**
Crofters, The M33: Sale 5B **90**
Crofters Hall Wlk. *M40: Man* *5D 41*
   (off Duncombe Dr.)
Croft Gates Rd. M24: Mid 2F **25**
Croft Hill Rd. M40: Man 3C **40**
Croft Ind. Est. BL9: Bury 1C **12**
Croftlands Rd. M22: Wyth 2A **110**
Croft La. BL9: Bury 1C **12**
Croftleigh Cl. M45: White 4A **12**
Crofton Av. WA15: Tim 2C **98**
Crofton St. M14: Man 2D **81**
   M16: Old T .1F **79**
   OL8: O'ham 1A **44**
   (not continuous)
Croft Rd. M33: Sale 1F **99**
CROFTS BANK **1E 75**
Crofts Bank Rd. M41: Urm 1E **75**
Croftside Av. M28: Walk 1A **32**
Croftside Cl. M28: Walk 1A **32**
Croftside Gro. M28: Walk 1A **32**

Croft St. M7: Sal 2E 51
   M11: Man 1D 69
   M35: Fail 3C 42
   SK14: Hyde 3E 87
Cromarty Av. OL9: Chad 1B 42
Cromarty Wlk. M11: Man 1B 68
                 (off Biscay Cl.)
Crombie Av. M22: Nor 4F 101
Cromer Av. M20: Man 2D 93
   M34: Dent 2C 84
Cromer Ind. Est. M24: Mid 5D 17
Cromer Rd. M33: Sale 5E 89
   SK8: Chea 5A 104
Cromer St. M11: Man 1F 69
   M24: Mid 5D 17
   SK1: Stoc 1D 107
Cromford Av. M32: Stre 2D 77
Cromford Bus. Cen. OL1: O'ham 1D 31
Cromford St. OL1: O'ham 1C 30
Cromhall Wlk. M8: Man 1C 52
             (off Starmoor Dr.)
Cromhurst St. M8: Man 4C 38
Crompton Cl. M26: Rad 1D 21
Crompton Ho. M27: Swin 4A 34
Crompton Rd. M19: Man 1C 94
   M26: Rad 1C 18
Crompton St. BL4: Farn 2A 18
   M27: Swin 4A 34
   M28: Walk 2B 32
   OL1: O'ham 1A 30
   OL6: A Lyme 3F 59
   OL9: Chad 2E 29
            (not continuous)
Cromwell Av. M16: W Ran 3E 79
   SK5: Dent 3C 84
   SK8: Gat 5C 102
Cromwell Bri. M6: Sal 2E 51
Cromwell Ct. M6: Sal 3D 51
         (off Cromwell Rd.)
   OL1: O'ham 5E 117
Cromwell Gro. M7: Sal 2E 51
   M19: Man 4C 82
Cromwell Range M14: Man 3F 81
Cromwell Rd. M6: Sal 3C 50
   M25: Pres 5E 23
   M27: Swin 3A 34
   M30: Ecc 5E 47
   M32: Stre 4A 78
   M45: White 4A 12
   SK6: Bred 2F 97
Cromwell St. OL1: O'ham . . .5E 117 (3B 30)
   SK4: Stoc 5F 95
Crondale Wlk. M13: Man 4E 67
           (off Watkin Cl.)
Crondall St. M14: Man 2C 80
Cronshaw St. M19: Man 5D 83
Crookhill Dr. M8: Man 5B 38
Crookilley Way SK1: Stoc 5C 96
   SK6: Bred 3F 97
Crook St. SK14: Hyde 3F 87
Croom Wlk. M40: Man 5F 53
           (off Marcer Rd.)
Crosby Av. M28: Walk 2B 32
Crosby Rd. M6: Sal 2F 49
   M40: Man 2F 55
Crosby St. SK2: Stoc 4B 106
Crosfield Gro. M18: Man 1F 83
Crossacres Rd. M22: Wyth 3F 109
Cross Av. M25: Pres 3C 22
Crossbank Cl. M13: Man 5F 67

Crossbank Ho. OL9: O'ham 3F 29
          (off Manchester St.)
Crossbank St. OL8: O'ham 5D 117 (3A 30)
           (not continuous)
Crossbank Way M24: Mid 5B 16
Crossby Cl. M24: Mid 4B 26
Cross Cliffe SK14: Hyde 5E 87
Crosscliffe St. M16: W Ran 1B 80
Crossdale Rd. M9: Man 5B 26
Crossfell Av. M9: Man 4D 25
Crossfield Cl. M34: Dent 3C 86
Crossfield Dr. M27: Swin 3A 34
   M28: Wors 5B 32
Crossfield Rd. SK9: Hand 5F 115
Crossfield St. BL9: Bury 2B 12
Crossford Ct. M33: Sale 2D 89
Crossford St. M32: Stre 4F 77
Crossgate Av. M22: Wyth 5F 101
Crossgate M. SK4: Stoc 1A 104
Cross Glebe St. OL6: A Lyme 4E 59
Cross Gro. WA15: Tim 3B 98
Crosshill St. M16: W Ran 1B 80
Cross Hope St. OL6: A Lyme 3F 59
Cross Keys St. M4: Man 3E 7 (5D 53)
Cross Knowle Vw. M41: Urm 1B 74
Crossland Rd. M21: Chor 5C 78
   M43: Droy 5D 57
Crosslands M25: Pres 1C 36
Cross La. M5: Sal 1C 64
   M18: Man 5F 69
   M43: Droy 3F 57
Crosslee Rd. M9: Man 5B 26
Crossley Ct. M4: Man 1F 67
          (off Pollard St.)
Crossley Cres. OL6: A Lyme 1F 59
Crossley Est. OL9: Chad 3D 29
Crossley Pk. SK4: Stoc 1D 95
Crossley Rd. M19: Man 1B 94
   M33: Sale 2C 88
   SK4: Stoc 1B 94
Crossley St. M18: Man 4D 69
   SK16: Duk 1F 73
Crossmead Dr. M9: Man 4A 26
Cross Rd. M21: Chor 5D 79
   SK8: H Grn 2D 115
Cross St. BL4: Farn 1A 18
   BL4: Kea 4D 19
   M2: Man 1B 10 (1B 66)
   M3: Sal 3F 5 (5A 52)
   M16: Old T 5F 65
   M24: Mid 1B 26
           (not continuous)
   M27: Clif 2F 35
   M28: Wors 5E 33
   M32: Stre 3F 77
   M33: Sale 3D 89
   M34: Dent 5A 72
   M41: Urm 4E 75
   M45: White 5A 12
   OL4: Lees 3F 31
   OL4: O'ham 2D 31
   OL6: A Lyme 3A 116 (5C 58)
   SK14: Hyde 3F 87
Crosswaite Rd. SK2: Stoc 5F 107
Crossway M20: Man 5D 93
   M43: Droy 3C 70
Crossway Rd. M33: Sale 2B 98
Crossways OL8: O'ham 3C 44
Croston Wlk. M11: Man 1A 68
Croton St. SK4: Stoc 1A 104

Croughton Cl. M11: Man 3F 69
Crowbank Wlk. *M40: Man* *2C 54*
               (off Bower St.)
Crowborough Wlk. *M15: Man* *5B 66*
            (off Arnott Cres.)
CROWCROFT PARK 3D 83
Crowcroft Rd. M12: Man 2C 82
  M13: Man 2C 82
Crowden Rd. M40: Man 2D 41
CROWHILL 3B 58
Crowhill Cotts. OL7: A Lyme 3C 58
Crow Hill Nth. M24: Mid 3B 26
Crowhill Rd. OL7: A Lyme 3B 58
Crow Hill Sth. M24: Mid 3B 26
Crowhurst Wlk. *M23: Wyth* *4A 100*
            (off Sandy La.)
Crowland Rd. M23: Wyth 3B 108
Crowley Rd. M9: Man 4B 40
  WA15: Tim 5D 99
Crown Bus. Cen. M35: Fail 4B 42
Crowngreen Rd. M30: Ecc 1A 62
Crownhill Ct. M43: Droy 5C 56
Crownhill Dr. M43: Droy 5C 56
Crown Ho. *M22: Shar* *5A 102*
           (off Lauriston Cl.)
Crown Ind. Est. M4: Man 5E 53
  SK5: Stoc 2A 84
  WA14: Tim 4A 98
Crown La. M4: Man 2D 7 (4C 52)
CROWN POINT 2B 86
       (Junc. of A57 with A6017)
Crown Point Av. M40: Man 2E 55
Crown Point Nth. Shop. Pk.
  M34: Dent 1A 86
Crown Point Sth. Ind. Pk. M34: Dent 2B 86
Crown Royal Ind. Pk.
  SK1: Stoc 5C 118 (3C 106)
Crown Sq. M3: Man 1F 9 (1A 66)
Crown St. M3: Sal 3E 5 (5A 52)
  M15: Man 4E 9 (3A 66)
  M34: Dent 1A 86
  M35: Fail .4B 42
  M40: Man 2E 55
  OL6: A Lyme 3B 116 (5D 59)
Crowther Av. M5: Sal 2C 64
Crowther St. M18: Man 5A 70
  SK1: Stoc 3B 118 (2B 106)
Crowthorn Dr. M23: Wyth 4C 108
Crowthorn Rd. OL7: A Lyme 1B 72
  SK4: Stoc 1F 95
Crowton Av. M33: Sale 1A 98
Croxdale Cl. OL7: A Lyme 2A 58
Croxdale Wlk. *M9: Man* *4F 25*
          (off Claygate Dr.)
Croxton Cl. M33: Sale 1A 98
Croxton Wlk. M13: Man 5F 11
Croyde Cl. M22: Wyth 2B 114
Croydon Cl. M5: Sal 2D 65
Croydon Dr. M40: Man 3E 55
Crummock Dr. M24: Mid 3A 16
Crummock Rd. M38: Gat 3D 111
CRUMPSALL .2B 38
CRUMPSALL GREEN 2C 38
Crumpsall La. M8: Man 3B 38
Crumpsall Stop (Metro) 3C 38
Crumpsall Va. M9: Man 2E 39
Crumpsall Way M8: Man 3D 39
Cryer St. M43: Droy 3E 57
Crystal Ho. M16: W Ran 2F 79
Cube 2C 10

Cube, The M11: Man 5B 54
Cubley Rd. M7: Sal 4A 38
Cuckoo Gro. M25: Pres 3D 23
Cuckoo La. M25: Pres 3D 23
  M45: White 3D 23
Cuckoo Nest M25: Pres 2D 23
Cuddington Av. M20: Man 5C 80
Cuddington Cres. SK3: Stoc 5F 105
Cuddington Way *SK9: Hand* *4F 115*
         (off Pickmere Rd.)
Cudworth Rd. M9: Man 4C 24
Cuerdon Wlk. M22: Nor 3A 102
Culand St. M12: Man 4A 68
Culbert Av. M20: Man 5E 93
CULCHETH 2E 55
Culcheth La. M40: Man 2E 55
Culcombe Wlk. *M13: Man* *5E 67*
           (off Corn Cl.)
Culford Cl. M12: Man 5A 68
Culgaith Wlk. *M9: Man* *5F 39*
         (off Ruskington Dr.)
Cullen Gro. M9: Man 1B 40
Cullercoats Wlk. M12: Man 2D 83
Culmere Rd. M22: Wyth 5F 109
Culmington Cl. M15: Man 5A 66
Culross Av. M40: Man 3A 42
Culvercliffe Wlk. M3: Man 2F 9
Culverden Wlk. M6: Sal 1B 50
Culver Rd. SK3: Stoc 5F 105
Culverwell Dr. M5: Sal 5D 51
Cumberland Av. M27: Clif 2B 34
  SK5: Stoc 4E 97
  SK16: Duk 2F 73
Cumberland Gro. OL7: A Lyme 3D 59
Cumberland Rd. M27: Clif 2C 34
Cumberland Rd. M9: Man 3F 39
  M33: Sale 1E 99
  M41: Urm 4E 75
Cumberland St. M7: Sal 1C 4 (3F 51)
Cumbrae Gdns. M5: Sal 1F 63
Cumbrae Rd. M19: Man 4E 83
Cumbria Ct. M25: Pres 3C 36
Cumbrian Cl. M13: Man 4E 67
Cumbria Wlk. M6: Sal 3D 51
Cummings St. OL8: O'ham 2E 43
Cunard Cl. M13: Man 4E 67
Cundall Wlk. M23: Wyth 2B 100
Cundiff Ct. M19: Man 4E 83
Cundiff Rd. M21: Chor 2D 91
        (not continuous)
Cundy St. SK14: Hyde 1F 87
Curlew Rd. OL4: O'ham 5F 31
Curlew Wlk. M12: Man 5A 68
Currier La. OL6: A Lyme 5E 59
Curtels Cl. M28: Wors 5E 33
Curtis Rd. SK4: Stoc 1C 104
Curtis St. M19: Man 4E 83
Curzon Ashton FC 3A 58
Curzon Av. M14: Man 1A 82
Curzon Dr. WA15: Tim 5D 99

Curzon Grn. SK2: Stoc 3F 107
Curzon Rd. M7: Sal 5F 37
   M32: Stre 2C 76
   M33: Sale 3D 89
   OL6: A Lyme 3F 59
   SK2: Stoc 4F 107
   SK8: H Grn 2D 115
Curzon St. OL1: O'ham 3E 117 (2B 30)
Curzon Urmston Cinema 2D 75
Cutgate Cl. M23: Wyth 2A 100
Cuthbert Av. M19: Man 3D 83
Cuthbert Bus. Cen. M11: Man 3E 69
               (off Ashton Old Rd.)
Cuthbert Rd. SK8: Chea 5A 104
Cuthill Wlk. M40: Man 3F 55
              (off Eastmoor Dr.)
Cutland St. M40: Man 1C 54
CUTLER HILL 5D 43
Cutler Hill Rd. M35: Fail 5D 43
Cutler St. OL9: Chad 2E 29
Cutter Cl. M5: Sal 2C 64
Cycle St. M11: Man 2D 69
Cyclone St. M11: Man 2B 68
Cygnus Av. M7: Sal 1B 4 (4E 51)
Cymbal Ct. SK5: Stoc 5B 96
Cypress Av. OL9: Chad 1D 29
Cypress Cl. SK3: Stoc 3E 105
Cypress Dr. BL4: Kea 2B 18
   M34: Dent 2C 86
Cypress Pl. M4: Man 1C 6 (4C 52)
Cypress Rd. M30: Ecc 3C 46
   M43: Droy 4C 56
   OL4: O'ham .1F 31
Cypress St. M9: Man 5F 39
   M24: Mid 1E 27
Cyprus Cl. M5: Sal 1B 64
   OL4: O'ham .4F 31
Cyprus St. M32: Stre 3F 77
Cyril St. M14: Man 2D 81
Cyrus St. M40: Man 5F 53

D

Daccamill Dr. M27: Swin 1B 48
Dacre Av. M16: W Ran 3D 79
Dacre Cl. M24: Mid 5D 15
Dagenham Rd. M14: Man 1E 81
Dagenham Rd. Ind. Est.
   M14: Man 2E 81
            (off Dagenham Rd.)
Dagnall Av. M21: Chor 2D 91
Dahlia Cl. M19: Man 2B 94
Daimler St. M8: Man 1C 52
Dain Cl. SK16: Duk 2F 73
Daine Av. M23: Wyth 2D 101
Dainton St. M12: Man 3F 67
Daintry Cl. M15: Man 5A 10 (4B 66)
Daintry Rd. OL9: O'ham 2E 29
Dairy St. OL9: Chad 2D 29
Daisy Av. M13: Man 1A 82
Daisy Bank M40: Man 2E 55
   SK14: Hyde .5E 87
Daisy Bank Av. M6: Sal 1E 49
   M27: Pen 1E 49
Daisy Bank Hall M14: Man 1F 81
Daisy Bank La. SK8: H Grn 5C 110
Daisy Bank Rd. M14: Man 1F 81
Daisy Bank Vs. M14: Man 1F 81
                (off Hope Rd.)
Daisyfield Cl. M22: Wyth 5E 109
Daisy Hill Cl. M33: Sale 4A 90
Daisy Hill Ct. OL4: O'ham 1F 31
               (off Howard St.)
DAISY NOOK 1F 57
Daisy Nook Country Pk. 1F 57
Daisy St. OL9: Chad 1C 28
   OL9: O'ham .2F 29
   SK1: Stoc 4B 106
Dakerwood Cl. M40: Man 2E 55
Dakota Av. M50: Sal 2A 64
Dakota Sth. M50: Sal 2B 64
Dalbeattie St. M9: Man 4A 40
Dalberg St. M12: Man 3F 67
Dalbury Dr. M40: Man 2E 53
Dalby Av. M27: Swin 5A 34
Dalby Gro. SK1: Stoc 2C 106
Dale Av. M30: Ecc 4E 47
Dalebank M. M27: Clif 4F 19
Dalebeck Cl. M45: White 1D 23
Dalebeck Wlk. M45: White 1E 23
Dale Brook Av. SK16: Duk 4F 73
Dalebrook Ct. SK4: Stoc 2E 105
Dalebrook Rd. M33: Sale 2E 99
Dale Ct. M34: Dent 3B 86
Dale End OL8: O'ham 2C 44
Daleford Sq. M13: Man 5F 11
Dale Gro. OL7: A Lyme 2C 58
   WA15: Tim .4B 98
Dalehead Cl. M18: Man 4B 70
Dale Ho. M24: Mid 5E 17
   SK1: Stoc 1B 118
Dale Rd. M24: Mid 4D 17
Dales Av. M8: Man 2B 38
   M45: White 5A 12
DALES BROW 1F 47
Dales Brow M27: Swin 1A 48
Dales Brow Av. OL7: A Lyme 2C 58
Dales Gro. M28: Walk 3B 32
Dales La. M45: White 5A 12
Dalesman Cl. M9: Man 4B 40
Dalesman Wlk. M15: Man 5C 10
Dales Pk. Dr. M27: Swin 1F 47
Dale St. BL4: Farn 1A 18
   M1: Man 5D 7 (1C 66)
   M24: Mid 2D 27
   M27: Swin 1A 48
   M45: White 5A 12
   SK3: Stoc 5A 106
Dale St. E.
   OL6: A Lyme 3A 116 (5C 58)
Dale St. W.
   OL6: A Lyme 4A 116 (5C 58)
Daleswood Av. M45: White 5A 12
Dale Vw. M34: Dent 5C 86
   SK14: Hyde .5F 87
Dalham Av. M9: Man 2C 40
Dalkeith Av. SK5: Stoc 1B 96
Dalkeith Rd. SK5: Stoc 1B 96
Dalkeith St. M18: Man 4D 69
Dallas Ct. M50: Sal 1F 63
Dalley Av. M7: Sal 1C 4 (3F 51)
Dallimore Rd. M23: Wyth 5A 100
Dalmahoy Cl. M40: Man 4E 41
Dalmain Cl. M8: Man 1B 52
Dalmorton Rd. M21: Chor 5F 79
Dalny St. M19: Man 4D 83
Dalry Wlk. M23: Wyth 5C 100
Dalston Av. M35: Fail 4D 43
Dalston Dr. M20: Man 1E 103

Dalton Av. M14: Man		3C **80**
M27: Clif		1E **35**
M32: Stre		1B **76**
M45: White		2C **22**
Dalton Ct. M40: Man		3D **53**
SK4: Stoc		4E **95**
Dalton Dr. M27: Pen		5F **35**
Dalton Ellis Hall *M14: Man*		*1F 81*
(off Conyngham Rd.)		
Dalton Gdns. M41: Urm		2D **75**
Dalton Gro. SK4: Stoc		4E **95**
Dalton Rd. M9: Man		4F **25**
M24: Mid		2D **25**
Dalton St. M4: Man		1F 7 (3D **53**)
M30: Ecc		4F **47**
M33: Sale		2E **89**
M35: Fail		4A **42**
M40: Man		1F 7 (3D **53**)
OL1: O'ham		2D **31**
OL9: Chad		2D **29**
Daltry St. OL1: O'ham		1C **30**
Dalveen Av. M41: Urm		1A **74**
Dalveen Dr. WA15: Tim		4B **98**
Damask Av. M3: Sal		3C 4 (5F **51**)
Dame Hollow		
SK8: H Grn		2F **115**
Dameral Cl. M8: Man		1C **52**
Dame St. OL9: O'ham		1F **29**
Dam Head Dr. M9: Man		1A **40**
Damien St. M12: Man		3D **83**
Damson Grn. M24: Mid		1F **27**
Danbury Wlk. M23: Wyth		3F **99**
Danby Ct. *OL1: O'ham*		*1A 30*
(off Bradford St.)		
Danby Wlk. *M9: Man*		*3A 40*
(off Polworth Rd.)		
Dancehouse, The		4C **10**
Dane Av. SK3: Stoc		3C **104**
DANE BANK		3D **85**
Dane Bank M24: Mid		1D **27**
Danebank M34: Dent		3D **85**
Danebank Wlk. M13: Man		5F **11**
Danebridge Cl. *BL4: Farn*		*1A 18*
(off Peel St.)		
Danefield Ct. SK8: H Grn		1F **115**
Danefield Rd. M33: Sale		2E **89**
Daneholme Rd. M19: Man		3A **94**
Dane Ho. *M33: Sale*		*4E 89*
(off Northenden Rd.)		
Dane M. M33: Sale		2D **89**
Dane Rd. M33: Sale		2E **89**
M34: Dent		3C **84**
Dane Rd. Ind. Est. M33: Sale		2E **89**
Danes, The M8: Man		3B **38**
Danesbury Ri. SK8: Chea		1F **111**
Daneshill M25: Pres		3D **23**
Daneshill Dr. *M23: Wyth*		*2C 108*
(off Chedlin Dr.)		
Danesmoor Rd. M20: Man		3C **92**
Danes Rd. M14: Man		3F **81**
Dane St. M11: Man		3A **70**
OL4: O'ham		2E **31**
Danesway M25: Pres		2F **37**
M27: Pen		5E **35**
Daneswood Av. M9: Man		5B **26**
Danett Cl. M12: Man		4D **69**
Dane Wlk. SK5: Stoc		4B **96**
Danforth Gro. M19: Man		5D **83**
Daniel Adamson Rd. M50: Sal		2F **63**

Daniel's La. SK1: Stoc		1B **118**
Daniel St. OL1: O'ham		1D **31**
Danisher La. OL8: O'ham		4B **44**
Dannywood Cl. SK14: Hyde		5E **87**
Danson St. M40: Man		4A **54**
Dantall Av. M9: Man		1C **40**
Dante Cl. M30: Ecc		3C **48**
Danty St. SK16: Duk		1D **73**
Dantzic St. M4: Man		4C 6 (5C **52**)
Danube, The M15: Man		4F **9**
Danwood Cl. M34: Dent		3E **87**
Dapple Gro. M11: Man		2C **68**
Darbyshire Ho. *WA15: Tim*		*4E 99*
(off Oakleigh Ct.)		
Darcy Wlk. M11: Man		1C **80**
Darden Cl. SK4: Stoc		5A **94**
Daresbury Av. M41: Urm		1A **74**
WA15: Alt		5A **98**
Daresbury Cl. M33: Sale		5B **90**
SK3: Stoc		5F **105**
Daresbury Rd. M21: Chor		4B **78**
Daresbury St. M8: Man		4C **38**
(not continuous)		
Darfield Wlk. *M40: Man*		*4F 53*
(off Burnell Cl.)		
Dargai St. M11: Man		1F **69**
Dargle Rd. M33: Sale		2D **89**
Darian Av. M22: Wyth		1F **113**
Dark La. M12: Man		2F **67**
SK6: Bred		5F **97**
Darlbeck Wlk. M21: Chor		3E **91**
Darley Av. BL4: Farn		1A **18**
M20: Man		4A **92**
M21: Chor		2D **91**
(not continuous)		
M30: Ecc		2E **61**
SK8: Gat		1D **111**
Darley Gro. BL4: Farn		1A **18**
DARLEY PARK		1E **79**
Darley Rd. M16: Old T		2E **79**
Darley St. BL4: Farn		1A **18**
M11: Man		1B **68**
M32: Stre		1F **77**
M33: Sale		4D **89**
SK4: Stoc		5E **95**
Darlington Rd. M20: Man		2C **92**
Darliston Av. M9: Man		4C **24**
Darlton Wlk. *M9: Man*		*4A 40*
(off Sequoia St.)		
Darnall Av. M20: Man		5C **80**
Darnbrook Dr. M22: Wyth		5D **109**
Darncombe Cl. M16: W Ran		1B **80**
Darnley St. M16: Old T		1F **79**
Darnton Gdns. OL6: A Lyme		4F **59**
Darnton Rd. OL6: A Lyme		3F **59**
Darras Rd. M18: Man		2E **83**
Darrell Wlk. M8: Man		1D **53**
Dart Cl. OL9: Chad		1B **28**
Dartford Av. M30: Ecc		5D **47**
SK5: Stoc		2D **97**
Dartford Cl. M12: Man		4F **67**
Dartford Rd. M41: Urm		4E **75**
Dartington Cl. M23: Wyth		5F **99**
Dartmouth Cl. OL8: O'ham		5B **30**
Dartmouth Cres. SK5: Stoc		3E **97**
Dartmouth Rd. M21: Chor		5E **79**
M45: White		2C **22**
Darton Av. M40: Man		4F **53**
Darwell Av. M30: Ecc		2E **61**
Darwen St. M16: Old T		5E **65**

Darwin St. OL4: O'ham 4E **31**
   OL7: A Lyme 4A **116** (5C **58**)
Dashwood Rd. M25: Pres 4C **22**
Dashwood Wlk. *M12: Man* 4C *68*
   (off Radbourne Cl.)
Dauntesy Av. M27: Pen 5F **35**
Davenfield Gro. *M20: Man* 5D *93*
   (off Davenfield Rd.)
Davenfield Rd. M20: Man 5D **93**
Davenham Rd. M33: Sale 2A **88**
   SK5: Stoc 3B **84**
   SK9: Hand 5F **115**
Davenhill Rd. M19: Man 5C **82**
DAVENPORT 5B **106**
Davenport Av. M20: Man 1D **93**
DAVENPORT GREEN 5A **108**
Davenport Pk. Rd. SK2: Stoc 5C **106**
Davenport Station (Rail) 5B **106**
Davenport St. M34: Aud 2A **72**
   M43: Droy 1A **70**
Davenport Ter. M9: Man 4A **40**
Daventry Rd. M21: Chor 5F **79**
David Cl. M34: Dent 4C **86**
David Cuthbert Ct. *M11: Man* 3E *69*
   (off Greenside St.)

David Lloyd Leisure
   Cheadle 4E **111**
   Urmston 3E **61**
David M. M14: Man 1E **93**
David Pegg Wlk. *M40: Man* 2D *55*
   (off Roger Byrne Cl.)
David's Farm Cl. M24: Mid 2D **27**
Davidson Dr. M24: Mid 3D **27**
David's Rd. M43: Droy 5A **56**
Davist St. M34: Dent 3C **86**
   OL1: O'ham 4D **117** (3A **30**)
   SK5: Stoc 5A **84**
Davies Av. SK8: H Grn 3D **115**
Davies Ct. *M32: Stre* 4F *77*
   (off Cyprus St.)
Davies Rd. SK6: Bred 5F **97**
Davies Sq. M14: Man 1C **80**
Davies St. BL4: Kea 2C **18**
   OL1: O'ham 1F **29**
   OL7: A Lyme 1B **72**
Davis Hall *M14: Man* 1F *81*
   (off Daisy Bank Hall)
Davis St. M30: Ecc 1A **62**
Davy Av. M27: Clif 2F **35**
DAVYHULME 1E **75**
Davyhulme Circ. M41: Urm 1E **75**
Davyhulme Millennium Pk. 5A **60**
Davyhulme Rd. M32: Stre 2E **77**
   M41: Urm 1A **74**
Davyhulme Rd. E. M32: Stre 2F **77**
Davylands M41: Urm 5A **60**
Davy St. M40: Man 1F **7** (3D **53**)
Daw Bank SK3: Stoc 3A **118** (2A **106**)
Dawlish Av. M43: Droy 1B **28**
   OL9: Chad 3E **97**
   SK5: Stoc 5E **79**
Dawlish Rd. M21: Chor 3A **88**
   M33: Sale 3D **69**
Dawnay St. M11: Man 1F **115**
Dawson Rd. SK8: H Grn 4F **31**
Dawson St. M3: Man 3C **8** (2F **65**)
   M3: Sal 3A **6** (5B **52**)
   M27: Pen 4C **34**
   OL4: Lees 4F **31**
   OL4: O'ham 3F **31**

Dawson St. SK1: Stoc 5D **97**
   SK14: Hyde 4F **87**
Day Dr. M35: Fail 1B **56**
Daylesford Cl. SK8: Chea 2F **111**
Daylesford Cres. SK8: Chea 2F **111**
Daylesford Rd. SK8: Chea 2F **111**
Daytona Karting 4A **64**
Deacon Av. M27: Swin 3A **34**
Deacons Cl. SK1: Stoc 2C **106**
Deacon's Dr. M6: Sal 1F **49**
Deal Av. SK5: Stoc 3D **97**
Deal Cl. M40: Man 2F **55**
Deal Wlk. OL9: Chad 3C **28**
Dean Av. M16: Old T 2D **79**
   M40: Man 1D **55**
Dean Bank Av. M19: Man 5B **82**
Dean Brook Cl. M40: Man 5D **41**
Dean Cl. M15: Man 4F **65**
Dean Ct. *M15: Man* 4F *65*
   (off Lucy St.)
   SK16: Duk 5C **116**
Deane Av. SK8: Chea 5B **104**
Deane Cl. M45: White 2F **21**
Deanery Ct. M8: Man 5C **38**
Deanery Gdns. M7: Sal 4F **37**
Deanery Way SK1: Stoc 1A **118** (1B **106**)
Dean Hall *M14: Man* 1F *81*
   (off Daisy Bank Hall)
Dean La. M40: Man 1D **55**
Dean Lane Station (Rail) 1D **55**
Dean Rd. M3: Sal 2F **5** (4A **52**)
   M18: Man 1A **84**
DEANS 5A **34**
Deanscourt Av. M27: Swin 5A **34**
Deansgate M3: Man 4F **9** (3A **66**)
   (not continuous)
Deansgate, The M14: Man 5F **81**
Deansgate La. WA14: Tim 4A **98**
   WA15: Tim 4A **98**
Deansgate M. M3: Man 3F **9**
Deansgate Quay M3: Man 4F **9**
Deansgate Station (Rail) 3F **9** (2A **66**)
Deanshut Rd. OL8: O'ham 2C **44**
Deans Rd. M27: Swin 5A **34**
Deans Rd. Ind. Est. M27: Swin 5A **34**
Dean St. M1: Man 5E **7** (1D **67**)
   M35: Fail 5F **41**
   OL7: A Lyme 2A **116** (4C **58**)
Deansway M27: Swin 4A **34**
Deanswood Dr. M9: Man 4C **24**
Dean Ter. OL6: A Lyme 2E **45**
Dean Av. M24: Mid 4F **15**
Deanwater Cl. M13: Man 5F **11** (3D **67**)
Deanwater Ct. M32: Stre 5E **77**
   SK8: H Grn 2F **115**
Deanway M40: Man 4C **40**
Dearden St. M15: Man 4A **66**
Dearman's Pl. M3: Sal 4F **5** (5A **52**)
Dearnalay Way OL9: Chad 5D **29**
Dearne Dr. M32: Stre 3A **78**
DEBDALE 1B **84**
Debdale Av. M18: Man 1B **84**
Debdale La. M18: Man 1B **84**
Debdale Outdoor Cen. 1A **84**
Debdale Pk. 1B **84**
Debenham Av. M40: Man 3E **55**
Debenham Rd. M32: Stre 4C **76**
De Brook Cl. M41: Urm 4A **74**
Dee Av. WA15: Tim 5F **99**
Dee Dr. BL4: Kea 4C **18**

Deepcar St. M19: Man 3C 82
Deepdale OL4: O'ham 3F 31
Deepdale Av. M20: Man 5C 80
Deepdale Cl. SK5: Stoc 4B 84
Deepdale Ct. M9: Man 1D 41
Deepdale Dr. M27: Pen 5F 35
Deepdene St. M12: Man 4B 68
Deeping Av. M16: W Ran 3F 79
Deeracre Av. SK2: Stoc 5E 107
Deerfold Cl. M18: Man 5F 69
Deerhurst Dr. M8: Man 1B 52
Deeroak Cl. M18: Man 4D 69
Deerpark Rd. M16: W Ran 2A 80
Deganwy Gro. SK5: Stoc 3B 96
Degas Cl. M7: Sal 4D 37
Deighton Av. M20: Man 5C 80
Delacourt Rd. M14: Man 5C 80
Delafield Av. M12: Man 3C 82
Delaford Av. M28: Wors 5A 32
Delaford Wlk. *M40: Man 3F 55*
(off Eastmoor Dr.)
Delahays Range M18: Man 1B 84
Delaine Rd. M20: Man 2E 93
Delamere Av. M6: Sal 1E 49
    M27: Clif .2D 35
    M32: Stre .3F 77
(not continuous)
    M33: Sale .5A 90
    M45: White 1F 21
Delamere Ct. M9: Man 4C 24
Delamere Rd. M19: Man 5D 83
    M34: Dent .3D 85
    M41: Urm .3B 74
    SK8: Gat 1D 111
    SK9: Hand .5F 115
Delamere St. M11: Man 3B 70
    OL6: A Lyme 2C 116 (5D 59)
    OL8: O'ham 4D 31
Delaunays Rd. M8: Man 3C 38
    M9: Man 3C 38
    M33: Sale .4B 88
Delaware Wlk. *M9: Man 5F 39*
Delbooth Av. M41: Urm 1A 74
Delft Wlk. M6: Sal 2C 50
Dell Av. M27: Pen 5F 35
Dellcot Cl. M6: Sal 2D 49
    M25: Pres .2F 37
Dellcot La. M28: Wors 2B 46
Dell Side SK6: Bred 5F 97
Dellside Gro. M28: Walk 1A 32
Delside Av. M40: Man 4C 40
Delta Point M34: Aud 3A 72
Delta Rd. M34: Aud 3A 72
Delta Wlk. M40: Man 5C 40
Delvino Wlk. M14: Man 1C 80
Delwood Gdns. M22: Wyth 2F 109
Demesne Rd. M16: W Ran 3A 80
Demmings, The SK8: Chea 5B 104
Demmings Rd. SK8: Chea 5B 104
Dempsey Dr. BL9: Bury 4D 13
Denbigh Pl. M5: Sal 5C 50
Denbigh Rd. M27: Clif 2C 34
    M34: Dent .4B 86
Denbigh St. OL8: O'ham 1B 44
    SK4: Stoc .5F 95
Denbigh Wlk. *M15: Man 5A 66*
(off Shearsby Cl.)
Denbury Wlk. *M9: Man 1E 53*
(off Mannington Dr.)
Denby La. SK4: Stoc 4F 95

Denby Rd. SK16: Duk 3E 73
Dencombe St. M13: Man 1B 82
Dene Brow M34: Dent 5D 87
Dene Ct. SK4: Stoc 1E 105
Dene Dr. M24: Mid 2B 26
Denefield Pl. M30: Ecc 4B 48
Deneford Rd. M20: Man 1C 102
Dene Hollow SK5: Stoc 4C 84
Dene Ho. SK4: Stoc 2A 104
Dene Pk. M20: Man 1C 102
Dene Rd. M20: Man 5C 92
Dene Rd. W. M20: Man 5B 92
Denes, The SK5: Stoc 4B 84
Deneside M40: Man 1F 53
Deneside Wlk. *M9: Man 3A 40*
(off Dalbeattie St.)
Denesway M33: Sale 5A 88
(not continuous)
Deneway SK4: Stoc 1E 105
Deneway Cl. SK4: Stoc 1E 105
Deneway M. SK4: Stoc 1E 105
Denewell Av. M13: Man 4F 67
Denham St. M13: Man 1F 81
Denhill Rd. M15: Man 1B 80
Denholm Rd. M20: Man 3E 103
Denis Av. M16: W Ran 3A 80
Denison Rd. M14: Man 2E 81
Denison St. M14: Man 2E 81
Deniston Rd. SK4: Stoc 3D 95
Denman Wlk. *M8: Man 1B 52*
(off Ermington Dr.)
Denmark Rd. M15: Man 5C 66
    M33: Sale .2D 89
Denmark St. OL4: O'ham 2D 31
    OL9: Chad .1E 29
Denmark Way OL9: Chad 1E 29
Denmore Rd. M40: Man 1E 41
Denning Pl. M27: Clif 2B 34
Dennington Dr. M41: Urm 1E 75
Dennis Ho. M34: Stoc 4D 95
Dennison Av. M20: Man 1D 93
Denshaw Av. M34: Dent 5F 71
Denshaw Cl. M19: Man 5A 94
Densmore St. M35: Fail 5B 42
Denson Rd. WA15: Tim 3D 99
Denstone Av. M30: Ecc 4A 48
    M33: Sale .5A 88
    M41: Urm .2E 75
Denstone Rd. M6: Sal 2F 49
    M41: Urm .2E 75
    SK5: Stoc .4B 84
Denstone Wlk. *M9: Man 1A 40*
(off Woodmere Dr.)
Dent Cl. SK5: Stoc 2E 97
Dentdale Wlk. M22: Wyth 1E 113
DENTON 2B 86
Denton Bus. Pk. M34: Dent 2F 85
Denton Ct. M34: Dent 5A 72
Denton Ent. Cen. *M34: Dent 2B 86*
(off Pitt St.)
Denton Hall Farm Rd. M34: Dent 3B 86
Denton La. OL9: Chad 4C 28
Denton Rd. M34: Aud 5A 72
Denton St Lawrence's Church *2B 86*
(off Town La.)
Denton Station (Rail) 1E 85
Denton Swimming Pool 2A 86
Denton Ter. M34: Aud 4A 72
Denver Av. M40: Man 4F 53
Denver Dr. WA15: Tim 5C 98

Denville Cres. M22: Wyth 3A 110
Denyer Ter. SK16: Duk 5C 116
Depleach Rd. SK8: Chea 1F 111
　　　　　　　　　　　　　　　　(not continuous)
Deptford Av. M23: Wyth 3C 108
De Quincey Cl. WA14: W Tim 2A 98
De Quincey Rd. WA14: W Tim 2A 98
Deramore St. M14: Man 2D 81
Derby Av. M6: Sal 5A 50
Derby Ct. M33: Sale 5E 89
　　OL9: O'ham 4D 83
Derby Gro. M19: Man 5D 67
Derby Ho. M15: Man 1F 61
　　　　　　　　　　　　　　　(off Dilworth St.)
Derby Range SK4: Stoc 4D 95
Derby Rd. M5: Sal 1A 64
　　M6: Sal 1E 93
　　M14: Man .1C 18
　　M26: Rad .2A 88
　　M33: Sale .2F 75
　　M41: Urm .3C 22
　　M45: White 4F 59
　　OL6: A Lyme 4E 95
　　SK4: Stoc .4E 95
Derbyshire Av. M32: Stre 2C 76
Derbyshire Cres. M32: Stre 2D 77
Derbyshire Grn. M32: Stre 3F 77
Derbyshire Gro. M32: Stre 2D 77
Derbyshire La. M32: Stre 3E 77
Derbyshire La. W. M32: Stre 2C 76
Derbyshire Rd. M33: Sale 3F 55
　　M40: Man .5E 89
Derbyshire Rd. Sth. M33: Sale 2E 69
Derbyshire St. M11: Man 2A 52
Derby St. M8: Man 5C 22
　　M25: Pres .2F 85
　　M34: Dent . . . .
　　　　　　　　　　　　　　　　(not continuous)
　　M35: Fail .3B 42
　　OL7: A Lyme 2C 58
　　OL9: Chad 1D 43
　　OL9: O'ham 4E 29
　　SK3: Stoc .3F 105
　　WA14: Alt .5A 98
Derby Ter. M34: Aud 2F 71
Derg St. M6: Sal 5B 50
Derker Station (Rail) 1C 30
Derker St. OL1: O'ham 1C 30
Dermot Murphy Cl. M20: Man 2B 92
Dernford Av. M19: Man 3B 94
Derry Av. M22: Wyth 2A 110
Derry St. OL1: O'ham 4E 117 (3B 30)
Derville Wlk. M9: Man 4F 39
　　　　　　　　　　　　　　　(off Alderside Rd.)
Derwen Rd. SK3: Stoc 4A 106
Derwent Av. M21: Chor 3F 91
　　M43: Droy .1A 70
　　M45: White 1D 58
　　OL7: A Lyme 3C 58
　　WA15: Tim .3F 91
Derwent Cl. M21: Chor 3F 91
　　M34: Dent .3D 85
　　M45: White 1D 23
Derwent Dr. BL4: Kea 4D 19
　　M33: Sale .1C 98
　　OL9: Chad 2C 28
　　SK9: Hand .4E 115
Derwent Rd. M24: Mid 3A 16
　　M32: Stre .2F 77
　　M41: Urm .3A 74

Derwent St. M5: Sal 3B 8 (2E 65)
　　M8: Man 1E 53
　　M43: Droy .1F 69
Derwent St. Ind. Est. M5: Sal 3B 8 (3E 65)
Derwent Wlk. M45: White 1D 23
　　OL4: O'ham 2F 31
Desford Av. M21: Chor 4E 79
Desmond Rd. M22: Wyth 2A 110
Destructor Rd. M27: Swin 3A 34
De Trafford Ho. M30: Ecc 1F 61
　　　　　　　　　　　　　　　(off Fintry Gro.)
Dettingen St. M6: Sal 1A 49
Deva Cen. M3: Sal 4E 5 (5A 52)
Deva Ct. M16: Old T 5E 65
Devaney Wlk. M34: Dent 4A 86
Deva Sq. OL9: O'ham 4E 29
Devas St. M15: Man 5D 67
　　　　　　　　　　　　　　　　(not continuous)
Deverill Av. M18: Man 1B 84
Devine Cl. M3: Sal 3C 4 (5F 51)
Devoke Av. M28: Walk 2A 32
Devoke Rd. M22: Wyth 4D 109
Devon Av. M19: Man 5B 82
　　M45: White 5A 12
Devon Cl. M6: Sal 4C 48
　　SK5: Stoc .4E 97
Devon M. M45: White 5A 12
Devon Rd. M35: Fail 1A 56
　　M41: Urm .4A 74
　　M43: Droy .4C 56
Devonshire Cl. M41: Urm 3A 76
Devonshire Ct. M7: Sal 4F 37
　　M33: Sale .5F 89
　　　　　　　　　　　　(off Derbyshire Rd. Sth.)
Devonshire Pk. Rd. SK2: Stoc 5C 106
Devonshire Pl. M25: Pres 4C 22
Devonshire Point M30: Ecc 5A 48
Devonshire Rd. M6: Sal 4C 48
　　M21: Chor .5E 79
　　M30: Ecc 5A 48
　　SK4: Stoc .1D 105
Devonshire St. M7: Sal 1F 51
　　M12: Man .4F 67
Devonshire St. E. M35: Fail 2F 55
Devonshire St. Nth. M12: Man 3F 67
Devonshire St. Sth. M13: Man 5F 67
Devon St. M27: Pen 2B 34
　　OL9: O'ham 5D 29
　　　　　　　　　　　　　　　　(not continuous)
Dewar Cl. M11: Man 1C 68
Dewberry Cl. M27: Swin 2A 34
Dewes Av. M27: Clif 2D 35
Dewey St. M11: Man 3F 69
Dewhurst St. M8: Man 1A 6 (3B 52)
Dewsnap Bri. SK16: Duk 4E 73
Dewsnap Cl. SK16: Duk 4E 73
Dewsnap La. SK16: Duk 4E 73
Dew Way OL9: O'ham 2F 29
Dexter Rd. M9: Man 4C 24
Deyne Av. M14: Man 1E 81
　　M25: Pres .5D 23
Deyne St. M6: Sal 5A 50
Dial Rd. SK2: Stoc 5E 107
Dialstone La. SK2: Stoc 4E 107
Dialstone Recreation Cen. 5F 107
Diamond Cl. OL6: A Lyme 3F 59
Diamond St. OL6: A Lyme 3F 59
　　SK2: Stoc .5C 106
Dibden Wlk. M23: Wyth 1C 108
Dickenson Rd. M14: Man 2E 81

Dickens Rd. M30: Ecc 1F 61
Dickinson Rd. M1: Man 2B 10 (2C 66)
  M3: Sal 1F 5 (3A 52)
  OL4: O'ham 2D 31
Didcot Rd. M22: Wyth 5E 109
Didley Sq. M12: Man 3C 68
DIDSBURY 5D 93
Didsbury Ct. M20: Man 4D 93
Didsbury Pk. M20: Man 1D 103
Didsbury Rd. SK4: Stoc 1F 103
Didsbury Sports Cen. & Swimming Pool
  . . . . .1D 103
Digby Wlk. M11: Man 1B 68
             (off Albert St.)
Digsby Ct. M20: Man 4D 93
Dillicar Wlk. M9: Man 5F 39
        (off Ravelston Dr.)
Dillmoss Wlk. M15: Man 4F 65
        (off Shawgreen Cl.)
Dillon Dr. M12: Man 5A 68
Dilworth Ho. M15: Man 5D 67
          (off Dilworth St.)
Dilworth St. M15: Man 5D 67
Dimora Ct. M27: Pen 1F 49
Dingle Av. M34: Dent 3D 87
Dingle Cl. M26: Rad 1D 21
Dingle Dr. M43: Droy 4D 57
Dingle Gro. SK8: Gat 5B 102
Dingle Rd. M24: Mid 3A 26
Dingle Ter. OL6: A Lyme 2D 45
Dinmore Ct. SK2: Stoc 5F 107
        (off Lisburne La.)
Dinmor Rd. M22: Wyth 5E 109
Dinnington Dr. M8: Man 1B 52
Dinorwic Cl. M8: Man 2C 38
Dinsdale Cl. M40: Man 5F 53
Dinslow Wlk. M8: Man 5B 38
       (off Winterford Rd.)
Dinting Av. M20: Man 1C 92
Dinton Ho. M5: Sal 1B 64
      (off Buckingham St.)
Dinton St. M15: Man 5B 8
Dipton Wlk. M8: Man 1E 53
        (off Lanhill Dr.)
Discovery Pk. SK4: Stoc 2D 95
Disley Av. M20: Man 2B 92
Disley Ho. SK3: Stoc 5A 118
Disley Wlk. M34: Dent 4C 86
Ditton Wlk. M23: Wyth 5B 100
Dixon Av. M7: Sal 1A 52
Dixon Cl. M33: Sale 1F 99
Dixon Ct. SK8: Chea 1F 111
Dixon Dr. M27: Clif 5A 20
Dixon Fold M45: White 5A 12
Dixon Rd. M34: Dent 4D 87
Dixon St. M6: Sal 1B 50
  M24: Mid 4C 16
  M40: Man 1D 55
        (not continuous)
  OL1: O'ham 1D 117 (1A 30)
  OL6: A Lyme 3F 59
Dobbinetts La. M23: Wyth 2A 108
  WA15: Hale 2A 108
Dob Brook Cl. M40: Man 1E 55
Dobcross Cl. M13: Man 3C 82
Dobroyd Ho. OL4: O'ham 1F 31
     (off Huddersfield Rd.)
Dobroyd St. M8: Man 4C 38
Dobson Ct. M40: Man 3D 55
Dock Office M50: Sal 3C 64

Doctor Fold La. OL10: H'ood 1D 15
Doddington La. M5: Sal 2C 64
Doddington Wlk. M34: Dent 4B 86
Dodd St. M5: Sal 5F 49
Dodge Fold SK2: Stoc 5F 107
Dodge Hill SK4: Stoc 1A 118 (1A 106)
Doe Brow M27: Clif 5A 20
Dolbey St. M5: Sal 1A 64
Dolefield M3: Man 5F 5 (1A 66)
D'Oliveira St. M24: Mid 4A 16
Dollond St. M9: Man 3A 40
Dolman Wlk. M8: Man 1B 52
     (off Felthorpe Dr.)
Dolphin Pl. M12: Man 3E 67
Dolphin St. M12: Man 3E 67
Dolwen Wlk. M40: Man 1D 55
     (off Harold Priestnall Cl.)
Dome, The M41: Urm 4F 61
     (off The Trafford Cen.)
Domestic App. M90: Man A 2E 113
Domett St. M9: Man 2E 39
Dominic Cl. M23: Wyth 2A 100
Donald St. M1: Man 3D 11 (2C 66)
Dona St. SK1: Stoc 3C 106
     (not continuous)
Don Av. M6: Sal 5E 49
Doncaster Av. M20: Man 1C 92
Doncaster Wlk. OL1: O'ham 2E 117
Donhead Wlk. M13: Man 4E 67
     (off Lauderdale Cres.)
Donleigh St. M40: Man 1F 55
Donnington Av. SK8: Chea 5B 104
Donnington Gdns. M28: Walk 1A 32
Donnington Rd. M18: Man 5A 70
Dennison St. M12: Man 4B 68
Donovan St. M40: Man 3E 53
Don St. M24: Mid 5E 17
Dorac Av. SK8: H Grn 2E 115
Dorchester Av. M25: Pres 2E 37
  M34: Dent 4B 86
  M41: Urm 2B 76
Dorchester Cl. M33: Sale 1D 99
Dorchester Dr. M23: Wyth 2A 100
Dorchester Rd. M27: Swin 1B 48
Dorclyn Av. M41: Urm 3F 75
Doric Av. SK6: Bred 5F 97
Doric Cl. M11: Man 1B 68
Doris Rd. SK3: Stoc 3E 105
Doris St. M24: Mid 4C 16
Dorking Av. M40: Man 3D 55
Dorking Cl. SK1: Stoc 4D 107
Dorlan Av. M18: Man 1B 84
Dorland Gro. SK2: Stoc 4D 107
Dorman St. M11: Man 3F 69
     (off Lees St.)
Dorning Rd. M27: Swin 5C 34
Dorning St. BL4: Kea 1B 18
  M30: Ecc .1F 61
Dornton Wlk. M8: Man 1B 52
     (off Dudley St.)
Dorothy St. M7: Sal 5B 38
Dorrington Rd. M33: Sale 4A 88
  SK3: Stoc 4C 104
Dorris St. M19: Man 5D 83
Dorset Av. M14: Man 3C 80
  M34: Aud 2E 71
  SK5: Stoc .3E 97
Dorset Rd. M19: Man 4E 83
  M35: Fail .1B 56
  M43: Droy 4B 56

Dorset St. M27: Pen 2B 34
    M32: Stre 4F 47
    OL6: A Lyme 1A 84
    OL9: O'ham 4E 29
Dorsey St. M4: Man 4E 7 (5D 53)
Dorstone Cl. M40: Man 3F 55
Dorwood Av. M9: Man 4C 68
Dougall Wlk. M12: Man 1F 51
(off Bridgend Cl.)
Doughty Av. M30: Ecc 4B 48
Douglas Av. M32: Stre 2F 77
Douglas Cl. M45: White 4E 13
Douglas Grn. M6: Sal 2C 50
Douglas Rd. M28: Wors 5E 33
Douglas St. M7: Sai 1F 51
    M27: Swin 5C 34
    M35: Fail 5C 42
    M40: Man 5C 40
    OL1: O'ham 1F 117 (1C 30)
    OL6: A Lyme 4F 59
    SK14: Hyde 3F 87
Douglas Wlk. M45: White 4E 13
Douglas Way M45: White 5E 13
Doulton St. M40: Man 4E 41
Dounby Av. M30: Ecc 4D 47
Douro St. M40: Man 2B 54
Dovecote M43: Droy 4F 57
Dovecote Bus. & Technology Pk.
    M33: Sale 4A 90
Dovecote M. M21: Chor 5C 78
Dovedale Av. M20: Man 1C 92
    M25: Pres 1A 38
    M30: Ecc 4A 48
    M41: Urm 3F 75
    M43: Droy 5A 56
Dovedale Ct. M24: Mid 4A 16
(off Grisdale Dr.)
Dovedale Rd. SK2: Stoc 5F 107
Dovedale St. M35: Fail 5A 42
Dovehouse Cl. M45: White 1F 21
Doveleys Rd. M6: Sal 3F 49
Dovercourt Av. SK4: Stoc 5B 94
Doveridge Gdns. M6: Sal 4B 50
Dover Pk. M41: Urm 1F 75
Dover Rd. M27: Clif 2C 34
Dover St. M13: Man 4D 67
    M30: Ecc 5D 47
    OL9: O'ham 4E 29
    SK5: Stoc 1A 96
Dovestone Wlk. M40: Man 3A 42
Doveston Gro. M33: Sale 2D 89
Doveston Rd. M33: Sale 2D 89
Dove St. OL4: O'ham 3E 31
Dove Wlk. M8: Man 2D 53
Dowland Cl. M23: Wyth 1B 100
Downcast Way M27: Pen 4F 35
(off Shearer Way)
Downes Way M22: Shar 5A 102
Downfields SK5: Stoc 4C 84
Downgate Wlk. M8: Man 1C 52
(off Tamerton Dr.)
Downham Chase WA15: Tim 5D 99
Downham Cres. M25: Pres 1F 37
Downham Gdns. M25: Pres 1A 38
Downham Gro. M25: Pres 1A 38
Downham Rd. SK4: Stoc 3F 95
Downham Wlk.
    M23: Wyth 3A 100
Downhill Cl. OL1: O'ham 1A 30
Downing Cl. OL7: A Lyme 1B 58

Downing St. M1: Man 4F 11 (3D 67)
    M13: Man 5F 11
    OL7: A Lyme 1B 58
Downing St. Ind. Est.
    M12: Man 4F 11 (3D 67)
Downley Dr. M4: Man 5E 53
Downs, The M24: Mid 3D 27
    M25: Pres 2C 36
    SK8: Chea 3F 111
Downs Dr. WA14: Tim 3A 98
Downshaw Rd. OL7: A Lyme 1C 58
Dowry St. OL8: O'ham 1B 44
Dowson Rd. SK14: Hyde 5F 87
Dow St. SK14: Hyde 5F 73
Doyle Av. SK6: Bred 5F 97
Drake Av. M22: Wyth 4D 109
Drake Cl. OL1: O'ham 1B 30
Drake Cl. SK5: Stoc 4A 96
Drayfields M43: Droy 5F 57
Drayford Cl. M23: Wyth 1B 100
Drayton Cl. M33: Sale 1A 98
Drayton Dr. SK8: H Grn 2D 115
Drayton Mnr. M20: Man 3D 103
Drayton St. M15: Man 5A 66
Drayton Wlk. M16: Old T 5F 65
(off Fernleigh Dr.)
Drefus Av. M11: Man 5E 55
Dresden St. M40: Man 4E 41
Dresser Cen., The M11: Man 3D 69
Drewett St. M40: Man 3A 54
Driffield St. M14: Man 2C 80
    M30: Ecc 2E 61
Drinkwater Rd. M25: Pres 3B 36
Driscoll St. M13: Man 2B 82
Drive, The M7: Sal 3E 37
    M20: Man 5E 93
    M25: Pres 5D 23
    M33: Sale 2A 98
    SK5: Stoc 4D 97
    SK6: Bred 5F 97
Droitwich Rd. M40: Man 3F 53
Dronfield Rd. M6: Sal 3F 49
    M22: Nor 3F 101
Droughts La. M25: Pres 1A 24
DROYLSDEN 1C 70
Droylsden FC (Butchers Arms Ground)
. . . . .1C 70
Droylsden Little Theatre 5D 57
(off Market St.)
Droylsden Rd. M34: Aud 1D 71
    M40: Man 1E 55
Drury La. OL9: Chad 1C 42
Drury St. M19: Man 4C 82
Dryad Cl. M27: Pen 2B 34
Drybrook Cl. M13: Man 5A 68
Dryden Av. M27: Swin 5F 33
    SK8: Chea 5B 104
Dryden Rd. M16: Old T 2E 79
Dryden St. M13: Man 4E 67
Dryden Way M34: Dent 5C 86
(off Spenser Av.)
Drygate Wlk. M9: Man 5A 40
(off Craigend Dr.)
Dryhurst Wlk. M15: Man 4C 66
Drymoss OL8: O'ham 3C 44
Drywood Av. M28: Wors 2E 15
Drywood Cotts. OL10: H'ood 1C 18
Ducal St. M4: Man 1E 7 (4D 53)
Duchess Rd. M8: Man 4D 39
Duchy Cvn. Pk. M6: Sal 2B 50

Duchy Rd. M6: Sal 1A 50
Duchy St. M6: Sal 4B 50
   SK3: Stoc 4F 105
Ducie Ct. M15: Man 5D 67
Ducie St. M1: Man 1E 11 (1D 67)
   M45: White 1B 22
   OL8: O'ham 2B 44
Duckworth Rd. M25: Pres 1B 36
Duddon Cl. M45: White 1D 23
Duddon Wlk. M24: Mid 4A 16
Dudley Av. M45: White 1B 22
Dudley Cl. M15: Man 5A 66
Dudley Ct. M16: W Ran 2F 79
Dudley Rd. M16: W Ran 3F 79
   M27: Pen 3B 34
   M33: Sale 2E 89
   WA15: Tim 4D 99
Dudley St. M7: Sal 5A 38
   M8: Man 1B 52
   M30: Ecc 1E 61
   OL4: O'ham 3F 31
Dudlow Wlk. M15: Man 4F 65
   (off Shawgreen Cl.)
Duffield Ct. M15: Man 5C 66
   (off Brennan Cl.)
   M24: Mid 4B 26
Duffield Gdns. M24: Mid 4B 26
Duffield Rd. M6: Sal 2F 49
   M24: Mid 4B 26
Dufton Wlk. M22: Wyth 5A 110
   M24: Mid 4A 16
Dugdale Av. M9: Man 5A 26
Duke Ct. M16: Old T 5F 65
Dukefield St. M22: Nor 1A 106
Duke Pl. M3: Man 3E 9 (2A 66)
Dukes Ct. M30: Ecc 5A 48
   (off Wellington Rd.)
Duke's Ter. SK16: Duk 5C 116 (1D 73)
Duke St. M3: Man 3E 9 (2A 66)
   M3: Sal 3A 6 (5B 52)
   M7: Sal 2F 51
   M28: Walk 2D 33
   M30: Ecc 3E 47
   M34: Dent 2A 86
   M35: Fail 4C 42
   OL6: A Lyme 2C 116 (4D 59)
   SK1: Stoc 3B 118 (2B 106)
Duke's Wharf M28: Wors 2B 46
DUKINFIELD 1D 73
Dukinfield Crematorium SK16: Duk 1F 73
DUKINFIELD HALL 3C 72
Dukinfield Rd. SK14: Hyde 5E 73
Dukinfield Swimming Pool 3F 73
Dulford Wlk. M13: Man 5E 67
   (off Plymouth Gro.)
Dulgar St. M11: Man 2C 68
Dulverton M40: Man 1D 55
Dulwich St. M4: Man 1E 7 (4D 53)
Dumbarton Cl. SK5: Stoc 2B 96
Dumbarton Rd. SK5: Stoc 2B 96
Dumbell St. M27: Pen 2B 34
Dumber La. M33: Sale 2B 88
Dumers Cl. M26: Rad 2A 12
Dumers La. BL9: Bury 2A 12
   M26: Rad 2A 12
DUMPLINGTON 3E 61
Dumvilles Brow
   SK1: Stoc 2B 118
Dunbar Av. M23: Wyth 3C 108
Dunbar St. OL1: O'ham 1A 30

Dunblane Av. SK4: Stoc 1F 105
Duncan Edwards Ct. M40: Man 2D 55
   (off Eddie Colman Cl.)
Duncan Edwards Ho. M6: Sal 4B 50
   (off Florin Gdns.)
Duncan Edwards Ter. M6: Sal 4B 50
   (off Doveridge Gdns.)
Duncan Rd. M13: Man 2B 82
   (not continuous)
Duncan St. M5: Sal 2A 8 (2E 65)
   M7: Sal 1E 51
   SK16: Duk 4E 73
Dunchurch Rd. M33: Sale 4A 88
Dun Cl. M3: Sal 3C 4 (5F 51)
Duncombe Dr. M40: Man 5D 41
Duncombe St. M7: Sal 1A 52
Dundee M30: Ecc 5A 48
   (off Monton La.)
Dundonald Rd. M20: Man 5E 93
Dundonald St. SK2: Stoc 5B 106
Dundraw Cl. M24: Mid 5D 15
Dunecroft M34: Dent 1C 86
Dunedin Dr. M6: Sal 2B 50
Dunelm Dr. M33: Sale 2F 99
Dunham Rd. SK9: Hand 4F 115
   SK16: Duk 4F 73
Dunham St. M15: Man 4A 66
   OL4: Lees 4D 31
Dunkeld Gdns. M23: Wyth 5C 100
Dunkeld Rd. M23: Wyth 5B 100
Dunkerley Av. M35: Fail 5B 42
Dunkerleys Cl. M8: Man 4B 38
   (off Grangeforth Rd.)
Dunkerley St. OL4: O'ham 1E 31
   OL7: A Lyme 2C 58
Dunkery Rd. M22: Wyth 5F 109
Dunkirk St. M34: Dent 3C 84
Dunkirk La. SK14: Hyde 5D 73
Dunkirk Rd. M45: White 5B 12
Dunkirk St. M43: Droy 1D 71
Dunley Cl. M12: Man 5C 68
Dunlop St. M3: Man 5A 6 (1B 66)
Dunmail Dr. M24: Mid 3A 16
Dunmaston Av. WA15: Tim 4F 99
Dunmere Wlk. M9: Man 1E 53
   (off Hendham Va.)
Dunmore Rd. SK8: Gat 5D 103
Dunmow Ct. SK2: Stoc 5F 107
Dunmow Wlk. M23: Wyth 1C 100
Dunnerdale Wlk. M18: Man 5E 69
   (off Beyer Cl.)
Dunnisher Rd. M23: Wyth 2D 109
Dunnollie Rd. M33: Sale 5A 90
Dunoon Rd. SK5: Stoc 1B 96
Dunoon Wlk. M9: Man 5F 39
   (off Kingsbridge Rd.)
Dunscar Cl. M45: White 2F 21
Dunsfold Dr. M23: Wyth 3F 99
Dunsley Av. M40: Man 2F 41
Dunsmore Cl. M16: W Ran 1F 79
Dunstable St. M19: Man 4D 83
Dunstall Rd. M22: Shar 1A 110
Dunstan Ct. M40: Man 4C 40
Dunstar Av. M34: Aud 3A 72
Dunster Av. M9: Man 5A 26
   M27: Clif 2D 35
   SK5: Stoc 3E 97
Dunster Cl. OL9: Chad 5C 28
Dunston St. M11: Man 2E 69
Dunton Grn. SK5: Stoc 2D 97

Dunton Towers. SK5: Stoc 2D **97**
    (off Dunton Grn.)
Dunworth St. M14: Man 2D **81**
Durant St. M4: Man 2E **7** (4D **53**)
Durban St. OL7: A Lyme 1A **72**
    OL8: O'ham 1E **43**
Durham Av. M41: Urm 2A **76**
Durham Cl. M27: Clif 2B **34**
    SK16: Duk 4F **73**
Durham Cres. M35: Fail 1C **56**
Durham Dr. OL6: A Lyme 4F **45**
Durham Ho. SK3: Stoc 5A **118** (3A **106**)
Durham Rd. M6: Sal 3E **49**
Durham St. M9: Man 5A **40**
    M43: Droy 2C **70**
    OL9: O'ham 5E **29**
    (not continuous)
    SK5: Stoc 3A **84**
Durham Wlk. *M34: Dent* 4B **86**
    (off Lancaster Rd.)
Durley Av. M8: Man 5D **39**
    WA15: Tim 4D **99**
Durling St. M12: Man 3C **76**
Durnford Av. M41: Urm 3E **67**
Durnford St. M24: Mid 5B **16**
Durnford Wlk. M22: Wyth 3D **109**
Durrington Wlk. *M40: Man* 1E **41**
    (off Moston La.)
Dutton St. M3: Man 1B **6** (4B **52**)
Duxford Lodge M8: Man 2B **38**
Duxford Wlk. *M40: Man* 1E **41**
    (off Moston La.)
Dyche St. M4: Man 3D **7** (4D **53**)
Dyche St. Trad. Est. M4: Man 2E **7**
Dyer St. M5: Sal 4B **8** (3E **65**)
Dymchurch Av. M26: Rad 2E **19**
Dymchurch St. M40: Man 3E **55**
Dysart St. OL6: A Lyme 5F **59**
Dyserth Gro. SK5: Stoc 4B **96**
Dyson Cl. BL4: Farn 1A **18**
Dyson Ho. *BL4: Farn* 1A **18**
    (off Hesketh Wlk.)

E

Eades St. M6: Sal 4C **50**
Eadington St. M8: Man 3C **38**
Eagar St. M40: Man 1E **55**
Eagle Ct. *M15: Man* 5A **66**
    (off Dudley Cl.)
Eagle Dr. M6: Sal 2C **50**
Eagles Nest M25: Pres 1C **36**
Eagle St. M4: Man 3D **7** (5C **52**)
    OL9: O'ham 3A **30**
Ealing Av. M14: Man 3E **81**
Ealinger Way M27: Pen 2B **34**
Ealing Pl. M19: Man 2C **94**
Ealing Rd. SK3: Stoc 3F **105**
Eames Av. M26: Rad 1C **18**
Eamont Wlk. *M9: Man* 5F **39**
    (off Ruskington Dr.)
Earby Gro. M9: Man 1B **40**
Earle Ct. *OL7: A Lyme* 1B **72**
    (off Graham St.)
Earle St. OL7: A Lyme 5B **58**
Earl Rd. SK4: Stoc 4E **95**
Earl's Lodge M35: Fail 1F **55**
Earlston Av.
    M34: Dent 2C **84**

Earl St. M7: Sal 3F **51**
    M25: Pres 5E **23**
    M34: Dent 1C **84**
    SK3: Stoc 3F **105**
Earls Way M35: Fail 1F **55**
Earlswood Rd. OL8: O'ham 1A **44**
Earlswood Wlk. *M18: Man* 4E **69**
    (off Briercliffe Rd.)
Earl Ter. SK16: Duk 5C **116** (1D **73**)
Earl Wlk. M12: Man 5B **68**
Earnshaw Av. SK1: Stoc 2D **107**
Earnshaw Cl. OL7: A Lyme 2B **58**
Easby Rd. M24: Mid 3B **16**
Easedale Cl. M41: Urm 2B **74**
Easington Wlk. M40: Man 1C **54**
East Av. M19: Man 1B **94**
    M45: White 4A **12**
    SK8: H Grn 5E **111**
Eastbourne St. OL8: O'ham 5D **31**
Eastburn Av. M40: Man 4E **53**
E. Central Dr. M27: Swin 5D **35**
Eastchurch Cl. BL4: Farn 2A **18**
Eastcombe Av. M7: Sal 5D **37**
Eastcote Av. M11: Man 2A **70**
Eastcote Rd. SK5: Stoc 3B **96**
Eastcote Wlk. *BL4: Farn* 1A **18**
    (off Darley St.)
East Ct. Wlk. M13: Man 4E **67**
East Cres. M24: Mid 2B **26**
Eastdale Pl. WA14: B'ath 4A **98**
EAST DIDSBURY 2E **103**
East Didsbury Station (Rail) 2E **103**
East Dr. BL9: Bury 2D **13**
    M6: Sal 2A **50**
    M21: Chor 4B **78**
    M27: Swin 5D **35**
Easterdale OL4: O'ham 3E **31**
Eastern Av. M27: Clif 1F **35**
    (not continuous)
Eastern By-Pass M11: Man 2F **69**
    (Crabtree La.)
    M11: Man 5E **55**
    (Stanton St.)
Eastern Circ. M19: Man 2C **94**
Eastfield M6: Sal 3A **50**
Eastfield Av. M24: Mid 2C **26**
    M40: Man 4A **54**
Eastford Sq. *M40: Man* 3E **53**
    (off Sand St.)
Eastgarth Wlk. *M9: Man* 1A **40**
    (off Greendale Dr.)
Eastgate St. OL7: A Lyme 5A **116** (1C **72**)
E. Grange Av. M11: Man 4E **55**
East Gro. M13: Man 4D **81**
Eastham Av. M14: Man 4F **115**
Eastham Way *SK9: Hand* 4E **115**
    (off Redesmere Dr.)
Easthaven Av. M11: Man 5E **55**
E. Hill St. OL4: O'ham 3C **30**
Eastholme Dr. M19: Man 1D **95**
Easthope Cl. M20: Man 1D **93**
E. Lancashire Rd.
    M27: Pen, Sal, Swin 4D **33**
    M28: Swin, Walk, Wors 4A **32**
East Lea M34: Dent 2C **86**
Eastleigh Av. M7: Sal 4A **38**
Eastleigh Dr. M40: Man 4F **53**
Eastleigh Rd. M25: Pres 1A **38**
    SK8: H Grn 5D **111**
E. Lynn Dr. M28: Walk 1C **32**

East Meade M21: Chor 1D 91
   M25: Pres 2F 37
   M27: Swin 1A 48
Eastmoor Dr. M40: Man 3F 55
E. Newton St. M4: Man 4E 53
   (off Rigel St.)
Eastnor Cl. M15: Man 4F 65
Easton Cl. M24: Mid 2E 27
Easton Dr. SK8: Chea 5C 104
Easton Rd. M43: Droy 5A 56
E. Ordsall La. M3: Sal 1C 8 (1F 65)
   M5: Sal 1C 8 (1F 65)
Eastpark Cl. M13: Man 4E 67
E. Philip St. M3: Sal 1F 5 (4A 52)
East Rd. M12: Man 2C 82
   M18: Man 2D 83
   M90: Man A 2E 113
Eastry Av. SK5: Stoc 2D 97
Eastside Valley M4: Man 1F 67
   (off Isaac Way)
East St. M34: Aud 3B 72
   OL6: A Lyme 3F 59
E. Union St. M16: Old T 4E 65
East Vw. M24: Mid 1B 26
   M33: Sale 5D 89
Eastville Gdns. M19: Man 3A 94
Eastway M24: Mid 5B 16
   M33: Sale 1A 98
   M41: Urm 2A 74
Eastwood M4: Man 4E 81
Eastwood Av. M40: Man 3B 42
   M41: Urm 3F 75
   M43: Droy 1A 70
Eastwood Rd. M40: Man 3A 42
Eastwood St. M34: Aud 3F 71
Eaton Cl. M27: Pen 2B 34
   SK16: Duk 4E 73
Eaton Dr. OL7: A Lyme 3B 58
   WA15: Tim 3C 98
Eaton Rd. M8: Man 3B 38
   M33: Sale 4C 88
Eaves La. SK9: Chad 4C 28
Ebbdale Cl. SK1: Stoc 5C 118 (3B 106)
Ebberstone St. M14: Man 3C 80
Ebden St. M1: Man 3E 11
Ebenezer St. M15: Man 5B 10 (3B 66)
Ebnall Wlk. M14: Man 1F 93
Ebor Ho. M32: Stre 4B 78
Ebor Rd. M22: Wyth 2A 110
Ebsworth St. M40: Man 4B 40
ECCLES 5B 48
Eccles Cl. M11: Man 2E 69
Eccles Crematorium M30: Ecc 2B 60
Eccles Dr. M27: Swin 1B 48
Eccles Fold M30: Ecc 5A 48
Eccleshall St. M11: Man 1D 69
   (not continuous)
Eccles New Rd. M5: Ecc, Sal 5C 48
   M50: Ecc, Sal 5C 48
Eccles Old Rd. M6: Sal 4D 49
Eccles St. M27: Swin 1B 48
Eccles Station (Metro) 5B 48
Eccles Station (Rail) 5B 48
Eccleston Av. M14: Man 4D 81
   M27: Swin 5F 33
Eccleston Pl. M7: Sal 4E 37
Eccleston St. M35: Fail 4C 42
Eccleston Way SK9: Hand 5F 115
   (off Henbury Rd.)
Echo St. M1: Man 3E 11 (2D 67)

Eckersley Cl. M23: Wyth 5B 100
Eckford St. M8: Man 1D 53
Edale Av. M34: Aud 3F 71
   M34: Dent 5B 86
   M40: Man 4C 40
   M41: Urm 4D 75
   SK5: Stoc 4C 84
Edale Cl. SK8: H Grn 2F 115
Edale Gro. M33: Sale 1A 98
Edale Rd. M32: Stre 2D 77
Edale St. M6: Sal 2D 51
Edbrook Wlk. M13: Man 5F 67
Eddie Colman Cl. M40: Man 2D 55
Eddie Colman Ct. M6: Sal 4C 50
   (off Belvedere Rd.)
Eddisbury Av. M20: Man 5B 80
   M41: Urm 1A 74
Eddystone Cl. M5: Sal 1C 64
Edenbridge Dr. M26: Rad 2D 19
Edenbridge Rd. M40: Man 3D 55
Eden Cl. M15: Man 4C 66
   SK1: Stoc 3C 106
Eden Ct. M19: Man 5C 82
Edendale Dr. M22: Wyth 5F 109
Edenfield Av. M21: Chor 4F 91
Edenfield La. M28: Wors 3B 46
Edenfield Rd. M25: Pres 1A 38
Edenhall Av. M19: Man 5B 82
Edenham Wlk. M40: Man 2F 41
   (off Enstone Dr.)
Edenhurst Dr. WA15: Tim 5D 99
Edenhurst Rd. SK2: Stoc 5D 107
Eden Pk. Rd. SK8: Chea H 1F 115
Eden Pl. M33: Sale 3D 89
   SK8: Chea 5F 103
Eden St. OL1: O'ham 2D 117 (2A 30)
Edgbaston Dr. M16: Old T 2C 78
EDGE, THE 2C 78
Edge, The M3: Sal 4A 6 (5A 52)
Edgecote Cl. M22: Shar 5B 102
Edgedale Av. M19: Man 3A 94
Edgefield Av. M9: Man 5A 26
Edge Fold Cres. M28: Walk 4A 32
Edge Fold Rd.
   M28: Walk, Wors 3A 32
Edgehill Cl. M5: Sal 5B 50
Edgehill Ct. M32: Stre 4A 78
Edgehill Rd. M6: Sal 4E 49
Edgehill St. M4: Man 4D 7
Edge La. M32: Stre 4F 77
   M43: Droy 5F 55
Edge La. Rd. OL1: O'ham 1F 117 (1C 30)
EDGELEY 4E 105
Edgeley Fold SK3: Stoc 4E 105
Edgeley Pk. .4A 106
Edgeley Rd. M41: Urm 5C 74
   SK3: Stoc 4C 104
Edgemoor Cl. OL4: O'ham 1F 31
Edge St. M4: Man 4D 7 (5C 52)
Edgeview Wlk. M13: Man 5F 11
Edgeware Av. M25: Pres 5B 24
Edgeware Rd. M30: Ecc 3C 46
   OL9: Chad 1A 42
Edgewater M5: Sal 5F 49
Edgeworth Dr. M14: Man 1A 94
Edgware Rd. M40: Man 3D 55
Edilom Rd. M8: Man 2A 38
Edinburgh M30: Ecc 5A 48
   (off Monton St.)
Edinburgh Cl. SK8: Chea 5B 104

Edinburgh Ho. M3: Sal 5D **5**	
(off Rocket St.)	
Edinburgh Sq. M40: Man 3A **54**	
(off Giltbrook Av.)	
Edison Rd. M30: Ecc 1E **61**	
Edison St. M11: Man 3A **70**	
Edith Av. M14: Man 2C **80**	
Edith Cavell Cl. M11: Man 1E **69**	
Edith Cliff Wlk. M40: Man 3B **42**	
Edith St. OL8: O'ham 1B **44**	
Edlin Cl. M12: Man 5A **68**	
Edlington Wlk. M40: Man 1E **55**	
Edmonds St. M24: Mid 5D **17**	
Edmonton Rd. M40: Man 3C **54**	
Edmund Cl. SK4: Stoc 5A **96**	
Edmund St. M6: Sal 4A **50**	
M35: Fail 4B **42**	
M43: Droy 1C **70**	
Edna St. SK14: Hyde 4F **87**	
Edson Rd. M8: Man 1B **38**	
Edward Av. M6: Sal 4E **49**	
M21: Chor .1B **90**	
Edward Charlton Rd. M16: Old T . . .3C **78**	
Edward Grant Ct. M9: Man 3A **40**	
Edward M. OL9: O'ham 4E **29**	
Edward Onyon Ct. M6: Sal 5A **50**	
Edward Pilkington Memorial Cotts.	
M27: Clif 1B **34**	
Edward Rd. M9: Man 4F **25**	
Edwards Ct. M22: Wyth 3F **109**	
Edwards Dr. M45: White 1D **23**	
Edward St. M7: Sal 1F **5** (3A **52**)	
M9: Man 4A **40**	
M24: Mid .4C **16**	
M25: Pres .4C **22**	
M26: Rad .1D **19**	
M33: Sale .4A **90**	
M34: Aud .3F **71**	
M34: Dent .1B **86**	
M43: Droy .2C **70**	
OL6: A Lyme 5F **59**	
OL9: Chad 1C **28**	
OL9: O'ham 3E **29**	
SK1: Stoc 4B **118** (3B **106**)	
SK14: Hyde 2E **87**	
(not continuous)	
SK16: Duk .4E **73**	
Edward Sutcliffe Cl. M14: Man 3C **80**	
Edwin Rd. M11: Man 1A **68**	
Edwin St. SK1: Stoc 3D **107**	
Edzell Wlk. M11: Man *1E **69***	
(off Kincraig Cl.)	
Eeasbrook M41: Urm 4F **75**	
Egbert St. M40: Man 5C **40**	
Egerton Cl. M14: Man *1E **81***	
(off Up. Park Rd.)	
M21: Chor .5B **78**	
M28: Wors 4C **32**	
M34: Dent *1C **86***	
(off Margaret Rd.)	
Egerton Cres. M20: Man 1D **93**	
Egerton Dr. M33: Sale 3D **89**	
Egerton Gro. M28: Walk 1A **32**	
Egerton Ho. M5: Sal *3C **64***	
(off Elmira Way)	
M15: Man .4D **9**	
SK4: Stoc .4C **94**	
Egerton Lodge M34: Dent *1C **86***	
(off Margaret Rd.)	
Egerton M. M43: Droy 2C **70**	

EGERTON PARK 5D **33**	
Egerton Pk. M28: Wors 5D **33**	
Egerton Pk. Art College Sports Hall . . .*1A **86***	
(off Boundary Grn.)	
Egerton Rd. M14: Man 5F **81**	
M28: Walk .1A **32**	
M30: Ecc 3F **47**	
M45: White 2B **22**	
Egerton Rd. Nth. M16: W Ran 3E **79**	
SK4: Stoc .3E **95**	
Egerton Rd. Sth. M21: Chor 5E **79**	
SK4: Stoc .3E **95**	
Egerton St. M3: Sal 5D **5** (1F **65**)	
M15: Man 4D **9** (3F **65**)	
M24: Mid .2E **25**	
M25: Pres .5E **23**	
M30: Ecc 5D **47**	
M34: Dent .5F **71**	
M43: Droy 1D **71**	
OL1: O'ham 3F **117** (2B **30**)	
OL6: A Lyme 4E **59**	
Egerton Ter. M14: Man 1F **93**	
Eggington St. M40: Man 2E **53**	
Egmont St. M6: Sal 1A **50**	
M8: Man 4C **38**	
Egremont Av. M20: Man 1C **92**	
Egremont Cl. M45: White 5C **12**	
Egremont Ct. M7: Sal *4E **37***	
(off Bury New Rd.)	
Egremont Gro. SK3: Stoc 3D **105**	
Egypt La. M25: Pres 5F **13**	
Eida Way M17: T Pk 2E **63**	
Eight Acre M45: White 2E **21**	
Eighth Av. OL8: O'ham 3F **43**	
Eighth St. M17: T Pk 4F **63**	
(not continuous)	
Eighth St. W. M17: T Pk 4E **63**	
Eileen Gro. M14: Man 3E **81**	
Eileen Gro. W. M14: Man 3D **81**	
Elaine Av. M9: Man 2D **41**	
Elbain Wlk. M40: Man *2E **55***	
(off Orford Rd.)	
Elberton Wlk. M8: Man *5B **38***	
(off Highshore Dr.)	
Elbe St. M12: Man 2E **67**	
Elbow St. M19: Man 4C **82**	
Elcot Cl. M40: Man 2E **53**	
Elder Cl. SK2: Stoc 3F **107**	
Elder Ct. SK4: Stoc 5D **95**	
Eldercroft Rd. WA15: Tim 5E **99**	
Elder Gro. M40: Man 2B **42**	
Elder Mt. Rd. M9: Man 2F **39**	
Elderwood OL9: Chad 2A **28**	
Eldon Cl. M34: Aud 3A **72**	
Eldon Pl. M30: Ecc 1E **61**	
Eldon Pct. OL8: O'ham 5D **117**	
Eldon Rd. SK3: Stoc 4E **105**	
Eldon St. OL8: O'ham 5E **117** (4B **30**)	
Eldon St. Est. OL8: O'ham 5E **117**	
Eldridge Dr. M40: Man 2C **54**	
Eldroth Av. M22: Wyth 3F **109**	
Eleanor Rd. M21: Chor 5C **78**	
Eleanor St. OL1: O'ham 1F **29**	
Electo St. M11: Man 3A **70**	
Electric Pk. M17: T Pk 5E **63**	
Elevator Rd. M17: T Pk 4A **64**	
Eleventh St. M17: T Pk 4E **63**	
Elf Mill Cl. SK3: Stoc 5A **106**	
Elf Mill Ter. SK3: Stoc 5A **106**	
Elford Gro. M18: Man 1C **84**	

Elgar St. M12: Man 1C **82**
Elgin Av. M20: Man 5F **93**
Elgin Dr. M33: Sale 5A **90**
Elgin Rd. OL4: O'ham 4E **31**
SK16: Duk 4E **73**
Elgin St. OL7: A Lyme 1B **116** (3C **58**)
(not continuous)
Elham Cl. M26: Rad 2E **19**
Eliot Rd. M30: Ecc 1F **61**
Eliot Wlk. M24: Mid 3E **17**
Elishaw Row M5: Sal 1B **64**
Eli St. OL9: Chad 1C **42**
Elitex Ho. M7: Sal 3A **52**
Eliza Ann St. M30: Ecc 1E **61**
M40: Man 3E **53**
Elizabeth Av. M34: Dent 5A **72**
OL9: Chad 1C **42**
SK1: Stoc 5C **118** (3B **106**)
Elizabeth Cl. M32: Stre 3F **77**
Elizabeth Ct. M14: Man 1F **93**
M18: Man 2B **84**
(off Reddish La.)
. . . . .1E **105**
SK4: Stoc 2D **105**
Elizabeth Ho. SK4: Stoc 2D **105**
Elizabeth Slinger Rd.
M20: Man 4A **92**
Elizabeth St. M8: Man 1B **52**
M25: Pres 5E **23**
M27: Pen 3B **34**
M34: Dent 2F **85**
M45: White 2B **22**
OL6: A Lyme 3D **59**
SK14: Hyde 2F **87**
Elizabeth St. Ind. Est. M34: Dent 2F **85**
(off Grey St.)
Elizabeth Yarwood Ct.
M13: Man 5F **11** (4D **67**)
Eliza St. M15: Man 5E **9** (4A **66**)
Elkanagh Gdns. M6: Sal 4B **50**
Elladene Pk. M21: Chor 5E **79**
Ellanby Cl. M14: Man 2D **81**
Elland Cl. BL9: Bury 4D **13**
Ellaston Dr. M41: Urm 3F **75**
Ellastone Rd. M6: Sal 3E **49**
Ellbourne Rd. M9: Man 1C **38**
Ellenbrook Cl. M12: Man 4D **69**
Ellenbrook Rd. M22: Wyth 1F **113**
Ellenbrook St. M12: Man 4D **69**
Ellen Gro. BL4: Kea 4E **19**
Ellenhall Cl. M9: Man 4F **39**
Ellen St. M43: Droy 2D **71**
OL9: O'ham 1F **29**
SK4: Stoc 5F **95**
Ellen Wilkinson Cres.
M12: Man 5C **68**
Elleray Rd. M6: Sal 2F **49**
M24: Mid 4B **26**
Ellerby Av. M27: Clif 1C **34**
Ellerslie Ct. M14: Man 2E **81**
Ellesmere Av. M30: Ecc 4A **48**
OL6: A Lyme 5E **45**
Ellesmere Circ. M41: Urm 3F **61**
Ellesmere Cl. SK16: Duk 3F **73**
Ellesmere Dr. SK8: Chea 5C **104**
Ellesmere Grn. M30: Ecc 4A **48**
Ellesmere Ho. M30: Ecc 4B **48**
(off Sandwich Rd.)
ELLESMERE PARK 3A **48**
Ellesmere Pk. M30: Ecc 3C **48**
(off Park Rd.)

Ellesmere Rd. M21: Chor 4E **79**
M30: Ecc 3A **48**
SK3: Stoc 4C **104**
WA14: Alt 5A **98**
Ellesmere Rd. Nth. SK4: Stoc 3E **95**
Ellesmere Rd. Sth. M21: Chor 4E **79**
Ellesmere Sports Club 4A **32**
Ellesmere St. BL4: Farn 1A **18**
M15: Man 5C **8** (3F **65**)
M27: Pen 3C **34**
M27: Swin 5F **33**
M30: Ecc 1F **61**
(not continuous)
M35: Fail 4B **42**
Ellesmere Ter. M14: Man 1F **93**
Ellesmere Wlk. BL4: Farn 1A **18**
Ellingham Cl. M11: Man 1B **68**
Elliot Sq. OL1: O'ham 1C **30**
Elliott Av. SK14: Hyde 5F **73**
Elliott Dr. M33: Sale 4A **88**
Ellis Bank Wlk. M13: Man 5F **11**
(off Deanwater Cl.)
Ellis Dr. M8: Man 3D **39**
Ellisland Wlk. M40: Man 1C **54**
(off Colebrook Dr.)
Ellis La. M24: Mid 1D **25**
Ellison Ho. OL7: A Lyme 4A **116**
Ellis St. M7: Sal 3A **52**
M15: Man 4A **66**
Elliston Sq. M12: Man 4C **68**
(off Bridgend Cl.)
Ellon Wlk. M11: Man 1E **69**
(off Edith Cavell Cl.)
Ellor St. M6: Sal 4B **50**
Ellwood Rd. SK1: Stoc 2D **107**
Elm Av. M26: Rad 1B **20**
Elmbank Av. M20: Man 4A **92**
Elmbank Rd. M24: Mid 1E **27**
Elmbridge Wlk. M40: Man 1C **54**
Elm Ct. SK1: Stoc 3D **107**
Elm Cres. M28: Wors 5C **32**
Elmdale Av. SK8: H Grn 4D **111**
Elmdale Wlk. M15: Man 5C **10**
Elm Dr. M32: Stre 4D **77**
Elmfield Av. M22: Nor 3A **102**
Elmfield Ct. SK3: Stoc 5B **106**
(off Elmfield Rd.)
Elmfield Rd. M34: Aud 2E **71**
SK3: Stoc 5B **106**
Elmfield St. M8: Man 1C **52**
Elmgate Gro. M19: Man 4C **82**
Elm Gro. M20: Man 5D **93**
M25: Pres 3C **22**
M27: Ward 3D **33**
M33: Sale 2D **89**
M34: Dent 5F **71**
M41: Urm 3A **76**
M43: Droy 5F **55**
OL6: A Lyme 2E **59**
SK9: Hand 5E **115**
(off Sagars Rd.)
Elmham Wlk. M40: Man 3E **53**
(off Rimworth Dr.)
Elmhurst Dr. M19: Man 3B **94**
Elmira Way M5: Sal 3C **64**
Elm Pk. Ct. M20: Man 4D **93**
Elm Rd. BL4: Kea 4B **18**
M20: Man 4C **92**
OL8: O'ham 3F **43**
SK8: Gat 1C **110**

Elm Rd. Sth. SK3: Stoc 4C **104**
Elms, The M45: White 4B **12**
Elms Cl. M45: White 4B **12**
Elmscott Wlk. M13: Man 5F **67**
              (off Bletchley Cl.)
Elmsdale Av. M9: Man 4F **25**
Elms Farm M45: White 4B **12**
Elmsleigh Cl. M30: Ecc 4B **48**
Elmsleigh Rd. SK8: H Grn 4C **110**
Elmsmere Rd. M20: Man 5F **93**
Elms Rd. M45: White 5B **12**
   SK4: Stoc 3D **95**
Elms Sq. M45: White 5A **12**
Elms St. M45: White 5A **12**
Elmstead Av. M20: Man 2C **92**
Elmstead Ho. M27: Swin 5B **34**
Elmstone Cl. M9: Man 2E **39**
Elm St. BL4: Farm 1A **18**
   M24: Mid 5E **17**
   M27: Swin 3A **34**
   M30: Ecc 1F **61**
   M35: Fail 4B **42**
Elmswood Av. M14: Man 3B **80**
Elmsworth Av. M19: Man 4D **83**
Elmton Rd. M9: Man 1A **40**
Elm Tree Cl. M35: Fail 5D **43**
Elm Tree Dr. M22: Wyth 3F **109**
Elmtree Dr. SK4: Stoc 1D **105**
Elm Tree Rd. SK6: Bred 5E **97**
              (not continuous)
Elmwood M28: Wors 2C **46**
Elmwood Cl. M32: Stre 5E **77**
Elmwood Gro. M9: Man 5B **40**
Elmwood Lodge M20: Man 4C **92**
Elrick Wlk. M11: Man 1D **69**
          (off Emily Beavan Cl.)
Elsa Rd. M19: Man 4E **83**
Elsdon Dr. M18: Man 4F **69**
Elsdon Rd. M13: Man 3B **82**
Elsham Gdns. M18: Man 1D **83**
Elsie St. M9: Man 4A **40**
Elsinore Bus. Cen. M16: Old T 1C **78**
Elsinore Cl. M35: Fail 5D **43**
Elsinore Rd. M16: Old T 1C **78**
Elsma Rd. M40: Man 3A **56**
Elsmore Rd. M14: Man 4C **80**
Elstead Wlk. M9: Man 1D **39**
Elstree Av. M40: Man 3D **55**
Elstree Ct. M41: Urm 3F **75**
Elswick Av. M21: Chor 3F **91**
Elsworth Cl. M26: Rad 1D **21**
Elsworth St. M3: Man 1C **6** (4C **52**)
Elterwater Cl. M24: Mid 3F **15**
Eltham Dr. M41: Urm 1E **75**
Eltham St. M19: Man 3C **82**
Elton Av. M19: Man 5C **82**
Elton Cl. M45: White 1C **22**
Elton Rd. M33: Sale 1A **98**
Elton St. M7: Sal 1D **5** (4F **51**)
   M32: Stre 5B **64**
Elton's Yd. M7: Sal 1D **5** (4F **51**)
Elvate Cres. M8: Man 2B **52**
Elverdon Cl. M15: Man 5A **66**
Elverston St. M22: Nor 2A **102**
Elverston Way OL9: Chad 1E **29**
Elvey St. M40: Man 2B **54**
Elvira Cl. M35: Fail 5D **43**
Elwick Cl. M16: W Ran 2B **80**
Elworth Way SK9: Hand 5F **115**
          (off Delamere Rd.)

Elwyn Av. M22: Nor 4F **101**
Ely Av. M32: Stre 2B **76**
Ely Cres. M35: Fail 2B **56**
Ely Gdns. M41: Urm 3A **76**
Elysian Flds. M6: Sal 4D **49**
Elysian St. M11: Man 2E **69**
Ely St. OL9: O'ham 4D **29**
Embankment Bus. Pk. SK4: Stoc 2B **104**
Embassy Wlk. M18: Man 1F **83**
Ember St. M11: Man 5F **55**
Embleton Wlk. M18: Man 4E **69**
          (off Peacock Cl.)
Emerald Rd. M22: Wyth 2B **114**
Emerald St. M34: Dent 2A **86**
Emerson Av. M30: Ecc 4C **48**
Emerson Dr. M24: Mid 5B **16**
Emerson Ho. M30: Ecc 5B **48**
Emerson St. M5: Sal 5F **49**
Emery Av. M21: Chor 2E **91**
Emery Cl. SK4: Stoc 4C **94**
   WA14: Alt 4A **98**
Emery Ct. SK4: Stoc 2B **104**
Emily Beavan Cl. M11: Man 1D **69**
Emily Cl. M35: Fail 3C **42**
Emily Pl. M43: Droy 1B **70**
Emley St. M19: Man 4D **83**
Emlyn Gro. SK8: Chea 5C **104**
Emlyn St. M27: Swin 4F **33**
   M28: Walk 1A **32**
Emmanuel Cl. OL6: A Lyme 3D **59**
Emma St. OL8: O'ham 1B **44**
Emmaus Wlk. M6: Sal 4B **50**
Emmeline Grange M6: Sal 5A **50**
Emmerson St. M27: Pen 3B **34**
Emmett St. E. M40: Man 2A **54**
Emmott Way OL1: O'ham 5E **117** (3B **30**)
Empire Rd. SK16: Duk 4E **73**
Empire St. M3: Man 1C **6** (3B **52**)
Empress Bus. Cen. M16: Old T 4E **65**
Empress Ct. M15: Man 4E **65**
Empress Dr. SK4: Stoc 4F **95**
Empress St. M8: Man 4B **38**
   M16: Old T 4E **65**
Emsworth Dr. M33: Sale 2E **99**
Ena St. OL1: O'ham 1E **31**
Enbridge St. M5: Sal 2C **64**
Encombe Pl. M3: Sal 4C **4** (5F **51**)
Endcott Cl. M18: Man 4D **69**
Enderby Rd. M40: Man 3E **41**
Endon Dr. M21: Chor 5B **80**
Endsleigh Rd. M20: Man 2E **93**
Energy St. M40: Man 4A **54**
Enfield Av. M19: Man 2C **94**
   OL8: O'ham 1A **44**
Enfield Cl. BL9: Bury 1B **12**
   M30: Ecc 2F **61**
Enfield Dr. M11: Man 5E **55**
Enfield Ho. M30: Ecc 2F **61**
            (off Enfield Cl.)
Enfield Rd. M27: Swin 1A **48**
   M30: Ecc 3F **47**
Enfield St. SK14: Hyde 5F **87**
Enford Av. M22: Wyth 4C **108**
Engell Cl. M18: Man 5F **69**
Engels Ho. M30: Ecc 2F **61**
          (off Trafford Rd.)
Engine St. OL9: Chad 5D **29**
England St. OL6: A Lyme 4E **59**
Englefield Gro. M18: Man 1F **83**
          (off Milkwood Gro.)

Enid Cl. M7: Sal 2F **51**
Ennerdale Av. M21: Chor 4F **91**
  M27: Swin 1B **48**
Ennerdale Dr. BL9: Bury 4C **12**
  M33: Sale 3A **88**
  SK8: Gat 3D **111**
  WA15: Tim 3C **98**
Ennerdale Gro. OL7: A Lyme 2B **58**
Ennerdale Rd. M24: Mid 4B **16**
  M32: Stre 2E **77**
  SK1: Stoc 4D **107**
Ennis Cl. M23: Wyth 1A **108**
Ennismore Av. M30: Ecc 5C **48**
Enstone Dr. M40: Man 3F **41**
Enterprise Cen. Two SK3: Stoc 2F **105**
             (off Chester St.)
Enterprise Ho. M50: Sal 3C **64**
Enterprise Trad. Est. M17: T Pk 2C **62**
Entwisle Av. M41: Urm 1D **75**
Entwisle St. BL4: Farn 1A **18**
  M27: Ward 3F **33**
Enver Rd. M8: Man 4D **39**
Enville Rd. M6: Sal 1A **50**
  M40: Man 3D **41**
Enville St. M9: Man 1F **39**
  M34: Aud 3B **72**
  OL6: A Lyme 4E **59**
Enys Wlk. M6: Sal 2C **50**
Epping Cl. OL6: A Lyme 5E **45**
  OL9: Chad 1A **28**
Epping Rd. M34: Dent 3D **85**
Epping St. M15: Man 5B **10** (4B **66**)
Eppleworth Ri. M27: Clif 1C **34**
Epsley Cl. M15: Man 4C **66**
Epsom Av. M19: Man 2B **94**
  SK9: Hand 5F **115**
Epsom M. M7: Sal 1F **51**
             (off Rigby St.)
Epsom Wlk. OL9: Chad 2E **29**
          (off Garforth St.)
Epworth Ct. SK4: Stoc 5D **95**
Epworth St. M1: Man 1E **67**
Equitable St. OL4: O'ham 1F **31**
Era St. M5: Sal 1B **64**
  OL4: O'ham 2E **31**
Erin Cl. OL9: Chad 4D **29**
Erindale Wlk. M40: Man 1F **53**
        (off Barnstaple Dr.)
Erin St. M11: Man 3A **70**
Erith Cl. SK5: Stoc 2D **97**
Erith Rd. OL4: O'ham 3E **31**
Erlesmere Av. M34: Dent 1C **86**
Erlington Av. M16: Old T 3D **79**
Ermen Rd. M30: Ecc 2E **61**
Ermington Dr. M8: Man 1B **52**
Erneley Cl. M12: Man 2D **83**
Ernest St. M25: Pres 5B **22**
  SK2: Stoc 5C **106**
  SK8: Chea 5E **103**
Ernocroft Gro. M18: Man 4A **70**
Errington Cl. SK2: Stoc 5F **107**
Errington Dr. M7: Sal 1C **4** (3F **51**)
Errol Av. M9: Man 4C **24**
  M22: Wyth 2E **109**

Errwood Cres. M19: Man 5C **82**
Errwood Pk. Works SK4: Stoc 2D **95**
Errwood Rd. M19: Man 3B **94**
Erskine Rd. M9: Man 4A **26**
Erskine St. M15: Man 4F **65**
Erwin St. M40: Man 1D **55**
Eryngo St. SK1: Stoc 2C **106**
Escott St. M16: W Ran 2B **80**
Esher Dr. M33: Sale 2E **99**
Esk Cl. M41: Urm 1C **74**
Eskdale Av. M20: Man 1C **92**
  OL8: O'ham 5F **29**
Eskdale Cl. BL9: Bury 3C **12**
Eskdale Dr. M24: Mid 3B **16**
  WA15: Tim 4E **99**
Eskdale Ho. M13: Man 1A **82**
Eskrigge Cl. M7: Sal 4B **38**
Esmond Rd. M8: Man 5C **38**
Esmont Dr. M24: Mid 3A **16**
Esporta Health & Fitness
    Denton 2E **85**
    Middleton 4D **15**
    Salford Quays 3B **64**
Essex Av. M20: Man 4D **93**
  M43: Droy 4C **56**
  SK3: Stoc 3D **105**
Essex Cl. M35: Fail 2B **56**
Essex Pl. M27: Clif 2B **34**
      (off Cumberland Av.)
Essex Rd. M18: Man 1B **84**
  SK5: Stoc 3E **97**
Essex St. M2: Man 1B **10** (1B **66**)
Essex Way M16: Old T 5F **65**
Essington Dr. M40: Man 1F **53**
Essington Wlk. M34: Dent 4A **86**
Essoldo Cl. M18: Man 5E **69**
Estate St. OL8: O'ham 5B **30**
Estate St. Sth. OL8: O'ham 5B **30**
Esther St. OL4: O'ham 2F **31**
Estonfield Dr. M41: Urm 3B **76**
Eston St. M13: Man 1F **81**
Eswick St. M11: Man 1E **69**
Etchells Rd. SK8: H Grn 5F **111**
  WA14: W Tim 3A **98**
Etchells St.
  SK1: Stoc 2B **118** (2B **106**)
Etchell St. M40: Man 2E **53**
Ethel Av. M9: Man 4F **25**
  M27: Pen 4D **35**
Ethel St. OL8: O'ham 1B **44**
Ethel Ter. M19: Man 4C **82**
Etherow Av. M40: Man 2B **42**
Etherow Ct. SK14: Hyde 3F **87**
        (off Ridling La.)
Etherstone St. M8: Man 4E **39**
Eton Av. OL8: O'ham 1A **44**
Eton Cl. M16: Old T 5F **65**
Eton Ct. M16: Old T 5F **65**
          (off Eton Cl.)
Eton Dr. SK8: Chea 4F **111**
Etruria Cl. M13: Man 5A **68**
Ettrick Cl. M11: Man 3F **69**
Euan Pl. M33: Sale 4E **89**
      (off Montague Rd.)
Euclid Cl. M11: Man 1A **68**
Europa Bus. Pk. SK3: Stoc 5D **105**
Europa Circ. M17: T Pk 5F **63**
Europa Ga. M17: T Pk 5F **63**
Europa Trad. Est. M26: Rad 2D **19**

Europa Way M17: T Pk 5F **63**
Eustace St. OL9: Chad 1D **29**
M26: Rad 2C **18**
SK3: Stoc 5D **105**
Euston Av. M9: Man 1C **40**
Evans Ct. M20: Man 5C **92**
Evans Rd. M30: Ecc 1C **60**
Evans St. M5: Sal 2F **5** (4A **52**)
M24: Mid 1D **27**
OL1: O'ham 1E **117** (1B **30**)
OL6: A Lyme 3F **59**
Evan St. M40: Man 2A **54**
Evanton Wlk. M9: Man 5A **40**
(off Nethervale Dr.)
Eva Rd. SK3: Stoc 4C **104**
Eva St. M14: Man 2E **81**
Evelyn St. M14: Man 5F **81**
OL1: O'ham 1D **31**
Evening St. M35: Fail 4B **42**
Evenly Cl. M11: Man 4A **70**
Eventhall Ho. M25: Pres 3C **36**
Everard St. M5: Sal 4B **8** (3E **65**)
Everest Av. OL7: A Lyme 2D **59**
Everest Cl. SK16: Duk 5B **116** (1D **73**)
Everett Ct. M20: Man 2D **93**
(off Aldborough Cl.)
Everett Rd. M20: Man 2C **92**
Everglade OL8: O'ham 3C **44**
Evergreen M. M7: Sal 5F **37**
Everleigh Dr. M7: Sal 1B **52**
Eversden Ct. M7: Sal 1E **5** (3A **52**)
Eversham Av. SK4: Stoc 5D **95**
Everside Dr. M8: Man 2A **52**
Eversley Cl. M33: Sale 1D **99**
Eversley Rd. M20: Man 5C **92**
Everton Rd. OL8: O'ham 1F **43**
SK5: Stoc 3B **84**
Everton St. M27: Swin 4A **34**
Every St. M4: Man 1F **67**
Evesham Av. M23: Wyth 4F **99**
Evesham Cl. M24: Mid 4D **27**
Evesham Gdns. M24: Mid 4C **26**
Evesham Gro. M33: Sale 4A **90**
OL6: A Lyme 5E **45**
Evesham Rd. M9: Man 2C **40**
M24: Mid 4C **26**
Evesham Wlk. M24: Mid 4D **27**
OL8: O'ham 4A **30**
Eve St. OL8: O'ham 2B **44**
Evington Av. M11: Man 3C **70**
Ewan St. M18: Man 4F **69**
Ewart Av. M5: Sal 1C **64**
Ewhurst Av. M27: Swin 1F **47**
Ewing Cl. M8: Man 3C **38**
Ewood OL8: O'ham 4C **44**
Ewood Ho. M30: Ecc 5B **48**
Exbourne Rd. M22: Wyth 5E **109**
Exbridge Wlk. M40: Man 3F **55**
(off Stansfield St.)
Exbury St. M14: Man 1F **93**
Exchange Ct. M4: Man 4C **6**
Exchange Quay M5: Sal 4C **64**
Exchange Quay Station (Metro) 4C **64**
Exchange Sq. M3: Man 4B **6** (5B **52**)
Exchange St. M2: Man 5B **6** (1B **66**)
OL4: O'ham 2D **31**
(off Gravel Walks)
SK3: Stoc 3A **118** (2A **106**)
Exeter Av. M30: Ecc 3C **48**
M34: Dent 4B **86**

Exeter Cl. SK16: Duk 4F **73**
Exeter Ct. M14: Man 1E **93**
(off Wilmslow Rd.)
M24: Mid 5B **16**
Exeter Dr. OL6: A Lyme 5F **45**
Exeter Rd. M41: Urm 1F **75**
SK5: Stoc 3E **97**
Exeter St. M6: Sal 5A **50**
(off Langton St.)
Exford Cl. M40: Man 4F **53**
SK5: Stoc 2B **96**
Exmoor Cl. OL6: A Lyme 5E **45**
Exmoor Wlk. M23: Wyth 3C **108**
Exmouth Av. SK5: Stoc 3E **97**
Exmouth Rd. M33: Sale 3A **88**
Express Trad. Est. BL4: Farn 3A **18**
Eycott Dr. M24: Mid 5F **15**
Eynford Av. SK5: Stoc 2D **97**
Eyre St. M15: Man 5C **66**

F

Faber St. M4: Man 1D **7** (4C **52**)
Factory Brow M24: Mid 2E **25**
Factory La. M5: Sal 5C **4**
M9: Man 3E **39**
Factory St. M24: Mid 1B **26**
FAILSWORTH 5B **42**
Failsworth Ind. Est. M35: Fail 1E **55**
Failsworth Pct. M35: Fail 5B **42**
Failsworth Rd. M35: Fail 5D **43**
Failsworth Sports Cen. 5C **42**
Failsworth Station (Rail) 4A **42**
Fairbairn Apartments M4: Man 4F **7**
Fairbank M43: Droy 2B **70**
Fairbank Av. M14: Man 1D **81**
Fairbank Dr. M24: Mid 4F **15**
Fairbottom St. OL1: O'ham 3F **117** (2B **30**)
Fairbottom Wlk. M43: Droy 2C **70**
(off Wood Sq.)
Fairbourne Dr. WA15: Tim 2D **99**
Fairbourne Rd. M19: Man 4E **83**
M34: Dent 3A **86**
Fairbourne Wlk. OL1: O'ham 1E **31**
Fairbrook Dr. M6: Sal 1A **50**
Fairbrother St. M5: Sal 5A **8** (3E **65**)
Fairburn Cl. M41: Urm 1C **74**
Fairclough St. M11: Man 5C **54**
Fairfax Av. M20: Man 4D **93**
WA15: Tim 5C **98**
Fairfax Rd. M25: Pres 4C **22**
FAIRFIELD 2C **70**
Fairfield Av. M43: Droy 2C **70**
Fairfield Ct. M14: Man 1F **81**
M43: Droy 2B **70**
Fairfield Ho. M43: Droy 1C **70**
(off Manchester Rd.)
Fairfield Rd. M11: Man 3A **70**
M24: Mid 5A **16**
M43: Droy 2A **70**
Fairfields OL8: O'ham 2A **44**
Fairfield Sq. M43: Droy 2C **70**
(not continuous)
Fairfield Station (Rail) 3C **70**
Fairfield St. M1: Man 2E **11** (2D **67**)
M6: Sal .2F **49**
M12: Man 2F **67**
Fairfield Vw. M34: Aud 3C **70**
Fairford Cl. SK5: Stoc 3B **96**

Fairford Way SK5: Stoc 3B 96
Fairham Wlk. M4: Man 1F 67
Fairhaven Av. M21: Chor 5D 79
   M45: White 2F 21
Fairhaven Cvn. Pk. SK14: Hyde 3E 87
Fairhaven St. M12: Man 4B 68
Fairholme Av. M41: Urm 4E 75
Fairholme Cvn. Pk. M8: Man 3D 53
Fairholme Rd. M20: Man 2E 93
   SK4: Stoc 5E 95
Fairhope Av. M6: Sal 3D 49
Fairhope Cl. M6: Sal 4E 49
                 (off Fairhope Av.)
Fairisle Cl. M11: Man 1B 68
Fairlands Rd. M33: Sale 1B 98
Fairlawn Sk4: Stoc 5F 95
Fairlawn Cl. M14: Man 1C 80
Fairlea M34: Dent 3C 86
Fairlea Av. M20: Man 1E 103
Fairlee Av. M34: Aud 1E 71
Fairleigh Av. M6: Sal 4E 49
Fairless Rd. M30: Ecc 1F 61
Fairlie Dr. WA15: Tim 3D 99
Fairman St. M16: W Ran 2B 80
Fairmead Rd. M23: Wyth 2E 101
Fairmile Dr. M20: Man 3E 103
Fairmount Rd. M27: Swin 1D 47
Fair Oak Rd. M19: Man 3B 94
Fairstead Wlk. M11: Man 3B 70
Fair St. M1: Man 1E 67
   M27: Pen 3C 34
Fairthorne Grange OL7: A Lyme 1B 72
                 (off Bennett St.)
Fairview M19: Man 3B 82
   M34: Dent 4C 84
Fairview Cl. OL9: Chad 1A 28
Fairview Rd. M34: Dent 3C 84
   WA15: Tim 5E 99
Fairway M25: Pres 2F 37
   M27: Pen 5E 35
   M43: Droy 2C 70
   SK8: Gat 2D 111
Fairway, The M40: Man 5E 41
   SK2: Stoc 4F 107
Fairway Av. M23: Wyth 4F 99
Fairway Ct. M34: Dent 1D 85
Fairway Dr. M33: Sale 1A 98
Fairway Ho. SK4: Stoc 4C 94
Fairway Rd. BL9: Bury 3C 12
   OL4: O'ham 5F 31
Fairways, The M45: White 3B 22
Fairwood Rd. M23: Wyth 4F 99
Fairy La. M8: Man 2A 52
   M33: Sale 4B 90
Fairywell Dr. M33: Sale 2C 98
Fairywell Rd. WA15: Tim 3D 99
Falcon Av. M41: Urm 3A 76
Falcon Bus. Cen. OL9: Chad 1E 29
Falcon Cl. M50: Sal 1E 63
Falcon Ct. M7: Sal 3A 52
   M15: Man 5A 66
   M50: Sal 2F 63
Falcon Cres. M27: Clif 2D 35
Falcon Dr. M24: Mid 3A 16
   OL9: Chad 1E 29
Falcon St. OL8: O'ham 5D 117 (4A 30)
Falcon's Vw. OL8: O'ham 1A 44
Falconwood Way M11: Man 2B 68
Falfield Dr. M8: Man 2D 53
Falkirk St. OL4: O'ham 2E 31

Falkirk Wlk. M23: Wyth 4C 108
Falkland Av. M40: Man 3F 53
Falkland Ho. M14: Man 4E 81
Fall Bank SK4: Stoc 2F 95
Fallons Rd. M28: Ward 3E 33
Fallow Av. M18: Man 3F 83
FALLOWFIELD .5E 81
Fallowfield Av. M5: Sal 2D 65
Fallow Flds. Dr. SK5: Stoc 4C 84
Fallowfield Shop. Cen. M14: Man 4A 82
Fallows, The OL9: Chad 4C 28
Falls Grn. Av. M40: Man 1C 54
Falls Gro. SK8: H Grn 3C 110
Falmer Cl. M18: Man 4B 70
Falmer Dr. M22: Wyth 5E 109
Falmouth Av. M33: Sale 3A 88
   M41: Urm 2A 74
Falmouth Cres. SK5: Stoc 3E 97
Falmouth St. M40: Man 3B 54
   OL8: O'ham 5B 30
Falsgrave Cl. M40: Man 2C 54
Falside Wlk. M40: Man 2E 55
Falston Av. M40: Man 2F 41
Falterley Rd. M23: Wyth 3B 100
Fane Wlk. M9: Man 1D 39
Faraday Av. M8: Man 1C 52
   M27: Clif .4E 35
Faraday St. M1: Man 4E 7 (1D 67)
Farcroft Cl. M23: Wyth 3B 100
Far Cromwell Rd. SK6: Bred 1F 97
Farden Dr. M23: Wyth 3F 99
Far La. M18: Man 1F 83
Farley Av. M18: Man 1C 84
Farley Rd. M33: Sale 1E 99
Farley Way SK5: Stoc 4A 84
Farm Av. M32: Stre 1C 76
Farm Cl. SK4: Stoc 2E 95
Farmers Cl. M33: Sale 5C 90
Farmer St. SK4: Stoc 5F 95
Farm Fold SK9: Sty 5B 114
Farm Hill M25: Pres 4A 22
Farm La. M25: Pres 1A 24
   M28: Wors 2B 46
   SK14: Hyde 5F 87
Farm Rd. OL8: O'ham 4E 43
Farm Side Pl. M19: Man 4C 82
Farmstead Cl. M35: Fail 1E 57
Farm St. M35: Fail 1F 55
Farmway M24: Mid 2C 26
Farm Yd. M19: Man 4C 82
Farn Av. SK5: Stoc 3A 84
Farnborough Av. OL4: O'ham 3F 31
Farnborough Rd. M40: Man 4F 53
Farncombe Cl. M23: Wyth 4F 99
           (off Petersfield Dr.)
Farndale Wlk. M9: Man 4A 40
          (off Caversham Dr.)
Farndon Cl. M33: Sale 5A 90
Farndon Dr. WA15: Tim 5C 98
Farndon Rd. SK5: Stoc 3A 84
Farnham Av. M9: Man 4F 25
Farnhill Wlk. M23: Wyth 2A 100
Farnsworth Av. OL7: A Lyme 2D 59
Farnsworth Cl. OL7: A Lyme 2D 59
Farnworth & Kearsley By-Pass
   BL4: Farn, Kea 1A 18
Farnworth Dr. M14: Man 3E 81

Farnworth Leisure Cen. 1A 18
Farnworth Station (Rail) 1D 18
Farrand Rd. OL8: O'ham 2D 43
Farrant Ho. M12: Man 1C 82
Farrant Rd. M12: Man 1C 82
Farrar Rd. M43: Droy 2B 70
Farrell St. M7: Sal 1E 5 (4A 52)
Farrer Rd. M13: Man 2B 82
Farrier Cl. M33: Sale 5B 90
Farringdon St. M6: Sal 4A 50
Farrington Av. M20: Man 1C 92
Farr St. SK3: Stoc 3F 105
Farwood Cl. M16: Old T 5E 65
(off Stanley Rd.)
Fastnet St. M11: Man 2C 68
Faulkenhurst M. OL1: Chad 1E 29
Faulkenhurst St. OL1: Chad 1E 29
Faulkner Rd. M32: Stre 3A 78
Faulkner St. M1: Man 2C 10 (2C 66)
Faversham Brow OL1: O'ham 1D 117
Faversham St. M40: Man 5D 41
Fawborough Rd. M23: Wyth 2B 100
Fawley Av. SK14: Hyde 4F 87
Fawley Gro. M22: Wyth 2F 109
Fay Av. M9: Man 1D 41
Fearnhead Cl. BL4: Farn 1A 18
Featherstall Ho. OL9: O'ham 4E 29
(off Featherstall Rd. Sth.)
Featherstall Rd. Nth. OL1: O'ham 1E 29
OL9: O'ham 2F 29
Featherstall Rd. Nth. Rdbt.
OL9: O'ham 1F 29
(off Featherstall Rd. Nth.)
Featherstall Rd. Sth. OL9: O'ham 4E 29
Federation St. M4: Man 3C 6 (5C 52)
M25: Pres 4B 22
Feldom Rd. M23: Wyth 1B 100
Fellbrigg Cl. M18: Man 2E 83
Felling Wlk. M14: Man 2D 81
(off Gt. Western St.)
Fellpark Rd. M23: Wyth 1C 100
Fells Gro. M28: Walk 3B 32
Fellside OL1: O'ham 2D 117 (2A 30)
Felltop Dr. SK5: Stoc 5C 84
Felskirk Rd. M22: Wyth 1E 113
Felt Ct. M34: Dent 3E 85
Feltham St. M12: Man 4C 68
Felthorpe Dr. M8: Man 1B 52
Felton Av. M22: Wyth 3F 109
Felton Cl. BL9: Bury 1C 12
Fencegate Av. SK4: Stoc 3F 95
Fenchurch Av. M40: Man 3E 55
Fencot Dr. M12: Man 1C 82
Fenella St. M13: Man 1A 82
Fenham Cl. M40: Man 2E 53
Fenmore Av. M18: Man 2D 83
Fennel St. M4: Man 3B 6 (5B 52)
Fenney St. M7: Sal 2F 51
Fenney St. E. M7: Sal 1A 52
Fenn St. M15: Man 4A 66
FENNY HILL 5D 31
Fenside Rd. M22: Shar 1A 110
Fenstock Wlk. M40: Man 3F 55
(off Assheton Rd.)
Fenton St. M12: Man 5C 68
OL4: O'ham 3D 31
Fenwick Dr. M24: Mid 5F 15
SK4: Stoc 5A 94
Fenwick St. M15: Man 4C 66
Ferdinand St. M40: Man 3F 53

Ferguson Ct. M19: Man 5B 82
Ferguson Way OL4: O'ham 1F 31
Fernacre M33: Sale 3E 89
Fernally St. SK14: Hyde 3F 87
Fern Av. M41: Urm 3C 74
Fern Bank M40: Man 5E 41
Fernbank M26: Rad 1C 20
Fern Bank Dr. M23: Wyth 3A 100
Fernbray Av. M19: Man 4F 93
Fernbrook Wlk. M8: Man 5B 38
(off Highshore Dr.)
Fern Cl. M24: Mid 1F 27
Fernclough Rd. M9: Man 5F 39
Ferndale SK9: Hand 5F 115
(off Station Rd.)
Ferndale Av. M45: White 2E 21
Ferndale Cl. OL4: O'ham 5F 31
Ferndale Gdns. M19: Man 2A 94
Ferndale Rd. M33: Sale 1D 99
Ferndene Gdns. M20: Man 3D 93
Ferndene Rd. M20: Man 3D 93
M25: Pres 2E 23
M45: White 2E 23
Ferndown Av. OL9: Chad 2F 27
Ferndown Rd. M23: Wyth 3F 99
Ferney Fld. Rd. OL9: Chad 2B 28
Ferngate Dr. M20: Man 2D 93
Fernhill OL4: O'ham 5F 31
Fernhill Dr. M18: Man 1D 83
Fernholme Ct. OL8: O'ham 5E 29
Fern Ho. M23: Wyth 2C 108
Fernhurst Rd. M20: Man 3E 93
Fernhurst St. OL1: Chad 1E 29
Fernie St. M4: Man 1C 6 (4C 52)
Fernlea SK4: Stoc 3E 95
SK8: H Grn 5D 111
Fernlea Av. OL1: Chad 1E 29
Fernlea Cres. M27: Swin 5A 34
Fernleaf St. M14: Man 1C 80
Fernlea Lodge BL4: Farn 2A 18
(off Longcauseway)
Fernleigh Av. M19: Man 4E 83
Fernleigh Dr. M16: Old T 5E 65
Fernley Av. M34: Dent 3C 86
Fernley Rd. SK2: Stoc 5D 107
Fern Lodge Dr. OL6: A Lyme 2F 59
Fernside M26: Rad 2D 19
Fernside Av. M20: Man 3F 93
Fernside Ct. M26: Rad 3E 19
Fernside Gro. M28: Walk 5A 18
Fern St. BL4: Farn 1C 6 (3C 52)
M4: Man 4F 29
OL8: O'ham 4F 29
OL9: Chad 1C 28
Fern Vw. WA15: Tim 1A 108
Fernwood Av. M18: Man 2F 83
Ferring Wlk. OL9: Chad 3D 29
Ferris St. M11: Man 2F 69
Ferry St. M11: Man 2A 68
Festival Village M41: Urm 4A 62
(off The Trafford Cen.)
Fettler Cl. M27: Swin 1B 48
Fiddick Ct. M6: Sal 5B 50
(off Newport St.)
Field Bank Gro. M19: Man 4E 83
Fielden Av. M21: Chor 4D 79
Fielden Ct. M21: Chor 3F 91
FIELDEN PARK 4B 92
Fielden Rd. M20: Man 4B 92
Fielders Way M27: Clif 5A 20

Fieldfare Av. M40: Man 3D 55
Fieldfare Way OL7: A Lyme 5C 44
Fielding Ind. Est. M34: Dent 3E 85
Fielding St. M24: Mid 4C 16
(not continuous)
M30: Ecc 1E 61
Fieldings Wharf *M43: Droy* 2C 70
(off Market St.)
Field La. OL6: A Lyme 2F 59
Field Pl. *M20: Man* 5D 93
(off Crossway)
Field Rd. M33: Sale 2A 88
Fields New Rd. OL9: Chad 5C 28
Field St. M6: Sal 5B 50
M18: Man 4A 70
M35: Fail 5A 42
M43: Droy 2B 70
SK14: Hyde 5F 73
Fieldsway OL8: O'ham 2A 44
Field Va. Dr. SK5: Stoc 4C 84
Fieldvale Rd. M33: Sale 2A 98
Field Vw. Wlk. M14: Man 3B 80
Fife Av. OL9: Chad 5B 28
Fifield Cl. OL8: O'ham 1C 44
Fifth Av. M11: Man 5E 55
M17: T Pk 5E 63
OL8: O'ham 2E 43
SK16: Duk 2C 72
Fifth St. M17: T Pk 5E 63
Filbert St. OL1: O'ham 1E 31
Filby Wlk. M40: Man 3A 54
Fildes St. M24: Mid 2F 27
Filey Av. M16: W Ran 3F 79
M41: Urm 1C 74
Filey Dr. M6: Sal 1F 49
Filey Rd. M14: Man 5F 81
SK2: Stoc 4E 107
Filton Wlk. *M9: Man* 1E 53
(off Westmere Dr.)
Finborough Cl. M16: W Ran 1A 80
Finchcroft OL1: O'ham 2A 30
Finchley Av. M40: Man 3E 55
Finchley Gro. M40: Man 3C 40
Finchley Rd. M14: Man 5D 81
Finchwood Rd. M22: Shar 1A 110
Findon Rd. M23: Wyth 5C 100
Finghall Rd. M41: Urm 3D 75
Finland Rd. SK3: Stoc 4F 105
Finlan Rd. M24: Mid 1F 27
Finlay St. BL4: Farn 1A 18
Finney Dr. M21: Chor 1C 90
Finney La. SK8: H Grn 1C 114
Finningley Rd. M9: Man 3D 25
Finny Bank Rd. M33: Sale 2C 88
Finsbury Av. M40: Man 3E 55
Finsbury Cl. OL8: O'ham 5D 31
Finsbury Rd. SK5: Stoc 5A 84
Finstock Cl. M30: Ecc 1D 61
Fintry Gro. M30: Ecc 1F 61
Firbank M25: Pres 5E 23
Firbank Cl. OL7: A Lyme 5B 58
Firbank Rd. M23: Wyth 1C 108
Firbeck Dr. M4: Man 5F 53
Fircroft Rd. OL8: O'ham 2C 44
Firdale Av. M40: Man 3A 42
Firdale Wlk. OL9: Chad 2E 29
Firdon Wlk. *M9: Man* 5A 40
(off Nethervale Dr.)
Firefly Cl. M3: Sal 5C 4
Fire Sta. Sq. M5: Sal 4A 4 (5E 51)

Firethorn Av. M19: Man 2B 94
Firfield Gro. M28: Walk 1B 32
Fir Gro. M19: Man 4C 82
OL9: Chad 1D 29
M34: Dent 2C 86
Firs Av. M16: Old T 3D 79
M35: Fail 5A 42
OL6: A Lyme 2D 59
Firsby St. *M19: Man* 4C 82
(off Barlow Rd.)
Firs Cl. SK8: Gat 3C 110
Firs Gro. SK8: Gat 2C 110
Firs Rd. M33: Sale 3A 88
(not continuous)
SK8: Gat 3C 110
First Av. M11: Man 5F 55
M17: T Pk 5F 63
M27: Swin 2F 47
OL8: O'ham 2F 43
Fir St. M6: Sal 5B 50
M16: Old T 1E 79
(off Worthington St.)
M30: Ecc 1F 61
M35: Fail 5A 42
M40: Man 3F 53
SK4: Stoc 1A 106
FIRSWOOD .2C 78
Firswood Dr. M27: Swin 1A 48
Firswood Mt. SK8: Gat 2C 110
Firth Cl. M7: Sal 1F 51
Firth Rd. M20: Man 3E 93
Firth St. OL1: O'ham 4E 117 (3B 30)
Fir Tree Av. OL8: O'ham 2B 44
Firvale Av. SK8: H Grn 5D 111
Firwood Av. M41: Urm 3C 76
(not continuous)
Firwood Cl. SK2: Stoc 3E 107
Firwood Ct. M30: Ecc 4A 48
Firwood Cres. M26: Rad 1D 21
Firwood Pk. OL9: Chad 1A 28
Fiscal Way M35: Fail 5A 42
Fishbourne Sq. *M14: Man* 2E 81
(off Claremont Rd.)
Fishbrook Ind. Est. BL4: Kea 2B 18
Fishermore Rd. M41: Urm 3A 74
Fisher St. OL1: O'ham 1F 117 (1B 30)
Fistral Av. SK8: H Grn 1E 115
Fitchfield Wlk. *M28: Walk* 1A 32
(off Malvern Gro.)
Fit City
Pendlebury 3A 34
Broughton Cen. 2F 51
Broughton Pool 1F 51
Clarendon 5C 50
Eccles 1B 62
(off Barton La.)
Ordsall 3C 64
Fitness First
Gorton 1A 84
Manchester Central 2B 10
Moston 1E 41
Whitefield 5C 12
Fitton Av. M21: Chor 2D 91
Fitton Cres. M27: Clif 1B 34
FITTON HILL 2C 44
Fitton Hill Rd. OL8: O'ham 5C 30
Fitton Hill Shop. Pct. OL8: O'ham . . .2C 44
Fitzgeorge St. M40: Man 2E 53
Fitzgerald Cl. M25: Pres 2B 36

Fitzgerald Ct. M34: Dent 5C 86
Fitzgerald Way M6: Sal 4B 50
     (off Salford Shop. City)
Fitzroy St. M43: Droy 2D 71
     OL7: A Lyme 2B 72
Fitzwarren Cl. M6: Sal 5B 50
Fitzwarren St. M6: Sal 4B 50
Fitzwilliam St. M14: Man 1F 81
Fitzwilliam St. M7: Sal 1D 5 (3F 51)
Five Fold Ind. Pk. OL9: O'ham 3F 29
Fiveways M43: Droy 5B 56
Flag Cft. Dr. M23: Wyth 1D 109
Flagship Av. M5: Sal 2D 65
     (off St Joseph's Dr.)
Flamborough Wlk. M14: Man 1D 81
     (off Gateshead Cl.)
Flamingo Cl. M12: Man 4C 68
Flamstead Av. M23: Wyth 5A 100
Flashfields M25: Pres 3B 36
Flash St. M40: Man 1E 55
Flatley Cl. M15: Man 4C 66
Flavian Wlk. M11: Man 2D 69
     (off Herne St.)
Flaxcroft Rd. M22: Wyth 3D 109
Flaxpool Cl. M16: W Ran 1A 80
     (not continuous)
Flax St. M3: Sal 2D 5 (4F 51)
Flaxwood Wlk. M22: Wyth 3D 109
Fleece St. OL4: O'ham 2D 31
     (off Honduras St.)
Fleeson St. M14: Man 2E 81
Fleet St. M18: Man 4B 70
     OL4: O'ham 2E 31
     OL6: A Lyme 4A 116 (5C 58)
     (not continuous)
Fleming Pl. OL9: O'ham 3F 29
Fleming Rd. M22: Wyth 4F 109
Flemish Rd. M34: Dent 3D 87
Fletcher Av. M27: Clif 1C 34
Fletcher Cl. OL9: O'ham 3F 29
Fletcher Ct. M26: Rad 1D 19
FLETCHER FOLD 1B 12
Fletcher Fold BL9: Bury 1B 12
Fletcher Fold Rd. BL9: Bury 1B 12
Fletcher Moss Botanical Gdns. 2D 103
Fletcher Sq. M1: Man 1E 67
     (off Longacre St.)
Fletcher St. M40: Man 2B 54
     OL6: A Lyme 4E 59
     SK1: Stoc 2B 118 (2B 106)
Flexbury Wlk. M40: Man 3F 55
     (off Eastmoor Dr.)
Flint Cl. M11: Man 5D 55
Flint St. M43: Droy 5D 57
     OL1: O'ham 1E 31
     SK3: Stoc 5A 118 (3A 106)
Flitcroft St. OL4: O'ham 5E 31
FLIXTON 4B 74
Flixton Rd. M13: Man 5F 67
     M31: C'ton 5A 74
     M41: Urm 4B 74
     (not continuous)
Flixton Station (Rail) 4B 74
Floatshall Rd. M23: Wyth 5B 100
Floats Rd. M23: Wyth 5A 100
Flora Dr. M7: Sal 1D 5 (3F 51)
Floral Ct. M7: Sal 1F 51
Flora St. M9: Man 1E 39
     OL1: O'ham 2D 117 (2A 30)
Florence Ct. SK3: Stoc 5D 105

Florence Pk. Ct. M20: Man 4E 93
Florence St. M30: Ecc 1D 61
     M33: Sale 2D 89
     M35: Fail 4B 42
     M43: Droy 2D 71
     SK4: Stoc : O'ham 1A 118 (1A 106)
Florian Ho. OL1: O'ham 2E 117 (2B 30)
Florida St. OL8: O'ham 4A 30
Florin Gdns. M6: Sal 4B 50
Florist St. SK3: Stoc 4A 106
Flowery Bank OL8: O'ham 5D 31
FLOWERY FIELD 5F 73
Flowery Fld. Grn. SK14: Hyde 1E 87
Flowery Fld. Ind. Pk.
     SK14: Hyde 5F 73
Flowery Field Station (Rail) 5F 73
Floyd Av. M21: Chor 2E 91
Floyer Rd. M9: Man 5A 26
Flynn Ct. M6: Sal 3A 50
     (off Monroe Cl.)
Fog La. M19: Man 4F 93
     M20: Man 4D 93
Fog Lane Pk. 4E 93
Fold, The M9: Man 1F 39
     M41: Urm 2C 74
Fold Av. M43: Droy 5D 57
Fold Grn. OL9: Chad 4C 28
Fold Rd. M26: Rad 2E 19
Fold St. M40: Man 4C 40
     OL1: O'ham 2C 44
Fold Vw. OL8: O'ham 5F 31
Fold Way OL7: A Lyme 4B 58
Foleshill Av. M9: Man 5F 39
Foley Wlk. M22: Wyth 1A 114
Foliage Cres. SK5: Stoc 4D 97
Foliage Gdns. SK5: Stoc 3E 97
Foliage Rd. SK5: Stoc 4D 97
Folkestone Rd. M11: Man 5F 55
Folkestone Rd. E. M11: Man 5F 55
Folkestone Rd. W.
     M11: Man 5E 55
Follows St. M18: Man 4F 69
Folly La. M27: Swin 2F 47
Folly Vw. M27: Swin 1F 47
Fonthill Gro. M33: Sale 2B 98
Fontwell Cl. M16: Old T 2E 79
Fontwell La. OL1: O'ham 1C 30
Fontwell Wlk. M40: Man 2F 43
Forbes Cres. M18: Man 2F 83
Forbes Cl. M33: Sale 1F 99
     SK1: Stoc 3D 107
Fordbank Rd. M20: Man 1C 102
Forde Cl. M24: Mid 4C 16
Ford La. M6: Sal 3C 50
     M20: Man 1C 102
     M22: Nor 2A 102
Ford Lodge M20: Man 1D 103
Ford St. M3: Man 4D 5 (5F 51)
     M12: Man 3F 67
     M26: Rad 1C 18
     SK3: Stoc 2F 105
     SK16: Duk 4E 73
Foreland Cl. M40: Man 2F 53
Forest Cl. SK16: Duk 4E 73
Forest Ct. M41: Urm 2A 74
Forest Dr. M33: Sale 1A 98
     WA15: Tim 5B 98
Foresters Grn. M17: T Pk 4A 64
     (off Wharfside Way)
Forest Range M19: Man 4C 82

Forest St. M30: Ecc 3C **46**
    OL6: A Lyme 3E **59**
    OL8: O'ham 2B **44**
Forge Ind. Est. OL4: O'ham 2D **31**
Forge St. OL4: O'ham 2D **31**
Formby Av. M21: Chor 1F **91**
Formby Dr. SK8: H Grn 1D **115**
Formby Rd. M6: Sal 2A **50**
Forrester Ho. *M12: Man* *4C 68*
    (off Blackwin St.)
Forrester St. M28: Wors 4C **32**
Forrest Rd. M34: Dent 4D **87**
Forshaw Av. M18: Man 4B **70**
Forshaw St. M34: Dent 1F **85**
Forston Wlk. M8: Man 1D **53**
Fortescue Rd. SK2: Stoc 4F **107**
Fortran Cl. M5: Sal 1C **64**
Fort Rd. M25: Pres 1F **39**
Fortrose Av. M9: Man 5B **82**
Fortuna Gro. M19: Man 5B **82**
Fortyacre Dr. SK6: Bred 5F **97**
Forum Gro. M7: Sal 2A **52**
Forum Leisure Cen. 3E **109**
Forum Sq. *M22: Wyth* *3F 109*
    (off Ainley Rd.)
Fosbrook Av. M20: Man 4E **93**
Foscarn Dr. M23: Wyth 1D **109**
Foster St. M5: Sal 1F **63**
    M34: Dent 2B **86**
    OL4: O'ham 2E **31**
Fotherby Dr. M9: Man 1F **39**
Foundry, The M1: Man 4B **10**
Foundry La. M4: Man 4E **7** (5D **53**)
    SK16: Duk 3A **30**
    (not continuous)
Fountain Pl. M45: White 2B **22**
Fountain Sq. *M27: Swin* *4B 34*
    (off Swinton Shop. Cen.)
Fountains Rd. M32: Stre 2B **76**
Fountain St. M2: Man 1C **10** (1C **66**)
    M24: Mid 1B **26**
    M30: Ecc 2F **61**
    OL1: O'ham 3D **117** (2A **30**)
    OL6: A Lyme 3F **59**
Fountains Wlk. OL9: Chad 4C **28**
    SK16: Duk 4E **73**
Fouracres Rd. M23: Wyth 1B **108**
Fourth Av. M11: Man 4E **55**
    M17: T Pk 5E **63**
    M27: Swin 2F **47**
    OL8: O'ham 3E **43**
    OL9: Chad 4C **28**
Fourways M17: T Pk 4C **62**
Fourways M40: Man 2D **41**
Four Yards M2: Man 1B **10** (1B **66**)
Fovant Cres. SK5: Stoc 4A **84**
Fowey Wlk. M23: Wyth 1C **108**
Fowler Av. M18: Man 3B **70**
Fowler St. OL8: O'ham 1E **43**
Fownhope Av. M33: Sale 5B **88**
Fownhope Rd. M33: Sale 5B **88**
Foxall Cl. M24: Mid 2E **25**
Foxall St. M24: Mid 2E **25**
Fox Bank Ct. SK3: Stoc 3F **105**
Foxbank St. M13: Man 1A **82**
Foxbench Wlk. M21: Chor 2F **91**
Fox Cl. WA15: Tim 5B **98**
Foxdale St. M11: Man 1E **69**
Foxdenton Dr. M32: Stre 2B **76**

Foxdenton La. M24: Mid 3A **28**
    OL9: Chad 3A **28**
Foxdenton Wlk. M34: Dent 4A **86**
Foxfield Dr. OL8: O'ham 3E **43**
Foxfield Rd. M23: Wyth 3B **108**
Foxford Wlk. M22: Wyth 4A **110**
Foxhall Rd. M34: Dent 1F **85**
    WA15: Tim 5A **98**
Foxham Wlk. *M7: Man* 1A **52**
Fox Hill Ct. SK4: Stoc 1C **104**
Foxhill Rd. M30: Ecc 1B **60**
Foxholes Rd. SK14: Hyde 5E **87**
Foxlair Ct. M22: Wyth 3D **109**
Foxlair Rd. M22: Wyth 3D **109**
Foxland Rd. SK8: Gat 2D **111**
Foxley Cl. M43: Droy 2A **70**
Foxley Wlk. M12: Man 5C **68**
Fox Pk. Rd. OL8: O'ham 2E **43**
Fox St. M30: Ecc 5B **48**
    OL8: O'ham 2E **43**
    SK3: Stoc 3F **105**
Foxton St. M24: Mid 2E **25**
Foxton Wlk. M23: Wyth 3C **108**
Foxwell Wlk. *M8: Man* *1D 53*
    (off Moordown Cl.)
Foxwood Dr. SK14: Hyde 1F **87**
Foxwood Gdns. M19: Man 3A **94**
Foynes Cl. M40: Man 2F **53**
Frame, The M11: Man 5C **54**
Framingham Rd.
    M33: Sale 5C **88**
Framley Rd. M21: Chor 1B **92**
Frampton Cl. M24: Wyth 2D **27**
Fram St. M6: Sal 5A **50**
    M9: Man 4B **40**
Frances Av. SK8: Gat 5C **102**
Francesca Wlk. *M18: Man* *4F 69*
    (off Briercliffe Cl.)
Frances St. *M13: Man* *4D 67*
    (off Cabot St.)
    OL1: O'ham 1C **30**
    SK3: Stoc 4A **118** (3A **106**)
    SK8: Chea 5A **104**
    SK14: Hyde 2E **87**
Frances St. W. SK14: Hyde 2E **87**
Francis Av. M28: Walk 2B **32**
    M30: Ecc 5A **48**
Francis Rd. M20: Man 3E **93**
Francis St. M3: Man 1A **6** (4B **52**)
    M30: Ecc 4F **47**
    M34: Dent 5D **87**
    M35: Fail 5B **42**
Francis Ter. *SK16: Duk* *1E 73*
    (off Astley St.)
Francis Thompson Dr.
    OL6: A Lyme 1B **116**
Frandley Wlk. M13: Man 4F **11**
Frankby Cl. M27: Pen 5E **35**
Frank Cowin Ct. M7: Sal 1D **5**
FRANK HILL 1D **117** (1A **30**)
Frank Hulme Ho. M32: Stre 4A **78**
Frankland Cl. M11: Man 5D **55**
Franklin Cl. OL1: O'ham 1D **117** (1A **30**)
Franklin St. M30: Ecc 5F **47**
    OL1: O'ham 1D **117** (1A **30**)
Franklyn Av. M41: Urm 3A **74**
Franklyn Cl. M34: Dent 3C **84**
Franklyn Rd. M18: Man 4A **70**
    M43: Droy 1C **70**
Frank Price Ct. M22: Wyth 3E **109**

Frank St. M1: Man 4C 10
   M6: Sal 3C 50
   M35: Fail .5A 42
   SK14: Hyde 3F 87
Frank Swift Wlk. M14: Man 2C 80
                (off Fred Tilson Cl.)
Frankton Rd. M45: White 2B 22
Franton Rd. M11: Man 5D 55
Fraser Av. M33: Sale 5A 90
Fraser Pl. M17: T Pk 1E 77
Fraser Rd. M8: Man 3B 38
Fraser St. M27: Pen 3C 34
   OL6: A Lyme 4E 59
Fraternitas Ter. M43: Droy 4A 56
Freckleton Av. M21: Chor 4F 91
Freda Wlk. M11: Man 1B 68
                   (off Doric Cl.)
Frederick Ct. BL4: Farn 1A 18
   SK15: A Lyme 5F 59
             (off Clarence St.)
Frederick Rd. M6: Sal 1A 4 (4D 51)
   M7: Sal .4D 51
Frederick St. BL4: Farn 1A 18
   M3: Sal 4E 5 (5A 52)
   M34: Dent 5A 72
   OL6: A Lyme 5F 59
   OL8: O'ham 4E 29
   OL9: Chad 1D 29
Frederick Ter. M9: Man 3F 39
                 (off Slack Rd.)
Fred Tilson Cl. M14: Man 2C 80
Freeland Wlk. M11: Man 2E 69
              (off Eccles Cl.)
Freeman Av. OL6: A Lyme 4F 59
   SK16: Duk 4E 73
Freeman Sq. M15: Man 4C 66
Freemantle Av. M18: Man 2F 83
Freemantle St. SK3: Stoc 3E 105
Freetown Cl. M14: Man 1C 80
French Av. OL1: O'ham 1E 31
French Barn La. M9: Man 1E 39
French St. OL6: A Lyme 3F 59
Frensham Wlk. M23: Wyth 5C 26
Freshfield M9: Man 5D 111
   SK8: H Grn 5D 117
Freshfield Av. M25: Pres 3E 23
   SK14: Hyde 4B 87
Freshfield Cl. M35: Fail 1C 56
Freshfield Rd. SK4: Stoc 1B 104
Freshfield Wlk. M11: Man 5E 55
Freshford Wlk. M22: Wyth 5D 109
Freshpool Way M22: Shar 5A 102
Freshwater Dr. M34: Dent 3F 59
   OL6: A Lyme 3F 59
Freshwater St. M18: Man 4A 70
Freshwinds Ct. OL4: O'ham 5F 31
Frew Ho. M40: Man 2D 41
Freya Gro. M5: Sal 3A 8 (2E 65)
Friar's Ct. M5: Sal 5D 49
Friar's Rd. M33: Sale 1A 84
Friendship Av. M18: Man 1A 84
Frieston Rd. WA14: Tim 3A 98
Frimley Gdns. M22: Wyth 3F 109
Frinton Av. M40: Man 1F 41
Frinton Cl. M33: Sale 2B 98
Frobisher Cl. M13: Man 5F 67
Frobisher Pl. SK5: Stoc 4A 96
Frodesley Wlk. M12: Man 4B 68
             (off Wenlock Way)
Frodsham Av. SK4: Stoc 5E 95

Frodsham Rd. M33: Sale 1A 100
Frodsham St. M14: Man 2D 81
Frodsham Way SK9: Hand 5F 115
Frogmore Av. SK14: Hyde 5F 87
Frome Av. M41: Urm 4D 75
Frome Dr. M8: Man 5D 39
Frome St. OL4: O'ham 3E 31
Frostlands St. M16: W Ran 2A 80
Frost St. M4: Man 1F 67
   OL8: O'ham 5A 30
Froxmer St. M18: Man 4E 69
Froxmer St. Ind. Est. M18: Man 4E 69
            (off Froxmer St.)
Fuchsia Gro. M7: Sal 1F 51
           (off Hilton St. Nth.)
Fulbeck Wlk. M7: Sal 2A 52
Fulford St. M16: Old T 1E 79
Fulham Av. M40: Man 2D 55
Fulham St. OL4: O'ham 3E 31
Fullerton Rd. SK4: Stoc 1D 105
Fulmead Wlk. M8: Man 1B 52
          (off Kilmington Dr.)
Fulmer Dr. M4: Man 5E 53
Fulmere Ct. M27: Swin 1F 47
Fulneck Sq. M43: Droy 2C 70
Fulshaw Wlk. M13: Man 5F 11
Fulstone M. SK2: Stoc 5D 107
Fulton Ct. M15: Man 5C 66
          (off Boundary La.)
Fulwood Av. M9: Man 5B 26
Furlong Rd. M22: Wyth 3D 109
Furnace St. SK14: Hyde 1E 87
   SK16: Duk 5C 116 (1D 73)
Furness Av. M45: White 1C 22
   OL7: A Lyme 3B 58
   OL8: O'ham 1E 45
Furness Gro. SK4: Stoc 2D 105
Furness Quay M50: Sal 3C 64
Furness Rd. M14: Man 4E 81
   M24: Mid 3B 16
   M41: Urm 2F 75
Furnival Cl. M34: Dent 3C 84
Furnival Rd. M18: Man 4E 69
Furnival St. SK5: Stoc 3B 84
Furrow Dr. M30: Ecc 3D 47
Furrows, The M32: Stre 1D 77
Furrow Sports Cen. 4E 15
Furze La. OL4: O'ham 1F 31
            (not continuous)
Fusion (1-9) M5: Sal 1B 8 (1E 65)
Fyfield Wlk. M8: Man 1D 53
          (off Moordown Cl.)
Fylde Av. SK8: H Grn 1E 115
Fylde Ct. M32: Stre 5E 77
          (off Highfield Rd.)
Fylde Rd. SK4: Stoc 1C 104

G

Gable Ct. M34: Dent 2B 86
Gable Dr. M24: Mid 5A 16
Gables, The M33: Sale 5D 89
           (Framingham Rd.)
   M33: Sale 3E 89
             (Irlam Rd.)
Gable St. M11: Man 2B 68
Gabriels Ter. M24: Mid 2E 27
Gaddum Rd. M20: Man 5E 93
Gadwall Cl. M28: Wors 4A 32

Gail Av. SK4: Stoc 1F **105**
Gail Cl. M35: Fail 2A **56**
Gainford Av. SK8: Gat 2D **111**
Gainford Gdns. M40: Man 3D **41**
Gainford Rd. SK5: Stoc 4B **84**
Gainsboro Rd. M34: Aud 1F **71**
Gainsborough Av. M20: Man 3E **93**
   M32: Stre 2B **78**
   OL8: O'ham 5A **30**
Gainsborough Dr. SK8: Chea 5B **104**
Gainsborough Ho. M33: Sale 5B **88**
Gainsborough Rd. OL9: Chad 5F **17**
Gainsborough St. M7: Sal 5A **38**
Gainsborough Wlk. M34: Dent 4A **86**
   (not continuous)
Gairloch Av. M32: Stre 3D **77**
Gair Rd. SK5: Stoc 4B **96**
Gairs St. SK14: Hyde 1F **87**
Gaitskell Cl. M12: Man 1A **68**
Gala Bingo
   Ashton-under-Lyne 1B **116** (4D **59**)
   Belle Vue 5D **69**
   Manchester 4A **40**
   Salford 4C **50**
   Stockport 2C **106**
   Wythenshawe 4F **109**
Galbraith Rd. M20: Man 5E **93**
Gale Dr. M24: Mid 4F **15**
Gale Rd. M25: Pres 1B **36**
Galgate Cl. M15: Man 5E **9** (3A **66**)
Galland St. OL4: O'ham 2F **31**
Gallery, The M3: Sal 4A **6**
   M16: W Ran 2A **80**
Gallery Oldham 4F **117**
Galloway Dr. M27: Clif 5B **20**
Galloway Rd. M27: Swin 1F **47**
Galston St. M11: Man 2C **68**
Galsworthy Av. M8: Man 1C **52**
Galvin Rd. M9: Man 1D **39**
Galway St.
   OL1: O'ham 4E **117** (3B **30**)
Galway Wlk. M23: Wyth 4B **108**
Gambrel Bank Rd. OL6: A Lyme 1D **59**
Gambrel Gro. OL6: A Lyme 1D **59**
Game St. OL4: O'ham 4E **31**
Games Wlk. M22: Wyth 5D **109**
Gamma Wlk. *M11: Man* 5D **55**
   (off John Heywood St.)
Gan Eden M7: Sal 4A **38**
Gantock Wlk. *M14: Man* 2E **81**
   (off Stenbury Cl.)
Ganton Av. M45: White 2F **21**
Garbo Ct. *M6: Sal* 3A **50**
   (off Monroe Cl.)
Garbrook Av. M9: Man 4E **25**
Garden Av. M32: Stre 2F **77**
   M43: Droy 5D **57**
Gardeners Way OL7: A Lyme 5A **58**
Gardenfold Ho. *M43: Droy* 5D **57**
   (off Fold Av.)
Garden La. M3: Man 5A **6** (1B **66**)
   M3: Sal 3F **5** (5A **52**)
   (not continuous)
Gardens, The M30: Ecc 3C **48**
Garden St. BL4: Kea 1A **18**
   M4: Man 4C **6** (5C **52**)
   M30: Ecc 1A **62**
   M34: Aud 4B **72**
   OL1: O'ham 2C **30**
Garden Vs. SK8: H Grn 2D **115**

Garden Wlk. M34: Dent 2C **86**
   OL6: A Lyme 3E **59**
Garden Wall Cl. M5: Sal 3A **8** (2E **65**)
Gardner Grange SK5: Stoc 4E **97**
Gardner Ho. *M30: Ecc* 5A **48**
   (off Church St.)
Gardner Rd. M25: Pres 5B **22**
Gardner St. M6: Sal 4C **50**
   M12: Man 4D **69**
Garfield Av. M19: Man 4D **83**
Garfield Cl. SK1: Stoc 1C **106**
Garfield St. M7: Man 5E **53**
Garforth Cres. M43: Droy 4D **57**
Garforth St. OL9: Chad 2E **29**
   OL4: O'ham 3D **31**
Gargrave St. M7: Sal 4B **36**
   OL4: O'ham 3D **31**
Garland Rd. M22: Wyth 3A **110**
Garlick St. M18: Man 5F **69**
   OL9: O'ham 3A **30**
   (not continuous)
Garnant Cl. *M9: Man* 4B **40**
   (off Gillford Av.)
Garner Av. WA15: Tim 2C **98**
Garner Dr. M5: Sal 4E **49**
   M30: Ecc 4E **47**
Garners La. SK3: Stoc 5A **106**
Garnett St. OL1: O'ham 1D **31**
   SK1: Stoc 3B **118** (2B **106**)
Garratt Way M18: Man 5E **69**
Garrett Wlk. SK3: Stoc 3E **105**
Garrick Cl. WA14: Alt 5A **98**
Garron Wlk. M22: Wyth 4C **108**
Garrowmore Wlk. *M9: Man* 1A **40**
   (off Greendale Dr.)
Garsden Wlk. M23: Wyth 2B **108**
Garside St. M34: Dent 3B **86**
   SK14: Hyde 4F **87**
Garstang Rd. M15: Man 5D **67**
Garston Cl. SK4: Stoc 5E **95**
Garswood Rd. M14: Man 3B **80**
Garth, The M5: Sal 5F **49**
Garth Av. WA15: Tim 5A **98**
Garthorne Cl. M16: W Ran 1F **79**
Garthorp Rd. M23: Wyth 2A **100**
Garth Rd. M22: Wyth 2F **109**
   SK2: Stoc 4E **107**
Garthwaite Av. OL8: O'ham 1A **44**
Gartland Wlk. M8: Man 4E **39**
Gartside St. M3: Man 1F **9** (1A **66**)
   (not continuous)
   OL4: O'ham 4D **31**
   OL7: A Lyme 1A **72**
Garwood St. M15: Man 5A **10** (3A **66**)
Gascoyne St. M14: Man 2D **81**
Gaskell Rd. M30: Ecc 1A **62**
   WA14: Alt 5A **98**
Gaskell St. M27: Pen 2B **34**
   M40: Man 2E **55**
   SK16: Duk 2D **73**
Gas St. OL6: A Lyme 2B **116** (4D **59**)
   SK4: Stoc 2A **106**
Gaston Wlk. *M9: Man* 4F **25**
   (off Claygate Dr.)
Gatcombe Sq. *M14: Man* 2F **81**
   (off Rusholme Gro.)
Gateacre Wlk. M23: Wyth 3A **100**
Gate Keeper Fold
   OL7: A Lyme 5C **44**
Gatesgarth Rd. M24: Mid 4E **15**
Gateshead Cl. M14: Man 1D **81**

Gateside Wlk. *M9:* Man 4A **26**
(off Crossmead Dr.)
Gate St. M11: Man 2E **69**
SK16: Duk 4C **72**
Gateway, The *M6: Sal* 3C **50**
(off Broughton Rd.)
M40: Man 1B **54**
Gateway Cres. OL9: Chad 4F **27**
Gateway Ho. M1: Man 1F **11**
Gateway Ind. Est. M1: Man . .1F **11** (1D **67**)
Gateway Rd. M18: Man 4E **69**
Gateways, The M27: Pen 3B **34**
Gathurst St. M18: Man 4A **70**
GATLEY .1D **111**
Gatley Av. M14: Man 4C **80**
Gatley Brow OL1: O'ham 1D **117**
Gatley Ct. M22: Nor 4A **102**
Gatley Grn. SK8: Gat 1C **110**
Gatley Rd. M33: Sale 5A **90**
SK8: Gat 1D **111**
Gatley Station (Rail) 5D **103**
Gatling Av. M12: Man 3D **83**
Gatwick Av. M23: Wyth 5D **101**
Gavel Wlk. M24: Mid 5A **16**
Gavin Av. M5: Sal 1C **64**
Gawsworth Av. M20: Man 2E **103**
Gawsworth Cl. SK3: Stoc 5F **105**
WA15: Tim 5F **99**
Gawsworth *M9: Man* 4C **24**
(off Deanswood Dr.)
Gawsworth M. SK8: Gat 1D **111**
Gawsworth Pl. M22: Wyth 5B **110**
Gawsworth Rd. M33: Sale 2A **100**
Gawsworth Way M34: Dent 4C **86**
SK9: Hand 5F **115**
Gawthorpe Cl. BL9: Bury 1C **12**
Gaydon Rd. M33: Sale 4A **88**
GAYTHORN 4A **10** (3B **66**)
Gaythorn St. M5: Sal 5B **4** (1E **65**)
Gayton Wlk. M40: Man 2F **41**
Gaywood Wlk. *M40: Man* 1E **53**
(off Westmount Cl.)
Gee La. M30: Ecc 4D **47**
OL8: O'ham 2D **43**
Gee St. SK3: Stoc 4F **105**
Gemini Rd. M6: Sal 3E **51**
Geneva Wlk. *M8: Man* 1D **53**
(off Moordown Cl.)
OL9: Chad 3E **29**
Genista Gro. *M7: Sal* 1F **51**
(off Hilton St. Nth.)
Geoff Bent Wlk. *M40: Man* 2D **55**
(off Roger Byrne Cl.)
George Ct. M40: Man 5C **116**
George Halstead Ct. *M8: Man* 3C **38**
(off Station Rd.)
George H Carnall Leisure Cen. 1A **76**
George Leigh St. M4: Man 4F **7** (5D **53**)
George Mann Cl.
M22: Wyth 5E **109**
George Parr Rd. M15: Man 4B **66**
George Sq. OL1: O'ham 4D **117** (3A **30**)
George's Rd. M33: Sale 5D **89**
SK4: Stoc 2F **105**
George St. M1: Man 2B **10** (2B **66**)
M25: Pres 3D **37**
M30: Ecc 1E **61**
M34: Dent 2C **86**
M35: Fail 4B **42**
M41: Urm 3A **76**

George St. M45: White 5A **12**
OL1: O'ham 4D **117** (3A **30**)
OL6: A Lyme 4E **59**
OL9: Chad 2C **28**
SK1: Stoc 2C **106**
George St. E. SK1: Stoc 3D **107**
George St. Nth. M7: Sal 4B **38**
George St. Sth. M7: Sal 4A **38**
George St. W. SK1: Stoc 3D **107**
George Ter. *M30: Ecc* 5F **47**
(off Byron St.)
George Thomas Ct. M9: Man 4F **39**
Georgette Dr. M3: Sal 2F **5** (4A **52**)
Georgia Av. M20: Man 3B **92**
Gerald Av. M8: Man 4C **38**
Gerald Rd. M6: Sal 2C **50**
Germain Cl. M9: Man 4E **25**
Germans Bldgs. SK2: Stoc 5C **106**
Gerrard Av. WA15: Tim 3C **98**
Gerrard Cl. OL7: A Lyme 1B **72**
Gerrards, The SK14: Hyde 5F **87**
Gerrards Gdns. SK14: Hyde 5F **87**
Gerrards Hollow SK14: Hyde 5F **87**
Gerrard St. BL4: Kea 1A **18**
M6: Sal 4D **51**
Gerrardswood SK14: Hyde 5F **87**
Gerry Wheale Sq. M14: Man 2C **80**
Gertrude Cl. M5: Sal 2C **64**
Gervis Cl. M40: Man 2F **53**
Ghyll Gro. M28: Walk 3A **32**
Giant's Seat M26: Rad 3A **20**
Giants Seat Gro. M27: Pen 4F **35**
Gibbon Av. M22: Wyth 4F **109**
Gibbon St. M11: Man 5C **54**
Gibb Rd. M28: Wors 5D **33**
Gibbs St. M3: Sal 5C **4** (1F **65**)
Gib La. M23: Wyth 4D **101**
Gib La. Cotts. *M23: Wyth* 4E **101**
(off Gib La.)
Gibraltar La. M34: Dent 5D **87**
Gibraltar St. OL4: O'ham 4F **31**
Gibsmere Cl. WA15: Tim 5F **99**
Gibson Av. M18: Man 3B **70**
Gibson Pl. M3: Man 1C **6** (4C **52**)
Gibsons Rd. SK4: Stoc 4D **95**
Gibson St. OL4: O'ham 3E **31**
Gibson Ter. OL7: A Lyme 2C **72**
Gibwood Rd. M22: Nor 3E **101**
Gidlow St. M18: Man 4A **70**
Gifford Av. M9: Man 5B **26**
Gilbert Ho. *M5: Sal* 3C **64**
(off Elmira Way)
Gilbert St. *M6: Sal* 1B **64**
(off Hodge La.)
M15: Man 4F **9** (3A **66**)
M30: Ecc 2D **61**
Gilda Brook Rd. M30: Ecc, Sal 1C **62**
Gilda Brook Rdbt. M30: Ecc 5C **48**
Gilda Cres. Rd. M30: Ecc 4C **48**
Gildenhall M35: Fail 5C **42**
Gildersdale Dr. M9: Man 3D **25**
Gildridge Rd. M16: W Ran 4A **80**
Gilesgate *M14: Man* 2E **81**
(off Viscount St.)
Giles St. M12: Man 1C **82**
Gillbrook Rd. M20: Man 5D **93**
Gillford Av. M9: Man 4B **40**
Gillingham Rd. M30: Ecc 5D **47**
Gillingham Sq. *M11: Man* 2B **68**
(off Glyneath Cl.)

Gill St. M9: Man 4B **40**
   SK1: Stoc 5D **97**
Gilman Cl. M9: Man 2E **39**
Gilman St. M9: Man 2E **39**
Gilmerton Dr. M40: Man 2E **55**
Gilmore Dr. M25: Pres 4D **23**
Gilmore St. SK3: Stoc 5A **118** (4A **106**)
Gilmour St. M24: Mid 1C **26**
Gilmour Ter. M9: Man 3B **40**
   (not continuous)
Gilpin Rd. M41: Urm 4B **76**
Gilpin Wlk. M24: Mid 5A **16**
Giltbrook Av. M40: Man 3F **53**
Gilwell Dr. M23: Wyth 2B **108**
Gilwood Gro. M24: Mid 2B **16**
Gipsey Moth Cl. WA15: Tim 5F **99**
Girton St. M7: Sal 1E **5** (3A **52**)
Girton Wlk. M40: Man 3F **41**
Girvan Av. M40: Man 2F **41**
Gisborne Dr. M6: Sal 2C **50**
Gisburne Av. M40: Man 2F **41**
Gissing Wlk. M9: Man 1F **53**
Givendale Dr. M8: Man 2C **38**
Givvons Fold OL4: O'ham 1F **31**
Glade, The SK4: Stoc 2C **104**
Gladeside Cl. M22: Wyth 2E **109**
Gladeside Rd. M22: Wyth 2E **109**
Glade Wood Dr. M35: Fail 4D **43**
Gladstone Bus. Pk.
   OL4: O'ham 3D **31**
Gladstone Cl. M15: Man 1A **80**
Gladstone Ct. OL7: A Lyme 4A **116**
   SK4: Stoc 5D **95**
Gladstone Gro. SK4: Stoc 5C **94**
Gladstone M. *SK4: Stoc* *5A 96*
   (off Short St.)
Gladstone Rd. M30: Ecc 5A **48**
   M41: Urm 3A **76**
   WA14: Alt 5A **98**
Gladstone St. M27: Pen 4C **34**
   OL4: O'ham 3D **31**
Gladville Dr. SK8: Chea 5C **104**
Gladwyn Av. M20: Man 4A **92**
Gladys St. M16: Old T 1E **79**
Glaisdale OL4: O'ham 3F **31**
Glamis Cl. M11: Man 4D **55**
   M32: Stre 3C **76**
Glamorgan Pl. OL9: O'ham 4E **29**
Glanford Av. M9: Man 1C **38**
Glanton Wlk. *M40: Man* *3F 41*
   (off Enstone Dr.)
Glanvor Rd. SK3: Stoc 3E **105**
Glass Box Gallery 4D **51**
Glasshouse St. M4: Man 2F **7** (4E **53**)
Glasson Wlk. OL9: Chad 3C **28**
Glass St. BL4: Farn 2A **18**
Glastonbury Av. M32: Stre 2B **76**
Glaswen Gro. SK5: Stoc 4B **96**
Glazebury Dr. M23: Wyth 1D **109**
Glaze Wlk. M45: White 4E **13**
Gleaves Rd. M30: Ecc 1A **62**
Gleave St. M33: Sale 2D **89**
Glebe Ho. *M24: Mid* *4C 16*
   (off Rochdale Rd.)
Glebelands Rd. M23: Wyth 5B **100**
   M25: Pres 4C **22**
   M33: Sale 2A **88**
Glebe Rd. M41: Urm 3F **75**
Glebe St. M34: Dent 1C **86**
   OL6: A Lyme 4E **59**

Glebe St. OL9: Chad 1C **42**
   SK1: Stoc 2C **106**
Gleden St. M40: Man 5A **54**
   (not continuous)
Gledhill Av. M5: Sal 3C **64**
Gledhill St. M20: Man 1D **93**
Glemsford Cl. M40: Man 1D **55**
Glen, The M24: Mid 3D **27**
Glenacre Gdns. M18: Man 1A **84**
Glenarm Wlk. M22: Wyth 4A **110**
Glenart M30: Ecc 4A **48**
Glen Av. BL4: Kea 3D **19**
   M9: Man 3A **40**
   M27: Swin 4F **33**
   M28: Wors 4C **32**
   M33: Sale 2C **88**
Glenbarry Cl. M13: Man 4D **67**
Glenbarry St. M12: Man 2F **67**
Glenbeck Rd. M45: White 5A **12**
Glenbrook Rd. M9: Man 4C **24**
Glenby Av. M22: Wyth 3B **110**
Glenby Est. OL9: Chad 3E **29**
Glencar Dr. M40: Man 2F **41**
Glencastle Rd. M18: Man 5E **69**
   (not continuous)
Glencoe St. OL8: O'ham 2E **43**
Glencross Av. M21: Chor 3C **78**
Glendale M27: Clif 2D **35**
Glendale Av. BL9: Bury 3B **12**
   M19: Man 2B **94**
Glendale Ct. OL8: O'ham 5B **30**
Glendale Rd. M30: Ecc 4C **48**
Glendene Av. M43: Droy 4E **57**
Glendevon Cl. M22: Wyth 1E **109**
Glendevon Pl. M45: White 2D **23**
Glendinning St. M6: Sal 5A **50**
Glendon Cres. OL6: A Lyme 5D **45**
Glendore M5: Sal 5E **49**
Glendower Dr. M40: Man 2E **53**
Gleneagles Av. M11: Man 5E **55**
Gleneagles Rd. M41: Urm 1A **74**
   SK8: H Grn 5E **111**
Glenfield Cl. OL4: O'ham 3F **31**
Glenfield Rd. SK4: Stoc 4F **95**
Glenfyne Rd. M6: Sal 2F **49**
Glen Gro. M24: Mid 2E **27**
Glenham Ct. *M15: Man* *1A 80*
   (off Moss La. W.)
Glenhaven Av. M41: Urm 3E **75**
Glenhurst Rd. M19: Man 3A **94**
Glenilla Av. M28: Wors 5A **32**
Glenlea Dr. M20: Man 3D **103**
Glenmay Ct. M32: Stre 3E **77**
Glen Maye M33: Sale 4E **89**
Glenmere Cl. M25: Pres 3B **22**
Glenmere Rd. M20: Man 3E **103**
Glenmoor Rd. SK1: Stoc 2C **106**
Glenmore Av. M20: Man 4A **92**
Glenmore Bungs. *SK16: Duk* *3E 73*
   (off Glenmore Gro.)
Glenmore Dr. M8: Man 5D **39**
   M35: Fail 1D **43**
Glenmore Gro. SK16: Duk 2E **73**
Glenolden St. M11: Man 5F **55**
Glenpark Wlk. *M9: Man* *5A 40*
   (off Craigend Dr.)
Glenridding Cl. OL1: O'ham 1C **30**
Glen Ri. WA15: Tim 5C **98**
Glen Rd. OL4: O'ham 3E **31**
Glensdale Dr. M40: Man 3A **42**

Glenshaw Way OL9: Chad 5C 28
Glenside Av. M18: Man 2F 83
Glenside Gdns. M35: Fail 5C 42
Glenside Gro. M28: Walk 1A 32
Glen St. M50: Sal 3C 64
Glenthorn Av. M9: Man 3F 25
Glenthorne Dr. OL7: A Lyme 3C 58
Glenthorn Gro. M33: Sale 5D 89
Glen Trad. Est. OL4: O'ham 3F 31
Glenville Rd. M8: Man 2B 52
Glenville Ter. M43: Droy 4A 56
     (off Greenside La.)
Glenville Way M34: Dent 3C 86
Glenwood Av. SK14: Hyde 5F 73
Glenwood Dr. M9: Man 5A 40
   M24: Mid 4E 17
Glenwyn Av. M9: Man 5A 26
Globe Cl. M16: Old T 5F 65
Globe La. SK16: Duk 3C 72
Globe La. Ind. Est. SK16: Duk 4D 73
Globe Sq. SK16: Duk 3C 72
Globe St. OL4: O'ham 2D 31
GLODWICK .4D 31
Glodwick OL4: O'ham 4D 31
GLODWICK BROOK 5B 30
Glodwick Rd. OL4: O'ham 4D 31
Glodwick Swimming Pool 3D 31
Glossop Ter. M40: Man 1F 41
Gloucester Av. M19: Man 5D 83
   M45: White 1C 22
Gloucester Cl. OL6: A Lyme 4F 45
Gloucester Ho. M7: Sal 1E 51
     (off Bk. Duncan St.)
Gloucester Pl. M6: Sal 4C 50
Gloucester Rd. M6: Sal 3E 49
   M24: Mid 3C 26
   M34: Dent 3C 84
   M41: Urm 3F 75
   M43: Droy 4C 56
   SK8: H Grn 2E 115
   SK14: Hyde 5F 87
Gloucester St. M1: Man 4B 10 (3B 66)
   M5: Sal 3A 8 (2E 65)
   M6: Sal .3C 50
   SK3: Stoc 4F 105
Gloucester St. Nth. OL9: O'ham 4E 29
Gloucester St. Sth. OL9: O'ham 4E 29
Glover Av. M8: Man 1D 53
Glover Ct. M7: Sal 4B 38
Glover Fld. M7: Sal 1F 51
Glyneath Cl. M11: Man 2B 68
Glynis Cl. SK3: Stoc 5B 106
Glynn Gdns. M20: Man 4F 91
Glynrene Dr. M27: Ward 3E 33
G Mex Cen. 3A 10 (2B 66)
G Mex Stop (Metro) 3A 10 (2B 66)
Goadsby St. M4: Man 3D 7 (5C 52)
Goats Ga. Ter. M45: White 4A 12
Godbert Av. M21: Chor 3E 91
Goddard St. OL8: O'ham 5B 30
Godfrey Av. M43: Droy 4F 55
Godfrey Mill SK14: Hyde 2F 87
Godfrey Range M18: Man 1B 84
Godfrey Rd. M6: Sal 5A 34
Godlee Dr. M27: Swin 2E 69
Godley Cl. M11: Man 3B 48
Godolphin Cl. M30: Ecc 3B 48
Godson St. OL1: O'ham 1D 117 (1A 30)
Godwin St. M18: Man 4A 70
Golborne Av. M20: Man 1B 92

Goldcrest Cl. M22: Shar 1B 110
Goldenhill Av. M11: Man 4E 55
Golden Sq. M30: Ecc 1F 61
     (off Golden St.)
Golden St. M30: Ecc 1F 61
Goldfinch Way M43: Droy 4E 57
Goldie Av. M22: Wyth 5B 110
Goldsmith Av. M5: Sal 5F 49
Goldsmith Rd. SK5: Stoc 4F 83
Goldsmith Way M34: Dent 5C 86
     (off Wordsworth Rd.)
Gold St. M1: Man 1D 11 (1C 66)
Goldsworthy Rd. M41: Urm 2A 74
Goldwick Wlk. M23: Wyth 2A 100
Golf Rd. M33: Sale 4B 90
Golfview Dr. M30: Ecc 3F 47
Gomer Wlk. M8: Man 1E 53
     (off Smedley Rd.)
Goodhope Mill OL6: A Lyme 3A 116
Goodiers Dr. M5: Sal 2C 64
Goodier St. M33: Sale 4C 88
   M40: Man 3B 54
Goodison Cl. BL9: Bury 3D 13
Goodman St. M9: Man 4A 40
Goodridge Av. M22: Wyth 5E 109
Goodwill Cl. M27: Swin 5B 34
Goodwin Ct. OL9: Chad 5E 29
Goodwin Sq. M9: Man 1E 39
Goodwood Av. M23: Wyth 3F 99
Goodwood Cl. M7: Sal 1F 51
Goodwood Cres. WA15: Tim 5E 99
Goodwood Dr. M27: Pen 5D 35
Goodworth Wlk. M40: Man 5D 41
     (off Egbert St.)
Goole St. M11: Man 2C 68
Goostrey Av. M20: Man 5C 80
Gordon Av. M19: Man 4D 83
   M33: Sale 2D 89
   OL4: O'ham 3D 31
   OL9: Chad 1C 42
Gordon Pl. M20: Man 3D 93
Gordon Rd. M27: Swin 1E 47
   M30: Ecc 4F 47
Gordon St. M7: Sal 3F 51
   M16: Old T 5F 65
   M18: Man 4A 70
   OL4: Lees 4F 31
   OL6: A Lyme 3F 59
   OL9: Chad 5B 28
   SK4: Stoc 1A 106
Gordon Ter. M9: Man 4A 40
     (off Kingscliffe St.)
Gore Av. M5: Sal 5F 49
   M35: Fail 5D 43
Gorebrook Ct. M12: Man 1C 82
Gore Cres. M5: Sal 4F 49
Goredale Av. M18: Man 2A 84
Gore Dr. M5: Sal 4F 49
Gorelan Rd. M18: Man 5F 69
Gore St. M1: Man 1E 11 (1D 67)
   M3: Sal 5E 5 (1A 66)
   M6: Sal .4C 50
     (off Up. Gloucester St.)
Goring Av. M18: Man 4F 69
Gorse Av. M32: Stre 2B 78
   M43: Droy 5E 57
   OL8: O'ham 1E 45
Gorse Cres. M32: Stre 2B 78
Gorse Dr. M32: Stre 2B 78
Gorsefield Dr. M27: Swin 5B 34
GORSE HILL .1A 78

Gorse La. M32: Stre 2B 78
Gorse Rd. M27: Swin 1A 48
   M28: Walk 2A 32
Gorse St. M32: Stre 2A 78
   OL9: Chad 5B 28
Gorseway SK5: Stoc 4D 97
Gorsey Av. M22: Wyth 1E 109
Gorsey Bank Rd. SK3: Stoc 3C 104
Gorsey Brow M41: Urm 3B 76
   SK1: Stoc 2C 106
Gorsey Dr. M22: Wyth 2E 109
Gorseyfields M43: Droy 2C 70
Gorsey Mt. St. SK1: Stoc 2C 106
                             (Hall St.)
   SK1: Stoc 2B 106
                    (Up. Brook St.)
Gorsey Rd. M22: Wyth 2E 109
Gorsey Way OL6: A Lyme 1F 59
Gorston Wlk. M22: Wyth 1E 113
Gort Cl. BL9: Bury 5C 12
GORTON 1F 83
Gorton Cres. M34: Dent 3E 85
Gorton Cross Cen. M18: Man 5F 69
Gorton Ind. Est. M18: Man 4E 69
Gorton La. M12: Man 4C 68
   M18: Man 4C 68
Gorton Mkt. M18: Man 5F 69
Gorton Parks M18: Man 4E 69
Gorton Rd. M11: Man 3B 68
   M12: Man 3B 68
   SK5: Stoc 5B 84
Gorton Station (Rail) 4F 69
Gorton St. M3: Sal 3A 6 (5B 52)
   M30: Ecc 1C 60
   OL7: A Lyme 1B 72
   OL9: Chad 3D 29
Gortonvilla Wlk. M12: Man 4B 68
                 (off Clowes St.)
Gosforth Wlk. M23: Wyth 2B 100
Goshen La. BL9: Bury 1B 12
Goshen Sports Cen. 1C 12
Gosport Sq. M7: Sal 2F 51
Gosport Wlk. M8: Man 1E 53
            (off Smeaton St.)
Goss Hall St. OL4: O'ham 3E 31
Gotha Wlk. M13: Man 4E 67
            (off Beamish Cl.)
Gough St. SK3: Stoc 2F 105
Goulden Rd. M20: Stoc 2C 92
Goulden St. M4: Man 3E 7 (5D 53)
   M6: Sal .5A 50
Goulder Rd. M18: Man 2A 84
Gould St. M4: Man 1D 7 (4D 53)
   M34: Dent 2A 86
   OL1: O'ham 1D 31
Govan St. M22: Nor 2A 102
Govind Ruia Ct. M16: W Ran 3A 80
Gowan Dr. M24: Mid 5F 15
Gowan Rd. M16: W Ran 4A 80
Gowerdale Rd. SK5: Stoc 3E 97
Gower Hey Gdns. SK14: Hyde 4F 87
Gower Rd. SK4: Stoc 4F 95
   SK14: Hyde 4F 87
Gower St. M27: Pen 3C 34
   OL1: O'ham 2C 30
   OL6: A Lyme 4E 59
Gowran Pk. OL4: O'ham 3F 31
Goyt Cres. SK1: Stoc 5D 97
Goyt Rd. SK1: Stoc 5D 97
Goyt Valley SK6: Bred 1F 107

Goyt Wlk. M45: White 4D 13
Grace Wlk. M4: Man 1F 67
Gracie Av. OL1: O'ham 1D 31
Gradwell St. SK3: Stoc 3F 105
Grafton Av. M30: Ecc 3C 48
Grafton Ct. M15: Man 5F 65
            (off Chorlton Rd.)
Grafton St. M13: Man 5D 67
   M35: Fail 4C 42
   OL6: A Lyme 5F 59
             (not continuous)
   SK4: Stoc 5A 96
   SK14: Hyde 2F 87
Graham Rd. M6: Sal 3E 49
   SK1: Stoc 3D 107
Graham St. M11: Man 2C 68
   OL7: A Lyme 1B 72
Grainger Av. M12: Man 2C 82
Grain Vw. M5: Sal 2C 64
Gralam Cl. M33: Sale 2A 100
Grammar School Rd.
   OL8: O'ham 2D 43
Grampian Cl. OL9: Chad 4C 28
Granada M. M16: W Ran 4A 80
Granada Rd. M34: Dent 2B 84
Granada Studios 2E 9 (2A 66)
Granada TV Cen. 1E 9 (1A 66)
Granary La. M28: Wors 3B 46
Granary Way M33: Sale 1B 98
Granby Ho. M1: Man 3D 11
Granby Rd. M27: Swin 5E 33
   M32: Stre 5F 77
   SK2: Stoc 5D 107
   WA15: Tim 4D 99
Granby Row M1: Man 3D 11 (2C 66)
             (not continuous)
Granby St. OL9: Chad 1C 42
Granby Village M1: Man 3D 11
Grandale St. M14: Man 2E 81
Grand Central Pools 3A 118 (2A 106)
Grand Central Sq.
   SK1: Stoc 3A 118 (2A 106)
Grand Union Way M30: Ecc 2F 61
Granford Cl. WA14: Alt 4A 98
Grange, The M14: Man 2E 81
   OL1: O'ham 1D 31
   SK3: Stoc 4E 105
             (off Edgeley Rd.)
Grange Arts Cen. 2A 30
Grange Av. M19: Man 5B 82
   M27: Swin 2F 33
   M30: Ecc 3F 47
   M32: Stre 3F 77
   M34: Dent 3D 87
   M41: Urm 3A 74
   OL8: O'ham 5E 29
   SK4: Stoc 3F 95
   WA15: Tim 4D 99
Grange Ct. OL8: O'ham 5F 29
Grange Cres. M41: Urm 4E 75
Grange Dr. M9: Man 1B 40
   M30: Ecc 3F 47
Grangeforth Rd. M8: Man 4B 38
Grange Gdns. M30: Ecc 4A 48
Grange Gro. M45: White 1B 22
Grange La. M20: Man 1D 103
Grange Mill Wlk. M40: Man 1D 55
Grange Pk. Av. SK8: Chea 1F 111
Grange Pk. Rd. M9: Man 1B 40
   SK8: Chea 1F 111

Grange Rd. M21: Chor 3C 78
  M30: Ecc 3B 46
  M33: Sale 4B 88
  M41: Urm 4E 75
  WA15: Tim .4D 99
Grange St. M6: Sal 5A 50
  M35: Fail 1F 55
  OL9: O'ham 2A 30
Grangethorpe Dr. M19: Man 1A 94
Grangethorpe Rd. M14: Man 3E 81
  M41: Urm 4E 75
Grange Wlk. M24: Mid 4A 16
Grangeway SK9: Hand 5E 115
Grangewood Dr. M9: Man 5F 39
Granite Ct. *M25: Pres* 4C 22
(off Longfield Cen.)
Granite St. OL1: O'ham 1D 31
Gransden Dr. M8: Man 1E 53
Granshaw St. M40: Man 4A 54
Gransmoor Av. M11: Man 3B 70
Gransmoor Rd. M11: Droy 3B 70
  M11: Man 3B 70
Grant Cl. M9: Man 2F 39
Grantham Ct. *M34: Dent* 4B 86
(off Stockport Rd.)
Grantham Rd. SK4: Stoc 1E 105
Grantham St. M14: Man 2C 80
  OL4: O'ham 4C 30
Granville Av. M7: Sal 4A 38
  M16: W Ran 2E 79
Granville Cl. OL9: Chad 2E 29
Granville Ct. M16: W Ran 2E 79
Granville Gdns. M20: Man 1C 102
Granville Rd. M14: Man 5E 81
  M34: Aud 1D 71
  M41: Urm 2A 76
  SK8: Chea H 5D 105
  WA15: Tim .5E 99
Granville St. M27: Swin 4B 34
  M30: Ecc 4F 47
  OL1: O'ham 1A 30
  OL6: A Lyme 5F 59
  OL9: Chad .1E 29
Granville Wlk. OL9: Chad 1E 29
Grasdene Av. M9: Man 1A 40
Grasmere Av. M27: Ward 2E 33
  M41: Urm 4A 74
  M45: White .2E 21
  SK4: Stoc 2A 96
Grasmere Cres. M30: Ecc 4D 47
Grasmere Gro. OL7: A Lyme 3B 58
Grasmere Rd. M27: Swin 1B 48
  M32: Stre 2F 77
  M33: Sale 1E 99
  OL4: O'ham 3E 31
  SK8: Gat 3D 111
  WA15: Tim .5E 99
Grasmere St. M12: Man 2D 83
Grasmere Wlk. M24: Mid 4B 16
Grasscroft SK5: Stoc 2E 97
Grasscroft Cl. M14: Man 3B 80
Grassfield Av. M7: Sal 1E 51
Grassingham Gdns. M6: Sal 4B 50
Grassington Av. M40: Man 3C 40
Grass Mead M34: Dent 5C 86
Gratrix Av. M5: Sal 5A 8 (3D 65)
Gratrix La. M33: Sale 5B 90
Gratrix St. M18: Man 1A 84
Gravel La. M3: Sal 4F 5 (5B 52)
Gravel Walks OL4: O'ham 2D 31

Gravenmoor Dr. M7: Sal 1A 52
Graver La. M40: Man 2F 55
(not continuous)
Grayrigg Wlk. *M9: Man* 5F 39
(off Ruskington Dr.)
Grayson Av. M45: White 1C 22
Graythorpe Wlk. M5: Sal 1C 64
Graythorp Wlk. *M14: Man* 2D 81
(off Whickham Cl.)
Greame St. M16: W Ran 2B 80
(not continuous)
Gt. Ancoats St. M4: Man 4E 7 (5D 53)
Gt. Arbor Way M24: Mid 5B 16
Gt. Bridgewater St. M1: Man 3F 9 (2B 66)
Gt. Cheetham St. E. M7: Sal 1A 52
Gt. Cheetham St. W. M7: Sal 2E 51
Gt. Clowes St. M7: Sal 1D 5 (2F 51)
(Cheetham)
  M7: Sal 1F 51
(Higher Broughton)
Gt. Cowes St. M3: Sal 1D 5 (4F 51)
Gt. Ducie St. M3: Man 1A 6 (4B 52)
Gt. Egerton St. SK1: Stoc . . .1A 118 (1A 106)
  SK4: Stoc .2A 106
Greater Manchester Police Mus.
. . . . .5E 7 (1D 67)
Greatfield Rd. M22: Wyth 3D 109
Gt. Gable Cl. OL1: O'ham 1F 117 (1C 30)
Gt. George St. M3: Sal 4C 4 (5F 51)
Gt. Heaton Cl. M24: Mid 2E 25
GREAT HORROCKS 3C 52
Gt. Jackson St. M15: Man 4E 9 (3A 66)
Gt. John St. M3: Man 2E 9 (2A 66)
Gt. Jones St. M12: Man 4C 68
Gt. Marlborough St. M1: Man . .4C 10 (3C 66)
Gt. Newton St. M40: Man 2E 55
Gt. Norbury St. SK14: Hyde 2E 87
Great Northern 2A 10 (2A 66)
Gt. Northern Sq. Amphitheatre
  M3: Man 2A 10
Gt. Portwood St. SK1: Stoc . .1C 118 (1B 106)
Gt. Southern St. M14: Man 2D 81
Greatstone Apartments *M32: Stre* 2A 78
(off Portland Rd.)
Gt. Stone Rd. M16: Old T 2C 78
  M32: Stre 1B 78
Great Underbank
  SK1: Stoc 2A 118 (2B 106)
Gt. Western St. M16: W Ran 1A 80
Greave Rd. SK1: Stoc 3E 107
Greaves Av. M35: Fail 1F 55
Greaves St. OL1: O'ham 3E 117 (2B 30)
Grecian St. M7: Sal 2E 51
  M7: Sal 2E 51
Grecian St. Nth. M7: Sal 2E 51
Grecian Ter. *M7: Sal* 2E 51
(off Albert Pk. Rd.)
Gredle Cl. M41: Urm 3B 76
Greeba Rd. M23: Wyth 5A 100
Greek St. M1: Man 5E 11
  SK3: Stoc 5A 118 (3A 106)
Green, The M27: Clif 2D 35
  M28: Wors .2B 46
  OL8: O'ham 1C 44
  SK4: Stoc 2E 95
  SK9: Hand .5F 115
  WA15: Tim 4D 99
(off Whitley Gdns.)
Greenacre SK8: H Grn 2E 115
Greenacre La. M28: Wors 3B 46
GREENACRES 2E 31

Greenacres Dr. M19: Man 4A **94**
GREENACRES HILL 1E **31**
GREENACRES MOOR 1E **31**
Greenacres Rd. OL4: O'ham 2D **31**
Green Av. M27: Swin 5B **34**
Green Bank SK4: Stoc 5C **94**
Greenbank Av. M27: Swin 1F **47**
   SK4: Stoc 1A **104**
   SK8: Gat 1C **110**
Greenbank Rd. M6: Sal 4A **50**
   M33: Sale 3A **88**
   SK8: Gat 5C **102**
Greenbank Ter. M24: Mid 5E **17**
   SK4: Stoc 1A **118**
Greenbrow Rd. M23: Wyth 1C **108**
                     (not continuous)
Green Bldg., The M1: Man 4B **10**
Green Cl. SK8: Gat 5C **102**
Greencourts Bus. Pk.
   M22: Wyth 1C **114**
Greencroft Rd. M30: Ecc 3D **47**
Greencroft Way M7: Salq 5F **37**
Greendale Dr. M9: Man 1A **40**
   M26: Rad 1D **21**
Greendale Gro. M34: Dent 5D **87**
Green Dr. M19: Man 4B **82**
   WA15: Tim 4C **98**
GREEN END 3B **94**
Green End M34: Dent 5D **87**
Green End Rd. M19: Man 3A **94**
Greenfield Av. M30: Ecc 2C **60**
   M41: Urm 3F **75**
Greenfield Cl. SK3: Stoc 5A **106**
   WA15: Tim 5E **99**
Greenfield St. M34: Aud 3F **71**
   SK14: Hyde 3F **87**
Greenfield Ter. M41: Urm 3A **74**
Green Fold M18: Man 4B **70**
Greenford Rd. M8: Man 5C **38**
Green Gables Cl. SK8: H Grn 5D **111**
Greengage M13: Man 4E **67**
Green Ga. WA15: Haleb 2A **112**
Greengate M3: Sal 2A **6** (4B **52**)
   M24: Man 1E **41**
   SK14: Hyde 5F **87**
Greengate E. M40: Man 1E **41**
Greengate Ind. Est. M24: Mid 4E **27**
Greengate La. M25: Pres 5C **22**
Greengate Rd. M34: Dent 1C **86**
Greengate Rdbt. M40: Man 1E **41**
Greengate St.
   OL4: O'ham 5F **117** (3C **30**)
                     (not continuous)
Greengate W. M3: Sal 2E **5** (4A **52**)
Greenhalgh St. M35: Fail 1E **55**
   SK4: Stoc 1A **118** (1A **106**)
Greenham Rd. M23: Wyth 1B **100**
Greenhaven Cl. M28: Walk 1B **32**
GREENHEYS 5C **66**
Greenheys M43: Droy 5C **56**
Greenheys Bus. Cen. M15: Man 5C **66**
               (off Pencroft Way)
Greenheys La. M15: Man 5B **66**
Greenheys La. W. M15: Man 5A **66**
GREEN HILL 2F **27**
Green Hill M25: Pres 5C **22**
Greenhill Av. M33: Sale 5C **88**
Greenhill Pas. OL1: O'ham 4F **117**
Green Hill Pl. SK3: Stoc 4F **105**

Greenhill Rd. M8: Man 5C **38**
   M24: Mid 2E **27**
   WA15: Tim 5E **99**
Green Hill St. SK3: Stoc 4F **105**
Green Hill Ter. SK3: Stoc 4F **105**
Greenhill Ter. M24: Mid 2E **27**
Greenhill Terraces OL4: O'ham 3C **30**
Greenholme Cl. M40: Man 3F **41**
Greenhow St. M43: Droy 2B **70**
Greenhurst Cres. OL8: O'ham 2C **44**
Greenhurst La. OL6: A Lyme 1F **59**
Greenhurst Rd. OL6: A Lyme 5F **45**
Greenhythe Rd. SK8: H Grn 3E **115**
Greening Rd. M19: Man 3D **83**
Greenland St. M6: Sal 5A **50**
   M8: Man 5B **38**
Green La. BL4: Kea 2C **18**
   M18: Man 4F **69**
   M24: Mid 2F **27**
                 (Grimshaw La.)
   M24: Mid 4D **17**
                (Hilton Fold La.)
   M30: Ecc 5E **47**
   M33: Sale 2A **88**
   M35: Fail 3A **56**
   M45: White 5B **12**
   OL6: A Lyme 2D **59**
   OL8: O'ham 2F **43**
   SK4: Stoc 5D **95**
Green La. Ind. Est. SK4: Stoc 1F **105**
Greenlaw Ct. M16: Old T 5E **65**
Greenlea Av. M18: Man 2F **83**
Greenleach La. M28: Wors 4A **32**
Green Mdws. Wlk. M22: Wyth 5A **110**
Greenmount Pk. BL4: Kea 2C **18**
Greenoak M26: Rad 2E **19**
Greenoak Dr. M33: Sale 2E **99**
Greenpark Rd. M22: Nor 2F **101**
Green Pastures SK4: Stoc 2F **103**
Greenroom Theatre 3B **10** (3B **66**)
GREENSIDE 5B **56**
Greenside M28: Wors 2C **46**
   SK4: Stoc 2C **104**
Greenside Av. BL4: Kea 3B **18**
Greenside Cl. M30: Ecc 4F **47**
Greenside Cres. M43: Droy 5B **56**
Greenside La. M43: Droy 4A **56**
Greenside Pl. M34: Dent 5C **86**
Greenside Shop. Cen.
   M43: Droy 1C **70**
Greenside St. M11: Man 1D **69**
Greenside Trad. Cen. M43: Droy 5C **56**
Greenside Way M24: Mid 4E **27**
Greenson Dr. M24: Mid 2A **26**
Greenstead Av. M8: Man 4C **38**
Greenstone Dr. M6: Sal 2B **50**
Green St. M14: Man 1F **93**
   M24: Mid 5D **17**
   M30: Ecc 2D **61**
   M32: Stre 5E **77**
   OL8: O'ham 3F **29**
   SK3: Stoc 5B **106**
   SK14: Hyde 4F **87**
Greenthorne Av. SK4: Stoc 1F **95**
Greenthorn Wlk. M15: Man 5B **66**
               (off Botham Cl.)
Greenvale Ct. SK8: Chea 5E **103**
Greenvale Dr. SK8: Chea 5E **103**
Green Vw. M7: Sal 5F **37**
Greenview Dr. M20: Man 3E **103**

Green Wlk. M16: W Ran 3E 79
   M32: Stre 3D 77
   SK8: Gat 5C 102
   WA15: Tim 4B 98
Green Walks M25: Pres 1E 37
Greenwatch Cl. M30: Ecc 1E 61
Greenway M22: Nor 3A 102
   M24: Mid 4B 26
   SK14: Hyde 4F 87
Greenway Av. M19: Man 5D 83
Greenway Cl. M33: Sale 5A 88
Greenway Rd. SK8: H Grn 2E 115
   WA15: Tim 3B 98
Greenways M40: Man 3F 41
   OL7: A Lyme 1B 58
Greenwich Cl. M40: Man 3F 55
Greenwood Av. M27: Clif 3D 35
   OL6: A Lyme 1E 59
              (not continuous)
   SK2: Stoc 5E 107
Greenwood Bus. Cen. M5: Sal 2C 64
Greenwood Cl. WA15: Tim 1A 108
Greenwood Pl. M30: Ecc 3A 48
Greenwood Rd. M22: Wyth 3D 109
Greenwood St. M6: Sal 3B 50
   OL4: O'ham 1E 31
              (not continuous)
   OL8: O'ham 3B 44
Greer St. M11: Man 2E 69
Greetland Dr. M9: Man 5B 26
Gregory St. M12: Man 4B 68
   OL8: O'ham 1E 43
   SK14: Hyde 5F 73
Gregory Way SK5: Stoc 2B 96
Gregson Rd. SK5: Stoc 2A 96
Gregson St. OL1: O'ham 4F 117 (3B 30)
Greg St. SK5: Stoc 3A 96
Greg St. Ind. Est. SK4: Stoc 3A 96
Grelley Wlk. M14: Man 2D 81
             (off Ellanby Cl.)
Grendale Av. SK1: Stoc 2D 107
Grendale Dr. M16: Old T 5E 65
Grendon Av. OL8: O'ham 5A 30
Grendon Wlk. M12: Man 4C 68
             (off Birch St.)
Grenfell Rd. M20: Man 5C 92
Grenham Av. M15: Man 4F 65
Grenville St. SK3: Stoc 3F 105
   SK16: Duk 2E 73
Grenville Ter. OL6: A Lyme 5F 59
Gresford Cl. M21: Chor 5C 78
Gresham Cl. M45: White 2F 21
Gresham Dr. OL9: O'ham 2E 29
Gresham St. M34: Dent 1B 86
Gresham Wlk. SK4: Stoc 5A 96
             (off Hesketh St.)
Gresham Way M33: Sale 2C 98
Gresty Av. M22: Wyth 5B 110
Greswell St. M34: Dent 1B 86
Greta Av. SK8: H Grn 3E 115
Greton Cl. M13: Man 1A 82
Greville St. M13: Man 1A 82
Greyfriars Ct. M3: Sal 1E 5 (4A 52)
Greyfriars Rd. M22: Wyth 4D 109
Greyhound Dr. M6: Sal 2E 51
Greylag Cres. M28: Wors 4A 32
Greylands Cl. M33: Sale 4B 88
Greylands Rd. M20: Man 3E 103
Grey Mare La. M11: Man 1B 68
Greysham Ct. M16: W Ran 3A 80

Greystoke Av. M19: Man 4E 83
   M33: Sale 5D 89
   WA15: Tim 5F 99
Greystoke Cres. M45: White 4A 12
Greystoke Dr. M24: Mid 4F 15
Greystoke La. M35: Fail 1F 55
Greystoke St. SK1: Stoc 2C 106
Greystone Av. M21: Chor 5B 80
Greystone Wlk. SK4: Stoc 1F 95
Grey St. M12: Man 4A 68
   M24: Mid 5B 16
   M25: Pres 5E 23
   M34: Dent 2F 85
   OL6: A Lyme 5E 59
Greyswood Av. M8: Man 5B 38
Greytown Cl. M6: Sal 2B 50
Grierson St. M16: W Ran 1A 80
Griffe La. BL9: Bury 3E 13
Griffin Gro. M19: Man 5C 82
Griffin La. SK8: H Grn 2F 115
Griffin Rd. M35: Fail 5F 41
Griffin St. M7: Sal 5D 37
Griffiths Cl. M7: Sal 1D 5 (3F 51)
Griffiths St. M40: Man 2E 55
Grimscott Cl. M9: Man 3B 40
Grimshaw Av. M35: Fail 4C 42
Grimshaw La. M24: Mid 1D 27
   M40: Man 2B 54
Grimshaw St. M35: Fail 4A 42
   SK1: Stoc 2C 106
Grimstead Cl. M23: Wyth 5A 100
Grindall Av. M40: Man 2D 41
Grindleford Wlk. M21: Chor 3F 91
Grindle Grn. M30: Ecc 2E 61
Grindleton Av. M22: Wyth 3F 109
Grindley Av. M21: Chor 3F 91
Grindlow St. M13: Man 5A 68
Grindon Av. M7: Sal 5C 36
Grinton Av. M13: Man 3A 82
Grisdale Dr. M24: Mid 4A 16
Grisebeck Way OL1: O'ham . . .2D 117 (2A 30)
Grisedale Cl. M18: Man 1E 83
   M24: Mid 3F 15
Gritley Wlk. M22: Wyth 5E 109
Grizebeck Cl. M18: Man 4E 69
Groby Rd. M21: Chor 5D 79
   M34: Aud 3A 72
Groby Rd. Nth. M34: Aud 2F 71
Groby St. OL8: O'ham 1C 44
Groom St. M1: Man 4E 11
Grosvenor Av. M45: White 1A 22
Grosvenor Casino
   Manchester 3A 52
   Salford 3C 8 (2F 65)
Grosvenor Ct. M7: Sal 4F 37
   M16: W Ran 2A 80
   M33: Sale 3B 88
   OL7: A Lyme 1C 72
   SK8: Chea 5F 103
Grosvenor Cres. SK14: Hyde 4E 87
Grosvenor Gdns. M7: Sal 3F 51
   M22: Shar 5A 102
Grosvenor Ho. M16: W Ran 4A 80
             (off Arnold Rd.)
   M33: Sale 4B 88
            (off Grosvenor Sq.)
   OL7: A Lyme 5A 116
Grosvenor Ho. M. M8: Man 2B 38
Grosvenor Ind. Est.
   OL7: A Lyme 5A 116 (1C 72)

Grosvenor Pl. M13: Man 5D **11** (3C **66**)
   OL7: A Lyme 1C **72**
Grosvenor Rd. M16: W Ran 3F **79**
   M27: Swin 5D **35**
   M30: Ecc .4C **46**
   M33: Sale 3B **88**
   M41: Urm 3E **75**
   M45: White 5A **12**
   SK4: Stoc 5C **94**
   (not continuous)
   SK14: Hyde 4F **87**
   WA14: Alt 5A **98**
Grosvenor Sq. M7: Sal 3F **51**
   M15: Man 5D **11** (3C **66**)
   M33: Sale 4C **88**
Grosvenor St. BL4: Kea 1A **18**
   M1: Man 5D **11** (3C **66**)
   M25: Pres 5E **23**
   M27: Pen 2B **34**
   M32: Stre 3F **77**
   M34: Dent 1F **85**
   OL7: A Lyme 5A **116** (1B **72**)
   (not continuous)
   SK1: Stoc 5B **118**
Grove, The M20: Man 2D **103**
   M30: Ecc 1B **62**
   M33: Sale 5D **89**
   M41: Urm 4B **74**
   SK2: Stoc 4A **106**
Grove Av. M35: Fail 2A **56**
Grove Cl. M14: Man 2E **81**
Grove Ct. M33: Sale 4F **89**
Grove Ho. M15: Man 5D **67**
   SK4: Stoc 2A **104**
Grovehurst M27: Swin 1D **47**
Grove La. M20: Man 5D **93**
   WA15: Tim 4B **98**
Grove M. M28: Walk 1A **32**
   (off Malvern Gro.)
Grove Pk. M33: Sale 4B **88**
Grove Rd. M24: Mid 4D **17**
Grove St. BL4: Kea 1A **18**
   M7: Sal .2A **52**
   M43: Droy 2B **70**
   OL7: A Lyme 2A **58**
   SK16: Duk 1F **73**
Grove Ter. OL4: O'ham 1F **31**
Grovewood Cl. OL7: A Lyme 2A **58**
Grundy Av. M25: Pres 2A **36**
Grundy Rd. BL4: Kea 2A **18**
Grundy St. M28: Walk 2B **32**
   SK4: Stoc 1A **104**
Guardian Ct. M33: Sale 3C **88**
Guardian Lodge SK8: Gat 1C **110**
Guardian M. M23: Wyth 2E **99**
Guernsey Cl. M19: Man 2C **94**
Guest Rd. M25: Pres 3C **22**
Guest St. M4: Man 1F **67**
GUIDE BRIDGE 2B **72**
Guide Bridge Station (Rail) 2B **72**
Guide Bridge Theatre 2A **72**
Guide Bri. Trad. Est.
   OL7: A Lyme 2A **72**
Guide La. M34: Aud 2B **72**
Guide Post Rd. M13: Man 4F **67**
Guide St. M50: Sal 1E **63**
Guido St. M35: Fail 5A **42**
Guildford Cl. SK1: Stoc 4D **107**
Guildford Dr. OL6: A Lyme 5E **45**
Guildford Gro. M24: Mid 3E **17**

Guildford Rd. M6: Sal 3D **49**
   M19: Man 3D **83**
   M41: Urm 1A **76**
Guildhall Cl. M15: Man 5C **66**
Guilford Rd. M30: Ecc 1D **61**
Guinness Circ. M17: T Pk 2C **62**
Guinness Rd. M17: T Pk 2B **62**
Guinness Rd. Trad. Est.
   M17: T Pk 2B **62**
Gullane Cl. M40: Man 5E **41**
Gulvain Pl. OL9: Chad 1B **28**
Gunson St. M40: Man 4E **53**
Gun St. M4: Man 4F **7** (5D **53**)
Gurner Av. M5: Sal 5A **8** (3D **65**)
Gurney St. M4: Man 1F **67**
Guy Fawkes St. M5: Sal 3D **65**
Gwelo St. M11: Man 5C **54**
Gwenbury Av. SK1: Stoc 2D **107**
Gwendor Av. M8: Man 1B **38**
Gwynant Pl. M20: Man 1E **93**
Gwyneth Morley Ct. SK9: Hand 5F **115**
Gypsy La. SK2: Stoc 5E **107**
   (not continuous)
Gypsy Wlk. SK2: Stoc 5E **107**
Gyte's La. M19: Man 3E **83**

H

Hacienda, The M1: Man 3A **10**
Hacking St. M7: Sal 1A **52**
   M25: Pres 5C **22**
Hackle St. M11: Man 5E **55**
Hackleton Cl. M4: Man 1F **67**
Hackness Rd. M21: Chor 5B **78**
Hackney Av. M40: Man 3E **55**
Hackwood Wlk. M8: Man 5B **38**
   (off Levenhurst Rd.)
Haddington Dr. M9: Man 1A **40**
Haddon Av. M40: Man 3B **42**
Haddon Cl. BL9: Bury 1C **12**
Haddon Gro. M33: Sale 5C **88**
   SK5: Stoc 1A **96**
   WA15: Tim 4B **98**
Haddon Hall Rd. M43: Droy 5A **56**
Haddon Ho. M5: Sal 4F **49**
Haddon Rd. M21: Chor 3F **91**
   M28: Wors 1E **47**
   M30: Ecc 2D **61**
   SK8: H Grn 2E **115**
Haddon St. M6: Sal 2D **51**
   M32: Stre 1F **77**
Haddon Way M34: Dent 4C **86**
Hadfield Av. OL9: Chad 5D **29**
Hadfield Cl. M14: Man 2F **81**
Hadfield Cres. OL6: A Lyme 2F **59**
Hadfield St. M7: Sal 1A **52**
   M16: Old T 5B **8** (4E **65**)
   OL8: O'ham 1A **44**
   SK16: Duk 3C **72**
Hadley Av. M13: Man 3A **82**
Hadley St. M6: Sal 2D **51**
Hadlow Grn. SK5: Stoc 2D **97**
Hadlow Wlk. M40: Man 4A **54**
   (off Sabden Cl.)
Hadrian Ho. OL1: O'ham 2E **117** (2B **30**)
Hafton Rd. M7: Sal 1D **51**
Hagley Rd. M5: Sal 4C **64**
Hags, The BL9: Bury 1C **12**

Hague Ct. M20: Man	3C 92
Hague Ho. OL8: O'ham	5E 117
Hague Rd. M20: Man	3C 92
Hague St. OL6: A Lyme	3E 59
Haigh Av. SK4: Stoc	3A 96
Haigh La. OL1: Chad	5F 17
Haigh Pk. SK4: Stoc	3A 96
Haig Rd. M32: Stre	2F 77
Halbury Gdns. OL9: Chad	3C 28
Haldane Rd. M1: Sal	1C 64
Haldene Wlk. M8: Man	1B 52
(off Felthorpe Dr.)
Haldon Rd. M20: Man	3F 93
Hale Bank Av. M20: Man	1B 92
HALEBARNS	2A 112
Hale La. M35: Fail	4A 42
Hale Rd. SK4: Stoc	5E 95
WA15: Hale	2A 112
Hales Cl. M43: Droy	4B 56
Halesden Rd. M44: Stoc	3F 95
Halesworth Wlk. M40: Man	3E 53
(off Talgarth Rd.)
Haletop M22: Wyth	4F 109
Haley Cl. SK5: Stoc	5B 84
Haley St. M8: Man	5D 39
HALF ACRE	3E 23
Halfacre Rd. M22: Wyth	2E 109
Half Edge La. M30: Ecc	4A 48
Half Lea Grange M30: Ecc	4A 48
(off Half Edge La.)
Half Moon La. SK2: Stoc	5F 107
Half Moon St. M2: Man	5B 6
Halford Dr. M40: Man	4E 41
Half St. M3: Sal	2F 5 (4A 52)
Halifax St. OL6: A Lyme	3D 59
Hallacres La. SK8: Chea H	1F 115
Hallam Mill SK2: Stoc	5C 106
(off Hallam St.)
Hallam Rd. M40: Man	2D 55
Hallams Pas. SK2: Stoc	5C 106
Hallam St. SK2: Stoc	5C 106
Hallas Gro. M23: Wyth	2D 101
Hall Av. M14: Man	2F 81
M33: Sale	2A 88
WA15: Tim	4B 98
Hall Bank M30: Ecc	5E 47
Hall Dr. M24: Mid	2B 26
Halle Sq. M4: Man	4C 6
Hall Farm Av. M41: Urm	2D 75
Hallgate Dr. SK8: H Grn	4C 110
Hallgate Rd. SK1: Stoc	3D 107
Hall Grn. Cl. SK16: Duk	1E 73
Hall Grn. Rd. SK16: Duk	1E 73
Hall Gro. M14: Man	2F 81
SK8: Chea	5E 103
Halliday Rd. M40: Man	3D 55
Halliford Rd. M40: Man	1C 54
Halliwell Av. OL8: O'ham	1A 44
Halliwell La. M8: Man	5B 38
Halliwell Rd. M25: Pres	3B 36
Halliwell St. W. M8: Man	5B 38
Halliwell Wlk. M25: Pres	3B 36
Hallkirk Wlk. M40: Man	2F 41
Hall La. M23: Wyth	5D 101
Hall Mdw. SK8: Chea H	5F 111
Hall Moss Rd. M9: Man	1C 40
Hall Rd. M14: Man	2F 81
OL6: A Lyme	2E 59
SK9: Hand	5F 115
Hallroyd Brow OL1: O'ham	1D 117

Hall St. M1: Man	2B 10 (2B 66)
M24: Mid	1C 26
M27: Pen	2B 34
M35: Fail	1F 55
OL4: O'ham	2D 31
(off Gravel Wlks.)
OL6: A Lyme	5F 59
SK1: Stoc	2C 106
SK8: Chea	5F 103
SK14: Hyde	2D 87
Hallsville Rd. M19: Man	4E 83
Hallsworth Rd. M30: Ecc	1C 60
Hallwood Av. M6: Sal	3E 49
Hallwood Rd. M23: Wyth	5C 100
Hallworth Av. M34: Aud	1D 71
Hallworth Rd. M8: Man	4D 39
Halmore Rd. M40: Man	5F 53
Halsbury Cl. M12: Man	4A 68
Halsey Cl. OL9: Chad	2A 42
Halsey Wlk. M8: Man	5B 38
(off Greywood Av.)
Halshaw La. BL4: Kea	2B 18
Halsmere Dr. M9: Man	1A 40
Halstead Av. M6: Sal	3F 49
M21: Chor	1C 90
Halstead Gro. SK8: Gat	2B 110
Halstock Wlk. M40: Man	2F 53
(off Foreland Cl.)
Halston St. M15: Man	4A 66
Halton Bank M6: Sal	3B 50
Halton Dr. WA15: Tim	2D 99
Halton Ho. M5: Sal	1B 64
(off Amersham St.)
Halton Rd. M11: Man	5E 55
Halvis Gro. M16: Old T	2D 79
Hamble Cft. M26: Rad	1D 19
(off Stoneclough Ri.)
Hambleton Rd. SK8: H Grn	1E 115
Hambridge Cl. M8: Man	5C 38
Hamer Dr. M16: Old T	5F 65
Hamer Hill M9: Man	1E 39
Hamerton Rd. M40: Man	3E 53
Hamilcar Av. M30: Ecc	5A 48
Hamilton Av. M30: Ecc	1A 62
Hamilton Cl. M25: Pres	1C 36
Hamilton Ct. M33: Sale	4D 89
Hamilton Cres. SK4: Stoc	2D 105
Hamilton Gro. M16: Old T	5F 65
(off Hamilton Rd.)
Hamilton Ho. WA14: Alt	5A 98
Hamilton Lodge M14: Man	2E 81
Hamilton M. M25: Pres	1C 36
M30: Ecc	4D 47
Hamilton Rd. M13: Man	2B 82
M25: Pres	1C 36
M45: White	1A 22
Hamilton Sq. SK4: Stoc	1A 106
Hamilton St. M7: Sal	5F 37
M16: Old T	5F 65
M27: Swin	3F 33
M30: Ecc	4D 47
OL4: O'ham	3C 30
OL7: A Lyme	1B 72
OL9: Chad	2C 28
Hamlet Dr. M33: Sale	2A 88
Hammerstone Rd.
M18: Man	4E 69
Hammett Rd. M21: Chor	5C 78
Hammond Av. SK4: Stoc	3A 96
Hammond Ct. SK4: Stoc	3A 96

Hamnett St. M11: Man 1F 69
　　M43: Droy 1F 69
　　SK14: Hyde .2F 87
Hampden Ct. M30: Ecc 5F 47
Hampden Cres. M18: Man 5E 69
　　　　　　　　　　　　　　　(not continuous)
Hampden Gro. M30: Ecc 5F 47
Hampden Rd. M25: Pres 5D 23
　　M33: Sale 5C 88
Hampshire Cl. SK5: Stoc 3E 97
Hampshire Ho. SK5: Stoc 3E 97
Hampshire Rd. M43: Droy 4C 56
　　OL9: Chad .4D 29
　　SK5: Stoc 3E 97
Hampshire Wlk. M8: Man 1D 53
　　　　　　　　　　　　　　(off Appleford Dr.)
Hampson Cl. M30: Ecc 1D 61
Hampson Cres. SK9: Hand 5E 115
Hampson Mill La. BL9: Bury 1B 12
Hampson Pl. OL6: A Lyme 1F 59
Hampson Rd. M32: Stre 3E 77
Hampson St. M5: Sal 1B 8 (1E 65)
　　M27: Pen 3C 34
　　M30: Ecc 1D 61
　　M33: Sale 4F 89
　　M40: Man 3F 53
　　M43: Droy 5C 56
　　SK1: Stoc .3D 107
Hampstead Av. M41: Urm 4A 74
Hampstead Dr. M45: White 5A 12
　　SK2: Stoc .5E 107
Hampstead La. SK2: Stoc 5E 107
Hampton Cl. SK9: Hand 4F 115
　　　　　　　　　　　　　　(off Wilmslow Rd.)
Hampton Gro. WA14: Tim 2B 98
Hampton Ho. M33: Sale 4E 89
　　　　　　　　　　　　　(off Northenden Rd.)
Hampton Rd. M21: Chor 4B 78
　　M35: Fail 4C 42
　　M41: Urm 4F 75
Hampton St. OL8: O'ham 5F 29
Hamsell Ct. M13: Man 5F 11 (3E 67)
Hamsell Rd. M13: Man 5F 11 (3E 67)
Hancock Cl. M14: Man 2D 81
Hancock St. M32: Stre 5F 77
Handel Av. M41: Urm 3C 74
Handel M. M33: Sale 4E 89
Handford Ho. M41: Urm 3A 76
　　　　　　　　　　　　　(off Cavendish Rd.)
HANDFORTH .5F 115
Handforth Gro. M13: Man 4A 82
Handforth Rd. SK5: Stoc 3B 96
Handforth Station (Rail) 5F 115
Handley Av. M14: Man 4D 81
Handley Cl. SK3: Stoc 5E 105
Handsworth St. M12: Man 3F 67
Hanging Birch M24: Mid 2D 25
Hanging Bri. M3: Man 4B 6
　　　　　　　　　　　　　(off Cateaton St.)
Hani Ct. M8: Man 3B 38
Hani Wells Bus. Pk. M19: Man 1D 95
Hankinson Way M6: Sal 4C 50
Hanley Cl. M24: Mid 4C 26
Hanlith M. M19: Man 5B 82
Hanlon St. M8: Man 3B 38
Hannah Baldwin Cl. M11: Man 2B 68
Hannah Lodge M20: Man 4C 92
　　　　　　　　　　　　　(off Palatine Rd.)
Hannah St. M12: Man 3C 82
Hannet Rd. M22: Wyth 4F 109

Hanover Ct. M28: Wors 1D 47
　　OL7: A Lyme 5A 116 (1C 72)
Hanover Cres. M14: Man 1F 81
Hanover Gdns. M7: Sal 4A 38
Hanover Ho. M14: Man 5F 81
　　　　　　　　　　　　　(off Ladybarn La.)
　　OL8: O'ham 3A 30
　　　　　　　　　　　　　　　　(off Lee St.)
Hanover St. M4: Man 3C 6 (5C 52)
Hanover St. Nth. M34: Aud 2A 72
Hanover St. Sth. M34: Aud 2A 72
Hanover Towers SK5: Stoc 5B 96
Hansby Cl. OL1: O'ham 1A 30
Hansdon Cl. M8: Man 1C 52
Hansen Wlk. M22: Wyth 4E 109
Hanslope Wlk. M9: Man 4A 40
　　　　　　　　　　　　　(off Swainsthorpe Dr.)
Hanson Cl. M24: Mid 5C 16
Hanson Cl. Ind. Est. M24: Mid 5C 16
Hanson M. SK1: Stoc 1D 107
Hanson Rd. M40: Man 5C 40
Hanson St. M24: Mid 5C 16
　　OL4: O'ham 2E 31
Hanworth Cl. M13: Man 5F 11 (3D 67)
Hapsford Wlk. M40: Norton 2C 54
Hapton Av. M32: Stre 4F 77
Hapton Pl. SK4: Stoc 5A 96
Hapton St. M19: Man 4C 82
Harbern Cl. M30: Ecc 3F 47
Harbord St. M33: Sale 5B 88
Harboro Gro. M33: Sale 4B 88
Harboro Rd. M33: Sale 3A 88
Harboro Way M33: Sale 4B 88
Harbour City Station (Metro) 2B 64
Harbour Farm Rd. SK14: Hyde 4F 73
Harbourne Wlk. M22: Wyth 1A 114
Harbury Cres. M22: Wyth 1E 109
Harcombe Rd. M20: Man 2E 93
Harcourt Av. M41: Urm 4B 76
Harcourt Cl. M41: Urm 4B 76
Harcourt Ind. Cen. M28: Walk 4A 18
Harcourt Rd. M33: Sale 2C 88
　　WA14: Alt 5A 98
Harcourt St. M32: Stre 2A 78
　　OL1: O'ham 1D 31
　　SK5: Stoc 5B 84
Hardberry Pl. SK2: Stoc 5F 107
Hardcastle Av. M21: Chor 2E 91
Hardcastle Rd. SK3: Stoc 4F 105
Hardcastle St. OL1: O'ham 3F 117 (2C 30)
Hardfield Rd. M24: Mid 4C 26
Hardicker St. M19: Man 1D 95
Harding St. M3: Sal 3A 6
　　M4: Man 1F 67
　　M6: Sal 3C 50
　　SK1: Stoc .2D 107
　　SK14: Hyde .5F 73
Hardman Av. M25: Pres 2F 37
Hardman Blvd. M3: Man 1F 9 (1A 66)
Hardman La. M35: Fail 4A 42
Hardman Rd. SK5: Stoc 5B 84
Hardman's M. M45: White 3B 22
Hardman Sq. M3: Man 1F 9 (1A 66)
Hardman's Rd. M45: White 3B 22
Hardman St. BL4: Farn 2A 18
　　M3: Man 1F 9 (1A 66)
　　M35: Fail 5F 41
　　OL9: Chad .1D 43
　　SK3: Stoc .2F 105
　　　　　　　　　　　　　　　(not continuous)

Hardon Gro. M13: Man 3B **82**
Hardrush Fold M35: Fail 1C **56**
Hardshaw Cl. M13: Man 5F **11** (4D **67**)
Hardwick St. OL7: A Lyme 5B **58**
Hardwood Cl. M8: Man 5C **38**
Hardy Av. M21: Chor 5C **78**
Hardy Cl. SK16: Duk 2E **73**
Hardy Dr. WA15: Tim 4B **98**
Hardy Farm M21: Chor 2D **91**
Hardy Gro. M27: Swin 2F **47**
      M28: Wors 4B **32**
Hardy La. M21: Chor 2D **91**
Hardy St. M30: Ecc 2D **61**
      OL4: O'ham 4C **30**
      OL6: A Lyme 1F **59**
Hardywood Rd. M34: Dent 5C **86**
Harecastle Av. M30: Ecc 2A **62**
Haredale Dr. M8: Man 1D **53**
Hare Dr. BL9: Bury 2D **13**
Harefield Dr. M20: Man 1C **102**
Harefield Rd. SK9: Hand 5F **115**
Harehill Cl. M13: Man 4F **11** (3D **67**)
Hare St. M4: Man 4D **7**
Harewood Av. M33: Sale 5A **88**
Harewood Cl. *M9: Man* *4C 24*
                                  (off Deanswood Dr.)
      M33: Sale 5E **89**
Harewood Gro. SK5: Stoc 5A **84**
Harewood Wlk. *M34: Dent* *4C 86*
                                      (off Tatton Rd.)
Harewood Way M27: Clif 2B **34**
Hargrave Cl. *M9: Man* 3E **25**
Hargreaves Rd. WA15: Tim 5E **99**
Hargreaves St. M4: Man 1D **7** (4C **52**)
      OL1: O'ham 2E **117** (2B **30**)
      OL9: O'ham 3E **29**
Harkerside Cl. M21: Chor 5E **79**
Harkness St. M12: Man 3E **67**
Harland Dr. M8: Man 5D **39**
Harlech Av. M45: White 3D **23**
Harleen Gro. SK2: Stoc 4F **107**
Harley Av. M14: Man 2A **82**
Harley Ct. M24: Mid 5B **16**
Harley Rd. M24: Mid 5B **16**
      M33: Sale 3D **89**
Harley St. M11: Man 2F **69**
      OL6: A Lyme 1C **116** (4D **59**)
Harling Rd. M22: Shar 4F **101**
Harlington Cl. *M23: Wyth* *4F 99*
                                  (off Petersfield Dr.)
Harlow Dr. M18: Man 2F **83**
Harmer Cl. M40: Man 2C **54**
Harmol Gro. OL7: A Lyme 1B **58**
Harmony Sq. M13: Man 5F **67**
Harmony St. OL4: O'ham 5F **117** (3C **30**)
Harmsworth Dr. SK4: Stoc 3D **95**
Harmsworth St. M6: Sal 5A **50**
Harold Av. M18: Man 1B **84**
      SK16: Duk 2F **73**
Harold Priestnall Cl. M40: Man 1D **55**
Harold St. M16: Old T 5B **8** (4E **65**)
      M24: Mid 5A **16**
      M25: Pres 5B **22**
      M35: Fail 5A **42**
      OL9: O'ham 2F **29**
      SK1: Stoc 3D **107**
Harper Ct. SK3: Stoc 4A **106**
Harper Ho. M19: Man 4B **82**
Harper Mill OL6: A Lyme 4E **59**
Harper Pl. OL6: A Lyme 4E **59**

Harper Rd. M22: Shar 4A **102**
Harper St. OL8: O'ham 5A **30**
      SK3: Stoc 5A **118** (4A **106**)
Harp Rd. M17: T Pk 2C **62**
Harp St. M11: Man 3A **70**
Harp Trad. Est. M17: T Pk 2C **62**
HARPURHEY .5F **39**
Harpurhey Leisure Cen. 4A **40**
Harpurhey Pools 3F **39**
Harpurhey Rd. M8: Man 4E **39**
      M9: Man 4E **39**
Harrier Cl. M22: Shar 1A **110**
Harriett St. M4: Man 5E **53**
Harringap Rd. M40: Man 2D **55**
Harrington St. M18: Man 5A **70**
Harris Av. M34: Dent 2D **85**
      M41: Urm 5F **61**
Harris Cl. M34: Dent 2D **85**
Harrison Av. M19: Man 3D **83**
Harrison St. M4: Man 1F **67**
      M7: Sal 1D **5** (3F **51**)
      M30: Ecc 2D **61**
      OL1: O'ham 4E **117** (3B **30**)
      SK1: Stoc 4B **106**
Harris St. M8: Man 1F **5** (3A **52**)
Harrogate Av. M25: Pres 2F **37**
Harrogate Cl. M11: Man 3A **70**
Harrogate Dr. SK5: Stoc 5A **84**
Harrogate Rd. SK5: Stoc 5A **84**
Harroll Ga. M27: Swin 5C **34**
Harrop Fold OL8: O'ham 3C **44**
Harrop St. M18: Man 4B **70**
      SK1: Stoc 4C **106**
      OL8: O'ham 1F **43**
Harrow Av. M19: Man 2C **94**
      OL8: O'ham 1F **43**
Harrowby Dr. M40: Man 2F **53**
Harrowby Rd. M27: Swin 5A **34**
Harrow Cl. BL9: Bury 1B **12**
Harrowdene Wlk. *M9: Man* *4F 39*
                                  (off Alderside Rd.)
Harrow Dr. M33: Sale 1C **98**
      SK8: Chea 4E **111**
Harrow Rd. M33: Sale 1C **98**
Harrow St. M8: Man 3D **39**
Harry Hall Gdns. M7: Sal 1B **4** (3E **51**)
Harry Piggott Ct. M9: Man 1E **39**
      Harry Rd. SK5: Stoc 5B **84**
Harry Rowley Cl. M22: Wyth 5E **109**
Harry St. OL9: O'ham 3E **29**
Harry Thorneycroft Wlk. *M11: Man* *2A 68*
                                  (off Rylance St.)
Hart Av. M33: Sale 5B **90**
      M43: Droy 1D **71**
Hart Dr. BL9: Bury 2D **13**
Harter St. M1: Man 2C **10** (2C **66**)
Hartfield Cl. M13: Man 5F **11** (4E **67**)
Hartford Av. SK4: Stoc 2F **95**
Hartford Gdns. WA15: Tim 5F **99**
Hartford Grange OL8: O'ham 5F **29**
Hartford Ind. Est. OL9: O'ham 3E **29**
Hartford Rd. M33: Sale 1A **98**
      M41: Urm 1A **76**
Hartford Sq. OL9: O'ham 3E **29**
Hartford St. M34: Dent 5A **72**
Hartford Wlk. *M9: Man* *1E 53*
                                  (off Mannington Dr.)
Hart Hill Dr. M5: Sal 4F **49**
Harthill St. M8: Man 2B **52**
Hartington Cl. M41: Urm 3A **76**

Hartington Dr. M11: Man 4D 55
Hartington Rd. M21: Chor 5D 79
   M30: Ecc 4C 46
   SK8: H Grn 1F 115
   WA14: B'ath 4A 98
Hartington St. M14: Man 2B 80
Hartis Av. M7: Sal 1A 52
Hartland Av. M41: Urm 3C 76
Hartland Cl. SK2: Stoc 3E 107
Hartlepool Cl. M11: Man 2D 81
Hartley Av. M25: Pres 1E 37
Hartley Hall Gdns. M16: W Ran 4A 80
Hartley Rd. M21: Chor 4C 78
Hartley St. M40: Man 4B 40
   SK3: Stoc 3F 105
Harton Av. M18: Man 2E 83
Hart Rd. M14: Man 3C 80
Hartshead Av. M6: A Lyme 1E 59
Hartshead Cl. M11: Man 3C 70
Hartshead Cres. M35: Fail 1E 55
Hartshead High School Sports Hall . . . 5F 45
              (off Greenhurst Rd.)
Hartshead Rd. OL6: A Lyme 1E 59
Hartsop Dr. M24: Mid 4E 15
Hartspring Av. M27: Swin 5C 34
Hart St. M1: Man 2C 10 (2C 66)
                 (Abingdon St.)
   M1: Man 1D 11 (1C 66)
                 (Minshull St.)
   M43: Droy 5C 56
   WA14: Alt 5A 98
Hartswood Cl. M34: Dent 1C 86
Hartswood Rd. M20: Man 2F 93
Hartwell Cl. M11: Man 2B 68
Harty Ho. M30: Ecc 5A 48
               (off Monton La.)
Harvard Gro. M6: Sal 4E 49
Harvard Rd. M18: Man 5D 69
Harvest Cl. M6: Sal 2A 50
   M33: Sale 5C 90
Harvey Cl. M11: Man 2C 68
Harvey St. SK1: Stoc 2C 118 (2B 106)
Harvin Gro. M34: Dent 3C 86
Harwich Cl. M19: Man 4D 83
   SK5: Stoc 2E 97
Harwood Cl. M6: Sal 3D 51
   SK4: Stoc 1A 104
Harwood Rd. M19: Man 2A 94
   SK4: Stoc 1A 104
Harwood St. M6: Sal 5A 96
Haselhurst Wlk. M23: Wyth 1B 100
Haslam Ct. M7: Sal 3F 37
Haslam Rd. SK3: Stoc 5A 106
Haslam St. M24: Mid 2E 27
Haslemere Rd. M20: Man 2F 93
   M41: Urm 4D 75
Haslington Rd. M22: Wyth 4A 110
Hasper Av. M20: Man 1C 92
Hassall Av. M20: Man 1B 92
Hassall St. M26: Rad 1A 12
Hassall Way SK9: Hand 4F 115
              (off Spath La.)
Hassop Av. M7: Sal 5C 36
Hassop Cl. M11: Man 1A 68
Hassop Rd. SK5: Stoc 4C 84
Hastings Av. M21: Chor 5C 78
   M45: White 2D 23
Hastings Cl. M45: White 2D 23
   SK1: Stoc 4D 107
Hastings Dr. M41: Urm 2A 74

Hastings Rd. M25: Pres 4E 23
   M30: Ecc 3C 46
Haston Cl. SK5: Stoc 4B 96
Hasty La. WA15: Ring 2A 112
             (not continuous)
Hatchett Rd. M22: Wyth 5F 109
Hatchley St. M13: Man 5F 67
Hatchmere Cl. WA15: Tim 5F 99
Hateley Rd. M16: Old T 3C 78
Hatfield Av. M19: Man 2B 94
Hathaway Cl. SK8: H Grn 2D 115
Hathaway Rd. BL9: Bury 3C 12
Hatherley Rd. M20: Man 2F 93
Hatherop Cl. M30: Ecc 1D 61
Hathersage Av. M6: Sal 4F 49
Hathersage Rd. M13: Man 1E 81
Hathersage St. OL9: O'ham 3E 29
Hathersage Way M34: Dent 5C 86
HATHERSHAW 1C 44
Hathershaw La. OL8: O'ham 1B 44
Hathershaw Sports Cen. 2B 44
Hatro Cl. M41: Urm 4C 76
Hatters Ct. SK1: Stoc 5C 118 (3B 106)
Hatter St. M4: Man 3F 5
Hatton Av. M7: Sal 1C 4 (4F 51)
Hattonfold M33: Sale 2E 99
Hattons Cl. M32: Stre 2E 77
Hattons Rd. M17: T Pk 4D 63
Hatton St. M12: Man 2C 82
   SK1: Stoc 1A 118 (1A 106)
   SK4: Stoc 1A 118 (1A 106)
Hatton Ter. SK16: Duk 5C 116
              (off Queen St.)
Hat Works (The Mus. of Hatting)
            . . . . 3A 118 (2A 106)
HAUGHTON DALE 5C 86
Haughton Dr. M22: Nor 2F 101
HAUGHTON GREEN 5D 87
Haughton Grn. Rd. M34: Dent 5C 86
Haughton Hall Rd. M34: Dent 2C 86
Haughton St. M34: Aud 5B 72
   SK14: Hyde 4F 87
Havana Cl. M11: Man 1B 68
Haveley Rd. M22: Wyth 1E 109
Havelock Dr.
   M7: Sal 1C 4 (3F 51)
Havelock St. OL8: O'ham 4B 30
Haven Dr. M43: Droy 5A 56
Havenscroft Av. M30: Ecc 2F 61
Haven St. M6: Sal 1A 64
Haverfield Rd. M9: Man 1A 40
Haverford St. M12: Man 4B 68
Haversham Rd. M8: Man 2A 38
Havers Rd. M18: Man 5A 70
Hawarden Av. M16: W Ran 3E 79
Hawarden Rd. WA14: Alt 5A 98
Hawdraw Grn. SK2: Stoc 5F 107
Hawes Av. M14: Man 1A 94
   M27: Swin 5B 34
Hawes Cl. SK2: Stoc 5C 106
Haweswater Cl. M34: Dent 3C 84
Haweswater Cres. BL9: Bury 1D 13
Haweswater Dr. M24: Mid 4A 16
Haweswater M. M24: Mid 4A 16
Hawkeshead Rd. M8: Man 1D 53
             (not continuous)
Hawkhurst Rd. M13: Man 2B 82
Hawkins St. SK5: Stoc 4A 96
Hawkridge Dr. M23: Wyth 1B 100
Hawkshaw Cl. M5: Sal 1C 64

Hawkshead Dr. M24: Mid 5A 16
Hawksley Ct. *OL8: O'ham* *1E 43*
     (off Maple St.)
Hawksley Ind. Est. OL8: O'ham 1E 43
Hawksley St. OL8: O'ham 1E 43
Hawkstone Av. M43: Droy 4A 56
    M45: White 2F 21
Hawkswick Dr. M23: Wyth 1C 100
Hawley St. M19: Man 5D 83
Haworth Dr. M32: Stre 2B 76
Haworth Rd. M18: Man 1E 83
Haworth St. OL1: O'ham 1A 30
Hawsworth Cl. M15: Man 5D 67
Hawthorn Av. M26: Rad 1D 21
    M28: Walk 3A 32
    M30: Ecc .4F 47
    M41: Urm .4B 76
    WA15: Tim 4B 98
Hawthorn Cl. WA15: Tim 4B 98
Hawthorn Ct. SK6: Bred 5F 97
Hawthorn Cres. OL8: O'ham 2B 44
Hawthornden *M20: Man* . . . .
    (off Palatine Rd.)
Hawthorn Dr. M6: Sal 3D 49
    M19: Man 1B 94
    M27: Pen .5E 35
Hawthorne Dr. M28: Wors 5C 32
Hawthorne Gro. OL9: Chad 1D 29
Hawthorn Gro. OL7: A Lyme 1B 72
    SK4: Stoc 5D 95
    SK14: Hyde 4F 87
Hawthorn La. M21: Chor 5B 78
    M32: Stre 5F 77
    M33: Sale 2A 88
Hawthorn Rd. BL4: Kea 4D 19
    M32: Stre *5F 77*
    (off Hancock St.)
    M34: Dent 1D 85
    M40: Man .3A 42
    M43: Droy 2D 43
    (not continuous)
    OL8: O'ham 2D 43
    SK4: Stoc 1B 104
    SK8: Gat .1C 110
Hawthorn Rd. Sth. M43: Droy 5E 57
Hawthorns, The M34: Aud 4F 71
    M34: Dent *1D 85*
    (off Hawthorn Rd.)
Hawthorn St. M18: Man 5A 70
    M34: Aud .4A 72
Hawthorn Ter. *SK4: Stoc* *5D 95*
    (off Hawthorn Gro.)
Haxby Rd. M18: Man 2F 83
Haybarn Rd. M23: Wyth 4D 101
Hayburn Rd. SK2: Stoc 3E 107
Hay Cft. SK8: Chea H 1F 115
Hayden Ct. *M40: Man* *2F 53*
    (off Sedgeford Rd.)
Haydn Av. M14: Man 1D 81
Haydock Cl. M32: Stre 1B 78
Haydock M. *M7: Sal* *1F 51*
    (off Rigby St.)
Haydock Wlk. OL9: Chad 2E 29
    (off Middleton Rd.)
Hayeswater Circ. M41: Urm 2E 75
Hayeswater Rd. M41: Urm 2E 75
Hayfield Cl. M12: Man 3A 68
    M24: Mid .3E 17
Hayfield Rd. M6: Sal 3D 49
Hayfield St. M33: Sale 3C 88

Hayfield Wlk. M34: Dent 5C 86
    WA15: Tim 5E 99
Haygrove Wlk. *M9: Man* *4F 39*
    (off Alfred St.)
Hay Ho. *OL4: O'ham* *1F 31*
    (off Huddersfield Rd.)
Hayley St. M13: Man 1A 82
Hayling Rd. M33: Sale 3A 88
Haymans Wlk. M13: Man 5F 11 (3D 67)
Haymarket St. M13: Man 5E 67
Haymond Cl. M6: Sal 1C 50
Haysbrook Cl. OL7: A Lyme 5C 44
Haythorp Av. M22: Wyth 3A 110
Hazel Av. M16: W Ran 3F 79
    M26: Rad .1C 18
    M27: Swin 5C 34
    M33: Sale 5D 89
    OL6: A Lyme 1F 59
    SK8: Chea 1F 111
Hazelbank Av. M20: Man 1D 93
Hazelbottom Rd. M8: Man 5D 39
Hazel Cl. M43: Droy 5E 57
Hazel Ct. *M16: W Ran* *2F 79*
    (off Dudley Rd.)
Hazeldene Rd. M40: Man 3A 42
Hazel Dr. M22: Wyth 1C 114
    SK2: Stoc 5F 107
Hazelfields M28: Wors 5D 33
Hazel Gro. M5: Sal 5E 49
    M26: Rad .1B 20
    M41: Urm .3A 76
    OL9: Chad 1D 29
Hazelhall Cl. M28: Wors 5D 33
HAZELHURST **5E 33**
Hazelhurst Dr. M24: Mid 2B 16
Hazelhurst Fold M28: Wors 5E 33
Hazelhurst M. OL9: Chad 1B 42
Hazelhurst Rd. M28: Wors 5D 33
Hazel La. OL8: O'ham 2F 43
Hazelmere Av. M30: Ecc 3D 47
Hazel Rd. M24: Mid 5D 17
    M45: White 1D 23
    WA14: Alt .5A 98
Hazel St. M34: Aud 4A 72
Hazel Ter. M9: Man 5F 25
Hazelwell M33: Sale 5D 89
Hazelwood OL9: Chad 1A 28
Hazelwood Ct. M41: Urm 2F 75
Hazelwood Dr. M34: Aud 4B 72
Hazelwood Rd. M22: Wyth 1F 113
Hazlemere BL4: Kea 2C 18
Headingley Dr. M16: Old T 2C 78
Headingley Rd. M14: Man 1F 93
Headlands Dr. M25: Pres 3C 36
HEALD GREEN **1D 115**
Heald Av. M14: Man 2D 81
Heald Grn. Ho. M22: Wyth 1C 114
Heald Green Station (Rail) **1C 114**
Heald Gro. M14: Man 1D 81
    SK8: H Grn 5C 110
Heald Pl. M14: Man 1D 81
Healey Cl. M7: Sal 4E 37
    M23: Wyth 1B 100
Heanor Av. M34: Dent 5C 86
Heapriding Bus. Pk. . . . .
    SK3: Stoc 2F 105
Heap St. M45: White 2B 22
    OL4: O'ham 2E 31
Heath, The M24: Mid 3D 27
    OL7: A Lyme 1C 58

Heath Av. M7: Sal 1B 4 (3E 51)
M41: Urm 2A 76
Heathbank Rd. M9: Man 5E 25
SK3: Stoc 4D 105
Heathcote Av. SK4: Stoc 5E 95
Heathcote Rd. M18: Man 1E 83
Heath Cres. SK2: Stoc 5B 106
Heather Av. M43: Droy 5E 57
Heather Ct. SK4: Stoc 3F 95
Heatherdale Dr. M8: Man 1C 52
Heather Gro. M43: Droy 2D 71
Heather Lea M34: Dent 3C 86
Heatherside SK5: Stoc 4C 84
Heather St. M11: Man 5D 55
Heatherway M14: Man 1D 81
(off Parkfield St.)
Heathfield BL4: Farn 1A 18
M28: Wors 2B 46
Heathfield Av. M34: Dent 3F 85
SK4: Stoc 3E 95
SK8: Gat 1D 111
Heathfield Cl. M33: Sale 4B 90
Heathfield Dr. M27: Swin 5C 34
Heathfield Rd. BL9: Bury 3B 12
M45: White 3B 12
SK2: Stoc 5B 106
Heathfield St. M40: Man 2E 55
Heathland Rd. M7: Sal 4D 37
Heathlands Dr. M25: Pres 3C 36
Heathlands Village M25: Pres 3C 36
Heathland Ter. SK3: Stoc 4A 106
Heath Rd. SK2: Stoc 5B 106
WA15: Tim 3B 98
Heathside Gro. M28: Walk 1A 32
Heathside Pk. Rd. SK3: Stoc 3B 104
Heathside Rd. M20: Man 3E 93
SK3: Stoc 4C 104
Heath St. M8: Man 5B 38
Heath Vw. M7: Sal 4C 36
Heathway Av. M11: Man 5F 55
Heathwood Rd. M19: Man 4A 94
Heatley Cl. M34: Dent 3D 85
Heatley Way SK9: Hand 5F 115
(off Delamere Rd.)
HEATON CHAPEL 3E 95
Heaton Chapel Station (Rail) 3E 95
Heaton Cl. BL9: Bury 1C 12
SK4: Stoc 5C 94
Heaton Ct. M25: Pres 1E 37
M33: Sale 4E 89
SK4: Stoc 4D 95
Heaton Dr. BL9: Bury 1C 12
Heaton Gdns. SK4: Stoc 4E 95
Heaton Hall 4A 24
Heaton La. SK4: Stoc 2A 118 (2F 105)
HEATON MERSEY 1A 104
Heaton Mersey Ind. Est.
SK4: Stoc 2A 104
HEATON MOOR 4D 95
Heaton Moor Rd. SK4: Stoc 5D 95
HEATON NORRIS 1F 105
HEATON PARK 5E 23
Heaton Pk. 4A 24
Heaton Pk. Bowling Pavilion 3E 23
Heaton Pk. Farm Cen. 4F 23
Heaton Pk. Horticultural Cen. 4F 23
Heaton Pk. Rd. M9: Man 4C 24
Heaton Pk. Rd. W. M9: Man 4C 24
Heaton Park Station (Metro) 5E 23
Heaton Pk. Tramway Mus. 4B 24

Heaton Rd. M20: Man 1E 93
SK4: Stoc 5E 95
Heatons Sports Club 5D 95
Heaton St. M7: Sal 5A 38
M24: Mid 2D 25
M25: Pres 5D 23
M34: Dent 2F 85
Heaton Towers SK4: Stoc 1A 118
HEAVILEY 5C 106
Heaviley Gro. SK2: Stoc 5C 106
Hebburn Wlk. M14: Man 1D 81
(off Gt. Western St.)
Hebden Av. M6: Sal 4E 49
Hebden Wlk. M15: Man 5B 66
(off Arnott Cres.)
Hebers Ct. M24: Mid 3B 16
Hector Rd. M13: Man 2B 82
Heddon Cl. SK4: Stoc 5A 94
Heddon Wlk. M8: Man 1E 53
(off Smedley St.)
Hedges St. M35: Fail 4C 42
Hedley Wlk. M8: Man 5B 38
(off Halliwell La.)
Heginbottom Cres. OL6: A Lyme 2E 59
Heightside WA15: Tim 5D 99
(off Edenhurst St.)
Helena St. M6: Sal 2E 49
Helen St. M7: Sal 2E 51
M30: Ecc 2D 61
Helensville Av. M6: Sal 2B 50
Helga St. M40: Man 3F 53
Hellidon Cl. M12: Man 4F 67
Helmet St. M1: Man 2E 67
Helmshore Wlk. M13: Man 5F 11 (3D 67)
Helsby Rd. M33: Sale 1A 100
Helsby Wlk. M12: Man 2F 67
Helsby Way SK9: Hand 5F 115
Helston Gro. SK8: H Grn 1E 115
Helton Wlk. M24: Mid 5E 15
Helvellyn Dr. M24: Mid 4F 15
Helvellyn Wlk. OL1: O'ham 1C 30
Hembury Av. M19: Man 2B 94
Hembury Cl. M24: Mid 4D 17
Hemlock Av. OL8: O'ham 1A 44
Hemming Dr. M30: Ecc 1A 62
Hemmington Dr. M9: Man 5F 39
Hemmons Rd. M12: Man 3D 83
Hempcroft Rd. WA15: Tim 5E 99
Hempshaw Bus. Cen. SK1: Stoc 4D 107
Hempshaw La.
SK1: Stoc 5C 118 (4B 106)
(not continuous)
SK2: Stoc 4B 106
Hemsley St. M9: Man 3A 40
Hemsley St. Sth. M9: Man 4A 40
Hemswell Cl. M6: Sal 3A 50
Hemsworth Rd. M18: Man 2F 83
Henbury Rd. SK9: Hand 5F 115
Henbury St. M14: Man 2C 80
Henderson Av. M27: Pen 3B 34
Henderson St. M19: Man 5D 83
Hendham Va. M9: Man 5E 39
Hendham Va. Ind. Est. M8: Man 5E 39
Hendon Dr. BL9: Bury 1B 12
SK3: Stoc 4C 104
Hendon Rd. M9: Man 5E 25
Henfield Wlk. M22: Wyth 3E 109
(off Cornfield Dr.)
Hengist St. M18: Man 1F 83
Henley Av. M16: Old T 2D 79

Henley Dr. OL7: A Lyme 3B 58
    WA15: Tim .4B 98
Henley Grange SK8: Chea 1E 111
Henley Pl. M19: Man 2C 94
Henley St. OL1: O'ham 1F 29
    OL9: Chad .1C 42
Henlow Wlk. M40: Man 2F 41
Henniker St. M27: Swin 1A 48
Henrietta St. M16: Old T 1E 79
    OL6: A Lyme 1C 116 (3D 59)
Henry Sq. OL6: A Lyme 4A 116
Henry St. M4: Man 4E 7 (5D 53)
                     (not continuous)
    M16: Old T 5E 65
    M24: Mid .1B 26
    M25: Pres .4E 23
    M30: Ecc .1E 61
    M34: Dent .5D 87
    M35: Fail 5B 42
    M43: Droy .1C 70
    SK1: Stoc .3D 107
    SK14: Hyde 3F 87
Henshaw Ct. M16: Old T 1D 79
Henshaw La. OL9: Chad 2B 42
Henshaw St. M32: Stre 3F 77
    OL1: O'ham 3D 117 (2A 30)
Henshaw Wlk. M13: Man 5F 11
Henthorn St. OL1: O'ham 1C 30
Henton Wlk. M40: Man 3E 53
                  (off Rimworth Dr.)
Henty Cl. M30: Ecc 1D 61
Henwood Rd. M20: Man 3E 93
Hepburn Ct. M6: Sal 3A 50
                 (off Monroe Cl.)
Hepple Cl. SK4: Stoc 5B 94
Heppleton Rd. M40: Man 3F 41
Hepple Wlk. OL7: A Lyme 2A 58
Heptonstall Wlk. M18: Man 5E 69
            (off Hampden Cres.)
Hepton St. OL1: O'ham 1A 30
Hepworth St. SK14: Hyde 5B 87
Heraldic Ct. M6: Sal 2C 50
Herbert St. M8: Man 2B 52
    M25: Pres .5B 22
    M32: Stre .3F 77
    M34: Dent .1C 86
    M43: Droy .1B 70
    OL4: O'ham 1F 31
    OL9: Chad 2D 29
    SK3: Stoc .4F 105
Hereford Cl. OL6: A Lyme 5F 45
Hereford Dr. M25: Pres 1E 37
    M27: Swin .1B 48
    SK9: Hand 5F 115
Hereford Gro. M41: Urm 3E 75
Hereford Rd. M30: Ecc 2C 48
    SK5: Stoc .3E 97
Hereford St. M33: Sale 5B 88
                (not continuous)
    OL9: Chad 4D 29
Hereford Wlk. M34: Dent 4B 86
              (off Norwich Av.)
Hereford Way M24: Mid 5E 17
Heristone Av. M34: Dent 2B 86
Heritage Gdns. M20: Man 1D 103
    SK4: Stoc .4E 95
          (off Heaton Moor Rd.)
Heritage Wharf OL7: A Lyme 5A 116
Herle Dr. M22: Wyth 5E 109
Hermitage Rd. M8: Man 3C 38

Hermon Av. OL8: O'ham 5A 30
Herne St. M11: Man 2C 68
Heron Av. SK16: Duk 3F 73
Heron Ct. M6: Sal 4D 49
    SK3: Stoc .4A 106
                (off Lomas St.)
Herondale Cl. M40: Man 2D 55
Heron Dr. M34: Aud 1E 71
Heron St. M15: Man 5A 66
    M27: Pen .3C 34
    OL8: O'ham 5E 29
    SK3: Stoc .3F 105
Herries St. OL6: A Lyme 3F 59
Herriots Bus. Pk. SK16: Duk 3C 72
Herristone Rd. M8: Man 2C 38
Herrod Av. SK4: Stoc 3A 96
Herschel St. M40: Man 4C 40
Hersey St. M6: Sal 5A 50
Hersham Wlk. M9: Man 4A 40
          (off Hemsley St. Sth.)
Hertford Ind. Est.
    OL7: A Lyme 5A 116 (1C 72)
Hertford Rd. M9: Man 3F 39
Hertford St. OL7: A Lyme 5A 116 (1C 72)
Hesford Av. M9: Man 5B 40
Hesketh Av. M20: Man 5C 92
Hesketh Ho. BL4: Farn 1A 18
             (off Hesketh Wlk.)
Hesketh Rd. M33: Sale 5B 88
Hesketh St. SK4: Stoc 4A 96
               (All Saints' Rd.)
    SK4: Stoc .5A 96
                (Belmont St.)
Hesketh Wlk. BL4: Farn 1A 18
    M24: Mid .4A 16
Hessel St. M50: Sal 1F 63
Hester Wlk. M15: Man 4B 66
               (off Brindle Pl.)
Heston Av. M13: Man 3A 82
Heston Dr. M41: Urm 2E 75
Heswall Av. M20: Man 1D 93
Heswall Rd. SK5: Stoc 4B 84
Hetherington Wlk. M12: Man 1C 82
             (off Norman Gro.)
Hethorn St. M40: Man 2E 55
Hetton Av. M13: Man 3A 82
Heversham Wlk. M18: Man 4E 69
           (off Grizebeck Cl.)
Hewart Cl. M40: Man 3E 53
Hewitt Av. M34: Dent 3A 86
Hewitt St. M15: Man 4F 9 (3A 66)
Hewlett Rd. M21: Chor 4C 78
Hexham Cl. M33: Sale 5A 88
    OL9: Chad 2E 29
    SK2: Stoc .5F 107
Hexham Rd. M18: Man 2E 83
Hexon Cl. M6: Sal 4A 50
Heybrook Cl. M45: White 1E 23
Heybrook Rd. M23: Wyth 1D 109
Heybrook Wlk. M45: White 1E 23
Heybury Cl. M11: Man 2B 68
Hey Cft. M45: White 2E 21
Heyes Av. WA15: Tim 4D 99
Heyes Dr. WA15: Tim 4D 99
Heyes La. WA15: Tim 4D 99
Heyes Leigh WA15: Tim 4D 99
Heyes Ter. WA15: Tim 3D 99
          (off The Old Orchard)
Heyford Av. M40: Man 2F 41
Heyland Rd. M23: Wyth 5C 100

Heylee OL7: A Lyme	2B **72**
(off South St.)	
Heyridge Dr. M22: Nor	2F **101**
Heyrod St. M1: Man	2E **67**
Heyrose Wlk. M15: Man	4F **65**
(off Shawheath Cl.)	
Heys, The M23: Wyth	2C **100**
OL6: A Lyme	3F **59**
SK5: Stoc	4C **84**
Heys Av. M23: Wyth	2C **100**
M27: Ward	2E **33**
Heys Cl. Nth. M27: Ward	2E **33**
Heys Ct. SK3: Stoc	3D **105**
Heyscroft Rd. M20: Man	2E **93**
SK4: Stoc	1C **104**
Heysham Av. M20: Man	1B **92**
Heyshaw Wlk. M23: Wyth	2B **100**
Heys Rd. M25: Pres	4C **22**
OL6: A Lyme	4F **59**
Heys Vw. M25: Pres	5D **23**
Heythrop Cl. M45: White	5A **12**
Heywood Av. M27: Clif	2D **35**
Heywood Ct. M24: Mid	2C **24**
Heywood Gdns. M25: Pres	5D **23**
Heywood Gro. M33: Sale	2C **88**
Heywood Ho. M6: Sal	4E **49**
(off Edgehill Rd.)	
OL8: O'ham	5E **117** (4B **30**)
Heywood M. M25: Pres	5D **23**
Heywood Old Rd. M24: Mid	4C **14**
OL10: H'ood	4C **14**
Heywood Rd. M25: Pres	4D **23**
M33: Sale	5D **89**
Heywood St. M8: Man	5C **38**
M27: Swin	4A **34**
M35: Fail	5F **41**
OL4: O'ham	1F **31**
Heywood Way M6: Sal	4B **50**
Heyworth St. M5: Sal	1A **64**
(off Bridson St.)	
Hibbert Av. M34: Dent	5A **72**
Hibbert Cres. M35: Fail	5C **42**
Hibbert St. M14: Man	2E **81**
SK4: Stoc	3A **96**
SK5: Stoc	3A **96**
Hibernia Way M32: Stre	5C **62**
Hidden Gem	
Manchester St Mary's Catholic Church	
	1A **10**
Higginshaw Rd.	
OL1: O'ham	1F **117** (1B **30**)
Higginson Rd. SK5: Stoc	1A **96**
Higgs Cl. OL4: O'ham	2F **31**
Higham Vw. M6: Sal	4C **50**
(off Broad St.)	
High Ash Gro. M34: Aud	3F **71**
High Bank M18: Man	5A **70**
M34: Dent	3D **85**
Highbank M27: Pen	5E **35**
High Bank Cres. M25: Pres	1E **37**
Highbank Dr. M20: Man	3D **103**
High Bank Gro. M25: Pres	1E **37**
High Bank Rd. BL9: Bury	3B **12**
M27: Pen	4D **35**
M43: Droy	2B **70**
High Bankside SK1: Stoc	2B **118** (2B **106**)
High Barn Rd. M24: Mid	2C **26**
Highbury SK4: Stoc	1B **104**
Highbury Av. M41: Urm	3A **74**
Highbury Ct. M25: Pres	4D **23**
Highbury Rd. M16: W Ran	4A **80**
SK4: Stoc	2E **95**
Highclere Av. M7: Sal	1B **52**
M8: Man	1B **52**
Highclere Rd. M8: Man	2B **38**
Highcliffe Rd. M9: Man	1C **38**
Highcrest Av. SK8: Gat	1B **110**
Highcroft Av. M20: Man	4A **92**
Highdales Rd. M23: Wyth	1D **109**
Highdown Wlk. M9: Man	4A **40**
(off Augustine Webster Cl.)	
High Elm Rd. WA15: Haleb	2A **112**
Higher Alt Hill OL6: A Lyme	3E **45**
Higher Ardwick M12: Man	3E **67**
Higher Barlow Row	
SK1: Stoc	4C **118** (3B **106**)
HIGHER BLACKLEY	5D **25**
HIGHER BOARSHAW	4E **17**
HIGHER BROUGHTON	1F **51**
Higher Bury St. SK4: Stoc	1F **105**
Higher Cambridge St.	
M15: Man	5C **10** (4C **66**)
Higher Chatham St.	
M15: Man	5C **10** (4C **66**)
Higher Cft. M30: Ecc	2E **61**
M45: White	3E **21**
HIGHER CRUMPSALL	3C **38**
Higher Fold M24: Mid	3D **17**
Higher Grn. OL6: A Lyme	3F **59**
Higher Henry St. SK14: Hyde	4F **87**
Higher Hillgate SK1: Stoc	4C **118** (3B **106**)
Higher Ho. Cl. OL9: Chad	5C **28**
Higher La. M45: White	1A **22**
Higher Lime Rd. OL8: O'ham	4E **43**
Higher Mkt. St. BL4: Farn	1A **18**
Higher Mdws. M19: Man	5E **83**
HIGHER OPENSHAW	3B **70**
Higher Ormond St. M15: Man	5D **11**
Higher Oswald St. M4: Man	3D **7**
(off Goadsby St.)	
Higher Rd. M41: Urm	3F **75**
HIGHER STAKE HILL	2F **17**
Higher Wharf St.	
OL7: A Lyme	4B **116** (5D **59**)
Higher Wood St. M24: Mid	5B **16**
(not continuous)	
Higher York St. M13: Man	4D **67**
Highfield M20: Man	1D **103**
M33: Sale	5E **89**
SK8: Chea	3E **111**
Highfield Av. M26: Rad	1E **21**
M33: Sale	5E **89**
Highfield Cl. M32: Stre	5E **77**
Highfield Ct. M25: Pres	4D **23**
Highfield Dr. M24: Mid	2B **26**
M27: Pen	5E **35**
M30: Ecc	3F **47**
M41: Urm	2E **75**
Highfield La. BL9: Bury	3B **12**
M45: White	3B **12**
Highfield Pk. SK4: Stoc	1B **104**
Highfield Pl. M18: Man	1B **84**
(off Debdale La.)	
Highfield Range M18: Man	1B **84**
Highfield Rd. M6: Sal	4B **50**
M19: Man	4E **83**
M25: Pres	3C **22**
M30: Ecc	3F **47**
M32: Stre	5E **77**

Highfield St. BL4: Kea 3C 18
   M8: Man .5B 38
   M24: Mid .1D 27
   M34: Aud .4B 72
   M34: Dent 5A 72
   OL9: O'ham 2F 29
                    (not continuous)
   SK3: Stoc .3E 105
   SK16: Duk 5C 116 (1D 73)
Highfield St. M16: SK16: Duk 1D 73
   OL7: A Lyme 5B 44
Highgate Av. M41: Urm 1C 74
Highgate Cres. M18: Man 2F 83
High Gates M33: Sale 3A 90
Highgrove M33: Sale 2C 98
Highgrove Ct. M9: Man 4C 24
High Gro. Rd. SK8: Chea 1E 111
High Hurst Cl. M24: Mid 1E 25
Highland Wlk. M40: Man 1F 55
High La. M21: Chor 5C 78
High Lea SK8: Chea 1E 111
High Lee Ho. M33: Sale 3F 89
                    (off Broad Rd.)
High Legh Rd. M11: Man 2F 69
High Mdw. M27: Swin 5D 35
Highmeadow M26: Rad 1B 20
Highmead St. M18: Man 5F 69
Highmead Wlk. M16: Old T 5F 65
                  (off Hamer Dr.)
Highmore Dr. M9: Man 1A 40
Highnam Wlk. M22: Wyth 5C 108
High Peak St. M40: Man 1D 55
Highshore Dr. M8: Man 5B 38
High Stile St. BL4: Kea 2A 18
Highstone Dr. M8: Man 1E 53
High St. M4: Man 5C 6 (1C 66)
   M24: Mid .4C 16
                    (not continuous)
   M43: Droy 1C 70
   OL1: O'ham 3E 117 (2B 30)
                    (not continuous)
   OL4: Lees 3F 31
   SK1: Stoc 2B 118 (2B 106)
   SK8: Chea 5F 103
   SK15: Stal 2F 73
Highgate Ho. OL8: O'ham 2F 43
                 (off Marple Cl.)
HIGHTOWN 5A 38
High Vw. M25: Pres 1D 37
Highview Wlk. M9: Man 1A 40
Highworth Dr. M40: Man 2F 41
Higson Av. M21: Chor 1D 91
   M30: Ecc .2E 61
Hilary Av. OL8: O'ham 3B 44
   SK8: H Grn 1F 115
Hilary Cl. SK4: Stoc 1F 105
Hilary Rd. M22: Wyth 5E 109
Hilbre Rd. M19: Man 5B 82
Hilbre Way SK9: Hand 5F 115
Hilbury Av. M9: Man 3F 39
Hilda Gro. SK5: Stoc 4B 96
Hilda Rd. SK14: Hyde 5F 87
Hilda St. OL9: O'ham 2F 29
                    (not continuous)
   SK5: Stoc .4B 96
Hilden Ct. M16: W Ran 1F 79
Hilditch Cl. M23: Wyth 5D 101
Hiley Rd. M30: Ecc 2B 60
Hillam Cl. M41: Urm 4B 76

Hillary Av. OL7: A Lyme 2D 59
Hillbank St. M24: Mid 1F 17
Hillbrook Av. M40: Man 2D 41
Hillbrook Rd. SK1: Stoc 3E 107
Hillbrow Wlk. M8: Man 5B 38
               (off Highshore Dr.)
Hill Cl. OL4: O'ham 4E 31
Hillcote Wlk. M18: Man 4D 69
                (off Marjorie Cl.)
Hillcourt St. M1: Man 5D 11 (3C 66)
Hill Cres. M9: Man 1C 38
Hillcrest M6: Sal 4C 48
   M24: Mid .3B 16
Hillcrest Av. SK4: Stoc 1C 104
Hillcrest Dr. M19: Man 1E 95
   M34: Dent 4D 87
Hillcrest Rd. M25: Pres 2B 36
   SK2: Stoc 5E 107
Hillcroft OL8: O'ham 3C 44
Hillcroft Cl. M8: Man 4C 38
Hilldale Av. M9: Man 5F 25
Hillel Ho. M15: Man 5C 66
Hillend Pl. M23: Wyth 1C 100
Hillend Rd. M23: Wyth 1C 100
Hill Farm Cl. OL8: O'ham 1C 44
Hillfield M5: Sal 1F 65
Hillfield Cl. M13: Man 5F 67
Hillfoot Wlk. M15: Man 4F 65
              (off Shawgreen Cl.)
Hillgate Av. M5: Sal 3D 65
Hillgate Bus. Cen. SK1: Stoc 5C 118
Hillgate St. OL6: A Lyme 3E 59
Hillhead Wlk. M8: Man 1C 52
              (off Barnsdale Dr.)
Hillier St. M9: Man 4A 40
Hillier St. Nth. M9: Man 4A 40
Hillingdon Cl. OL8: O'ham 4D 43
Hillingdon Dr. M9: Man 2D 41
Hillingdon Rd. M32: Stre 4A 78
   M45: White 2E 21
Hillington Rd. M33: Sale 4A 88
   SK3: Stoc 3E 105
Hillkirk St. M11: Man 1A 68
Hill La. M9: Man 1F 39
Hillman Cl. M40: Man 2F 53
Hillsborough Dr. BL9: Bury 4D 13
Hillside Av. M7: Sal 4C 36
   M45: White 4A 12
   OL4: O'ham 2E 31
Hillside Cl. M40: Man 3C 40
   M25: Pres 1C 36
Hillside Dr. M24: Mid 5D 17
   M27: Pen .1F 49
Hillside Rd. SK2: Stoc 5F 107
Hillside Vw. M34: Dent 5C 86
Hills La. BL9: Bury, White 4E 13
Hill St. M7: Sal 1F 51
                    (not continuous)
   M20: Man 1D 93
   M24: Mid .3C 16
   OL4: O'ham 2D 31
   OL7: A Lyme 4A 116 (5C 58)
   SK16: Duk 5C 116 (1D 73)
Hill Top Av. M25: Pres 5D 23
Hilltop Av. M9: Man 1F 39
   M45: White 1D 23
Hilltop Ct. M8: Man 2B 38
   M14: Man 4F 81
Hilltop Gro. M45: White 1D 23
Hill Top Rd. M28: Walk 5A 18

Hillview Rd. M34: Dent 4C 84
Hillwood Av. M8: Man 1B 38
Hilrose Av. M41: Urm 3B 76
Hilson Ct. M43: Droy 1C 70
Hilton Arc. OL1: O'ham 3E 117
Hilton Av. M41: Urm 3F 75
Hilton Ct. SK3: Stoc 3A 106
Hilton Cres. M25: Pres 2D 37
   OL6: A Lyme 2E 59
Hilton Dr. M25: Pres 2D 37
Hilton Fold La. M24: Mid 5D 17
Hilton Ho. SK1: Stoc . . . 3B 118 (2B 106)
Hilton La. M25: Pres 3B 36
Hilton Lodge M25: Pres 2D 37
HILTON PARK 2D 37
Hilton Rd. M22: Shar 1A 110
Hiltons Cl. OL8: O'ham 4A 30
Hiltons Farm Cl. M34: Aud 4A 72
Hilton Sq. M27: Pen 4C 34
Hilton St. M1: Man 5E 7 (1D 67)
   M4: Man 4D 7 (5C 52)
   M7: Sal 1F 51
   M24: Mid 4B 16
   OL1: O'ham 1E 31
   SK3: Stoc 3F 105
Hilton St. Nth. M7: Sal 1F 51
Hilton Wlk. M24: Mid 1E 25
Himley Rd. M11: Man 4E 55
Hincaster Wlk. M18: Man 5E 69
                  (off Hampden Cres.)
Hinchley Rd. M9: Man 2D 41
Hinchley Way M27: Pen 2B 34
Hinckley St. M11: Man 2B 68
Hindburn Cl. M45: White 5D 13
Hindburn Wlk. M45: White 5D 13
Hinde St. M40: Man 4C 40
Hindhead Wlk. M40: Man 3F 55
                  (off Thaxmead Dr.)
Hindley Av. M22: Wyth 4D 109
Hindley Cl. OL7: A Lyme 1B 72
Hindley Cl. OL7: A Lyme 1B 72
                  (not continuous)
   SK1: Stoc 5C 118 (3B 106)
Hindsford Cl. M23: Wyth 2F 99
Hinstock Cres. M18: Man 5F 69
Hinton M. SK1: Stoc 2D 107
Hinton St. M4: Man 2F 7 (4D 53)
   OL8: O'ham 5E 117 (4B 30)
Hitchen St. M13: Man 5E 67
Hives, The M17: T Pk 3D 63
Hive St. OL8: O'ham 2D 43
HMP Forest Bank M27: Pen 3A 36
HMP Manchester
   M3: Man 1A 6 (3B 52)
Hobart St. M18: Man 5F 69
Hobson Ct. M34: Aud 4A 72
Hobson Cres. M34: Aud 4A 72
Hobson St. M11: Man 3C 70
   M35: Fail 1E 55
   OL1: O'ham 4E 117 (3B 30)
   SK5: Stoc 3B 84
Hockenhull Cl. M22: Wyth 4A 110
Hockerley Cl. M33: Sale 3A 88
Hockley Rd. M23: Wyth 1B 108
Hodder Bank SK2: Stoc 5F 107
Hodder Way M45: White 1E 13
                  (not continuous)
Hoddesdon St. M8: Man 5D 39
Hodge La. M5: Sal 1B 64
Hodge Rd. M28: Walk 2A 32

Hodge St. M9: Man 3B 40
Hodgson Dr. WA15: Tim 3C 98
Hodgson St. M8: Man 2B 52
   OL6: A Lyme 4A 116 (5C 58)
Hodnett Av. M41: Urm 4A 74
Hodnet Wlk. M34: Dent 4A 86
Hodson Fold OL8: O'ham 3C 44
Hodson Rd. M27: Swin 2A 34
Hodson St. M3: Sal 3E 5 (5A 52)
Hogarth Wlk. M8: Man 1E 53
                  (off Smeaton St.)
Hoggs Bri. Cl. M27: Pen 4F 35
Holbeck Gro. M14: Man 1A 82
Holbeton Cl. M8: Man 2A 52
Holborn Av. M35: Fail 5D 43
Holborn Dr. M8: Man 2D 53
Holbrook St. M1: Man 3D 11
Holcombe Ct. BL4: Kea 3C 18
   M6: Sal 5C 50
Holcombe Cres. BL4: Kea 3C 18
Holcombe Gdns. M19: Man 3A 94
Holcombe Rd. M14: Man 1A 94
Holcombe Wlk. SK4: Stoc 1F 95
Holden Av. M16: W Ran 4A 80
Holden Clough Dr.
   OL7: A Lyme 5C 44
Holden Gallery 5D 11
Holden St. OL6: A Lyme 3E 59
                  (not continuous)
   OL8: O'ham 1B 44
Holdgate Cl. M15: Man 5A 66
Holdsworth St. M27: Swin 5F 33
Holebottom OL6: A Lyme 1E 59
Holford Av. M14: Man 3D 81
Holford Ct. M34: Dent 2B 86
Holker Cl. M13: Man 5F 67
Holker Way M34: Dent 4C 86
                  (off Two Trees La.)
Holkham Cl. M4: Man 5E 53
Holland Ct. M8: Man 2B 38
   SK1: Stoc 4C 106
Holland Gro. OL6: A Lyme 1D 59
Holland Rd. M8: Man 2B 38
Holland St. M6: Sal 2C 50
   M34: Dent 1F 85
   M40: Man 5F 53
Holland St. E. M34: Dent 1F 85
Holland Wlk. M34: Dent 1F 85
Holland Wlk. M6: Sal 2C 50
Hollies, The M6: Sal 4D 49
   M20: Man 5B 92
   M27: Swin 5D 35
                  (Manchester Rd.)
   M27: Swin 1F 47
                  (Moorfield Cl.)
   OL8: O'ham 5F 29
   SK4: Stoc 5D 95
   SK8: Gat 1D 111
Hollies Cl. M33: Sale 4D 89
Hollin Bank SK4: Stoc 1F 95
Hollinhey Rd. M22: Wyth 5B 110
Hollingworth Av.
   M40: Man 2B 42
Hollingworth Cl. SK1: Stoc 4B 118
Hollingworth Cl. OL9: Chad 1D 43
Hollinhall St. OL4: O'ham 2E 31
Hollin Ho. M24: Mid 3C 16
Hollin La. M24: Mid 1A 16
   SK9: Sty 3B 114

HOLLINS
BL9 .1C 12
M24 .3C 16
OL8 .1E 43
Hollins Brook Cl. BL9: Bury 1D 13
Hollins Brook Way BL9: Bury 1D 13
Hollins Brow BL9: Bury 2B 12
Hollins Cl. BL9: Bury 2D 13
Hollinsclough Cl. M22: Shar 1A 110
Hollinscroft Av. WA15: Tim 5F 99
Hollins Dr. M24: Mid 2A 16
HOLLINS GREEN 2A 44
Hollins Grn. M24: Mid 3C 16
Hollins Gro. M12: Man 2C 82
M33: Sale 4C 88
Hollinshead M7: Sal 1A 52
(off Wilmur Av.)
Hollins La. BL9: Bury 1C 12
Hollins M. BL9: Bury 2E 13
Hollins Rd. OL8: O'ham 1E 43
Hollins Sq. BL9: Bury 3D 13
HOLLINS VALE 1C 12
Hollins Wlk. M22: Wyth 4F 109
Hollin Well Cl. M24: Mid 2B 16
HOLLINWOOD 2E 43
Hollinwood Av. M40: Man 1F 41
OL9: Chad 1F 41
Hollinwood Bus. Cen. OL8: O'ham . .3D 43
Hollinwood Station (Rail) 2C 42
Holloway Dr. M28: Ward 3E 33
Hollow End SK5: Stoc 1D 97
Hollow End Towers SK5: Stoc 1D 97
Hollowgate M27: Swin 1E 47
Hollow Mdws. M26: Rad 3E 19
Hollows, The SK8: H Grn 5E 111
Hollows Av. M21: Chor 3E 91
Hollows Dr. SK14: Hyde 3F 87
(off Ridling La.)
Hollow Va. Dr. SK5: Stoc 4B 84
Holly Av. M28: Walk 2A 32
M41: Urm 3D 75
SK8: Chea 1F 111
Holly Bank M33: Sale 5E 89
M40: Man 5E 41
OL6: A Lyme 5F 59
Hollybank M43: Droy 4E 57
Holly Bank Cl. M15: Man 4E 65
Hollybush St. M18: Man 4A 70
Holly Cl. WA15: Tim 5C 98
Holly Ct. M20: Man 2D 93
SK3: Stoc 5A 106
Hollycroft Av. M22: Wyth 5F 101
Holly Dr. M33: Sale 4C 88
Hollyedge Dr. M25: Pres 2C 36
Holly Fold M45: White 5B 12
Hollygate, The SK3: Stoc 2F 105
(off Chestergate)
Holly Gro. M33: Sale 4F 89
M34: Dent 2C 86
OL9: Chad 1D 29
Hollyhedge Av. M22: Wyth 1F 109
Hollyhedge Ct. M22: Shar 1A 110
Hollyhedge Ct. Rd. M22: Shar 1A 110
Hollyhedge Rd. M22: Shar, Wyth . . .1E 109
M23: Wyth 1B 108
Hollyhey Dr. M23: Wyth 2E 101
Holly Ho. Dr. M41: Urm 3B 74
Hollyhurst M28: Wors 1D 47
Holly La. OL8: O'ham 2E 43
SK9: Sty 5A 114

Hollymount M16: Old T 1D 79
Hollymount Av. SK2: Stoc 5E 107
Hollymount Dr. SK2: Stoc 5E 107
Hollymount Gdns. SK2: Stoc 5E 107
Hollymount Rd. SK2: Stoc 5E 107
Holly Rd. M27: Swin 1F 47
SK4: Stoc 3E 95
Holly Royde Cl. M20: Man 2D 93
Holly St. M11: Man 2A 68
M43: Droy 5F 55
SK1: Stoc 2C 106
Holly Vw. M22: Shar 2A 110
Hollyway M22: Nor 3A 102
Hollywood Bowl
Ashton-under-Lyne 4B 58
Hollywood Towers SK3: Stoc 3F 105
(off Hardman St.)
Hollywood Way SK4: Stoc 2F 105
Holm Ct. M6: Sal 5C 50
(off Mulberry Rd.)
Holmcroft Rd. M18: Man 2F 83
Holmdale Av. M19: Man 3A 94
Holmdale Ct. M33: Sale 4E 89
Holmebrook Wlk. M8: Man 1C 52
(off Heywood St.)
Holmefield M33: Sale 4D 89
Holme Pk. Way M35: Fail 5D 43
Holme Rd. M20: Man 5B 92
Holmes St. SK1: Stoc 3C 118
Holmes St. SK2: Stoc 4A 106
SK8: Chea 5A 104
Holme St. SK14: Hyde 3F 87
Holmes Way M34: Dent 5B 86
Holmfield Av. M9: Man 5B 40
M25: Pres 1E 37
Holmfield Av. W. M9: Man 5B 40
Holmfield Cl. M9: Man 5F 95
Holmfirth St. M13: Man 1B 82
Holmfoot Wlk. M9: Man 5F 39
(off Foleshill Av.)
Holmlea Rd. M43: Droy 5A 56
Holmleigh Av. M9: Man 3A 40
Holmpark Rd. M11: Man 3B 70
Holmside Gdns. M19: Man 4A 94
Holmwood Ct. M20: Man 4D 93
Holmwood Rd. M20: Man 3D 93
Holroyd St. M11: Man 2C 68
Holst Av. M8: Man 1C 52
Holstein St. M13: Man 5F 67
Holtby St. M9: Man 3A 40
Holt La. M35: Fail 5D 43
HOLT LANE END 5D 43
Holt La. M. M35: Fail 5D 43
HOLTS .5F 31
Holts La. OL4: O'ham 5F 31
SK9: Sty 5B 114
(not continuous)
Holt St. M27: Clif 2B 34
M30: Ecc 2E 61
M34: Aud 2A 72
M40: Man 2B 54
OL4: O'ham 5F 31
SK1: Stoc 5C 118 (3B 106)
HOLT TOWN 5A 54
Holt Town M40: Man 5F 53
Holt Town Ind. Est. M11: Man 5A 54
Holtwood Wlk. SK5: Stoc 1E 97
Holway Wlk. M9: Man 5E 39
(off Hendham Va.)
Holwick Rd. M23: Wyth 1B 100

Holwood Dr. M16: W Ran 5A 80	Hope Rd. M33: Sale 5D 89
Holybourne Wlk. M23: Wyth 3F 99	Hopes Carr SK1: Stoc 3C 118 (2B 106)
Holyoake Rd. M28: Walk 2A 32	Hope St. BL4: Farn 1A 18
Holyoake St. M43: Droy 5E 57	M1: Man 1D 11 (1C 66)
Holyoak St. M40: Man 1E 55	M5: Sal 5A 4 (1E 65)
Holyrood Cl. M25: Pres 3E 23	M7: Sal 5F 37
Holyrood Ct. M25: Pres 3D 23	M27: Pen .4C 34
Holyrood Dr. M25: Pres 3E 23	M27: Swin 5F 33
M27: Swin 5F 33	M30: Ecc .5B 48
Holyrood Gro. M25: Pres 3E 23	M34: Aud .5A 72
Holyrood Rd. M25: Pres 4E 23	OL1: O'ham 2D 31
Holyrood St. M40: Man 3A 56	OL6: A Lyme 3F 59
OL1: O'ham 1C 30	SK4: Stoc 2F 105
Holywood St. M14: Man 2D 81	SK16: Duk 2D 73
Homebeck Ho. SK8: Gat 1C 110	(not continuous)
Homebury Dr. M11: Man 5D 55	Hope Ter. SK3: Stoc 5A 118 (3A 106)
Home Dr. M24: Mid 2B 26	SK16: Duk 2D 73
Home Front Mus. (by appointment only)	(off Hope St.)
. . . . .3E 89	Hopgarth Wlk. M40: Man 2F 55
(off Broad Rd.)	(off Terence St.)
Homelands Cl. M33: Sale 1B 98	Hopkin Av. OL1: O'ham 1D 31
Homelands Rd. M33: Sale 1B 98	Hopkinson Av. M34: Dent 5F 71
Homelands Wlk. M9: Man 5F 39	Hopkinson Rd. M9: Man 4F 25
(off Shiredale Dr.)	Hopkins St. M12: Man 2C 82
Homelaurel Ho. M33: Sale 1D 99	Hopkin St. OL1: O'ham 3F 117 (2B 30)
Homerton Rd. M40: Man 3D 55	Hoppet La. M43: Droy 5E 57
Homestead, The M33: Sale 3B 88	Hopton Av. M22: Wyth 3A 110
Homestead Cres. M19: Man 5F 93	Hopton Ct. M15: Man 4C 66
Homewood Av. M22: Nor 2F 101	(off Booth St. W.)
Homewood Rd. M22: Nor 2E 101	Hopwood Av. M30: Ecc 4F 47
Honduras St. OL4: O'ham 2D 31	Hopwood Cl. BL9: Bury 3B 12
Honeycombe Cotts. SK8: Chea 1F 111	Hopwood Ct. M24: Mid 2C 16
(off Oak Rd.)	Hopwood Rd. M24: Mid 2C 16
Honey St. M8: Man 1D 7 (3D 53)	Hopwood St. M27: Pen 4C 34
Honeysuckle Cl. M23: Wyth 2F 99	M40: Man 1D 55
Honeywell La. OL8: O'ham 1B 44	Horace Barnes Cl.
Honford Rd. M22: Wyth 2E 109	M14: Man 2C 80
Hong Kong Av. M90: Man A 1C 112	Horace Gro. SK4: Stoc 4A 96
Honister Dr. M24: Mid 4B 16	Horatio St. M18: Man 4B 70
Honister Rd. M9: Man 5B 40	Horbury Av. M18: Man 2F 83
Honiton Cl. OL9: Chad 1A 28	Horlock Ct. M5: Sal 2A 4 (4D 51)
Honiton Ho. M6: Sal 4C 48	Hornbeam Cl. WA15: Tim 1A 108
(off Devon Cl.)	Hornbeam Ct. M6: Sal 4C 50
Honor St. M13: Man 2B 82	Hornbeam Rd. M19: Man 3D 83
Honsham Wlk. M23: Wyth 2A 100	Hornbeam Way M4: Man 1C 6 (4C 52)
Hood St. M4: Man 4F 7 (5D 53)	Hornby Av. M9: Man 4A 26
Hood Wlk. M34: Dent 5C 86	Hornby Lodge M25: Pres 1D 37
HOOLEY HILL 3B 72	(off Prestwich Pk. Rd. Sth.)
Hooley Range SK4: Stoc 5D 95	Hornby Rd. M32: Stre 1B 78
Hooper St. M12: Man 2F 67	Hornby St. M8: Man 1A 6 (3B 52)
OL4: O'ham 3C 30	M24: Mid 1C 26
SK1: Stoc 3A 118 (2A 106)	OL8: O'ham 4F 29
Hooton St. M40: Man 4B 54	Horncastle Rd. M40: Man 2D 41
Hooton Way SK9: Hand 4F 115	Hornchurch Ct. M15: Man 4B 66
(off Beeston Rd.)	(off Bonsall St.)
Hopcroft Cl. M9: Man 3D 25	Hornchurch Ho. SK2: Stoc 5C 106
Hope Av. M32: Stre 2D 77	Hornchurch St. M15: Man 4A 66
SK9: Hand 5E 115	Horniman Ho. M13: Man 5D 67
Hope Chapel OL6: A Lyme 3F 59	Hornsea Cl. OL9: Chad 1B 28
(off Curzon Rd.)	Hornsea Wlk. M11: Man 1C 68
Hopecourt Cl. M6: Sal 3E 49	(off Grey Mare La.)
Hope Cres. M6: Sal 4E 49	Horsedge St. OL1: O'ham 1E 117 (1D 30)
Hopedale Cl. M11: Man 1B 68	Horsefield Av. M21: Chor 1A 92
Hopedale Rd. SK5: Stoc 2B 96	Horseshoe La. M24: Mid 3B 28
Hopefold Dr. M28: Walk 4A 32	Horsham St. M6: Sal 5A 50
Hopelea St. M20: Man 1D 93	Horstead Wlk. M19: Man 3C 82
Hope Pk. Cl. M25: Pres 1D 37	(off Deepcar St.)
Hope Pk. Rd. M25: Pres 1D 37	Horticultural Cen. in Wythenshawe Pk.
Hope Rd. M14: Man 1F 81	. . . . .3B 100
M25: Pres 2C 36	Horton Rd. M14: Man 3C 80

Horton St. SK1: Stoc 4C 106
Hortree Rd. M32: Stre 3A 78
Horwood Cres. M20: Man 3F 93
Hoscar Dr. M19: Man 1B 94
Hoskins Cl. M12: Man 5C 68
Hospital Av. M30: Ecc 5A 48
Hospital Rd. M23: Wyth 1A 108
   M27: Pen 5D 35
Hotel Rd. M90: Man A 2E 113
Hothersall Rd. SK5: Stoc 1B 96
Hothersall St. M7: Sal 1E 5
Hotspur Cl. M14: Man 5C 80
Hough Cl. OL8: O'ham 2C 44
Hough End Av. M21: Chor 2E 91
Hough End Cen., The
   M21: Chor 1A 92
Houghend Cres. M21: Chor 1A 92
Hough Hall Rd. M40: Man 4B 40
Hough Rd. M20: Man 1C 92
Houghton Av. OL8: O'ham 2F 43
Houghton La. M27: Swin 2F 47
Houghton Rd. M8: Man 3C 38
Houghton St. M27: Pen 1F 49
Hough Wlk. M7: Sal 1B 4 (4E 51)
   (not continuous)
Houldsworth Av. WA14: Tim 4A 98
Houldsworth Sq. SK5: Stoc 1A 96
Houldsworth St. M1: Man 4E 7 (5D 53)
   SK5: Stoc 1A 96
Houseley Av. OL9: Chad 1C 42
Houson St. OL8: O'ham 5E 117 (4B 30)
Houston Pk. M50: Sal 1B 64
Hoveden St. M8: Man 3B 52
Hove Dr. M14: Man 1A 94
Hovey Cl. M8: Man 5B 38
Hoviley SK14: Hyde 2F 87
Hovington Gdns. M19: Man 2A 94
Hovis St. M11: Man 2E 69
Howard Av. BL4: Kea 2B 18
   M30: Ecc 4F 47
   SK4: Stoc 2E 95
Howard Cl. OL6: A Lyme 4E 59
Howard Hill BL9: Bury 1C 12
Howardian Cl. OL8: O'ham 1A 44
Howard La. M34: Dent 1B 86
Howard Pl. SK14: Hyde 3F 87
   (off Rutherford Way)
Howard Rd. M22: Nor 2F 101
Howard Spring Wlk. M8: Man 4B 38
   (off Absalom Dr.)
Howard St. M5: Sal 2C 64
   M8: Man 3B 52
   M32: Stre 3F 77
   M34: Aud 4B 72
   M34: Dent 5A 72
   OL4: O'ham 1F 31
   OL7: A Lyme 1A 116 (3C 58)
   SK1: Stoc 1B 118 (1B 106)
Howarth Av. M28: Wors 5E 33
Howarth Cl. M11: Man 1C 68
Howarth St. M16: Old T 1E 79
Howbro Dr. OL7: A Lyme 2A 58
Howbrook Wlk. M15: Man 4B 66
   (off Brindle Pl.)
Howclough Cl. M28: Walk 2B 32
How Clough Dr. M28: Walk 2B 32
Howden Cl. SK5: Stoc 3A 84
   (not continuous)
Howden Rd. M9: Man 4E 25
Howells Av. M33: Sale 3D 89

Howe St. M7: Sal 5E 37
   OL7: A Lyme 2B 72
Howgill Cres. OL8: O'ham 1A 44
Howgill St. M11: Man 1F 69
Howton Cl. M12: Man 1C 82
Hoy Dr. M41: Urm 5F 61
Hoylake Cl. M40: Man 4F 41
Hoylake Rd. M33: Sale 1B 100
   SK3: Stoc 3C 104
Hoyland Cl. M12: Man 4B 68
Hoyle Av. OL8: O'ham 4A 30
Hoyle St. M12: Man 2E 67
   M24: Mid 3E 27
Hoyle St. Ind. Est. M12: Man 3E 67
   (off Hoyle St.)
Hoyle Wlk. M13: Man 4E 67
   (off Glenbarry Cl.)
Hucclecote Av. M22: Wyth 4E 109
Hucklow Av. M23: Wyth 4C 108
Huddart Cl. M5: Sal 3A 8 (2D 65)
Huddersfield Rd. OL1: O'ham 2D 31
   OL4: Lees, O'ham 2D 31
Hudson Ct. M9: Man 1E 39
Hudson Rd. SK14: Hyde 5F 87
Hudson St. OL9: Chad 3C 42
Hudswell Cl. M45: White 1A 22
Hughes Av. M35: Fail 4A 42
Hughes St. M11: Man 2A 68
Hughes Way M30: Ecc 1C 60
Hugh Oldham Dr. M7: Sal 1E 51
Hugo St. M40: Man 5C 40
Hulbert St. M24: Mid 5D 17
Hull Sq. M3: Sal 3C 4 (5F 51)
HULME 4B 66
Hulme Ct. M15: Man 5E 9
Hulme Dr. WA15: Tim 4E 99
Hulme Hall La. M40: Man 3A 54
Hulme Hall M14: Man 1E 81
Hulme Hall Rd. M15: Man 5C 8 (3F 65)
Hulme High St. M15: Man 5B 66
Hulme Mkt. Hall M15: Man 5B 66
Hulme Pl. M5: Sal 5B 4 (1E 65)
Hulme Rd. M26: Rad 2E 19
   M33: Sale 5F 89
   M34: Dent 2D 85
   SK4: Stoc 2F 95
Hulme's La. M34: Dent 5A 86
Hulmes Rd. M35: Fail 3B 56
   M40: Man 3A 56
   (not continuous)
Hulme St. M1: Man 5A 10 (3B 66)
   M5: Sal 5B 4 (1E 65)
   M15: Man 5B 10 (3B 66)
   (Cambridge St.)
   M15: Man 5F 9 (3A 66)
   (Jackson Cres.)
   OL6: A Lyme 3F 59
   OL8: O'ham 5A 30
   SK1: Stoc 4D 107
Hulmeswood Ter. M34: Dent 5C 86
   (off Tennyson Av.)
Hulme Wlk. M15: Man 4B 66
   (off Stretford Rd.)
Hulton St. M5: Sal 3C 64
   M16: W Ran 1A 80
   M34: Dent 1A 86
   M35: Fail 5F 41
Humberstone Av. M15: Man 5F 9 (4B 66)
Humber St. M8: Man 5D 39
   M50: Sal 1F 63

Hume St. M19: Man 5D 83
Humphrey Booth Gdns. M6: Sal 4A 50
Humphrey Cres. M41: Urm 3C 76
Humphrey La. M41: Urm 3C 76
Humphrey Pk. M41: Urm 3C 76
Humphrey Park Station (Rail) 2C 76
Humphrey Rd. M16: Old T 5D 65
Humphrey St. M8: Man 4B 38
Humphries Ct. M40: Man 3E 53
Huncoat Av. SK4: Stoc 3F 95
Huncote Dr. M9: Man 3A 40
(off Hemsley St. Sth.)
Hungerford Wlk. M23: Wyth 4F 99
(off Butcher La.)
Hunmanby Av. M15: Man 5A 10 (3B 66)
Hunston Rd. M33: Sale 5B 88
Hunt Av. OL7: A Lyme 2D 59
Hunters Hill BL9: Bury 2D 13
Hunters La. OL1: O'ham 3F 117 (2B 30)
Hunters M. M33: Sale 3C 88
Hunterston Av. M30: Ecc 5C 48
Hunters Vw. SK9: Hand 5E 115
Huntingdon Av. OL9: Chad 4D 29
Huntingdon Cres. SK5: Stoc 3E 97
Huntingdon Way M34: Dent 4B 86
Huntington Av. M20: Man 1C 92
Hunt La. OL9: Chad 1B 28
Huntley Rd. M8: Man 2A 38
SK3: Stoc 4D 105
Hunt's Bank M3: Man 3B 6 (5B 52)
Huntsman Rd. M9: Man 4B 40
Hunts Rd. M6: Sal 2F 49
Hunt St. M9: Man 3F 39
Hurdlow Av. M7: Sal 5C 36
Hurdlow Wlk. M9: Man 5F 39
Hurford Av. M18: Man 4F 69
Hurlbote Cl. SK9: Hand 4F 115
HURST 2F 59
Hurstbank Av. M19: Man 4F 93
Hurst Bank Rd. OL6: A Lyme 3F 59
Hurstbourne Av. M11: Man 4D 55
HURST BROOK 3E 59
Hurst Brook Cl. OL6: A Lyme 3E 59
Hurstbrook Dr. M32: Stre 3B 76
Hurst Ct. M23: Wyth 2B 108
OL6: A Lyme 2F 59
Hurst Cross OL6: A Lyme 2F 59
Hurstead Ct. M8: Man 1C 52
Hurstfield Ind. Est.
SK5: Stoc 2A 96
Hurstfold Av. M19: Man 5F 93
Hurst Gro. OL6: A Lyme 2F 59
Hurst Hall OL6: A Lyme 2F 59
Hursthead Wlk. M13: Man 5F 11
Hurst Hill Cres. OL6: A Lyme 2F 59
HURST KNOLL 3F 59
Hurst Mdw. OL6: A Lyme 2F 59
Hurstmead Ter. M20: Man 1D 103
(off South Rd.)
HURST NOOK 1F 59
Hurst St. OL9: O'ham 2F 29
SK5: Stoc 1A 96
Hurstvale Av. SK8: H Grn 5D 111
Hurstville Rd. M21: Chor 2D 91
Hurst Wlk. M22: Wyth 4C 108
Hurstway Dr. M9: Man 1A 40
Hurstwood Cl. OL8: O'ham 5E 31
Hus St. M43: Droy 2B 70
Hutchins La. OL4: O'ham 1F 31
Hutton Av. OL6: A Lyme 5F 59

Hutton Lodge M20: Man 1E 93
(off Wilmslow Rd.)
Hutton Wlk. M13: Man 4E 67
(off Glenbarry Cl.)
Huxley Av. M8: Man 1C 52
Huxley St. OL4: O'ham 4E 31
Ilford St. M11: Man 5D 55
HYDE 3F 87
HYDE, THE 4D 115
Hyde Central Station (Rail) 3E 87
Hyde Festival Theatre 3F 87
Hyde Fold Cl. M19: Man 2B 94
Hyde Gro. M13: Man 5E 67
M33: Sale 4D 89
Hyde Ho. SK4: Stoc 3E 95
Hyde North Station (Rail) 5E 73
Hyde Pl. M13: Man 5E 67
Hyde Point SK14: Hyde 1E 87
Hyde Rd. M12: Man 3E 67
M24: Mid 3A 28
M34: Dent 1B 86
Hyde's Cross M4: Man 3C 6
Hyde Sq. M24: Mid 5A 16
Hyde St. M43: Droy 3E 57
SK16: Duk 4C 36
Hydra Cl. M7: Sal 1B 4 (4E 51)
Hyldavale Av. SK8: Gat 5D 103
Hylton Dr. OL7: A Lyme 2B 58
Hyman Goldstone Wlk. M8: Man 5B 38
(off Carstairs Cl.)
Hyndman Ct. M5: Sal 5F 49
(off Sheader Dr.)
Hythe Cl. M14: Man 2E 81
Hythe Rd. SK3: Stoc 3D 105
Hythe Wlk. OL9: Chad 3D 29

I

Ibberton Wlk. M9: Man 3B 40
(off Carnaby St.)
Iceland St. M6: Sal 5A 50
Ifco Cen. M14: Man 2E 81
Ilex Gro. M7: Man 1F 51
Ilford St. M11: Man 5D 55
Ilfracombe Rd. SK2: Stoc 3F 107
Ilfracombe St. M40: Man 1F 55
Ilkeston Wlk. M34: Dent 5C 86
M40: Man 1C 54
(off Halliford Rd.)
Ilkley Cl. OL9: Chad 3D 29
Ilkley Cres. SK5: Stoc 5A 84
Ilkley Dr. M41: Urm 1C 74
Ilkley St. M40: Man 3C 40
Ilk St. M11: Man 5D 55
Illona Dr. M7: Sal 4C 36
Ilminster Wlk. M9: Man 4A 26
(off Crossmead Dr.)
Ilthorpe Wlk. M40: Man 1C 54
Imax Cinema
Manchester 3C 6
(within The Printworks)
Imex Bus. Pk. M13: Man 2B 82
Imogen Ct. M5: Sal 3B 8 (2E 65)
Imperial Point M50: Sal 3B 64
Imperial Ter. M33: Sale 2C 88
(off Woodfield Gro.)
Imperial War Mus. North 3A 64
Ince Cl. M20: Man 1D 93
SK4: Stoc 5A 96
Ince St. SK4: Stoc 5A 96

Inchcape Dr. M9: Man 5D 25
Inchfield Rd. M40: Man 3C 40
Inchley Rd. M13: Man 5E 11 (3D 67)
Incline Rd. OL8: O'ham 2D 43
Independent Ho. SK8: Chea 3E 111
India Ho. M1: Man 3C 10 (2C 66)
Indigo St. M6: Sal 2B 50
Indigo St. M6: Sal 2B 50
Indus Pl. M7: Sal 1B 4 (3E 51)
Infant St. M25: Pres 5E 23
Ingham Rd. WA14: W Tim 3A 98
Ingham St. M40: Man 3A 56
    OL1: O'ham 2C 30
Inghamwood Cl. M7: Sal 5B 38
Ingleby Av. M9: Man 5B 26
Ingleby Ct. M32: Stre 4A 78
Ingledene Av. M7: Sal 3A 38
Ingledene Ct. M7: Sal 3A 38
Ingle Dr. SK2: Stoc 4E 107
Inglehead Cl. M34: Dent 3C 86
Ingle Rd. SK8: Chea 5C 104
Inglesham Cl. M23: Wyth 5D 101
Ingleton Av. M8: Man 2D 39
Ingleton Cl. SK8: Chea 5E 103
Ingleton Rd. SK3: Stoc 4E 105
Inglewood Cl. OL7: A Lyme 2B 58
Inglewood Rd. OL9: Chad 5F 17
Inglewood Wlk. M13: Man 5F 11
Ingoldsby Av. M13: Man 1F 81
Ingram Dr. SK4: Stoc 5A 94
Inkerman St. M40: Man 1F 53
    SK14: Hyde 1F 87
Inman St. M34: Dent 2B 86
Innes St. M12: Man 2D 83
Innis Av. M40: Man 2E 55
Institute of Gymnastics 5E 69
Instow Cl. OL9: Chad 1B 28
International App. M90: Man A 2E 113
Invar Rd. M27: Swin 3F 33
Invergarry Wlk. M11: Man 1E 69
                                    (off Bob Massey Cl.)
Inverness Av. M9: Man 5C 26
Inverness Rd. SK16: Duk 3E 73
Inver Wlk. M40: Man 2F 41
Inwood Wlk. M8: Man 1E 53
                                    (off Smedley Rd.)
Inworth Wlk. M8: Man 5B 38
                                    (off Highshore Rd.)
Iona Way M41: Urm 5F 61
Ionian Gdns. M7: Sal 2E 51
Ipswich Wlk. M12: Man 5A 68
                                    (off Chipstead Av.)
    M34: Dent 4C 86
                                    (off Lancaster Rd.)
Iqbal Cl. M12: Man 5C 68
Ireby Cl. M24: Mid 4E 15
Iredine St. M11: Man 1E 69
Irene Av. SK14: Hyde 1F 87
Iris Av. BL4: Kea 4B 18
                                    (not continuous)
    M11: Man 2F 69
Iris St. OL8: O'ham 2B 44
Irkdale St. M8: Man 1E 53
Irk St. M4: Man 1D 7 (4C 52)
Irk Va. Dr. OL1: Chad 5F 17
Irk Way M45: White 4D 13
Irlam Av. M30: Ecc 1F 61
Irlam Rd. M33: Sale 3E 89
    M41: Urm 3A 74
IRLAMS O'TH' HEIGHT 1E 49

Irlam Sq. M6: Sal 2F 49
Irlam St. M40: Man 2A 54
Irmass Ind. Est. M17: T Pk 4F 63
Iron St. M40: Man 4A 54
Irvin Dr. M22: Wyth 1C 114
Irving St. OL8: O'ham 2D 43
Irvin St. M40: Man 1E 55
Irwell Av. M30: Ecc 1B 62
Irwell Gro. M30: Ecc 1B 62
Irwell Ho. M15: Man 4D 9
Irwell Pk. Way M30: Ecc 1B 62
Irwell Pl. M5: Sal 4A 4 (5E 51)
    M26: Rad 1D 19
    M30: Ecc 1B 62
Irwell Sq. M3: Man 5E 5 (1A 66)
Irwell St. M3: Man 5E 5 (1A 66)
    M6: Sal .1C 50
    M8: Man 1F 5 (3A 52)
    M26: Rad 1C 18
Irwell Wlk. OL8: O'ham 1E 43
Irwin Dr. SK9: Hand 4E 115
Irwin St. M34: Dent 2A 86
Isaac Cl. M5: Sal 2C 64
Isaac Way M4: Man 1F 67
Isabella Cl. M16: Old T 1E 79
Isaiah St. OL8: O'ham 5B 30
Isca St. M11: Man 1B 68
Isel Wlk. M24: Mid 4F 15
Isis Cl. M7: Sal 4B 36
Islington St. M3: Sal 4D 5 (1F 65)
Islington Way M3: Sal 5C 4 (1F 65)
Isobel Baillie Lodge M16: Old T 5F 65
                                    (off Whitchurch Dr.)
Isobel Cl. M16: W Ran 1B 80
                                    (off Crosshill St.)
    M30: Ecc 1D 61
Ivanhoe St. OL1: O'ham 1E 31
Iver Ho. M5: Sal 1B 64
                                    (off Amersham St.)
Ivybridge Cl. M13: Man 5F 67
Ivy Cl. M43: Droy 4B 56
Ivy Cotts. M34: Dent 5C 86
Ivy Ct. M21: Chor 1D 91
Ivy Dr. M24: Mid 2B 26
Ivygreen Rd. M21: Chor 5B 78
Ivy Gro. BL4: Kea 2B 18
Ivy Leaf Sq. M7: Sal 1A 52
Ivylea Rd. M19: Man 4A 94
Ivy St. M30: Ecc 1F 61
    M40: Man 4C 40

J

Jack Brady Cl. M23: Wyth 2A 108
Jackie Brown Wlk. M40: Man 2F 53
                                    (off Thornton St. Nth.)
Jack La. M41: Urm 3A 76
    M43: Droy 5D 57
                                    (not continuous)
Jackson Av. SK16: Duk 2F 73
Jackson Cl. OL8: O'ham 4A 30
    WA15: Tim 4E 99
Jackson Ct. M21: Chor 4B 78
    M41: Urm 2C 74
Jackson Cres. M15: Man 5E 9 (4A 66)
Jackson Gdns. M34: Dent 3F 85
Jackson M. OL4: O'ham 1F 31
Jackson Pit OL1: O'ham 4D 117 (3A 30)
Jackson's Row M2: Man 1A 10 (1B 66)

Jackson St. BL4: Kea 2B 18
  M24: Mid .5D 17
  M32: Stre .3E 77
  M33: Sale .4F 89
  M35: Fail 1F 55
  M45: White 2B 22
  OL4: O'ham 2D 31
  OL6: A Lyme 1C 116 (3D 59)
  SK8: Chea 5A 104
  SK14: Hyde 3F 87
Jacobite Cl. M11: Sal 3E 37
James Andrew St. M24: Mid 5D 17
James Bentley Wlk. *M40: Man* 2E 55
       (off Lastingham St.)
James Brindley Basin M1: Man 1E 67
James Cl. SK16: Duk 2F 73
James Corbett Rd. M50: Sal 1E 63
James Ct. *M18: Man* 5F 69
       (off Wellington St.)
James Henry Av. M5: Sal 2D 65
James Leech St.
  SK3: Stoc 4A 118 (3A 106)
James Leigh St. M1: Man 3C 10
James Nasmyth Way M30: Ecc 5E 47
Jameson Cl. M8: Man 2A 52
James St. BL4: Kea 1B 18
  M3: Sal 5C 4 (1F 65)
  M25: Pres .4C 22
       (not continuous)
  M33: Sale .4F 89
  M34: Aud .2A 72
  M34: Dent .1C 86
  M35: Fail 4C 42
  M40: Man .4F 53
  M43: Droy .5D 57
  SK3: Stoc 5A 118 (4A 106)
  SK15: Stal .2F 73
James St. Sth. OL9: Chad 2C 28
Jammy La. OL9: Chad 3E 29
Jane Barter Ho. *BL4: Farn* 1A 18
       (off Hesketh Wlk.)
Jane St. OL9: Chad 3D 29
Japan St. M7: Sal 4B 38
Jardine Way OL9: Chad 5B 28
Jarvis St. OL4: O'ham 3C 30
Jasmine Av. M43: Droy 5E 57
Jasmine Cl. M23: Wyth 2A 100
Jayton Av. M20: Man 3D 103
Jean Cl. M19: Man 3C 82
Jefferson Pl. M4: Man 1C 6
Jeffreys Dr. SK16: Duk 2F 73
Jehlum Cl. M8: Man 5D 39
Jenkinson St. M15: Man 5D 11 (4C 66)
Jenkyn Wlk. *M11: Man* *1B 68*
       (off Newcombe Cl.)
Jennings Av. M5: Sal 2C 64
Jennings St. SK3: Stoc 4F 105
Jennison Cl. M18: Man 4D 69
Jenny St. OL8: O'ham 2E 43
Jepson St. SK2: Stoc 5C 106
Jersey Cl. M19: Man 1B 94
Jersey Rd. SK5: Stoc 4B 96
Jersey St. M4: Man 4F 7 (5D 53)
  OL4: A Lyme 1C 116 (3D 59)
Jerusalem Pl. M2: Man 2A 10
Jesmond Av. M25: Pres 2D 37
Jesmond Wlk. *M9: Man* *4F 25*
       (off Claygate Dr.)
Jessamine Av. M7: Sal 1C 4 (3F 51)
Jessel Cl. M13: Man 5F 11 (4E 67)

Jessie St. M40: Man 1C 54
Jessup St. M18: Man 5F 69
Jetson St. M18: Man 4B 70
Jevington Wlk. M13: Man 4E 67
Jewel Cl. M41: Urm 3D 75
Jimmy McMullen Wlk. *M14: Man* 2C 80
       (off Fred Tilson Cl.)
Jinnah Cl. M11: Man 2E 69
  OL4: O'ham 4E 31
JJB Soccer Dome
  Manchester 4D 61
JJ Thomson M. M14: Man 5F 81
Joan St. M40: Man 5C 40
Jobling St. M11: Man 2B 68
Jocelyn St. M40: Man 1A 54
Joddrell St. M3: Man 1F 9 (1A 66)
Johannesburg Dr. M23: Wyth 2B 108
Johannesburg Gdns. M23: Wyth 2B 108
John Atkinson Ct. M5: Sal 5F 49
John Av. SK8: Chea 1F 111
John Beeley Av. M11: Man 2F 69
John Clynes Av. M40: Man 4E 52
John Dalton St. M2: Man 1A 10 (1B 66)
John Derby Ho. M16: Old T 1C 78
John Foran Cl. M40: Man 1D 55
John Gilbert Way M17: T Pk 5F 63
John Grundy Ho. *SK14: Hyde* *3F 87*
       (off Reynold St.)
John Heywood St. M11: Man 5D 55
John Howarth Countryside Cen. 1A 58
JOHN LEE FOLD 5D 17
John Lee Fold M24: Mid 5C 16
John Lester Ct. *M6: Sal* *4C 50*
       (off Belvedere Rd.)
Johnny King Cl. M40: Man 2F 53
John Paine Ct. *M27: Pen* *2B 34*
       (off Pott St.)
John Robinson Wlk. *M40: Man* *5C 40*
       (off Shelderton Cl.)
Johns Cl. M21: Chor 5D 79
John Shepley St. SK14: Hyde 3F 87
John Smeaton Ct. M1: Man 1E 67
Johnsonbrook Rd. SK14: Duk, Hyde . .5E 73
Johnson Gro. M24: Mid 1A 26
Johnson's Sq. M40: Man 3F 53
Johnson St. M3: Sal 4F 5 (5A 52)
  M15: Man .4F 65
  M27: Pen .1F 49
       (off Hill St.)
Johnson Ter. *SK16: Duk* *5C 116*
       (off Hill St.)
John Stone Ct. M32: Stre 2C 76
John St. BL4: Farn 1A 18
  M3: Sal 3F 5 (5A 52)
  M4: Man 4D 7 (5C 52)
  M7: Sal 3F 51
       (not continuous)
  M25: Pres .1A 24
  M27: Swin .4C 34
  M30: Ecc .1D 61
  M33: Sale .3D 89
  M34: Dent .1B 86
  M35: Fail 3B 42
  M43: Droy .2B 70
  OL7: A Lyme 2B 70
  OL8: O'ham 3A 30
  SK1: Stoc 4B 118 (3B 106)
       (not continuous)
  SK14: Hyde 2F 87
       (not continuous)
John St. W. OL7: A Lyme 2B 72

John William St. M11: Man 1E 69
  M30: Ecc 5B 48
Joiner St. M4: Man 5D 7 (1C 66)
  M5: Sal 5B 4 (1E 65)
Join Rd. M33: Sale 4F 89
Jonas St. M7: Sal 1E 5 (4A 52)
  M9: Man 4A 40
Jones Sq. SK1: Stoc 4C 106
Jones St. M6: Sal 4B 50
  OL1: O'ham 1C 30
Jopson St. M24: Mid 5D 17
Jordan St. M15: Man 4F 9 (3A 66)
Joseph Adamson Ind. Est.
  SK14: Hyde 3E 87
Joseph Dean Ct. M40: Man 5C 40
Josephine Dr. M27: Swin 5C 34
Joseph Jennings Ct.
  OL7: A Lyme 1C 58
Joseph Johnson M. M22: Nor 2A 102
Joseph Mamlock Ho. M8: Man 3A 38
Joseph St. M24: Mid 5B 16
  M30: Ecc 1D 61
  M35: Fail 4B 42
Joshua La. M24: Mid 2F 27
Josslyn Rd. M5: Sal 4F 49
Jo St. M5: Sal 1C 64
Joule Cl. M5: Sal 2C 64
Joules Ct. SK1: Stoc 3C 118 (2B 106)
Joule St. M9: Man 3A 40
Jowett St. SK5: Stoc 4B 96
Jowett's Wlk. OL7: A Lyme 5B 58
Joyce St. M40: Man 5D 41
Joynson Av. M7: Sale 3F 51
Joynson St. M33: Sale 3D 89
Jubilee Av. SK16: Duk 1F 73
Jubilee Cl. M30: Ecc 4F 47
Jubilee Ct. M16: Old T 1D 79
  SK5: Stoc 3B 84
  SK9: Hand 4F 115
            (off Chelford Rd.)
Jubilee Rd. M24: Mid 5D 17
Jubilee Sq. M34: Dent 24 86
            (off Market St.)
Jubilee St. M6: Sal 5B 50
  OL7: A Lyme 1B 72
Jubilee Ter. M24: Mid 5D 17
Judson Av. M21: Chor 2E 91
Julian Ho. OL1: O'ham 2E 117 (2B 30)
Julia St. M3: Man 1A 6 (4B 52)
Julius St. M19: Man 5D 83
July St. M13: Man 5F 67
Jumping Jack's Adventure Land 2F 87
         (off Dukinfield Rd.)
Junction 22 Bus. Pk. OL9: Chad 3B 42
Junction Ho. M1: Man 1F 11
Junction Rd.
  SK1: Stoc 5B 118 (4B 106)
           (not continuous)
Junction St. SK14: Hyde 5E 73
Junction Works M1: Man 1F 11
June Av. SK4: Stoc 1D 105
June St. OL7: A Lyme 4A 116 (5C 58)
Juniper Bank SK5: Stoc 5C 84
Juniper Cl. M33: Sale 2C 88
Juniper Cres. M43: Droy 2B 70
Jupiter Wlk. M40: Man 2C 54
Jura Cl. SK16: Duk 2F 73
Jura Dr. M41: Urm 5A 62
Jurby Av. M9: Man 5F 25
Jury St. M8: Man 3B 52

Justin Cl. M13: Man 5E 11 (3D 67)
Jutland Ho. M1: Man 1F 11
Jutland St. M1: Man 1F 11 (1D 67)

K

Kale St. M13: Man 5F 11 (3D 67)
Kalmia Gro. M7: Sal 1F 51
Kansas Av. M50: Sal 2A 64
Kara St. M6: Sal 5A 50
Karting 2000 . . . . .4E 69
Katherine Ct. M16: Old T 5E 65
         (off Humphrey Rd.)
Katherine Ho. OL6: A Lyme . . .2A 116 (4C 58)
Katherine Rd. SK2: Stoc 5E 107
Katherine St. OL6: A Lyme . . .2B 116 (4D 59)
  OL7: A Lyme 3A 116 (5B 58)
Kathkin Av. M8: Man 2D 39
Kathleen Gro. M14: Man 5F 67
         (off Stanley Av.)
Kay Av. SK6: Bred 5F 97
Kayes Av. SK1: Stoc 2D 107
Kayley Ind. Est. OL7: A Lyme 4B 58
Kay Lodge M14: Man 5E 81
         (off Lombard Gro.)
Kays Gdns. M3: Sal 3D 5 (5F 51)
Kay St. M6: Sal 1B 50
  M11: Man 3B 68
Keadby Cl. M30: Ecc 2F 61
Keane Ct. M8: Man 5C 38
Keane St. OL7: A Lyme 1A 116 (4C 58)
Kean Pl. M30: Ecc 1F 61
KEARSLEY 3C 18
Kearsley Community Leisure Cen. 3A 18
Kearsley Grn. M26: Rad 3E 19
Kearsley Hall Rd. M26: Rad 2E 19
Kearsley Mt. Shop. Pct. BL4: Kea . . .3D 19
Kearsley Rd. M8: Man 2C 38
  M26: Rad 1E 19
Kearsley Station (Rail) 2C 18
Kearsley St. M30: Ecc 5D 47
Kearsley Va. M26: Rad 1D 19
Kearton Dr. M30: Ecc 1C 62
Keary Cl. M18: Man 4F 69
Keasdon Av. M22: Wyth 2F 109
Keaton Cl. M6: Sal 3A 50
Keats Av. M34: Dent 5C 86
  M43: Droy 5C 56
Keats Ho. SK5: Stoc 5A 84
Keats M. M23: Wyth 3E 99
Keats Rd. M30: Ecc 1F 61
Keb La. OL8: O'ham 4C 44
Keble Av. OL8: O'ham 1A 44
Kedington Cl. M40: Man 2E 53
         (off Ribblesdale Dr.)
Kedleston Av. M14: Man 1A 82
Kedleston Grn. SK2: Stoc 4F 107
Kedleston Wlk. M34: Dent 4B 86
Keele Cl. M40: Man 4E 53
  SK2: Stoc 5D 107
Keeley Cl. M40: Man 3E 55
Keighley Av. M43: Droy 4C 56
Keith Dr. SK3: Stoc 4D 105
Keith Wlk. M40: Man 4A 54
Kelboro Av. M34: Aud 3F 71
Kelbrook Rd. M11: Man 2D 69
Kelby Av. M23: Wyth 4D 101
Kelday Wlk. M8: Man 1E 53
         (off Smedley Rd.)

Keld Wlk. *M18: Man* 5E **69**
      (off Hampden St.)
Kelfield Av. M23: Wyth 1C **100**
Kelham Wlk. M40: Man 3E **41**
Kellbrook Cres. M7: Sal 3D **37**
      (not continuous)
Kellett Wlk. *M11: Man* 5D **55**
      (off Trimdon Cl.)
Kelling Wlk. M15: Man 5D **9**
Kelmarsh Cl. M11: Man 3F **69**
Kelmscott Lodge M41: Urm 2D **75**
      (off Cornhill Rd.)
Kelsall Cl. SK3: Stoc 5F **105**
Kelsall Dr. M43: Droy 4B **56**
    WA15: Tim 5E **99**
Kelsall St. M12: Man 4B **68**
    M33: Sale 4D **89**
    OL9: O'ham 3F **29**
Kelsall Way SK9: Hand 4F **115**
      (off Spath La.)
Kelsey Wlk. M9: Man 4D **25**
Kelso Cl. OL8: O'ham 3B **44**
Kelson Av. OL7: A Lyme 2C **58**
Kelso Pl. M15: Man 4C **8** (3F **65**)
Kelstern Av. M13: Man 2A **82**
Kelstern Sq. M13: Man 2A **82**
Kelton Cl. SK5: Stoc 3B **96**
Kelverlow St. OL4: O'ham 2E **31**
Kelvin Av. M24: Mid 3D **25**
    M33: Sale 4D **89**
Kelvindale Dr. WA15: Tim 4E **99**
Kelvin Gro. M8: Man 1C **52**
Kelvington Dr. M9: Man 1F **53**
Kelvin St. M4: Man 4D **7**
    OL7: A Lyme 2A **72**
Kemball M30: Ecc 5B **48**
Kemble Av. M23: Wyth 2E **101**
Kemmel Av. M22: Shar 1A **110**
Kemnay Wlk. *M11: Man* 1E **69**
      (off Edith Cavell Cl.)
Kempley Cl. M12: Man 4B **68**
Kempnough Hall Rd.
    M28: Wors 5A **32**
Kempsey Ct. OL9: Chad 2D **29**
Kempsey Wlk. *M40: Man* 3F **41**
      (off Enstone Dr.)
Kempsford Cl. M23: Wyth 5D **101**
Kempster St. M7: Sal 3F **51**
Kemp St. M24: Mid 1B **26**
Kempton Cl. M43: Droy 5E **57**
Kempton Ho. *M7: Sal* 1E **51**
      (off Griffin St.)
Kempton Rd. M19: Man 5C **82**
Kempton Way OL9: Chad 2E **29**
Kemsing Wlk. M5: Sal 1C **64**
Kenchester Av. M11: Man 2F **69**
Kendal Av. M33: Sale 5E **89**
    M34: Dent 4C **86**
    M41: Urm 1A **74**
    OL7: A Lyme 3B **58**
    SK14: Hyde 5E **73**
Kendal Cl. WA15: Tim 1A **108**
Kendal Ct. *M22: Shar* 5A **102**
      (off Downes Way)
    M30: Ecc 1D **61**
      (off New La.)
Kendal Dr. SK8: Gat 2E **111**
Kendal Gdns. M28: Walk 2B **32**
    M45: White 1B **22**
Kendall Rd. M8: Man 1B **38**

Kendal Rd. M6: Sal 2E **49**
    M32: Stre 2F **77**
Kendal Ter. *SK16: Duk* 1E **73**
      (off Astley St.)
Kendal Wlk. M24: Mid 5A **16**
Kendon Gro. M34: Dent 2A **86**
Kendrew Wlk. *M9: Man* 3A **40**
      (off Shepherd St.)
Kenford Wlk. *M8: Man* 1B **52**
      (off Ermington Dr.)
Kenilworth Av. M20: Man 3B **92**
    M27: Clif 1D **35**
    M45: White 3C **22**
    OL9: Chad 5F **17**
    SK9: Hand 5F **115**
Kenilworth Gro. M34: Aud 2E **71**
Kenilworth Rd. M33: Sale 4A **88**
    SK3: Stoc 4B **104**
Kenley Wlk. *M8: Man* 1E **53**
      (off Gransden Dr.)
Kenmere Gro. M40: Man 3D **41**
Kenmore Cl. M45: White 1D **23**
Kenmore Rd. M22: Nor 4F **101**
    M45: White 1D **23**
Kenmore Way
    M45: White 1D **23**
Kennard Cl. M9: Man 3B **40**
Kennard Pl. WA14: Alt 5A **98**
Kennedy Dr. BL9: Bury 4D **13**
Kennedy Rd. M5: Sal 5E **49**
Kennedy St. M2: Man 1B **10** (1B **66**)
    OL8: O'ham 4A **30**
Kennedy Way M34: Dent 3F **85**
    SK4: Stoc 1E **105**
Kennerley Ct. SK2: Stoc 5C **106**
Kennerley Rd. SK2: Stoc 5C **106**
Kenneth Collis Ct. M22: Wyth 3E **109**
Kenneth Sq. M7: Sal 1A **52**
Kennett Rd. M23: Wyth 3C **108**
Kenninghall Rd. M22: Wyth 3F **109**
Kennington Av. M40: Man 3D **55**
Kenny Cl. OL4: Lees 4F **31**
Kenside St. M16: W Ran 2B **80**
Kensington, The M20: Man 3D **93**
Kensington Av. M14: Man 1F **81**
    OL6: A Lyme 3F **59**
    OL9: Chad 1A **28**
Kensington Cl. M7: Sal 4E **37**
    M34: Dent 1D **85**
Kensington Dr. M5: Sal 4F **49**
Kensington Gro. M34: Dent 1D **85**
    WA14: Tim 3A **98**
Kensington Rd. M21: Chor 3C **78**
    M35: Fail 4D **43**
    OL8: O'ham 5F **29**
    SK3: Stoc 4D **105**
Kensington St. M14: Man 2C **80**
Kenslow Av. M8: Man 2B **38**
Kensworth Cl. M23: Wyth 5F **99**
Kent Av. M43: Droy 1A **70**
    OL9: Chad 3D **28**
Kent Ct. M14: Man 2E **81**
Kent Dr. BL4: Kea 3D **19**
Kentford Dr. M40: Man 3E **53**
Kent Gro. M35: Fail 1A **56**
Kentmere Cl. SK8: Gat 3D **111**
Kentmere Dr. M9: Man 5C **26**
Kentmere Dr. M24: Mid 3A **16**
Kentmere Rd. WA15: Tim 5F **99**
      (not continuous)

Kentmore Cl. M12: Man 3C **68**
   SK4: Stoc 1A **104**
Kenton Av. M18: Man 2E **83**
Kenton Cl. M34: Aud 3F **71**
Kenton St. OL8: O'ham 4D **31**
Kent Rd. M34: Dent 3C **84**
   SK3: Stoc 3D **105**
Kent Rd. E. M14: Man 2F **81**
Kent Rd. W. M14: Man 2E **81**
Kentstone Av. SK4: Stoc 5F **93**
Kent St. M2: Man 5B **6**
   M7: Sal .3F **51**
   M27: Pen 2B **34**
   OL8: O'ham 5B **30**
Kentucky St. OL4: O'ham 3E **31**
Kentwell Cl. SK16: Duk 3D **73**
Kenwick Dr. M40: Man 2A **42**
Kenwood Av. M19: Man 2B **94**
   SK8: Gat 5C **102**
Kenwood Cl. M32: Stre 3A **78**
Kenwood Ct. M32: Stre 4A **78**
Kenwood La. M28: Wors 2B **46**
Kenwood Rd. M32: Stre 4A **78**
   SK5: Stoc 2A **84**
KENWORTHY 1D **101**
Kenworthy Av. OL6: A Lyme 2F **59**
Kenworthy La. M22: Nor 1F **101**
Kenwright St. M4: Man 3D **7** (5C **52**)
Kenwyn St. M40: Man 4A **54**
Kenyon Av. M33: Sale 1A **100**
   OL8: O'ham 1B **44**
   SK16: Duk 3F **73**
Kenyon Ho. *SK16: Duk* 1D **73**
            (off Astley St.)
Kenyon La. M24: Mid 1E **27**
   M25: Pres 5E **23**
   M40: Man 4C **40**
   SK16: Duk 3F **73**
            (off Kenyon Av.)
Kenyon St. M18: Man 4A **70**
   OL6: A Lyme 2A **116** (4C **58**)
   SK16: Duk 2D **73**
Keppel Rd. M21: Chor 4D **79**
Keppel St. OL6: A Lyme 4E **59**
Kepwick Dr. M22: Wyth 5A **110**
Kerfield Wlk. M13: Man 5F **11**
Kerfoot Cl. M22: Nor 3A **102**
Kerne Gro. M23: Wyth 2C **100**
Kerrera Dr. M5: Sal 1F **63**
Kerrier Cl. *M30: Ecc* 5C **48**
            (off Kearton Dr.)
Kerris Cl. M22: Wyth 5A **110**
Kerr St. M9: Man 1F **39**
Kerry Wlk. M23: Wyth 3B **108**
KERSAL 4C **36**
Kersal Av. M27: Pen 4E **35**
Kersal Bank M7: Sal 3E **37**
Kersal Cell *M7: Sal* 4B **36**
       (off White Water Dr.)
Kersal Cl. M7: Sal 3E **37**
   M25: Pres 3C **36**
Kersal Crag M7: Sal 3E **37**
KERSAL DALE 4E **37**
Kersal Dr. WA15: Tim 4E **99**
Kersal Gdns. M7: Sal 3E **37**
Kersal Hall Av. M7: Sal 4C **36**
Kersal Rd. M7: Sal 4C **36**
   M25: Pres 3C **36**
Kersal Va. M25: Pres 4B **36**

Kersal Va. Ct. M7: Sal 4C **36**
Kersal Va. Rd. M25: Pres 3B **36**
Kersal Way M7: Sal 5D **37**
Kerscott Rd. M23: Wyth 2A **100**
Kersh Av. M19: Man 5D **83**
Kershaw Av. M25: Pres 2B **36**
          (not continuous)
   M33: Sale 1F **99**
Kershaw Dr. OL9: Chad 1F **41**
Kershaw Gro. M34: Aud 2D **71**
Kershaw La. M34: Aud 2D **71**
Kershaw Rd. M35: Fail 5B **42**
Kershaw St. M43: Droy 1B **70**
   OL7: A Lyme 2B **72**
Kershaw Wlk. *M12: Man* 4F **67**
             (off Aked Cl.)
Kershope Gro. M5: Sal 2C **64**
Kersley St. OL4: O'ham 3C **30**
Kerswell Wlk. *M40: Man* 2C **54**
        (off Troydale Dr.)
Kerwin Wlk. *M11: Man* 2C **68**
             (off Mill St.)
Kesteven Rd. M9: Man 5F **39**
Keston Av. M9: Man 1C **40**
   M43: Droy 1A **70**
Keston Cres. SK5: Stoc 2D **97**
Keston Rd. OL1: O'ham 1E **31**
Kestrel Av. M27: Clif 2D **35**
   M34: Aud 1E **71**
   OL4: O'ham 4E **31**
Kestrel Cl. M45: White 3C **22**
   SK14: Hyde 1F **87**
Kestrel Ct. M50: Sal 2F **63**
Kestrel Rd. M17: T Pk 2B **62**
Kestrel Wlk. *M12: Man* 4C **68**
         (off Flamingo Cl.)
Keswick Av. M34: Dent 1F **85**
   M41: Urm 4A **74**
   OL7: A Lyme 2B **58**
   OL8: O'ham 5C **30**
   OL9: Chad 2C **28**
   SK8: Gat 3D **111**
   SK14: Hyde 1E **87**
Keswick Cl. M13: Man 5F **67**
   M24: Mid 4F **15**
Keswick Ct. *M22: Shar* 5A **102**
         (off Downes Way)
   M24: Mid 4F **15**
Keswick Gro. M6: Sal 4B **50**
Keswick Rd. M28: Walk 2B **32**
   M32: Stre 2E **77**
   SK4: Stoc 1F **95**
   WA15: Tim 5F **99**
Ketley Wlk. M22: Wyth 3B **110**
Kettering Rd. M19: Man 3D **83**
Kettlewell Wlk. *M18: Man* 5E **69**
       (off Hampden Cres.)
Ketton Cl. M11: Man 3A **70**
Kevin St. M19: Man 5C **82**
Kew Dr. M41: Urm 1C **74**
Kew Gdns. M40: Man 3C **40**
Kew Rd. M35: Fail 4C **42**
   OL4: O'ham 3D **31**
          (not continuous)
Key Ct. M34: Dent 5C **86**
Keyhaven Wlk. *M40: Man* 2F **53**
       (off Glendower Dr.)
Keymer St. M11: Man 5A **54**
Keynsham Rd. M11: Man 4D **55**
Keystone Cl. M6: Sal 3A **50**

Key W. Cl. M11: Man 1B **68**
Keyworth Wlk. *M40: Man* *3A* **54**
 (off Kirkhaven Sq.)
Khartoum St. M11: Man 5F **55**
 M16: Old T 1F **79**
Kibworth Cl. M45: White 1F **21**
Kibworth Wlk. *M9: Man* *4A* **26**
 (off Crossmead Dr.)
Kidacre Wlk. *M40: Man* *5C* **40**
 (off Rudd St.)
Kidderminster Way OL9: Chad 1B **28**
Kidnall Wlk. M9: Man 3B **40**
Kid St. M24: Mid 5B **16**
Kiel Cl. M30: Ecc 2A **62**
Kielder Hill M24: Mid 2B **16**
Kielder Sq. M5: Sal 1B **64**
Kilburn Av. M9: Man 4F **25**
Kilburn Cl. SK8: H Grn 2D **115**
Kilburn Ct. *M14: Man* *1F* **81**
 (off Hope Rd.)
Kilburn Rd. SK3: Stoc 4E **105**
Kilcoby Av. M27: Pen 4F **35**
Kildare Rd. M21: Chor 5F **79**
 M27: Swin 5A **34**
Kilmane Av. M9: Man 1D **41**
Kilmarsh Wlk. *M8: Man* *5B* **38**
 (off Halliwell La.)
Kilmington Dr. M8: Man 1B **52**
Kilner Cl. BL9: Bury 2D **13**
Kilner Wlk. *M40: Man* *3E* **53**
 (off Talgarth Rd.)
Kilnsey Wlk. *M18: Man* *5E* **69**
 (off Hampden Cres.)
Kilnside Dr. M9: Man 5F **39**
Kilnwick Dr. M18: Man 2D **83**
Kilrush Av. M30: Ecc 2F **61**
Kilsby Wlk. M40: Man 3F **53**
Kilton Wlk. *M40: Man* *3E* **53**
 (off Rimworth Dr.)
Kilvert Dr. M33: Sale 3B **88**
Kilworth Av. M33: Sale 3B **88**
Kimberley St. M7: Sal 5A **38**
 OL8: O'ham 1E **43**
 SK3: Stoc 4A **106**
Kimberley Wlk. M15: Man 5D **9**
Kimbolton Ct. M12: Man 3C **68**
Kinburn Rd. M19: Man 1F **103**
Kinbury Wlk. *M40: Man* *3E* **53**
 (off Kingsfold Av.)
Kincardine Ct. M13: Man 5F **11**
Kincardine Rd. M13: Man 5E **11** (3D **67**)
Kincraig Cl. M11: Man 1E **69**
Kinder Av. OL4: O'ham 4F **31**
Kinder Ct. SK3: Stoc 5A **118**
Kinder Ho. *M5: Sal* *4F* **49**
 (off Medway Cl.)
Kinder St. SK3: Stoc 4A **106**
Kinderton Av. M20: Man 1D **93**
Kinder Way M24: Mid 4B **16**
Kineton Wlk. *M13: Man* *4E* **67**
 (off Lauderdale Cres.)
Kingcombe Wlk. *M9: Man* *4A* **40**
 (off Thornsett St.)
King Edward Rd. SK14: Hyde 5F **87**
King Edwards Bldgs. *M7: Sal* *4B* **38**
 (off Bury Old Rd.)
King Edward St. M5: Sal 3A **8** (2D **65**)
 M19: Man 4D **83**
 M30: Ecc 5E **47**
Kingfisher Av. M34: Aud 1E **71**

Kingfisher Cl. M12: Man 5A **68**
Kingfisher Ct. M50: Sal 2F **63**
King George Rd. SK14: Hyde 4F **87**
Kingham Dr. M4: Man 5E **53**
Kings Av. M8: Man 4C **38**
 M45: White 4A **12**
 SK8: Gat 2C **110**
Kingsbridge Ct. M9: Man 5E **39**
Kingsbridge Dr. SK16: Duk 3D **73**
Kingsbridge Rd. M9: Man 5E **39**
 OL8: O'ham 4D **31**
Kingsbrook Ct. *M16: W Ran* *5A* **80**
 (off St Austell Rd.)
Kingsbrook Rd. M16: W Ran 5A **80**
Kingsbury Rd. M11: Man 5E **55**
Kingscliffe St. M9: Man 4A **40**
Kings Cl. M18: Man 4B **70**
 M25: Pres 4E **23**
Kings Ct. *M6: Sal* *3C* **50**
 (off St Georges Way)
 SK5: Stoc 5B **96**
King's Cres. M16: Old T 2D **79**
Kingsdale Rd. M18: Man 1C **84**
Kingsdown Rd. M22: Wyth 5E **109**
Kingsdown Wlk. SK5: Stoc 3D **97**
King's Dr. M24: Mid 1A **26**
 SK4: Stoc 5C **94**
Kingsfield Dr. M20: Man 1E **103**
Kingsfold Av. M40: Man 3E **53**
Kingsford St. M5: Sal 5F **49**
Kingsgate Rd. M22: Wyth 5E **109**
Kings Gro. M32: Stre 2B **78**
Kingsheath Av. M11: Man 4D **55**
Kingshill Rd. M21: Chor 5C **78**
Kingsholme Rd. M22: Wyth 4E **109**
Kingsland Cl. M40: Man 4F **53**
Kingsland Rd. SK3: Stoc 4C **104**
Kings La. M32: Stre 2B **78**
Kingslea Rd. M20: Man 3E **93**
Kingsleigh Rd. SK4: Stoc 5A **94**
Kingsley Av. M7: Sal 5C **36**
 M9: Man 5B **40**
 M32: Stre 2B **78**
 M41: Urm 3D **75**
 M45: White 2C **22**
 SK4: Stoc 4A **96**
Kingsley Cl. M34: Dent 4F **85**
Kingsley Ct. M5: Sal 1C **64**
Kingsley Gro. M34: Aud 2E **71**
Kingsley Rd. M22: Nor 3F **101**
 M24: Mid 4D **17**
 M27: Swin 3F **33**
 OL4: O'ham 3E **31**
 WA15: Tim 5D **99**
Kings Lynn Cl. M20: Man 5D **93**
Kingsmead M. M9: Man 4E **25**
Kingsmere Av. M19: Man 4B **82**
Kingsmill Av. M19: Man 5D **83**
Kingsnorth Rd. M41: Urm 1A **74**
Kings Pk. M17: T Pk 5D **63**
King Sq. OL8: O'ham 4D **117** (3A **30**)
Kings Reach Bus. Pk.
 SK4: Stoc 2E **105**
Kings Rd. M16: Old T 2C **78**
 M21: Chor 5E **79**
 M25: Pres 4E **23**
 M32: Stre 4A **78**
 M33: Sale 4B **88**
 M34: Aud 5C **70**
 OL6: A Lyme 3E **59**

Kings Rd. OL8: O'ham 5F 117 (4B 30)
   OL9: Chad 1A 42
Kings Ter. M32: Stre 2B 78
   SK16: Duk 5C 116
KINGSTON 2D 87
Kingston Av. M20: Man 2D 103
   OL1: O'ham 1D 31
   OL9: Chad 5C 28
Kingston Cl. M7: Sal 4F 37
Kingston Ct. M20: Man 2D 103
           (off Kingston Rd.)
Kingston Dr. M33: Sale 3F 89
   M41: Urm 5D 75
Kingston Gdns. SK14: Hyde 2D 87
Kingston Gro. M9: Man 5B 26
Kingston Hill SK8: Chea 2F 111
Kingston M. M35: Fail 5D 43
Kingston Mill SK3: Stoc 2F 105
Kingston Rd. M20: Man 2D 103
   M35: Fail 5D 43
   SK9: Hand 5E 115
Kingston St. SK3: Stoc 2F 105
King St. BL4: Farn 1A 18
   M2: Man 3F 5 (5A 52)
           (not continuous)
   M3: Sal 3F 5 (5A 52)
   M6: Sal 2F 49
   M7: Sal 5A 38
   M24: Mid 5C 16
   M30: Ecc 1B 62
   M32: Stre 4F 77
   M34: Aud 4B 72
   M34: Dent 2B 86
   M35: Fail 1F 55
   M43: Droy 2C 70
           (not continuous)
   OL8: O'ham 5D 117 (3A 30)
   OL9: O'ham 4D 117 (3A 30)
   SK14: Hyde 2F 87
   SK16: Duk 5C 116 (1D 73)
King St. E. SK1: Stoc 1B 118 (1B 106)
King St. Rdbt. OL1: O'ham 3A 30
   OL4: O'ham 3A 30
   OL8: O'ham 5D 117 (3A 30)
King St. W. M3: Man 3A 6 (1B 66)
   SK3: Stoc 2A 106
Kings Vw. SK4: Stoc 2E 105
Kings Wlk. M43: Droy 2C 70
           (off King St.)
   OL6: A Lyme 2F 59
           (off King's Rd.)
Kingsway BL4: Kea 3B 18
   M19: Man 1F 103
   M20: Man 5E 103
   M24: Mid 3B 26
   M27: Pen 1E 49
   M28: Walk 4A 32
   M32: Stre 4E 77
   SK8: Chea, H Grn 4F 111
   SK8: Gat 5E 103
Kingsway Av. M19: Man 4B 82
Kingsway Bldgs. M19: Man 3A 94
Kingsway Cl. OL8: O'ham 4A 30
Kingsway Cres. M19: Man 3A 94
Kingsway Pk. M41: Urm 5E 61
Kingswood Gro. SK5: Stoc 4B 84
Kingswood Rd. M14: Man 5F 81
   M24: Mid 3B 16
   M25: Pres 4B 22
   M30: Ecc 3D 47

King William Ent. Pk. M50: Sal 2C 64
King William St. M30: Ecc 4C 46
   M50: Sal 2C 64
Kinlett Wlk. M40: Man 2F 41
Kinley Cl. M12: Man 4B 68
           (off Clowes St.)
Kinloch Gdns. OL8: O'ham 5B 30
Kinloch St. M11: Man 5C 54
   OL8: O'ham 5C 30
Kinmel Av. SK5: Stoc 4E 97
Kinmel Wlk. M23: Wyth 5B 100
Kinmount Wlk. M9: Man 1F 53
         (off Lathbury Rd.)
Kinnaird Cres. SK1: Stoc 3D 107
Kinnaird Rd. M20: Man 3E 93
Kinross M30: Ecc 5B 48
           (off Peel St.)
Kinross Rd. M14: Man 2A 82
Kinsale Wlk. M23: Wyth 3B 108
Kinsey Av. M23: Wyth 4B 100
Kintore Wlk. M40: Man 2E 53
        (off Ribblesdale Dr.)
Kinver Rd. M40: Man 2E 41
Kipling Av. M34: Dent 5C 86
   M43: Droy 4C 56
Kipling St. M7: Sal 1F 51
Kippax St. M14: Man 2D 81
Kirby Av. M27: Swin 2F 47
   OL9: Chad 1F 41
Kirkbank St. OL9: O'ham 1F 29
          (not continuous)
Kirkby Av. M33: Sale 1E 99
   M40: Man 5D 41
Kirkby Dr. M33: Sale 1F 99
Kirkdale Av. M40: Man 2F 41
Kirkfell Wlk. OL1: O'ham 1B 30
          (not continuous)
Kirkgate Cl. M40: Man 4E 53
         (off Bothwell Rd.)
Kirkham Av. M18: Man 4F 69
Kirkham St. M34: Dent 2B 86
Kirkham Rd. SK8: H Grn 5E 111
KIRKHAMS 2D 23
   OL9: O'ham 2F 29
Kirkham St. M5: Man 1A 64
Kirkhaven Sq. M40: Man 3A 54
Kirkhill Wlk. M40: Man 2F 41
         (off Blandford Dr.)
Kirkholt Wlk. M9: Man 1A 40
        (off Woodmere Dr.)
Kirklands M33: Sale 1C 98
Kirklee Av. OL9: Chad 1C 28
Kirklees Wlk. M45: White 5D 13
Kirkley St. SK14: Hyde 4F 87
Kirklinton Dr. M9: Man 1F 53
Kirkman Av. M30: Ecc 2E 61
Kirkman Cl. M18: Man 1A 84
Kirkmanshulme La. M12: Man 1B 82
Kirkman St. BL9: Bury 3B 12
Kirk Rd. M19: Man 1D 95
Kirkstall Rd. M24: Mid 3B 16
   M41: Urm 2A 76
Kirkstall Sq. M13: Man 4E 67
Kirkstead Cl. M11: Man 2C 68
Kirkstile Pl. M27: Clif 3A 20
Kirkstone Av. M28: Walk 3B 32
Kirkstone Cl. OL1: O'ham 1B 30

Kirkstone Dr. M24: Mid 4A 16
Kirkstone Rd. M40: Man 2E 41
   SK14: Hyde 5E 73
Kirk St. M18: Man 5F 69
Kirktown Wlk. M11: Man 2E 69
   (off Greenside St.)
Kirkway M9: Man 5C 26
   M24: Mid 2C 26
Kirkwood Dr. M40: Man 3E 53
Kirtley Av. M30: Ecc 4F 47
Kirton Lodge M25: Pres 5E 23
Kirton Wlk. M9: Man 4E 25
Kitepool St. M30: Ecc 3C 46
Kitty Wheeldon Gdns.
   M33: Sale 3C 88
   (off Ashton La.)
Kiwi St. M6: Sal 5C 50
Knaresborough Cl. SK5: Stoc 4A 84
Knight Cres. M24: Mid 2F 15
Knightley Wlk. M40: Man 2F 53
   (off Thornton St. Nth.)
Knightsbridge
   SK1: Stoc 1B 118 (1B 106)
Knightsbridge Cl. M7: Sal 4F 37
Knightsbridge M. M20: Man 4D 93
Knights Cl. M25: Pres 4D 23
Knights Ct. M5: Sal 5C 48
Knight St. M20: Man 1D 103
   OL7: A Lyme 5B 58
Knightswood Rd. M8: Man 5C 38
Kniveton Cl. M12: Man 4B 68
   (off Kniveton Rd.)
Kniveton Rd. M12: Man 4B 68
Knob Hall Gdns. M23: Wyth 3B 108
Knoll St. M7: Sal 5F 37
Knoll St. Ind. Pk. M7: Sal 5F 37
   (off Knoll St.)
Knott Fold SK14: Hyde 5F 87
Knott La. SK14: Hyde 5F 87
KNOTT LANES 5A 44
Knott Lanes OL8: O'ham 4B 44
KNOTT MILL 5F 9 (3A 66)
Knowe Av. M22: Wyth 5F 109
Knowl Cl. M34: Dent 3D 85
Knowldale Way M12: Man 5A 68
   (off Dillon Dr.)
Knowle Av. OL7: A Lyme 3B 58
Knowle Dr. M25: Pres 2C 36
Knowle Pk. SK9: Hand 5E 115
Knowles Ct. M6: Sal 4D 49
Knowles Pl. M15: Man 5B 10
Knowls, The OL8: O'ham 3D 43
Knowl St. OL8: O'ham 2E 43
Knowsley Av. M5: Sal 2D 65
   M41: Urm 1E 75
Knowsley Cres. SK1: Stoc 3D 107
Knowsley Dr. M27: Swin 5F 21
Knowsley Rd. M45: White 1B 22
   SK1: Stoc 3D 107
Knowsley St. M8: Man 1C 6 (3B 52)
Knowsley Ter. SK1: Stoc 3D 107
   (off Knowsley Rd.)
Knutsford Av. M16: Old T 1F 79
   M33: Sale 4A 90
   SK4: Stoc 1F 95
Knutsford Rd. M18: Man 5E 69
Knutsford St. M6: Sal 5A 50
Knypersley Av. SK2: Stoc 4E 107
Krokus Sq. OL9: Chad 2C 28
Kynder St. M34: Dent 2B 86

L

Labrador Quay M50: Sal 3C 64
Labtec St. M27: Pen 3D 35
Laburnum Av. M27: Swin 1A 48
   M30: Ecc 2C 60
   (off Wilfred Rd)
   M34: Aud 1E 71
   M35: Fail 1B 56
   M45: White 3B 22
   OL6: A Lyme 1E 59
   OL9: Chad 1D 29
   SK14: Hyde 5F 87
Laburnum Cl. WA15: Tim 5D 99
Laburnum Dr. BL9: Bury 5C 12
Laburnum Gro. M25: Pres 4C 22
Laburnum Rd. M18: Dent 2B 84
   M18: Man 1F 83
   M24: Mid 1E 27
   M28: Walk 2A 32
   M34: Dent 2B 84
   M41: Urm 1D 75
   OL8: O'ham 4E 43
Laburnum St. M6: Sal 5B 50
Laburnum Vs. OL8: O'ham 3C 44
   (off Simkin Way)
Laburnum Way SK3: Stoc 3D 105
Lacerta M. M7: Sal 1B 4 (4E 51)
Lackford Dr. M40: Man 3E 53
Lacrosse Av. OL8: O'ham 5E 29
Lacy Gro. M32: Stre 4F 77
Lacy St. M32: Stre 4F 77
   SK1: Stoc 4B 118 (3B 106)
Lacy Wlk. M12: Man 2A 68
   (off Alderman Sq.)
Ladbrooke Cl. OL6: A Lyme 3E 59
Ladbrooke Rd. OL6: A Lyme 2E 59
LADYBARN 1F 93
Ladybarn Cres. M14: Man 1F 93
Ladybarn Ho. M14: Man 4F 81
Ladybarn La. M14: Man 5F 81
Ladybarn Rd. M14: Man 5F 81
Ladybrook Av. WA15: Tim 4D 99
Ladylands Av. M11: Man 5E 55
Ladyshore Cl. M5: Sal 1B 64
Ladysmith Cen.
   OL6: A Lyme 2C 116 (4D 59)
Ladysmith Rd. M20: Man 5E 93
Ladysmith St. OL8: O'ham 1E 43
   SK3: Stoc 4A 106
Ladythorne Av. M25: Pres 2C 36
Ladythorne Ct. M25: Pres 2C 36
   (off Ladythorne Dr.)
Ladythorne Dr. M25: Pres 2C 36
Ladywell Station (Metro) 5C 48
Ladywell Trad. Est. M50: Sal 5D 49
LA Fitness
   Sale 1D 99
Lagan Wlk. M22: Wyth 4A 110
Lagos Cl. M14: Man 1C 80
Laindon Rd. M14: Man 1A 82
Lainton Ct. SK3: Stoc 3E 105
Lake Dr. M24: Mid 2B 26
Lake Ho. M15: Man 5C 8 (3F 65)
Lakeland Ct. M24: Mid 4F 15
Lake Rd. M17: T Pk 3E 63
   M34: Dent 1B 86
Lakeside BL9: Bury 1B 12
   SK8: Chea 3E 111

Lakeside Av. OL7: A Lyme 3B 58
Lakeside Bldg. SK8: Chea 3E 111
Lakeside Cl. M18: Man 4B 70
Lakeside Ct. M7: Sal 3F 37
Lakeside Grn. SK2: Stoc 5E 107
Lakeside Ri. M9: Man 1C 38
Lakes Rd. SK16: Duk 2E 73
Lake St. SK2: Stoc 5D 107
Lakeswood SK16: Duk 2D 73
Lake Vw. M7: Man 2C 40
Lakin St. M40: Man 5C 40
Lamb Cl. M12: Man 5B 68
Lamb Ct. M3: Sal 4E 5 (5A 52)
Lambert Dr. M33: Sale 2A 88
Lambert Hall M1: Man 3E 11
(off Granby Row)
Lamberton Dr. M23: Wyth 5A 100
Lambert St. OL7: A Lyme 1B 72
Lambeth Av. M35: Fail 4D 43
Lambeth Rd. M40: Man 3E 55
SK5: Stoc 1B 96
Lamb La. M1: Man 4E 5 (5A 52)
Lambourne Cl. M22: Wyth 1F 113
Lambourn Rd. M41: Urm 1A 74
Lambrook Wlk. M40: Man 3F 55
(off Eastmoor Dr.)
Lambs Fold SK4: Stoc 3F 95
Lambton Rd. M21: Chor 5F 79
M28: Wors 5E 33
Lambton St. M30: Ecc 3D 47
Lamburn Av. M40: Man 2F 41
Lamb Wlk. M34: Dent 5C 86
(off Wordsworth Rd.)
Lamorna Cl. M7: Sal 4D 37
Lamplight Way M27: Pen 5A 36
Lamport Cl. M1: Man 4E 11 (3D 67)
Lamport Ct. M1: Man 4E 11
Lampson St. M8: Man 3A 52
Lampton Cl. WA14: Alt 4A 98
Lamsholme Cl. M19: Man 3C 82
Lanark Av. M22: Nor 3F 101
Lanbury Dr. M8: Man 5B 38
Lancashire Aero Club 3A 60
Lancashire County Cricket Club Mus.
. . . . .1C 78
Lancashire County Cricket Ground 1B 78
Lancashire Ct. OL9: O'ham 4E 29
LANCASHIRE HILL 5A 96
Lancashire Hill SK4: Stoc 1A 118 (5A 96)
SK5: Stoc 1B 118 (5A 96)
Lancaster Av. M24: Mid 2E 27
M35: Fail 5A 42
M41: Urm 2A 76
M45: White 2C 22
Lancaster Ct. M19: Man 5B 82
M40: Man 3D 55
Lancaster Dr. M25: Pres 2E 37
Lancaster Ho. M1: Man 5F 11
SK3: Stoc 5A 118
Lancaster Lodge M27: Swin 1D 49
Lancaster Rd. M6: Sal 1D 49
M20: Man 5C 92
M34: Dent 4B 86
M43: Droy 4B 56
Lancaster St. OL9: Chad 5C 28
SK1: Stoc 1C 106
Lancelot Rd. M22: Wyth 4B 110
Lanchester St. M40: Man 4A 54
Lancing Av. M20: Man 5F 93
Lancing Wlk. OL9: Chad 3C 28

Landcross Rd. M14: Man 4E 81
Landells Wlk. M40: Man 2C 54
(off Peckford Dr.)
Lander Gro. M9: Man 1B 40
Landkey Cl. M23: Wyth 1B 100
Landor Ct. M34: Dent 2B 84
Landos Ct. M40: Man 4E 53
Landos Rd. M40: Man 4E 53
Landsberg Rd. M35: Fail 4D 43
Landsberg Ter. M35: Fail 4D 43
Landseer St. OL4: O'ham 5F 117 (4C 30)
(not continuous)
Lands End Rd. M24: Mid 2D 25
Landstead Dr. M40: Man 5A 54
Lane End M30: Ecc 1B 62
Lane End Cl. M35: Fail 1C 56
Lane End Rd. M19: Man 4F 93
Lanegate SK14: Hyde 5F 87
Lanesfield Wlk. M8: Man 4E 39
(off Stakeford Dr.)
Laneside Rd. M20: Man 3E 103
Lanfield Dr. M8: Man 5B 38
Langbourne Cl. M26: Rad 1D 19
Langcliffe Pl. M26: Rad 1E 19
Langcliffe Wlk. M18: Man 5E 69
(off Hampden Cres.)
Langcroft Dr. M40: Man 2E 55
Langdale Av. M19: Man 5D 83
OL8: O'ham 5F 29
Langdale Cl. M34: Dent 4A 86
SK8: Gat 3E 111
WA15: Tim 5A 98
Langdale Ct. M8: Man 1D 53
Langdale Dr. BL9: Bury 3C 12
M24: Mid 3B 16
M28: Walk 3B 32
Langdale Hall M14: Man 2E 81
(off Upper Pk. Rd.)
Langdale Rd. M14: Man 1F 81
M32: Stre 2E 77
M33: Sale 2A 98
SK4: Stoc 2E 95
Langfield Av. M16: W Ran 2F 79
Langfield Cres. M43: Droy 5E 57
Langfield Wlk. M6: Sal 5C 50
Langford Rd. M20: Man 2C 92
SK4: Stoc 4E 95
Langford St. M34: Dent 2B 86
Langham Ct. M20: Man 4B 92
M32: Stre 1C 76
Langham Gro. WA15: Tim 3D 99
Langham Rd. M6: Sal 5B 50
OL8: O'ham 5A 30
SK4: Stoc 2D 105
Langham St. OL7: A Lyme 2C 58
Langham St. Ind. Est. OL7: A Lyme 2C 58
Langholme Cl. M15: Man 5D 9
Langholme Pl. M30: Ecc 5D 47
Langland Cl. M9: Man 5A 26
(off Leconfield Dr.)
M19: Man 4F 83
Langland Dr. M30: Ecc 3E 61
LANGLEY 5A 16
Langley Av. M24: Mid 2A 16
M25: Pres 4D 23
Langley Cl. M41: Urm 3A 76
Langley Cr. M7: Sal 3A 38
Langley Cres. M25: Pres 3D 23
Langley Gdns. M25: Pres 3D 23
Langley Grange M25: Pres 3D 23

Langley Gro. M25: Pres 3D **23**
Langley Hall Rd. M25: Pres 3D **23**
Langley Ho. M24: Mid 3C **16**
Langley La. M24: Mid 2E **15**
  OL10: H'ood 2E **15**
Langley Rd. M6: Sal 4B **36**
  M14: Man 4E **81**
  M25: Pres 4C **22**
  M27: Pen 4B **36**
  M33: Sale 5A **88**
Langley Rd. Sth. M6: Sal 1B **50**
Langness St. M11: Man 1E **69**
Lango St. *M16: Old T* 5E **65**
  (off Howarth St.)
Langport Av. M12: Man 4A **68**
Langroyd Wlk. *M8: Man* 5B **38**
  (off Highshore Dr.)
Langsett Av. M6: Sal 4E **49**
Langshaw St. M6: Sal 1B **64**
  M16: Old T 1E **79**
Langside Av. M9: Man 5A **26**
Langston St. M3: Man 1A **6** (4B **52**)
Langthorne St. M19: Man 5D **83**
Langton Cl. M35: Fail 4D **43**
Langton St. M6: Sal 5A **50**
  M24: Mid 1C **26**
Langworthy Rd. M6: Sal 3B **50**
  M40: Man 5C **40**
Langworthy Station (Metro) 1A **64**
Lanhill Dr. M8: Man 1E **53**
Lankro Way M30: Ecc 1B **62**
Lanreath Wlk. *M8: Man* 1D **53**
  (off Moordown Cl.)
Lansbury Ho. *M16: W Ran* 2F **79**
  (off Whalley Rd.)
Lansdale Gdns. M19: Man 3A **94**
Lansdale St. BL4: Farn 1A **18**
  M30: Ecc 2C **60**
Lansdowne Av. M34: Aud 1E **71**
Lansdowne Cl. OL9: Chad 3D **29**
Lansdowne Ho. *M20: Man* 1D **103**
  (off Wilmslow Rd.)
Lansdowne Rd. M8: Man 3C **38**
  M30: Ecc 4F **47**
  M33: Sale 2C **88**
  M41: Urm 5A **74**
  OL9: Chad 3E **29**
Lansdowne Rd. Nth. M41: Urm 4A **74**
Lapwing Cen. 2E **97**
Lapwing Ct. M20: Man 3C **92**
Lapwing La. M20: Man 3C **92**
  OL7: A Lyme 1F **71**
  SK5: Stoc 1D **97**
Larch Av. M26: Rad 1D **21**
  M27: Swin 1E **47**
  M32: Stre 4F **77**
Larch Cl. M23: Wyth 3E **99**
  M35: Fail 1B **56**
Larch Gdns. M8: Man 2C **52**
Larch Gro. M27: Ward 2D **33**
  OL9: Chad 1D **29**
Larch Ho. *M14: Man* 1E **81**
  (off Rusholme Pl.)
Larch Rd. M30: Ecc 3C **46**
  M34: Dent 2C **86**
Larch St. OL8: O'ham 4F **29**
Larchview Rd. M24: Mid 1E **27**
Larchwood OL9: Chad 1F **29**
  SK8: Chea 5F **103**
Larchwood Av. M9: Man 5B **40**

Larden Wlk. *M8: Man* 1B **52**
  (off Greyswood Av.)
Largs Wlk. M23: Wyth 5B **100**
Larke Ri. M20: Man 5B **92**
Larkfield Cl. OL7: A Lyme 5D **45**
Larkhall Ri. M22: Shar 1A **110**
LARK HILL .1C **26**
Lark Hill BL4: Farn 2A **18**
Larkhill Cl. WA15: Tim 5D **99**
Lark Hill Ct. M24: Mid 1C **26**
Lark Hill Rd. SK3: Stoc 3E **105**
Larkhill Wlk. *M8: Man* 1D **53**
  (off Appleford Dr.)
Larkside Av. M28: Walk 1A **32**
Larks Ri. M43: Droy 4F **57**
Lark St. BL4: Farn 2A **18**
Larmuth Av. M21: Chor 2E **91**
Larne Av. M32: Stre 3E **77**
  SK3: Stoc 4D **105**
Larne St. M11: Man 2C **68**
Larwood Av. SK4: Stoc 2D **105**
Lascar Av. M5: Sal 2C **64**
Laser Quest & The Rock 4F **61**
Lashbrook Cl. M40: Man 3F **53**
Lassell St. M11: Man 3B **70**
  (not continuous)
Lastingham St. M40: Man 1E **55**
Latchford St. OL7: A Lyme 3C **58**
Latchmere Rd. M14: Man 5E **81**
Latham St. M11: Man 3B **70**
Lathbury Rd. M9: Man 1F **53**
  M40: Man 1F **53**
Lathom Gro. M33: Sale 5A **90**
Lathom Rd. M20: Man 1F **93**
Latimer St. OL4: O'ham 3C **30**
Latrigg Cres. M24: Mid 4E **15**
Latrobe St. M43: Droy 2C **70**
Lauderdale Cres. M13: Man 4E **67**
Launceston Cl. OL8: O'ham 5E **31**
Laundry St. M6: Sal 3B **50**
Laureate Way M34: Dent 5C **86**
Laurel Av. M14: Man 3C **80**
  OL9: Chad 1F **27**
  SK8: Chea 1F **111**
Laurel Bank SK14: Hyde 5E **87**
Laurel Bank Gdns. M9: Man 1F **39**
Laurel Ct. M20: Man 2D **93**
  SK4: Stoc 4D **95**
Laurel End La. SK4: Stoc 5C **94**
Laurel Grn. M34: Dent 3C **86**
Laurel Gro. M5: Sal 5E **49**
Laurel Ho. M6: Sal 3D **49**
  SK4: Stoc 4D **95**
Laurel Rd. SK4: Stoc 4D **95**
Laurel St. M24: Mid 1F **27**
  OL4: O'ham 3D **31**
  SK4: Stoc 1A **106**
Laurence Cl. M12: Man 4D **69**
Laurence Lowry Ct. *M27: Pen* 3B **34**
  (off Lowry Dr.)
Laurieston Ct. SK8: Chea 1E **111**
Lauriston Cl. M22: Shar 5A **102**
Lauriston Gallery, The 3D **89**
  (within Waterside Arts Cen.)
Lausanne Rd. M20: Man 1D **93**
Lavender Cl. M23: Wyth 2A **100**
Lavender Rd. OL4: O'ham 5F **31**
Lavenders Brow
  SK1: Stoc 2C **118** (2B **106**)

Lavenham Av. M11: Man	1F **69**
Lavenham Bus. Pk. OL9: O'ham	3E **29**
(off Parsons St.)	
Lavenham Cl. BL9: Bury	3B **12**
Lavington Av. SK8: Chea	5C **104**
Lavington Gro. M18: Man	1F **83**
Lavinia St. M30: Ecc	5D **47**
Lavister Av. M19: Man	5F **93**
Lawefield Cres. M27: Clif	4F **19**
Lawers Av. OL9: Chad	1C **28**
Lawler Av. M5: Sal	4D **65**
Lawnbank Cl. M24: Mid	5A **16**
Lawn Closes OL8: O'ham	1E **45**
Lawn Dr. M27: Swin	5A **34**
WA15: Tim	5A **98**
Lawngreen Av. M21: Chor	1C **90**
Lawnhurst Av. M23: Wyth	3B **100**
Lawnhurst Trad. Est. SK3: Stoc	5D **105**
Lawnside M. M20: Man	3C **92**
Lawnswood Dr. M27: Swin	1D **49**
Lawnswood Pk. Rd. M27: Swin	1C **48**
Lawrence Rd. M41: Urm	2A **74**
Lawrence St. BL9: Bury	2B **12**
SK1: Stoc	3A **118** (2A **106**)
Lawson Av. SK8: Gat	1D **111**
Lawson Cl. M24: Mid	2C **16**
M28: Wors	5E **33**
Lawson Dr. WA15: Tim	5C **98**
Lawson Gro. M33: Sale	2C **88**
Lawson St. M9: Man	2E **39**
OL1: O'ham	1C **30**
(off Mortimer St.)	
Lawson Wlk. M34: Dent	5B **86**
Lawton Moor Rd. M23: Wyth	2C **100**
Lawton Rd. SK4: Stoc	4E **95**
Lawton St. M11: Man	3F **69**
M43: Droy	5D **57**
Laxey Cl. OL9: Chad	4D **29**
Laxey St. M40: Man	5D **41**
Layard St. OL6: A Lyme	2A **116** (4C **58**)
Laycock Cres. M35: Fail	5B **42**
Laycock Gro. M35: Fail	5B **42**
Laycock Way M34: Dent	5B **86**
Laystall St. M1: Man	5F **7** (1D **67**)
Layton Av. SK14: Hyde	2E **87**
Layton Cl. SK1: Stoc	3C **106**
Layton Dr. BL4: Kea	3B **18**
Layton St. M40: Man	5F **53**
Lazonby Wlk. M13: Man	1B **82**
(off Bates St.)	
Leabank St. M19: Man	4C **82**
Leabrook Dr. M40: Man	4A **42**
Leaburn Dr. M19: Man	4A **94**
Leach M. M25: Pres	5B **22**
Leach St. BL4: Farn	1A **18**
M18: Man	4D **69**
M25: Pres	5B **22**
Leach Wlk. OL4: O'ham	1F **31**
Leaconfield Dr. M28: Wors	5B **32**
Lea Ct. M35: Fail	5A **42**
SK4: Stoc	4D **95**
Leacroft Rd. M21: Chor	3F **91**
Lea Dr. M9: Man	1B **40**
Leafield Av. M20: Man	4F **93**
Leaford Av. M34: Dent	1F **85**
Leaford Cl. M34: Dent	1F **85**
Leaf St. M15: Man	5A **10** (4B **66**)
SK5: Stoc	1A **96**
Leagate M41: Urm	4A **74**
Leaholme Cl. M40: Man	2F **55**

Leak St. M16: Old T	4E **65**
(off Hadfield Cl.)	
Leamington Av. M20: Man	4B **92**
Leamington Ct. SK5: Stoc	1A **96**
Leamington Ho. M15: Man	5D **67**
(off Denmark Rd.)	
Leamington Rd. M30: Ecc	4D **47**
M41: Urm	2D **75**
SK5: Stoc	1A **96**
(not continuous)	
Leamington St. M11: Man	3F **69**
OL4: O'ham	1E **31**
Leamore Wlk. M9: Man	1A **40**
(off Leconfield Dr.)	
Leam St. OL6: A Lyme	3F **59**
Leander Cl. M9: Man	2A **40**
Lea Rd. SK4: Stoc	4D **95**
SK8: H Grn	5D **111**
Leaside Dr. M20: Man	3F **93**
Leaside Gro. M28: Walk	1A **32**
Leaton Av. M23: Wyth	5C **100**
Le Bas Ho. M20: Man	2B **92**
Lecester Rd. M8: Man	1D **53**
Leconfield Dr. M9: Man	5A **26**
Leconfield Rd. M30: Ecc	3B **46**
Ledbroke Cl. M5: Sal	2D **65**
Ledburn Cl. M15: Man	5D **9** (4F **65**)
Ledburn Ct. M15: Man	5D **9**
Ledbury Av. M41: Urm	2E **75**
Ledbury Cl. M24: Mid	3C **26**
Ledbury Rd. M35: Fail	3A **56**
Ledbury Wlk. M9: Man	1E **39**
Ledsham Av. M9: Man	4C **24**
Ledson Rd. M23: Wyth	1B **108**
Leech Av. OL6: A Lyme	2F **59**
Leech Brook Av. M34: Aud	4A **72**
Leech Brook Cl. M34: Aud	4A **72**
Lee Ct. M22: Nor	3A **102**
Lee Cres. M32: Stre	2A **78**
Lee Dale Cl. M34: Dent	3C **86**
Leedale Cl. M12: Man	3C **82**
Leeds Cl. BL9: Bury	3D **13**
Leegate Cl. SK4: Stoc	4B **94**
Leegate Dr. M9: Man	5B **26**
Leegate Gdns. SK4: Stoc	4B **94**
Leegate Ho. SK4: Stoc	4C **94**
Leegate Rd. SK4: Stoc	4B **94**
(not continuous)	
Leegrange Rd. M9: Man	3A **40**
Lee Rd. M9: Man	4A **40**
LEES	3F **31**
Lees Av. M34: Dent	3A **86**
LEESBROOK	3F **31**
Lees Brook Pk. OL4: O'ham	3F **31**
Lee's Ct. SK1: Stoc	3B **118** (2B **106**)
LEESFIELD	4F **31**
Leesfield OL6: A Lyme	1C **116** (3D **59**)
Lees Gro. OL4: O'ham	4F **31**
Lees Hall Ct. M14: Man	5F **81**
Lees Hall Cres. M14: Man	5F **81**
Leeside SK4: Stoc	2C **104**
Lees New Rd. OL4: O'ham	2F **45**
Lees Pk. Av. M43: Droy	5E **57**
Lees Pk. Way M43: Droy	5E **57**
Lees Rd. OL4: O'ham	2C **30**
OL6: A Lyme	1F **59**
Lees Sq. OL6: A Lyme	4E **59**
Lees St. M11: Man	3F **69**
M24: Mid	1F **27**
M27: Pen	3B **34**

Lees St. M43: Droy 5D 57
  OL6: A Lyme 1C 116 (3D 59)
  OL8: O'ham 4C 44
Lees St. Ent. Trad. Est. M18: Man ...4A 70
Leestone Rd. M22: Shar 5A 102
Lee St. M24: Mid 3B 16
  OL8: O'ham 3F 29
  SK1: Stoc 3B 118 (2B 106)
Leesway OL4: Lees 4F 31
Leesway Dr. M34: Dent 3C 86
Leeswood Av. M21: Chor 2E 91
Leewood M27: Clif 5F 19
Leewood Ct. SK4: Stoc 5D 95
Left Bank M3: Man 5F 5 (1A 66)
Legh Ct. M33: Sale 5F 89
Legh Dr. M34: Aud 1D 71
Leghorn Wlk. M11: Man 1B 68
             (off Yeoman Wlk.)
Legh Rd. M7: Sal 4F 37
  M33: Sale 5A 90
Legh St. M7: Sal 5F 37
  M30: Ecc 1E 61
Legion Gro. M7: Sal 1A 52
Legwood Ct. M41: Urm 3E 75
Leicester M7: Sal 4B 38
  M34: Dent 4B 86
  M43: Droy 4B 56
  WA15: Tim 3C 98
Leicester Ct. M7: Sal 3A 38
Leicester Rd. M7: Sal 1A 52
  M33: Sale 3D 89
  M35: Fail 2C 56
  M45: White 5A 12
Leicester St. OL4: O'ham 3D 31
  OL7: A Lyme 1B 116 (3D 59)
  SK5: Stoc 3B 84
Leicester Wlk. M7: Sal 1A 52
          (off Brighton Av.)
Leigh Av. M27: Swin 2F 47
Leighbrook Rd. M14: Man 5D 81
Leigh Fold SK14: Hyde 5F 73
Leigh Rd. M28: Wors 1A 46
         (not continuous)
Leigh St. BL4: Farn 1A 18
Leighton Rd. M16: Old T 1E 79
Leighton St. M40: Man 4C 40
Leinster Rd. M27: Swin 5A 34
Leith Av. M33: Sale 4A 90
Leith Pl. OL8: O'ham 2A 44
Leith Rd. M33: Sale 4A 90
Lemnos St. OL1: O'ham 2C 30
Lena St. M1: Man 1E 11 (1D 67)
Len Cox Wlk. M4: Man 4E 7
Leng Rd. M40: Man 2F 55
Lenham Av. M30: Ecc 5D 47
         (off Dover St.)
Lenham Cl. SK5: Stoc 2D 97
Lenham Towers SK5: Stoc 2D 97
Lenham Wlk. M22: Wyth 1F 113
Lennox Ho. OL6: A Lyme ...1C 116 (3D 59)
Lennox St. M34: Aud 4A 72
  OL6: A Lyme 4E 59
Lenthall Wlk. M8: Man 5B 38
         (off Crookhill Dr.)
Lentmead Dr. M40: Man 3C 40
Lenton Gdns. M22: Shar 1A 110
Leominster Dr. M22: Wyth 3A 110
Leominster Rd. M24: Mid 3D 27
Leopold Av. M20: Man 3C 92
Leroy Dr. M9: Man 2F 39

Lesley Rd. M32: Stre 4C 76
Leslie Av. BL9: Bury 3B 12
  OL9: Chad 1D 43
Leslie Gro. WA15: Tim 5C 98
Leslie Hough Way M6: Sal 1A 4 (3D 51)
Leslie St. M14: Man 2D 81
Lester St. M32: Stre 3F 77
Letchworth St. M14: Man 2D 81
Letham St. OL8: O'ham 2B 44
Levedale Rd. M9: Man 5A 26
Leven Cl. BL4: Kea 3D 19
Levenhurst Rd. M8: Man 5B 38
Levens Cl. SK8: Gat 2D 111
LEVENSHULME 4C 82
Levenshulme Rd. M18: Man 1F 83
Levenshulme Station (Rail) 4C 82
Levenshulme Swimming Pools 4D 83
Levenshulme Ter. M19: Man 4C 82
        (off Stockport Rd.)
Levenshulme Trad. Est.
  M19: Man 3E 83
Levens St. M6: Sal 2D 51
  M40: Man 5C 40
Levens Wlk. OL9: Chad 4C 28
Leven Wlk. M23: Wyth 5C 100
  M45: White 1E 23
Lever Av. M27: Clif 2D 35
Lever Ct. M7: Sal 4C 36
Lever St. M1: Man 5D 7 (1D 67)
  M24: Mid 5C 16
Levington Dr. OL8: O'ham 2B 26
Lewes Av. M34: Dent 4C 44
Lewes Wlk. OL9: Chad 4B 86
Lewis Av. M9: Man 3D 29
  M41: Urm 3A 40
Lewisham Av. M40: Man 5F 61
Lewis Rd. M43: Droy 3D 55
  SK5: Stoc 4B 84
Lewis St. M30: Ecc 1F 61
  M40: Man 4F 53
  SK14: Hyde 2F 87
Lewtas St. M30: Ecc 1A 62
Lexton Av. M8: Man 2D 39
Leybourne Av. M19: Man 3D 83
Leybourne M. M7: Sal 1A 52
      (off Gt. Cheetham St. E.)
Leybrook Rd. M22: Wyth 3E 109
Leyburn Av. M32: Stre 2E 77
  M41: Urm 4C 74
Leyburn Cl. M45: White 1A 22
Leyburn Rd. SK2: Stoc 5F 107
Leyburn Ho. M13: Man 1F 81
Leyburn Rd. M40: Man 2E 41
Leycett Dr. M23: Wyth 2C 100
Leycroft St.
  M1: Man 2F 11 (2D 67)
Leyden Wlk. M23: Wyth 2C 108
Leyland Av. M20: Man 5F 93
  SK8: Gat 5D 103
Leyland St. BL9: Bury 2A 12
  SK4: Stoc 2A 118 (2A 106)
Leys Rd. WA14: Tim 3A 98
Leyton Av. M40: Man 5D 41
Leyton Dr. BL9: Bury 1B 12
Leywell Rd. M9: Man 4B 40
Library La. OL9: O'ham 1F 29
Library Theatre 2B 10
       (off St Peter's Sq.)
Library Wlk. M2: Man 1B 10

Lichens Cres. OL8: O'ham 1C **44**
Lichfield Av. OL6: A Lyme 5F **45**
　　　SK5: Stoc 1A **96**
Lichfield Dr. M8: Man 5D **39**
　　　M25: Pres 2E **37**
　　　M27: Swin 1B **48**
Lichfield Rd. M30: Ecc 3B **48**
　　　M41: Urm 1F **75**
Lichfield St. M6: Sal 2C **50**
Lidbrook Wlk. M12: Man 4A **68**
Lidgate Gro. M20: Man 5C **92**
Lidiard St. M8: Man 3C **38**
Lieutenant Wlk. M5: Sal 3A **8**
Liffey Av. M22: Wyth 3A **110**
Lifton Av. M40: Man 3A **54**
Lightborne Av. M33: Sale 4A **88**
Lightbourne Av. M27: Swin 5B **34**
LIGHTBOURNE GREEN **5B 34**
Lightbowne Rd. M40: Man 1C **54**
Lightfoot Wlk. *M11: Man* *1B 68*
　　　　　　　　　　(off Newcombe Cl.)
Lighthorne Av. SK3: Stoc 4B **104**
Lighthorne Gro. SK3: Stoc 4B **104**
Lighthorne Rd. SK3: Stoc 4B **104**
Light Oaks Rd. M6: Sal 3D **49**
Lignum Av. OL9: Chad 1D **29**
Lilac Av. M27: Swin 4C **34**
　　　SK14: Hyde 5F **87**
Lilac Ct. M6: Sal 5C **50**
Lilac Gro. M25: Pres 3C **22**
　　　M40: Man 3C **40**
　　　OL9: Chad 1D **29**
Lilac La. OL8: O'ham 2F **43**
Lilac St. SK2: Stoc 5B **106**
Lila St. M9: Man 5B **40**
Lilford Cl. M12: Man 4C **68**
Lilian St. M16: Old T 1E **79**
Lillian Gro. SK5: Stoc 5B **84**
Lilmore Av. M40: Man 1E **55**
Lilstock Wlk. *M9: Man* *1A 40*
　　　　　　　　　(off Woodmere Dr.)
LILY HILL **4B 12**
Lily Hill St. M45: White 4A **12**
Lily La. M9: Man 5B **40**
LILY LANES **4F 45**
Lily Lanes OL6: A Lyme 4F **45**
Lily St. M24: Mid 1E **27**
　　　M30: Ecc 1D **61**
　　　OL1: O'ham 1A **30**
Lily Thomas Ct. M11: Man 3F **69**
Lime Av. M27: Swin 1E **47**
　　　M41: Urm 3D **75**
　　　M45: White 2B **22**
Lime Bank St. M12: Man 2F **67**
Limebrook Cl. M11: Man 3A **70**
Lime Cl. M6: Sal 4C **50**
　　　SK16: Duk 4F **73**
Lime Ct. M6: Sal 4C **50**
Lime Cres. M16: Old T 1D **79**
Limeditch Rd. M35: Fail 3C **42**
LIME FIELD **1A 26**
Limefield M24: Mid 1A **26**
Limefield Cl. M7: Sal 3F **37**
Limefield Rd. M7: Sal 3F **37**
Limefield Ter. M19: Man 4C **82**
Lime Gdns. M24: Mid 1A **26**
　　　SK16: Duk 2D **73**
LIME GATE **3E 43**
Lime Ga. OL8: O'ham 2E **43**
Lime Grn. OL8: O'ham 3F **43**

Lime Grn. Pde. *OL8: O'ham* *3F 43*
　　　　　　　　　　(off Lime Grn.)
Lime Grn. Rd. OL8: O'ham 4E **43**
Lime Gro. M15: Man 5D **67**
　　　M16: Old T 1D **79**
　　　M20: Man 5C **92**
　　　M25: Pres 3C **22**
　　　M28: Walk 3A **32**
　　　M34: Dent 1B **86**
　　　OL6: A Lyme 2E **59**
　　　SK8: Chea 5F **103**
　　　WA15: Tim 1D **99**
LIMEHURST **1C 58**
Limehurst Av. M20: Man 5B **80**
　　　OL7: A Lyme 1C **58**
Limehurst Ct. OL8: O'ham 3F **43**
Limehurst Rd. OL7: A Lyme 1C **58**
Limekiln La. M12: Man 2F **67**
Lime Kilns, The M28: Wors 2C **46**
Lime La. M35: Fail 5E **43**
　　　OL8: O'ham 3E **43**
　　　　　　　　　　　(not continuous)
Lime Pl. *SK16: Duk* *2D 73*
　　　　　　　　　　(off Railway St.)
Lime Rd. M32: Stre 4F **77**
Limerston Dr. M40: Man 2B **54**
Limes, The SK3: Stoc 4F **105**
LIME SIDE **3F 43**
Limeside Rd. OL8: O'ham 2E **43**
Limestead Av. M8: Man 4C **38**
Lime St. BL4: Farn 1A **18**
　　　M30: Ecc 1F **61**
　　　OL1: Chad 1E **29**
　　　SK16: Duk 2D **73**
　　　　　　　　　　　(not continuous)
Lime Tree Cl. M41: Urm 4A **76**
Lime Tree Gro. M35: Fail 5D **43**
Limetrees Rd. M24: Mid 1B **26**
Limetree Wlk. *M11: Man* *1B 68*
　　　　　　　　　　(off Albert St.)
Limley Gro. M21: Chor 1E **91**
Linby St. M15: Man 5E **9** (3A **66**)
Lincoln Av. M19: Man 4D **83**
　　　M32: Stre 2B **76**
　　　M34: Dent 4B **86**
　　　M43: Droy 4C **56**
　　　SK8: H Grn 2D **115**
Lincoln Cl. OL6: A Lyme 4F **45**
Lincoln Ct. M7: Sal 3A **38**
　　　M40: Man 3D **55**
Lincoln Dr. M25: Pres 2C **22**
Lincoln Grn. SK5: Stoc 2D **97**
Lincoln Gro. M13: Man 5E **67**
　　　M33: Sale 4A **90**
Lincoln Minshull Cl. M23: Wyth 1B **100**
Lincoln Pl. M1: Man 4C **10**
Lincoln Rd. M24: Mid 4E **27**
　　　M27: Swin 5A **34**
　　　M35: Fail 1C **56**
Lincoln Sq. *M2: Man* *1A 10*
　　　　　　　　　　(off Brazennose St.)
Lincoln St. M13: Man 1B **82**
　　　M30: Ecc 1E **61**
　　　OL9: O'ham 4D **29**
Lincoln Towers
　　　SK1: Stoc 4C **118** (3B **106**)
Lincombe Rd. M22: Wyth 1E **113**
Lindale SK14: Hyde 5E **73**
Lindale Av. BL9: Bury 3C **12**
　　　M40: Man 2F **41**

Lindale Av. M41: Urm 2B 74
　　OL9: Chad 3C 28
Lindale Dr. M24: Mid 3A 16
Lindbury Av. SK2: Stoc 4E 107
Linden Av. M6: Sal 1A 50
　　M27: Swin 5F 33
　　M33: Sale 4B 88
　　M34: Aud 3F 71
　　OL4: O'ham 1F 31
　　WA15: Alt 5A 98
Linden Cl. M34: Dent 2C 86
Linden Dr. M5: Sal 2C 64
Linden Gro. M14: Man 5F 81
Linden Lea M33: Sale 1D 99
Linden Pk. M19: Man 5D 82
Linden Rd. M20: Man 4C 92
　　M34: Dent 2C 86
Linden Way M43: Droy 2A 70
Lindenwood OL9: Chad 1A 28
Lindeth Av. M18: Man 1F 83
Lindfield Rd. SK5: Stoc 4B 84
Lindinis Av. M6: Sal 5C 50
Lindisfarne Cl. M33: Sale 2D 99
Lindisfarne Rd. OL7: A Lyme 2A 58
Lindley Gro. SK3: Stoc 5F 105
Lindley St. BL4: Kea 3D 49
Lindleywood Rd. M14: Man 5A 82
Lindon Av. M34: Dent 5F 85
Lindow Ct. M33: Sale 5B 90
　　　　　　　　(off Northenden Rd.)
　　SK6: Bred 5F 97
Lindow Rd. M16: Old T 3D 79
Lindow St. M33: Sale 5B 90
Lindrick Av. M45: White 3F 21
Lindrick Cl. M40: Man 5E 41
Lindsay Av. M19: Man 4B 82
　　M27: Swin 5A 34
Lindsay Rd. M19: Man 5B 82
Lindsgate Dr. WA15: Tim 4D 99
Lindside Wlk. M9: Man 1A 40
　　　　　　　　(off Woodmere Dr.)
Lind St. M40: Man 3A 54
Lindum Av. M16: Old T 1E 79
Lindum St. M14: Man 2D 81
Lindwall Cl. M23: Wyth 1D 101
Lindy Av. M27: Clif 1B 34
Linear Walkway M30: Ecc 4F 47
Linebank Grn. WA14: Alt 5A 98
　　　　　　　　(off Grosvenor Rd.)
Linehan Cl. SK4: Stoc 1F 103
Linen Cl. M3: Sal 2C 4 (4F 51)
Lines Rd. M43: Droy 1D 71
Linfield St. M11: Man 1D 69
Linford Av. M40: Man 2E 41
Lingard Cl. M34: Aud 2E 71
Lingard La. SK6: Bred 3F 97
Lingard Rd. M22: Nor 2F 101
Lingard St. SK5: Stoc 5B 84
Lingard Ter. M34: Aud 2E 71
Lingcrest Cl. M19: Man 1E 95
Lingdale Wlk. M40: Man 5C 40
Lingfield M16: W Ran 2F 79
　　　　　　　　(off Whalley Rd.)
Lingfield Rd. M11: Man 5E 55
Lingfield Wlk. OL9: Chad 2E 29
　　　　　　　　(off Kempton Way)
Lingholme Dr. M24: Mid 4E 15
Lingmell Cl. M24: Mid 4F 15
　　M41: Urm 1B 74
Lingmoor Cl. M24: Mid 4E 15

Lingmoor Wlk. M15: Man 5B 66
　　　　　　　　(off Arnott Cres.)
Lings Wlk. M22: Wyth 5A 110
Linhope Cl. SK4: Stoc 5A 94
Link, The SK5: Stoc 2E 97
　　SK9: Hand 5F 115
Link Av. M41: Urm 4C 76
Link La. OL8: O'ham 2A 44
Links, The M40: Man 5E 41
Links Av. M35: Fail 2B 56
Links Cres. M25: Pres 2A 38
Linksfield M34: Dent 5B 72
Links Pl. OL6: A Lyme 1F 59
Links Ri. M41: Urm 1C 74
Links Vw. M25: Pres 3C 36
Links Vw. Ct. M45: White 2F 21
Links Way OL9: Chad 1E 29
Linksway M25: Pres 2F 37
　　M27: Swin 1C 48
　　SK8: Gat 2C 110
Linksway Cl. SK4: Stoc 3C 94
Linksway Dr. BL9: Bury 3C 12
Linkway Ind. Est. M24: Mid 1D 27
Linley Dr. OL4: O'ham 5F 31
Linley Rd. M33: Sale 3D 89
Linley St. M26: Rad 1A 12
Linnet Cl. M34: Aud 1E 71
Linnets Wood M. M28: Walk 1A 32
Linnett Cl. M12: Man 1B 82
Linn St. M8: Man 3C 38
LINNYSHAW 1A 32
Linnyshaw Ind. Est. M28: Walk 1B 32
Linnyshaw La. M28: Walk 5A 18
Linslade Ho. M5: Sal 1B 64
　　　　　　　(off Buckingham St.)
Linslade Wlk. M9: Man 5F 39
　　　　　　　(off Carisbrook St.)
Linstead Dr. M8: Man 1B 52
Linton Av. M34: Dent 2C 84
Linton Cl. M4: Man 2F 67
Linton Rd. M33: Sale 2E 89
Linton Vw. M26: Rad 1D 19
Linton Wlk. M7: Sal 4B 36
　　　　　　　　(not continuous)
Linwood Gro. M12: Man 3C 82
Linwood St. M35: Fail 1E 55
Lion Brow M9: Man 2F 39
Lion Fold La. M9: Man 1F 39
Lions Dr. M27: Swin 5C 34
Lion St. M9: Man 2F 39
Lisburn Av. M21: Chor 4E 79
　　M33: Sale 5C 88
Lisburne Av. SK2: Stoc 5F 107
Lisburne Cl. SK2: Stoc 5F 107
Lisburne Ct. SK2: Stoc 5F 107
Lisburne La. SK2: Stoc 5E 107
Liscard Av. M40: Man 4C 40
Liscard Av. M14: Man 4D 81
Lisetta Av. OL4: O'ham 5B 44
Lismore Av. SK3: Stoc 4D 105
Lismore Rd. SK16: Duk 3F 73
Lismore Wlk. M22: Wyth 1A 114
Lismore Way M41: Urm 5C 59
Lissadel Science Pk. M6: Sal . . .1A 4 (4D 51)
Lissadel St. M6: Sal 3C 50
Lister Rd. M24: Mid 3D 25
Litcham Cl. M1: Man 4E 11 (3D 67)
Litchfield Ct. M24: Mid 2D 25
Litchfield Gro. M28: Wors 5C 32
Litherland Av. M22: Wyth 4A 110

Litherland Rd. M33: Sale 5A 90
Lit. Ancoats St. M1: Man 4E 7 (5D 53)
Littlebank Cl. OL4: O'ham 3D 31
LITTLE BOLTON 1D 63
Lit. Bolton Ter. M5: Sal 5E 49
Lit. David St. M1: Man 2D 11 (2C 66)
Lit. Ees La. M33: Sale 3B 88
Lit. Egerton St. SK1: Stoc 1A 118 (1A 106)
LITTLE GREEN 5E 17
Littlegreen Gdns. M6: Sal 4B 50
Littleham Wlk. M18: Man 5E 69
   (off Hampden Cres.)
Littlehaven Cl. M12: Man 5A 68
Littlehills Cl. M24: Mid 5A 16
Lit. Holme St. M4: Man 5F 53
Lit. John St. M3: Man 2E 9 (1A 66)
Little La. M9: Man 5D 25
Lit. Lever St. M1: Man 5E 7 (1D 67)
   (not continuous)
Lit. Moor Cotts. SK1: Stoc 3D 107
   (off Hampson St.)
Littlemoor Ho. OL4: O'ham 1E 31
Littlemoor La. OL4: O'ham 1E 31
LITTLEMOSS 5E 57
Littlemoss Bus. Pk. M43: Droy 4E 57
Lit. Moss La. M27: Clif 2B 34
Littlemoss Rd. M43: Droy 4E 57
Lit. Nelson St.
   M4: Man 2D 11 (4C 52)
LITTLE PARK 1B 26
Lit. Peter St. M15: Man 4F 9 (3A 66)
Lit. Pitt St. M1: Man 5F 7
Lit. Quay St. M3: Man 1A 10 (1B 66)
Littler Av. M21: Chor 3E 91
Littlers Point M17: T Pk 5F 63
Little St. SK2: Stoc 3D 107
Littleton Rd. M6: Sal 4B 36
   M7: Sal 4B 36
Little Town OL8: O'ham 5E 29
Little Underbank
   SK1: Stoc 2B 118 (2B 106)
Littlewood Rd. M22: Wyth 2E 109
Littlewood St. M6: Sal 5A 50
Liverpool Cl. SK5: Stoc 1A 96
Liverpool Rd. M3: Man 2D 9 (2F 65)
   M30: Ecc .4A 60
Liverpool Road Steam Railway 2A 66
   (off Liverpool Rd.)
Liverpool St. M5: Sal 5F 49
   M6: Sal 5A 4 (5F 49)
   SK5: Stoc .1A 96
Liverstudd Av. SK5: Stoc 5B 84
Liverton Ct. M9: Man 4D 25
   (off Liverton Dr.)
Liverton Dr. M9: Man 4D 25
Livesey St. M4: Man 1F 7 (4E 53)
   M19: Man .5D 83
   OL1: O'ham 1E 31
Livingston Av. M22: Wyth 4D 109
Livingstone Pl. M16: Old T 5D 65
   (off Carver St.)
Livsey St. M45: White 1B 22
Lizard St. M1: Man 5E 7
Lizmar Ter. M9: Man 1F 41
Llanberis Rd. SK8: Chea H 5F 111
Llanfair Rd. SK3: Stoc 4B 106
Lloyd Av. SK8: Gat 5C 102
Lloyd Ct. M12: Man 4B 68
   (off Kelsall St.)
Lloyd Rd. M19: Man 1D 95

Lloyd St. M2: Man 1A 10 (1B 66)
   (not continuous)
   M43: Droy .1B 70
   SK4: Stoc .5F 95
   (not continuous)
Lloyd St. Nth. M14: Man 1C 80
   M15: Man .1C 80
Lloyd St. Sth. M14: Man 4C 80
Lloyd Wright Av. M11: Man 2A 68
Lock Bldg., The M1: Man 3B 10 (2B 66)
Lockes Yd. M1: Man 4B 10
Lockett Gdns. M3: Sal 3D 5 (5F 51)
Lockett St. M6: Sal 2C 50
   M8: Man 3A 52
Lockhart Cl. M12: Man 5C 68
Lockingate St. OL6: A Lyme 1D 59
Locking Ga. Ri. OL4: O'ham 1F 31
Lock Keepers M. M27: Pen 4F 35
Locksley Cl. SK4: Stoc 1E 105
Lockton Cl. M1: Man 4F 11 (3D 67)
   SK5: Stoc .2A 96
Lockton Ct. M1: Man 4E 11
Lock Vw. M26: Rad 1D 19
Lockwood St. M12: Man 2D 83
Loddon Wlk. M9: Man 4A 40
   (off Hillier St.)
Lodge Av. M41: Urm 3A 76
Lodge Cl. SK16: Duk 3F 73
Lodge Ct. SK14: Stoc 1B 104
Lodge Fold M43: Droy 5D 57
Lodge La. SK14: Hyde 1F 87
   SK16: Duk .2F 73
Lodgepole Cl. M30: Ecc 2B 60
Lodges, The M28: Wors 4C 32
Lodgeside Cl. M43: Droy 5D 57
Lodge St. M24: Mid 5C 16
   M40: Man .2A 54
   OL7: A Lyme 1B 72
   SK14: Hyde 5F 73
Lodge Vw. M43: Droy 5D 57
Loganberry Av. M6: Sal 4C 50
Lok Fu Gdns. M8: Man 2A 52
Lomas Cl. M19: Man 5A 94
Lomas Ct. OL6: A Lyme 2A 116 (4C 58)
Lomas St. M24: Mid 5D 17
   M35: Fail 3C 42
   SK3: Stoc .4F 105
Lomax St. M1: Man 5F 7 (1E 67)
   M45: White .4A 12
Lombard Gro. M14: Man 5E 81
Lombard St. OL1: O'ham 2D 117 (2A 30)
Lombardy Ct. M6: Sal 4C 50
Lomond Av. M32: Stre 2F 77
Lomond Lodge M8: Man 2B 38
Lomond Rd. M22: Wyth 4B 110
   SK8: H Grn 4B 110
London Pl. SK1: Stoc 3B 118 (2B 106)
London Rd. M1: Man 1E 11 (2D 67)
   OL1: O'ham 1D 31
London Sq. SK1: Stoc 3B 118 (2B 106)
London St. M6: Sal 3D 51
   M45: White .2B 22
Longacre St. M1: Man 1E 67
Longbow Ct. M7: Sal 2F 51
Longbridge Rd. M17: T Pk 4C 62
Longcauseway BL4: Farn 2A 18
Longcrag Wlk. M15: Man 5C 66
   (off Botham Cl.)
Longcroft Gro. M23: Wyth 4C 100
   M34: Aud .2D 71

Longdell Wlk. *M9:* Man 4A **40**
(off Dalbeattie St.)
Longden Rd. M12: Man 3C **82**
Longfellow Wlk. *M34:* Dent 5C **86**
(off Wordsworth Rd.)
Longfield M25: Pres 4C **22**
Longfield Av. M41: Urm 4E **75**
SK8: H Grn 2E **115**
WA15: Tim 5E **99**
Longfield Cen. M25: Pres 4C **22**
Longfield Cl. SK14: Hyde 4F **73**
Longfield Cotts. *M41:* Urm 3D **75**
(off Stamford Rd.)
Longfield Dr. OL4: O'ham 1E **31**
Longfield Dr. M41: Urm 3D **75**
Longfield La. OL4: O'ham 1F **31**
Longfield Rd. M23: Wyth 3B **100**
Longford Av. M32: Stre 3A **78**
Longford Cl. M32: Stre 2A **78**
Longford Cotts. M32: Stre 3B **78**
Longford Ho. M21: Chor 4B **78**
Longford Pk. 3B **78**
Longford Pl. M14: Man 1A **82**
Longford Rd. M21: Chor 4C **78**
M32: Stre 2A **78**
SK5: Stoc 4B **84**
Longford Rd. W. M19: Man 4F **83**
SK5: Stoc 4F **83**
Longford St. M18: Man 4F **69**
Longford Trad. Est. M32: Stre 2F **77**
Longford Wharf M32: Stre 3A **78**
Longham Cl. M11: Man 1A **68**
Longhey Rd. M22: Wyth 1F **109**
Longhill Wlk. *M40:* Man 1C **54**
(off Halliford Rd.)
Longhope Rd. M22: Wyth 3D **109**
Longhurst Rd. M9: Man 5D **25**
Long La. OL9: Chad 1B **42**
Longlevens Rd. M22: Wyth 4E **109**
Longley Dr. M28: Wors 1D **47**
Longley La. M22: Nor 3F **101**
Longley St. OL1: O'ham 5E **117**
Longmeadow Gro. M34: Dent 3A **86**
Long Mdw. Pas. SK14: Hyde 2F **87**
Longmead Rd. M6: Sal 2F **49**
Longmead Way M24: Mid 5D **17**
Longmere Av. M22: Wyth 3F **109**
Long Millgate M3: Man 3B **6** (5B **52**)
Longnor Rd. SK8: H Grn 2F **115**
Longport Av. M20: Man 1C **92**
Longshaw Av. M27: Pen 3C **34**
Longshut La. SK1: Stoc 5C **118** (4B **106**)
Longshut La. W.
SK2: Stoc 5B **118** (4B **106**)
LONGSIGHT 1C **82**
Longsight Ind. Est. M12: Man 1B **82**
Longsight Rd. M18: Man 2D **83**
Longsight Shop. Cen. M12: Man 1B **82**
Longsons, The *SK5:* Stoc 5B **96**
(off Lancashire Hill)
Long St. M18: Man 4A **70**
M24: Mid 5C **16**
M27: Swin 5B **34**
Longthwaite Cl. M24: Mid 4F **15**
Longton Av. M20: Man 3C **92**
Longton Rd. M6: Sal 2E **49**
M9: Man 4E **25**
Longton St. BL9: Bury 2B **12**
Longview Dr. M27: Ward 3F **33**
Longwood Av. SK2: Stoc 5D **107**

Long Wood Rd. M17: T Pk 4D **63**
Longwood Rd. M22: Wyth 3A **110**
Long Wood Rd. Est. M17: T Pk 4D **63**
Longworth La. M41: Urm 4A **74**
Longworth St. M3: Man 2F **9** (2A **66**)
Lonsdale Av. M27: Swin 2F **47**
M41: Urm 1D **75**
SK5: Stoc 2B **84**
Lonsdale Ct. M24: Mid 2E **27**
Lonsdale Rd. M19: Man 3D **83**
OL8: O'ham 2E **43**
Loom St. M4: Man 4F **7** (5D **53**)
Loonies Ct. SK1: Stoc 3B **118** (3B **106**)
Lord Byron Sq. M50: Sal 1B **64**
Lord Kitchener Ct. M33: Sale 2D **89**
Lord La. M35: Fail 3A **56**
Lord La. M. M35: Fail 1B **56**
Lord Napier Dr. M5: Sal 3D **65**
Lord Nth. St. M40: Man 3A **54**
Lord's Av. M5: Sal 5F **49**
Lordsfield Av. OL7: A Lyme 3D **59**
Lord Sheldon Way
OL6: A Lyme 1A **116** (4B **58**)
OL7: A Lyme 1F **71**
Lordship Cl. M9: Man 3B **40**
Lordsmead St. M15: Man 5D **9** (4F **65**)
Lord St. BL4: Kea 1A **18**
M3: Man 1B **6** (3B **52**)
M4: Man 1B **6** (3B **52**)
M7: Sal 3E **51**
M24: Mid 4C **16**
M34: Dent 1C **84**
OL1: O'ham 1E **117** (1B **30**)
(not continuous)
OL6: A Lyme 1C **116** (3D **59**)
SK1: Stoc 3A **118** (2B **106**)
Loretto Rd. M41: Urm 4B **76**
Loring St. M40: Man 2E **55**
Lorland Rd. SK3: Stoc 4D **105**
Lorna Gro. SK8: Gat 5B **102**
Lorne Gro. M41: Urm 3A **76**
SK3: Stoc 5A **106**
Lorne Rd. M14: Man 5E **81**
Lorne St. M30: Ecc 2D **61**
OL8: O'ham 5A **30**
Lorraine Rd. WA15: Tim 5C **98**
Lorton Cl. M24: Mid 4E **15**
Lostock Av. M19: Man 4D **83**
M33: Sale 4A **90**
M41: Urm 2D **75**
Lostock Circ. M41: Urm 1B **76**
Lostock Ct. M32: Stre 1B **76**
SK9: Hand 5F **115**
Lostock Gro. M32: Stre 2D **77**
Lostock Rd. M5: Sal 5A **50**
M41: Urm 1E **75**
SK9: Hand 5F **115**
Lostock St. M40: Man 4F **53**
Lostock Wlk. M45: White 5E **13**
Lothian Av. M30: Ecc 4D **47**
Lottery St. SK3: Stoc 2F **105**
Lottie St. M27: Pen 4C **34**
Loughborough Cl. M33: Sale 5A **88**
Loughfield M41: Urm 3C **74**
Louisa St. M11: Man 2E **69**
Louvaine Cl. M18: Man 4A **70**
Louvain St. M35: Fail 5A **42**
Love La. SK4: Stoc 1A **106**
Lovell Ct. M8: Man 2B **38**

Lovett Wlk. M22: Nor 3A **102**
Lowbrook Av. M9: Man 1D **41**
Lowcock St. M7: Sal 1E **5** (3A **52**)
Lowcroft Cres. OL9: Chad 1B **28**
Lowcross Rd. M40: Man 1C **54**
Lwr. Albion St. M1: Man 3E **11** (2D **67**)
Lwr. Alma St. SK16: Duk 1D **73**
Lwr. Alt Hill OL6: A Lyme 4E **45**
Lwr. Bamford Cl. M24: Mid 4C **16**
Lowerbank M34: Dent 5B **72**
Lwr. Bennett St. SK14: Hyde 1E **85**
LOWER BREDBURY 1F **107**
Lwr. Brooklands Pde. *M8: Man* 2A **38**
(off Counthill Dr.)
Lwr. Brook La. M28: Wors 2C **46**
LOWER BROUGHTON 1B **4** (3A **52**)
Lwr. Broughton Rd.
M7: Sal 1B **4** (2E **51**)
Lwr. Bury St. SK4: Stoc 1F **105**
Lwr. Byrom St. M3: Man 2E **9** (2A **66**)
Lower Carrs OL6: A Lyme 2F **59**
SK1: Stoc 3C **118** (2B **106**)
Lwr. Chatham St. M1: Man 4C **10** (3C **66**)
M15: Man 5C **10** (3C **66**)
Lower Cft. M45: White 3E **21**
LOWER CRUMPSALL 4E **39**
Lwr. Edge Av. OL1: O'ham 1D **117** (1A **30**)
Lowerfields OL8: O'ham 5D **31**
Lower Fold M34: Dent 2C **86**
Lower Grn. M24: Mid 4B **26**
OL6: A Lyme 3E **59**
Lower Hillgate SK1: Stoc . . .2B **118** (2B **106**)
Lower Ho. St. OL1: O'ham 1D **31**
LOWER KERSAL 1D **51**
Lwr. Lime Rd. OL8: O'ham 4E **43**
Lwr. Meadow Rd. SK9: Hand 5F **115**
Lwr. Moat Cl. SK4: Stoc 5A **96**
Lwr. Monton Rd. M30: Ecc 5A **48**
LOWER MOOR 1C **30**
Lwr. Mosley St.
M2: Man 3A **10** (2B **66**)
Lwr. Moss La. M15: Man 5D **9** (3F **65**)
M45: White 1B **22**
Lwr. Ormond St.
M1: Man 4C **10** (3C **66**)
M15: Man 5C **10** (3C **66**)
Lwr. Park Rd. M14: Man 1E **81**
Lwr. Rawson St. BL4: Farn 1A **18**
Lwr. Seedley Rd. M6: Sal 4A **50**
Lwr. Sutherland St. M27: Swin 4A **34**
Lwr. Vickers St. M40: Man 4F **53**
Lwr. Victoria St. OL9: Chad 2D **29**
Lwr. Wharf St.
OL6: A Lyme 3C **116** (5D **59**)
Lowestead Rd. M11: Man 5E **55**
Lowestoft St. M14: Man 3D **81**
Lowe St. M34: Dent 2D **87**
SK1: Stoc 3B **118** (2B **106**)
Loweswater Rd. SK8: Gat 3D **111**
Lowfell Wlk. M18: Man 2F **83**
Lowfield Av. M43: Droy 4B **56**
Lowfield Gro. SK2: Stoc 4B **106**
Lowfield Rd. SK2: Stoc 4B **106**
SK3: Stoc 5A **106**
Lowfield Wlk. *M9: Man* 1A **40**
(off Normanton Dr.)
Lowgill Wlk. *M18: Man* 5E **69**
(off Beyer Cl.)
Lowland Gro. OL7: A Lyme 1C **58**
Lowlands Cl. M24: Mid 4E **27**

Lowndes Cl. SK2: Stoc 5D **107**
Lowndes La. SK2: Stoc 4D **107**
Lowndes Wlk. *M13: Man* 4E **67**
(off Copeman Cl.)
Lownorth Rd. M22: Wyth 1A **114**
Lowood Av. M41: Urm 1B **74**
Lowrey Wlk. *M9: Man* 5A **40**
(off Craigend Dr.)
Lowry, The 3A **64**
Lowry, The M14: Man 5E **81**
Lowry Dr. M27: Pen 3B **34**
Lowry Ho. *M30: Ecc* 5A **48**
(off Monton La.)
Lowry Lodge *M16: Old T* 5F **65**
(off Hamer Dr.)
Lowry Outlet Mall M50: Sal 3B **64**
Lows, The OL4: O'ham 4D **31**
(not continuous)
LOW SIDE .5E **31**
Lowside Dr. OL4: O'ham 4D **31**
Lowther Av. M18: Man 2D **83**
WA15: Tim 5C **98**
Lowther Cl. M25: Pres 1C **36**
Lowther Ct. M25: Pres 1B **36**
Lowther Cres. M24: Mid 5A **16**
Lowther Gdns. M41: Urm 2A **74**
Lowther Rd. M8: Man 3C **38**
M25: Pres 1B **36**
Lowthorpe St. M14: Man 3C **80**
Lowton Av. M9: Man 5B **40**
Lowton Rd. M33: Sale 1A **98**
Low Wood Rd. M34: Dent 1C **84**
Loxford St. M15: Man 5B **10**
Loxford St. M15: Man 5B **10** (4B **66**)
Loxley Wlk. *M40: Man* 3A **54**
(off Filby Wlk.)
Lubeck St. M9: Man 4A **40**
Lucas St. OL4: O'ham 2D **31**
Lucas Wlk. M11: Man 2B **68**
Lucerne Cl. OL9: Chad 3E **29**
Lucien Cl. M12: Man 5A **68**
Lucy St. M7: Sal 2F **51**
M15: Man 4F **65**
SK3: Stoc 3A **106**
Ludford Gro. M33: Sale 1B **98**
Ludgate Hill M4: Man 2E **7** (4D **53**)
Ludgate Rd. M40: Man 3E **55**
Ludgate St. M4: Man 2D **7** (4C **52**)
Ludlow Av. M27: Clif 2C **34**
M45: White 3D **23**
Ludlow Pk. *OL4: O'ham* 3F **31**
(off Lees Brook Pk.)
Ludlow Rd. SK2: Stoc 3E **107**
Ludlow Towers SK5: Stoc 1E **97**
Ludwell Wlk. *M8: Man* 1C **52**
(off Barnsdale Dr.)
Luke Kirby Ct. M27: Pen 3B **34**
Luke Rd. M43: Droy 1D **71**
Luke Wlk. *M8: Man* 1D **53**
(off Appleford Dr.)
Lullington Cl. M22: Wyth 5E **109**
Lullington Rd. M6: Sal 3F **49**
Lulworth Av. M41: Urm 3B **74**
Lulworth Cres. M35: Fail 4D **43**
Lulworth Gdns. M23: Wyth 3B **100**
Lulworth Rd. M24: Mid 4C **16**
M30: Ecc 4E **47**
Lumber La. M28: Wors 4A **32**
Lumb Cl. M34: Aud 1E **71**
(not continuous)

Lumb La. M43: Droy 4E 57
                      (not continuous)
    OL7: Droy 4E 57
Lumley Cl. M14: Man 1D 81
Lumn's La. M27: Clif 2E 35
Lumsdale Rd. M32: Stre 3A 84
Luna St. M4: Man 4E 7 (5D 53)
Lundale Wlk. M40: Man 1C 54
                (off Craiglands Av.)
Lund Av. M26: Rad 1D 21
Lund St. M16: Old T 4E 65
Lundy Av. M21: Chor 3E 91
Lune Cl. M45: White 1C 22
Lunedale Grn. SK2: Stoc 5F 107
Lune Dr. M45: White 5C 12
Lune St. OL8: O'ham 5A 30
Lune Wlk. M43: Droy 2D 71
                   (off Ellen St.)
    M45: White 1C 22
Lune Way SK5: Stoc 3B 96
Lunn Av. M18: Man 4B 70
Lupton St. M34: Dent 1B 86
Lurden Wlk. OL9: Chad 5C 28
Lurgan Av. M33: Sale 5E 89
Luton Dr. M23: Wyth 2C 108
Luton Rd. SK5: Stoc 5B 84
Luxhall Wlk. M40: Man 3D 55
Luxor Gro. M34: Dent 2B 84
Lyceum Pl.
    M15: Man 5C 10 (3C 66)
Lychgate M. M21: Chor 5C 78
    SK4: Stoc 1A 104
Lydden Av. M11: Man 4F 55
Lydford St. M6: Sal 3D 51
Lydford Wlk. M13: Man 4E 67
            (off Beckhampton Cl.)
Lydgate Cl. M34: Dent 4D 87
    M45: White 5C 12
Lydgate Dr. OL4: O'ham 4E 31
Lydgate Rd. M33: Sale 1E 99
    M43: Droy 4A 56
Lydgate Wlk. M45: White 5C 12
Lydney Av. SK8: H Grn 2E 115
Lyme Clough Way M24: Mid 2B 16
Lymefield Ct. SK2: Stoc 4F 107
Lymefield Gro. SK2: Stoc 5D 107
Lyme Gro. M33: Sale 5E 89
    M43: Droy 1B 70
    SK2: Stoc 4B 106
Lyme Ho. SK4: Stoc 2A 104
Lyme Pl. SK16: Duk 2D 73
Lyme St. SK4: Stoc 1A 104
Lyme Ter.
    SK16: Duk 5C 116 (1D 73)
Lymington Cl. M24: Mid 4D 27
Lymington Dr. M23: Wyth 2F 99
Lymm Cl. SK3: Stoc 5F 105
Lyndale Av. M27: Swin 1F 47
    SK5: Stoc 2B 84
Lyndene Av. M28: Wors 4C 32
Lyndene Gdns. SK8: Gat 5D 103
Lyndene Rd. M22: Wyth 1F 109
Lyndhurst Av. M25: Pres 1A 38
    M33: Sale 5B 88
    M34: Dent 2A 86
    M41: Urm 1E 75
    OL6: A Lyme 2D 59
    OL9: Chad 4B 28
Lyndhurst Gdns.
    M24: Mid 1A 26

Lyndhurst Rd. M20: Man 4C 92
    M32: Stre 3D 77
    OL8: O'ham 1F 43
    SK5: Stoc 3A 84
Lyndhurst St. M6: Sal 5A 50
Lyndhurst Vw. SK16: Duk 1E 73
Lyndon Cft. OL8: O'ham 5E 29
Lyneham Wlk. M7: Sal 1B 52
               (off Highclere Av.)
Lyngarth Ho. WA14: Alt 5A 98
            (off Grosvenor Rd.)
Lyngate Cl. SK1: Stoc 3C 106
Lynmouth Av. M20: Man 2C 92
    M41: Urm 5D 75
    OL8: O'ham 1B 44
    SK5: Stoc 1A 96
Lynmouth Ct. M25: Pres 1B 36
Lynmouth Gro. M25: Pres 1B 36
Lynn Av. M33: Sale 2E 89
Lynn Dr. M43: Droy 5A 56
Lynnfield Ho. WA14: Alt 5A 98
Lynnwood Rd.
    M19: Man 1F 103
Lynside Wlk. M22: Wyth 2F 113
Lynthorpe Rd. M40: Man 2F 41
Lynton Av. M27: Pen 3B 34
    OL8: O'ham 2E 43
Lynton Cl. OL9: Chad 1B 28
Lynton Dr. M19: Man 1B 94
    M25: Pres 3E 23
Lynton Gro. WA15: Tim 5B 98
Lynton Rd. M21: Chor 4C 78
    M27: Pen 3B 34
    SK4: Stoc 3E 95
    SK8: Gat 1E 111
Lynton St. M14: Man 3D 81
Lynton Ter. M26: Rad 2D 19
Lyntonvale Av. SK8: Gat 5D 103
Lyn Town Trad. Est.
    M30: Ecc 5F 47
Lynway Dr. M20: Man 3D 93
Lynway Gro. M24: Mid 4D 17
Lynwell Rd. M30: Ecc 5F 47
Lynwood Av. M16: W Ran 3E 79
    M30: Ecc 5F 47
Lynwood Cl. OL7: A Lyme 5C 44
Lynwood Ct. M8: Man 2B 38
Lynwood Dr. OL4: O'ham 1F 31
Lynwood Gro. M33: Sale 3E 89
    M34: Aud 1E 71
    SK4: Stoc 2E 95
Lyon Gro. M28: Wors 4C 32
Lyon Rd. BL4: Kea 3A 18
Lyon Rd. Ind. Est. BL4: Kea 3A 18
Lyon's Fold M33: Sale 2D 89
Lyons Rd. M17: T Pk 3C 62
Lyon St. M27: Swin 5A 34
Lyon Way SK5: Stoc 2A 96
Lyra Pl. M7: Sal 1B 4 (4E 51)
Lyric Theatre 3A 64
               (in The Lowry)
Lysander Cl. M14: Man 5D 81
Lytham Av. M21: Chor 1C 91
Lytham Rd. M14: Man 4A 82
    SK8: H Grn 5D 111
Lytham St. SK3: Stoc 5B 106
Lyth St. M14: Man 1F 93
Lytton Av. M8: Man 1C 52
Lytton Rd. M43: Droy 5C 56

M

Mabel Av. M28: Wors 5C 32
Mabel Rd. M35: Fail 3C 42
Mabel's Brow BL4: Kea 2A 18
Mabel St. M40: Man 2F 55
Mabfield Rd. M14: Man 4E 81
Mabledon Cl. SK8: H Grn 1F 115
Mabs Ct. OL6: A Lyme 5F 59
Macauley Rd. M16: Old T 3D 79
    SK5: Stoc 4F 83
Macauley Way M34: Dent 5C 86
Mc Bride Riverside Pk.
    M24: Mid 1B 26
McCall Wlk. M11: Man 5D 55
                          (off Trimdon Cl.)
McConnell Rd. M40: Man 5C 40
McCready Dr. M5: Sal 2D 65
Macdonald St. OL8: O'ham 5B 30
McDonough Cl. OL8: O'ham 1C 44
McDowall Wlk. M8: Man 2D 39
Macefin Av. M21: Chor 4F 91
Macfarren St. M12: Man 2C 82
McGinty Pl. M1: Man 3C 10
Macintosh Mills
    M15: Man 4B 10 (3B 66)
Mackenzie Ind. Pk. SK3: Stoc 5D 105
Mackenzie Rd. M7: Sal 1D 51
Mackenzie St. M12: Man 2C 82
Mackeson Dr. OL6: A Lyme 3F 59
Mackeson Rd. OL6: A Lyme 3F 59
McKie Cl. OL8: O'ham 1C 44
Mackintosh Way
    OL1: O'ham 2E 117 (2B 30)
Mackworth St. M15: Man 5A 66
McLaren Ct. M21: Chor 4C 78
Maclaren Dr. M8: Man 3A 38
Mconnel Apartments M4: Man 4F 7
Maddison Rd. M43: Droy 2B 70
Madeira Pl. M30: Ecc 5D 47
Madeley Dr. OL9: Chad 3D 29
Maden Wlk. OL9: Chad 1D 29
Madison Apartments M16: Old T 5D 65
Madison Av. M34: Aud 2E 71
Madison Gdns. M35: Fail 5A 42
Madison St. M18: Man 4A 70
Madras Rd. SK3: Stoc 4E 105
Mafeking St. OL8: O'ham 1E 43
Magdala St. OL1: O'ham 1D 117 (1A 30)
Magna Carta St. M6: Sal 1D 49
Magnetic Ho. M50: Sal 3B 64
Magnolia Ct. M6: Sal 5C 50
Magnolia Dr. M8: Man 1C 52
Magpie Cl. M43: Droy 4E 57
Magpie La. OL4: O'ham 5F 31
Magpie Wlk. M11: Man 1B 68
                        (off Newcombe St.)
Maher Gdns. M15: Man 1A 80
Mahood St. SK3: Stoc 4F 105
Maida St. M12: Man 3D 83
Maiden Cl. OL7: A Lyme 1C 58
Maiden M. M27: Swin 5B 34
Maidford Cl. M4: Man 1F 67
    M32: Stre 3A 78
Maidstone Av. M21: Chor 4C 78
Maidstone M. M21: Chor 4C 78
Maidstone Rd. SK4: Stoc 5F 93
Maidstone Wlk. M34: Dent 4C 86
                        (off Worcester Av.)

Main Av. M17: T Pk 5E 63
    M19: Man 1B 94
Maine Rd. M14: Man 2C 80
                          (not continuous)
Mainhill Wlk. M40: Man 2E 55
                        (off Marlinford Dr.)
Mainprice Cl. M6: Sal 4B 50
Main Rd. M27: Clif 1E 35
    OL9: O'ham 2E 29
Main St. M35: Fail 4B 42
    SK14: Hyde 1F 87
Mainwaring Ter. M23: Wyth 1C 100
Mainway M24: Mid 3B 26
Mainway E. M24: Mid 3E 27
Mainwood Rd. WA15: Tim 5E 99
Mainwood Sq. M13: Man 5F 11
Maismore Rd. M22: Wyth 5C 108
Maitland Av. M21: Chor 3E 91
Maitland Cl. SK1: Stoc 4D 107
Maitland Wlk. OL9: Chad 1D 29
Maizefield Cl. M33: Sale 4B 90
Major St. M1: Man 2C 10 (2C 66)
Major Wlk. M5: Sal 2D 65
                        (off Robert Hall St.)
Makepeace Wlk. M8: Man 2A 38
Makin St. M1: Man 3C 10 (2C 66)
Makkah Cl. M40: Man 2C 54
Malaga Av. M90: Man A 2D 113
Malakoff St. SK15: Stal 2F 73
Malbern Ind. Est. M34: Dent 1F 85
Malbrook Wlk. M13: Man 4E 67
                             (off Jessel Cl.)
Malby St. OL1: O'ham 1E 117 (1B 30)
Malcolm Av. M27: Clif 1C 34
Malcolm Dr. M27: Clif 2C 34
Malden Gro. M23: Wyth 4C 100
Maldon Cres. M27: Swin 1B 48
Maldon Dr. M30: Ecc 3A 48
Maldon St. M11: Man 4C 68
Maldwyn Av. M8: Man 2C 38
Malford Dr. M8: Man 1B 52
Malgam Dr. M20: Man 3D 103
Malham Ct. SK2: Stoc 5F 107
Malham Dr. M45: White 1C 22
Malimson Bourne M7: Sal 1F 51
                        (off Hilton St. Nth.)
Mall, The M30: Ecc 5B 48
    M33: Sale 4D 89
    SK14: Hyde 3F 87
Mallaig Wlk. M11: Man 2E 69
                          (off Brigham St.)
Mallard Cl. OL8: O'ham 2F 43
    SK16: Duk 3F 73
Mallard Ct. M50: Sal 2F 63
    SK8: H Grn 1E 115
Mallard St. M1: Man 4C 10 (2C 66)
Malley Wlk. M9: Man 1A 40
                        (off Greendale Dr.)
Malling Rd. M23: Wyth 2C 108
Mallory Av. OL7: A Lyme 2D 59
Mallory Wlk. M23: Wyth 3F 99
Mallowdale Av. M14: Man 5D 81
Mallowdale Rd. SK2: Stoc 5F 107
Mallow St. M15: Man 4A 66
Malpas Dr. WA14: Tim 3A 98
Malpas St. M12: Man 4C 68
    OL1: O'ham 2F 117 (2B 30)
Malpas Wlk. M16: Old T 5F 65
                           (off Clifton Cl.)
Malsham Rd. M23: Wyth 1B 100
Malta Cl. M24: Mid 2F 27

Malta St. M4: Man 1F 67
   OL4: O'ham 3F 31
Maltby Rd. M23: Wyth 5B 100
Malton Av. M21: Chor 5D 79
   M45: White 4B 12
Malton Cl. M45: White 4B 12
   OL9: Chad 1B 28
Malton Rd. SK4: Stoc 4C 94
Malton St. OL8: O'ham 4F 29
Malt St. M15: Man 5C 8 (3G 66)
Malus Ct. M6: Sal 4C 50
Malvern Av. M41: Urm 2D 75
   M43: Droy 5E 57
   OL6: A Lyme 5E 45
   SK8: Gat 1B 110
Malvern Cl. M25: Pres 4E 23
   M27: Pen 1F 49
   SK4: Stoc 5F 95
Malvern Dr. M27: Pen 1F 49
Malvern Gro. M6: Sal 4E 49
   M20: Man 2C 92
   M28: Walk 1A 32
Malvern Rd. M24: Mid 4B 26
Malvern Row M15: Man 4F 65
   (off Cornbrook Pk. Rd.)
Malvern St. M15: Man 4F 65
   OL8: O'ham 4F 29
Manby Rd. M18: Man 1D 83
Manby Sq. M18: Man 1D 83
Mancentral Trad. Est. M5: Sal . . .5D 5 (1F 65)
MANCHESTER 5C 6 (1B 66)
Manchester Airport Eastern Link Rd.
   SK8: Chea H 3F 115
   SK9: Hand 3F 115
Manchester Airport Station (Rail)
   . . . . .2D 113
Manchester Apollo 4E 67
Manchester Aquatics Cen. . . .5D 11 (3D 67)
Manchester Art Gallery 1C 10 (1C 66)
Manchester Bus. Pk. M22: Wyth 1F 113
Manchester Cathedral 3B 6 (5B 52)
Manchester Cathedral Vis. Cen. 4B 6
Manchester Chambers
   OL1: O'ham 3D 117 (2A 30)
Manchester City FC 5B 54
Manchester Climbing Cen. 3B 68
Manchester Craft & Design Cen. 4D 7
   (off Oak St.)
Manchester Crematorium M21: Chor . . .2E 91
Manchester Evening News Arena
   .2B 6 (4B 52)
Manchester Fort Shop. Pk. M8: Man . .2D 53
Manchester Ind. Cen.
   M3: Man 2D 9 (2F 65)
   (not continuous)
Manchester Ind. Pk. M40: Man 2B 54
MANCHESTER INTERNATIONAL AIRPORT
   . . . . .3D 113
Manchester Intl. Bus. Cen.
   M22: Wyth 2C 114
Manchester International Convention Cen.
   . . . . .2A 10 (2B 66)
Manchester Jewish Mus. 3C 52
Manchester Leisure Sports
   Development Cen., The 1C 80
Manchester Maccabi Community &
   Sports Club 1F 37
Manchester Metropolitan University
   All Saints Building 3C 66
   Aytoun Building 2D 11 (2D 67)

Manchester Metropolitan University
   Bellhouse Building 5C 10
     (off Lwr. Ormond St.)
   Chatham Building 5D 11 (4C 66)
   Didsbury Campus 1D 103
   Elizabeth Gaskell Campus 1E 81
   Geoffrey Manton Building 4C 66
     (off Rosamond Rd. W.)
   Grosvenor Building 5C 10
   Hollings Campus 3F 81
   John Dalton Building 4C 10 (3C 66)
   Loxford Tower 5C 10
   Mabel Tylecote Building 5C 10
   St Augustine's 5C 10
     (off Lower Chatham St.)
Manchester Mus., The 4D 67
Manchester New Rd. M24: Mid 4A 26
Manchester Old Rd. M24: Mid 2D 25
Manchester Rd. BL4: Kea, Swin 3C 18
   BL9: Bury 1A 12
   (not continuous)
   M16: W Ran 4D 79
   M21: Chor 4D 79
   (Barlow Moor Rd.)
   M21: Chor 5C 78
   (Wilbraham Rd.)
   M27: Pen, Swin 5C 34
   M27: Ward 2D 33
   M28: Walk 2A 32
   M34: Aud 3C 70
   M34: Dent 1C 84
   (not continuous)
   M43: Droy 1A 70
   OL7: A Lyme 4A 116 (5B 58)
   OL8: O'ham 2D 43
   OL9: O'ham 2D 43
   OL10: H'ood 1E 15
   SK4: Stoc 3E 95
   SK8: Chea 3F 103
   SK14: Hyde 2D 87
   WA14: Alt, B'ath, Tim 3A 98
Manchester Rd. Nth. M34: Dent 1E 85
Manchester Rd. Sth. M34: Dent 2E 85
Manchester St Mary's Catholic Church
   Hidden Gem 1A 10
Manchester Science Pk. M15: Man . . .5C 66
Manchester St. M16: Old T 5E 65
   OL1: O'ham 4D 117 (3A 30)
   OL8: O'ham 4F 29
   (not continuous)
   OL9: O'ham 3A 30
Manchester St. Rdbt. OL9: O'ham . . .3F 29
   (off Manchester St.)
Manchester Tennis Cen. 5B 54
Manchester United FC 5B 64
Manchester United Mus. & Tour 5B 64
Manchester Velodrome
   (National Cycling Cen.) 5C 54
Mancroft Wlk. M1: Man 4E 11
Mancunian Rd. M34: Dent 5C 86
Mancunian Way M1: Man 5A 10 (3C 66)
   M15: Man 5E 9 (3A 66)
Mandarin Wlk. M6: Sal 4D 51
   (off Milton Pl.)
Mandeville St. M19: Man 5D 83
Mandley Av. M40: Man 2F 41
Mandley Pk. Av. M7: Sal 5A 38
Manesty Cl. M24: Mid 4E 15
Manet Cl. M7: Sal 4D 37
Mangle St. M1: Man 5E 7 (1D 67)

Mango Pl. M6: Sal 5C **50**
Manifold St. M6: Sal 2D **51**
Manilla Wlk. *M11: Man* *1B **68***
(off Abernant Cl.)
Manipur St. M11: Man 2B **68**
Manley Av. M27: Clif 5A **20**
MANLEY PARK 3E **79**
Manley Rd. M16: W Ran 4D **79**
M21: Chor 4D **79**
M33: Sale 2A **98**
OL8: O'ham 5A **30**
Manley St. M7: Sal 1F **51**
Mannington Dr. M9: Man 5E **39**
Mannock St. OL8: O'ham 3F **29**
Manor Av. M16: W Ran 3F **79**
M41: Urm 4F **75**
Manor Cl. M34: Dent 3D **87**
OL9: Chad 1E **29**
Manor Ct. M32: Stre 4D **77**
SK1: Stoc *2C **106***
(off Hall St.)
Manordale Wlk. *M40: Man* *1E **53***
(off Westmount Cl.)
Manor Dr. M21: Chor 4F **91**
Mnr. Farm Cl. OL7: A Lyme 1B **58**
Mnr. Farm Ri. OL4: O'ham 2F **31**
Manor Ind. Est. M32: Stre 5E **77**
Manor Lodge M27: Pen 4F **35**
Manor Pk. M41: Urm 4F **75**
Manor Rd. M6: Sal 3F **49**
M19: Man 3D **83**
M24: Mid 3B **26**
M27: Swin 1B **48**
M32: Stre 3D **77**
M33: Sale 3D **89**
M34: Aud 3D **71**
M34: Dent 3D **87**
M43: Droy 1A **70**
OL4: O'ham 5E **31**
SK5: Stoc 3D **97**
Manor St. BL4: Kea 4D **19**
M12: Man 4F **11** (2E **67**)
M24: Mid 4C **16**
M34: Aud 3B **72**
Manor Wlk. *M34: Aud* *3B **72***
(off Mt. Pleasant St.)
Mansfield Av. M9: Man 5F **25**
M34: Dent 1F **85**
Mansfield Cl. M34: Dent 5F **71**
OL7: A Lyme 1B **72**
Mansfield Cres. M34: Dent 1F **85**
Mansfield Dr. M9: Man 5A **26**
Mansfield Rd. M9: Man 5F **25**
M41: Urm 4D **75**
OL8: O'ham 4D **31**
Mansfield St. OL7: A Lyme 2A **72**
Mansford Dr. M40: Man 2B **54**
Manshaw Cres. M34: Aud 3C **70**
Manshaw Rd. M11: Man 3C **70**
Mansion Av. M45: White 3A **12**
Manstead Wlk. M40: Man 5A **54**
Manston Lodge SK2: Stoc 5D **107**
Manswood Dr. M8: Man 5C **38**
Mantell Wlk. *M40: Man* *2C **54***
(off Bower St.)
Manthorpe Av. M28: Wors 5C **32**
Manton Av. M9: Man 2D **41**
M34: Dent 2C **84**
Manton Cl. M7: Sal 1B **52**

Manton Ho. SK5: Stoc 4D **97**
Manvers St. SK5: Stoc 5A **96**
Manwaring St. M35: Fail 4A **42**
Manway Bus. Pk. WA14: Tim 3A **98**
Maple Av. M21: Chor 5D **79**
M30: Ecc 3C **46**
M32: Stre 4F **77**
M34: Aud 1D **71**
M34: Dent 2A **86**
M45: White 2B **22**
Maple Cl. BL4: Kea 4B **18**
M6: Sal 4B **50**
M24: Mid 1F **27**
OL9: Chad 1D **29**
SK2: Stoc 5D **107**
Maple Ct. M16: Old T 1D **79**
SK4: Stoc 4E **95**
Maplecroft SK1: Stoc 3D **107**
Mapledon Rd. M9: Man 4B **40**
Maple Dr. WA15: Tim 1A **108**
Maple Gro. M25: Pres 3C **22**
M28: Walk 4A **32**
M35: Fail 2A **56**
M40: Man 2A **42**
Maple Ho. M14: Man 1E **81**
Maple Rd. M23: Wyth 4B **99**
M27: Swin 1A **48**
OL9: Chad 1D **29**
Maple Rd. W. M23: Wyth 3E **99**
Maple St. OL8: O'ham 1E **43**
Maplewood Cl. M9: Man 2E **39**
Maplewood Ct. M7: Sal 5F **37**
Mapley Av. M22: Nor 3F **101**
Maplin Cl. M13: Man 5F **11** (3E **67**)
Maranatha Ct. M30: Ecc 2F **61**
Marble St. M2: Man 5C **6** (1C **66**)
OL1: O'ham 1D **31**
Marbury Av. M14: Man 4D **81**
Marbury Cl. M41: Urm 2A **74**
SK3: Stoc 4C **104**
Marbury Dr. WA14: Tim 2A **98**
Marbury Rd. SK4: Stoc 2F **95**
Marcer Rd. M40: Man 5F **53**
March Av. SK4: Stoc 1D **105**
Marchbank Dr. SK8: Chea 5E **103**
Marchers M. M30: Ecc 1D **61**
Marchioness St. M18: Man 4B **70**
Marchmont Cl. M13: Man 4F **67**
Marchwood Av. M21: Chor 4F **79**
Marcliffe Dr. M19: Man 4E **83**
Marcliff Gro. SK4: Stoc 1D **105**
Marcus Garvey Ct. M16: W Ran . . .3A **80**
Marcus Gro. M14: Man 2E **81**
Mardale Av. M20: Man 3E **93**
M27: Ward 2E **33**
M41: Urm 2B **74**
Mardale Cl. M25: Pres 2E **23**
OL4: O'ham 1F **31**
Mardale Dr. M24: Mid 5A **16**
SK8: Gat 5D **103**
Marden Rd. M27: Swin 1F **47**
Marden Rd. M23: Wyth 1C **108**
Marfield Av. OL9: Chad 4C **28**
Marfield Ct. M41: Urm 4A **74**
Marford Cl. M22: Wyth 5F **101**
Marford Cres. M33: Sale 1B **98**
Margaret Ashton Cl. M9: Man 5B **40**
Margaret Ho.
OL6: A Lyme 3A **116** (5C **58**)

Margaret Rd. M34: Dent 1C 86
    M43: Droy 5A 56
Margaret Sands St. M15: Man 4F 65
Margaret St. OL6: A Lyme 3A 116 (4C 58)
    OL7: A Lyme 4A 116 (5C 58)
    OL8: O'ham 2D 43
    SK5: Stoc 1A 96
Margaret Ter. OL6: A Lyme 3A 116
Margate Av. M40: Man 2D 55
Margate Rd. SK5: Stoc 1B 96
Margrove Cl. M35: Fail 5E 43
Margrove Rd. M6: Sal 3E 49
Marguerita Rd. M40: Man 3F 55
                     (not continuous)
Marham Cl. M21: Chor 2A 92
Marie Cl. M34: Dent 3B 86
Marie St. M7: Sal 5A 38
Marigold Ter. M24: Mid 2F 27
                    (off Sundew Pl.)
Mariman Dr. M8: Man 2C 38
Marina Av. M34: Dent 4C 86
Marina Cl. SK9: Hand 5F 115
Marina Cres. M11: Man 4D 55
Marina Rd. M43: Droy 5D 57
Marion St. OL8: O'ham 1B 44
Maritime Cl. M33: Sale 4B 88
Marjorie Cl. M18: Man 4D 69
Mark Av. M6: Sal 3D 51
Market Av. OL6: A Lyme 2C 116 (4D 59)
Market Pl. BL4: Farn 1A 18
    M22: Wyth 3F 109
    M24: Mid 5C 16
    M27: Pen 3C 34
    M34: Dent 2A 86
    M43: Droy 1C 70
    OL1: O'ham 3D 117 (2A 30)
    OL6: A Lyme 2C 116 (4D 59)
    SK1: Stoc 1B 118 (1B 106)
                    (not continuous)
    SK14: Hyde .3F 87
                    (not continuous)
Market Pct. BL4: Farn 1A 18
Market St. BL4: Farn 1A 18
    M2: Man 4B 6 (1B 66)
    M24: Mid 5B 16
                    (not continuous)
    M26: Rad 1D 19
    M27: Pen 3C 34
    M34: Dent 2A 86
                    (not continuous)
    M43: Droy 2C 70
    OL6: A Lyme 4D 59
    SK14: Hyde .2F 87
Market Street Stop (Metro) 5C 6 (1C 66)
Market Wlk. M33: Sale 4D 89
Market Way M6: Sal 4B 50
Markfield Av. M13: Man 5F 67
Markham Cl. M12: Man 2A 68
    SK14: Hyde .4F 73
Markham St. SK14: Hyde 4F 73
Markington St. M14: Man 2C 80
Mark Jones Wlk. M40: Man 2D 55
                  (off Mitchell St.)
Markland St. SK14: Hyde 4F 87
                    (not continuous)
Mark La. M4: Man 4C 6
Mark St. OL9: O'ham 2F 29
Marland Av. OL8: O'ham 3C 44
Marland Cres. SK5: Stoc 5B 84
Marland Fold La. OL8: O'ham 3B 44

Marland St. OL9: Chad 1C 42
Marland Way M32: Stre 2F 77
Marlborough Av. M16: W Ran 3E 79
Marlborough Cl. M34: Dent 2B 86
    OL7: A Lyme 2A 72
Marlborough Ct. M9: Man 4C 24
Marlborough Dr. M35: Fail 1A 56
    SK4: Stoc 4F 95
Marlborough Gro. M43: Droy 5E 57
Marlborough Rd. M7: Man, Sal 1B 52
    M7: Sal 1B 52
    M30: Ecc 3C 48
    M32: Stre 2E 77
    M33: Sale 4D 89
    M41: Urm 2B 74
    SK14: Hyde .5F 87
Marlborough St.
    OL4: O'ham 5F 117 (3C 30)
    OL7: A Lyme 2A 72
                    (not continuous)
Marlcroft Av. SK4: Stoc 1D 105
Marlcroft Dr. M23: Wyth 4C 100
Marle Cft. M45: White 3E 21
Marle Rd. SK14: Hyde 1F 87
Marley Cl. WA15: Tim 4B 98
Marley Rd. M33: Sale 2C 88
Marleyer Cl. M40: Man 5E 41
Marley Rd. M19: Man 5D 83
Marlfield Rd. WA15: Haleb 2A 112
Marlfield St. M9: Man 3A 40
Marlhill Cl. SK2: Stoc 5F 107
Marlhill Cl. SK2: Stoc 5F 107
Marlinford Dr. M40: Man 2E 55
Marlor St. M34: Dent 1A 86
Marlow Cl. M41: Urm 1D 75
Marlow Dr. M27: Swin 1A 48
    SK9: Hand .4E 115
Marlowe Dr. M20: Man 4D 93
Marlowe Wlk. M34: Dent 5B 86
Marlow Ho. M5: Sal 1B 64
                  (off Hodge La.)
Marlow Rd. M9: Man 3B 40
Marlton Wlk. M9: Man 5A 26
              (off Leconfield Dr.)
Marmion Dr. M21: Chor 5C 78
Marne Av. M22: Shar 1A 110
Maroon Rd. M22: Wyth 2B 114
Marple Cl. OL8: O'ham 2F 43
Marple Gro. M32: Stre 2E 77
Marple Rd. SK2: Stoc 4F 107
Marple St. M15: Man 5F 65
Marquis Dr. SK8: H Grn 2F 115
Marquis St. M19: Man 4F 83
Marrick Av. SK8: Chea 1E 111
Marriott St. M20: Man 2D 93
    SK1: Stoc 5C 118 (3B 106)
Marryat Ct. M12: Man 4B 68
                  (off Gregory St.)
Marsden Cl. OL7: A Lyme 2A 58
Marsden Dr. WA15: Tim 5E 99
Marsden St. M2: Man 5B 6 (1B 66)
    M24: Mid 2E 27
               (off Lancaster Av.)
    M28: Walk 2D 33
    M30: Ecc 4E 47
Marsett Wlk. M23: Wyth 1B 100
Marshall Ct. OL1: O'ham 1A 30
                 (off Bradford St.)
    OL6: A Lyme 5F 59

Marshall Rd. M19: Man 4C 82
Marshall Stevens Way M17: T Pk 5D 63
Marshall St. M4: Man 3E 7 (5D 53)
  M12: Man .4E 67
Marsham Cl. M13: Man 5A 68
Marshbrook Dr. M9: Man 2E 39
Marshbrook Rd. M41: Urm 2E 75
Marsh Cl. SK3: Stoc 5F 105
Marshfield Rd. WA15: Tim 5E 99
Marshfield Rd. M13: Man 4E 67
Marshfield Wlk. M13: Man 4E 67
               (off Lauderdale Cres.)
Marsh St. M28: Walk 2B 32
Marsland Av. WA15: Tim 3D 99
Marsland Cl. M34: Dent 2D 85
Marsland Rd. M33: Sale 5C 88
  WA15: Tim 5D 99
Marsland St. SK1: Stoc 5B 96
               (not continuous)
Marsland St. Nth. M7: Sal 5B 38
Marsland St. Sth. M7: Sal 5B 38
Marsland Ter. SK1: Stoc 3D 107
Mars St. OL9: O'ham 2E 29
Marston Cl. M35: Fail 1E 57
  M45: White 1E 23
Marston Ho. M5: Sal 1B 64
                (off Cypress Cl.)
Marston Rd. M7: Sal 4A 38
  M32: Stre .3B 78
Marthall Dr. M33: Sale 1A 100
Marthall Way SK9: Hand 4F 115
Martha St. OL1: O'ham 1F 29
Martin Av. OL4: O'ham 3E 31
Martin Cl. M34: Dent 5B 72
Martindale Cres. M12: Man 4A 68
  M24: Mid .3F 15
Martingale Cl. M8: Man 5C 38
Martingale Way M43: Droy 4F 57
Martin Gro. BL4: Kea 2B 18
Martin Rd. M27: Clif 2D 35
Martinscroft Rd. M23: Wyth 1D 109
Martin St. M5: Sal 5A 50
  M34: Aud .3B 72
  SK14: Hyde 3F 87
Martlesham Wlk. M4: Man 4D 7
Martlet Cl. M14: Man 4D 81
Martlock Av. M22: Wyth 3A 110
Marton Av. M20: Man 1E 103
Marton Grange M25: Pres 1F 37
Marton Grn. SK3: Stoc 5F 105
Marton Gro. SK4: Stoc 2A 96
Marton Pl. M33: Sale 4C 88
Marton Way SK9: Hand 4F 115
               (off Spath La.)
Marvic Ct. M13: Man 2A 82
Marwood Cl. M26: Rad 1C 18
Marwood Dr. M23: Wyth 3B 108
Maryfield Cl. M16: W Ran 5A 80
Mary France St.
  M15: Man 5E 9 (4A 66)
Marylon Dr. M22: Nor 3A 102
Maryport Dr. WA15: Tim 4F 99
Mary St. M3: Man 1F 5 (4B 52)
  M34: Dent 1C 86
  M43: Droy 1D 71
  SK1: Stoc 1C 106
  SK8: Chea 5F 103
  SK14: Hyde 2E 87
  SK16: Duk 1D 73

Masboro St. M8: Man 5B 38
Masefield Av. M25: Pres 1B 36
Masefield Cres. M43: Droy 1C 70
Masefield Dr. SK4: Stoc 1C 104
Masefield Gro. SK5: Stoc 4A 84
Masefield Rd. M43: Droy 1C 70
Mason St. M4: Man 3E 7 (5D 53)
  OL7: A Lyme 1B 72
Massey Av. M35: Fail 4D 43
  OL6: A Lyme 1E 59
Massey Rd. M33: Sale 4A 90
Massey St. M5: Sal 5B 4 (1E 65)
  SK1: Stoc 3B 118 (2B 106)
Massey Wlk. M22: Wyth 5B 110
Massie St. SK8: Chea 5F 103
Masson Pl. M4: Man 1C 6
Matham Wlk. M15: Man 5C 10
Mather Av. M25: Pres 3E 37
  M30: Ecc .5A 48
  M45: White 4B 12
Mather Cl. M45: White 5B 12
Mather Rd. M30: Ecc 5A 48
Mather St. BL4: Kea 1A 18
  M35: Fail .5F 41
Mather Way M6: Sal 4C 50
            (off Salford Shop. City)
Matisse Way M7: Sal 4D 37
Matley Grn. SK5: Stoc 2E 97
Matlock Av. M7: Sal 5C 36
  M20: Man .2B 92
  M34: Dent .5C 86
  M41: Urm .5D 75
Matlock Cl. BL4: Farn 1A 18
  M33: Sale .4E 89
Matlock M. WA14: Alt 5A 98
             (off Renshaw St.)
Matlock Rd. M32: Stre 2C 76
  SK5: Stoc .4C 84
  SK8: H Grn 2E 115
Matlock St. M30: Ecc 2E 61
Matson Wlk. M22: Wyth 4C 108
Matt Busby Cl. M27: Pen 5D 35
Matthew Cl. OL8: O'ham 5E 31
Matthews Av. BL4: Kea 2B 18
Matthews La. M12: Man 3C 82
  M18: Man .3E 83
  M19: Man .3C 82
Matthew's St. M12: Man 3B 68
Matthias Ct. M3: Sal 2C 4 (4F 51)
Mattison St. M11: Man 1B 52
Maudsley Cl. M7: Sal 5C 94
Mauldeth Cl. SK4: Stoc 5C 94
Mauldeth Rd. M14: Man 1E 93
  M19: Man .2A 94
             (Broadhill Rd.)
  M19: Man .4B 94
             (Leegate Rd.)
  M20: Man .1E 93
  SK4: Stoc .1B 104
Mauldeth Road Station (Rail) 2A 94
Mauldeth Rd. W. M20: Man 5B 80
  M21: Chor .2E 91
Maureen Av. M8: Man 4C 38
Maurice Cl. SK16: Duk 2F 73
Maurice Dr. M6: Sal 3B 50
Maurice Pariser Wlk. M8: Man 5B 38
               (off Squire Rd.)
Maurice St. M6: Sal 3B 50
Mawdsley Dr. M8: Man 4E 39

Maxton Ho. *BL4:* Farn 1A **18**
 (off Bridgewater St.)
Mayall St. E. OL4: O'ham 2E **31**
Mayan Av. M3: Sal 3C **4** (5F **51**)
May Av. SK4: Stoc 1E **105**
Mayberth Av. M8: Man 2C **38**
Maybrook Wlk. *M9:* Man 4F **39**
 (off Alfred St.)
Mayburn Cl. M24: Mid 4E **27**
Maybury St. M18: Man 4A **70**
May Ct. M16: W Ran 2F **79**
Maycroft SK5: Stoc 2D **97**
Maycroft Av. M20: Man 3E **93**
May Dr. M19: Man 2B **94**
Mayer St. SK2: Stoc 4E **107**
Mayes Ct. *M14:* Man 1F **93**
 (off Sheringham Rd.)
Mayes Gdns. M4: Man 1F **67**
Mayes St. M4: Man 3C **6** (5C **52**)
 (not continuous)
Mayfair M7: Sal 3E **37**
Mayfair, The M20: Man 3D **93**
Mayfair Av. M6: Sal 4D **49**
 M41: Urm 3D **75**
 M45: White 2B **22**
Mayfair Ct. M14: Man 5E **81**
 WA15: Tim 4D **99**
 (Park Rd.)
 WA15: Tim 4D **99**
 (Stockport Rd.)
Mayfair Cres. M35: Fail 4D **43**
Mayfair Dr. M33: Sale 1A **98**
Mayfair Gdns. *M45:* White 2B **22**
 (off Bury New Rd.)
Mayfair Gro. M45: White 2C **22**
Mayfair Pk. M20: Man 4B **92**
Mayfair Rd. M22: Wyth 3A **110**
Mayfield Av. M27: Swin 1E **47**
 M32: Stre 4D **77**
 M33: Sale 4A **90**
 M34: Dent 5C **86**
 SK5: Stoc 3B **96**
Mayfield Cl. WA15: Tim 5D **99**
Mayfield Gro. M18: Man 2B **84**
 SK5: Stoc 3B **96**
Mayfield Mans. M16: W Ran 2A **80**
Mayfield Rd. M7: Sal 3E **37**
 M16: W Ran 2A **80**
 OL1: O'ham 1D **31**
 WA15: Tim 5D **99**
Mayfield St. M34: Aud 5A **72**
Mayflower Av. M5: Sal 5A **72**
Mayford Rd. M19: Man 2C **64**
Maygate OL9: O'ham 3C **82**
May Gro. M19: Man 1F **29**
Mayhill Rd. M6: Sal 3D **83**
 M28: Wors 3C **48**
Mayhurst Av. M21: Chor 4C **32**
Mayorlowe Av. SK5: Stoc 5F **91**
Mayor St. OL9: O'ham 2E **29**
Mayo St. M12: Man 2F **67**
Maypole, The *M6:* Sal 3C **50**
 (off Broughton Rd.)
Maypool Dr. SK5: Stoc 2B **96**
May Rd. M16: W Ran 2F **79**
 M27: Pen 1D **49**
Maysmith M. M7: Sal 1F **51**
May St. M30: Ecc 3E **47**
 M40: Man 2E **55**
 (not continuous)

May St. OL8: O'ham 5E **29**
Mayton St. M11: Man 2C **68**
Mayville Dr. M20: Man 3D **93**
Maywood Av. M20: Man 3D **103**
Meachin Av. M21: Chor 3E **91**
Mead, The M5: Sal 5F **49**
Meade, The M21: Chor 1D **91**
Meade Cl. M41: Urm 3E **75**
Meade Gro. M13: Man 2B **82**
Meade Hill Rd. M8: Man 1A **38**
 M25: Pres 1A **38**
Meadfoot Av. M25: Pres 1E **37**
Meadfoot Rd. M18: Man 4F **69**
Meadon Av. M27: Clif 3D **35**
Meadow Bank M21: Chor 1C **90**
 SK4: Stoc 1D **105**
 WA15: Tim 4C **98**
Meadowbank OL7: A Lyme 1C **58**
Meadowbank Cl. M35: Fail 1C **56**
Meadow Bank Ct. M32: Stre 4D **77**
Meadowburn Nook M30: Ecc 3D **47**
Meadow Cl. M32: Stre 4A **78**
 M34: Dent 5C **86**
Meadow Cft. M6: Sal 4D **49**
 M21: Chor 5B **78**
Meadow Cft. M45: White 3E **21**
Meadowcroft La. OL1: O'ham 1D **31**
Meadowfield Ct. SK14: Hyde 1F **87**
Meadowgate M28: Wors 4B **32**
 M41: Urm 4F **75**
Meadowgate Rd. M6: Sal 4D **49**
Meadow Ind. Est. M35: Fail 1E **55**
 M35: 3A **56**
 SK1: Stoc 5B **96**
Meadow La. M28: Wors 2B **46**
 M34: Dent 5C **86**
 OL8: O'ham 2A **44**
 SK16: Duk 2F **73**
Meadow Mill SK1: Stoc 5B **96**
Meadow Rd. M7: Sal 1B **4** (4E **51**)
 M24: Mid 3A **26**
 M41: Urm 4F **75**
Meadows, The M24: Mid 3D **27**
 M25: Pres 5D **23**
 M45: White 2E **21**
 (off Old Hall La.)
Meadowside Av. M22: Wyth 2F **109**
 M28: Walk 5A **18**
Meadowside Gro. M28: Walk 1A **32**
Meadows Rd. M33: Sale 2E **89**
 SK4: Stoc 1E **95**
 (not continuous)
 SK8: H Grn 5D **111**
Meadow Way M40: Man 3C **40**
Meads, The OL9: Chad 3C **28**
Meads Ct. M27: Swin 4B **34**
Mead Way M34: Dent 5B **86**
Meadway BL4: Kea 1B **18**
 BL9: Bury 1B **12**
 M33: Sale 5A **88**
 OL9: Chad 2A **42**
Meadway Cl. M33: Sale 1A **98**
Mealhouse Brow SK1: Stoc 2B **118**
Meal St. SK4: Stoc 5A **96**
Mecca Bingo
 Bank Top 4D **117** (3A **30**)
 Sale 4C **88**
 West Gorton 4C **68**
Medlock Ct. M11: Man 3D **69**

Medlock Dr. OL8: O'ham 3C 44
Medlock Gates M35: Fail 3B 56
Medlock Ho. M15: Man 4D 9
Medlock Leisure Cen. 5D 57
Medlock Rd. M35: Fail 3B 56
Medlock St. M15: Man 4A 10 (3B 66)
   M43: Droy 5C 56
   OL1: O'ham 2C 30
MEDLOCK VALE 3B 56
Medlock Way M45: White 1E 23
   OL8: O'ham 5E 117
Medtia Sq. OL1: O'ham 5E 117
Medway Cl. M5: Sal 4F 49
   OL8: O'ham 1E 43
Medway Dr. BL4: Kea 4D 19
Medway Rd. OL8: O'ham 1E 43
Medway Wlk. M40: Man 4F 53
                 (off Naylor St.)
Meech St. M11: Man 2E 69
Meerbrook Rd. SK3: Stoc 3C 104
Mee's Sq. M30: Ecc 2F 61
Megabowl
   Stockport 4A 118 (3A 106)
Megna Cl. OL9: O'ham 2F 29
Melanie Dr. SK5: Stoc 5B 84
Melba St. M11: Man 2A 70
Melbecks Rd. M23: Wyth 1B 100
Melbourne Av. M34: Dent 3F 77
   M90: Man A 1C 112
   OL9: Chad 2C 28
Melbourne M. M7: Sal 2F 51
                 (off Arrow St.)
   OL9: Chad 2D 29
Melbourne St. M7: Sal 2A 52
   M9: Man 4A 40
   M15: Man 5F 9 (3A 66)
   M27: Pen .4D 35
   M34: Dent 3A 86
   OL9: Chad 2D 29
   SK5: Stoc 5B 84
Melbourne St. Nth. OL6: A Lyme 3E 59
Melbourne St. Sth. OL6: A Lyme 3E 59
Melbury Av. M20: Man 4F 93
Meldon Rd. M13: Man 3A 82
Meldreth Dr. M12: Man 1B 82
Meldrum St. OL8: O'ham 5B 30
Melford Av. M40: Man 3A 42
Melford Gro. OL4: O'ham 3F 31
Melfort Av. M32: Stre 4A 78
Melia Ho. M4: Man 1D 7
Meliden Cres. M22: Wyth 3A 110
Melksham Cl. M5: Sal 5D 51
            (off Culverwell Dr.)
Mellalieu St. M24: Mid 5A 16
Melland Av. M21: Chor 3E 91
Melland Rd. M18: Man 2E 83
Mellands Ct. M18: Man 2F 83
        (off Levenshulme Rd.)
Melland Sports Cen. 2E 83
Meller Rd. M13: Man 3B 82
Melling Av. OL9: Chad 5F 17
   SK4: Stoc 2A 96
Melling Rd. OL4: O'ham 3E 31
Melling St. M12: Man 1C 82
Mellington Av. M20: Man 3D 103
Mellor Cl. OL6: A Lyme 5F 59
Mellors Rd. M17: T Pk 3D 63
Mellor St. M25: Pres 5B 22
   M30: Ecc .1F 61
   M32: Stre .1A 78
   M35: Fail .1F 55

Mellor St. M40: Man 4F 53
   M43: Droy 1B 70
   OL8: O'ham 2E 43
       (off Limeside Rd., not continuous)
Mellor Way OL9: Chad 5D 29
Mellowstone Dr. M21: Chor 5B 80
Melloy Pl. M8: Man 3C 52
Melmerby Ct. M5: Sal 1B 64
Melon Pl. M6: Sal 5D 51
Melrose Apartments M13: Man 1E 81
           (off Hathersage Rd.)
Melrose Av. M20: Man 5E 93
   M30: Ecc .3C 46
   M33: Sale 4D 89
   SK3: Stoc 4B 104
Melrose Cl. M45: White 4B 12
Melrose Ct. OL9: Chad 5C 28
Melrose St. M40: Man 2E 55
   OL1: O'ham 1D 31
Melsomby Rd. M23: Wyth 1C 100
Meltham Av. M20: Man 2C 92
Meltham Cl. SK4: Stoc 2A 104
Meltham Rd. SK4: Stoc 2A 104
Melton Av. M34: Dent 2C 84
Melton Dr. BL9: Bury 1C 12
Melton Rd. M8: Man 3A 38
Melton St. M9: Man 3B 40
             (off Gilmour Ter.)
   SK5: Stoc 4B 96
Melverley Rd. M9: Man 4C 24
Melville Cl. M11: Man 3A 70
Melville Rd. BL4: Kea 3B 18
   M32: Stre .2D 77
Melville St. OL4: Lees 4F 31
   OL6: A Lyme 1C 116 (4D 59)
Melvin Av. M22: Wyth 2A 110
Memorial Rd. M28: Walk 2A 32
Menai Gro. SK8: Chea 5C 104
Menai Rd. SK3: Stoc 5A 106
Mendip Av. M22: Wyth 2B 110
Mendip Cl. OL9: Chad 4C 28
   SK4: Stoc 5A 96
   SK8: H Grn 2D 115
Mendip Ct. SK4: Stoc 5A 96
Mendip Rd. OL8: O'ham 1F 43
Menston Av. M40: Man 3A 42
Mentone Cres. M22: Wyth 2A 110
Mentone Rd. SK4: Stoc 5D 95
Mentor St. M13: Man 2B 82
Menzies Ct. M21: Chor 4D 79
           (off Ransfield Rd.)
Mercer Rd. M18: Man 5F 69
Mercer St. M19: Man 4D 83
   M43: Droy 5D 57
Merchants Quay M50: Sal 4B 64
Merchants Quay Ct. M30: Ecc 4E 47
Mercian Rd. OL6: A Lyme 2C 116 (4D 59)
Mercian Way SK3: Stoc 5A 118 (4F 105)
Mercury Bldgs. M1: Man 1E 11
Mercury Bus. Pk. M41: Urm 4B 62
Mercury Way M41: Urm 5B 62
Mere, The OL6: A Lyme 1F 59
Mere Av. M6: Sal 5A 50
   M24: Mid .3C 26
   M43: Droy 2A 70
Mere Cl. BL9: Bury 1D 13
   M33: Sale 5B 90
   M34: Dent 3D 85
Mereclough Av. M28: Walk 3B 32
Meredew Av. M27: Swin 1A 48

Meredith Ct. M15: Man 4C 66
                    (off Epsley Cl.)
Meredith St. M14: Man 1F 93
Mere Dr. M20: Man 4D 93
  M27: Clif .2C 34
Merefield Rd. WA15: Tim 5E 99
Mere Ho. M15: Man 5B 8 (3F 65)
  SK4: Stoc 2A 104
Mereland Av. M20: Man 4E 93
Meremanor M28: Walk 3B 32
Mereside Gro. M28: Walk 1A 32
Mereside Wlk. M15: Man 4F 65
             (off Mosshall Cl.)
Merewood Dr. M22: Wyth 5F 101
Meridian Cen. OL8: O'ham 5D 117
Meridian Pl. M20: Man 4C 92
Meriton Rd. SK9: Hand 5E 115
Meriton Wlk. M18: Man 1D 83
Merlewood Av. M19: Man 1E 95
  M34: Aud 1D 71
Merlewood Dr. M27: Swin 1E 47
Merlin Cl. OL8: O'ham 4C 44
             (not continuous)
Merlin Dr. M27: Clif 2D 35
Merlin Av. M20: Man 4F 93
Merlyn Av. M20: Man 4E 93
  M33: Sale 2E 89
  M34: Dent 3A 86
Merlyn Ct. M20: Man 4E 93
              (off Milden Cl.)
Merrick Av. M22: Wyth 2A 110
Merridale Rd. M40: Man 3E 41
Merridge Wlk. M8: Man 1B 52
           (off Brentfield Av.)
Merrill St. M4: Man 1F 67
Merriman St. M16: W Ran 1A 80
Merrow Wlk. M1: Man 4E 11
Merrybower Rd. M7: Sal 4A 38
Merrydale Av. M30: Ecc 3A 48
Merseybank Av. M21: Chor 4F 91
Mersey Cl. M45: White 5D 13
Mersey Ct. M33: Sale 3A 90
Mersey Cres. M20: Man 5F 91
Mersey Dr. M45: White 5D 13
Mersey Ferries Terminal 3B 64
Mersey Mdws. M20: Man 5B 92
Mersey Rd. M20: Man 5B 92
  M33: Sale 2D 89
  SK4: Stoc 1B 104
Mersey Rd. Ind. Est. M35: Fail 3D 43
Mersey Rd. Nth. M35: Fail 3C 42
Mersey Sq. M45: White 5D 13
  SK1: Stoc 2A 118 (2A 106)
             (not continuous)
Mersey St. M11: Man 3A 70
             (not continuous)
  SK1: Stoc 1C 106
Mersey Valley Vis. Cen. 2B 90
Mersey Vw. M41: Urm 5A 74
Merseyway SK1: Stoc 2A 118 (2A 106)
Merston Dr. M20: Man 3E 103
Merton Av. OL8: O'ham 1F 43
Merton Dr. M43: Droy 1A 70
Merton Gro. OL9: Chad 1F 41
  WA15: Tim 5D 99
Merton Rd. M25: Pres 4E 23
  M33: Sale 3C 88
  SK3: Stoc 3D 105
Merton Wlk. M9: Man 5A 40
          (off Nethervale Dr.)

Merville Av. M40: Man 3B 40
Mervyn Rd. M7: Sal 1C 50
Merwell Rd. M41: Urm 4A 74
Merwood Av. SK8: H Grn 1F 115
Merwood Gro. M14: Man 1A 82
Meshaw Cl. M23: Wyth 1A 100
Mesnefield Rd. M7: Sal 4C 36
Mesne Lea Gro. M28: Wors 4A 32
Mesne Lea Rd. M28: Walk 4A 32
Metfield Wlk. M40: Man 2F 41
Methodist Intl. Ho. M14: Man 1A 82
          (off Daisy Bank Rd.)
Methuen St. M12: Man 2D 83
Metroplex Bus. Pk. M50: Sal 2A 64
Mevagissey Wlk. OL4: O'ham 1E 31
Mews, The M25: Pres 1D 37
  M28: Wors 1A 46
  M33: Sale 5E 89
  M40: Man 4B 54
  M45: White 1F 21
  SK8: Gat 1D 111
Mexborough St. OL4: O'ham 1F 31
Meyer St. SK3: Stoc 5B 106
Meyrick Rd. M6: Sal 4C 50
Michael Ct. M19: Man 1F 103
Michaels Hey Pde. M23: Wyth 3E 99
Michael St. M24: Mid 1B 26
Michigan Av. M50: Sal 2B 64
Michigan Pk. M50: Sal 2B 64
Mickleby Wlk. M40: Man 4F 53
          (off Landos Rd.)
Micklehurst Av. M20: Man 4A 92
Midbrook Wlk. M22: Wyth 4D 109
          (off Plowden Rd.)
Middlebourne St. M6: Sal 5A 50
Middlefield OL8: O'ham 4C 44
Middlegate M40: Man 1F 41
Middle Grn. OL6: A Lyme 3E 59
Middleham St. M14: Man 3C 80
Middle Hillgate SK1: Stoc . .3C 118 (2B 106)
Middlesex Rd. M9: Man 2F 39
  SK5: Stoc 2D 97
Middlesex Wlk. OL9: O'ham 3F 29
Middlestone Dr. M9: Man 5F 39
MIDDLETON 4C 16
Middleton Av. M35: Fail 5B 42
Middleton Cen. Ind. Est. M24: Mid 1B 26
Middleton Dr. BL9: Bury 3B 12
Middleton Gdns. M24: Mid 1B 26
MIDDLETON JUNCTION 3F 27
Middleton Leisure Cen. 1C 26
Middleton Old Rd. M9: Man 2F 39
Middleton Rd. M8: Man 3B 38
  M24: Mid 3C 24
             (not continuous)
  OL1: Chad 5F 17
  OL9: Chad 5F 17
             (not continuous)
  OL10: H'ood, Mid 1A 16
  SK5: Stoc 3B 84
Middleton Shop. Cen. M24: Mid 1B 26
Middleton Swimming Baths 1C 26
Middleton Vw. M24: Mid 1D 27
Middleton Way M24: Mid 1B 26
Middlewich Wlk. M18: Man 5E 69
          (off Peacock Cl.)
Middlewood Ct. OL9: Chad 2C 28
Middlewood Dr. SK4: Stoc 2C 104
Middlewood Grn. OL9: Chad 1C 28

Middlewood St. M5: Sal 1B **8** (1E **65**)
Middlewood Wlk. *M9:* Man 5F **39**
(off Fernclough Rd.)
Midfield Ct. M7: Sal 5A **38**
Midford Av. M30: Ecc 5D **47**
Midford Wlk. *M8:* Man 1C **52**
(off Barnsdale Dr.)
Midgley Av. M18: Man 4A **70**
Midgley Cres. OL6: A Lyme 3F **59**
Midgley St. M27: Swin 1F **47**
Midhurst Av. M40: Man 3D **55**
Midhurst Way *OL9:* Chad 3D **29**
(off Petworth Rd.)
Midland Rd. SK5: Stoc 3B **84**
Midland St. M12: Man 3F **67**
Midlothian St. M11: Man 5D **55**
Midmoor Wlk. *M9:* Man 1A **40**
(off Stockfield Dr.)
MID REDDISH 1B **96**
Midville Rd. M11: Man 4E **55**
Midway St. M12: Man 3C **82**
Midwood Hall *M6:* Sal 4B **50**
(off Eccles Old Rd.)
Milan St. M7: Sal 1A **52**
Milburn Av. M23: Wyth 1D **101**
Milden Cl. M20: Man 4E **93**
Mildred Av. M25: Pres 3E **37**
Mildred St. M7: Sal 2E **51**
Mild St. M9: Man 1F **39**
MILE END .5D **107**
Mile End La. SK2: Stoc 5D **107**
MILES PLATTING 4A **54**
Miles Platting Swimming Pool & Fitness Cen.
. . . . .4F **53**
Miles St. M12: Man 3C **68**
OL1: O'ham 1D **31**
Milford Av. OL8: O'ham 2E **43**
Milford Dr. M19: Man 1D **95**
Milford Gro. SK2: Stoc 4E **107**
Milford St. M6: Sal 1A **64**
M9: Man 5D **25**
Milk St. M2: Man 5C **6** (1C **66**)
OL4: O'ham 2E **31**
SK14: Hyde 3F **87**
Milkwood Gro. M18: Man 1F **83**
Millais St. M40: Man 4C **40**
Millard St. OL9: Chad 2C **28**
Millard Wlk. M18: Man 1F **83**
Millbank St. M1: Man 1F **11** (1E **67**)
Millbeck Ct. M24: Mid 4F **15**
Millbeck Rd. M24: Mid 4F **15**
Millbeck St. M15: Man 4C **66**
Millbrook Av. M34: Dent 4F **85**
Millbrook Ho. *BL4:* Farn 1A **18**
(off Lime St.)
Mill Brook Ind. Est. M23: Wyth 5A **100**
Millbrook Rd. M23: Wyth 3C **108**
Millbrook St.
SK1: Stoc 4B **118** (3B **106**)
Millbrook Towers
SK1: Stoc 4B **118** (3B **106**)
Mill Brow M9: Man 2E **39**
M28: Wors 1B **46**
OL6: A Lyme 3E **45**
Mill Ct. M41: Urm 3A **76**
Mill Ct. Dr. M26: Rad 1D **19**
Millennium Ho. *M16: Old T* 4E **65**
(off Chester Rd.)
M34: Dent 3E **85**
Millennium Tower M50: Sal 2B **64**

Miller Rd. OL8: O'ham 1A **44**
Millers Cl. M33: Sale 5C **90**
Miller's Ct. M5: Sal 5C **48**
Millers La. M30: Ecc 1E **61**
Miller St. M4: Man 2C **6** (5C **52**)
OL6: A Lyme 3D **59**
Millfield Wlk. *M40:* Man 2E **41**
(off Pleasington Dr.)
Mill Fold Rd. M24: Mid 1B **26**
Millford Av. M41: Urm 3A **74**
(not continuous)
Millford Gdns. M41: Urm 3A **74**
Mill Ga. OL8: O'ham 1F **43**
Millgate SK1: Stoc 1B **118** (1B **106**)
Millgate La. M20: Man 3C **102**
(Parrs Wood Rd.)
M20: Man 2D **103**
(Wilmslow Rd.)
Mill Grn. St. M12: Man 2F **67**
Millhalf Cl. M15: Man 5A **66**
Millhead Av. M40: Man 5A **54**
Millhouse Av. M23: Wyth 2C **108**
Milliner Ct. SK2: Stoc 4F **107**
Milliners Wharf M4: Man 4G **53**
Milling St. M1: Man 3B **10** (2B **66**)
Millington Rd. M17: T Pk 3E **63**
Millington Wlk. *M15:* Man 4F **65**
(off Mosshall Cl.)
Mill La. M22: Nor 2A **102**
M34: Dent 4D **87**
M35: Fail 5E **41**
OL6: A Lyme 3B **116** (5D **59**)
OL9: Chad 5E **29**
SK5: Stoc 4B **84**
SK8: Chea 5F **103**
(not continuous)
SK14: Hyde 3E **87**
WA15: Alt 5A **112**
Millom Av. M23: Wyth 2D **101**
Millom Ct. WA15: Tim 5F **99**
Millom Dr. BL9: Bury 4C **12**
Millom Pl. SK8: Gat 3D **111**
Millow St. M4: Man 2C **6** (4C **52**)
Millpool Wlk. *M9:* Man 4F **39**
(off Alderside Rd.)
Millrise OL1: O'ham 1D **117**
Mills Farm Cl. OL8: O'ham 3C **44**
MILLS HILL 1A **28**
Mills Hill Rd. M24: Mid 5F **17**
Mills Hill Station (Rail) 5F **17**
Millside *OL6: A Lyme* 4E **59**
(off Mossley Rd.)
Millstream La. M40: Man 4A **56**
Mill St. M6: Sal 3C **50**
M11: Man 2C **68**
(not continuous)
M35: Fail 5E **41**
WA14: Alt 5A **98**
Mill Vw. Ct. OL8: O'ham 1F **43**
Millwain Ho. SK4: Stoc 4C **94**
Millwall Cl. M18: Man 5F **69**
Millway Wlk. *M40:* Man 2E **55**
(off Orford Rd.)
Millwood Ct. BL9: Bury 1B **12**
Millwood Ter. SK14: Hyde 3F **87**
Millwright St. M40: Man 2D **55**
Milne Ct. M12: Man 4C **68**
SK16: Duk 2E **73**
Milner St. M16: Old T 1F **79**
M27: Swin 4B **34**

Milne St. M12: Man 4C **68**
(off Milne Cl.)
OL9: Chad 2D **29**
(Brook St.)
OL9: Chad 1E **29**
(Burnley La.)
OL9: O'ham 4E **29**
Milnrow Cl. M13: Man 4F **11** (3D **67**)
Milnthorpe St. M6: Sal 2D **51**
Milnthorpe Way M12: Man 4A **68**
Milstead Wlk. M40: Man 2C **54**
(off Peckford Dr.)
Milston Wlk. M8: Man 1C **52**
(off Barnsdale Dr.)
Milton Av. M5: Sal 5F **49**
M43: Droy 1C **70**
Milton Cl. M32: Stre 2A **78**
Milton Ct. M7: Sal 3A **98**
M19: Man 4A **94**
M30: Ecc 5F **47**
Milton Cres. SK8: Chea 1E **111**
Milton Dr. M33: Sale 2C **88**
OL9: Chad 3C **28**
WA15: Tim 2C **98**
Milton Gro. M16: W Ran 3E **79**
M33: Sale 2C **88**
Milton Lodge M16: W Ran 3E **79**
Milton Mt. M18: Man 1F **83**
(off Old Hall Dr.)
Milton Pl. M6: Sal 4D **51**
Milton Rd. M25: Pres 1C **37**
M27: Swin 4E **23**
M32: Stre 3F **33**
M34: Aud 2A **78**
Milton St. M7: Sal 3A **52**
M24: Mid 5B **16**
M30: Ecc 5F **47**
SK14: Hyde 1F **87**
Milverton Rd. M14: Man 1F **81**
Milwain Dr. SK4: Stoc 2E **95**
Milwain Rd. M19: Man 2E **95**
M32: Stre 5B **82**
Mimosa Dr. M27: Pen 2B **34**
Mincing St. M4: Man 2D **7** (4C **52**)
Minden Cl. M20: Man 4E **93**
Minden St. M6: Sal 1A **50**
Minehead Av. M20: Man 1B **92**
M41: Urm 5D **75**
Minerva Rd. OL6: A Lyme 5E **59**
Minford Cl. M40: Man 2D **55**
Minoan Gdns. M7: Sal 2E **51**
Minorca Av. M11: Man 5F **55**
Minor St. M35: Fail 4C **42**
(not continuous)
Minshull St. M1: Man 1D **11** (1C **66**)
Minshull St. Sth. M1: Man 2E **11** (2D **67**)
Minsmere Cl. M8: Man 1C **52**
Minstead Wlk. M22: Wyth 4D **109**
Minster Cl. SK16: Duk 4F **73**
Minster Dr. M41: Urm 2C **74**
SK8: Chea 2C **74**
Minster Rd. M9: Man 5C **104**
Minster Way OL9: Chad 4B **40**
Minstrel Cl. M27: Swin 1C **28**
Minton St. M40: Man 5A **34**
OL4: O'ham 4E **41**
Minto St. OL7: A Lyme 1A **116** (3C **58**)
(not continuous)
Mintridge Cl. M11: Man 4C **30**
Mirabel St. M3: Man 2A **6** (4B **52**)

Miranda Ct. M5: Sal 3B **8** (2E **65**)
Mirfield Av. M9: Man 5F **25**
OL8: O'ham 5A **30**
SK4: Stoc 1D **105**
Mirfield Dr. M24: Mid 5B **16**
M30: Ecc 3F **47**
M41: Urm 1E **75**
Mirfield Rd. M9: Man 5F **25**
Miriam St. M35: Fail 1F **55**
Missenden Ho. M5: Sal 1B **64**
(off Cyprus Cl.)
Missouri Av. M50: Sal 1A **64**
Misterton Wlk. M23: Wyth 4A **100**
(off Sandy La.)
Mistletoe Gro. M3: Sal 2D **5**
Mistral Ct. M30: Ecc 4A **48**
Mitcham Av. M9: Man 1C **40**
Mitchell Cl. SK8: Gat 5B **102**
Mitchell Gdns. M22: Shar 1A **110**
Mitchell Ho. SK8: Gat 5B **102**
(off Mitchell Cl.)
Mitchells Quay M35: Fail 5A **42**
M30: Ecc 4E **47**
M40: Man 2D **55**
OL1: O'ham 1A **30**
Mitcheson Gdns. M6: Sal 4B **50**
Mitford Ct. M14: Man 1E **93**
Mitford Rd. M14: Man 1E **93**
Mitford St. M32: Stre 4E **77**
Mitre Rd. M13: Man 1B **82**
Mitre St. M35: Fail 4B **42**
Moat Av. M22: Wyth 1E **109**
Moat Gdns. M22: Wyth 2E **109**
Moat Hall Av. M30: Ecc 2C **60**
Moat Rd. M22: Wyth 1E **109**
Moat Wlk. SK5: Stoc 1E **97**
Mobberley Cl. M19: Man 4A **94**
Moberly Hall M15: Man 5D **67**
(off Burlington St. E.)
Mocha Pde. M7: Sal 1D **5** (4F **51**)
Modbury Ct. M26: Rad 2C **18**
Modbury Wlk. M8: Man 1C **52**
(off Brinsworth Dr.)
Mode Hill La. M45: White 1E **23**
Mode Hill Wlk. M45: White 1E **23**
Model Lodging Ho. M3: Sal 4E **5**
Mode Wheel Circ. M17: T Pk 3E **63**
Mode Wheel Rd. M5: Sal 1F **63**
Mode Wheel Rd. Sth. M50: Sal 2F **63**
Modwen Rd. M5: Sal 4D **65**
Moffat Ct. SK16: Duk 1D **73**
Moison Ho. SK2: Stoc 5C **106**
(off Canada St.)
Mold St. OL1: O'ham 1D **117** (1A **30**)
Mollets Wood M34: Dent 5C **72**
Mollington Rd. M22: Wyth 1A **114**
Molyneux Rd. M19: Man 4E **83**
Mona Av. M32: Stre 2E **77**
SK8: H Grn 5F **111**
Mona Dr. M22: Nor 1F **101**
Mona Rd. OL9: Chad 4D **29**
Monart Rd. M9: Man 3A **40**
Mona St. M6: Sal 3C **50**
(off Gloucester St.)
SK14: Hyde 3F **87**
Monde Trad. Est. M17: T Pk 4C **62**
Monica Av. M8: Man 1B **38**
Monica Ct. M30: Ecc 4B **48**
Monica Gro. M19: Man 5B **82**

Monks Cl. M8: Man 2D 39
Monks Ct. M5: Sal 5D 49
Monksdale Av. M41: Urm 3D 75
Monkswood OL1: O'ham 2D 117 (2A 30)
Monkton Av. M18: Man 2E 83
Monkwood Dr. M9: Man 4A 40
(off Dalbeattie St.)
Monmouth Av. M33: Sale 3B 88
Monmouth St. M18: Man 4A 70
M24: Mid 1E 27
OL9: O'ham 4E 29
Monroe Cl. M6: Sal 3A 50
Monsal Av. M7: Sal 5C 36
SK2: Stoc 4F 107
Monsall Cl. BL9: Bury 4C 12
Monsall Rd. M40: Man 1A 54
Monsall St. M40: Man 2F 53
OL8: O'ham 1A 44
Montague Bus. Pk. M16: Old T 1C 78
Montague Cl. M33: Sale 4E 89
(off Montague Rd.)
Montague Ho. SK3: Stoc 2F 105
(off East St.)
Montague Rd. M16: Old T 5C 64
M33: Sale 4D 89
OL6: A Lyne 5F 59
Montagu Rd. SK2: Stoc 4F 107
Montana Sq. M11: Man 3A 70
Montcliffe Cres. M16: W Ran 4B 80
Monteagle St. M9: Man 5D 25
Montford Ent. Cen. M50: Sal 1B 64
(off Wynford Sq.)
Montford St. M50: Sal 1B 64
Montgomery Dr. BL9: Bury 4D 13
Montgomery Ho. M16: W Ran 3B 80
OL8: O'ham 3D 43
Montgomery Rd. M13: Man 3B 82
Montgomery St. OL8: O'ham 2D 43
Montmano Dr. M20: Man 2B 92
MONTON .3F 47
Monton Av. M30: Ecc 4A 48
Monton Bri. Ct. M30: Ecc 3E 47
Montondale M30: Ecc 4E 47
Montonfields Rd. M30: Ecc 3F 47
Monton Grn. M30: Ecc 3F 47
Monton La. M30: Ecc 5A 48
Montonmill Gdns. M30: Ecc 4E 47
Monton Rd. M30: Ecc 4F 47
(not continuous)
SK5: Stoc 4E 97
Monton St. M14: Man 1C 80
Montpelier M. M7: Sal 3A 38
Montpellior Rd. M22: Wyth 4F 109
Montreal St. M19: Man 4D 83
OL8: O'ham 5B 30
Montrose M30: Ecc 5A 48
(off Monton La.)
Montrose Av. M20: Man 3C 92
M32: Stre 3D 77
SK16: Duk 3E 73
Montrose Cres. M19: Man 4B 82
Moon Gro. M14: Man 2F 81
Moorby Av. M19: Man 4A 94
Moorby St. OL1: O'ham 1C 30
MOORCLOSE 2E 27
Moorclose St. M24: Mid 1E 27
Moorclose Wlk. M9: Man 5F 39
(off Conran St.)

Moorcock Av. M27: Pen 4D 35
Moorcot Ct. M23: Wyth 3B 100
Moorcroft Dr. M19: Man 4B 94
Moorcroft Rd. M23: Wyth 2B 100
Moorcroft St. M43: Droy 2C 70
OL8: O'ham 2E 43
Moorcroft Wlk. M19: Man 4A 94
Moordale Av. M20: Man 3C 92
Moordown Cl. M8: Man 1D 53
Moore Ho. M30: Ecc 2F 61
Moor End M22: Nor 3F 101
Moor End Av. M7: Sal 4E 37
Moor End Ct. M7: Sal 4E 37
Moore Wlk. M34: Dent 5C 86
(off Wordsworth Rd.)
Moorfield M7: Sal 3E 37
(off Moor La.)
M28: Wors 4B 32
Moorfield Av. M20: Man 1E 93
M34: Dent 4C 86
Moorfield Chase BL4: Farn 2A 18
Moorfield Cl. M27: Swin 1F 47
M30: Ecc 5F 47
Moorfield Gro. M33: Sale 5F 89
SK4: Stoc 4D 95
Moorfield Rd. M6: Sal 3F 49
M20: Man 4B 92
M27: Swin 1E 47
OL8: O'ham 2D 43
Moorfield St. M20: Man 1D 93
(not continuous)
Moorfield Wlk. M41: Urm 3F 75
Moorgate Av. M20: Man 1B 92
Moorhead St. M4: Man 2F 7 (4D 53)
MOORHEY 3D 31
Moorhey Ind. Est.
OL4: O'ham 3D 31
Moorhey St. OL4: O'ham 3D 31
Moorhill Ct. M7: Sal 3E 37
Moorings, The M28: Wors 2C 46
Moorings Rd. M17: T Pk 2D 63
Moorland Av. M20: Man 2B 38
M33: Sale 5E 89
M43: Droy 1A 70
Moorland Dr. M27: Swin 5B 34
(off Worsley Rd.)
Moorland Rd. M20: Man 5D 93
Moorlands Av. M41: Urm 2D 75
Moor La. M7: Sal 4C 36
M23: Wyth 1C 100
M41: Urm 2C 74
Moorlea M35: Fail 4B 42
Moor Lodge SK4: Stoc 4D 95
Moor Nook M33: Sale 5F 89
Moor Pk. Rd. M20: Man 3E 103
Moor Platt M33: Sale 5F 89
(off Derbyshire Rd. Sth.)
Moor Rd. M23: Wyth 2A 100
Moorsholme Av. M40: Man 5C 40
MOORSIDE 4E 33
Moorside Av. M43: Droy 5E 57
Moorside Cl. M33: Sale 4D 89
(off Sibson Rd.)
M34: Dent 1B 86
Moorside Cres. M43: Droy 5E 57
Moorside Ho. WA15: Tim 4E 99
(off Oakleigh Ct.)
Moorside La. M34: Dent 1C 86
(not continuous)
Moorside Lodge M27: Swin 4F 33

Moorside Rd. M7: Sal 4E **37**
    M8: Man 3C **38**
    M27: Swin 5E **33**
    M41: Urm 2A **74**
    SK4: Stoc 1C **104**
Moorside Station (Rail) 3F **33**
Moorside St. M43: Droy 5D **57**
Moorsley Dr. M9: Man 5B **26**
Moor St. M27: Swin 5B **34**
    M30: Ecc 1D **61**
    OL1: O'ham 2D **31**
Moorton Av. M19: Man 1B **94**
Moorton Pk. M19: Man 1B **94**
Moortop Cl. M9: Man 4E **25**
Moor Top Pl. SK4: Stoc 5D **95**
Moorville Rd. M6: Sal 2E **49**
Moorway Dr. M9: Man 5C **26**
Moorwood Dr. M33: Sale 5A **88**
    OL8: O'ham 5E **31**
Mora Av. OL9: Chad 1D **29**
Moran Wlk. M15: Man 4B **66**
(off Crediton Rd.)
Morar Rd. SK16: Duk 3F **73**
Mora St. M9: Man 4B **40**
Moravian Cl. SK16: Duk 1E **73**
Moravian Fld. M43: Droy 2C **70**
Moray Rd. OL9: Chad 5C **28**
Morbourne Cl. M12: Man 4A **68**
Morden Av. M11: Man 5E **55**
Morecombe Cl. M40: Man 1D **55**
Moresby Dr. M20: Man 3D **103**
Morestead Wlk. M40: Man 4E **53**
(off New Allen St.)
Moreton Cl. M32: Stre 3F **77**
    M33: Sale 5A **88**
    M45: White 5B **12**
(not continuous)
Moreton Cl. SK16: Duk 4F **73**
Moreton La. SK2: Stoc 4F **107**
Moreton St. OL9: Chad 1B **28**
Moreton Wlk. SK2: Stoc 4E **107**
Morgan Pl. SK5: Stoc 4B **96**
Morland Rd. M16: Old T 1E **79**
Morley Av. M14: Man 4C **80**
    M27: Swin 1A **48**
Morley St. M45: White 1B **22**
    OL4: O'ham 1F **31**
Morna Wlk. M12: Man 2F **67**
Morningside Cl. M43: Droy 3C **70**
Morningside Dr. M20: Man 3E **103**
Mornington Av. SK8: Chea 2F **111**
Mornington Ct. OL1: O'ham 1A **30**
(off Bradford St.)
Mornington Cres. M14: Man 5C **80**
Mornington Rd. M33: Sale 3F **89**
    SK8: Chea 2F **111**
Morpeth Cl. M12: Man 5A **68**
    OL7: A Lyme 3A **58**
Morpeth St. M27: Swin 1A **48**
Morrell Rd. M22: Nor 3F **101**
Morris Gro. M41: Urm 5A **74**
Morris Hall M14: Man 1F **81**
(off Daisy Bank Hall)
Morrison Wlk. M40: Man 2C **54**
(off Eldridge St.)
Morris St. M20: Man 1D **93**
    M26: Rad 1A **12**
    OL4: O'ham 4C **30**
Morrowfield Av. M8: Man 5B **38**
Morse Rd. M40: Man 2D **55**

Mortar St. OL4: O'ham 1E **31**
(not continuous)
Mortimer Av. M9: Man 5A **26**
Mortimer St. OL1: O'ham 1C **30**
Mortlake Dr. M40: Man 2D **55**
Morton St. M24: Mid 4C **16**
    M35: Fail 1E **55**
    SK4: Stoc 4A **96**
Morton Ter. M34: Dent 4C **86**
(off Tatton Rd.)
Morven Dr. M23: Wyth 1C **108**
Morville Rd. M21: Chor 4F **79**
Moscow Rd. SK3: Stoc 4F **105**
Moscow Rd. E. SK3: Stoc 4F **105**
Mosedale Cl. M23: Wyth 5A **100**
Mosedale Rd. M24: Mid 4F **15**
Moseldene Rd. SK2: Stoc 5F **107**
Moseley Ct. M19: Man 4B **82**
Moseley Rd. M14: Man 5F **81**
    M19: Man 5B **82**
Moseley St. SK3: Stoc 5A **118** (3A **106**)
Mosley Arc. M1: Man 1C **10**
(off Parker St.)
Mosley Cl. WA15: Tim 4B **98**
Mosley St. M17: T Pk 1E **77**
    WA15: Tim 5D **99**
Mosley St. M2: Man 2B **10** (1C **66**)
Mosley Street Stop (Metro) . .1C **10** (1C **66**)
Moss, The M24: Mid 3D **27**
Mossack Av. M22: Wyth 5F **109**
Moss Bank M8: Man 4C **38**
Moss Bank Av. M43: Droy 5E **57**
Moss Bank Ct. M43: Droy 5E **57**
Moss Bank Gro. M27: Ward 2F **33**
Moss Bank Rd. M27: Ward 2F **33**
Moss Bank Trad. Est. M28: Walk . . .5A **18**
Mossbray Av. M19: Man 4F **93**
Moss Brook Ct. M40: Man 3E **53**
(off Kentford Dr.)
Moss Brook Rd. M9: Man 5A **40**
Mossclough Ct. M9: Man 5A **40**
Moss Colliery Rd. M27: Clif 1A **34**
Moss Cft. Cl. M41: Urm 2A **74**
Mossdale Rd. M23: Wyth 2B **100**
    M33: Sale 2A **98**
Moss Farm Cl. M24: Mid 3D **27**
Mossfield Cl. SK4: Stoc 1D **105**
Mossfield Rd. BL4: Kea 4B **18**
    M27: Swin 2A **34**
    WA15: Tim 5F **99**
Moss Fold OL6: A Lyme 2A **58**
(off Ripon St.)
Moss Grange Av. M16: W Ran 1F **79**
MOSS GROVE 2F **43**
Moss Gro. Cl. M15: Man 1A **80**
(off Moss La. W.)
Mossgrove Rd. WA15: Tim 4B **98**
Mossgrove St. OL8: O'ham 2F **43**
Mosshall Cl. M15: Man 4F **65**
Moss Hall Rd. OL10: H'ood, Mid . . .1B **14**
Moss Hey Dr. M23: Wyth 2D **101**
Moss Ho. Ter. M9: Man 3E **39**
Moss La. BL4: Kea 4D **19**
    M9: Mid 4C **26**
    M24: Mid 4B **26**
(not continuous)
    M27: Ward 3F **33**
    M28: Walk 5A **18**
(not continuous)
    M33: Sale 5A **88**

Moss La. M41: Urm 5F **61**
   M45: White 1B **22**
   OL7: A Lyme 3F **57**
   SK9: Sty 4F **113**
   WA15: Tim 4B **98**
Moss La. E. M15: Man 1B **80**
Moss La. Ind. Est. M45: White 5B **12**
Moss La. Trad. Est. M45: White 5C **12**
Moss La. W. M15: Man 1A **80**
Mosslee Av. M8: Man 1B **38**
Mossley Rd. OL6: A Lyme 4E **59**
Moss Lodge La. OL7: A Lyme 5F **57**
Moss Mnr. M33: Sale 5A **88**
Moss Mdw. Rd. M6: Sal 3E **49**
MOSS NOOK 2B **114**
Moss Nook Ind. Area M22: Wyth . . .1B **114**
Moss Pk. Rd. M32: Stre 3C **76**
Moss Rd. BL4: Farn 2A **18**
   M32: Stre 1E **77**
MOSS SIDE 1C **80**
Moss Side Leisure Cen. 5B **66**
Moss St. BL4: Farn 1A **18**
   M7: Sal 2F **51**
   M34: Aud 1D **71**
   M43: Droy 5D **57**
   OL4: O'ham 1F **31**
Moss St. E. OL6: A Lyme 2B **116** (4D **59**)
Moss St. W. OL7: A Lyme . . .3A **116** (5B **58**)
Moss Ter. OL6: A Lyme 3A **116** (5C **58**)
Moss Va. Cres. M32: Stre 1B **76**
Moss Va. Rd. M41: Urm 3A **76**
   (not continuous)
Moss Vw. M40: Man 2E **41**
Moss Way M33: Sale 4A **88**
   OL7: A Lyme, Aud 1A **72**
Mossway M24: Mid 4B **26**
Mosswood Pk. M20: Man 3D **103**
Mossylea Cl. M24: Mid 4D **27**
MOSTON 4C **40**
Moston Bank Av. M9: Man 5A **40**
Moston Fairway Nature Reserve 4E **41**
Moston La. M9: Man 4A **40**
   M40: Man 4A **40**
      (Kenyon La.)
   M40: Man 2E **41**
      (Leyburn Rd.)
Moston La. E. M40: Man 2F **41**
Moston Rd. M24: Mid 4F **27**
Moston Station (Rail) 2F **41**
Moston St. M7: Sal 5B **38**
   SK5: Stoc 1B **96**
Mostyn Av. M14: Man 5A **82**
Motcombe Farm Rd. SK8: H Grn . . .5D **111**
Motcombe Gro. SK8: H Grn 3C **110**
Motcombe Rd. SK8: H Grn 4C **110**
Motherwell Av. M19: Man 4C **82**
Mottershead Rd. M22: Wyth 2E **109**
Mottram Av. M21: Chor 3E **91**
Mottram Dr. WA15: Tim 5C **98**
Mottram Fold SK1: Stoc 4B **118** (3B **106**)
Mottram M. M33: Sale 3F **87**
Mottram St. SK1: Stoc 4C **118** (3B **106**)
      (Bamford St.)
   SK1: Stoc 4B **118** (3B **106**)
      (Millbrook St.)

Mottram Towers
   SK1: Stoc 4B **118** (3B **106**)
Mottram Way SK1: Stoc 4B **118**
Mough La. OL9: Chad 1F **41**

Mouldsworth Av. M20: Man 1C **92**
   SK4: Stoc 2F **95**
Moulton St. M8: Man 3A **52**
Moulton St. Pct. M8: Man 3A **52**
Mount, The M7: Sal 4E **37**
   OL6: A Lyme 4F **59**
   SK5: Stoc 4D **97**
Mountain St. M40: Man 3F **55**
   SK1: Stoc 1C **106**
Mountbatten Cl. BL9: Bury 4D **13**
Mountbatten St. M18: Man 5E **69**
Mt. Carmel Ct. *M5: Sal* *4A 8*
   (off Mt. Carmel Cres.)
Mt. Carmel Cres. M5: Sal 4A **8** (3E **65**)
Mount Dr. M41: Urm 3B **76**
Mountfield M25: Pres 5D **23**
Mountfield Rd. SK3: Stoc 4E **105**
Mountfield Wlk. *M11: Man* *1B 68*
   (off Hopedale Cl.)
Mountfold M24: Mid 2D **27**
Mountford Av. M8: Man 2B **38**
Mount Gro. SK8: Gat 5B **102**
Mountheath Ind. Pk. M25: Pres 3D **37**
Mt. Pleasant M24: Mid 1E **25**
   M25: Pres 1A **24**
Mt. Pleasant Bus. Cen. OL4: O'ham . .2D **31**
Mt. Pleasant Ho. M27: Swin 4C **34**
Mt. Pleasant St. M34: Dent 3B **86**
Mt. Pleasant St. M34: Aud 3B **72**
      (not continuous)
   OL4: O'ham 2D **31**
   OL6: A Lyme 3E **59**
      (not continuous)
Mt. Pleasant Trad. Est. *OL6: A Lyme* . .*3E 59*
   (off Pleasant St.)
Mount Rd. M18: Man 5E **69**
   M19: Man 1E **83**
   M24: Mid 2B **26**
   M25: Pres 2E **23**
   SK4: Stoc 1E **105**
Mountside Cres. M25: Pres 5B **22**
Mount St. M2: Man 2B **10** (2B **66**)
   M3: Sal 3D **5** (5F **51**)
   M27: Swin 5B **34**
   M30: Ecc 2E **61**
   M34: Dent 4D **87**
   SK14: Hyde 3F **87**
Mount Ter. M43: Droy 4A **56**
Mt. Zion Rd. BL9: Bury 1B **12**
Mousell St. M8: Man 3C **52**
Mowbray Av. M25: Pres 2E **37**
   M33: Sale 5E **89**
Mowbray St. OL1: O'ham 4F **117** (3B **30**)
   OL7: A Lyme 5C **58**
   SK1: Stoc 4C **118** (3B **106**)
Mowbray Wlk. M24: Mid 4A **16**
Moxley Rd. M8: Man 3A **38**
Mozart Cl. M4: Man 5E **53**
Muirfield Cl. M25: Pres 4D **23**
   M40: Man 4E **41**
Muirhead Ct. M6: Sal 2C **50**
Mulberry Cl. SK8: H Grn 2E **115**
Mulberry Ct. *M6: Sal* *4C 50*
   (off Mulberry Rd.)
   M41: Urm 3A **76**
   WA14: Alt *5A 98*
   (off Gaskell Rd.)
Mulberry M. SK4: Stoc 1F **105**
Mulberry Mt. St.
   SK3: Stoc 5A **118** (3A **106**)

Mulberry Rd. M6: Sal 5C **50**
Mulberry St. M2: Man 1A **10** (1B **66**)
   OL6: A Lyme 4E **59**
Mulberry Wlk. M43: Droy 2A **70**
Mulgrave Rd. M28: Wors 4C **32**
Mulgrave St. M27: Swin 3F **33**
Mulgrove Wlk. M9: Man 1A **40**
               (off Haverfield Rd.)
Mullacre Rd. M22: Wyth 5F **101**
Mull Av. M12: Man 5B **68**
Mullineux St. M28: Walk 2A **32**
Mullion Cl. M19: Man 3F **83**
Mullion Dr. WA15: Tim 4A **98**
Mullion Wlk. M8: Man 1D **53**
Mulmount Cl. OL8: O'ham 1E **43**
MUMPS 2C **30**
Mumps OL1: O'ham 2C **30**
Mumps M. OL1: O'ham 2C **30**
               (off Garden St.)
Mumps Rdbt. OL1: O'ham 2C **30**
   OL4: O'ham 2C **30**
Munday St. M4: Man 1F **67**
Munn Rd. M9: Man 4D **25**
Munro Av. M22: Wyth 4B **110**
Munslow Wlk. M9: Man 1B **40**
Munster St. M4: Man 2C **6** (4C **52**)
Muriel St. M7: Sal 2F **51**
Murray St. M4: Man 4F **7** (5D **53**)
   M7: Sal .1F **51**
Murrow Wlk. M9: Man 4F **39**
             (off Alderside Rd.)
Muscle & Fitness Gymnasium 2B **34**
              (off Station Rd.)
Musden Wlk. SK4: Stoc 1F **95**
Mus. of Science & Industry . . . 2E **9** (2A **66**)
Mus. of the Manchester Regiment, The
   . . . . .2C **116** (4D **59**)
Mus. of Transport 1D **53**
Museum St. M2: Man 2A **10** (2B **66**)
Musgrave Rd. M22: Wyth 3F **109**
Muslin St. M5: Sal 1B **8** (1E **65**)
Muter Av. M22: Wyth 4B **110**
Myerscroft Cl. M40: Man 3A **42**
Myrtle Bank M25: Pres 3C **36**
Myrtle Cl. OL8: O'ham 4A **30**
Myrtle Gro. M25: Pres 2D **37**
   M34: Dent 2B **84**
   M43: Droy 5E **57**
   M45: White 4A **12**
Myrtleleaf Gro. M5: Sal 5F **49**
Myrtle Pl. M7: Sal 3E **51**
Myrtle Rd. M24: Mid 4E **17**
Myrtle St. M11: Man 2A **68**
   M16: Old T 1E **79**
             (off Langshaw St.)
   SK3: Stoc 3D **105**
My St. M5: Sal 1A **64**
Mythorn Wlk. M40: Man 2C **54**
              (off Harmer Cl.)
Mytton St. M15: Man 5B **66**

N

Naburn Cl. SK5: Stoc 2E **97**
Naburn St. M13: Man 1F **81**
Nada Lodge M8: Man 3B **38**
          (off St Mary's Hall Rd.)
Nada Rd. M8: Man 3B **38**
Naden Wlk. M45: White 1C **22**

Nadine St. M6: Sal 4A **50**
Nadin St. OL8: O'ham 1A **44**
Nairn Cl. M40: Man 4A **54**
            (off Eastfield Av.)
Nall St. M19: Man 1D **95**
Nameplate Cl. M30: Ecc 5C **46**
Nancy St. M15: Man 5C **8** (4F **65**)
Nangreave Rd. SK2: Stoc 5C **106**
Nangreave St. M5: Sal 1C **8** (1F **65**)
Nan Nook Rd. M23: Wyth 2B **100**
Nansen Av. M30: Ecc 4E **47**
Nansen Cl. M32: Stre 1A **78**
Nansen Dr. SK8: Gat 2C **110**
Nansen St. M6: Sal 5A **50**
   M11: Man 2A **68**
   M32: Stre 2F **77**
Nantwich Rd. M14: Man 4C **80**
Nantwich Way SK9: Hand 4F **115**
             (off Spath La.)
Napier Ct. M15: Man 4E **65**
             (off City Rd.)
   SK4: Stoc 5D **95**
Napier Grn. M5: Sal 3D **65**
Napier Rd. M21: Chor 5D **79**
   M30: Ecc 4E **47**
   SK4: Stoc 5D **95**
Napier St. M27: Swin 5F **33**
Napier St. E. OL8: O'ham 4F **29**
Napier St. W. OL8: O'ham 4E **29**
Naples Rd. SK3: Stoc 5D **105**
Naples St. M4: Man 2D **7** (4C **52**)
Narbonne Av. M30: Ecc 3C **48**
Narborough Wlk. M40: Man 2E **53**
           (off Westmount Cl.)
Narbuth Dr. M8: Man 5B **38**
Naseby Av. M9: Man 5B **26**
Naseby Ct. M25: Pres 4E **23**
Naseby Pl. M25: Pres 5E **23**
Naseby Rd. SK5: Stoc 5A **84**
Naseby Wlk. M45: White 1E **23**
Nash Rd. M17: T Pk 2A **62**
Nash St. M15: Man 4A **66**
Nasmyth Av. M34: Dent 1C **86**
Nasmyth Bus. Cen. M30: Ecc 4E **47**
Nasmyth Rd. M30: Ecc 2E **61**
Nasmyth St. M8: Man 2E **53**
Nathan Dr. M3: Sal 3E **5** (5A **52**)
Nathans Rd. M22: Wyth 2E **109**
National Dr. M5: Sal 2C **64**
National Ind. Est. OL7: A Lyme 5B **58**
National Squash Cen. 5B **54**
Naunton Rd. M24: Mid 2D **27**
Naunton Wlk. M9: Man 4A **40**
             (off Jonas St.)
Naval St. M4: Man 3F **7** (5E **53**)
Nave Ct. M6: Sal 3B **50**
Navenby Av. M16: Old T 1E **79**
Navigation Ho. M1: Man 1F **11**
Navigation Rd. WA14: Alt 5A **98**
Navigation Road Station (Rail & Metro)
   . . . . .5A **98**
Navigation Trad. Est.
   M40: Man 2B **54**
Naylor Ct. M40: Man 4E **53**
Naylor St. M40: Man 4F **53**
   OL1: O'ham 2D **117** (2A **30**)
Nazeby Wlk. OL9: O'ham 4E **29**
Naze St. OL1: O'ham 1A **30**
           (off Bradford St.)
Naze Wlk. SK5: Stoc 2E **97**

Neal Av. OL6: A Lyme 4F 59
   SK8: H Grn .1C 114
Neale Rd. M21: Chor 1C 90
Nearbrook Rd. M22: Wyth 2E 109
Nearcroft Rd. M23: Wyth 4C 100
Nearmaker Av. M22: Wyth 2E 109
Nearmaker Rd. M22: Wyth 2E 109
Neary Way M41: Urm 5E 61
Neath Av. M22: Nor 4F 101
Neath Cl. M45: White 2E 23
Neath St. OL9: O'ham 2F 29
Neden Cl. M11: Man 2D 69
Needham Av. M21: Chor 5D 79
Needham Ct. M45: White 2B 22
Needwood Cl. M40: Man 2F 53
Neem Ho. M14: Man 1E 81
   (off Rusholme Pl.)
Neenton Sq. M12: Man 4C 68
Neild St. M1: Man 3F 11 (2E 67)
   OL8: O'ham .5A 30
Neill St. M7: Sal .3A 52
Neilson Cl. M24: Mid 2E 27
Neilson Cl. M23: Wyth 5C 100
Neilston Av. M40: Man 5D 41
Nell La. M21: Chor 1E 91
Nelson Av. M30: Ecc 4F 47
Nelson Bus. Cen. M34: Dent 1B 86
Nelson Cl. M15: Man 1A 80
Nelson Ct. M40: Man 3F 53
   (off Droitwich Rd.)
Nelson Dr. M43: Droy 5F 55
Nelson Fold M27: Pen 3C 34
Nelson Mandela Ct. M16: W Ran 2A 80
   (off Range Rd.)
Nelson Rd. M9: Man 4F 25
Nelson St. BL4: Farn 1A 18
   M5: Sal 1A 64
   M7: Sal 2F 51
   M13: Man 5D 67
   M24: Mid 2E 27
   M30: Ecc 5F 47
   M32: Stre 4F 77
   M34: Aud 4B 72
   M34: Dent 1B 86
      (not continuous)
   M40: Man 4A 54
   OL4: Lees 4F 31
   SK14: Hyde .3F 87
Nelson Way OL9: Chad 5D 29
Nelstrop Cres. SK4: Stoc 2F 95
Nelstrop Rd. SK4: Stoc 2E 95
Nelstrop Rd. Nth. M19: Man 4F 83
   SK4: Stoc 1E 95
Nelstrop Wlk. SK4: Stoc 2E 95
Nepaul Rd. M9: Man 3A 40
Neptune Gdns. M7: Sal 2E 51
Nesfield Rd. M23: Wyth 1B 100
Neston Av. M20: Man 2C 92
   M33: Sale 1A 100
Neston Gro. SK3: Stoc 5F 105
Neston St. M11: Man 3B 70
Neswick Wlk. M23: Wyth 1B 100
Netherbury Cl. M18: Man 2E 83
Nethercote Av. M23: Wyth 5D 101
Nethercroft Rd. WA15: Tim 5E 99
Netherfield Cl. OL8: O'ham 5E 29
Nether Hey St. OL8: O'ham 4D 31
      (not continuous)
Netherland St. M5: Sal 2C 64
NETHER LEES 4F 31

Netherlees OL4: Lees 4F 31
Netherlow Ct. SK14: Hyde 3F 87
   (off Union St.)
Nether St. M12: Man 3F 11 (2E 67)
Netherton Rd. M14: Man 4C 80
Nethervale Dr. M9: Man 5A 40
Netherwood M35: Fail 4D 43
Netherwood Rd. M22: Nor 4E 101
Netley Rd. M23: Wyth 2C 108
Nettlebarn Rd. M22: Wyth 1E 109
Nettleford Rd. M16: W Ran 5A 80
Nettleton Gro. M9: Man 3B 40
Nevada St. M13: Man 5F 67
Nevendon Dr. M23: Wyth 2B 108
Nevile Ct. M7: Sal 4D 37
Nevile Rd. M7: Sal 4D 37
Neville Cardus Wlk. M14: Man 3E 81
   (off Taylor St.)
Neville St. OL9: Chad 2E 29
Nevin Rd. M40: Man 3F 41
New Allen St. M40: Man 4E 53
NEWALL GREEN 2C 108
Newall Rd. M23: Wyth 3B 108
Newall St. OL9: Chad 2D 43
Newark Av. M14: Man 2D 81
Newark Rd. M27: Clif 2D 35
   SK5: Stoc 3B 96
New Bailey St. M3: Sal 4E 5 (1A 66)
Newbank Chase OL9: Chad 1C 28
Newbank Cl. M24: Mid 2E 27
New Bank St. M12: Man 4A 68
Newbank Twr. M3: Sal 1E 5 (4A 52)
New Barn Rd. OL8: O'ham 2C 44
New Barns Av. M21: Chor 2E 91
New Barton St. M6: Sal 2E 49
Newbeck St. M4: Man 3D 7
New Beech Rd. SK4: Stoc 1A 104
      (not continuous)
New Belvedere Cl. M32: Stre 3F 77
Newberry Gro. SK3: Stoc 5F 105
Newbold Cl. SK16: Duk 2E 73
Newbold Wlk. M15: Man 5B 10
Newboult Rd. SK8: Chea 5A 104
Newbreak Cl. OL4: O'ham 1F 31
Newbreak St. OL4: O'ham 1F 31
New Bri. Gdns. BL9: Bury 1A 12
New Bri. La. SK1: Stoc 2C 118 (2B 106)
New Bri. St. M3: Sal 2A 6 (4B 52)
Newbrook Av. M21: Chor 5F 91
Newburn Av. M9: Man 5B 26
Newbury Ct. WA15: Tim 4B 98
   (off Tulip Dr.)
Newbury Dr. M30: Ecc 4D 47
   M41: Urm 5E 61
Newbury Pl. M7: Sal 5F 37
Newbury Rd. SK8: H Grn 2D 115
Newbury Wlk. M9: Man 1F 53
   (off Ravelston Dr.)
   OL9: Chad 2E 29
   (off Kempton Way)
Newby Dr. M24: Mid 3B 16
   M33: Sale 5A 90
   SK8: Gat 5C 102
Newby Rd. SK4: Stoc 1E 105
Newcastle St. M15: Man 5B 10 (3B 66)
      (not continuous)
Newcastle Wlk. M34: Dent 4C 86
   (off Trowbridge Rd.)
New Cathedral St. M1: Man 4B 6 (5B 52)
New Century Ho. M34: Dent 2E 85

Newchurch OL8: O'ham 4C **44**
New Church Ct. *M45: White* *2B 22*
(off Elizabeth St.)
Newchurch St. M11: Man 2B **68**
(off Blackrock St.)
Newcliffe Rd. M9: Man 5B **26**
New College St. M3: Man 1E **9** (1A **66**)
Newcombe Cl. M11: Man 1B **68**
Newcombe Ct. *M33: Sale* *4B 88*
(off Beech Gro.)
Newcombe St. M3: Man 1B **6** (4B **52**)
New Ct. St. M3: Man 1F **9** (1A **66**)
Newcroft M35: Fail 1D **57**
Newcroft Cres. M41: Urm 4B **76**
Newcroft Dr. M9: Man 3E **39**
  M41: Urm 4C **76**
  SK3: Stoc 5F **105**
Newcroft Rd. M41: Urm 4B **76**
New Cross M4: Man 4E **7** (5D **53**)
New Cross St. M5: Sal 5E **49**
  M27: Swin 5C **34**
Newdale Rd. M12: Man 3D **83**
NEW EARTH .4E **31**
New Earth St. OL4: O'ham 4E **31**
New Elm Rd. M3: Man 2D **9** (2F **65**)
New Forest Rd. M23: Wyth 3E **99**
New Gartside St. M3: Man 1E **9** (1A **66**)
New George St. M4: Man 3D **7** (5C **52**)
New Hall Av. M7: Sal 4F **37**
  SK8: H Grn 2D **115**
Newhall Av. M30: Ecc 3C **60**
New Hall Cl. *M33: Sale* 4B **90**
New Hall Dr. M23: Wyth 1C **100**
New Hall Rd. M7: Sal 4F **37**
Newhall Rd. SK5: Stoc 3C **84**
Newham Av. M11: Man 5D **55**
Newhaven Av. M11: Man 3B **70**
Newhaven Bus. Pk. M30: Ecc 1A **62**
New Herbert St. M6: Sal 2E **49**
Newhey Av. M22: Wyth 1F **109**
New Hey Rd. SK8: Chea 5A **104**
Newhey Rd. M22: Wyth 2F **109**
Newholme Ct. M32: Stre 3A **78**
Newholme Rd. M20: Man 3B **92**
Newick Wlk. *M9: Man* *1A 40*
(off Leconfield Dr.)
Newington Av. M8: Man 1B **38**
New Islington M4: Man 5E **53**
New Kings Head Yd. M3: Sal . . .3A **6** (5B **52**)
Newlands M35: Fail 3A **56**
Newlands Av. M30: Ecc 2B **60**
  M45: White 5A **12**
Newlands Dr. M20: Man 3E **103**
  M25: Pres 4C **22**
  M27: Pen 1E **49**
Newlands Rd. M23: Wyth 3B **100**
  SK8: Chea 5F **103**
Newland St. M8: Man 3D **39**
Newlands Wlk. M24: Mid 2A **16**
New La. M24: Mid 5C **16**
  M30: Ecc 1D **61**
New Lawns SK5: Stoc 4C **84**
New Lees St. OL6: A Lyme 2F **59**
(not continuous)
Newlyn Dr. M33: Sale 2E **99**
Newlyn St. M14: Man 3D **81**
New Mansion Ho. SK1: Stoc 5B **118**
Newman St. OL6: A Lyme 2A **116** (4C **58**)
New Mkt. M2: Man 5B **6** (1B **66**)
Newmarket Gro. OL7: A Lyme 2A **58**

New Mkt. La. M2: Man 5C **6** (1C **66**)
Newmarket M. M7: Sal 1F **51**
Newmarket Rd. OL7: A Lyme 2A **58**
New Medlock Ho. M15: Man . . .5B **10** (3B **66**)
Newmill Wlk. *M8: Man* *1C 52*
(off Brentfield Av.)
NEW MOSTON 3A **42**
New Mount St. M4: Man 2D **7**
New Oak Cl. M35: Fail 4E **43**
New Pk. Rd. M5: Sal 3D **65**
Newpark Wlk. *M8: Man* *1C 52*
(off Tamerton Dr.)
Newport Av. SK5: Stoc 1A **96**
Newport M. *BL4: Farn* *2A 18*
(off Newport St.)
Newport Rd. M21: Chor 4C **78**
  M34: Dent 5D **87**
Newport St. BL4: Farn 2A **18**
  M6: Sal .5A **50**
  M14: Man 2D **81**
  M24: Mid 5E **17**
  OL8: O'ham 4F **29**
Newquay Av. SK5: Stoc 1A **96**
New Quay St. M3: Man 1E **9** (1A **66**)
New Radcliffe St.
  OL1: O'ham 3D **17** (2A **30**)
New Ridd Ri. SK14: Hyde 5F **87**
New Rd. OL8: O'ham 5A **30**
Newry Rd. M30: Ecc 2A **62**
Newry Wlk. *M9: Man* *1D 39*
(off Riverdale Rd.)
Newsham Rd. SK3: Stoc 5A **106**
Newsham Wlk. M12: Man 2D **83**
Newsholme St. M8: Man 5B **38**
New Smithfield Mkt. M11: Man 3E **69**
Newstead Av. M20: Man 3F **93**
  OL6: A Lyme 5E **45**
Newstead Rd. M41: Urm 2A **76**
Newstead Ter. WA15: Tim 4B **98**
New St. M27: Pen 3C **34**
  M30: Ecc 1E **61**
  M40: Man 3A **54**
  M43: Droy 2C **70**
  OL4: Lees 3F **31**
New Thomas St. M6: Sal 3C **50**
Newton Av. M12: Man 1B **82**
  M20: Man 2C **92**
Newton Ct. *SK14: Hyde* *5F 73*
(off Markham St.)
Newton Cres. M24: Mid 4F **15**
Newton Hall .1E **87**
Newton Hall Ct. SK14: Hyde 5E **73**
Newton Hall Rd. SK14: Hyde 5E **73**
NEWTON HEATH 1D **55**
Newtonmore Wlk. *M11: Man* *1D 69*
(off Kincraig Cl.)
Newton Rd. M24: Mid 2D **25**
  M35: Fail 3A **56**
  M41: Urm 3E **75**
  WA14: Alt 4A **98**
Newton St. M1: Man 5E **7** (1D **67**)
  M32: Stre 4F **77**
  M35: Fail 1E **55**
  M40: Man 1E **55**
  M43: Droy 4D **57**
  OL6: A Lyme 4E **59**
  SK3: Stoc 5A **118** (3A **106**)
  SK14: Hyde 2F **87**
Newton Ter. SK16: Duk 5C **116**
NEWTON WOOD 4E **73**

Newton Wood Rd. SK16: Duk 4D **73**
NEWTOWN
    M4 . . . . .4D **53**
    M27 . . . . .2A **34**
Newtown Av. M34: Dent 3C **86**
Newtown Cl. M11: Man 2D **69**
    M27: Pen 2B **34**
Newtown Ct. M25: Pres 5E **23**
    M40: Man 1F 7 (3E **53**)
Newtown M. M25: Pres 5E **23**
Newtown St. M25: Pres 5E **23**
New Union St. M4: Man 5E **53**
New Viaduct St. M11: Man 5A **54**
Newville Dr. M20: Man 1D **83**
New Vine St. M15: Man 5A **10** (4B **66**)
New Wakefield St. M1: Man . .4C **10** (3C **66**)
New Welcome St. M15: Man 4B **66**
NEW WINDSOR 5A 4 (5D **51**)
New York St. M1: Man 1C **10** (1C **66**)
New Zealand Rd. SK1: Stoc 2C **106**
Ney St. OL7: A Lyme 1B **58**
Niagara St. SK2: Stoc 5C **106**
Nicholas Cft. M4: Man 4D 7 (5C **52**)
Nicholas Owen Cl. M11: Man 2E **69**
Nicholas Rd. OL8: O'ham 5A **30**
Nicholas St. M1: Man 1C **10** (1C **66**)
Nicholson Rd. SK14: Hyde 5E **73**
Nicholson Sq. SK16: Duk 2D **73**
Nicholson St. OL4: Lees 3F **31**
    SK4: Stoc 1A **106**
Nichols St. M6: Sal 4D **51**
                     (off Gerrard St.)
Nico Ditch M18: Man 3E **83**
Nicolas Rd. M21: Chor 4B **78**
Nield Rd. M34: Dent 2B **86**
Nigel Rd. M9: Man 5B **40**
Nightingale Dr. M34: Aud 5E **57**
Nightingale Gdns. M23: Wyth 2C **100**
Nightingale St. M3: Man 2A 6 (4B **52**)
Nile, The M15: Man 4A **10**
Nile St. OL1: O'ham 1D **117** (1A **30**)
    OL7: A Lyme 2B **72**
Nile Ter. M7: Sal 2F **51**
NIMBLE NOOK 4C **28**
Nimble Nook OL9: Chad 4C **28**
Nina Dr. M40: Man 1E **41**
Nine Acre Ct. M5: Sal 3D **65**
              (off Taylorson St.)
Nine Acre Dr. M5: Sal 3D **65**
Ninfield Rd. M23: Wyth 2D **109**
Ninian Ct. M24: Mid 5B **16**
Ninth Av. OL8: O'ham 3F **43**
Nipper La. M45: White 5A **12**
Nisbet Av. M22: Wyth 3A **110**
Niven St. M12: Man 3E **67**
Nixon St. M35: Fail 5A **42**
    SK3: Stoc 5A **118** (3A **106**)
Noble St. OL8: O'ham 5B **30**
Noel Dr. M33: Sale 4F **89**
Nolan St. M9: Man 5A **40**
Nona St. M6: Sal 5A **50**
Nook, The M28: Wors 4B **32**
    M30: Ecc 4C **46**
    M41: Urm 4F **75**
Nook La. OL6: A Lyme 2F **59**
Norbet Wlk. M9: Man 5A **40**
             (off Broadwell Dr.)
Norbreck Av. M21: Chor 1D **91**
    SK8: Chea 5C **104**
Norburn Rd. M13: Man 3B **82**

Norbury Av. M6: Sal 2F **49**
    M33: Sale 4B **88**
    SK14: Hyde 3F **87**
Norbury Cl. M40: Man 3A **54**
              (off Giltbrook Av.)
Norbury Gro. M27: Pen 3B **34**
Norbury Ho. OL4: O'ham 4D **31**
Norbury La. OL8: O'ham 1F **45**
Norbury St. M7: Sal 1A **52**
    SK1: Stoc 3B **118** (2B **106**)
Norbury Way SK9: Hand 4F **115**
            (off Chelford Rd.)
Norcliffe Hall M. SK9: Sty 5F **113**
Norcliffe Wlk. M18: Man 1D **83**
Norcot Wlk. M15: Man 4F **65**
             (off Royce Rd.)
Norcross Cl. SK2: Stoc 5F **107**
Norden Av. M20: Man 2C **92**
Nordens Rd. OL9: Chad 1B **28**
Nordens St. OL9: Chad 1C **28**
Noreen Av. M25: Pres 4E **23**
Norfield Cl. SK16: Duk 2E **73**
Norfolk Av. M18: Man 1E **83**
    M34: Dent 2B **84**
    M43: Droy 4B **56**
    M45: White 1C **22**
    SK4: Stoc 2E **95**
Norfolk Cres. M35: Fail 1A **56**
Norfolk Gdns. M41: Urm 2A **74**
Norfolk Ho. M7: Sal 3A **38**
    M33: Sale 4F **89**
Norfolk Rd. M18: Man 1E **83**
Norfolk St. M2: Man 5B 6 (1B **66**)
    M6: Sal 2C **50**
    OL9: O'ham 5D **29**
             (not continuous)
    SK14: Hyde 3F **87**
Norgate St. M20: Man 5D **93**
Norlan Av. M34: Aud 3A **72**
Norland Wlk. M40: Man 2C **54**
             (off Bower St.)
Norleigh Rd. M22: Nor 3F **101**
Norley Av. M32: Stre 2B **78**
Norley Dr. M19: Man 3E **83**
    M33: Sale 4A **90**
Normanby Gro. M27: Swin 3A **34**
Normanby St. M14: Man 1C **80**
    M27: Swin 3A **34**
Norman Cl. M24: Mid 5E **17**
Norman Gro. M12: Man 1B **82**
    SK5: Stoc 1A **96**
Norman Rd. M7: Sal 5A **38**
    M14: Man 3E **81**
    M33: Sale 5D **89**
    OL6: A Lyme 1E **59**
    SK4: Stoc 5D **95**
Norman Rd. W. M9: Man 5B **40**
Norman St. M12: Man 5D **69**
    M24: Mid 5D **17**
    M35: Fail 3C **42**
    OL1: O'ham 1F **29**
Normanton Av. M6: Sal 4E **49**
Normanton Dr. M9: Man 5A **26**
Normanton Rd. SK3: Stoc 4C **104**
Norman Weall Ct. M24: Mid 4C **16**
Normington St. OL4: O'ham 2E **31**
Norreys Av. M41: Urm 2A **74**
Norris Av. SK4: Stoc 2E **105**
NORRIS BANK 1E **105**
Norris Bank Ter. SK4: Stoc 2E **105**

NORRIS HILL 1D 105
Norris Hill Dr. SK4: Stoc 1E 105
Norris Rd. M33: Sale 1D 99
Norris Towers SK4: Stoc 1A 118
Northallerton Rd. M7: Sal 1C 50
Northampton Rd. M40: Man 1B 54
Northampton Way M34: Dent 4C 86
(off Leicester Av.)
North Av. BL9: Bury 2D 13
M19: Man 1B 94
Northavon Cl. M30: Ecc 1C 62
(off Andoc Av.)
Northbank Gdns. M19: Man 2A 94
Northbank Rd. M28: Wors 2C 46
Northbank Wlk. M20: Man 5F 91
Nth. Blackfield La. M7: Sal 4E 37
Northbourne St. M6: Sal 5A 50
Northbrook Av. M8: Man 5B 24
Nth. Broughton St. M3: Sal 4E 5
North Circ. M45: White 3C 22
Nth. City Shop. Cen. M9: Man 4A 40
Nth. Clifden La. M7: Sal 1A 52
Northcliffe Rd. SK2: Stoc 3E 107
Northcote Av. M22: Wyth 2F 109
North Cres. M11: Man 4F 55
North Cft. OL8: O'ham 1C 44
Northdale Rd. M9: Man 4D 25
Nth. Dean St. M27: Pen 3C 34
Northdown Av. M15: Man 4F 65
North Dr. M27: Swin 5D 35
M34: Aud 1E 71
NORTHENDEN 2F 101
Northenden Pde. M22: Nor 2F 101
Northenden Rd. M33: Sale 3D 89
SK8: Gat 5C 102
Northenden Vw. M20: Man 1D 103
(off South Rd.)
Northen Gro. M20: Man 4B 92
Northerly Cres. M40: Man 1F 41
Northern,
(Tennis & Squash Club) 4C 92
Northern Av. M27: Clif 1E 35
NORTHERN MOOR 2B 100
Northfield Av. M40: Man 2B 42
Northfield Rd. M40: Man 2B 42
Northfleet Rd. M30: Ecc 2B 60
North Ga. OL8: O'ham 2A 44
Northgate Rd. SK3: Stoc 3E 105
Nth. George St. M3: Sal 2C 4 (5F 51)
North Gro. M13: Man 5F 67
M41: Urm 3E 75
Nth. Harvey St.
SK1: Stoc 2C 118 (2B 106)
Nth. Hill St. M3: Sal 2D 5 (4F 51)
Northland Rd. M9: Man 1C 40
Northleigh Dr. M25: Pres 1F 37
Northleigh Ho. M16: Old T 3D 79
Northleigh Rd. M16: Old T 2D 79
Nth. Lonsdale St. M32: Stre 2A 78
Nth. Manchester Bus. Pk. M40: Man . .1A 54
North Meade M21: Chor 1D 91
NORTH MOOR 2F 29
Northmoor Rd. M12: Man 1C 82
Northolme Gdns. M19: Man 3A 94
Northolt Ct. M11: Man 5F 55
Northolt Rd. M23: Wyth 2B 100
North Pde. M3: Man 5A 6
M33: Sale 1F 99
Nth. Phoebe St. M5: Sal 1D 65
North Pl. SK1: Stoc 2B 118 (2B 106)

Northpoint Ind. Est.
SK16: Duk 4D 73
NORTH REDDISH 4A 84
Northridge Rd. M9: Man 3F 25
North Rd. M11: Man 5D 55
M25: Pres 4B 22
M34: Aud 1F 71
M43: Droy 5D 55
Northside Av. M41: Urm 4B 74
North Stage M50: Sal 2B 64
Nth. Star Dr. M3: Sal 5C 4 (1F 65)
Northstead Av. M34: Dent 3D 87
North St. M8: Man 2C 52
M24: Mid 1A 28
OL6: A Lyme 2A 116 (4D 59)
(Oldham Rd.)
OL6: A Lyme 3A 116 (5C 58)
(Welbeck St. Nth.)
Northumberland Av. OL7: A Lyme . . .3D 59
Northumberland Cl. M16: Old T 5E 65
Northumberland Cres. M16: Old T . . .5E 65
(off Henry St.)
Northumberland Ho. OL9: O'ham 4E 29
(off Milne St.)
Northumberland Rd. M16: Old T 1E 79
SK5: Stoc 1D 97
Northumberland St. M7: Sal 5F 37
Northumberland Way M22: Shar 5A 102
Northurst Dr. M8: Man 1B 38
Nth. Vale Rd. WA15: Tim 5B 98
North Vw. M45: White 4A 12
North Way SK5: Stoc 2E 97
Northway M30: Ecc 5B 48
M43: Droy 2C 70
WA14: Alt 5A 98
Nth. Western St. M1: Man 2E 67
M12: Man 3F 67
M19: Man 5C 82
Northwold Dr. M9: Man 1D 41
Northwood Av. M40: Man 1D 41
Northwood Gro. M33: Sale 4D 89
North Woodley M26: Rad 1E 21
Norton Av. M12: Man 2D 83
M33: Sale 2A 88
M34: Dent 2C 84
M41: Urm 1F 75
Norton Grange M25: Pres 1F 37
Norton Gro. SK4: Stoc 2D 105
Norton St. M1: Man 1B 6
M3: Sal 3A 6 (5B 52)
M7: Sal 5A 38
M16: Old T 1E 79
M40: Man 3A 54
Norview Dr. M20: Man 4D 103
Norville Av. M40: Man 1F 41
Norway Gro. SK5: Stoc 4B 96
Norway St. M6: Sal 5A 50
M32: Stre 2A 78
Norwell Rd. M22: Shar 1A 110
Norwich Av. M34: Dent 4B 86
Norwich Cl. OL6: A Lyme 4F 45
Norwich Rd. M32: Stre 2B 76
Norwood M25: Pres 2D 37
Norwood Av. M7: Sal 4D 37
M20: Man 4F 93
Norwood Cl. M28: Walk 4A 32
Norwood Ct. M32: Stre 4A 78
(off Norwood Rd.)
Norwood Dr. M27: Swin 5E 33
WA15: Tim 1A 108
Norwood Lodge M7: Sal 4E 37

Norwood Rd. M32: Stre 4A 78
   SK8: Gat 5D 103
Nottingham Av. SK5: Stoc 2E 97
Nottingham Cl. SK5: Stoc 3E 97
Nottingham Dr. M35: Fail 2C 56
   OL6: A Lyme 5D 45
Nottingham Ter. SK5: Stoc 2E 97
Nottingham Way
   M34: Dent 4C 86
Nowell Ct. M24: Mid 3C 16
Nowell Ho. M24: Mid 3C 16
Nowell Rd. M24: Mid 3C 16
Nuffield Rd. M22: Wyth 2A 110
Nugget St. OL4: O'ham 3D 31
No. 2 Passage SK3: Stoc 2F 105
Nuneaton Dr. M40: Man 4F 53
Nuneham Av. M20: Man 1E 93
Nunfield Cl. M40: Man 2D 41
Nunthorpe Dr. M8: Man 4E 39
Nursery Brow M45: White 1D 21
Nursery Cl. M33: Sale 4F 89
   SK2: Stoc 4F 107
Nursery La. SK3: Stoc 4C 104
Nursery Rd. M25: Pres 3C 22
   M35: Fail 5C 42
   M41: Urm 1C 74
   SK4: Stoc 1E 105
   SK14: Hyde 2E 87
Nursery St. M6: Sal 4B 50
   M16: W Ran 2B 80
Nutbank La. M9: Mid 3A 26
Nuthurst Rd. M40: Man 2E 41
NUTSFORD VALE 1D 83
Nutsford Va. M12: Man 1D 83
Nuttall Av. M45: White 1B 22
Nuttall M. M45: White 1B 22
Nuttall Sq. BL9: Bury 1B 12
Nuttall St. M11: Man 3C 68
   M16: Old T 5E 65
   OL8: O'ham 5D 31
Nutt La. M25: Pres 1A 24
Nutwood Cl. SK5: Stoc 1A 96
NW Regional Basketball Cen. 5C 84

O

Oadby Cl. M12: Man 1C 82
Oadby Pl. SK5: Stoc 3B 84
Oak Av. M21: Chor 5D 79
   M24: Mid 2C 26
   M45: White 2B 22
   SK4: Stoc 1D 105
OAK BANK .1C 22
Oak Bank M9: Man 4F 39
   M25: Pres 3B 36
   (Hilton La.)
   M25: Pres 4C 22
   (Stanhope Av.)
Oak Bank Av. M9: Man 3B 40
Oakbank Av. OL9: Chad 1A 28
Oak Bank M. M45: White 1D 23
Oakcliffe Rd. M23: Wyth 4C 100
Oak Cotts. SK9: Sty 5A 114
Oakcroft Way M22: Shar 5A 102
Oakdale Cl. M45: White 1F 21
Oakdale Dr. M20: Man 2E 103
   SK8: H Grn 4D 111
Oakden Dr. M34: Dent 3E 85
Oakdene M27: Swin 1D 47

Oakdene Av. SK4: Stoc 3F 95
   SK8: H Grn 2D 115
Oakdene Rd. M24: Mid 1E 27
   WA15: Tim 3D 99
Oakdene St. M9: Man 4B 40
Oak Dr. M14: Man 4F 81
   M34: Dent 1C 84
Oaken Bank Rd. OL10: H'ood 1B 16
Oaken Clough OL7: A Lyme 1B 58
Oakenclough M11: Man 2D 117
Oaken Clough Dr. OL7: A Lyme 1B 58
Oaken Clough Ter. OL7: A Lyme 1B 58
Oaken St. OL7: A Lyme 1C 58
Oaker Av. M20: Man 4A 92
Oakes St. BL4: Kea 2B 18
Oakfield M25: Pres 1F 37
   M33: Sale 3C 88
Oakfield Av. M16: Old T 2C 78
   M16: W Ran 2F 79
   M43: Droy 1B 70
   SK8: Chea 5A 104
Oakfield Ct. WA15: Tim 5B 98
Oakfield Gro. M18: Man 1F 83
Oakfield M. M33: Sale 4C 88
   SK3: Stoc 5B 106
Oakfield Rd. M20: Man 5C 92
   SK3: Stoc 5B 106
Oakfield St. M8: Man 1C 52
Oakfield Trad. Est. WA15: Alt 5A 98
Oakfold Av. OL6: A Lyme 1F 59
Oakford Av. M40: Man 4E 53
Oak Gro. M30: Ecc 1D 61
   M41: Urm 3A 76
   OL6: A Lyme 1F 59
   SK8: Chea 1F 111
Oakham Av. M20: Man 5C 80
Oakham M. M7: Sal 3E 37
Oakham Rd. M34: Dent 4C 86
Oakhill Ct. M7: Sal 5A 38
Oakhill Way M8: Man 5B 38
   (off Greenland St.)
Oak Ho. M14: Man 4F 81
Oakhouse Dr. M21: Chor 1D 91
Oakhurst Dr. SK3: Stoc 5D 105
Oakhurst Gdns. M25: Pres 5C 22
Oakington Av. M14: Man 2D 81
   (off Heald Pl.)
Oakland Av. M6: Sal 3C 48
   M16: Old T 1C 78
   M19: Man 4A 94
   SK2: Stoc 5E 107
Oakland Ho. M16: Old T 5C 64
Oaklands Dr. M25: Pres 5D 23
   M33: Sale 3C 88
Oaklands Ho. M14: Man 4E 81
Oaklands Rd. M7: Sal 5C 36
   M27: Swin 1F 47
Oak La. M45: White 1D 23
Oaklea M16: Old T 2E 79
   (off Up. Chorlton Rd.)
Oaklea Rd. M33: Sale 3A 88
Oakleigh SK4: Stoc 5D 95
   (off Heaton Moor Rd.)
Oakleigh Av. M19: Man 1B 94
   WA15: Tim 4C 98
Oakleigh Ct. WA15: Tim 4E 99
Oakleigh Ho. M33: Sale 5A 88
Oakleigh M. M33: Sale 5A 88
Oakley Cl. M26: Rad 1C 20
   M40: Man 2E 55

Oakley Vs. SK4: Stoc 5D **95**
Oakmere Av. M30: Ecc 3E **47**
Oakmere Cl. M22: Wyth 2F **109**
Oakmere Rd. SK9: Hand 4F **115**
Oakmoor Dr. M7: Sal 4C **36**
Oakmoor Rd. M23: Wyth 5C **100**
Oakridge Wlk. *M9: Man* *5F 39*
(off Carisbrook St.)
Oak Rd. M7: Sal 1E **51**
M20: Man 3D **93**
M33: Sale 4F **89**
M35: Fail 1B **56**
OL8: O'ham 2E **43**
SK8: Chea 5A **104**
Oaks, The SK8: H Grn 4C **110**
Oaks Bus. Pk., The
M23: Wyth 3A **100**
Oakshaw Cl. M9: Man 2F **39**
Oakside Cl. SK8: Chea 5A **104**
Oak St. M4: Man 4D **7** (5C **52**)
(not continuous)
M24: Mid 2F **27**
M26: Rad 1E **21**
M27: Pen 3C **34**
M30: Ecc 1F **61**
M34: Aud 4B **72**
SK3: Stoc 3D **105**
Oak Tree Cl. SK2: Stoc 3F **107**
Oak Tree Ct. SK8: Chea 1F **111**
Oakville Dr. M6: Sal 3C **48**
Oakville Ter. M40: Man 3B **40**
Oak Wlk. M34: Aud 4A **72**
Oakway M20: Man 3E **103**
M24: Mid 2B **16**
Oakwell Dr. BL9: Bury 3D **13**
M7: Sal 3A **38**
Oakwell Mans. M7: Sal 3A **38**
Oakwood M27: Clif 5A **20**
OL9: Chad 2A **28**
Oakwood Av. M27: Clif 5A **20**
M28: Walk 2B **32**
M34: Aud 3A **72**
M40: Man 3F **41**
SK8: Gat 1C **110**
Oakwood Dr. M6: Sal 2D **49**
M28: Walk 2B **32**
Oakwood Est. M5: Sal 1F **63**
Oakwood Ho. M21: Chor 5E **79**
Oakworth St. M9: Man 2E **39**
Oatlands Rd. M22: Wyth 5E **109**
Oat St. SK1: Stoc 4C **106**
Oban Av. M40: Man 3D **55**
OL1: O'ham 1D **31**
Oban Dr. M33: Sale 5A **90**
Oberlin St. OL4: O'ham 2F **31**
Oberon Cl. *M30: Ecc* *5F 47*
(off Shakespeare Cres.)
Occleston Cl. M33: Sale 2A **100**
Ocean Ho. *M15: Man* *5C 66*
(off Boundary La.)
Ocean Wlk. *M15: Man* *5B 66*
(off Crediton St.)
Ockendon Dr. M9: Man 5A **40**
Octavia Dr. M40: Man 3E **55**
Oddfellow Hall OL6: A Lyme 3B **116**
Odell St. M11: Man 3D **69**
Odeon Cinema
Manchester 3C **6** (5C **52**)
The Trafford Cen. 4A **62**
Odessa Av. M6: Sal 3D **49**

Odette St. M18: Man 1E **83**
OFFERTON 5F **107**
Offerton Dr. SK2: Stoc 5F **107**
Offerton Fold SK2: Stoc 4E **107**
Offerton Ind. Est. SK2: Stoc 4E **107**
Offerton La. SK2: Stoc 3D **107**
Offerton St. SK1: Stoc 1D **107**
Off Green St. M24: Mid 5D **17**
Off Vaudrey La. M34: Dent 3C **86**
Ogbourne Wlk. *M13: Man* *4E 67*
(off Lauderdale Cres.)
Ogden Cl. M45: White 5C **12**
Ogden Ct. *SK14: Hyde* *3F 87*
(off Frank St.)
Ogden Gdns. SK16: Duk 2F **73**
Ogden Gro. SK8: Gat 2B **110**
Ogden La. M11: Man 3F **69**
Ogden Rd. M35: Fail 1B **56**
Ogden Sq. SK16: Duk 2D **73**
Ogden St. M20: Man 5D **93**
M24: Mid 1C **26**
M25: Pres 5E **23**
M27: Swin 5B **34**
OL4: O'ham 3F **31**
OL9: Chad 1D **29**
Ogden Wlk. M45: White 1C **22**
Ogmore Wlk. M40: Man 2E **41**
Ogwen Dr. M25: Pres 4D **23**
Ohio Av. M50: Sal 2B **64**
O'Kane Ho. *M30: Ecc* *1F 61*
(off Cawdor St.)
Okehampton Cres. M33: Sale 3A **88**
Okeover Rd. M7: Sal 4F **37**
Olanyian Dr. M8: Sal 2A **52**
Old Bank St. M2: Man 5B **6** (1B **66**)
Old Barton Rd. M41: Urm 3F **61**
Old Birley St. M15: Man 5B **66**
Old Boat Yd., The M28: Wors 2C **46**
Old Broadway M20: Man 3D **93**
Oldbury Cl. M40: Man 4F **53**
Old Chapel St. SK3: Stoc 5A **118** (4E **105**)
Oldcastle Av. M20: Man 5C **80**
Old Church M. SK16: Duk 2F **73**
Old Church St. M40: Man 1D **55**
OL1: O'ham 3F **117** (2B **30**)
Old Clough La. M28: Walk 3B **32**
(not continuous)
Old Ct. House, The M3: Sal 4C **4**
Old Ct. St. SK14: Hyde 3F **87**
Old Courtyard, The M22: Shar 1A **110**
Oldcroft M. SK1: Stoc 4D **107**
Old Crofts Bank M41: Urm 1E **75**
Old Cross St. OL6: A Lyme 4E **59**
Old Dairy M. SK14: Hyde 5E **73**
Old Edge La. OL2: O'ham 1B **30**
(not continuous)
Old Elm St. M12: Man 4E **67**
Oldershaw Dr. M9: Man 1F **53**
Old Farm Cres. M43: Droy 2B **70**
Oldfield Dr. WA15: Tim 5B **98**
Oldfield Gro. M33: Sale 3E **89**
Oldfield Rd. M5: Sal 4A **8** (3E **65**)
M25: Pres 2E **23**
M33: Sale 3E **89**
Oldfield St. M11: Man 1D **69**
Old Fold M30: Ecc 3E **47**
Old Garden, The WA15: Tim 4D **99**
Old Gdns. St. SK1: Stoc 4C **118** (3B **106**)
Oldgate Wlk. *M15: Man* *4F 65*
(off Shawheath Cl.)

Old Hall Ct. M33: Sale	4A **90**
M45: White	2E **21**
Old Hall Dr. M18: Man	1F **83**
Old Hall La. M13: Man	4F **81**
M14: Man	4F **81**
M24: Man	3C **24**
M25: Pres	1B **24**
(not continuous)	
M28: Wors	5A **32**
M45: White	2E **21**
Old Hall Rd. M7: Sal	3F **37**
M32: Stre	1C **76**
M33: Sale	4A **90**
M40: Man	5D **41**
M45: White	2E **21**
SK8: Gat	5C **102**
Old Hall St. BL4: Farn	2A **18**
M11: Man	3A **70**
M24: Mid	1B **26**
SK16: Duk	3C **72**
OLDHAM	3E **117** (2B **30**)
Oldham Av. SK1: Stoc	2D **107**
Oldham B'way. Bus. Pk. OL9: Chad	5A **28**
Oldham Bus. Cen. OL1: O'ham	5E **117**
Oldham Central Trad. Pk.	
OL1: O'ham	1C **30**
Oldham Coliseum Theatre	3F **117** (2B **30**)
Oldham Ct. M40: Man	4E **53**
Oldham Crematorium OL8: O'ham	3E **43**
OLDHAM EDGE	1E **117** (1B **30**)
Oldham Mumps Station (Rail)	3C **30**
Oldham Rd. M4: Man	3F **7** (5D **53**)
M24: Mid	1C **26**
M35: Fail	1D **55**
M40: Man	5D **53**
OL6: A Lyme	1B **116** (4D **59**)
OL7: A Lyme	1A **116** (5C **44**)
Oldham Sports Cen.	3E **117** (2B **30**)
Oldham St. M1: Man	5D **7** (1C **66**)
M5: Sal	1C **8** (1F **65**)
M34: Dent	3E **85**
M43: Droy	5D **57**
SK5: Stoc	1A **96**
SK14: Hyde	3F **87**
Oldham Way OL1: O'ham	5E **117** (3B **30**)
OL4: O'ham	5E **117** (3B **30**)
OL8: O'ham	3A **30**
OL9: O'ham	1F **29**
Oldham Werneth Station (Rail)	3F **29**
Old Heyes Rd. WA15: Tim	3D **99**
Old Ho. Ter. OL6: A Lyme	2F **59**
Old La. M11: Man	2F **69**
OL9: Chad	5D **29**
Old Lansdowne Rd. M20: Man	4B **92**
Old Lees St. OL6: A Lyme	2F **59**
Old Market St. M9: Man	2E **39**
Old Meadow Dr. M34: Dent	5B **72**
Old Medlock St. M3: Man	2D **9** (2F **65**)
Old Mill Cl. M27: Pen	5F **17**
Old Mills Hill M24: Mid	1E **67**
Old Mill St. M4: Man	1C **92**
Old Moat La. M20: Man	3F **97**
Oldmoor Rd. SK6: Bred	5F **47**
Old Mount St. M4: Man	2D **7** (4D **53**)
Old Oak Dr. M34: Dent	2C **86**
Old Oake Cl. M28: Walk	5D **93**
Old Oak St. M20: Man	3D **99**
Old Orchard, The WA15: Tim	3D **99**
Old Park La. M30: Urm	4E **61**
Old Parrin La. M30: Ecc	4D **47**
Old Rectory Gdns. SK8: Chea	5F **103**
Old Rd. M9: Man	2F **39**
M35: Fail	5A **42**
SK4: Stoc	5A **96**
SK8: Chea	5B **104**
SK9: Hand	5F **115**
SK14: Hyde	5F **73**
SK16: Duk	1E **73**
(not continuous)	
Old School Ct. M9: Man	2E **39**
(off Old School Dr.)	
M30: Ecc	3F **47**
Old School Dr. M9: Man	2E **39**
Old School M. SK16: Duk	2F **73**
(off Vicarage Dr.)	
Old Shaw St. M5: Sal	2C **64**
Old Sq. OL6: A Lyme	4E **59**
Old Stables, The M34: Aud	4B **72**
Old Station St. M30: Ecc	1E **61**
Oldstead Wlk. M9: Man	1F **53**
(off Kelvington Dr.)	
Old St. OL4: O'ham	4F **31**
OL6: A Lyme	3A **116** (5C **58**)
OLD TRAFFORD	5D **65**
Old Trafford Cricket Ground	2B **78**
Old Trafford Football Ground	5B **64**
Old Trafford Station (Metro)	1C **78**
Old Vicarage Gdns. M28: Walk	1A **32**
Oldway Wlk. M40: Man	2D **55**
Old Wellington Rd. M30: Ecc	5F **47**
Oldwood Rd. M23: Wyth	3C **108**
Old York St. M15: Man	4A **66**
Olive Rd. WA15: Tim	3C **98**
Oliver St. SK1: Stoc	5B **118** (3B **106**)
Olive Shapley Av. M20: Man	5D **93**
Olive St. M35: Fail	4A **42**
Olivia Ct. M5: Sal	3B **8** (2E **65**)
Olivia Gro. M14: Man	2F **81**
Ollerenshaw Hall M14: Man	1F **81**
(off Daisy Bank Hall)	
Ollerton Av. M16: Old T	2E **79**
M33: Sale	2A **88**
Ollerton Cl. M22: Nor	2A **102**
Ollerton Ct. M16: Old T	3D **79**
(off Manchester Rd.)	
Ollerton Dr. M35: Fail	1B **56**
Ollerton Rd. SK9: Hand	4F **115**
Ollier Av. M12: Man	3C **82**
Olmpic St. M11: Man	2A **68**
Olney Av. M22: Wyth	5F **101**
Olney St. M13: Man	1F **81**
Olwen Av. M12: Man	5C **68**
Olwen Cres. SK5: Stoc	5B **84**
Olympia Trad. Est. M15: Man	4F **9** (3A **66**)
Olympic Cl. M50: Sal	2B **64**
Olympic Ho. M90: Man A	2E **113**
Omer Av. M13: Man	3B **82**
Omer Dr. M19: Man	1A **94**
Onchan Av. OL4: O'ham	3D **31**
Ongar Wlk. M9: Man	1D **39**
Onslow Av. M40: Man	3A **42**
Onslow Cl. OL1: O'ham	1A **30**
Onslow Rd. SK3: Stoc	3E **105**
Ontario Ho. M50: Sal	3C **64**
Onward St. SK14: Hyde	3F **87**
Opal Ct. M14: Man	5F **81**
Opal Gdns. M14: Man	1F **81**
Opal Hall M15: Man	5C **10** (4C **66**)
Opal St. M19: Man	5D **83**
OPENSHAW	2D **69**

Openshaw Ct. M27: Clif	2C **34**
Openshaw Wlk. *M11: Man*	1E **69**
(off Greenside St.)	
Opera House	1F 9 (1A 66)
Orama Av. M6: Sal	3C **48**
Orange Hill Rd. M25: Pres	4E **23**
Orbital 24 M34: Dent	2F **85**
Orbital Way M34: Dent	2F **85**
Orbit Ho. *M30: Ecc*	5B **48**
(off Albert St.)	
Orchard, The OL8: O'ham	1E **45**
Orchard Av. *M18: Man*	1A **84**
(off Woodland St.)	
Orchard Ct. SK2: Stoc	5F **107**
WA15: Tim	4D **99**
Orchard Gdns. SK8: Gat	5B **102**
Orchard Gro. M20: Man	3B **92**
Orchard Ind. Est. M6: Sal	3C **50**
Orchard Pl. M33: Sale	3D **89**
WA15: Tim	4D **99**
Orchard Rd. M35: Fail	5B **42**
WA15: Alt	5A **98**
Orchard Rd. E. M22: Nor	1F **101**
Orchard Rd. W. M22: Nor	1F **101**
Orchard St. BL4: Farn	2A **18**
M6: Sal	2C **50**
(not continuous)	
M20: Man	3B **92**
SK1: Stoc	3C **118** (2B **106**)
Orchard Trad. Est. M6: Sal	2B **50**
Orchard Va. SK3: Stoc	5E **105**
Orchid Cl. OL1: O'ham	1F **29**
Orchid St. M9: Man	5F **39**
Ordell Wlk. M9: Man	1A **40**
Ordnance St. M30: Ecc	5F **47**
ORDSALL	3D **65**
Ordsall District Cen. M5: Sal	2D **65**
Ordsall Hall Mus.	4D **65**
Ordsall La. M5: Sal	5A **8** (4C **64**)
Oregon Cl. M13: Man	5F **11** (4E **67**)
Orford Rd. M25: Pres	4D **23**
M40: Man	2E **55**
Oriel Av. OL8: O'ham	1A **44**
Oriel Cl. OL9: Chad	4C **28**
SK2: Stoc	5D **107**
Oriel Ct. M33: Sale	3D **89**
Oriel Rd. M20: Man	4C **92**
Orient, The *M41: Urm*	4F **61**
(off The Trafford Cen.)	
Orient Dr. OL7: A Lyme	4B **58**
Orient Ho. M1: Man	3D **11**
Orient Rd. M6: Sal	3C **48**
Orient St. M7: Sal	5B **38**
Oriole Ho. M19: Man	5F **93**
Orion Bus. Pk. SK3: Stoc	5E **105**
Orion Pl. M7: Sal	1B **4** (3E **51**)
Orion Trad. Est. M17: T Pk	2C **62**
Orkney Cl. M23: Wyth	2C **108**
Orkney Dr. M41: Urm	5F **61**
Orlanda Av. M6: Sal	3C **48**
Orlanda Dr. M7: Sal	1B **52**
Orleans Way OL1: O'ham	2D **117** (2A **30**)
Orme Av. M6: Sal	2D **49**
M24: Mid	2C **26**
Orme Cl. M11: Man	1A **68**
M41: Urm	3B **76**
Ormeston Lodge M41: Urm	4F **75**
Orme St. M11: Man	1A **68**
OL4: O'ham	4C **30**
Ormonde Av. M6: Sal	3D **49**

Ormonde Ct. OL6: A Lyme	3E **59**
Ormonde St. OL6: A Lyme	3E **59**
Ormsby Av. M18: Man	1D **83**
Ormsgill Cl. M15: Man	5B **66**
Orms Gill Pl. SK2: Stoc	5F **107**
Ormskirk Av. M20: Man	2B **92**
Ormskirk Rd. SK5: Stoc	2B **96**
Ornsay Wlk. *M11: Man*	1E **69**
(off Bob Massey Cl.)	
Oronsay Gro. M5: Sal	1F **63**
Orphanage St. SK4: Stoc	5A **96**
Orpington Rd. *M9: Man*	5A **40**
(off Vernon St.)	
Orrell St. M11: Man	2F **69**
Orrel St. M6: Sal	5A **50**
Orsett Cl. M40: Man	4E **53**
Orthes Gro. SK4: Stoc	3F **95**
Orton Av. M23: Wyth	2C **100**
Orton Rd. M23: Wyth	2C **100**
Orvietto Av. M6: Sal	3C **48**
Orville Dr. M19: Man	1B **94**
Orwell Av. M22: Wyth	5F **101**
M34: Dent	2C **84**
Osborne Dr. M27: Pen	5E **35**
Osborne Gro. SK8: H Grn	3C **110**
Osborne Ho. *M30: Ecc*	5E **47**
(off Queen Victoria St.)	
Osborne Rd. M6: Sal	5C **48**
M9: Man	5A **40**
M19: Man	4B **82**
M34: Dent	1B **86**
OL8: O'ham	4F **29**
SK2: Stoc	4B **106**
WA15: Alt	5A **98**
Osborne St. M6: Sal	4B **50**
M20: Man	5C **92**
M40: Man	3E **53**
OL9: O'ham	1E **29**
SK6: Bred	5F **97**
Osborne Ter. M33: Sale	4D **89**
OL6: A Lyme	4E **59**
(off Union St.)	
Osborne Trad. Est. OL9: O'ham	1E **29**
Osbourne Cl. BL4: Farn	1A **18**
Oscar St. M40: Man	5C **40**
Oscroft Cl. M8: Man	1B **52**
Oscroft Wlk. *M14: Man*	1F **93**
(off Lyth St.)	
Osmond St. OL4: O'ham	2E **31**
Osprey Cl. M15: Man	5A **66**
SK16: Duk	3F **73**
Osprey Cl. *M15: Man*	5A **66**
(off Osprey Cl.)	
Osprey Dr. M43: Droy	4E **57**
Osprey Ho. M50: Sal	2E **63**
Ossington Wlk. M23: Wyth	1C **100**
Ossory St. M14: Man	2D **81**
Osterley Rd. M9: Man	1B **40**
Ostlers Ga. M43: Droy	5F **57**
Ostrich La. M25: Pres	1E **37**
Oswald Cl. M6: Sal	2C **50**
Oswald La. M21: Chor	4D **79**
Oswald Rd. M21: Chor	4C **78**
Oswald St. M4: Man	1F **67**
(Every St.)	
M4: Man	2C **6** (4C **52**)
(Miller St.)	
OL9: O'ham	1F **29**
SK5: Stoc	2B **84**
Otago St. OL4: O'ham	1E **31**

Othello Dr. M30: Ecc 5F 47
Otley Av. M6: Sal 4E 49
Otley Cl. OL9: Chad 3D 29
Otranto Av. M6: Sal 3D 49
Ottawa Cl. M23: Wyth 2B 108
Otterburn Ho. M30: Ecc 4A 48
Otterburn Pl. SK2: Stoc 5F 107
Otter Dr. BL9: Bury 2D 13
    M8: Man 2A 52
Ottersham Wlk. M40: Man 2F 55
Ottery Wlk. M40: Man 2F 41
Oulton Av. M33: Sale 3A 90
Oulton Wlk. M40: Man 4F 53
                                (off Dinsdale Cl.)
Oundle Cl. M14: Man 2E 81
Ouse St. M50: Sal 1E 63
Outline Fitness & Leisure Cen. 2A 110
Outram Ho. M1: Man 1E 67
                                (off Millbank St.)
Outram Rd. SK16: Duk 4D 73
Outram Sq. M43: Droy 2C 70
Outrington Dr. M11: Man 2C 68
OUTWOOD 1B 20
Outwood Av. M27: Clif 5F 19
Outwood Dr. SK8: H Grn 1C 114
Outwood La. M90: Man A 1E 113
Outwood La. M. M90: Man A 1D 113
Outwood Rd. M26: Rad 1C 20
    SK8: H Grn 1D 115
Oval, The SK8: H Grn 1D 115
Oval Dr. SK16: Duk 3D 73
Overbridge Rd. M3: Sal 3A 52
    M7: Sal 1F 5 (3A 52)
    M8: Man .3A 52
Overbrook Av. M40: Man 2F 53
Overbrook Dr. M25: Pres 1D 37
Overcombe Wlk. M40: Man 2E 53
                                (off Glendower Dr.)
Overdale M27: Swin 1C 48
Overdale Cres. M41: Urm 3B 74
Overdale Ho. M6: Sal 3D 49
Overdale Rd. M22: Wyth 1F 109
Overens St. OL4: O'ham 2D 31
Overhill Rd. OL9: Chad 1B 28
Overlea Dr. M19: Man 3A 94
Overlinks Dr. M6: Sal 2D 49
Overman Way M27: Pen 5A 36
Overstone Dr. M8: Man 5B 38
Overton Av. M22: Wyth 1F 109
Overton Cres. M33: Sale 1A 98
Overton Rd. M22: Wyth 1F 109
Overton Way SK9: Hand 4F 115
Overwood Rd. M22: Nor 3F 101
Ovington Wlk. M40: Man 2E 53
                                (off Ribblesdale Dr.)
Owens Cl. OL9: Chad 1A 28
Owens Farm Dr. SK2: Stoc 4F 107
Owens Pk. M14: Man 4F 81
Owen St. M6: Sal 2C 50
    M30: Ecc 1D 61
    SK3: Stoc 2F 105
Owler La. OL9: Chad 1F 41
Owls Ga. OL4: Lees 3F 31
Oxbow Way M45: White 1C 22
Oxbridge Cl. M33: Sale 5A 88
Oxendale Dr. M24: Mid 5F 15
Oxendon Av. M11: Man 4D 55
Oxenholme Wlk. M18: Man 5F 69
                                (off Borwell St.)
Oxenhurst Grn. SK2: Stoc 5F 107

Oxford Av. M33: Sale 4A 88
    M43: Droy 4B 56
    M45: White 1C 22
Oxford Ct. M2: Man 2B 10 (2B 66)
    M15: Man 5B 10 (4B 66)
    M16: Old T 5F 65
                                (off Globe Cl.)
Oxford Dr. M24: Mid 4E 17
Oxford Ho. OL9: O'ham 3C 29
Oxford Pk. Community Sports Cen. 2B 72
Oxford Pl. M14: Man 1E 81
Oxford Rd. M1: Man 4C 10 (3C 66)
    M6: Sal .3C 48
    M13: Man 5D 11 (3C 66)
    M15: Man 3C 66
    SK16: Duk 2F 73
Oxford Road Station (Rail) 4C 10 (3C 66)
Oxford St. M2: Man 2B 10 (2B 66)
    M16: Old T 1A 62
    M30: Ecc 2B 72
    OL7: A Lyme 2B 72
    OL9: O'ham 4D 29
Oxford St. E. OL7: A Lyme 5A 116 (2B 72)
Oxford St. W. OL7: A Lyme 2B 72
Oxford Wlk. M34: Dent 4C 86
                                (off Worcester Av.)
Oxford Way SK4: Stoc 5F 95
Oxhill Wlk. M40: Man 2F 41
                                (off Blandford Dr.)
Oxney Rd. M14: Man 1E 81
Oxted Wlk. M8: Man 1C 52
                                (off Dinnington Dr.)
Oxton Av. M22: Wyth 2E 109
Oxton St. M11: Man 3B 70
Ozanam Ct. M7: Sal 5F 37

P

PACIFIC QUAYS 2F 63
Pacific Way M50: Sal 2E 63
Packwood Chase OL9: Chad 1B 28
Padbury Cl. M41: Urm 2A 74
Padbury Ho. M5: Sal 1B 64
                                (off Cypress Cl.)
Padbury Wlk. M40: Man 2B 54
                                (off Mansford Dr.)
Paddington Av. M40: Man 2D 55
Paddington Cl. M6: Sal 5C 50
Paddison St. M27: Swin 5A 34
Paddock, The M28: Wors 5A 32
    M45: White 2E 21
    SK9: Hand 5F 115
Paddock Av. M35: Fail 2B 56
Paddock Fld. M5: Sal 2D 65
Paddock La. M35: Fail 2B 56
Paddock Rd. SK14: Hyde 3E 87
Padstow St. M40: Man 4A 54
Padworth Wlk. M23: Wyth 3F 99
Paget St. M40: Man 2F 53
    OL6: A Lyme 3E 59
Pagnall Ct. OL9: Chad 4D 29
Paignton Av. M19: Man 5B 82
Paignton Dr. M33: Sale 3A 88
Paignton Gro. SK5: Stoc 1A 96
Pailin Dr. M43: Droy 5E 57
Painswick Rd. M22: Wyth 5D 109
Palace Rd. M33: Sale 3C 88
    OL6: A Lyme 2F 59

Palace St. OL9: O'ham 2E 29
Palace Theatre 3C 10 (2D 66)
Palatine Av. M20: Man 2D 93
Palatine Ct. M34: Dent 5A 72
Palatine Cres. M20: Man 3D 93
Palatine Ho. SK3: Stoc 5A 118
Palatine M. M20: Man 2D 93
    M34: Dent 1A 86
Palatine Rd. M22: Nor 2F 101
Palatine St. M34: Dent 5A 72
                                    (not continuous)
Palfrey Pl. M12: Man 3E 67
Palgrave Av. M40: Man 2F 53
Pall Mall M2: Man 5B 6 (1B 66)
                                    (not continuous)
Pall Mall Ct. M2: Man 5B 6
Palma Av. M90: Man A 1C 112
Palm Bus. Cen. OL9: Chad 3D 29
Palmer Av. SK8: Chea 5B 104
Palmer Cl. M8: Man 2D 39
    OL8: O'ham 5B 30
Palmerston Av. M16: W Ran 3F 79
Palmerston Cl. M34: Dent 2D 85
Palmerston Rd. M34: Dent 2D 85
Palmerston St. M12: Man 2F 67
Palmer St. M7: Sal 2E 51
    M33: Sale .4C 88
    SK16: Duk .1D 73
Palm Gro. OL9: Chad 1D 29
Palm St. M13: Man 2B 82
    M43: Droy .5F 55
    OL4: O'ham 1E 31
Pamir Dr. OL7: A Lyme 5B 58
Pandora St. M20: Man 3C 92
Panfield Rd. M22: Wyth 2E 109
Pangbourne Av. M41: Urm 2A 76
Pangbourne Cl. SK3: Stoc 5E 105
Pankhurst Cen., The 5D 67
Pankhurst Wlk. M14: Man 2D 81
                                    (off Ellanby Cl.)
Panmure St. OL8: O'ham 5B 30
Paprika Cl. M11: Man 3F 69
Parade, The M27: Swin 4B 34
Parade Rd. M90: Man A 2E 113
Paradise St. M34: Aud 3B 72
Paradise Wlk. M1: Man 1F 11
Paradise Wharf M1: Man 1F 11 (1D 67)
Parbold Av. M20: Man 2C 92
Pardoner's Ct. M5: Sal 5D 49
Parham Wlk. M9: Man 1A 40
                                (off Stockfield Dr.)
Paris Av. M5: Sal 3D 65
Parish Vw. M5: Sal 2D 65
Park, The M32: Stre 1A 78
Park Av. M7: Sal 4B 38
    M16: Old T .5E 65
    M19: Man 4C 82
    M25: Pres .5D 23
    M27: Swin .5C 34
    M33: Sale .2C 88
    M35: Fail 4F 41
    M41: Urm 3E 75
    M45: White .3F 21
    OL9: Chad .1D 29
    SK3: Stoc .4B 104
    SK14: Hyde .1F 87
    WA14: Tim .3A 98
Park Bank M5: Sal 5F 49
PARK BRIDGE .2E 45
Park Bridge Heritage Cen. 3E 45

Park Bri. Rd. OL6: A Lyme 3D 45
    OL7: A Lyme .5C 44
Parkbridge Wlk. M13: Man 5F 11
Parkbrook Rd. M23: Wyth 4D 101
Park Brow Cl. M21: Chor 5E 79
Park Cl. M45: White 3B 22
    OL9: Chad .1D 29
    WA14: Tim .3B 98
Park Ct. M22: Wyth 3F 109
    M28: Walk .3A 32
    M33: Sale .3C 88
Park Ct. M. SK8: Chea 2F 111
Park Cres. M14: Man 2E 81
    OL6: A Lyme 2E 59
    OL9: Chad .1B 28
Parkdale OL9: Chad 1D 29
Parkdale Av. M18: Man 5E 69
    M34: Aud 3F 71
Park Dr. M16: W Ran 3E 79
    M30: Ecc 3F 47
    SK4: Stoc .1D 105
    SK14: Hyde .1F 87
    WA15: Tim .4C 98
Parker Arc. M1: Man 1C 10
                                    (off Parker St.)
Parker St. M1: Man 1D 11 (1C 66)
Parkfield M5: Sal 5F 49
    M24: Mid 1B 26
    M43: Droy .5C 56
Parkfield Av. M14: Man 2D 81
    M25: Pres .1F 37
    M41: Urm 4D 75
    OL8: O'ham 2D 43
Parkfield Dr. M24: Mid 1A 26
Parkfield Est. M27: Swin 1C 48
Parkfield Ind. Est. M24: Mid 1A 26
Parkfield Rd. Nth. M40: Man 2A 42
Parkfield Rd. Sth. M20: Man 4C 92
Parkfield St. M14: Man 2D 81
                                (Claremont Rd.)
    M14: Man .1D 81
                                    (Moss La. E.)
Park Ga. Av. M20: Man 2D 93
Park Ga. Cl. SK6: Bred 3F 99
Parkgate Dr. M27: Swin 5C 34
Parkgate Way SK9: Hand 5F 115
                                (off Davenham Rd.)
Park Gro. M19: Man 3C 82
    M28: Walk .4A 32
    SK4: Stoc .4D 95
Park Hall M14: Man 2E 81
                                (off Thurloe St.)
Park Hill M25: Pres 3F 37
Parkhill Av. M8: Man 2D 39
Park Hill Dr. M45: White 1A 22
Park Ho. M23: Wyth 4E 99
                                    (off Bridge Rd.)
    M43: Droy .2C 70
Park Ho. Bri. Est. M6: Sal 5A 36
Park Ho. Bri. Rd. M6: Sal 1A 50
Parkhouse St. M11: Man 2D 69
Parkhouse St. Ind. Est.
    M11: Man 2D 69
Parkhurst Av. M40: Man 3A 42
Parkin Cl. SK16: Duk 2E 73
Parkin St. M12: Man 2C 82
Parklake Av. M7: Sal 4A 38
Parklands M33: Sale 3E 89
                                (off Charlton Dr.)

Parklands M45: White 1A **22**
　　　　　　　　　　　　　　　　　(Higher La.)
　　M45: White .4B **12**
　　　　　　　　　　　　　　　　　(Well La.)
Parklands, The M26: Rad 2D **19**
　　SK4: Stoc 4A **96**
Parklands Rd. M23: Wyth 4B **100**
Parklands Sports Cen. 3E **109**
PARK LANE 2F **21**
Park Lane 3A **22**
Park La. M6: Sal 2E **49**
　　M7: Sal 4F **37**
　　M27: Pen 5F **35**
　　M45: White .2F **21**
　　OL8: O'ham .2B **44**
　　SK1: Stoc .3D **107**
　　SK16: Duk 2E **73**
Park La. Ct. M7: Sal 4F **37**
　　M45: White .2F **21**
Park La. W. M27: Pen 5F **35**
Park Lea Ct. M7: Sal 3A **38**
Parkleigh Dr. M40: Man 2A **42**
Park Lodge M7: Sal 4F **37**
　　M16: W Ran .3A **80**
　　M19: Man 4C **82**
Park Lodge Cl. SK8: Chea 2F **111**
Park M. M7: W Ran 3E **79**
Park Mt. SK8: Gat 1C **110**
Parkmount Rd. M9: Man 3A **40**
Park Pde. OL6: A Lyme 4A **116** (5C **58**)
Park Pde. Ind. Est.
　　OL6: A Lyme 4A **116** (5C **58**)
Park Pl. M4: Man 1C **6** (4C **52**)
　　M6: Sal 4C **48**
　　M25: Pres 4E **23**
　　SK4: Stoc .1B **104**
Park Range M14: Man 2F **81**
Park Rd. M6: Sal 3C **48**
　　M8: Man 1F **37**
　　M24: Mid 1B **26**
　　M25: Pres 1F **37**
　　M28: Walk 2C **33**
　　M30: Ecc 3C **48**
　　　　　　　　　　　　　　　(Ellesmere Pk.)
　　M30: Ecc 3F **47**
　　　　　　　　　　　　　　　　　　(Monton)
　　M32: Stre 1D **79**
　　M33: Sale 2C **88**
　　M34: Aud 2F **71**
　　M34: Dent 2A **86**
　　OL4: O'ham 5E **117** (3A **30**)
　　OL8: O'ham 5E **117** (3A **30**)
　　SK4: Stoc 3D **95**
　　SK8: Chea .5A **104**
　　SK8: Gat 5B **102**
　　SK14: Hyde .1F **87**
　　SK16: Duk 1E **73**
　　WA14: Tim 3A **98**
　　WA15: Tim 3A **98**
Park Rd. Nth. M41: Urm 2E **75**
Park Rd. Sth. M41: Urm 3E **75**
Park Row SK4: Stoc 2A **104**
Park Seventeen M45: White 5B **12**
Parkside M14: Man 4E **81**
　　M24: Mid 3A **26**
Parkside Av. M7: Sal 4A **38**
　　M28: Walk 3A **32**
　　M30: Ecc 1E **61**
　　M35: Fail 2A **56**
Parkside Cl. M26: Rad 2A **12**

Parkside M. M45: White 5B **12**
Parkside Rd. M14: Man 3B **80**
　　M33: Sale 5F **89**
Park Sq. M16: Old T 3C **78**
Parkstead Dr. M9: Man 1F **53**
Parkstone Av. M18: Man 4B **70**
　　M45: White .3F **21**
Parkstone Dr. M27: Swin 1D **49**
Parkstone La. M28: Wors 3B **46**
Park St. BL4: Farn 1A **18**
　　M3: Man 1B **6** (4B **52**)
　　M3: Man 5C **4**
　　M7: Sal 4F **37**
　　M25: Pres 5E **23**
　　M27: Swin 5C **34**
　　M34: Dent 2F **85**
　　M43: Droy 5E **57**
　　OL6: A Lyme 4B **116** (5C **58**)
　　OL7: A Lyme 4A **116** (5C **58**)
　　OL8: O'ham .4A **30**
　　　　　　　　　　　　　　　(not continuous)
　　SK1: Stoc 1B **118** (1B **106**)
Parksway M9: Man 4D **25**
　　M25: Pres 2E **37**
　　M27: Pen 1E **49**
Park Ter. M45: White 2F **21**
Park Vw. BL4: Farn 1A **18**
　　BL4: Kea 2B **18**
　　M9: Man 1E **53**
　　M14: Man 1D **81**
　　　　　　　　　　　　　　　(Fairbank Av.)
　　M14: Man 1A **94**
　　　　　　　　　　　　　　　　　(Green St.)
　　M34: Aud 2F **71**
　　OL9: Chad 1C **28**
　　SK1: Stoc .4D **107**
　　SK3: Stoc 4B **104**
　　SK6: Bred 5E **97**
　　SK8: Gat 5C **102**
Park Vw. Ct. M21: Chor 4B **78**
　　M25: Pres 1D **37**
Parkview Ct. M32: Stre 1B **78**
Park Vw. Rd. M25: Pres 1D **37**
Parkville Rd. M20: Man 3E **93**
　　M25: Pres 2E **23**
Park Way M17: T Pk 5B **62**
　　M32: Stre 5B **62**
　　M41: Urm 1B **76**
Parkway M34: Dent 5C **72**
　　OL9: Chad 1C **28**
　　SK3: Stoc 4B **104**
Parkway Bus. Cen. M14: Man 3B **80**
Parkway Circ. M17: T Pk 4C **62**
Parkway Four Ind. Est. M17: T Pk 4C **62**
Parkway Ind. Est. M17: T Pk 4C **62**
Parkway Trad. Est. M32: Stre 5C **62**
Parkwood Cotts. M25: Pres 1B **24**
Parkwood Rd. M23: Wyth 4E **101**
Parlane St. M4: Man 1E **7** (4D **53**)
Parndon Dr. SK2: Stoc 4E **107**
Parnell Av. M22: Nor 3F **101**
Parrbrook Cl. M45: White 5C **12**
Parrbrook Wlk. M45: White 5D **13**
Parrenthorn Rd. M25: Pres 2E **23**
Parrfield Rd. M28: Wors 5C **32**
Parr Fold BL9: Bury 4D **13**
Parr Ho. OL8: O'ham 4B **30**
　　　　　　　　　　　　　　　　(off Eldon St.)
Parrin La. M30: Ecc 4D **47**
Parr La. BL9: Bury 5C **12**

Parrot St. M11: Man 1E **69**
Parrs Mt. M. SK4: Stoc 1B **104**
Parr St. M11: Man 3A **70**
    M30: Ecc .1F **61**
Parrs Wood Av. M20: Man 1E **103**
Parrs Wood Ct. M20: Man 2E **103**
Parrs Wood Entertainment Cen. 2F **103**
Parrs Wood La. M20: Man 2E **103**
Parrs Wood Rd. M20: Man 3D **103**
Parrs Wood Sports Cen. 2F **103**
Parry Rd. M12: Man 1C **82**
Parry Wlk. OL6: A Lyme 3F **59**
Parslow Av. M8: Man 4C **38**
Parsonage M3: Man 5A **6** (1B **66**)
Parsonage CI. M5: Sal 3A **8**
Parsonage Ct. M20: Man 2D **93**
    SK4: Stoc 4D **95**
Parsonage Gdns. M3: Man 5A **6**
Parsonage La. M3: Man 4A **6**
Parsonage Rd. M20: Man 1E **93**
    M26: Rad .2E **19**
    M41: Urm .4A **74**
                 (not continuous)
    SK4: Stoc 4D **95**
Parsonage St. M8: Man 3B **38**
    M15: Man 5A **66**
    SK4: Stoc 1A **106**
    SK14: Hyde 3F **87**
Parson's Dr. M24: Mid 4B **16**
Parsons Fld. M6: Sal 2C **50**
Parsons St. OL9: O'ham 3E **29**
Parsons Way M9: Man 5A **40**
Partington La. M27: Swin 5A **34**
Partington Pl. M33: Sale 3D **89**
                 (off School Rd.)
Partington St. M28: Wors 5E **33**
    M30: Ecc .4F **47**
               (off Monton Rd.)
    M35: Fail .5B **42**
    M40: Man 2B **54**
    OL1: O'ham 2C **30**
Partridge Av. M23: Wyth 5D **101**
Partridge Ri. M43: Droy 1E **57**
Partridge Rd. M35: Fail 1E **57**
Partridge St. M32: Stre 5B **64**
Partridge Way OL9: Chad 1F **27**
Parvet Av. M43: Droy 4B **56**
Pascal St. M19: Man 5C **82**
Pass St. OL9: O'ham 3F **29**
Paston Rd. M22: Shar 4F **101**
Pasturefield Cl. M33: Sale 5B **90**
Pasture Fld. Rd. M22: Wyth 5B **110**
Patch Cft. Rd. M22: Wyth 5B **110**
Patchett St. M12: Man 4B **68**
Patey St. M12: Man 2C **82**
Pathfield Wlk. M9: Man 4F **39**
              (off Smallfield Dr.)
Paton St. M1: Man 1E **11** (1D **67**)
Patricia Dr. M28: Walk 2A **32**
Patrick Roddy Ct. M18: Man 5E **69**
PATRICROFT .1F **61**
Patricroft Bri. M30: Ecc 1E **61**
Patricroft Rd. M30: Ecc 5E **47**
Patricroft Station (Rail) 5E **47**
Patten St. M20: Man 2D **93**
Patterdale SK8: Chea 1E **111**
Patterdale Av. M41: Urm 1D **75**
    OL7: A Lyme 2B **58**
Patterdale Cl. OL1: O'ham 1C **30**
Patterdale Dr. M24: Mid 4A **16**

Patterdale Rd. M22: Nor 3A **102**
    OL7: A Lyme 2B **58**
    SK1: Stoc 4D **107**
Patterdale Wlk. WA15: Tim 5F **99**
            (off Bowness Rd.)
Patterson Av. M21: Chor 4C **78**
Patterson St. M34: Dent 1B **86**
Pattishall Cl. M4: Man 1F **67**
Patton Cl. BL9: Bury 4D **13**
Patton Ct. M7: Sal 3E **51**
Paul Ct. SK1: Stoc 2C **106**
                 (off Hall St.)
Paulden Av. M23: Wyth 5D **101**
    OL4: O'ham 1F **31**
Paulden Dr. M35: Fail 5C **42**
Paulhan Rd. M20: Man 4F **93**
Pavilion Dr. OL6: A Lyme 2F **59**
Pavilion Lodge M16: Old T 2C **78**
          (off Edgbaston Dr.)
Pavilions, The M21: Chor 4E **79**
    SK8: Chea 2F **111**
Paxton St. M35: Fail 2A **68**
Peace St. M35: Fail 3C **42**
Peacehaven Av. M11: Man 5E **55**
Peaceville Rd. M19: Man 4B **82**
Peach Bank M24: Mid 1C **26**
Peach Bank Ho. M24: Mid 1C **26**
Peach St. M25: Pres 4E **23**
Peach Tree Cl. M7: Sal 1B **52**
         (off Brakenhurst Dr.)
Peach Tree Ct. M6: Sal 5C **50**
Peacock Av. M6: Sal 2F **49**
Peacock Cl. M18: Man 4E **69**
Peacock Dr. SK8: H Grn 3D **115**
Peacock Gro. M18: Man 1F **83**
Peacock Way SK9: Hand 4F **115**
          (off Pickmere Rd.)
Peakdale Av. M9: Man 4D **39**
    SK8: H Grn 5D **111**
Peakdale Rd. M43: Droy 4A **56**
Peaknaze Cl. M27: Pen 4D **35**
Peak St. M1: Man 1F **11** (1D **67**)
    OL1: O'ham 3E **29**
    SK1: Stoc 2C **106**
Pear Cl. M24: Mid 3D **27**
Peardale Cl. M30: Ecc 2E **61**
Pear Ind. Est. SK6: Bred 1E **107**
Pearl Av. M7: Sal 3A **38**
Pearl Mill Cl. OL8: O'ham 5D **31**
Pearl St. M34: Dent 2A **86**
Pearn Av. M19: Man 3B **94**
Pearn Rd. M19: Man 3B **94**
Pearson Ho. M30: Ecc 2F **61**
Pearson St. SK5: Stoc 5B **96**
    SK16: Duk 5A **72**
Pear Tree Cl. M6: Sal 5C **50**
Pear Tree Ct. M6: Sal 5C **50**
Peartree Wlk. M22: Wyth 2D **109**
Peart St. M34: Dent 2A **86**
Peary St. M4: Man 1F **7** (4D **53**)
Peatfield Av. M27: Ward 2F **33**
Peatfield Wlk. M15: Man 5B **66**
             (off Botham Cl.)
Pebworth Cl. M24: Mid 4B **26**
Peckford Dr. M40: Man 2C **54**
Peckforton St. SK8: Gat 1C **110**
Pedley Wlk. M13: Man 4F **11**
Peebles Dr. M40: Man 3F **55**
Peel Av. M41: Urm 4F **61**
         (off The Trafford Cen.)

Peel Cen., The SK1: Stoc 1C 118 (1C 106)
Peel Circ. M41: Urm 4A 62
Peel Ct. SK2: Stoc 5C 106
         (off Peel St.)
Peel Cross Rd. M5: Sal 1C 64
Peel Dr. M33: Sale 4A 90
Peelgate Dr. SK8: H Grn 4C 110
PEEL GREEN 2D 61
Peel Grn. Rd. M30: Ecc 2D 61
Peel Grn. Trad. Est. M30: Ecc 2D 61
Peel Gro. M12: Man 1C 82
   M28: Wors 4A 32
PEEL HALL .4B 110
Peel Hall Rd. M22: Wyth 3A 110
Peel Ho. M30: Ecc 5B 48
Peel La. M8: Man 3C 52
Peel Moat Ct. SK4: Stoc 3E 95
Peel Moat Rd. SK4: Stoc 3D 95
Peel Moat Sports and Target Fitness Cen.
              . . . . .3D 95
Peel Mt. M6: Sal 1A 4 (4B 51)
Peel Sq. M18: Man 1F 83
Peel St. BL4: Farn 1A 18
   M30: Ecc 5B 48
   M34: Aud 4A 72
   M34: Dent 1A 86
   M35: Fail 1F 55
   M43: Droy 2B 70
   OL6: A Lyme 2B 116 (4D 59)
   OL9: Chad 3D 29
   SK2: Stoc 5B 106
   SK16: Duk 1E 73
Peel Ter. SK16: Duk 5C 116
Peerglow Pk. Est. WA14: Tim 3A 98
Peers Cl. M41: Urm 1A 74
Pegasus Ct. M33: Sale 3F 89
         (off Broad Rd.)
Pegasus Sq. M7: Sal 1B 4 (4E 51)
Pegwell Dr. M7: Sal 2A 52
Pekin St. OL6: A Lyme 3E 59
Pelham Pl. M8: Man 2D 53
Pelham St. OL7: A Lyme 2A 72
   OL8: O'ham 1A 44
Pellowe Rd. OL8: O'ham 2F 33
Pelton Av. M27: Pen 2F 53
Pelton Wlk. M40: Man 2F 53
       (off Pitsford Rd.)
Pemberton St. M16: Old T 1E 79
Pembridge Fold M24: Mid 1E 23
Pembridge Rd. M9: Man 5B 26
Pembroke Av. M30: Ecc 3B 88
   M33: Sale 4F 67
Pembroke Cl. M13: Man 1A 68
Pembroke Ct. M27: Pen 4D 35
Pembroke Ho. SK3: Stoc 3A 106
         (off York St.)
Pembroke St. M6: Sal 1A 64
   M7: Sal 1A 52
   OL8: O'ham 3F 29
Pembroke Way M34: Dent 4C 86
       (off Worcester Av.)
Pembry Cl. SK5: Stoc 3D 97
Pembury Cl. M22: Wyth 3E 109
Penarth Rd. M22: Nor 3F 101
Pencarrow Cl. M20: Man 5B 92
Pencombe Cl. M12: Man 5C 68
Pencroft Way M15: Man 5C 66
Pendeen Cl. M22: Wyth 5A 110
Pendennis Rd. SK4: Stoc 5E 95
PENDLEBURY 4D 35

Pendlebury Cl. M25: Pres 2B 36
Pendlebury Ct. M27: Pen 3C 34
Pendlebury Rd. M27: Swin, Pen 4B 34
   SK8: Gat 5C 102
Pendlebury Towers SK5: Stoc 5B 96
Pendle Cl. OL4: O'ham 4F 31
Pendlecroft Av. M27: Pen 5E 35
Pendle Ho. M34: Dent 3B 86
Pendle Rd. M34: Dent 3B 86
PENDLETON .4C 50
Pendleton Grn. M6: Sal 4B 50
       (off Nursery St.)
Pendleton Ho. M6: Sal 4C 50
      (off Broughton Rd.)
Pendleton Way M6: Sal 4B 50
Pendle Wlk. M40: Man 4F 53
   SK5: Stoc 3C 96
Pendleway M27: Pen 3C 34
Pendragon Pl. M35: Fail 5C 42
Pendrell Wlk. M9: Man 1A 40
      (off Sanderstead Dr.)
Penelope Rd. M6: Sal 2F 49
Penerley Dr. M9: Man 1F 53
Penfair Cl. M11: Man 1C 68
Penfield Cl. M1: Man 4E 11 (3D 67)
Penfold Wlk. M12: Man 4B 68
      (off Witterage Cl.)
Pengham Wlk. M23: Wyth 2C 100
Penhall Wlk. M40: Man 2C 54
      (off Mansford Dr.)
Peninsula M7: Sal 5D 37
Penistone Av. M6: Sal 4E 49
   M9: Man 1C 40
Penketh Av. M18: Man 1D 83
Penmere Gro. M33: Sale 2A 98
Pennant Dr. M25: Pres 4C 22
Pennant Ind. Est. OL1: O'ham 1D 31
Pennant St. OL1: O'ham 1D 31
Pennell St. M11: Man 1F 69
Pennine Av. OL9: Chad 4C 28
Pennine Cl. M9: Man 5B 26
Pennine Ct. M27: Pen 3C 34
Pennine Ter. SK16: Duk 1E 73
        (off Peel St.)
Pennine Vw. M34: Aud 5A 72
Pennington St. M12: Man 3C 82
   M28: Walk 2A 32
   OL9: Chad 1D 43
Pennon Cl. M7: Sal 1A 52
Penn St. M40: Man 4B 40
   OL8: O'ham 4F 29
Penny Black Chambers M28: Wors 2B 46
      (off Barton Rd.)
Penny Bri. La. M41: Urm 4C 74
      (not continuous)
Penny La. SK5: Stoc 1B 106
      (not continuous)
Penny Mdw. OL6: A Lyme 4E 59
Penrhos Av. SK8: Gat 1B 110
Penrhyn Av. M24: Mid 2C 26
   SK8: Chea H 5F 111
Penrhyn Dr. M25: Pres 5D 23
Penrhyn Rd. SK3: Stoc 3D 105
Penrith Av. M11: Man 4D 55
   M28: Walk 2B 32
   M33: Sale 1E 99
   M45: White 2D 23
   OL7: A Lyme 2B 58
   OL8: O'ham 5E 29
   SK5: Stoc 4B 84

Penrod Pl. M6: Sal 3D 51
Penrose Cl. M8: Man 1C 52
Penrose Gdns. M24: Mid 5D 17
Penrose Wlk. M24: Mid 2C 16
Penroy Av. M20: Man 5F 91
Penroyson Cl. M12: Man 4B 68
Penruddock Wlk. M13: Man 1B 82
(off Bates St.)
Penryn Av. M33: Sale 2E 99
Penryn Cl. M7: Sal 3F 37
Pensarn Av. M14: Man 5A 82
Pensarn Gro. SK5: Stoc 4B 96
Pensby Cl. M27: Pen 5E 35
Pensby Wlk. M40: Man 2F 53
(off Tollard Av.)
Pensford Rd. M23: Wyth 3B 108
Penshurst Rd. SK5: Stoc 2D 97
Penshurst Wlk. M34: Dent 4C 86
(off Two Trees La.)
Pentland Av. M40: Man 2E 41
Pentlands Av. M7: Sal 2F 51
Pentwyn Gro. M23: Wyth 4D 101
Penwell Fold OL1: O'ham 1A 30
Penzance St. M40: Man 4A 54
Peoples History Mus. 5E 5
Peover Av. M33: Sale 4A 90
Peover Rd. SK9: Hand 4F 115
Pepler Av. M23: Wyth 1D 101
Peploe Wlk. M23: Wyth 2F 99
Pepper Cl. M22: Wyth 5F 101
Pepperhill Rd. M16: W Ran 1B 80
Percival Cl. M8: Man 1B 52
Percival Rd. M43: Droy 1D 71
Percy Dr. M5: Sal 3D 65
Percy Rd. M34: Dent 3A 86
Percy St. BL4: Farn 2A 18
    M15: Man 4F 65
    OL4: O'ham 2E 31
    SK1: Stoc 1B 118 (1B 106)
Peregrine Cres. M43: Droy 4E 57
Peregrine St. M15: Man 5B 66
Peregrine Vw. M43: Droy 4E 57
(off Bittern Dr.)
Periton Wlk. M9: Man 1A 40
(off Leconfield Dr.)
Perivale Dr. OL8: O'ham 5D 31
Perkins Av. M7: Sal 2A 52
Pernham St. OL4: O'ham 2E 31
Perrin St. SK14: Hyde 3F 87
Perrygate Av. M20: Man 2C 92
Perrymead M25: Pres 3E 23
Perry Rd. WA15: Tim 5D 99
Pershore Rd. M24: Mid 3C 16
Perth M30: Ecc 5A 48
(off Monton La.)
Perth Av. OL9: Chad 5C 28
Perth St. M27: Swin 5F 33
Peru St. M3: Sal 3C 4 (5F 51)
Peterborough Cl. OL6: A Lyme 1D 59
Peterborough St. M18: Man 4B 70
Peterchurch Wlk. M11: Man 2E 69
(off Eccles Cl.)
Peterhead Wlk. M5: Sal 1C 64
Peterloo Ct. M6: Sal 5A 50
(off St Luke's Rd.)
Peterloo Ter. M24: Mid 4C 16
Petersburg Rd. SK3: Stoc 5E 105
Peters Ct. WA15: Tim 1A 108
Petersfield Dr. M23: Wyth 4F 99

Peter St. M2: Man 2A 10 (2B 66)
    M3: Man 2A 10 (2B 66)
    M30: Ecc 1F 61
    M34: Dent 2C 86
    OL1: O'ham 4E 117 (3B 30)
    SK1: Stoc 1C 106
(not continuous)
Peterswood Cl. M22: Wyth 3D 109
Peter Wood Gdns.
    M32: Stre 4C 76
Petheridge Dr. M22: Wyth 5D 109
Petrel Cl. M43: Droy 4E 57
    SK3: Stoc 5F 105
Petrel Ho. M19: Man 4F 93
Petrie Ct. M6: Sal 3D 51
Petrock Wlk. M40: Man 2E 55
(off Gaskell St.)
Petworth Cl. M22: Shar 1A 110
Petworth Rd. OL9: Chad 3D 29
Pevensey Cl. M9: Man 2C 40
Pevensey Rd. M6: Sal 2A 50
Pevensey Wlk. OL9: Chad 3D 29
Peveril Cl. M45: White 2E 23
Peveril Cres. M21: Chor 3C 78
Peveril Rd. M5: Sal 5F 49
Peversham Cl. M30: Ecc 3B 48
Pewsey Rd. M22: Wyth 3B 110
Pexhill Ct. SK4: Stoc 1C 104
Pexwood OL1: Chad 1A 28
Pheasant Dr. M21: Chor 1F 91
Phelan Cl. M40: Man 2E 53
Philip Av. M34: Dent 5A 72
Philip Dr. M33: Sale 1D 99
Philip Godlee Lodge
    M20: Man 1D 103
Philips Av. BL4: Farn 2A 18
Philips Ct. M14: Man 1F 81
(off Hope Rd.)
Philips Dr. M45: White 3F 21
PHILIPS PARK 4C 54
Philips Pk.
    Bank Bri. Rd. 4C 54
    Philips Pk. Rd. W. 4F 21
Philips Pk. Rd. M11: Man 5A 54
Philips Pk. Rd. E. M45: White 3A 22
Philips Pk. Rd. W. M45: White 4E 21
Philips Sports Cen. 2A 22
Philip St. M30: Ecc 1F 61
    OL4: O'ham 1E 31
Phillimore St. OL4: Lees 4F 31
Phillip & Pauline Gordon Ho.
    M25: Pres 3D 37
Phillips Pl. M45: White 2B 22
Phoebe St. M5: Sal 2C 64
Phoenix, The M7: Sal 2F 51
Phoenix Ct. SK4: Stoc 3A 96
Phoenix Ind. Est. M35: Fail 4C 42
Phoenix St. BL4: Farn 2A 18
    M2: Man 5C 6 (1C 66)
    OL1: O'ham 4E 117 (3B 30)
Phoenix Way M15: Man 5B 66
    M41: Urm 4A 62
Phyllis St. M24: Mid 2E 27
Piccadilly M1: Man 5D 7 (1C 66)
    SK1: Stoc 2B 118 (2B 106)
Piccadilly Gdns. 5D 7 (1C 66)
Piccadilly Gardens Stop (Metro)
    . . . . .1D 11 (1C 66)
Piccadilly Pl. M1: Man 2E 11 (2D 67)
Piccadilly Plaza M1: Man 1C 10

Piccadilly Sth. M1: Man 1E 11 (1D 67)
Piccadilly Station (Rail & Metro)
. . . . 2F 11 (2D 67)
Piccadilly Trad. Est. M1: Man 2E 67
PICCADILLY VILLAGE 1F 11 (1E 67)
Piccard Cl. M40: Man 2F 53
Pickering Cl. M26: Rad 3D 75
    M41: Urm 1C 98
    WA15: Tim 5A 66
Pickering St. M15: Man 5A 66
Pickford Cl. M15: Man 5A 66
    SK16: Duk 2E 73
Pickford St. M15: Man 2E 73
Pickford M. SK16: Duk 2E 73
                                    (off Pickford La.)
Pickford's Brow SK1: Stoc 2B 118
Pickford St. M4: Man 4F 7 (5D 53)
Pickmere Av. M20: Man 5D 81
Pickmere Cl. M33: Sale 1B 100
    M43: Droy 1D 71
    SK3: Stoc 5E 105
Pickmere Rd. SK9: Hand 4F 115
Pickmere Ter. SK16: Duk 5C 116 (1D 73)
Picton Cl. M3: Man 3E 5 (5A 52)
Picton Sq. OL4: O'ham 3C 30
    OL7: A Lyme 1D 5
Picton St. M7: Sal 1C 58
Picton Wlk. M16: W Ran 2B 80
                                    (off Bedwell St.)
Piercy Av. M7: Sal 3F 51
Piercy St. M4: Man 1F 67
    M35: Fail 5A 42
Pigeon St. M1: Man 5F 7 (1D 67)
Pike Av. M35: Fail 1E 57
Pike Fold La. M9: Man 1E 39
Pike Vw. Cl. OL4: O'ham 4D 31
Pilgrim Dr. M11: Man 1B 68
Pilkington Dr. M45: White 4D 13
Pilkington Rd. BL4: Kea 3B 18
    M9: Man 2C 40
Pilkington St. M24: Mid 5D 17
    M34: Dent 2B 86
Pilling Wlk. OL9: Chad 3C 28
Pilsworth Cotts. BL9: Bury 1E 13
Pilsworth Rd. BL9: Bury 1C 12
                                    (not continuous)
Pilsworth Rd. Ind. Est. BL9: Bury 1C 12
Pilsworth Way BL9: Bury 1C 12
Pimblett St. M3: Man 1B 6 (4B 52)
Pimlico Cl. M7: Sal 1F 51
                                    (off Hilton St. Nth.)
Pimlott Gro. M25: Pres 2A 38
    SK14: Hyde 5F 73
Pimmcroft Way M33: Sale 5B 90
Pincher Wlk. M11: Man 1E 69
                                    (off Edith Cavell Cl.)
Pinder Wlk. M15: Man 4B 66
                                    (off Brindle Pl.)
Pine Av. M45: White 2B 22
Pine Cl. M34: Aud 4A 72
Pine Ct. M20: Man 4C 92
Pine Gro. M14: Man 1A 82
    M25: Pres 3C 22
    M27: Swin 5F 33
    M28: Wors 4C 48
    M30: Ecc 3A 48
    M33: Sale 3A 90
    M34: Dent 2C 86
Pinehurst Rd. M40: Man 2A 54
Pine Mdws. M26: Rad 3D 19

Pine Rd. M20: Man 4C 92
Pines, The M33: Sale 1D 99
Pine St. M1: Man 1C 10 (1C 66)
    M24: Mid 2E 27
    OL6: A Lyme 3D 59
    OL9: Chad 1C 28
    SK14: Hyde 5F 73
Pinetop Cl. M21: Chor 2F 91
Pine Tree Rd. OL8: O'ham 3F 43
Pinetree St. M18: Man 5E 69
Pinewood OL9: Chad 2A 28
Pinewood Cl. SK4: Stoc 5C 94
    SK16: Duk 1E 73
Pinewood Ct. M33: Sale 3F 89
Pinewood Rd. M21: Chor 1C 90
Pinfold Av. M9: Man 2C 40
Pinfold Cl. M32: Stre 4E 77
                                    (off Barton Rd.)
    M45: White 1A 22
Pinfold Dr. M25: Pres 4B 22
Pinfold La. M45: White 1A 22
    M90: Man a 3B 112
Pingot Av. M23: Wyth 2D 101
Pinhigh Pl. M6: Sal 1D 49
Pink Bank La. M12: Man 1C 82
                                    (not continuous)
Pin Mill Brow M12: Man 2F 67
Pinner Pl. M19: Man 2C 94
Pinnington La. M32: Stre 3F 77
Pinnington Rd. M18: Man 4F 69
Pintail Av. SK3: Stoc 5F 105
Pioneer Ct. OL7: A Lyme 5A 116
                                    (not continuous)
Pioneer Rd. M27: Clif 2F 35
Pioneer St. M11: Man 4D 55
    M24: Mid 1F 17
Piperhill Av. M22: Nor 1F 101
Pipewell Av. M18: Man 5E 69
Pipit Cl. M34: Aud 5E 57
Pirie Wlk. M40: Man 1E 55
                                    (off Queensferry St.)
Pitcairn Ho. M30: Ecc 1F 61
                                    (off Adelaide St.)
Pitchcombe Rd. M22: Wyth 4D 109
Pitfield Cotts. SK14: Hyde 2E 87
Pitfield Gdns. M23: Wyth 4B 100
Pitman Cl. M11: Man 2C 68
Pitmore Wlk. M40: Man 2F 41
PITSES 5F 31
Pitsford Rd. M40: Man 2A 54
Pit St. OL9: Chad 5D 29
Pittbrook St. M12: Man 3F 67
Pitt St. M34: Dent 2B 86
    OL4: O'ham 3C 30
    SK3: Stoc 3F 105
    SK14: Hyde 2F 87
Pitt St. E. OL4: O'ham 4D 31
Place, The M1: Man 1F 11 (1D 67)
Plain Pitt St. SK14: Hyde 5E 73
                                    (not continuous)
Plainsfield St. M16: W Ran 1A 80
Plane Cl. M6: Sal 5C 50
Plane Rd. M35: Fail 2B 56
Plane St. OL4: O'ham 2E 31
Planetree Wlk. M23: Wyth 3E 99
Planet Way M34: Aud 5A 72
Plantagenet Wlk. M40: Man 3F 55
                                    (off Marguerita Rd.)
Plantation Gro. BL9: Bury 2E 13
Plantation Ind. Est. OL6: A Lyme 5F 59

Plantation St. M18: Man 5A 70
  OL6: A Lyme 5F 59
Plant Cl. M33: Sale 3C 88
Plant Hill Rd. M9: Man 4E 25
  M19: Man 4E 83
Plasman Ind. Cen.
Plate St. OL1: O'ham 3F 117 (2B 30)
Platinum Rd. M41: Urm 5B 62
Plato St. OL9: O'ham 2F 29
Platt Av. OL6: A Lyme 1E 59
Plattbrook Cl. M14: Man 4D 81
Platt Ct. M14: Man 3E 81
Platt Fields Pk. 3E 81
Platt Hall
  (The Gallery of Costume) 3E 81
Platt Ho. M5: Sal 4C 64
                (off Elmira Way)
Platting Gro. OL7: A Lyme 3D 58
Platt La. M14: Man 4C 80
Platt Lane Complex 3D 81
Platt St. SK8: Chea 5A 104
  SK16: Duk 3C 72
Platt Wlk. M34: Dent 4A 86
Plattwood Wlk. M15: Man 4F 65
           (off Shawgreen Cl.)
Playfair St. M14: Man 1D 81
Playgolf Manchester 4E 61
Pleachway SK4: Stoc 1B 104
Pleasant Rd. M30: Ecc 1A 62
Pleasant St. M9: Man 5F 39
Pleasant Ter. SK16: Duk 1E 73
              (off Peel St.)
Pleasant Vw. M9: Man 5D 25
  M26: Rad 1D 21
Pleasington Dr. M40: Man 2E 41
Ploughbank Dr. M21: Chor 1F 91
Plough St. SK16: Duk 2F 73
Plover Ter. M21: Chor 1F 91
Plowden Rd. M22: Wyth 4D 109
Plowley Cl. M20: Man 1D 103
Plumbley Dr. M16: Old T 2E 79
Plumbley St. M11: Man 3A 70
Plumley Cl. M33: Sale 1F 99
Plumley Rd. SK9: Hand 4F 115
Plummer Av. M21: Chor 2D 91
Plumpton Wlk. M13: Man 1B 82
Plum St. OL8: O'ham 4F 29
Plumtree Cl. M30: Ecc 5A 48
Pluto Cl. M6: Sal 3E 51
Plymouth Av. M13: Man 5D 45
Plymouth Cl. OL6: A Lyme 5D 45
Plymouth Gro. M13: Man 4E 67
  SK3: Stoc 4D 105
Plymouth Gro. W. M13: Man 4E 67
Plymouth Rd. M33: Sale 3A 88
Plymouth St. OL8: O'ham 5B 30
          (not continuous)
Plymouth Vw. M13: Man 4E 67
Plymouth Village M13: Man 5F 67
        (off Plymouth Gro.)
Plymtree Cl. M8: Man 2A 38
Pochin St. M40: Man 4A 54
Pocklington Dr. M23: Wyth 4B 100
Podsmead Rd. M22: Wyth 4D 109
Point, The OL6: A Lyme 5E 59
         (off Scotland St.)
Poland St. M4: Man 3F 7 (5E 53)
  M34: Aud 2A 72
Poland St. Ind. Est. M4: Man 5E 53
Polden Cl. M23: Wyth 4A 44

Polden Wlk. M9: Man 3B 40
          (off Glen Av.)
Polebrook Av. M12: Man 4F 67
Polefield App. M25: Pres 3D 23
Polefield Circ. M25: Pres 3D 23
Polefield Gdns. M25: Pres 3D 23
Polefield Grange M25: Pres 3D 23
Polefield Gro. M25: Pres 3D 23
Polefield Hall Rd. M25: Pres 3D 23
Polefield Rd. M9: Man 2F 39
  M25: Pres 3E 23
Pole La. BL9: Bury 3E 13
  M35: Fail 4B 42
Pole La. Ct. BL9: Bury 3E 13
Pole St. OL7: A Lyme 1B 116 (3D 59)
Polesworth Cl. M12: Man 4C 68
Police St. M2: Man 5A 6 (1B 66)
  M6: Sal .4C 50
  M30: Ecc 5E 47
Pollard Ct. OL1: O'ham 1A 30
         (off Bradford St.)
Pollard St. M4: Man 1E 67
Pollard St. E. M40: Man 5F 53
Pollen Cl. M33: Sale 1F 99
Polletts Av. SK5: Stoc 2E 97
Pollitt Av. OL6: A Lyme 2E 59
Pollitt Cl. M12: Man 4B 68
Pollitts Cl. M30: Ecc 5D 47
Polo Rd. M17: T Pk 2C 62
Polonia Ct. OL8: O'ham 1E 43
Polruan Rd. M21: Chor 3C 78
Polworth Rd. M9: Man 3A 40
Polygon, The M7: Sal 1E 51
  M30: Ecc 5C 48
Polygon Av. M13: Man 4E 67
Polygon Rd. M8: Man 3B 38
Polygon St. M13: Man 3E 67
Pomfret St. M6: Sal 2E 49
  M12: Man 4C 68
Pomona Cres. M5: Sal 3D 65
Pomona Docks M16: Old T 5A 8 (4E 65)
Pomona Station (Metro) 4D 65
         (not continuous)
Pomona Strand M16: Old T 5A 8 (5C 64)
         (not continuous)
Ponds Cl. M21: Chor 4D 79
Ponsford Av. M9: Man 1C 40
Ponsonby Rd. M32: Stre 2F 77
Pontefract Cl. M27: Swin 5D 35
Pool Bank St. M24: Mid 2D 25
         (not continuous)
Poolcroft M33: Sale 5B 90
Pooley Cl. M24: Mid 5D 15
Pool Fold M35: Fail 1C 56
Pool St. OL8: O'ham 5B 30
Poolton Rd. M9: Man 5D 25
Poorfield St. OL8: O'ham 5D 117
Pope Way M34: Dent 5C 86
         (off Kipling Av.)
Poplar Av. M19: Man 1D 95
  OL8: O'ham 2F 43
  WA14: Alt 5A 98
Poplar Cl. SK8: Gat 1D 111
Poplar Ct. M34: Aud 4B 72
  SK3: Stoc 5B 106
         (off Garners La.)
Poplar Dr. M25: Pres 2C 36
Poplar Gro. M18: Man 1F 83
  M33: Sale 5D 89
  M41: Urm 3A 76
  OL6: A Lyme 2E 59

Poplar Rd. M19: Man 5F 93
   M27: Swin 5F 33
   M28: Walk 3A 42
   M30: Ecc .5E 77
   M32: Stre . . . .
Poplar St. M24: Mid 2F 27
   M34: Aud 3B 72
   M35: Fail .1F 55
   SK4: Stoc 1A 104
Poplar Wlk. M34: Aud 4B 72
                (off Poplar St.)
   OL9: Chad 1D 29
Poplin Dr. M3: Sal 2F 5 (4A 52)
Poppy Cl. M23: Wyth 2A 100
   OL9: Chad 2F 27
Poppythorn La. M25: Pres 4C 22
Poppythorn La. M25: Pres 4C 22
              (not continuous)
Porchfield Sq. M3: Man 2F 9 (2A 66)
Porlock Av. M34: Aud 2E 71
Porlock Cl. SK1: Stoc 3E 107
Porlock Rd. M23: Wyth 5D 101
   M41: Urm 5C 74
Portal Ct. M24: Mid 1E 27
Portal Gro. M34: Dent 4D 87
Portal Wlk. M9: Man 4F 39
            (off Alderside Rd.)
Porter Dr. M40: Man 1F 53
Porter St. OL9: O'ham 4E 29
Portfield Wlk. M40: Man 2D 55
            (off Harmer Cl.)
Portgate Wlk. M13: Man 5F 67
         (off St Stephens Cl.)
Porthleven Dr. M23: Wyth 5A 100
Portico Library & Gallery, The
             . . . . .1C 10 (1C 66)
Portland, The M14: Man 5F 81
Portland Arc. M1: Man 1D 11
            (off Parker St.)
Portland Basin Mus. 5A 116 (1C 72)
Portland Ct. M20: Man 5D 93
Portland Cres. M13: Man 5F 67
Portland Gro. SK4: Stoc 4D 95
Portland Ho. M6: Sal 4C 48
   OL6: A Lyme 3A 116 (5C 58)
Portland Mill OL6: A Lyme 3A 116
Portland Pl.
   OL7: A Lyme 4A 116 (5C 58)
Portland Rd. M13: Man 2B 82
   M27: Swin 5C 34
   M30: Ecc 4B 48
   M32: Stre 1A 78
Portland St. M1: Man 2C 10 (2C 66)
Portland St. Nth.
   OL6: A Lyme 2A 116 (4C 58)
Portland St. Sth.
   OL6: A Lyme 3A 116 (5C 58)
   OL7: A Lyme 4A 116 (5C 58)
Portland Ter. OL6: A Lyme 3A 116
Portloe Rd. SK8: H Grn 2D 115
Portman Rd. M16: W Ran 2A 80
Porton Wlk. M22: Wyth 5D 109
Portree Cl. M30: Ecc 5D 47
Portrush Rd. M22: Wyth 4A 110
Portslade Wlk. M23: Wyth 1B 108
Portsmouth Cl. M7: Sal 2F 51
Portsmouth St. M13: Man 5D 67
            (not continuous)
Port Soderick Av. M5: Sal 1C 64
Portstone Cl. M16: W Ran 1A 80

Port St. M1: Man 5E 7 (1D 67)
   OL8: O'ham 5B 30
   SK1: Stoc 1A 118 (2A 106)
   SK14: Hyde 3F 87
            (off Market St.)
Portugal Rd. M25: Pres 2D 37
Portugal St. M4: Man 3F 7 (5E 53)
           (not continuous)
   OL7: A Lyme 1B 72
Portugal St. E. M1: Man 2F 11 (2E 67)
Portville Rd. M19: Man 3C 82
Portway M22: Wyth 4D 109
PORTWOOD 5D 97
Portwood Ind. Est. SK1: Stoc 1D 107
            (not continuous)
Portwood Pl. SK1: Stoc 1B 106
Portwood St. M9: Man 5F 39
          (off Shiredale Dr.)
Posnett St. SK3: Stoc 3E 105
Postal St. M1: Man 5E 7
Potato Wharf M3: Man 3D 9 (2F 65)
Pot Hill OL6: A Lyme 3E 59
Pot Hill Sq. OL6: A Lyme 3E 59
Potter Ho. OL8: O'ham 5E 117
Potter's La. M9: Man 5A 40
Pottery La. M11: Man 5B 68
   M12: Man 5B 68
Pottinger St. OL7: A Lyme 1B 72
Pott St. M27: Pen 2B 34
   M40: Man 2F 55
Poulton St. M11: Man 3A 70
Poundswick La. M22: Wyth 3E 109
Powell St. M11: Man 5F 55
   M16: Old T 1E 79
Powerhouse Health & Fitness Cen. . . .2F 87
          (off Borough Arc.)
Powerleague Soccer Cen.
   Alexandra Pk. 5B 80
   Ardwick 3F 67
   Norris Bank 2D 105
Pownall Av. M20: Man 5C 80
Poynings Dr. M22: Wyth 5E 109
Poynter St. M40: Man 3E 41
Poynton St. M15: Man 4B 66
Praed Rd. M17: T Pk 5E 63
Pratt Wlk. M11: Man 1B 68
          (off Raglan Cl.)
Precinct, The SK2: Stoc 5F 107
   SK3: Stoc 4F 105
Precinct Cen. M13: Man 4C 66
Preesall Av. SK8: H Grn 1D 115
Premier Rd. M8: Man 3B 52
Premier St. M16: Old T 1F 79
Prentice Wlk. M11: Man 1C 68
Prenton St. M11: Man 2A 70
Prescot Rd. M9: Man 5F 39
Prescott Wlk. M34: Dent 4D 87
Press St. M11: Man 3F 69
Presswood Ct. M6: Sal 1E 49
         (off Swinton Pk. Rd.)
Prestage St. M12: Man 3D 83
   M16: Old T 5E 65
Prestbury Av. M14: Man 4B 80
   WA15: Alt 5A 98
Prestbury Dr. SK6: Bred 5F 97
Prestfield Rd. M45: White 2C 22
PRESTOLEE 1C 18
Prestolee Rd. M26: Rad 1C 18
Preston Av. M30: Ecc 4C 48
Preston Cl. M30: Ecc 4C 48

Preston Rd. M19: Man 5C **82**
Preston St. M18: Man 4E **69**
  M24: Mid 1C **26**
  OL4: O'ham 3C **30**
Presto St. BL4: Farn 1A **18**
PRESTWICH 4C **22**
Prestwich Cl. SK2: Stoc 4D **107**
Prestwich Forest Pk. 5E **21**
Prestwich Hills M25: Pres 1C **36**
PRESTWICH PARK 2B **36**
Prestwich Pk. Rd. Sth. M25: Pres . . .1C **36**
Prestwich Station (Metro) 4C **22**
Prestwick Wlk. M40: Man 2E **41**
                (off Pleasington Dr.)
Prestwood Rd. M6: Sal 3E **49**
Pretoria Rd. OL8: O'ham 1E **43**
Price St. M4: Man 1F **67**
  SK16: Duk 2E **73**
Pridmouth Rd. M20: Man 2E **93**
Priest Av. SK8: Gat 2C **110**
Priest Hill OL1: O'ham 3D **117**
Priest Hill St. OL1: O'ham 3D **117** (2A **30**)
Priestley Rd. M28: Ward 4E **33**
Priestnall Rd. SK4: Stoc 5B **94**
                (off Priestnall Rd.)
Priestnall Recreation Cen. 5B **94**
Priestnall Rd. SK4: Stoc 5B **94**
Priest St. OL9: Chad 5D **29**
Primley Wlk. M9: Man 4A **40**
                (off Edward St.)
Primrose Av. M41: Urm 3F **75**
  SK14: Hyde 5F **87**
PRIMROSE BANK 4A **30**
Primrose Bank OL8: O'ham 4A **30**
Primrose Cl. M5: Sal 5B **50**
Primrose Cres. SK14: Hyde 5F **87**
Primrose Dr. M43: Droy 4E **57**
Primrose St. BL4: Kea 2A **18**
  M4: Man 3F **7**
Primrose Wlk. OL8: O'ham 4A **30**
Prince Albert Av. M19: Man 3C **82**
                (off Belvoir Av.)
Prince Charlie St. OL1: O'ham 1D **31**
Princedom St. M9: Man 4A **40**
Prince Edward Av. M34: Dent 3B **86**
  OL4: O'ham 2E **31**
Princemead Pl. M17: T Pk 5D **63**
Prince of Wales Ind. Units
  OL1: O'ham 1E **31**
Princes Av. M30: Ecc 4E **93**
Prince's Bri. M3: Man 2D **9** (2F **65**)
Princes Ct. M30: Ecc 4F **47**
Princes Dr. M33: Sale 5F **89**
Princes Rd. M33: Sale 5E **89**
  SK4: Stoc 4C **94**
Princess Av. BL4: Kea 3B **18**
  M25: Pres 2E **37**
  M34: Dent 2A **86**
Princess Cl. SK16: Duk 2F **73**
Princess Ct. M15: Man 4F **65**
           (off Cornbrook Pk. Rd.)
  M25: Pres 1D **37**
Princess Dr. M24: Mid 1A **26**
Princess Pde. M14: Man 4B **80**
Princess Parkway M22: Nor 3E **101**
  M23: Wyth 3E **101**
Princess Rd. M14: Man 1B **80**
  M15: Man 5A **10** (4B **66**)
  M16: W Ran 1B **80**
  M20: Man 5F **91**

Princess Rd. M21: Chor 5F **91**
  M25: Pres 5E **23**
  M41: Urm 2D **75**
  OL9: Chad 1A **42**
Princess St. M1: Man 2C **10** (1B **66**)
  M2: Man 1B **10** (1B **66**)
  M6: Sal 3C **50**
            (off Cheltenham Dr.)
  M15: Man 5B **8** (4E **65**)
  M27: Swin 5C **34**
  M30: Ecc 5E **47**
  M35: Fail .5A **42**
  OL4: Lees 3F **31**
  OL6: A Lyme 3F **59**
Prince's St. SK1: Stoc 2A **118** (2A **106**)
Princeton Cl. OL8: O'ham 2C **30**
Princeton Cl. M6: Sal 4E **49**
Prinknash Rd. M22: Wyth 4F **109**
Printers Cl. SK4: Stoc 1F **103**
Printer St. M11: Man 2F **69**
  OL1: O'ham 4E **117** (3B **30**)
Printon Av. M9: Man 5D **25**
Printworks, The M4: Man 3C **6** (5C **52**)
Printworks La. M19: Man 4E **83**
Prior St. OL8: O'ham 4D **31**
Priory, The M7: Sal 1E **51**
  M21: Chor 5D **79**
Priory Av. M7: Sal 1E **51**
  SK5: Stoc 5A **84**
Priory Cl. M33: Sale 2F **89**
  OL8: O'ham 1F **43**
  SK16: Duk 4F **73**
Priory Ct. M30: Ecc 5A **48**
            (off Abbey Gro.)
  SK5: Stoc 5A **84**
Priory Gdns. M20: Man 4D **93**
Priory Gro. M7: Sal 1E **51**
  OL9: Chad 5C **28**
Priory La. SK5: Stoc 5A **84**
Priory Pl. M7: Sal 1E **51**
Priory Rd. M27: Swin 3A **34**
  M33: Sale 3E **89**
Pritchard St. M1: Man 3D **11** (2C **66**)
  M32: Stre 3F **77**
Privet St. OL4: O'ham 1F **31**
Proctor Way M30: Ecc 3B **60**
            (not continuous)
Progress Av. M34: Aud 4B **72**
Progressive Bus. Pk. M34: Aud 2A **72**
Progress St. OL6: A Lyme 2A **116** (4C **58**)
Progress Way M34: Dent 3E **85**
Propps Hall Dr. M35: Fail 1F **55**
Prospect Dr. M35: Fail 2B **56**
Prospect Ho. M9: Man 5A **40**
            (off Church La.)
Prospect Pl. M27: Swin 5C **34**
           (off Manchester Rd.)
  OL6: A Lyme 2F **59**
Prospect Rd. OL6: A Lyme 2F **59**
  OL9: O'ham 2E **29**
  SK16: Duk 1F **73**
Prospect Va. SK8: H Grn 5D **111**
Prospect Vw. M27: Swin 5C **34**
            (off Manchester Rd.)
Prospect Vs. M9: Man 3B **40**
Prout St. M12: Man 2C **82**
Providence Ho. OL4: O'ham 1F **31**
           (off Huddersfield Rd.)
Providence St. M4: Man 1F **67**
  M34: Aud 3B **72**
  OL6: A Lyme 3F **59**

Provident Av. M19: Man 4E 83
Provident Way WA15: Tim 4C 98
Provis Rd. M21: Chor 1D 91
Prubella Av. M34: Dent 5A 72
Pryme St. M15: Man 4E 9 (3A 66)
Pugin Wlk. M9: Man 1F 53
(off Oldershaw Dr.)
Pulford Av. M21: Chor 4E 91
Pulford Rd. M33: Sale 1E 99
Pullman Cl. M19: Man 5D 83
Pullman Dr. M32: Stre 3B 76
Pump St. OL9: O'ham 2D 43
Pump Yd. M4: Man 3C 6
Purbeck Cl. M22: Wyth 5E 109
Purcell St. M12: Man 2C 82
Purdy Ho. OL8: O'ham 5D 117 (4A 30)
Puritan Wlk. M40: Man 2E 53
(off Ribblesdale Dr.)
Purley Av. M23: Wyth 2D 101
Purslow Cl. M12: Man 1A 68
Purton Wlk. M9: Man 5A 40
(off Broadwell Dr.)
Puzzletree Ct. SK2: Stoc 4E 107
Pymgate Dr. SK8: H Grn 4C 110
Pymgate La. SK8: H Grn 4C 110
Pym St. M30: Ecc 5F 47
M40: Man 4B 40
Pyramid Ct. M7: Sal 1F 51
Pyrus Cl. M30: Ecc 2B 60
Pytha Fold Rd. M20: Man 3E 93

Q

Quadrant, The M9: Man 1C 40
M43: Droy 1B 70
SK1: Stoc 2D 107
Quail St. OL4: O'ham 4E 31
Quainton Ho. M5: Sal 1B 64
(off Amersham St.)
Quantock Cl. SK4: Stoc 1A 106
Quantock Dr. OL8: O'ham 1B 44
Quantock St. M16: W Ran 1A 80
Quarmby Rd. M18: Man 1B 84
Quarry Bank Rd. SK9: Sty 5B 114
Quarrymans Vw. WA15: Tim 5D 99
Quarry Rd. BL4: Kea 2C 18
Quarry Wlk. M11: Man 1B 68
(off Redfield Cl.)
Quay 5 M5: Sal 5A 8 (3D 65)
Quays, The M50: Sal 3B 64
Quays Reach M50: Sal 1A 64
Quays Theatre 3A 64
(in The Lowry)
Quay St. M3: Man 1E 9 (1A 66)
M3: Sal 4F 5 (5A 52)
Quayview M5: Sal 2C 64
Quay W. M17: T Pk 4A 64
Quebec Bldg. M3: Sal 3F 5
Quebec St. M34: Dent 1A 86
OL9: O'ham 1E 29
Queen Alexandra Cl. M5: Sal 3A 8
Queen Anne Cl. BL9: Bury 2E 13
Queenhill Rd. M22: Nor 2A 102
Queens Av. M18: Man 5D 69
Queensbury Ct. M40: Man 4A 54
(off Wardle St.)
Queensbury Pde. M40: Man 4A 54
(off Eastfield Av.)
Queens Cl. SK4: Stoc 1C 104

Queens Ct. M20: Man 4C 92
M40: Man 2F 53
M41: Urm 3A 74
SK4: Stoc 1C 104
Queenscroft M30: Ecc 4A 48
Queen's Dr. M25: Pres 2E 37
SK4: Stoc 1C 104
Queensferry St. M40: Man 1E 55
Queens Gdns. SK8: Chea 5A 104
Queen's Gro. M12: Man 1C 82
Queensland Rd. M18: Man 5D 69
Queensmead Pl. M17: T Pk 5D 63
Queens Pk. 1E 53
Queens Pk. Mus. & Art Gallery ..1E 53
Queen Sq. OL6: A Lyme 4F 59
Queens St. M8: Man 2C 52
M9: Man 1E 53
M33: Sale 3B 88
M40: Man 1F 53
M41: Urm 4F 75
OL6: A Lyme 2F 59
OL8: O'ham 5F 117 (4B 30)
OL9: Chad 2C 28
Queens Ter. SK9: Hand 5F 115
SK16: Duk 5C 116 (1D 73)
Queenston Rd. M20: Man 4C 92
Queen St. BL4: Farn 1A 18
M2: Man 1A 10 (1B 66)
M3: Sal 3F 5 (5A 52)
M6: Sal 2F 49
M24: Mid 1E 27
M34: Aud 4B 72
M34: Dent 1A 86
M35: Fail 5A 42
OL1: O'ham 3F 117 (2B 30)
OL6: A Lyme 4E 59
SK8: Chea 5B 104
SK14: Hyde 4F 87
SK16: Duk 5C 116 (1D 73)
Queen St. W. M20: Man 1D 93
Queen's Wlk. M43: Droy 1C 70
Queensway BL4: Kea 4B 18
M19: Man 1F 103
M27: Clif 2C 34
M41: Urm 1A 76
SK8: H Grn 1D 115
Queen Victoria St. M30: Ecc ...5E 47
Quenby St. M15: Man 5D 9 (3F 65)
Quendon Av. M7: Sal 3A 52
Quickwood M34: Dent 1C 86
(off Herbert Sth.)
Quilter Gro. M9: Man 2E 39
Quince Ho. M6: Sal 4D 51
(off Milton Pl.)
Quinney Cres. M16: W Ran 1A 80
Quinn St. M11: Man 1C 68
Quinton Wlk. M13: Man 5F 11

R

Raby St. M14: Man 1B 80
M16: W Ran 1A 80
Rachel Rosing Wlk. M8: Man 4B 38
Rachel St. M12: Man 2E 67
Rackhouse Rd. M23: Wyth 2D 101
Radbourne Cl. M12: Man 4C 68
Radcliffe New Rd. M45: White ...4A 12
Radcliffe Pk. Cres. M6: Sal 2E 49
Radcliffe Pk. Rd. M6: Sal 2D 49

Radcliffe St. OL1: O'ham 1E **117** (1B **30**)
(not continuous)
Radcliffe Vw. M5: Sal 3D **65**
(off Ordsall Dr.)
Radclyffe St. M24: Mid 4C **16**
OL9: Chad 1D **29**
Radclyffe Ter. M24: Mid 4C **16**
Radford Cl. SK2: Stoc 4F **107**
Radford Dr. M9: Man 4A **40**
(off Hemsley St. Sth.)
Radford Ho. SK2: Stoc 4F **107**
Radford St. M7: Sal 4E **37**
Radium St. M4: Man 3F **7** (5E **53**)
Radlet Dr. WA15: Tim 3C **98**
Radlett Wlk. M13: Man 5E **67**
(off Plymouth Gro.)
Radley Cl. M33: Sale 5A **88**
Radley St. M16: W Ran 2B **80**
M43: Droy 2A **70**
Radnor Av. M34: Dent 2D **85**
Radnor Ho. SK3: Stoc 5A **118**
Radnor St. M15: Man 5B **66**
M18: Man 1E **83**
M32: Stre 3F **77**
OL9: O'ham 4E **29**
Radstock Cl. M14: Man 4D **81**
Radstock Rd. M32: Stre 3E **77**
Rae St. SK3: Stoc 3E **105**
Raglan Av. M27: Clif 2D **35**
M45: White 2D **23**
Raglan Cl. M11: Man 1B **68**
Raglan Dr. WA14: Tim 3A **98**
Raglan Rd. M32: Stre 2D **77**
M33: Sale 5B **88**
Raglan St. SK14: Hyde 3E **87**
Raglan Wlk. M15: Man 4B **66**
(off Eden Cl.)
Railside Ter. M30: Ecc 5C **48**
(off St Mary's Rd.)
Railton Av. M16: W Ran 2F **79**
Railton Ter. M9: Man 5B **40**
Railway Bank SK14: Hyde 3E **87**
(off Bowling Grn. St.)
Railway Rd. M32: Stre 5A **64**
M41: Urm 3F **75**
OL9: Chad 2C **42**
OL9: O'ham 3F **29**
SK1: Stoc 4A **118** (3A **106**)
Railway St. BL4: Farn 1A **18**
M18: Man 4E **69**
SK4: Stoc 1A **106**
SK14: Hyde 3F **87**
SK16: Duk 5B **116** (1D **73**)
Railway St. Ind. Est. M18: Man 4F **69**
Railway Ter. M21: Chor 3D **79**
(off Manchester Rd.)
Railway Vw. SK5: Stoc 3A **84**
Rainbow Cl. M21: Chor 1D **91**
Raincliff Av. M13: Man 3B **82**
Rainford Av. M20: Man 5C **80**
WA15: Tim 5C **98**
Rainforth St. M13: Man 2B **82**
Rainham Dr. M8: Man 5C **38**
Rainham Way OL9: Chad 3D **29**
SK5: Stoc 2D **97**
Rainhill Wlk. M40: Man 3F **55**
(off Eastmoor Dr.)
Rainow Av. M43: Droy 1A **70**
Rainow Rd. SK3: Stoc 5E **105**
Rainshaw St. OL4: O'ham 1F **31**

RAINSOUGH 3C **36**
Rainsough Av. M25: Pres 3C **36**
Rainsough Brow M25: Pres 3B **36**
Rainsough Cl. M25: Pres 3C **36**
Rainsough Hill M25: Pres 3B **36**
Rainton Wlk. M40: Man 2F **41**
(off Enstone Dr.)
Rainwood OL9: Chad 1A **28**
Raja Cl. M8: Man 5D **39**
Rakehead Wlk. M15: Man 5C **66**
(off Botham Cl.)
Rake La. M27: Clif 1C **34**
Raleigh Cl. M20: Man 3C **92**
OL1: O'ham 1E **117** (1B **30**)
Raleigh St. M32: Stre 3F **77**
SK5: Stoc 4A **96**
Ralli Courts M3: Sal 5E **5** (1A **66**)
Ralli Quays M3: Sal 5E **5** (1A **66**)
Ralph Grn. St. OL9: O'ham 1D **43**
Ralphs La. SK16: Duk 3E **73**
Ralph St. M11: Man 1F **69**
Ralston Cl. M7: Sal 4B **38**
Ramage Wlk. M12: Man 1A **68**
Ralstone Av. OL8: O'ham 5B **30**
Ramp Rd. E. M90: Man A 2E **113**
Ramp Rd. Sth. M90: Man A 2E **113**
(off Outwood La.)
Ramp Rd. W. M90: Man A 2D **113**
Ramsbottom Row M25: Pres 5C **22**
Ramsbury Dr. M40: Man 2F **41**
Ramsdale St. OL9: Chad 2C **28**
Ramsden Cl. OL1: O'ham 2A **30**
Ramsden Cres. OL1: O'ham 2A **30**
Ramsden Fold M27: Clif 2B **34**
Ramsden St. OL1: O'ham 2A **30**
OL6: A Lyme 3D **59**
Ramsey Av. M19: Man 4F **83**
Ramsey St. M40: Man 5D **41**
OL1: O'ham 1D **31**
OL9: Chad 4D **29**
Ramsgate Rd. M40: Man 3E **55**
SK5: Stoc 1B **96**
Ramsgate St. M7: Sal 2A **52**
Ramsgill Cl. M23: Wyth 2B **100**
Ramsgte St. M8: Man 3A **52**
Ranby Av. M9: Man 5B **26**
Randale Dr. BL9: Bury 3C **12**
Randall Wlk. M11: Man 1B **68**
(off Raglan Cl.)
Randal St. SK14: Hyde 5C **72**
Randerson St. M12: Man 3E **67**
(off Paddock St.)
Randlesham St. M25: Pres 5E **23**
Randolph Pl. SK3: Stoc 5A **118** (4A **106**)
Randolph Rd. BL4: Kea 2B **18**
Randolph St. M19: Man 3D **83**
OL8: O'ham 2E **43**
Ranelagh Rd. M27: Pen 5E **35**
Ranelagh St. M11: Man 5D **55**
Ranford Rd. M19: Man 5C **82**
Range Hall Ct. SK1: Stoc 2C **106**
(off Hall St.)
Rangemore Av. M22: Nor 3A **102**
Range Rd. M16: W Ran 2A **80**
SK3: Stoc 5A **106**
Range Stadium 5B **80**
Range St. M11: Man 2E **69**
Rankin Cl. M15: Man 5A **66**
Ranmore Av. M11: Man 2F **69**
Ransfield Rd. M21: Chor 4D **79**

Ranulph Ct. M6: Sal 2F **49**
(off King St.)
Ranworth Av. SK4: Stoc 1B **104**
Ranworth Cl. M11: Man 2C **68**
Raper St. OL4: O'ham 1E **31**
Rastell Wlk. M9: Man 1A **40**
(off Ravenswood Dr.)
Ratcliffe St. M19: Man 4D **83**
SK1: Stoc 5B **118** (3B **106**)
Ratcliffe Towers
SK1: Stoc 4B **118** (3B **106**)
Rathan Rd. M41: Urm 1E **75**
Rathbourne Av. M9: Man 5F **25**
Rathen Rd. M20: Man 3D **93**
Rathmell Rd. M23: Wyth 1B **100**
Rathmore Av. M40: Man 1E **113**
Rathvale Dr. M22: Wyth 2A **54**
Rath Wlk. M40: Man 2E **55**
(off Orford Rd.)
Rattenbury Ct. M6: Sal 2E **49**
Raveley Av. M14: Man 5F **81**
Ravelston Dr. M9: Man 1F **53**
Raven Av. OL9: Chad 4C **28**
Raven Cl. M43: Droy 4E **57**
Raven Ct. M15: Man 5A **66**
(off Dudley Cl.)
Ravenglass Dr. M24: Mid 3F **15**
Ravenhead Cl. M14: Man 5F **81**
Ravenhurst M7: Sal 3A **38**
(off Up. Park Rd.)
M7: Sal .3A **38**
(Bury Old Rd.)
Ravenna Av. M23: Wyth 4F **99**
Ravenoak Av. M19: Man 5E **83**
Ravenoak Dr. M35: Fail 4C **42**
Raven Rd. WA15: Tim 2D **99**
Ravensbury St. M11: Man 5D **55**
Ravenscar Cres. M22: Wyth 1F **113**
Ravenscar Wlk. BL4: Farn 2A **18**
(off Norris St.)
Ravens Cl. M25: Pres 2A **38**
Ravensdale Gdns. M30: Ecc 4A **48**
Ravensdale St. M14: Man 2E **81**
Ravensfield Ind. Est.
SK16: Duk 5B **116** (1C **78**)
Ravenside Pk. OL9: Chad 4C **28**
Ravens Pl. M25: Pres 2A **38**
Ravenstone Dr. M33: Sale 3A **90**
Raven St. M12: Man 2E **67**
Ravensway M25: Pres 2F **37**
Ravenswood M20: Man 4B **92**
Ravenswood Av. SK4: Stoc 2C **104**
Ravenswood Dr. M9: Man 1A **40**
Ravenswood Rd. M32: Stre 5B **64**
Raven Ter. SK16: Duk 1E **73**
(off Peel St.)
Raven Way M8: Man 4B **50**
(off Salford Shop. City)
Ravenwood OL9: Chad 2F **27**
Ravenwood Dr. M34: Aud 4A **72**
Ravine Av. M9: Man 5A **40**
(not continuous)
Rawcliffe St. M14: Man 2D **81**
Rawdon Cl. M19: Man 4D **83**
Rawpool Gdns. M23: Wyth 4C **100**
Rawson Av. BL4: Farn 1A **18**
Rawson St. BL4: Farn 1A **18**
Rawsthorne Av. M18: Man 3F **83**
Rayburn Way M8: Man 2C **52**
Raycroft Av. M9: Man 2C **40**

Raydon Av. M40: Man 2F **53**
(off Sedgeford Rd.)
Rayleigh Av. M11: Man 3B **70**
Raymond Av. OL9: Chad 5D **29**
Raymond Rd. M23: Wyth 1D **101**
Raymond St. M27: Pen 3B **34**
Rayner La. OL7: A Lyme 1F **71**
Rayner St. SK1: Stoc 3D **107**
Raynham Av. M20: Man 5D **93**
Raynham St. OL6: A Lyme 4E **59**
Raysonhill Dr. M9: Man 2E **39**
Reabrook Av. M12: Man 4B **68**
Reach, The M28: Walk 2A **32**
Reade Av. M41: Urm 4A **74**
Reade Ho. M41: Urm 4B **74**
(off Flixton Rd.)
Reading Cl. M11: Man 2E **69**
Reading Dr. M33: Sale 4A **88**
Reading St. M6: Sal 2D **51**
Reading Wlk. M34: Dent 4B **86**
Readitt Wlk. M11: Man 5D **55**
(off Coghlan Cl.)
Read St. SK14: Hyde 2E **87**
Read St. W. SK14: Hyde 2E **87**
Reaney Wlk. M12: Man 4C **68**
(off Stonehurst Cl.)
Reather Wlk. M40: Man 4E **53**
(off Orsett Cl.)
Rebecca St. M8: Man 4C **38**
Recreation Rd. M35: Fail 3C **42**
Recreation St. M25: Pres 5E **23**
Rectory Av. M8: Man 3C **38**
M25: Pres 5D **23**
Rectory Ct. M34: Dent 3C **86**
Rectory Flds. SK1: Stoc 2C **106**
Rectory Gdns. M25: Pres 5D **23**
Rectory Grn. M25: Pres 4C **22**
SK1: Stoc 2C **106**
Rectory Gro. M25: Pres 1D **37**
Rectory La. M25: Pres 4C **22**
Rectory Rd. M8: Man 3B **38**
Rectory St. M24: Mid 5B **16**
Redacre Rd. M18: Man 4A **70**
Red Bank M4: Man 1C **6** (4C **52**)
M8: Man 1C **6** (4C **52**)
Redbourne Dr. M41: Urm 1B **74**
Redbrick Ct.
OL7: A Lyme 5A **116** (1C **72**)
Redbridge Gro. M21: Chor 5C **78**
(off Crossland Rd.)
Redbrook Av. M40: Man 2A **54**
Redbrook Cl. BL4: Farn 1A **18**
Redbrook Rd. WA15: Tim 5F **99**
Redburn Rd. M23: Wyth 4D **101**
Redby St. M11: Man 2D **93**
Redcar Av. M20: Man 4D **93**
M41: Urm 5E **35**
Redcar Lodge M27: Pen 1C **74**
(off Redcar Rd.)
Redcar Rd. M27: Pen 5E **35**
Redcliffe Ct. M25: Pres 2D **37**
Redclyffe Av. M14: Man 2E **81**
Redclyffe Circ. M41: Urm 4E **61**
Redclyffe Rd. M20: Man 3C **92**
M41: Urm 3F **61**
Redcot Ct. M45: White 2E **21**
Redcote St. M40: Man 4C **40**
Redcourt Av. M20: Man 4D **93**
Redcroft Gdns. M19: Man 4A **94**
Redcroft Rd. M33: Sale 2A **88**

Reddaway Cl. M6: Sal 2C 50
REDDISH 1A 96
REDDISH GREEN 1F 95
Reddish La. M18: Man 1A 84
Reddish Leisure Cen. 1A 96
Reddish North Station (Rail) 3B 84
Reddish Rd. SK5: Stoc 4B 96
Reddish South Station (Rail) 1B 96
REDDISH VALE 1C 96
Reddish Vale Country Pk. 1D 97
Reddish Vale Country Pk.
    Local Nature Reserve 5D 85
Reddish Vale Farm 1C 96
Reddish Va. Rd. SK5: Stoc 1B 96
Reddish Vale Sports Cen.
    (NW Regional Basketball Cen.)
    ....5C 84
Reddish Vale Vis. Cen. 1D 97
Reddley Wlk: Droy 3F 99
    WA15: Tim 5F 99
Redesmere Cl. M43: Droy 1D 71
Redesmere Pk. M41: Urm 5D 75
Redesmere Rd. SK9: Hand 4F 115
Redfern Av. M33: Sale 5A 90
Redfern St. M4: Man 3C 6 (5C 52)
Redfield Cl. M11: Man 1B 68
Redford Rd. M8: Man 5B 24
Red Gables OL7: A Lyme 3C 58
Redgate SK14: Hyde 5F 87
Redgate La. M12: Man 4B 68
                            (not continuous)
Redgates Wlk: M21: Chor 4D 79
                        (off Ransfield Rd.)
Redgrave Pas. OL4: O'ham 1F 31
Redgrave St. OL4: O'ham 1E 31
Redgrave Wlk. M19: Man 4E 83
Red Hall St. OL4: O'ham 3E 31
Redhill Dr. SK6: Bred 5F 97
Redhill St. M4: Man 5F 7 (1D 67)
Redland Av. SK5: Stoc 3B 96
Redland Cres. M21: Chor 2D 91
Red Lion St. M4: Man 4D 7 (5C 52)
Redlynch Wlk. M8: Man 5C 38
Redmans Ct. M30: Ecc 1D 61
Redmere Gro. M14: Man 5E 81
Redmires Ct. M5: Sal 1C 64
Redmond Cl. M34: Aud 3A 72
Redmoor Sq. M13: Man 4F 11
Redmoss Row M27: Pen 4F 35
Red Pike Wlk.
    OL1: O'ham 1F 117 (1C 30)
    ....4D 31
Red Rock La. M26: Rad 3F 19
Red Rose Cres. M19: Man 1E 95
Red Rose Gdns. M33: Sale 2D 89
Red Rose Retail Cen.
    M5: Sal 2A 8 (1D 65)
Redruth St. M14: Man 3D 81
Redscar Rd. M24: Mid 5A 16
Redshaw Cl. M14: Man 4F 81
Redstone Rd. M19: Man 5F 93
Redthorn Av. M19: Man 1B 94
Redvale Dr. M7: Sal 1A 52
REDVALES 1A 12
Redvers St. OL1: O'ham 1F 29
Redwing Cen. M17: T Pk 4E 63
Redwood OL9: Chad 2F 27
Redwood Cl. SK3: Stoc 3D 105
Redwood Dr. M8: Man 2D 53
    M34: Aud 4A 72
Redwood Ho. M22: Nor 2A 102
Redwood St. M6: Sal 3B 50

Reece Ct. SK16: Duk 2F 73
Reedbank M26: Rad 1C 20
Reede Ct. OL1: O'ham 1A 30
                          (off Bradford St.)
Reedham Wlk. M40: Man 3A 54
                         (off Giltbrook Av.)
    OL9: O'ham 5E 29
Reedmace Cl. M28: Walk 3A 32
Reedmaker Pl. M27: Swin 4F 33
Reedshaw Rd. M9: Man 1E 53
Reed St. M18: Man 4F 69
    OL1: O'ham 3F 117
Reeve's Cl. M5: Sal 5C 48
Reeves Rd. M21: Chor 1D 91
Reform Wlk. M11: Man 2D 69
Regal Cl. M45: White 1D 23
Regal Ind. Est. M12: Man 3C 68
Regal Wlk. M40: Man 1E 55
                      (off Lastingham St.)
Regan Av. M21: Chor 1F 91
Regatta Cl. OL9: Chad 1C 42
Regatta St. M6: Sal 1B 50
Regency Cl. M40: Man 2F 53
    OL8: O'ham 5F 29
Regency Ct. M33: Sale 4B 88
    SK2: Stoc 5C 106
Regency Gdns. SK8: Chea H 1F 115
Regency Lodge M25: Pres 5C 22
Regent Av. M14: Man 3C 80
Regent Bri. M5: Sal 2F 65
Regent Cvn. Pk. M6: Sal 3B 50
Regent Ct. M7: Sal 3F 37
    SK4: Stoc 3E 95
Regent Cres. M35: Fail 1A 56
    M41: Urm 4F 61
                      (off The Trafford Cen.)
Regent Dr. M34: Dent 4F 85
Regent Ho. M14: Man 2F 81
    SK4: Stoc 2A 118
Regent Pl. M14: Man 1E 81
Regent Retail Pk. M5: Sal ...2B 8 (2E 65)
Regent Rd. M5: Man 2A 8 (1D 65)
    SK2: Stoc 5C 106
Regents Pl. M5: Sal 1D 65
Regent Sq. M5: Sal 3A 8 (2D 65)
                            (not continuous)
Regent St. M24: Mid 4B 16
    M30: Ecc 5B 48
    M40: Man 2F 55
    OL1: O'ham 2C 30
Regent Trad. Est. M5: Sal ...5C 4 (1F 65)
Regent Wlk. BL4: Farn 1A 18
Regina Ct. M6: Sal 4C 48
Reginald Latham Ct. M40: Man 4F 53
                        (off Berkshire Rd.)
Reginald St. M11: Man 3B 70
    M27: Swin 3F 33
    M30: Ecc 2C 60
Reid Cl. M34: Dent 5C 86
Reigate Rd. M41: Urm 5A 74
Reilly St. M15: Man 5A 10 (4B 66)
Reins Lee Av. OL8: O'ham 2C 44
Reins Lee Rd. OL7: A Lyme 1C 58
Reliance St. M40: Man 5E 41
Reliance St. Ent. Pk. M40: Man ...1E 55
Reliance Trad. Est. M40: Man 1E 55
Rena Cl. SK4: Stoc 5F 95
Rena Ct. SK4: Stoc 5F 95
Rendel Cl. M32: Stre 3F 77
Rennie Cl. M32: Stre 3A 78

Renolds Ho. M5: Sal 4B 8
Renshaw Av. M30: Ecc 1F 61
Renshaw St. M30: Ecc 1F 61
  WA14: Alt 5A 98
Renton Rd. M22: Wyth 2F 109
  M32: Stre 3A 78
Repton Av. M34: Dent 2C 84
  M40: Man 3A 42
  M43: Droy 4F 55
  OL8: O'ham 1F 43
  SK14: Hyde 2F 87
Repton Cl. M33: Sale 5B 90
Reservoir Rd. SK3: Stoc 4F 105
Reservoir St. M3: Sal 2F 5 (4A 52)
  M6: Sal 5B 50
Residences, The
  M25: Pres 1E 37
Retford St. OL4: O'ham 4D 31
Retiro St. OL1: O'ham 3F 117 (2B 30)
Retley Pas. OL1: O'ham 3D 117
Retreat, The M28: Wors 4B 32
Reuben St. SK4: Stoc 4A 96
Reynard Ct. M13: Man 1A 82
Reynard Rd. M21: Chor 1D 91
Reynard St. SK14: Hyde 2F 87
Reynell Rd. M13: Man 3B 82
Reyner St. M1: Man 2C 10
  OL6: A Lyme 5F 59
Reynolds Dr. M18: Man 4F 69
Reynolds Rd. M16: Whal T 1E 79
Reynold St. SK14: Hyde 3F 87
Rhine, The M15: Man 4A 10
Rhine Dr. M8: Man 2A 52
RHODES 2E 25
RHODES BANK 4F 117 (3B 30)
Rhodes Bank
  OL1: O'ham 4F 117 (3B 30)
Rhodes Bus. Pk. M24: Mid 2E 25
Rhodes Dr. BL9: Bury 4C 12
RHODES GREEN 1D 25
Rhodes St. OL1: O'ham 2C 30
  SK14: Hyde 2E 87
Rhodes St. Nth. SK14: Hyde 5A 82
Rhos Av. M14: Man 2C 26
  M24: Mid 4C 66
Rial Pl. M15: Man 4C 66
              (off Eden Cl.)
Rialto Gdns. M7: Sal 1A 52
Ribble Av. OL9: Chad 1A 28
Ribble Dr. BL4: Kea 4C 18
  M45: White 5C 12
               M45: White 1E 19
Ribblehead Ct. M26: Rad 1E 43
Ribble Rd. OL8: O'ham 2E 53
Ribblesdale Dr. M40: Man 2C 70
Ribble Wlk. M43: Droy 2C 70
               (off Ellen St.)
Ribston St. M15: Man 4A 66
Rice St. M3: Man 2E 9 (2A 66)
Richards Cl. M34: Aud 3A 72
Richardson Cl. M45: White 5A 48
Richardson Rd. M30: Ecc 3A 70
Richardson St. M11: Man 4C 106
  SK1: Stoc
Richard St. SK1: Stoc 1C 118 (5B 96)
Richborough Cl.
  M7: Sal 2A 52
Richmond Av. M25: Pres 3E 37
  M41: Urm 3A 76
  OL9: Chad 5C 28
  SK9: Hand 4F 115

Richmond Cl. M33: Sale 5B 90
  M45: White 2F 21
  SK16: Duk 4F 73
Richmond Ct. M3: Sal 3C 4
  M9: Man 4C 24
         (off Deanswood Dr.)
  M13: Man 1F 81
  M34: Aud 4A 72
  SK2: Stoc 5F 107
Richmond Dr. M28: Wors 4E 33
Richmond Gro. M13: Man 1F 81
  M30: Ecc 4A 48
Richmond Gro. E. M12: Man 5A 68
Richmond Hill M3: Man 2E 5
Richmond Hill Rd. SK8: Chea 1E 111
Richmond Ho. M27: Pen 2B 34
            (off Berry St.)
Richmond Pk. M14: Man 4F 81
Richmond Rd. M14: Man 5F 81
  M17: T Pk 3C 62
  M34: Dent 2C 84
  M35: Fail 4C 42
  SK4: Stoc 1B 104
  SK16: Duk 4F 73
Richmond St. M1: Man 2D 11 (2C 66)
  M3: Sal 2E 5 (4A 52)
  M34: Aud 4A 72
  M43: Droy 5E 57
  OL6: A Lyme 3A 116 (4B 58)
  OL7: A Lyme 3B 58
Richmond Wlk. OL9: O'ham 3F 29
Riddell Ct. M5: Sal 5E 49
Ridding Av. M22: Wyth 3A 110
Ridding Cl. SK2: Stoc 5F 107
Riddings Ct. WA15: Tim 3B 98
Riddings Rd. WA15: Tim 3B 98
Ridge Cres. M45: White 1D 23
Ridgecroft OL7: A Lyme 1D 59
Ridgefield M3: Man 1A 10 (1B 66)
Ridgefield St. M35: Fail 5F 41
         (not continuous)
Ridge Gro. M45: White 1D 23
Ridgemont Av. SK4: Stoc 1D 105
Ridgemont Wlk. M23: Wyth 1B 100
Ridge Wlk. M9: Man 1F 39
Ridgeway M27: Clif 3D 35
Ridgeway Av. WA15: Tim 1A 108
Ridgewood Av. M40: Man 2F 53
  OL9: Chad 1A 28
Ridgway St. M40: Man 5F 53
Ridgway St. E. M4: Man 5F 53
Riding Cl. M33: Sale 4B 90
Riding Fold M43: Droy 4F 57
Ridingfold La.
  M28: Wors 2C 46
Ridings St. M11: Man 2D 69
  M40: Man 2B 54
Ridings Way OL9: Chad 3D 29
Ridley Dr. WA14: Tim 2A 98
Ridley Gro. M33: Sale 5B 90
Ridley St. OL4: O'ham 3C 30
Ridley Wlk. M15: Man 5C 66
          (off Wellhead Cl.)
Ridling La. SK14: Hyde 3F 87
Ridsdale Av. M20: Man 2C 92
Ridsdale Cl. M6: Sal 2C 50
         (off Langley Rd. Sth.)
Rifle Rd. M33: Sale 3B 90
Rifle St. OL1: O'ham 1E 117 (1B 30)
Riga Rd. M14: Man 4E 81

Riga St. M4: Man 3D **7** (5C **52**)
Rigby St. M7: Sal 5F **37**
Rigby Wlk. M7: Sal 1A **52**
Rigel Pl. M7: Sal .1B **4**
Rigel St. M4: Man 4E **53**
Righton Gallery 5C **10**
Rigton Cl. M12: Man 5C **68**
Rileys Snooker Club 5D **69**
Rimington Fold M24: Mid 3F **15**
Rimmer Cl. M11: Man 2A **68**
Rimmington Cl. M9: Man 2C **40**
Rimsdale Cl. SK8: Gat 3C **110**
Rimsdale Dr. M40: Man 4E **41**
Rimworth Dr. M40: Man 3E **53**
Ringcroft Gdns. M40: Man 3D **41**
Ringford Wlk. M40: Man 2A **54**
RINGLEY 2F **19**
RINGLEY BROW 1F **19**
Ringley Chase M26: Rad 1D **19**
    M45: White 1F **21**
Ringley Cl. M45: White 1F **21**
Ringley Dr. M45: White 1F **21**
Ringley Hey M45: White 1F **21**
Ringley Mdws. M26: Rad 2E **19**
Ringley M. M26: Rad 1D **21**
Ringley Old Brow M26: Rad 2E **19**
Ringley Pk. M45: White 1F **21**
Ringley Rd. M26: Rad 1D **19**
    M45: White 1E **21**
                                        (not continuous)
Ringley Rd. W. M26: Rad 1A **20**
Ringley St. M9: Man 4F **39**
Ringlow Av. M27: Swin 5E **33**
Ringlow Pk. Rd. M27: Swin 1E **47**
Ringmer Dr. M22: Wyth 5E **109**
Ringmere Ct. OL1: O'ham 1D **117**
Rings Cl. M35: Fail 1B **56**
Ringstead Dr. M40: Man 3E **53**
Ringstone Cl. M25: Pres 1C **36**
RINGWAY 3B **112**
Ringway Gro. M33: Sale 1A **100**
Ringway M. M22: Shar 1A **110**
Ringway Rd. M22: Wyth 2A **114**
    M90: Man A 2E **113**
Ringway Rd. W. M22: Man A 1E **113**
    M90: Man A 1E **113**
Ringway Trad. Est.
    M22: Wyth 1A **114**
Ringwood Av. M12: Man 3D **83**
    M26: Rad .1D **21**
    M34: Aud 1E **71**
Ringwood Way OL9: Chad 1E **29**
Rink St. M14: Man 1F **93**
Ripley Cl. M4: Man 2F **67**
Ripley Cres. M41: Urm 5B **60**
Ripley Way M34: Dent 5B **86**
Ripon Av. M45: White 4B **12**
Ripon Cl. M26: Rad 1A **12**
    M45: White 4B **12**
    OL9: Chad .3D **29**
    SK1: Stoc 5B **118** (3B **106**)
Ripon Cres. M32: Stre 2B **76**
Ripon Gro. M33: Sale 2B **88**
Ripon Rd. M32: Stre 2B **76**
Ripon St. M15: Man 5C **66**
    OL1: O'ham 1F **29**
    OL6: A Lyme 4E **59**
Rippenden Av. M21: Chor 3C **78**
Rippingham Rd. M20: Man 1D **93**
Rippleton Rd. M22: Wyth 2A **110**

Ripponden Rd. OL1: O'ham 1E **31**
    OL4: O'ham 1E **31**
Ripton Wlk. *M9: Man* 5D **25**
                                        (off Selston Rd.)
Risbury Wlk. *M40: Man* 1E **55**
                                    (off Bridlington Cl.)
Rishworth Cl. SK2: Stoc 5F **107**
Rishworth Dr. M40: Man 4A **42**
Rising La. OL8: O'ham 2A **44**
Rising La. Cl. OL8: O'ham 2A **44**
Risley Av. M9: Man 4F **39**
Risley St. OL1: O'ham 1E **117** (1B **30**)
Rissington Av. M23: Wyth 5D **101**
Rita Av. M14: Man 2D **81**
Ritson Cl. M18: Man 4D **69**
Riva Rd. M19: Man 1F **103**
River Bank, The M26: Rad 1C **18**
Riverbank Lawns M3: Sal 1E **5**
Riverbank Twr. M3: Sal 2E **5** (4A **52**)
Riverbank Wlk. M20: Man 5F **91**
Riverdale Rd. M9: Man 1C **38**
River Ho. *M43: Droy* 5C **56**
                                     (off Medlock St.)
River La. M34: Dent 2D **87**
Rivermead Cl. M34: Dent 5C **86**
Rivermead Rd. M34: Dent 5C **86**
Rivermead Way M45: White 1C **22**
Riverpark Rd. M40: Man 4C **54**
River Pl. M15: Man 4F **9** (3A **66**)
Riversdale Ct. M25: Pres 5C **22**
Riversdale Dr. OL8: O'ham 3C **44**
Rivershill M33: Sale 2C **88**
Rivershill Dr. SK8: Chea 5E **103**
Riverside M7: Sal 2B **4** (4E **51**)
    OL1: Chad .5F **17**
    SK16: Duk .1E **73**
Riverside Av. M21: Chor 5F **91**
Riverside Cl. M26: Rad 2A **12**
Riverside Ct. M20: Man 5B **92**
    M50: Sal 2C **64**
Riverside Dr. M26: Rad 1D **19**
    M41: Urm 5D **75**
Riverside M15: Man 4F **9**
Riverside Pk. Cvn. Site M22: Nor 2A **102**
Riverside Rd. M26: Rad 2A **12**
Rivers La. M41: Urm 5D **61**
Riverstone Dr. M23: Wyth 4F **99**
River St. M1: Man 4B **10**
    M12: Man 2E **67**
    M15: Man 5A **10** (3B **66**)
    SK1: Stoc 5D **97**
Riverton Rd. M20: Man 3D **103**
River Vw. M24: Mid 3E **27**
    SK5: Stoc 1C **96**
Riverview SK4: Stoc 3B **104**
River Vw. Cl. M25: Pres 2B **36**
Riverview Ct. M7: Sal 4E **37**
Rivington Av. M27: Pen 4E **35**
    M45: White 2E **21**
Rivington Cres. M27: Pen 4E **35**
Rivington Gro. M34: Aud 2E **71**
Rivington Rd. M6: Sal 3E **49**
Rivington St. OL1: O'ham 1B **30**
Rivington Wlk. M12: Man 5B **68**
Rixton Ct. *M16: Old T* 2D **79**
                                     (off Basford Rd.)
Roach Ct. *M40: Man* 3E **53**
                                   (off Hamerton Rd.)
Roach St. BL9: Bury 2B **12**

Roachwood Cl. OL9: Chad 2A 28
Roaring Ga. La. WA15: Hale, Ring . . .3A 108
Robert Bolt Theatre, The 3D 89
(within Waterside Arts Cen.)
Robert Hall St. M5: Sal 3A 8 (2D 65)
Robert Harrison Av. M20: Man 2B 92
Robert Lawrence Ct. M41: Urm 4C 74
Robert Malcolm Cl. M40: Man 2F 53
Robert Owen Gdns. M22: Nor 3F 101
Robert Owen St. M43: Droy 5E 57
Robert Powell Theatre 4D 51
Robert Salt Ct. WA14: Alt 5A 98
Roberts Av. M14: Man 1D 81
Robertscroft Cl. M22: Wyth 2E 109
Robertshaw Av. M21: Chor 2D 91
Robertson Cl. M18: Man 5E 69
Roberts St. M30: Ecc 1F 61
Robert St. M3: Man 1B 6 (4B 52)
　　M25: Pres 5E 23
　　M33: Sale 4A 90
　　M35: Fail 3C 42
　　OL8: O'ham 1D 43
　　SK14: Hyde 2E 87
　　SK16: Duk 2D 73
Robeson Way M22: Shar 5A 102
Robe Wlk. *M18: Man* 4F 69
(off Briercliffe Cl.)
Robin Cft. SK6: Bred 5F 97
Robin Hood St. M8: Man 4B 38
Robinia Cl. M30: Ecc 2B 60
Robin La. M45: White 2B 22
Robinsbay Rd. M22: Wyth 1A 114
Robins Cl. M43: Droy 4E 57
Robinson St. OL6: A Lyme 1B 116 (3D 59)
　　OL9: Chad 3D 29
　　SK3: Stoc 4F 105
　　SK15: Stal 2F 73
Robin St. OL1: O'ham 1A 30
Robinswood Rd. M22: Wyth 4F 109
Robson Av. M41: Urm 3A 62
Robson St. OL1: O'ham 4F 117 (3B 30)
Roby Rd. M30: Ecc 2E 61
Roby St. M1: Man 1E 11
Roch Bank M9: Man 1B 38
Roch Cl. M45: White 5D 13
Roch Cres. M45: White 4D 13
Rochdale Ho. M15: Man 3E 9
Rochdale Rd. M4: Man 3E 7 (4D 53)
　　M9: Man 4D 53
　　M24: Mid 4C 16
　　M40: Man 3E 7 (4D 53)
　　OL1: O'ham 1A 30
　　OL9: O'ham 1A 30
Rochester Av. M21: Chor 2F 91
　　M25: Pres 2E 37
Rochester Cl. OL6: A Lyme 5E 45
Rochester Dr. WA14: Tim 2A 98
Rochester Rd. M41: Urm 1F 75
Rochester Way OL9: Chad 3D 29
Rochford Av. M45: White 2F 21
Rochford Cl. M45: White 2F 21
Rochford Ho. *M34: Aud* 4A 72
(off Denton Rd.)
Rochford Rd. M30: Ecc 2B 60
Roch Wlk. M45: White 5D 13
Roch Way M45: White 5D 13
Rockall Wlk. *M11: Man* 1B 68
(off Fairisle Cl.)
Rock Bank M7: Sal 1E 51
Rockdove Av. M15: Man 5A 10 (3B 66)

Rocket St. M3: Sal 5D 5 (1F 65)
Rockfield Dr. *M9: Man* 4A 40
(off Dalbeattie St.)
Rockhampton St. M18: Man 5F 69
Rockhouse Cl. M30: Ecc 2E 61
Rockingham Cl. M12: Man 4F 67
Rockland Wlk. M40: Man 2E 41
Rockley Gdns. M6: Sal 3D 51
Rocklyn Av. M40: Man 2E 41
Rockmead Dr. M9: Man 1A 40
Rock Rd. M41: Urm 3B 76
Rock St. M7: Sal 1F 51
　　M11: Man 2A 70
　　OL1: O'ham 3E 117 (2B 30)
(not continuous)
　　OL7: A Lyme 2C 58
(not continuous)
Rock Ter. SK16: Duk 1E 73
Rocky La. M27: Swin 2F 47
　　M30: Ecc 2F 47
Roda St. M9: Man 5B 40
Rodborough Gdns. M23: Wyth 3B 108
Rodborough Rd. M23: Wyth 3B 108
Rodenhurst Dr. M40: Man 5C 40
Rodmell Av. M40: Man 2F 53
Rodmill Ct. M14: Man 4E 81
Rodmill Dr. SK8: Gat 2C 110
Rodney Ct. *M4: Man* 4E 53
(off Wadeford Cl.)
Rodney St. M3: Sal 5D 5 (1F 65)
　　M4: Man 5E 53
　　OL6: A Lyme 3F 59
Roebuck Ct. M33: Sale 4C 88
Roebuck La. M33: Sale 4C 88
Roebuck M. M33: Sale 5D 89
Roeburn Wlk. M45: White 1E 23
ROE GREEN .4C 32
Roe Grn. M28: Wors 4B 32
Roe Grn. Av. M28: Wors 4C 32
Roe La. OL4: O'ham 4F 31
Roe St. M4: Man 4E 53
Rogate Dr. M23: Wyth 1C 108
Roger Byrne Cl. M40: Man 2D 55
Rogerson Cl. WA15: Tim 4E 99
Roger St. M4: Man 1D 7 (4C 52)
Rokeby Av. M32: Stre 4F 77
Roker Av. M13: Man 3B 82
Roker Pk. Av. M34: Aud 3F 71
Roland Rd. SK5: Stoc 1B 96
Rolla St. M3: Sal 3F 5 (5A 52)
Rolleston Av. M40: Man 5F 53
Rolls Cres. M15: Man 4A 66
Rollswood Dr. M40: Man 1C 54
Romana Sq. WA14: Tim 3A 98
Roman Ct. M7: Sal 2F 51
Roman Rd. M25: Pres 3C 36
　　M35: Fail 4C 42
　　OL8: O'ham 4C 42
　　SK4: Stoc 1A 118 (1A 106)
(not continuous)
Roman St. M4: Man 4D 7
Romer Av. M40: Man 3A 42
Rome Rd. M40: Man 4E 53
Romford Av. M34: Dent 1C 86
Romford Cl. OL8: O'ham 4A 30
Romford Rd. M33: Sale 2A 88
Romford Wlk. M9: Man 1C 38
Romiley St. M6: Sal 2F 49
　　SK1: Stoc 1D 107
Romley Rd. M41: Urm 1F 75

Romney St. M6: Sal 2D 51
   M40: Man .4C 40
   OL6: A Lyme 4E 59
Romney Towers SK5: Stoc 2D 97
Romney Wlk. OL9: Chad 3D 29
Romney Way SK5: Stoc 2D 97
Romsey Av. M24: Mid 3B 16
Romsey Gdns. M23: Wyth 5C 100
Romsley Cl. M12: Man 4C 68
Ronaldsay Gdns. M7: Sal 1A 64
Ronald St. M11: Man 1F 69
   OL4: O'ham 2E 31
Rona Wlk. M12: Man 5B 68
Rondin Rd. M12: Man 2A 68
Ronnis Mt. OL7: A Lyme 5B 44
Ronton Wlk. *M8: Man* 5E 49
(off Mawdsley Dr.)
Rooden Ct. M25: Pres 5E 23
Rookery Av. M18: Man 4B 70
Rooke St. M30: Ecc 2C 60
Rookfield M33: Sale 3E 89
Rookfield Av. M33: Sale 3E 89
Rookley Wlk. *M14: Man* 2E 81
(off Whitecliffe Cl.)
Rook St. M15: Man 5A 66
   OL4: O'ham 4E 31
Rookway M24: Mid 2C 26
Rookwood OL1: Chad 5F 17
Rookwood Av. M23: Wyth 4B 100
Roosevelt Rd. BL4: Kea 2B 18
Rooth St. SK4: Stoc 1F 105
Ropewalk M3: Sal 2F 5 (4A 52)
Ropley Wlk. *M9: Man* *3B 40*
(off Oak Bank Av.)
Rosa Gro. M7: Sal 1F 51
Rosalind Ct. M5: Sal 3B 8 (2E 65)
Rosamond Dr. M3: Sal 4D 5 (5F 51)
Rosamond St. M15: Man 4D 66
Rosamond St. W. M15: Man . .5C 10 (4C 66)
Rosary Cl. OL8: O'ham 3B 44
Rosary Rd. OL8: O'ham 3C 44
Roscoe St. OL1: O'ham 4F 117 (3B 30)
(not continuous)
   SK3: Stoc 3F 105
Roscow Rd. BL4: Kea 2C 18
Roseacre Dr. SK8: H Grn 5E 111
Rose Bank M40: Man 3D 55
Roseberry Av. OL1: O'ham 1D 31
Roseberry St. OL8: O'ham 3F 29
Rosebery St. M14: Man 2B 80
Rose Cott. M14: Man 5D 81
Rose Cotts. *M14: Man* *5F 81*
(off Ladybarn La.)
Rosedale Cl. OL1: O'ham 1D 31
Rosedale M34: Dent 2A 86
Rosedale Rd. M14: Man 3C 80
   SK4: Stoc 3F 95
Rosedale Way SK16: Duk 4E 73
Rosefield Ct. SK3: Stoc 5A 106
Rosegarth Av. M20: Man 4F 91
Rose Gro. BL4: Kea 2B 18
Rosehay Av. M34: Dent 3B 86
Rose Hey La. M35: Fail 3A 56
Rose Hill M34: Dent 2F 85
Rose Hill Av. M40: Man 3D 55
Rosehill Cl. M6: Sal 5B 50
Rosehill Ct. M6: Sal 5B 50
   OL4: O'ham 1F 31
Rosehill M. *M27: Clif* *2B 34*
(off Lit. Moss La.)

Rosehill Rd. M27: Pen 2B 34
(not continuous)
Roseland Av. M20: Man 4D 93
Roseland Dr. M25: Pres 3E 23
Roselands Av. M33: Sale 1B 98
Rose Leigh *M41: Urm* 2F 75
(off Crofts Bank Rd.)
Roseleigh Av. M19: Man 1B 94
Rosemary Dr. SK14: Hyde 5F 87
Rosemary Gro. M7: Sal 2E 51
Rosemary La. SK1: Stoc 2C 106
Rosemead Ct. OL9: Chad 1A 28
Rosemead Ct. SK5: Stoc 2B 96
Rosemount M24: Mid 4B 16
   SK14: Hyde 5F 73
Rosemount Cres. SK14: Hyde 5E 73
Roseneath Av. M19: Man 4E 83
Roseneath Rd. M41: Urm 2F 75
Rosen Sq. OL9: Chad 2D 29
Rose St. M24: Mid 1E 27
   OL9: Chad 1C 42
   SK5: Stoc 5B 96
Rosethorns Cl. M24: Mid 2B 16
Rosevale Av. M19: Man 3A 94
Roseville M. M33: Sale 4D 89
Rosewall Cl. M40: Man 3F 53
Rosewood M34: Dent 2F 85
Rosewood Av. M43: Droy 5D 57
   SK4: Stoc 2C 104
Rosewood Cl. SK16: Duk 4F 73
Rosewood Cres. OL9: Chad 1D 29
Rosewood Gdns. *M33: Sale* 5B 90
(off Hart Av.)
   SK8: Gat 5B 102
Rosewood M. M9: Man 4F 25
Rosford Av. M23: Wyth 3E 99
Rosford Av. M14: Man 3D 81
Rosgill Cl. SK4: Stoc 1A 104
Rosgill Dr. M24: Mid 5F 15
Rosgill Wlk. *M18: Man* 5E 69
(off Hampden Cres.)
Rosina St. M11: Man 3B 70
Roslin St. M11: Man 5F 55
Roslyn Av. M41: Urm 4A 74
Roslyn Rd. SK3: Stoc 5A 106
Rossall Av. M26: Rad 1E 21
   M32: Stre 2E 77
Rossall Way M6: Sal 4C 50
Ross Av. M19: Man 4B 82
   M45: White 3B 22
   OL9: Chad 1B 42
   SK3: Stoc 5A 106
Ross Dr. M27: Clif 5A 20
Rossendale Av. M9: Man 3B 40
Rossendale Rd. SK8: H Grn 1E 115
Rossett Av. M22: Wyth 1F 113
   WA15: Tim 3C 98
Rossett Dr. M41: Urm 1B 74
Rossetti Wlk. *M34: Dent* 5C 86
(off Wordsworth Cl.)
Ross Gro. M41: Urm 3E 75
Rosshill Wlk. *M15: Man* 4F 65
(off Shawgreen Cl.)
Rossington St. M40: Man 2F 55
Rosslare Rd. M22: Wyth 4A 110
Ross Lave La. M34: Dent 5D 85
   SK5: Dent 5D 85
Rosslave Wlk. SK5: Stoc 1E 97

Rosslyn Gro. WA15: Tim 5C **98**
Rosslyn Rd. M16: Old T 3C **78**
   M40: Man 3C **40**
   SK8: H Grn 5F **111**
Ross St. OL8: O'ham 4F **29**
Rostherne Av. M14: Man 4C **80**
   M16: Old T 2E **79**
Rostherne Rd. M33: Sale 5B **90**
   SK3: Stoc 5A **106**
Rostherne St. *M6: Sal* *5A 50*
   (off White St.)
Rosthwaite Cl. M24: Mid 5E **15**
Roston Ct. M7: Sal 4A **38**
Roston Rd. M7: Sal 4A **38**
Rostrevor Rd. SK3: Stoc 5A **106**
   (not continuous)
Rostron Av. M12: Man 4A **68**
Rostron Brow SK1: Stoc 2B **118**
Rostron St. M19: Man 4D **83**
Rothay Cl. M45: White 1E **23**
Rothay Dr. M24: Mid 3A **16**
   SK5: Stoc 5B **84**
Rothbury Av. OL7: A Lyme 3A **58**
Rotherby Rd. M22: Shar 1A **110**
Rotherdale Av. WA15: Tim 5F **99**
Rothermere Wlk. *M23: Wyth* *4A 100*
   (off Sandy La.)
Rotherwood Av. M32: Stre 2A **78**
Rothesay Av. SK16: Duk 3E **73**
Rothesay Rd. M8: Man 2A **38**
   M27: Pen 5E **35**
   OL1: O'ham 1E **31**
Rothiemay Rd. M41: Urm 4A **74**
Rothley Av. M22: Wyth 1F **109**
Rothman Cl. M40: Man 1E **55**
Rothwell St. M28: Walk 1B **32**
   M35: Fail 1B **56**
   M40: Man 1E **55**
Rottingdene Dr. M22: Wyth 5E **109**
Roughey Gdns. M22: Wyth 2F **109**
Roughlee Av. M27: Swin 4A **40**
Roundham Wlk. *M9: Man* *4A 40*
   (off Hillier St.)
Roundhey SK8: H Grn 1D **115**
ROUNDTHORN
   M23 . . . .**5A 100**
   OL4 . . . .**5F 31**
   (not continuous)
Roundthorn Ind. Est. M23: Wyth 5A **100**
Roundthorn Rd. M23: Wyth 5B **100**
   M24: Mid 2D **27**
   OL4: O'ham 3D **31**
Roundwood Rd. M22: Nor 4F **101**
Rowntree Ho. *OL9: O'ham* *3F 29*
   (off Manchester St.)
Rousdon Cl. M40: Man 2F **53**
Rouse Cl. M11: Man 1B **68**
Routledge Wlk. M9: Man 4A **40**
Roving Bri. Ri. M27: Pen 4F **35**
Rowan Av. M16: W Ran 2F **79**
   M33: Sale 1C **99**
   M41: Urm 2F **75**
Rowan Cl. M35: Fail 1B **56**
Rowan Ct. M14: Man 1F **93**
Rowandale St. M1: Man 3A **10**
Rowan Ho. OL6: A Lyme 3C **116**
Rowanlea M25: Pres 5E **23**
Rowan Pl. M25: Pres 1D **37**
Rowan Tree Dr. M33: Sale 2D **99**
Rowan Tree Rd. OL8: O'ham 3F **43**

Rowan Way M7: Sal 5F **37**
Rowanwood OL9: Chad 2A **28**
Rowany Cl. M25: Pres 2C **36**
Rowarth Av. M34: Dent 5C **86**
Rowarth Rd. M23: Wyth 4B **108**
Rowbottom Wlk. OL8: O'ham 4A **30**
Rowcon Cl. M34: Aud 5A **72**
   (not continuous)
Rowdell Wlk. M23: Wyth 1D **101**
Rowden Rd. OL4: O'ham 5F **31**
Rowe Grn. M34: Dent 2B **86**
Rowfield Dr. M23: Wyth 3B **108**
Rowland Av. M41: Urm 2A **76**
Rowland St. M5: Sal 2C **64**
Rowlands Way M22: Wyth 4F **109**
Rowley Cl. OL6: A Lyme 1F **59**
Rowood Av. M8: Man 1D **53**
   SK5: Stoc 3B **84**
Rowrah Cres. M24: Mid 5D **15**
Rowsley Av. M20: Man 4A **92**
Rowsley Gro. SK5: Stoc 1A **96**
Rowsley Rd. M30: Ecc 2E **61**
   M32: Stre 2C **76**
Rowsley St. M6: Sal 2D **51**
   M11: Man 5B **54**
Rowson Ct. *M33: Sale* *4F 89*
   (off Oak Rd.)
Roxburgh St. M18: Man 5F **69**
ROXBURY **4E 31**
Roxbury Av. OL4: O'ham 4F **31**
Roxby Wlk. *M40: Man* *2F 41*
   (off Blandford Dr.)
Roxholme Wlk. M22: Wyth 1E **113**
Roxton Rd. SK4: Stoc 2E **95**
Roxwell Wlk. *M9: Man* *4F 39*
   (off Alderside Rd.)
Royal, The M3: Sal 4C **4**
Royal Av. M21: Chor 1C **90**
   M41: Urm 3F **75**
   M43: Droy 5D **57**
Royal Cres. SK8: Chea 4E **111**
Royal Exchange M2: Man 5B **6** (1B **66**)
Royal Exchange Arc. *M2: Man* *5B 6*
   (within Royal Exchange)
Royal Exchange Theatre 5B **6** (1B **66**)
Royal George St.
   SK3: Stoc 5A **118** (3A **106**)
   (not continuous)
Royal Oak Ind. Est. SK1: Stoc 5C **118**
Royal Oak Rd. M23: Wyth 4B **100**
   (not continuous)
Royal Oak Yd. SK1: Stoc 2B **118**
Royalthorn Av. M22: Wyth 5E **101**
Royalthorn Dr. M22: Wyth 5E **101**
Royalthorn Rd. M22: Wyth 5E **101**
Royce Av. WA15: Alt 5A **98**
Royce Ct. *M15: Man* *4F 65*
   (off Erskine St.)
Royce Rd. M15: Man 5F **9** (4A **66**)
Royce Trad. Est. M17: T Pk 3A **62**
Roydale St. M40: Man 4A **54**
Royden Av. M9: Man 4F **25**
Roydes St. M24: Mid 4D **17**
Royds Cl. M13: Man 5A **68**
Roy St. OL8: O'ham 5E **29**
Roy Grainger Ct. M16: W Ran 2A **80**
Royle Cl. OL8: O'ham 1B **44**
   SK2: Stoc 5C **108**
Royle Grn. Rd. M22: Nor 3A **102**
Royle Higginson Ct. M41: Urm 4E **75**

Royles Cotts. M33: Sale	.5D **89**
Royle St. M6: Sal	.1B **64**
M14: Man	.1F **93**
M28: Walk	.2A **32**
Royle St. M34: Dent	.5B **72**
SK1: Stoc	.4B **106**
Royley Rd. OL8: O'ham	.5A **30**
Royon Dr. SK3: Stoc	.4D **105**
Royston Av. M16: W Ran	.2F **79**
M34: Dent	.2C **84**
Royston Ct. M16: W Ran	.2F **79**
Royston Rd. M16: Old T	.2D **79**
M41: Urm	.2A **76**
Royton Av. M33: Sale	.1A **100**
Rozel Sq. M3: Man	.2F **9** (2A **66**)
Ruabon Rd. M20: Man	.1E **103**
Ruby St. M15: Man	.4C **66**
M34: Dent	.3A **86**
Rudcroft Cl. M13: Man	.5F **11** (4D **67**)
Ruddpark Rd. M22: Wyth	.5F **109**
Rudd St. M40: Man	.5C **40**
Rudheath Av. M20: Man	.1C **92**
Rudman Dr. M5: Sal	.3A **8** (2E **65**)
Rudman St.	
OL7: A Lyme	.5A **116** (1C **72**)
Rudston Av. M40: Man	.2D **41**
Rudyard Av. M24: Mid	.3E **17**
Rudyard Gro. M33: Sale	.1A **98**
SK4: Stoc	.2F **95**
Rudyard Rd. M6: Sal	.1B **64**
Rudyard St. M7: Sal	.1F **51**
Rufford Cl. M45: White	.4C **12**
OL6: A Lyme	.5E **45**
Rufford Dr. M45: White	.4B **12**
Rufford Pde. M45: White	.4B **12**
Rufford Pl. M18: Man	.1B **84**
Rufford Rd. M16: W Ran	.2F **79**
Rufus St. M14: Man	.1A **94**
Rugby Dr. M33: Sale	.1C **98**
Rugby Pk. SK4: Stoc	.2A **104**
Rugby Rd. M6: Sal	.4C **48**
Rugby St. M8: Man	.3A **52**
Rugeley St. M6: Sal	.2D **51**
Ruislip Av. M40: Man	.2A **54**
Ruislip Cl. OL8: O'ham	.5D **31**
Rumbold St. M18: Man	.4A **70**
Runcorn St. M15: Man	.5B **8**
Runger La. M90: Man A	.2B **112**
Runhall Cl. M12: Man	.4C **68**
Runnymeade M6: Sal	.1C **48**
M27: Swin	.1C **48**
Runnymede Cl.	
SK3: Stoc	.4E **105**
Runnymede Ct. SK3: Stoc	.5E **105**
Rupert St. M26: Rad	.1D **21**
M40: Man	.3A **56**
SK5: Stoc	.1A **96**
Rupert Ter. SK5: Stoc	.1A **96**
Ruscombe Fold M24: Mid	.3F **15**
Rushall Wlk. M23: Wyth	.4B **108**
Rushberry Av. M40: Man	.2E **41**
Rushbrooke Av. M11: Man	.5E **55**
Rushcroft Ct. M9: Man	.2C **40**
Rushden Rd. M19: Man	.3D **83**
Rushen St. M11: Man	.1E **69**
Rushey Av. M22: Wyth	.5E **101**
Rushey Cl. WA15: Haleb	.2A **118**
Rushey Rd. M22: Wyth	.1E **109**
Rushfield Dr. M13: Man	.2B **82**
Rushford Av. M19: Man	.3C **82**

Rushford Ct. M19: Man	.3C **82**
	(off Rushford Av.)
RUSHFORD PARK	.3C **82**
Rushford St. M12: Man	.1C **82**
Rushley Av. M7: Sal	.1D **51**
Rushmere OL6: A Lyme	.1F **59**
Rushmere Av. M19: Man	.4D **83**
Rushmere Wlk. M16: Old T	.5F **65**
RUSHOLME	.2F **81**
Rusholme Gdns. M14: Man	.3E **81**
	(off Wilmslow Rd.)
Rusholme Gro. M14: Man	.2E **81**
Rusholme Gro. W. M14: Man	.2E **81**
Rusholme Pl. M14: Man	.1E **81**
Rushton Gro. M11: Man	.3A **70**
Rushton Rd. SK3: Stoc	.4D **105**
Rushton St. M20: Man	.1D **103**
M28: Walk	.2A **32**
Rushway Av. M9: Man	.2D **41**
Rushwick Av. M40: Man	.2A **54**
Rushworth Ct. SK4: Stoc	.3E **95**
Ruskin Av. BL4: Kea	.2B **18**
M14: Man	.1D **81**
M34: Aud	.3E **71**
M34: Dent	.4F **85**
OL9: Chad	.1B **42**
Ruskin Cres. M25: Pres	.1B **36**
Ruskington Dr. M9: Man	.5F **39**
Ruskin Rd. M16: Old T	.2E **79**
M25: Pres	.1C **36**
M43: Droy	.5C **56**
SK5: Stoc	.4A **84**
Ruskin St. OL1: O'ham	.1F **29**
Rusland Ct. M9: Man	.1C **40**
M33: Sale	.3C **88**
SK2: Stoc	.4D **107**
	(off Sylvester Av.)
Rusland Wlk. M22: Wyth	.4E **109**
Russborne Av. M16: W Ran	.3F **79**
M33: Sale	.3F **89**
Russell Ct. BL4: Farn	.1A **18**
	(off Russell St.)
M16: W Ran	.2E **79**
Russell Fox Ct. SK5: Stoc	.1A **96**
	(off Broadstone Rd.)
Russell Gdns. SK4: Stoc	.2D **105**
Russell Pl. M33: Sale	.3D **89**
Russell Rd. M6: Sal	.2D **49**
M16: W Ran	.2F **79**
Russell St. BL4: Farn	.1A **18**
M8: Man	.3A **52**
M16: W Ran	.2B **80**
M25: Pres	.5D **23**
M30: Ecc	.5B **48**
OL6: A Lyme	.3F **59**
OL9: Chad	.2D **29**
SK2: Stoc	.5C **106**
SK14: Hyde	.2F **87**
SK16: Duk	.2E **73**
Russet Rd. M9: Man	.3F **39**
Rustons Wlk. M40: Man	.3A **42**
	(off Glensdale Dr.)
Ruth Av. M40: Man	.3A **42**
Ruthen La. M16: Old T	.1D **79**
Rutherford Av. M14: Man	.2D **81**
Rutherford Cl. SK14: Hyde	.3F **87**
Rutherford Way SK14: Hyde	.3F **87**
	(Birchfield M.)
SK14: Hyde	.3F **87**
	(The Mall)

Rutherglade Cl. M40: Man 1E 53
Rutherglen Wlk. M40: Man 2A 54
Ruthin Av. M9: Man 4E 25
   M24: Mid .3C 26
Ruthin Cl. M6: Sal 5C 50
   OL8: O'ham 2D 43
Ruthin Ct. M6: Sal 5C 50
Ruth St. M18: Man 2F 83
   OL1: O'ham 1F 117 (1B 30)
Rutland Av. M16: Old T 2C 78
   M20: Man 2C 92
   M27: Pen .2B 34
   M34: Dent 3C 86
   M41: Urm .2A 76
Rutland Cl. OL6: A Lyme 5F 59
   SK8: Gat 5D 103
Rutland Ct. M20: Man 3D 93
   SK2: Stoc 5C 106
Rutland Cres. SK5: Stoc 3F 97
Rutland Dr. M7: Sal 4E 37
Rutland La. M33: Sale 4B 90
                (not continuous)
Rutland Rd. M30: Ecc 3B 48
   M43: Droy 5A 56
Rutland St. M18: Man 4A 70
   M27: Swin 3A 34
   M35: Fail .4B 42
   OL6: A Lyme 5F 59
   OL9: O'ham 4E 29
   SK14: Hyde 5F 73
Ryall Av. M5: Sal 2D 65
Ryall Av. Sth. M5: Sal 2D 65
Ryan St. M11: Man 3A 70
Rydal Av. M24: Mid 3B 26
   M30: Ecc .3D 47
   M33: Sale 3B 88
   M41: Urm .5C 74
   M43: Droy 1A 70
   OL9: Chad 5F 17
   SK14: Hyde 5E 73
Rydal Cl. M34: Dent 3D 85
   SK8: Gat 2D 111
Rydal Cres. M27: Swin 1B 48
   M28: Walk 3A 32
Rydal Gro. M45: White 3C 58
   OL7: A Lyme 1C 22
Rydal Ho. M28: Walk 4A 32
             (off Sandwich St.)
Rydal Mt. SK5: Stoc 3B 84
   OL4: O'ham 2F 29
Rydal Rd. M32: Stre 2F 77
   OL4: O'ham 2F 29
Rydal Wlk. OL4: O'ham 5D 87
Ryde Av. M34: Dent 1D 105
   SK4: Stoc 1D 105
Ryder Av. WA14: Alt 4A 98
RYDER BROW .2F 83
Ryder Brow M18: Man 1F 83
Ryder Brow Rd.
   M18: Man 1F 83
Ryder Brow Station (Rail) 1F 83
Ryder St. M40: Man 3E 53
Ryebank Gro. OL6: A Lyme 2F 59
Ryebank M. M21: Chor 3C 78
Rye Bank Rd. M16: Old T 4B 78
Ryebank Rd. M21: Chor 3C 78
Ryeburn Av. M22: Wyth 3F 109
Ryeburne St. OL4: O'ham 2E 31
Ryeburn Wlk. M41: Urm 1B 74
Ryecroft M45: White 2E 21
Ryecroft Av. M6: Sal 4E 49

Ryecroft Bus. Cen.
   OL7: A Lyme 1B 72
               (off Ryecroft St.)
Ryecroft Cl. OL9: Chad 1B 42
             (not continuous)
Ryecroft Gro. M23: Wyth 4C 100
Ryecroft Ho. OL7: A Lyme 5A 116
Ryecroft La. M28: Wors 3B 46
   M34: Aud .3A 72
Ryecroft Rd. M32: Stre 4E 77
Ryecroft St. OL7: A Lyme 1B 72
Ryecroft Vw. M34: Aud 2E 71
Ryedale Av. M40: Man 2A 54
Ryedale Cl. SK4: Stoc 5D 95
Ryefield OL7: A Lyme 1B 72
Ryefield Av. WA15: Tim 5E 99
Ryefield Cl. WA15: Tim 5E 99
Rye Wlk. M13: Man 5E 67
             (off Carmoor Rd.)
   OL9: Chad 3C 28
Rygate Wlk. M8: Man 1B 52
          (off Felthorpe Dr.)
Rylance St. M11: Man 1A 68
Ryland Cl. SK5: Stoc 4B 84
Rylands Ct. M15: Man 4F 65
          (off Stretford Rd.)
Rylands St. M18: Man 4A 70
Rylane Wlk. M40: Man 2A 54
Rylatt Ct. M33: Sale 3B 88
           (off Ashton La.)
Rylstone Av. M21: Chor 5F 91
Ryther Gro. M9: Man 4D 25
Ryton Av. M18: Man 2E 83

S

Sabden Cl. M40: Man 4A 54
Sabrina St. M8: Man 2A 52
Sack St. SK14: Hyde 5F 73
Sackville Pl. M1: Man 3D 11
Sackville St. M1: Man 2D 11 (2C 66)
   M3: Sal 4E 5
   OL6: A Lyme 1C 116 (4D 59)
Saddlecote M28: Wors 3C 46
Saddlecote Cl. M8: Man 4D 39
Saddle Gro. M43: Droy 4F 57
Saddlewood Av.
   M19: Man 1F 103
Sadie Av. M32: Stre 1C 76
Sadler Cl. M15: Man 5A 66
Sadler St. M24: Mid 5B 16
Safflower Av. M27: Swin 4F 33
Saffron Wlk. M22: Wyth 1F 113
Sagars Rd. SK9: Sty 5D 115
Sagar St. M8: Man 3B 52
Sahal Ct. M7: Sal 3F 51
St Agnes Rd. M13: Man 3B 82
St Agnes St. SK5: Stoc 2B 84
St Aidans Cl. M26: Rad 1B 20
St Aidan's Gro. M7: Sal 1D 51
St Albans Av. M40: Man 2D 55
   OL6: A Lyme 1D 59
   SK4: Stoc .3E 95
St Albans Cl. OL8: O'ham 5B 30
St Alban's Ter. M8: Man 2A 52
St Aldwyn's Rd. M20: Man 3D 93
St Ambrose Cl. OL1: O'ham 1E 31
St Ambrose Gdns. M6: Sal 5B 50
          (off Blodwell St.)
St Ambrose Rd. OL1: O'ham 1E 31

St Andelm Hall M14: Man 2F 81
St Andrews Av. M30: Ecc 1A 62
    M43: Droy .1A 70
    WA15: Tim 4A 98
St Andrews Cl. SK4: Stoc 4D 95
St Andrews Cl. SK1: Stoc 2C 106
St Andrews Rd. M32: Stre 3D 77
    SK4: Stoc .4D 95
    SK8: H Grn 5E 111
St Andrew's Sq. M1: Man 2E 67
St Andrew's St. M1: Man 2E 67
St Annes Av. M6: Sal 4A 50
St Annes Av. M6: Sal 3B 50
                    (off Brindle St.)
    M33: Sale .4E 89
    M34: Aud .4A 72
St Anne's Dr. M34: Dent 1C 86
St Annes Rd. M21: Chor 1D 91
    M34: Dent 5B 72
St Annes's Rd. M34: Aud 4B 72
St Ann's All. M2: Man 5A 6
St Ann's Arc. M2: Man 5B 6
St Ann's Chyd. M2: Man 5B 6
St Anns Cl. M25: Pres 1C 36
St Ann's Pas. M2: Man 5B 6
St Ann's Pl. M2: Man 5A 6
St Ann's Rd. M25: Pres 5A 6
St Ann's Rd. Nth. SK8: H Grn 5E 111
St Ann's Rd. Sth.
    SK8: H Grn 5E 111
St Ann's Sq. M2: Man 5B 6 (1B 66)
    SK8: H Grn 1E 115
St Ann's St. M27: Swin 4A 34
    M33: Sale .5B 90
St Ann St. M2: Man 5A 6 (1B 66)
St Asaph's Dr. M7: Sal 4B 38
    OL6: A Lyme 1D 59
St Augustine's Rd. SK3: Stoc 3D 105
St Augustine St. M40: Man 2F 53
St Austell Dr. SK8: H Grn 1D 115
St Austell Rd. M16: W Ran 4A 80
St Austells Dr. M25: Pres 4D 23
    M27: Pen .5E 35
St Barnabas Sq. M11: Man 2D 69
St Bartholomew's Dr.
    M5: Sal 2A 8 (2E 65)
St Bees Cl. M14: Man 1C 80
    SK8: Gat 3D 111
St Bees Wlk. M24: Mid 4A 16
St Benedict's Av. M12: Man 4B 68
St Bernards Av. M6: Sal 2E 51
St Bernards Cl. M6: Sal 2E 51
St Boniface Rd. M7: Sal 3E 51
St Brannock's Rd. M21: Chor 4E 79
St Brelades Dr. M7: Sal 4B 38
St Brendan's Rd. M20: Man 1D 93
St Brendan's Rd. Nth. M20: Man 1D 93
St Bride St. M16: Old T 5F 65
St Brides Way M16: Old T 5F 65
St Catherine's Rd. M20: Man 1D 93
St Chads Cres. OL8: O'ham 3F 43
St Chads Rd. M20: Man 1F 93
St Chad's St. M4: Man 1C 6 (3C 52)
St Christopher's Av. OL6: A Lyme 1F 59
St Christophers Ct. M20: Man 2B 92
St Christophers Ho. SK1: Stoc 5C 118
St Christopher's Rd.
    OL6: A Lyme 1F 59
St Clement Cl. M41: Urm 4F 75
                    (off Manor Av.)

St Clements Ct. M25: Pres 5E 23
    OL8: O'ham 5E 117
St Clements Dr. M5: Sal 5A 8 (3D 65)
St Clements Fold M41: Urm 3A 76
St Clement's Rd. M21: Chor 5C 78
St Cuthbert's Fold OL8: O'ham 3C 44
St Davids Cl. M33: Sale 5C 88
    OL6: A Lyme 5F 45
St Davids Ct. M8: Man 2C 52
St David's Rd. SK8: Chea 5C 104
St David's Wlk. M32: Stre 3C 76
St Domingo St. OL9: O'ham 2A 30
St Dominics Way M24: Mid 2C 26
St Dunstan Wlk. M40: Man 1C 54
               (off Craiglands Av.)
St Edmund's Rd. M40: Man 1A 54
St Elisabeth's Way
    SK5: Stoc 1A 96
St Elizabeth Pk. M34: Dent 2F 85
St Elmo Av. SK2: Stoc 4F 107
St Gabriel's Hall M14: Man 1E 81
St Gabriels M. M24: Mid 2E 27
ST GEORGES 5C 8 (4F 65)
St George's Av. M15: Man 5C 8 (4F 65)
    WA15: Tim 4C 98
St Georges Ct. BL9: Bury 3E 13
    M15: Man .5D 9
                  (off Angela St.)
    M30: Ecc .1B 62
              (off Bentcliffe Way)
    M32: Stre .4E 77
    SK14: Hyde 3F 87
St George's Cres. M6: Sal 4C 48
    WA15: Tim 3C 98
St Georges Dr. M40: Man 5D 41
    SK14: Hyde 4F 87
St George's Gdns. M34: Dent 4C 86
St Georges Pl. M6: Sal 2C 50
                  (off Gerald Rd.)
St Georges Rd. BL9: Bury 2E 13
    M14: Man .1A 94
    M32: Stre .3E 77
    M43: Droy .4B 56
St George's Sq. OL9: Chad 1F 41
St Georges Way M6: Sal 3C 50
St Gregory's Rd. M12: Man 3E 67
St Helier's Dr. M7: Sal 4B 38
St Helier Sq. M19: Man 3B 94
St Herberts Ct.
    OL9: Chad 2D 29
St Hilda's Cl. M22: Nor 2A 102
St Hilda's Dr. OL1: O'ham 1F 29
St Hilda's Rd. M16: Old T 5E 65
    M22: Nor .2F 101
    M34: Aud .4A 72
St Hilda's Vw. M34: Aud 5A 72
St Hugh's Cl. WA14: Tim 3A 98
St Ignatius Wlk. M5: Sal 2D 65
             (off King Edward St.)
St Ives Av. SK8: Chea 5C 104
St Ives Cres. M33: Sale 2C 98
St Ives Rd. M14: Man 3D 81
St James Cl. M6: Sal 4D 49
St James Ct. M6: Sal 4D 49
    M20: Man .5D 93
              (off Moorland Rd.)
    M20: Man 2D 103
               (Millgate La.)
    OL4: O'ham 1E 31
St James Dr. M33: Sale 5C 88

St James Gro. WA14: Tim 2B **98**
St James Ho. *M6: Sal* *4B* **50**
    (off Pendleton Way)
  SK4: Stoc .5F **95**
St James Rd. M7: Sal 1A **52**
  SK4: Stoc .3D **95**
St James's Sq.
  M2: Man .1B **10**
St James St. M1: Man 2B **10** (2C **66**)
  M30: Ecc .5A **48**
  OL1: O'ham 2D **31**
  OL6: A Lyme 5F **59**
St Johns Av. M43: Droy 5D **57**
St John's Ct. *M6: Sal* *3B* **50**
    (off Milford St.)
                     .1F **51**
    (off Wellington St. W.)
St John's Pas. M3: Man 2F **9** (2A **66**)
St John's Pl. SK4: Stoc 1A **104**
St John's Rd. M13: Man 1B **82**
  M16: Old T 1E **79**
  M34: Dent 5B **72**
  SK4: Stoc 1A **104**
St Johns Sq. M3: Sal 4D **5**
St John's St. BL4: Kea 1A **18**
  M7: Sal 1F **51**
  OL9: O'ham 4E **29**
St John St. M3: Man 2F **9** (2A **66**)
  M27: Pen .1F **49**
  M30: Ecc .1F **61**
  SK16: Duk 2F **73**
    (not continuous)
St Johns Wlk. OL9: O'ham 3E **29**
  SK3: Stoc *3D* **105**
    (off Oak St.)
St Joseph's Av. M45: White 2D **23**
St Joseph's Dr. M5: Sal 2D **65**
St Kilda Av. BL4: Kea 3B **18**
St Kilda's Av. M43: Droy 4B **56**
St Kilda's Dr. M7: Sal 4B **38**
St Lawrence Ct. M34: Dent 3B **86**
St Lawrence Quay M50: Sal 3B **64**
St Lawrence Rd. M34: Dent 2B **86**
St Leonard's Ct. M33: Sale 4F **65**
St Leonards Dr. WA15: Tim 5B **98**
St Leonards Rd. SK4: Stoc 3F **95**
St Leonards Sq. *M24: Mid* *5C* **16**
    (off Clarke Brow)
St Leonards St. M24: Mid 5C **16**
St Lesmo Ct. SK3: Stoc 4E **105**
St Lesmo Rd. SK3: Stoc 3D **105**
St Lukes Ct. OL9: Chad 2C **28**
St Lukes Cres. SK16: Duk 2E **73**
St Luke's Rd. M6: Sal 5F **49**
St Lukes Wlk. *M40: Man* *1C* **54**
    (off Rollswood Dr.)
St Margaret's Av. M19: Man 2B **94**
St Margarets Cl. M25: Pres 3E **23**
St Margaret's Gdns. OL8: O'ham 1E **43**
St Margaret's Rd. M25: Pres 3E **23**
  M40: Man 1F **41**
  SK8: Chea 5C **104**
St Marks Ct. *M22: Wyth* *4E* **109**
    (off Stoneacre Rd.)
  OL9: Chad 1D **29**
  SK16: Duk 5C **116** (1D **73**)
St Marks Cres. M28: Walk 3A **32**
St Mark's La. M7: Sal 5B **38**
  M8: Man .5B **38**

St Marks St. M19: Man 4E **83**
  SK16: Duk 5B **116** (1D **73**)
St Martin's Av. SK4: Stoc 1E **105**
St Martin's Cl.
  M43: Droy 4B **56**
St Martin's Dr. M7: Sal 4B **38**
St Martins Rd. M33: Sale 2A **88**
  OL8: O'ham 2C **44**
St Mary's Apartments *M25: Pres* *5C* **22**
    (off The Coppice)
St Mary's Av. M34: Dent 5C **86**
St Mary's Cl. M25: Pres 5C **22**
St Marys Cl. SK1: Stoc 2C **106**
St Marys Ct. *M8: Man* *3B* **38**
    (off St Mary's Hall Rd.)
  M19: Man *4C* **82**
    (off Elbow St.)
  M25: Pres 5C **22**
  M40: Man 4D **41**
  OL1: O'ham 2D **117**
St Mary's Dr. SK5: Stoc 2B **96**
  SK8: Chea 5B **104**
St Mary's Est. OL1: O'ham 2E **117**
St Mary's Ga. M1: Man 4B **6** (5B **52**)
  SK1: Stoc 2C **118** (1B **106**)
St Mary's Hall Rd. M8: Man 3B **38**
St Mary's Parsonage M3: Man . . .5F **5** (1A **66**)
St Marys Rd. M25: Pres 5C **22**
  M30: Ecc .5B **48**
  M33: Sale 3B **88**
  M40: Man 5D **41**
St Mary's St. M3: Man 5A **6** (1B **66**)
  M15: Man 5A **66**
  OL1: O'ham 1E **117** (1B **30**)
St Mary St. M3: Sal 4D **5**
St Marys Way OL1: O'ham 2D **117** (2A **30**)
  SK1: Stoc 1C **106**
St Matthews Cl. M32: Stre 4E **77**
St Matthew's Rd. SK3: Stoc 3F **105**
St Matthew's Ter. SK3: Stoc 3F **105**
St Michael's & All Angels Church *5E* **59**
    (off Park Pde.)
St Michaels Ct. M27: Ward 2F **33**
  M30: Ecc .2C **60**
  M33: Sale 2A **88**
St Michaels Gdns. M45: White 5D **13**
St Michael's Pl. M4: Man 1D **7**
St Michael's Sq. M4: Man 2D **7** (4C **52**)
  OL6: A Lyme 4E **59**
St Modwen Rd. M32: Stre 5B **62**
St Nicholas Rd. M15: Man 5E **9** (3A **66**)
St Oswalds Rd. M19: Man 3D **83**
St Pauls Cl. M26: Rad 1C **20**
St Pauls Ct. *M7: Sal* *3E* **37**
  M28: Walk 1A **32**
  OL8: O'ham 5B **30**
St Paul's Gdns. *M7: Sal* *3E* **37**
    (off St Paul's Rd.)
St Paul's M. *SK1: Stoc* *5D* **97**
    (off St Paul's St.)
St Paul's Ri. *M7: Sal* *3E* **37**
    (off St Paul's Rd.)
St Paul's Rd. M7: Sal 3E **37**
  M20: Man 2E **93**
  M28: Walk 2A **32**
  SK4: Stoc 4D **95**
St Paul's St. SK1: Stoc 5C **96**
St Petersburgh Way
  M22: Wyth 3E **109**
St Peters Cl. OL7: A Lyme 5B **58**

St Peter's Ct. *M32*: Stre 2A **78**
    (off Burleigh Rd.)
St Petersgate SK1: Stoc 3A **118** (2A **106**)
St Peter's Rd. M27: Swin 5A **34**
St Peter's Sq. M2: Man 2B **10** (2B **66**)
  SK1: Stoc 2A **118** (2A **106**)
St Peters St. OL6: A Lyme 4A **116** (5C **58**)
St Philip's Pl. M3: Sal 4C **4** (5F **51**)
St Philip's Rd. M18: Man 1F **83**
St Philips Sq. *M3: Sal* 4C **4**
    (off Bank St.)
Saintsbridge Rd. M22: Wyth 4E **109**
St Simons Cl. SK2: Stoc 3E **107**
St Simon St. M3: Sal 1D **5** (4F **51**)
St Stephen's Av. M34: Aud 2A **72**
St Stephens Cl. M13: Man 5F **67**
St Stephens Ct. *M9: Man* 5F **39**
    (off Shieldborn Dr.)
St Stephens Gdns. BL4: Kea 3C **18**
  M24: Mid 4C **16**
St Stephens St. BL4: Kea 3C **18**
  OL1: O'ham 1C **30**
St Stephen St. M3: Sal 4D **5** (5F **51**)
St Stephens Vw. M43: Droy 5C **56**
St Teresa's Cl. M16: Old T 2C **78**
St Thomas Circ. OL8: O'ham 4F **29**
St Thomas' Pl. M8: Man 3C **52**
St Thomas's Pl.
  SK1: Stoc 5B **118** (3B **106**)
St Thomas St. Nth. OL8: O'ham 4F **29**
St Thomas St. Sth. OL8: O'ham 4F **29**
St Vincent St. M4: Man 5E **53**
St Werburgh's Rd. M21: Chor 4E **79**
St Wilfrid's St. M15: Man 5E **9** (4A **66**)
Salcombe Cl. M33: Sale 3A **88**
Salcombe Rd. M11: Man 2F **69**
  SK2: Stoc 3E **107**
Salcot Wlk. *M40: Man* 4E **53**
    (off Eastburn Av.)
SALE 2D **89**
Sale Circ. M23: Wyth 1D **101**
Sale Heys Rd. M33: Sale 5B **88**
Sale Leisure Cen. 3E **89**
SALEM 4F **31**
Salem Gro. OL4: O'ham 3F **31**
Sale Rd. M23: Wyth 1B **100**
Sale Sharks RUFC 4A **106**
Sale Station (Metro) 4D **89**
Sale Water Pk. 1F **89**
SALFORD 4D **5** (2D **65**)
Salford App. M3: Sal 3A **6** (5B **52**)
Salford Central Station (Rail)
. . . . .5E **5** (1A **66**)
Salford City Reds RLFC 5F **49**
Salford Crescent Station (Rail) 5D **51**
Salford Ent. Cen. M50: Ecc 1E **63**
Salford Foyer M6: Sal 4B **50**
Salford Mus. & Art Gallery 3A **4** (5E **51**)
SALFORD QUAYS 3B **64**
Salford Quays Station (Metro) 3C **64**
Salford Roman Catholic Cathedral 4D **5**
Salford Shop. City M6: Sal 4B **50**
Salford Sports Village 5C **36**
Salford St. OL4: O'ham 4F **31**
Salford University Bus. Pk.
  M6: Sal 1A **4** (4D **51**)
Salford University Climbing Wall 2A **4**
Salford Watersports Cen. 3B **64**
Salisbury Cres. OL6: A Lyme 5F **45**
Salisbury Dr. M25: Pres 2E **37**

Salisbury Ho. M1: Man 3D **11**
  M3: Sal 3E **5**
Salisbury Rd. M21: Chor 4D **79**
  M27: Swin .5A **34**
  M30: Ecc 3B **48**
  M41: Urm 1F **75**
  OL4: O'ham 3D **31**
  WA14: B'ath 4A **98**
Salisbury St. M14: Man 1C **80**
  M24: Mid 5D **17**
Salisbury St. M45: White 1B **22**
  SK5: Stoc .5B **84**
Salix Ct. M6: Sal 4C **50**
Sally's Yd. M1: Man 4C **10**
Salmon St. M4: Man 4D **7** (5C **52**)
Salop St. M6: Sal 3C **50**
Saltash Cl. M22: Wyth 5F **109**
Saltdene Rd. M22: Wyth 5E **109**
Saltergate M. *M5: Sal* 1C **64**
    (off Cavell Way)
Salterton Wlk. *M40: Man* 5D **40**
    (off Hugo St.)
Salteye Rd. M30: Ecc 1C **60**
Saltford Av. M4: Man 5E **53**
Saltford Ct. M4: Man 5F **53**
Salthill Dr. M22: Wyth 4A **110**
Saltire Gdns. M7: Sal 4A **38**
Saltney Av. M20: Man 1B **92**
Saltrush Rd. M22: Wyth 4F **109**
Salutation St. M15: Man 4B **66**
Salvin Wlk. *M9: Man* 1A **40**
    (off Rockmead Dr.)
Sam Cowan Cl. M14: Man 2C **80**
Samian Gdns. M7: Sal 2E **51**
Samlesbury Cl. M20: Man 5B **92**
Sammy Cookson Cl. M14: Man 2C **80**
Samouth Cl. M40: Man 4F **53**
Sampson Sq. M14: Man 1C **80**
Sam Swire St. M15: Man 5B **66**
Samuel Ogden St. M1: Man 3D **11** (2C **66**)
Samuel St. M19: Man 5D **83**
  M24: Mid 4C **16**
  M35: Fail 4B **42**
  SK4: Stoc .5F **95**
Sanby Av. M18: Man 1E **83**
Sanby Rd. M18: Man 1E **83**
Sanctuary, The M15: Man 5F **9** (4A **66**)
Sanctuary Cl. M15: Man 5D **67**
Sandacre Rd. M23: Wyth 4D **101**
Sandal St. M40: Man 4A **54**
Sandbach Av. M14: Man 5B **80**
Sandbach Rd. M33: Sale 5B **90**
  SK5: Stoc .3A **84**
Sandbrook Way M34: Dent 5B **72**
Sanderling Dr. M8: Man 2A **52**
Sanderson Cl. M28: Wors 4D **33**
Sanderson Ct. *M40: Man* 2A **54**
    (off Redbrook Av.)
Sanderson St. M40: Man 2A **54**
Sanderstead Dr. M9: Man 1A **40**
Sandfold SK5: Stoc 3A **84**
Sandfold La. M19: Man 3E **83**
  SK5: Stoc .3A **84**
Sandford Av. M18: Man 4F **69**
Sandford Rd. M33: Sale 5B **90**
Sandford St. M3: Sal 2E **5** (4A **52**)
Sandgate Av. M11: Man 5F **55**
  M26: Rad 2D **19**

Sandgate Dr. M41: Urm 1E **75**
Sandgate Rd. M45: Pres, White . . .2D **23**
    OL9: Chad 3D **29**
Sandheys M34: Dent 5B **72**
Sandheys Gro. M18: Man 1A **84**
Sandhill Wlk. M22: Wyth 4D **109**
Sandhole Rd. BL4: Kea 3C **18**
Sandhurst Av. M20: Man 2C **92**
Sandhurst Rd. M20: Man 1D **103**
    SK2: Stoc 5D **107**
Sandhurst St. OL8: O'ham 5E **31**
Sandhutton St. Man 3F **39**
Sandilands Rd. M23: Wyth 3F **99**
Sandilea Ct. M7: Sal 3C **36**
Sandileigh Av. M20: Man 3D **93**
    SK5: Stoc 4D **97**
    SK8: Chea 5C **104**
Sandimoss Ct. M33: Sale 4B **88**
Sandiway Dr. M20: Man 5C **92**
Sandiway Pl. WA14: Alt 5A **98**
Sandiway Rd. M33: Sale 4B **88**
    SK9: Hand 4F **115**
    WA14: Alt 5A **98**
Sandmere Wlk. M9: Man 1A **40**
    (off Rockmead Dr.)
Sandown Av. M6: Sal 5A **50**
Sandown Cl. OL1: O'ham 1C **30**
Sandown Cres. M18: Man 2F **83**
Sandown Dr. M33: Sale 5A **88**
    M34: Dent 5D **87**
Sandown Rd. BL9: Bury 3C **12**
    SK3: Stoc 3D **105**
Sandown St. M18: Man 4A **70**
Sandpiper Cl. SK16: Duk 3F **73**
Sandpiper Dr. SK3: Stoc 5F **105**
Sandray Gro. M5: Sal 1A **64**
Sandridge Cl. BL4: Kea 1A **18**
Sandridge Wlk. M12: Man 4A **68**
    (off Martindale Cres.)
Sandringham Av. M34: Aud 4F **71**
    M34: Dent 2C **84**
Sandringham Cl. M9: Man 4C **24**
    (off Deanswood Dr.)
    M23: Wyth 3E **99**
Sandringham Dr. SK4: Stoc 2C **104**
Sandringham Grange M25: Pres 1A **38**
Sandringham Rd. SK6: Bred 5E **97**
    SK14: Hyde 5F **87**
Sandringham St. M18: Man 1E **83**
Sands Av. OL9: Chad 3A **52**
Sandsend Cl. M8: Man 2E **75**
Sandsend Rd. M41: Urm 1F **91**
Sandstone Way M21: Chor 3E **53**
Sand St. M40: Man 2D **89**
Sandwell Dr. M33: Sale 2D **89**
Sandwich Rd. M30: Ecc 4B **48**
Sandwich St. M28: Walk 2A **32**
Sandy Bank Rd. M8: Man 4B **38**
Sandybrook Dr. M9: Man 2E **39**
Sandy Brow M9: Man 2F **39**
Sandy Cl. BL9: Bury 2B **12**
Sandycroft Av. M22: Wyth 3F **109**
Sandygate Cl. M27: Swin 5A **34**
Sandy Gro. M6: Sal 4A **50**
    M27: Swin 4B **34**
    SK16: Duk 2F **73**
Sandyhill Ct. M9: Man 1C **38**
Sandyhill Rd. M9: Man 1C **38**
Sandylands Dr. M25: Pres 3C **36**

Sandy La. M6: Sal 4A **50**
    M21: Chor 5D **79**
    M23: Wyth 4A **100**
    M24: Mid 1E **27**
    M25: Pres 1B **36**
    M32: Stre 1A **80**
    M43: Droy 4E **57**
    SK5: Stoc 5A **96**
    SK16: Duk 2F **73**
Sandy Meade M25: Pres 1C **36**
Sandys Av. OL8: O'ham 1F **43**
Sandyshot Wlk. M22: Wyth 3B **110**
Sandy Va. SK16: Duk 1F **73**
Sandyway M25: Pres 1C **36**
Sandywell Cl. M11: Man 3F **69**
Sandywell St. M11: Man 2F **69**
Sandywood M6: Sal 4A **50**
Sangster Ct. M5: Sal 2C **64**
Sankey Gro. M9: Man 1D **39**
Santiago St. M14: Man 2D **81**
Santley St. M12: Man 2C **82**
Santon Av. M14: Man 5A **82**
Sapling Gro. M33: Sale 1A **98**
Sapling Rd. M27: Swin 2F **47**
SARAH MOOR 1B **30**
Sarah St. M11: Man 2B **68**
    M24: Mid 1B **26**
    M30: Ecc 1D **61**
    OL8: O'ham 2F **43**
Sargent Dr. M16: W Ran 1A **80**
Sargent Rd. SK6: Bred 1F **107**
Sark Rd. M21: Chor 3C **78**
Sarn Av. M22: Wyth 2F **109**
Sarnesfield Cl. M12: Man 1C **82**
Sarnia Ct. M7: Sal 5F **37**
    (off Bk. Hope St.)
Satinwood Wlk. M3: Sal 2E **5**
Saturn Gro. M6: Sal 3E **51**
Saunton Rd. M11: Man 2F **69**
Saville Rd. SK8: Gat 5D **103**
Saville St. M24: Mid 2F **27**
Savio Way M24: Mid 2C **26**
Savoy Cinema
    Stockport 5D **95**
Savoy Ct. M45: White 4A **12**
Savoy St. OL4: O'ham 4D **31**
Sawley Av. M45: White 4B **12**
    OL4: O'ham 5F **31**
Sawley Rd. M40: Man 3F **53**
Sawston Wlk. M40: Man 1E **41**
Saxbrook Wlk. M22: Wyth 3B **110**
Saxby St. M6: Sal 2E **49**
Saxelby Dr. M8: Man 1D **53**
Saxfield Dr. M23: Wyth 5E **101**
Saxholme Wlk. M22: Wyth 4E **109**
Saxon Av. M8: Man 3C **38**
    SK16: Duk 2E **73**
Saxon Cl. M33: Sale 5D **89**
Saxon Dr. M34: Aud 3A **72**
    M43: Droy 5D **57**
    OL9: Chad 1A **28**
Saxon Ho. M16: W Ran 2F **79**
Saxonside M24: Mid 3A **16**
Saxon St. M24: Mid 1D **27**
    M34: Dent 2B **86**
    M40: Man 4A **54**
    M43: Droy 5D **57**
    OL4: O'ham 2E **31**
Saxthorpe Wlk. M12: Man 5A **68**
    (off Britnall Av.)

Saxwood Av. M9: Man 3F **39**
Scafell Av. OL7: A Lyme 3B **58**
Scafell Cl. OL1: O'ham 1B **30**
 (not continuous)
Scalby Wlk. M22: Wyth 5F **109**
Scale St. *M5: Sal* *1C 64*
 (off Christopher St.)
Scarborough St. M40: Man 4C **40**
Scarcroft Rd. M12: Man 5C **68**
Scargill Cl. M14: Man 5E **81**
Scarisbrick Av. M20: Man 5F **93**
Scarisbrick Rd. M19: Man 5B **82**
Scarr Wheel M7: Sal 5E **37**
Scarsdale Rd. M14: Man 1A **82**
Scarsdale St. M6: Sal 4D **51**
Scawton Wlk. M9: Man 4D **25**
Schofield Cl. M24: Mid 3C **16**
Schofield Rd. M30: Ecc 1C **60**
 M43: Droy 1D **71**
Schofield St. M11: Man 1E **69**
 M35: Fail 4B **42**
 OL8: O'ham 1A **44**
Scholar Grn. Rd. M32: Stre 5C **62**
Scholars Ct. M27: Clif 1A **34**
Scholars Dr. M20: Man 1C **92**
Scholar's Way M24: Mid 5B **16**
Scholes Cl. M7: Sal 4B **38**
Scholes Dr. M40: Man 2A **42**
Scholes La. M25: Pres 1D **37**
Scholes St. M27: Swin 4C **34**
 M35: Fail 3C **42**
 OL1: O'ham 3F **117** (2C **30**)
 OL9: Chad 5C **28**
Scholes Wlk. M25: Pres 1D **37**
Scholfield Av. M41: Urm 4B **76**
School Av. M32: Stre 2B **78**
School Brow M28: Wors 1B **46**
School Ct. M4: Man 3F **7** (5E **53**)
 SK3: Stoc 5B **106**
School Gro. M20: Man 2E **93**
 M25: Pres 2C **36**
School Ho. Flats OL8: O'ham 2D **43**
School Ho. Rd. OL4: O'ham 4E **31**
School La. M9: Man 2E **39**
 M19: Man 5D **93**
 M20: Man 5D **93**
 SK4: Stoc 3E **95**
School Rd. M30: Ecc 2E **61**
 M32: Stre 3E **77**
 M33: Sale 3D **89**
 (not continuous)
 M35: Fail 5B **42**
 OL8: O'ham 2D **43**
 SK9: Hand 5F **115**
Schools Hill SK8: Chea 3F **111**
Schoolside Cl. M8: Man 1D **53**
Schoolside La. M24: Mid 2D **25**
Schools Rd. M18: Man 5A **70**
School St. M4: Man 2E **7** (4C **52**)
 M7: Sal 1E **5** (3A **52**)
 M30: Ecc 4D **47**
 OL8: O'ham 4F **29**
School Wlk. M16: Old T 5F **65**
School Yd. SK4: Stoc 1A **104**
Schuster Rd. M14: Man 2F **81**
Schwabe St. M24: Mid 1E **25**
Scoltock Way
 OL1: O'ham 2E **117** (2B **30**)
Score St. M11: Man 1C **68**

Scorton Wlk. *M40: Man* *2F 41*
 (off Blandford Dr.)
Scotforth Cl. M15: Man 5E **9** (3A **66**)
Scotland Hall Rd. M40: Man 2D **55**
Scotland Rd. M4: Man 2C **6** (4C **52**)
Scotland St. M40: Man 2E **55**
 OL6: A Lyme 4E **59**
Scotta Rd. M30: Ecc 2D **61**
Scott Av. BL9: Bury 1B **12**
 M21: Chor 3D **79**
 M30: Ecc 4E **47**
Scott Cl. SK5: Stoc 4B **96**
Scottfield OL8: O'ham 4A **30**
Scottfield Rd. OL8: O'ham 4B **30**
Scott Ga. M34: Aud 3A **72**
Scott Pl. M3: Man 1A **10** (1A **66**)
Scott Rd. M25: Pres 1B **36**
 M34: Dent 4A **86**
 M43: Droy 1C **70**
Scott St. M26: Rad 2F **19**
 OL8: O'ham 4B **30**
Scout Dr. M23: Wyth 2B **108**
Scout Grn. M24: Mid 3C **16**
Scovell St. M7: Sal 1F **51**
Scropton St. M40: Man 1F **53**
Seabright Wlk. *M11: Man* *1B 68*
 (off Pilgrim Dr.)
Seabrook Cres. M41: Urm 1E **75**
Seabrook Rd. M40: Man 3E **55**
Seacombe Av. M14: Man 4C **80**
Seacombe Gro. SK3: Stoc 3D **105**
Seaford Rd. M6: Sal 2D **51**
Seaford Wlk. M9: Man 1E **39**
 OL9: Chad 3D **29**
Seaham Dr. *M14: Man* *2D 81*
 (off Head Pl.)
Sealand Cl. M33: Sale 1A **100**
Sealand Dr. M30: Ecc 2C **60**
Sealand Ho. M25: Pres 4E **23**
Sealand Rd. M23: Wyth 1B **100**
Sealand Way SK9: Hand 5F **115**
 (off Henbury Rd.)
Seale Av. M34: Aud 3F **71**
Sealey Wlk. *M40: Man* *3A 54*
Searby Rd. M18: Man 1D **83**
Searness Rd. M24: Mid 4E **15**
Seascale Av. M11: Man 4D **55**
Seascale Wlk. M24: Mid 4A **16**
Seathwaite Cl. M24: Mid 4F **15**
Seathwaite Wlk. *M18: Man* *5E 69*
 (off Hampden Cres.)
Seatoller Dr. M24: Mid 6E **15**
Seaton M. OL7: A Lyme 3A **58**
Seaton Way M14: Man 1C **80**
Second Av. M11: Man 4F **55**
 M17: T Pk 5F **63**
 M27: Swin 2F **47**
 OL8: O'ham 2E **43**
Sedan Cl. M5: Sal 1C **64**
Sedburgh Cl. M33: Sale 5A **88**
Sedbury Cl. M23: Wyth 2B **100**
Seddon Av. M18: Man 4F **69**
 M26: Rad 1A **12**
Seddon Gdns. M26: Rad 1C **18**
Seddon La. M26: Rad 1C **18**
Seddon St. M12: Man 3D **83**
Sedgeborough Rd. M16: W Ran 1A **80**
Sedge Cl. SK5: Stoc 5C **84**
Sedgefield Cl. M5: Sal 5B **50**

Sedgefield Pk. OL4: O'ham 3F 31
Sedgefield Rd. M26: Rad 1B 20
Sedgefield Wlk. M23: Wyth 1B 100
Sedgeford Rd. M40: Man 2F 53
Sedgemoor Way
    OL1: O'ham 2D 117 (2A 30)
Sedgley Av. M25: Pres 2E 37
Sedgley Bldgs. M43: Droy 2C 70
Sedgley Cl. M24: Mid 2E 27
SEDGLEY PARK 2F 37
Sedgley Pk. Rd. M25: Pres 2E 37
Sedgley Pk. RUFC 3A 22
Sedgley Pk. Trad. Est. M25: Pres 3D 37
Sedgley Rd. M8: Man 4C 38
Sedgley St. M24: Mid 2E 27
Sedley Av. M25: Pres 4B 22
SEEDLEY 5A 50
Seedley Pk. Rd. M6: Sal 5A 50
Seedley Rd. M6: Sal 4A 50
Seedley St. M14: Man 2D 81
Seedley Ter. M6: Sal 4A 50
Seedley Vw. Rd. M6: Sal 5F 11 (4D 67)
Sefton Cl. M13: Man 5F 11 (4D 67)
    M24: Mid 1A 26
Sefton Cres. M33: Sale 2D 89
Sefton Dr. M27: Swin 1F 47
    M28: Wors 2C 46
Sefton Rd. M21: Chor 5D 79
    M24: Mid 1A 26
    M27: Pen 3B 34
    M33: Sale 3D 89
Sefton St. M8: Man 4C 38
    M45: White 2B 22
    OL9: O'ham 2D 43
Segal Cl. M7: Sal 5F 37
Selborne Rd. M21: Chor 4D 79
Selbourne Cl. SK5: Stoc 3A 84
Selbourne St. OL8: O'ham 3C 44
Selby Av. M45: White 4B 12
    OL9: Chad 1B 28
Selby Cl. M26: Rad 1A 12
    M32: Stre 2C 76
Selby Dr. M6: Sal 4D 49
    M41: Urm 5B 60
Selby Rd. M24: Mid 3B 16
    M32: Stre 2C 76
Selby St. M11: Man 4F 95
    SK4: Stoc 4E 95
Selden St. OL8: O'ham 4F 29
Selham Wlk. M13: Man 5F 11
Selhurst Av. M11: Man 5F 29
Selkirk Av. OL8: O'ham 3B 44
Selkirk Dr. M9: Man 1B 40
Selkirk Rd. OL9: Chad 2C 70
Sellars Sq. M43: Droy 2C 70
Selsby Av. M30: Ecc 5D 47
Selsey Av. M33: Sale 4B 104
    SK3: Stoc 5B 88
Selsey Dr. M20: Man 3E 103
Selside Wlk. M14: Man 1D 19
                 (off Boland Dr.)
Selstead Rd. M22: Wyth 5E 109
Selston Rd. M9: Man 5D 25
Selwood Wlk. M9: Man 5F 39
           (off Carisbrook St.)
Selworth Av. M33: Sale 4A 90
Selworth Cl. WA15: Tim 5A 98
Selworthy Rd. M16: W Ran 1A 80
Selwyn Av. M9: Man 4F 39

Selwyn St. OL8: O'ham 4A 30
Seminar Cen. 2B 66
     (in Manchester International
                Convention Cen.)
Senior Av. M14: Man 1A 94
Senior Rd. M30: Ecc 2B 60
Senior St. M3: Sal 2F 5 (4A 52)
Sepal Cl. SK5: Stoc 4C 84
Sepia Gro. M24: Mid 5B 16
Sequoia St. M9: Man 4A 40
Sergeants La. M45: White 2E 21
Service St. SK3: Stoc 3D 105
Setantii Vis. Cen. 2C 116
Sevenoaks Av. M41: Urm 1F 75
    SK4: Stoc 3C 94
Sevenoaks Dr. M27: Swin 1C 48
Sevenoaks Rd. SK8: Gat 5D 103
Sevenoaks Wlk. M13: Man 5E 67
          (off Beckhampton Cl.)
Seventh Av. OL8: O'ham 3E 43
Severn Rd. OL8: O'ham 3D 43
              (not continuous)
    OL9: Chad 1B 28
Severnside Trad. Est. M17: T Pk 5D 63
Severn Way BL4: Kea 3D 19
    SK5: Stoc 3C 96
Sewerby St. M16: W Ran 1B 80
Sexa St. M11: Man 2F 69
Seymour Av. M11: Man 5F 55
Seymour Cl. M16: Old T 5E 65
Seymour Ct. M7: Sal 4E 38
    SK4: Stoc 1A 104
Seymour Gro. M16: Old T 5D 65
    M33: Sale 4D 89
    WA15: Tim 5C 98
Seymour Pl. M16: Old T 5D 65
Seymour Rd. M8: Man 3B 38
    SK2: Stoc 5D 107
Seymour Rd. Sth. M11: Man 5F 55
Seymour St. M18: Man 4F 69
    M34: Dent 2F 85
Shackleton Ct. M40: Man 3E 55
Shackleton St. M30: Ecc 4E 47
Shackliffe Rd. M40: Man 2D 41
Shadowbrook Av. M23: Wyth 2C 108
Shadowbrook Cl. OL1: O'ham 1A 30
Shadow Moss Rd. M22: Wyth 2A 114
Shady La. M23: Wyth 4F 99
    WA15: Tim 5C 98
Shaftesbury Av. M30: Ecc 2E 61
    WA15: Tim 5C 98
Shaftesbury Rd. M8: Man 5C 38
    M27: Swin 5B 34
    SK3: Stoc 5C 104
Shafton Wlk. M40: Man 2F 41
           (off Blandford Dr.)
Shakespeare Av. M34: Dent 5B 86
Shakespeare Cres. M30: Ecc 5F 47
    M43: Droy 5C 56
Shakespeare Dr. SK8: Chea 5B 104
             (not continuous)
Shakespeare Rd. M25: Pres 1B 36
    M27: Swin 4F 33
    M43: Droy 5C 56
Shakespeare Wlk. M13: Man 4E 67
Shakleton Av. M9: Man 1C 40
Shaldon Dr. M40: Man 3A 56
Shandon Av. M22: Nor 2F 101
Shanklin Cl. M21: Chor 4C 78
    M34: Dent 5D 87
Shanklin Ho. M21: Chor 4C 78

Shanklyn Av. M41: Urm 3E **75**
Shanley Ct. OL9: Chad 1D **29**
Shannon Rd. M22: Wyth 3A **110**
Shap Av. WA15: Tim 5F **99**
Shap Cres. M28: Walk 3B **32**
Shap Dr. M28: Walk 2B **32**
Shapwick Cl. M9: Man 4F **39**
(off Coningsby Dr.)
Sharcott Cl. M16: W Ran 1B **80**
Shardlow Cl. M40: Man 3F **53**
(off Thornden Rd.)
Sharnbrook Wlk. M8: Man 2A **38**
Sharnford Sq. M12: Man 4C **68**
(off Bridgend Cl.)
Sharon Cl. OL7: A Lyme 1A **72**
Sharples Hall St. OL4: O'ham 1F **31**
Sharples St. SK4: Stoc 5A **96**
Sharp St. M4: Man 2E **7** (4D **53**)
M24: Mid 1C **26**
M25: Pres 5C **22**
M28: Walk 1A **32**
Sharrington Dr. M23: Wyth 5A **100**
Sharrow Wlk. M9: Man 5F **39**
(off Broadwell Dr.)
SHARSTON 5A **102**
Sharston Grn. Bus. Pk. M22: Shar . . .5B **102**
Sharston Ind. Area M22: Shar 4F **101**
(not continuous)
Sharston Rd. M22: Shar 4A **102**
Shaving La. M28: Walk 3A **32**
Shawbrook Rd. M19: Man 2B **94**
Shawbury Gro. M33: Sale 1B **98**
Shawbury Rd. M23: Wyth 2D **109**
Shawbury St. M24: Mid 2E **27**
Shawcross Fold SK1: Stoc 1B **118**
Shawcross La. M22: Nor 3B **102**
Shawcross St. M6: Sal 1B **64**
SK1: Stoc 5C **118** (3C **106**)
Shawdene Rd. M22: Nor 3E **101**
Shawe Hall Av. M41: Urm 5C **74**
Shawe Hall Cres. M41: Urm 5C **74**
Shawe Rd. M41: Urm 3C **74**
Shawe Vw. M41: Urm 3C **74**
Shawfield Cl. M14: Man 5C **80**
Shawfield Ct. SK2: Stoc 5F **107**
Shawford Cres. M40: Man 2E **41**
Shawford Rd. M40: Man 2E **41**
Shawgreen Cl. M15: Man 4F **65**
Shaw Hall M14: Man 1F **81**
(off Daisy Bank Hall)
Shaw Head Dr. M35: Fail 1B **56**
SHAW HEATH 4F **105**
Shaw Heath SK2: Stoc 4B **106**
SK3: Stoc 5A **118** (3A **106**)
Shawheath Cl. M15: Man 4F **65**
Shawhill Wlk. M40: Man 5A **54**
(off Millhead Av.)
Shaw Ho. BL4: Farn 2A **18**
(off Moorfield Chase)
Shawlea Av. M19: Man 2A **94**
Shaw Rd. OL1: O'ham 1C **30**
SK4: Stoc 3D **95**
Shaw Rd. Sth. SK3: Stoc 5A **106**
(not continuous)
Shaws Fold SK9: Sty 5B **114**
Shaw St. M3: Man 2B **6** (4B **52**)
OL1: O'ham 2F **117** (1B **30**)
OL6: A Lyme 4F **59**
Shaw Ter. SK16: Duk 1E **73**
Shay Av. WA15: Haleb 5A **108**

Shayfield Av. M22: Wyth 1F **109**
OL9: Chad 2A **28**
Shayfield Dr. M22: Wyth 5F **101**
Shayfield Rd. M22: Wyth 1F **109**
Shay La. WA15: Haleb 5A **108**
Sheader Dr. M5: Sal 5E **49**
Sheard Av. OL6: A Lyme 1F **59**
Shearer Way M27: Pen 4F **35**
Shearsby Cl. M15: Man 5A **66**
Shearwater Gdns. M30: Ecc 2C **60**
Shearwater Ho. M19: Man 4F **93**
Sheepfoot La. M25: Pres 1F **37**
Sheerness St. M18: Man 5F **69**
Sheffield St. M1: Man 2F **11** (2D **67**)
SK4: Stoc 5A **96**
Shefford Cl. M11: Man 2B **68**
Shelderton Cl. M40: Man 5C **40**
Sheldon Av. M41: Urm 3D **75**
Sheldon Cl. OL7: A Lyme 2D **59**
Sheldon St. M11: Man 5D **55**
Sheldrake Cl. SK16: Duk 3F **73**
Shelford Av. M18: Man 1D **83**
Shelley Av. M24: Mid 4D **17**
Shelley Gro. M43: Droy 5C **56**
SK14: Hyde 5F **73**
Shelley Rd. M25: Pres 1B **36**
M27: Swin 4F **33**
OL9: Chad 1B **42**
SK5: Stoc 4F **83**
Shelley St. M40: Man 4E **41**
Shelley Way M34: Dent 5B **86**
Shelmerdine Gdns. M6: Sal 3E **49**
Shelton Av. M33: Sale 4A **88**
Shenfield Wlk. M40: Man 4F **53**
(off Farnborough Rd.)
Shentonfield Rd. M22: Shar 5A **102**
Shenton St. SK14: Hyde 1E **87**
Shepherd St. M9: Man 3A **40**
Shepherd Wlk. M34: Dent 5B **86**
Shepley Cl. SK16: Duk 2F **73**
(off Jeffreys Dr.)
Shepley Ind. Est. Nth. M34: Aud 3C **72**
Shepley Ind. Est. Sth. M34: Aud 4C **72**
Shepley Rd. M34: Aud 4B **72**
Shepley St. M34: Aud 3B **72**
M35: Fail 3C **42**
Shepton Dr. M23: Wyth 4C **108**
Shepway Ct. M30: Ecc 5D **47**
Sheraton Rd. M22: Shar 5A **30**
Sherborne Ho. M24: Mid 3C **16**
Sherborne Rd. SK3: Stoc 4C **104**
Sherborne St. M3: Man 1F **5** (3B **52**)
M8: Man 3B **52**
Sherborne St. Trad. Est. M8: Man . . .2C **52**
Sherborne St. W. M3: Sal . . .1F **5** (4A **52**)
Sherbourne Cl. OL8: O'ham 5E **31**
Sherbourne Rd. M25: Pres 5C **22**
Sherbourne Rd. M24: Mid 3C **16**
M41: Urm 2A **76**
Sherbrooke Cl. M25: Pres 5C **22**
Sherbrooke Rd. M33: Sale 5B **88**
Sherdley Cl. M8: Man 3C **38**
Sherdley Rd. M8: Man 3C **38**
Sheridan Ct. M40: Man 2A **54**
(off Ridgewood Av.)
Sheridan Way M34: Dent 5B **86**
OL9: Chad 1A **28**
Sheringham Dr. M27: Swin 1B **48**
Sheringham Rd. M14: Man 1F **93**
Sherlock St. M14: Man 1F **93**

Sherratt St. M4: Man 3F 7 (5D 53)
Sherrington St. M12: Man 2C 82
Sherway Dr. WA15: Tim 4E 99
Sherwell Rd. M9: Man 1D 39
Sherwood Av. M7: Sal 5D 37
   M14: Man 5E 81
   M33: Sale 3E 89
   M43: Droy 5E 57
   SK4: Stoc 2C 104
Sherwood Cl. M5: Sal 4F 49
   OL6: A Lyme 5E 45
Sherwood Dr. M27: Pen 5D 35
Sherwood M. OL6: A Lyme 3F 59
(off Board St.)
Sherwood Rd. M34: Dent 2D 85
Sherwood St. M14: Man 5E 81
   OL1: O'ham 1F 29
Shetland Circ. M41: Urm 5E 61
Shetland Rd. M40: Man 4F 53
Shetland Way M41: Urm 5E 61
Shevington Gdns. M23: Wyth 2D 101
Shieldborn Dr. M9: Man 5F 39
Shield Cl. OL8: O'ham 3A 30
Shield Dr. M28: Ward 4E 33
Shield St. SK3: Stoc 3A 106
Shiel St. M28: Walk 1A 32
Shiers Dr. SK8: Chea 2F 111
Shilford Dr. M4: Man 2F 7 (4E 53)
Shillingford Rd. OL9: Chad 5C 28
Shilton Wlk. M40: Man 2F 41
(off Blandford Dr.)
Ship Canal Ho.
   M15: Man 3E 9 (2A 66)
Shipla Cl. OL9: O'ham 2A 30
Shipley Av. M6: Sal 4E 49
Shipley Vw. M41: Urm 5B 60
Shippey St. M14: Man 1F 93
Shiredale Dr. M9: Man 5F 39
Shiregreen Av. M40: Man 2E 53
Shirehills M25: Pres 1C 36
Shireoak Rd. M20: Man 1F 93
Shires, The M43: Droy 4F 57
Shirley Av. M7: Sal 5C 36
   M27: Pen 5E 35
   M30: Ecc 2E 61
   M32: Stre 2B 78
   M34: Aud 2E 71
   M34: Dent 2B 84
   OL9: Chad 2A 42
   SK8: H Grn 2E 115
   SK14: Hyde 5F 73
Shirley Ct. M33: Sale 4E 89
Shirley Gro. SK3: Stoc 5A 106
Shirley Rd. M8: Man 5C 38
Shoecroft Av. M34: Dent 2A 86
Shone Av. M22: Wyth 4B 110
Shoreditch Cl. M8: Man 3D 95
Shoreham Cl. M16: W Ran 1A 80
Shoreham Wlk. OL9: Chad 3C 28
Shore St. OL1: O'ham 2C 30
Shorland St. M27: Swin 5E 33
Short Av. M43: Droy 2B 70
Shortcroft St. M15: Man 4A 10 (3B 66)
Shortland Cres. M19: Man 5E 83
Short St. M4: Man 5D 7 (1C 66)
   M7: Sal 1E 5 (4A 52)
   SK4: Stoc 5F 95
Short St. E. SK4: Stoc 5A 96
Shortwood Cl. M40: Man 2C 54
(off Harmer Cl.)

Shotton Wlk. M14: Man 2D 81
(off Ellanby Cl.)
Showcase Cinema
   Belle Vue 5D 69
Shrewsbury Ct. M16: Old T 5F 65
Shrewsbury Rd. M25: Pres 1C 36
   M33: Sale 1C 98
   M43: Droy 5C 56
Shrewsbury St. M16: Old T 5E 65
   OL4: O'ham 1E 31
Shrewsbury Way M34: Dent 4C 86
(off Trowbridge Rd.)
Shrivenham Wlk. M23: Wyth 4B 100
(off Pitfield Gdns.)
Shropshire Av. SK5: Stoc 2E 97
Shropshire Rd. M35: Fail 1C 56
Shropshire Sq. M12: Man 4B 68
(off St Benedict's Av.)
Shrowbridge Wlk. M12: Man 4C 68
(off Clowes St.)
Shude Hill M4: Man 4C 6 (5C 52)
Shude Hill Stop (Metro) 3C 6 (5C 52)
Shuttle St. M26: Rad 1E 21
   M30: Ecc 5B 48
Shuttleworth Cl. M16: W Ran 5A 80
Siam St. M11: Man 2B 68
Sibley Rd. SK4: Stoc 5D 95
Sibley St. M18: Man 5F 69
Siblies Wlk. M22: Wyth 5D 109
Sibson Ct. M21: Chor 4C 78
Sibson Rd. M21: Chor 4C 78
   M33: Sale 4C 88
Sickle St. M2: Man 5C 6 (1C 66)
   OL4: O'ham 4C 30
Sidbury Rd. M21: Chor 5E 79
Sidcup Rd. M23: Wyth 1B 108
Siddall St. M12: Man 3C 82
   M34: Dent 2B 86
   OL1: O'ham 1E 117 (1B 30)
Siddington Av. M20: Man 1C 92
   SK3: Stoc 5E 105
Siddington Rd. SK9: Hand 4F 115
   OL4: O'ham 1F 31
Sidebottom St. M43: Droy 1B 70
   OL8: O'ham 2E 43
Side St. M11: Man 5D 55
   OL8: O'ham 2E 43
Sidings, The M28: Wors 2C 46
Sidlaw Cl. OL8: O'ham 2B 44
Sidley Av. M9: Man 5B 26
Sidmouth Av. M41: Urm 2A 74
Sidmouth Dr. M9: Man 2F 39
Sidmouth Rd. M33: Sale 3A 88
Sidmouth St. M34: Aud 3F 71
(not continuous)
   OL9: O'ham 4E 29
Sidney Rd. M9: Man 3F 39
Sidney St. M1: Man 5D 11 (3C 66)
   M3: Man 1A 10 (1B 66)
   M3: Sal .4D 5
   OL1: O'ham 1C 30
Sidwell Wlk. M4: Man 1F 67
(off Merrill St.)
Siemens Rd. M20: Man 3A 92
Sienna Cl. OL9: Chad 1C 28
Sighthill Wlk. M9: Man 4F 39
(off Coningsby Dr.)
Signal Cl. M30: Ecc 5D 47
Signal Dr. M40: Man 1F 53
Signet Wlk. M8: Man 2D 53
Silas St. OL6: A Lyme 2F 59

Silburn Way M24: Mid 2E **25**
Silbury Wlk. *M8: Man* *2B* **52**
(off Barrow Hill Rd.)
Silchester Dr. M40: Man 1F **53**
Silchester Wlk. OL1: O'ham 2E **117**
Silfield Cl. M11: Man 1A **68**
Silkhey Gro. M28: Walk 3A **32**
Silkin Cl. M13: Man 5E **11**
Silkin Cl. M13: Man 5E **11**
Silk Mill Way M24: Mid 1B **26**
Silk St. M3: Sal 2C **4** (4F **51**)
    M4: Man 3F **7** (5E **53**)
    M24: Mid .1B **26**
    M30: Ecc .1B **62**
    M40: Man .1E **55**
Silsden Av. M9: Man 4D **25**
Silsden Wlk. M7: Sal 4B **36**
Silton St. M9: Man 5B **40**
Silvamere Cl. M6: Sal 4A **50**
Silverbirch Cl. M33: Sale 1A **98**
Silver Birches M34: Dent 4D **87**
Silver Birch Gro. M27: Pen 1D **49**
Silverbirch Way M35: Fail 5B **42**
Silver Cl. SK16: Duk 3D **73**
Silver Ct. M45: White 5A **12**
Silvercroft St.
    M15: Man 4E **9** (3A **66**)
Silverdale M27: Clif 2C **34**
Silverdale Av. M25: Pres 2C **38**
    M34: Dent 3C **86**
    OL9: Chad 3C **28**
Silverdale Rd. M21: Chor 4E **79**
    SK4: Stoc 4E **95**
    SK8: Gat 2D **111**
Silverdale St. M11: Man 3B **70**
Silver Jubilee Wlk. M4: Man 4E **7**
Silverlea Dr. M9: Man 2E **39**
Silverstone Dr. M40: Man 3F **55**
Silver St. M1: Man 2C **10**
    (Abingdon St.)
    M1: Man 1D **11** (1C **66**)
    (Chorlton St.)
    M45: White 5A **12**
    OL1: O'ham 4D **117** (3A **30**)
Silverton Gro. M24: Mid 2F **15**
Silverton Ho. *M6: Sal* *4C* **48**
    (off Devon Cl.)
Silverwell St. M40: Man 2F **55**
Silverwood OL9: Chad 2A **28**
Silverwood Av. M21: Chor 5D **79**
Silvine Wlk. M40: Man 3F **53**
Simeon St. M4: Man 2E **7** (4D **53**)
SIMISTER 1A **24**
Simister Dr. BL9: Bury 4C **12**
Simister Grn. M25: Pres 1A **24**
Simister La. M24: Man 5C **14**
    M25: Pres 1F **23**
Simister Rd. M35: Fail 5B **42**
Simister St. M9: Man 4A **40**
Simkin Way OL8: O'ham 3B **44**
Simmons Ct. M16: W Ran 2A **80**
Simms Cl. M3: Sal 4C **4** (5F **51**)
Simon Freeman Cl.
    M19: Man 1E **95**
Simon Ho. SK4: Stoc 2E **95**
Simon La. M24: Mid 4C **14**
Simons Cl. M33: Sale 5C **88**
Simonsway M23: Wyth 3D **109**
Simpson Av. M27: Clif 2E **35**
Simpson Sq. OL9: Chad 1E **43**

Simpson St. M4: Man 2D **7** (4C **52**)
    M11: Man 1C **68**
    OL9: Chad 5D **29**
    SK14: Hyde 3F **87**
Sinclair Av. M8: Man 3B **38**
Sindsley Ct. *M27: Ward* *3F* **33**
    (off Moss La.)
Sindsley Rd. M27: Ward 2F **33**
Singapore Av. M90: Man A 1C **112**
Singleton Cl. M7: Sal 3F **37**
Singleton Lodge *M7: Sal* *3F* **37**
    (off Cavendish Rd.)
Singleton Rd. M7: Sal 3E **37**
    SK4: Stoc 4D **95**
Sir Charles Groves Hall *M15: Man* *4C* **66**
    (off Booth St. W.)
Sirdar St. M11: Man 2B **70**
Sirius Pl. M7: Sal 1C **4** (4F **51**)
Sir Matt Busby Way M16: Old T 5B **64**
Sir Richard Fairey Rd. SK4: Stoc 2C **94**
Sir Robert Thomas Ct. *M9: Man* *4F* **39**
    (off Coningsby Dr.)
Sir Williams Ct. M23: Wyth 5C **100**
Sisley Cl. M7: Sal 4D **37**
Sisson St. M35: Fail 5B **42**
Sisters St. M43: Droy 2C **70**
Sixth Av. OL8: O'ham 3E **43**
Sixth St. M17: T Pk 5F **63**
SK14 Ind. Pk. SK14: Hyde 5E **73**
Skaife Rd. M33: Sale 4A **90**
Skarratt Cl. M12: Man 4B **68**
Skelton Gro. M13: Man 3B **82**
Skelton Rd. M32: Stre 2F **77**
    WA14: Tim 4A **98**
Skelwith Cl. M41: Urm 1C **74**
Skerry Cl. M13: Man 5F **11** (3D **67**)
Skerton Rd.
    M16: Old T 5D **65**
Skiddaw Cl. M24: Mid 3F **15**
Skilgate Wlk. *M40: Man* *1E* **55**
    (off Queensferry St.)
Skip Pl. M3: Man 1C **6** (4C **52**)
Skipton Av. M40: Man 3F **41**
    OL9: Chad 1B **28**
Skipton Cl. SK5: Stoc 5A **84**
Skipton Dr. M41: Urm 5B **60**
Skipton St. OL8: O'ham 5D **31**
Skye Rd. M41: Urm 5F **61**
Skye Wlk. M23: Wyth 2C **108**
Slackey Brow BL4: Kea 3E **19**
Slack La. M27: Pen 3C **34**
Slack Rd. M9: Man 3E **39**
Slade Gro. M13: Man 3B **82**
Slade Hall Rd. M12: Man 3C **82**
Slade La. M13: Man 4B **82**
    M19: Man 5B **82**
Slade Mt. M19: Man 5B **82**
Slaithwaite Dr. M11: Man 5E **55**
Slate La. M34: A Lyme 2A **72**
    M34: Aud .2E **71**
Slater Ho. M5: Sal 4B **8** (3E **65**)
Slater St. BL4: Farn 1A **18**
    M30: Ecc .5D **47**
    M35: Fail .3B **42**
    OL8: O'ham *3A* **30**
    (off Foundry St.)
    OL9: O'ham *3A* **30**
    (off Bloom St.)
Slate Wharf M15: Man 3D **9** (2F **65**)
SLATTOCKS 1F **17**

Slattocks Link Rd. M24: Mid 1F **17**
Sleaford Cl. M40: Man 4F **53**
Sleddale Cl. SK2: Stoc 5F **107**
Sledmere Cl. M11: Man 1C **68**
Sledmoor Rd. M23: Wyth 2B **100**
Sloane St. OL6: A Lyme 4E **59**
Slough Ind. Est. M5: Sal 3B **8** (2E **65**)
Smalldale Av. M16: W Ran 2B **80**
Smallfield Dr. M9: Man 4F **39**
Smallridge Cl. M40: Man 4F **53**
SMALLSHAW 2E **59**
Smallshaw Fold OL6: A Lyme 2D **59**
Smallshaw La. OL6: A Lyme 2E **59**
Smallshaw Sq. OL6: A Lyme 2D **59**
Smallwood St. M40: Man 1E **55**
Smart St. M12: Man 2C **82**
Smeaton Cl. M32: Stre 3A **78**
Smeaton St. M8: Man 1E **53**
SMEDLEY 1D **53**
Smedley Av. M8: Man 1D **53**
Smedley La. M8: Man 1D **53**
Smedley Rd. M8: Man 1D **53**
Smedley St. M8: Man 1C **52**
Smethurst St. M9: Man 3F **39**
    M24: Mid 2F **27**
Smithfield Bldgs. M4: Man 5D **7**
Smithfield Ent. Est. M11: Man 3F **69**
                                (off Press St.)
Smithies Av. M24: Mid 4C **16**
Smith St. M16: Old T 4E **65**
    M34: Dent 3B **86**
    OL7: A Lyme 1B **72**
    SK8: Chea 5B **104**
    SK14: Hyde 5F **73**
    SK16: Duk .2C **72**
Smithy Gro. OL6: A Lyme 3E **59**
Smithy La. M3: Man 5A **6** (1B **66**)
Smyrna St. M5: Sal 1A **64**
    OL4: O'ham 3E **31**
Snell St. M4: Man 1F **67**
Snipe Retail Pk. OL7: A Lyme 2F **71**
Snipe Rd. OL8: O'ham 2D **45**
Snipeway OL7: A Lyme 2F **71**
Snowden Av. M41: Urm 5D **75**
Snowden St. OL8: O'ham 5B **30**
Snowden Wlk. M40: Man 2E **41**
                            (off Pleasington Dr.)
Snowdon Rd. M30: Ecc 4C **48**
Snowdrop Wlk. M7: Sal 1F **51**
                            (off Bury New Rd.)
Soap St. M4: Man 4D **7**
Soho St. OL4: O'ham 2D **31**
Solent Av. M8: Man 2C **38**
Solway Cl. M27: Clif 5A **20**
    OL8: O'ham 4A **30**
Solway Rd. M22: Wyth 2A **110**
Somerby Dr. M22: Wyth 5E **109**
Somerfield Rd. M9: Man 3F **39**
Somerford Av. M20: Man 5C **80**
Somerford Rd. SK5: Stoc 3B **84**
Somerford Way SK9: Hand 4F **115**
                            (off Spath Rd.)
Somerset Cl. SK5: Stoc 4E **97**
Somerset Pl. M33: Sale 2D **89**
Somerset Rd. M30: Ecc 3C **48**
    M35: Fail .1A **56**
    M43: Droy .4B **56**
Somerset St. OL4: O'ham 3E **31**
Somers Rd. SK5: Stoc 4B **84**
Somers Wlk. M9: Man 1D **39**

Somerton Av. M22: Wyth 3E **109**
    M33: Sale .5E **89**
Somerton Ct. M9: Man 1C **40**
Somerville Gdns. WA15: Tim 4B **98**
Somerwood Wlk. M12: Man 4B **68**
                            (off Kelsall St.)
Sommerville Ct. M7: Sal 4F **37**
                            (off Park La.)
Sonning Wlk. M8: Man 1D **53**
Sopwith Dr. M14: Man 4C **80**
Sorrel Bank M6: Sal 3B **50**
Sorrell Bank SK5: Stoc 4C **84**
Sorrel St. M15: Man 5E **9** (4A **66**)
Sorton St. M1: Man 4D **11** (3C **66**)
Souchay Ct. M20: Man 4D **93**
                            (off Clothorn Rd.)
Soudan Rd. SK2: Stoc 5C **106**
Soudan St. M24: Mid 5E **17**
Southacre Dr. SK9: Hand 5F **115**
Southall St. M3: Man 1A **6** (4B **52**)
Southampton Cl. M7: Sal 2F **51**
Southam St. M7: Sal 5B **38**
South Av. BL4: Kea 3B **18**
    M19: Man .1B **94**
    M27: Swin .2F **47**
    M45: White 5A **12**
Southbank Rd. M19: Man 3F **93**
Southbourne Av. M41: Urm 3B **76**
Southbourne St. M6: Sal 5A **50**
Southbrook Av. M8: Man 1B **38**
Southchurch Pde. M40: Man 3E **53**
                            (off Whitley Rd.)
Southcliffe Rd. SK5: Stoc 2B **96**
Sth. Cliffe St. M11: Man 3B **70**
South Cl. BL9: Bury 3C **12**
Southcombe Wlk. M15: Man 5B **66**
South Cres. M11: Man 5F **55**
South Cft. OL8: O'ham 1D **45**
Southcross Rd. M18: Man 2F **83**
Sth. Croston St. M16: Old T 1F **79**
Southdene Av. M20: Man 4A **92**
Southdown Cl. SK4: Stoc 1F **105**
Southdown Cres. M9: Man 2C **40**
South Dr. M21: Chor 2D **91**
    M41: Urm .5B **60**
    SK8: Gat .2C **110**
    WA15: Tim .4C **98**
Southend Av. M15: Man 4F **65**
Southerly Cres. M40: Man 1F **41**
Southern App. M27: Clif 2E **35**
Southernby Cl. M13: Man 1B **82**
                            (off Holmfirth St.)
Southern Cl. M34: Dent 5B **86**
Southern Ind. Est. M28: Walk 4A **18**
Southern Rd. M33: Sale 2C **88**
Southern St. M3: Man 3F **9** (2A **66**)
    M6: Sal 5A **50**
    M28: Walk .4A **18**
Southey Cl. M34: Dent 5C **86**
Southey Wlk. M34: Dent 5C **86**
                            (off Burns Rd.)
Southfield Cl. SK9: Hand 5E **115**
                            (off Knowle Pk.)
    SK16: Duk .4F **73**
South Fld. Ind. Est. M17: T Pk 4E **63**
Southfields Av. M11: Man 5E **55**
Southfields Dr. WA15: Tim 4D **99**
Southgarth Rd. M6: Sal 4A **50**
Southgate M3: Man 5A **6** (1B **66**)
    M21: Chor .1D **91**

Southgate M41: Urm 5D 75
  SK4: Stoc 3E 95
Southgate Av. M40: Man 3C 54
Southgate Ct. M33: Sale 3E 89
Southgate M. SK4: Stoc 3E 95
Southgate Rd. BL9: Bury 3B 12
  OL9: Chad 1A 42
Southgate St. OL1: O'ham 4F 117 (3B 30)
Southgate Way OL7: A Lyme 1C 72
(off John St.)
South Gro. M13: Man 5F 67
  M33: Sale 5D 89
Sth. Hall St. M5: Sal 3B 8 (2E 65)
Sth. Hill St. OL4: O'ham 3C 30
Sth. King St. M2: Man 5A 6 (1B 66)
  M30: Ecc 5D 47
Southlands Av. M30: Ecc 2B 60
Southlands St. SK3: Stoc 5B 106
Sth. Langworthy Rd. M50: Sal 2A 64
Southlea Rd. M19: Man 3F 93
  M20: Man 3F 93
Southlink OL4: O'ham 3C 30
Southlink Bus. Pk. OL4: O'ham 3C 30
Southlink Bus. Pk. Workshops
  OL4: O'ham 3C 30
Southlink Ind. Pk. OL4: O'ham 2D 31
Sth. Lonsdale St. M32: Stre 2A 78
South Manchester Gymnastics Cen.
. . . . .1A 110
South Meade M21: Chor 1D 91
  M25: Pres 2F 37
  M27: Swin 1A 48
  WA15: Tim 4C 98
Southmere Cl. M40: Man 1E 41
Sth. Mesnefield Rd. M7: Sal 5C 36
Southmill St. M2: Man 2A 10 (2B 66)
Southmoor M23: Wyth 4B 100
Southmoor Bus. Pk. M23: Wyth 4A 100
Southmoor Ind. Est. M23: Wyth 5B 100
Southmoor Rd. M23: Wyth 4B 100
Southolme Gdns. M19: Man 4A 94
South Pk. Rd. SK8: Gat 5D 103
Southpoint SK4: Stoc 1C 104
Sth. Pump St. M1: Man 2E 11 (2D 67)
Sth. Radford St. M7: Sal 5C 36
SOUTH REDDISH 2B 96
South Ridge M34: Dent 5B 72
South Rd. M20: Man 1D 93
  M27: Clif 2F 35
South Row M25: Pres 3B 36
Southsea St. M11: Man 3F 69
South Stage M50: Sal 2B 64
South St. M11: Man 2D 69
(not continuous)
  M12: Man 5A 68
  OL7: A Lyme 2A 72
  OL8: O'ham 2D 43
South Va. Cres. WA15: Tim 5B 98
South Vw. M14: Man 3E 81
(off Taylor St.)
  SK5: Stoc 2B 84
  SK16: Duk 5C 116 (1E 73)
South Vw. Gdns. SK8: Chea 3E 111
Southwark Dr. SK16: Duk 4F 73
Southway M30: Ecc 5B 48
  M40: Man 2B 42
  M43: Droy 2C 70
  OL7: A Lyme 1D 59
  OL8: O'ham 1A 44
  WA14: Alt 5A 98

Southwell Ct. M32: Stre 4E 77
Southwell Gdns. OL6: A Lyme 5D 45
Southwick Rd. M23: Wyth 1C 100
Sth. William St. M3: Sal 5C 4
Southwold Cl. M19: Man 4E 83
Sth. Woodley Gdns. M26: Rad 1E 21
Southworth Ct. M3: Sal 4C 4
Southyard St. M19: Man 5D 83
Sovereign Ent. Pk. M50: Sal 2C 64
Sovereign Ho. SK8: Chea 5B 104
Sovereign Point M50: Sal 3B 64
Sovereign St. M6: Sal 3C 50
Sowerby Wlk. M9: Man 5D 25
(off Chapel La.)
Spa Cl. SK5: Stoc 5A 84
Spa La. OL4: Lees 4F 31
Spalding Dr. M23: Wyth 4C 108
Sparkford Av. M23: Wyth 2F 99
Sparkle St. M1: Man 1F 11 (1D 67)
Spark Rd. M23: Wyth 4B 100
Sparrow Cl. SK5: Stoc 3A 84
Sparrow St. M13: Man 5F 67
Sparta Wlk. M11: Man 2C 68
(off Mill St.)
Sparth Ct. SK4: Stoc 5F 95
Sparthfield Rd. SK4: Stoc 5F 95
Sparth Hall SK4: Stoc 5F 95
Sparth La. SK4: Stoc 5F 95
Sparth Rd. M40: Man 2F 55
Spa St. M15: Man 5D 67
Spathfield Ct. SK4: Stoc 5F 95
Spath Holme M20: Man 5C 92
Spath La. SK9: Hand 4F 115
Spath Rd. M20: Man 4B 92
Spaw St. M3: Sal 4E 5 (5A 52)
Spean Wlk. M11: Man 1E 69
(off Bill Williams Cl.)
Spear St. M1: Man 5D 7 (1C 66)
Spectator Av. M4: Man 1F 67
Specton Wlk. M12: Man 2D 83
Spectrum Bus. Pk. SK3: Stoc 5D 105
Spectrum Way SK3: Stoc 5E 105
Speke Wlk. M34: Dent 4A 86
Spencer Av. M16: W Ran 3E 79
  M45: White 4A 12
  SK14: Hyde 5F 73
Spencer St. M30: Ecc 1E 61
  OL1: O'ham 2C 30
  OL9: Chad 5D 29
  SK5: Stoc 5B 84
  SK16: Duk 2E 73
Spender Av. M8: Man 1C 52
Spennithorne Rd.
  M41: Urm 3D 75
Spenser Av. M34: Dent 5C 86
Spenser Av. M34: Dent 5C 86
Spey Ho. SK5: Stoc 3B 84
Speyside Cl. M45: White 1C 22
Spindle Cft. BL4: Farn 1A 18
Spindle Shop. Cen.
  OL1: O'ham 4D 117 (3A 30)
Spinks St. OL4: O'ham 4D 31
Spinney, The M28: Wors 2D 47
  M41: Urm 3C 74
  M45: White 2E 21
Spinney Cl. SK9: Hand 5E 115
Spinney Dr. M33: Sale 5A 88
Spinney Gro. M34: Dent 5B 72
Spinney Rd. M23: Wyth 4D 101

Spire Wlk. *M12:* Man 2A **68**
(off Aden Cl.)
Spodden Wlk. M45: White 5E **13**
Spooner Rd. M30: Ecc 1E **61**
SPORTCITY 5B **54**
Sportside Av. M28: Walk 1A **32**
Sportside Cl. M28: Walk 5A **18**
Sportside Gro. M28: Walk 5A **18**
Sportsmans Dr. OL8: O'ham 1C **44**
Spreadbury St. M40: Man 5C **40**
Spring Av. M45: White 4A **12**
Spring Bank M6: Sal 4A **50**
Springbank Av. M34: Aud 3F **71**
OL6: A Lyme .2D **59**
Springbank Ct. M48: Man 2B **38**
Springbank Pl. SK1: Stoc 4A **118** (3A **106**)
Spring Bank St. OL8: O'ham 5E **29**
Spring Bank Ter. M34: Aud 3E **71**
Springbridge Ct. M16: W Ran 4B **80**
Spring Bri. Rd. M16: W Ran 3B **80**
Spring Cl. OL4: Lees 4F **31**
Spring Clough M28: Wors 2D **47**
OL7: A Lyme .1C **58**
Spring Clough Av. M28: Walk 2B **32**
Spring Clough Dr. M28: Walk 2B **32**
Springclough Dr. OL8: O'ham 5D **31**
Springdale Gdns. M20: Man 5C **92**
Springfield M26: Rad 3E **19**
M41: Urm 3E **75**
OL4: O'ham 2E **31**
(off Moorgate St.)
Springfield Av. M8: Man 4D **39**
SK5: Stoc 1A **96**
Springfield Cl. M35: Fail 4A **42**
Springfield Gdns. BL4: Kea 3C **18**
Springfield Ind. Est. M35: Fail 4A **42**
Springfield La. SK1: Stal 2F **5** (4A **52**)
Springfield Rd. BL4: Kea 3A **18**
M24: Mid 5B **16**
M33: Sale 4D **89**
M43: Droy 5B **56**
SK8: Gat 2D **111**
WA14: Alt 3A **98**
Springfield St. M34: Aud 4B **72**
OL6: A Lyme .2F **59**
Spring Gdns. M2: Man 5C **6** (1C **66**)
M6: Sal 4B **50**
M24: Mid 4C **16**
SK1: Stoc 2C **106**
SK14: Hyde 1F **87**
WA15: Tim 5E **99**
Spring Gro. M45: White 4A **12**
Springhead Av. M20: Man 1C **92**
SPRING HILL 1F **31**
Spring Hill Ct. OL4: O'ham 1F **31**
Spring La. OL4: Lees 4F **31**
Spring Rd. SK3: Stoc 3E **105**
Springside SK4: Stoc 1F **95**
Springside Av. M28: Walk 1A **32**
Springside Cl. M28: Walk 1A **32**
Springside Gro. M28: Walk 1A **32**
Springside Wlk. *M15:* Man 4F **65**
(off Shawgreen Cl.)
Springs Rd. M24: Mid 3A **28**
Spring St. M12: Man 3C **82**
OL4: O'ham 1E **31**
Spring Ter. OL9: Chad 2C **28**
Spring Va. M24: Mid 1C **26**
M25: Pres 2C **36**

Springvale Cl. OL7: A Lyme 2B **58**
Springvale Cl. M24: Mid 5D **17**
Spring Vw. BL4: Kea 3C **18**
Springville Av. M9: Man 5B **40**
Springwater La. M45: White 4A **12**
Springwell Cl. M6: Sal 5A **50**
Springwood Av. M27: Pen 1D **49**
OL9: Chad 5F **17**
Springwood Hall OL7: A Lyme 5C **44**
Springwood Hall OL8: O'ham 2C **44**
Springwood Way OL7: A Lyme 1C **58**
Spruce Cl. M6: Sal 5D **51**
Spruce Lodge SK8: Chea 5F **103**
Spruce St. M15: Man 4A **66**
Sprucewood OL9: Chad 1F **27**
Spur, The OL8: O'ham 1C **44**
Spur Wlk. *M8:* Man 5B **38**
(off Broomfield Dr.)
Square, The M27: Swin 2A **48**
M45: White 1F **21**
SK4: Stoc 5E **95**
SK14: Hyde 3F **87**
Square Fold M43: Droy 5D **57**
Squire Rd. M8: Man 5B **38**
Squire's Ct. M5: Sal 5C **48**
Stablefold M28: Wors 2C **46**
Stableford Av. M30: Ecc 3E **47**
Stables, The M25: Pres 1F **37**
M43: Droy 4F **57**
Stable St. OL1: O'ham 1D **31**
OL9: Chad 2C **42**
Stafford Rd. M27: Swin 4B **34**
M30: Ecc 4A **48**
M35: Fail 2C **56**
Stafford St. OL9: O'ham 5E **29**
Stafford Wlk. *M34:* Dent 4C **86**
(off Lancaster Rd.)
Stag Pasture Rd. OL8: O'ham 3F **43**
Stainburne Rd. SK2: Stoc 5E **107**
Stainburn Rd. M11: Man 2D **69**
Staindale OL4: O'ham 3F **31**
Stainer St. M12: Man 2C **82**
Stainforth St. M11: Man 2B **68**
Stainmoor Ct. SK2: Stoc 5F **107**
Stainmore Av. OL6: A Lyme 5F **45**
Stainton Av. M18: Man 1A **84**
Stainton Dr. M24: Mid 3F **15**
Staircase House (Mus.) 1B **118**
Staithes Rd. M22: Wyth 1F **113**
Stakeford Dr. M8: Man 4E **39**
STAKEHILL 1F **17**
Stake Hill Ind. Est. M24: Mid 2F **17**
Stakehill Ind. Est. M24: Mid 1F **17**
Stakehill La. M24: Mid 1F **17**
Staley St. OL4: O'ham 3D **31**
Stalham Cl. M40: Man 4F **53**
Stalmine Av. SK8: H Grn 1D **115**
Stamford Arc. *OL6: A Lyme* 4E **59**
(off Stamford St.)
Stamford Brook Rd. WA14: W Tim 3A **98**
Stamford Ct. OL6: A Lyme 5F **59**
Stamford Dr. M35: Fail 1D **57**
SK15: Stal 4E **61**
Stamford Pl. M33: Sale 4E **89**
Stamford Rd. M7: Sal 1D **51**
M13: Man 2A **82**
M34: Aud 3F **71**
M41: Urm 3D **75**
Stamford St. SK15: Stal 5F **59**
(not continuous)

Stamford Sq. OL6: A Lyme 5F 59
Stamford St. M16: Old T 5E 65
(not continuous)
  M27: Pen 3C 34
  M33: Sale 2C 88
  OL6: A Lyme 3B 116 (5D 59)
Stamford St. Central OL6: A Lyme 4E 59
Stamford St. E. OL6: A Lyme 4E 59
(not continuous)
Stamford St. W.
  OL6: A Lyme 4A 116 (5C 58)
Stampstone St. OL1: O'ham 1D 31
Stanage Av. M9: Man 5B 26
Stanbank St. SK4: Stoc 4A 96
Stanbridge Ct. SK4: Stoc 1A 106
Stanbrook St. M19: Man 5E 83
Stanbury Dr. SK16: Duk 2F 73
Stanbury Wlk. M40: Man 4F 53
(off Berkshire Rd.)
Stancliffe Rd. M22: Shar 1A 110
Stancross Rd. M23: Wyth 2E 99
STAND 2E 21
Standall Wlk. M9: Man 3A 40
(off Dalbeattie St.)
Stand Av. M45: White 5A 12
Stand Cl. M45: White 1E 21
Standish Rd. M14: Man 5F 81
Standish Wlk. M34: Dent 4A 86
Stand La. M26: Rad 1E 21
  M45: White 1E 21
Standmoor Ct. M45: White 2F 21
Standmoor Rd. M45: White 2F 21
Standon Wlk. M40: Man 2F 41
(off Blandford Dr.)
Stand Ri. M26: Rad 1D 21
Stanford Cl. M26: Rad 2E 19
Stanhope Av. M25: Pres 4C 22
  M34: Aud 4A 72
Stanhope Cl. M34: Dent 5A 72
Stanhope Ct. M25: Pres 3C 22
Stanhope Rd. M6: Sal 2A 50
Stanhope St. M19: Man 4D 83
  M34: Aud 5A 72
  OL6: A Lyme 3F 59
  SK5: Stoc 1A 96
Stanhope Way M35: Fail 4A 42
Stanhorne Av. M8: Man 2C 38
Stanhurst M30: Ecc 4A 48
Stanier Av. M30: Ecc 4F 47
Stanier St. M9: Man 4A 40
Stanion Gro. SK16: Duk 2F 73
Stan Jolly Wlk. M11: Man 2E 69
Stanlaw Ho. M30: Ecc 1A 62
Stanley Av. M14: Man 2E 81
Stanley Av. Nth. M25: Pres 3C 22
Stanley Av. Sth. M25: Pres 3C 22
Stanley Cl. M16: Old T 5E 65
  M45: White 5B 12
Stanley Dr. M45: White 3B 22
  WA15: Tim 5C 98
Stanley Grn. Bus. Pk.
  SK8: Chea H 4F 115
Stanley Gro. M12: Man 1B 82
  M18: Man 1B 82
  M21: Chor 5C 78
(off Crossland Rd.)
  M41: Urm 3F 75
  SK4: Stoc 4D 95
Stanley Mt. M33: Sale 5C 88
Stanley Pk. Grange SK9: Hand 4F 115

Stanley Rd. M7: Sal 4A 38
  M16: Old T 5D 65
  M16: W Ran 3A 80
  M27: Swin 4C 34
  M30: Ecc 1E 61
  M34: Dent 2D 85
  M45: White 5B 12
  OL9: Chad 5D 29
  SK4: Stoc 4D 95
  SK8: Chea H 3F 115
  SK9: Hand 3F 115
Stanley Rd. Ind. Est. M45: White 5B 12
Stanley St. M3: Sal 1E 9 (1A 66)
(not continuous)
  M8: Man 1D 7 (3C 52)
  M11: Man 3F 69
Stanley St. M25: Pres 5E 23
  M40: Man 2B 54
  M45: White 5B 12
  OL4: Lees 4F 31
  OL9: Chad 2D 29
  SK1: Stoc 1C 106
Stanlo Ho. M1: Man 3D 11
Stanmore Av. M32: Stre 3D 77
Stanmore Ho. M34: Aud 2E 71
Stannard Rd. M30: Ecc 1B 60
Stanneylands Rd. SK9: Sty 5D 115
Stannybrook Rd. M35: Fail 5F 43
Stansbury Pl. SK2: Stoc 5F 107
Stansby Gdns. M12: Man 4A 68
Stansfield Rd. M35: Fail 4C 42
  SK14: Hyde 1F 87
Stansfield St. M11: Man 2F 69
  M40: Man 3F 55
  OL1: O'ham 1A 30
  OL9: Chad 4D 29
Stansted Wlk. M23: Wyth 2F 99
Stanthorne Av. M20: Man 1C 92
Stanton Av. M7: Sal 1D 51
  M20: Man 4A 92
Stanton Ct. M32: Stre 1F 77
Stanton Gdns. M20: Man 4B 92
  SK4: Stoc 1D 105
Stanton St. M11: Man 5E 55
  M32: Stre 1F 77
  OL9: Chad 1D 43
Stanway Cl. M24: Mid 3D 27
Stanway Rd. M45: White 1D 23
Stanway St. M9: Man 4A 40
  M32: Stre 2F 77
Stanwell Rd. M27: Swin 5B 34
  M40: Man 3E 41
Stanwick Av. M9: Man 5C 24
Stanworth Cl. M16: W Ran 2A 80
Stanyard Ct. M5: Sal 2C 64
STANYCLIFFE 3E 17
Stanycliffe La. M24: Mid 3D 17
Stapleford Cl. M23: Wyth 2B 108
  M33: Sale 3A 90
Stapleford Wlk. M34: Dent 4A 86
Staplehurst Rd. M40: Man 3C 54
Staplers Wlk. M14: Man 2E 81
(off Stenbury Cl.)
Stapleton St. M6: Sal 2E 49
Starcross Wlk. M40: Man 1D 55
(off Morecambe Cl.)
Star Gro. M7: Sal 1A 52
Star Ind. Est.
  OL8: O'ham 5E 117 (4B 30)
Starkie St. M28: Wors 5C 32

Starling Cl. M22: Shar 5A **102**
   M43: Droy .4F **57**
Starmoor Dr. M8: Man 1C **52**
Starry Wlk. M7: Sal 1A **4** (3E **51**)
Stash Gro. M23: Wyth 4D **101**
Statham Cl. M34: Dent 2C **86**
Statham Wlk. M13: Man 4F **11**
Station App. M1: Man 1E **11** (1D **67**)
                      (Ducie St.)
   M1: Man 3C **10** (2C **66**)
                  (Whitworth St.)
   SK8: H Grn 1C **114**
Station Bri. M41: Urm 3F **75**
Station Cl. SK14: Hyde 3E **87**
Station Lofts OL6: A Lyme 3C **116**
Station M. M35: Fail 4A **42**
Station Rd. BL4: Kea 2B **18**
   M8: Man 3C **38**
   M27: Swin, Pen 4B **34**
   M30: Ecc 1F **61**
   M32: Stre 2F **77**
   M41: Urm 3F **75**
   SK1: Stoc 4A **118** (3A **106**)
   SK3: Stoc 4A **118** (4B **106**)
   SK4: Stoc 2A **104**
   SK5: Stoc 3A **84**
   SK9: Hand 5F **115**
   SK9: Sty 5C **114**
Station Rd. Ind. Est. SK5: Stoc 3A **84**
Station St. SK16: Duk 5B **116** (1D **73**)
Station Vw. M19: Man 4C **82**
   M43: Droy 3C **70**
Staton St. M11: Man 2E **69**
Statter St. BL9: Bury 2C **12**
Staveleigh Mall
   OL6: A Lyme 2C **116** (4D **59**)
Staveley Cl. M24: Mid 4A **16**
Staverton Cl. M13: Man 5F **11** (3E **67**)
Staycott St. M16: W Ran 1B **80**
Stedman Cl. M11: Man 1A **68**
Steele Ho. M5: Sal 4B **8** (3E **65**)
Steeple Cl. M8: Man 2B **52**
Steeple Dr. M5: Sal 1C **64**
Stelfox Av. M14: Man 4C **80**
   WA15: Tim 4E **99**
Stelfox La. M34: Aud 3A **72**
Stelfox St. M30: Ecc 2D **61**
Stella St. M9: Man 5D **25**
Stelling St. M18: Man 5F **69**
Stenbury Cl. M14: Man 2E **81**
Stenner La. M20: Man 1C **102**
Stenson Sq. *M11: Man* . . . . *.3F **69***
                    (off Ettrick Cl.)
Stephen Lowry Wlk. *M40: Man* *5C **40***
              (off McConnell Rd.)
Stephen Oake Cl. M8: Man 2B **52**
Stephenson Av. M43: Droy 1C **70**
Stephenson Ct. SK5: Stoc 3B **84**
Stephenson Rd. M32: Stre 3F **77**
Stephenson St. M35: Fail 3C **42**
   OL4: O'ham 1F **31**
Stephens Rd. M20: Man 3E **93**
Stephens Ter. *M20: Man* *5D **93***
             (off Kings Lynn Cl.)
Stephen St. M3: Man 1B **6** (3B **52**)
   M41: Urm 3A **76**
   SK1: Stoc 3D **107**
Stephen Wlk. *SK1: Stoc* *3D **107***
                 (off Stephen St.)
Stern Av. M5: Sal 2C **64**

Sterndale Rd. SK3: Stoc 5A **106**
Steven Ct. M21: Chor 5E **79**
Stevenson Ct. *BL4: Kea* *2A **18***
                    (off Bent Ct.)
Stevenson Pl. M1: Man 5E **7**
Stevenson Rd. M27: Swin 4A **34**
Stevenson Sq. M1: Man 5E **7** (1D **67**)
Stevenson St. M3: Sal 5C **4** (1F **65**)
Stewart St. OL7: A Lyme 5B **58**
Stillwater Dr. M11: Man 5C **54**
Stilton Dr. M11: Man 2C **68**
Stirling *M30: Ecc* *5A **48***
                 (off Monton La.)
Stirling Av. M20: Man 5B **80**
Stirling Cl. SK5: Stoc 5E **105**
Stirling Ct. SK4: Stoc 3E **95**
Stirling Gro. M45: White 1C **22**
Stirling Rd. OL9: Chad 5B **28**
Stirling St. OL9: O'ham 2E **29**
Stirrup Ga. M28: Wors 2C **46**
Stitch La. SK4: Stoc 5F **95**
Stobart Av. M25: Pres 2E **37**
STOCK BROOK 2C **28**
Stockburn Dr. M35: Fail 5E **43**
Stockdale Av. SK3: Stoc 5B **106**
Stockdale Rd. M9: Man 5A **26**
Stockfield Mt. OL9: Chad 3D **29**
Stockfield Rd. OL9: Chad 2D **29**
Stockholm Rd. SK3: Stoc 5F **105**
Stockholm St. M11: Man 5D **55**
Stockland Cl. M13: Man 5E **11** (3D **67**)
Stock La. OL9: Chad 2D **29**
Stockley Wlk. *M15: Man* *4F **65***
                (off Shawgreen Cl.)
STOCKPORT 3A **118** (2A **106**)
Stockport Air Raid Shelters 2B **118**
Stockport Art Gallery 4B **118** (3B **106**)
Stockport Cemetery & Crematorium
   SK1: Stoc 4C **106**
Stockport County FC 4A **106**
Stockport Garrick Theatre
             .3A **118** (2A **106**)
STOCKPORT LITTLE MOOR 3D **107**
Stockport Mus. 1D **107**
Stockport Rd. M12: Man 4E **67**
   M13: Man 4F **67**
   M19: Man 1A **82**
   M34: Dent 2B **86**
   OL7: A Lyme 4A **116** (2B **72**)
   SK3: Stoc 4B **104**
   SK8: Chea 5F **103**
   SK14: Hyde 5F **87**
   WA15: Alt, Tim 5A **98**
Stockport Rd. W. SK6: Bred 5E **97**
Stockport Station (Rail) 4A **118** (3A **106**)
Stockport Trad. Est. SK4: Stoc 2D **105**
Stockport Viaduct 1F **105**
Stockport Village SK1: Stoc 2A **118**
Stocksfield Dr. M9: Man 1A **40**
Stocks Ho. M41: Urm 5B **74**
Stocks Ind. Est. M30: Ecc 5E **47**
Stocks St. M8: Man 1C **6** (4C **52**)
Stocks St. E. M8: Man 1C **6** (4C **52**)
Stockton Av. SK3: Stoc 3D **105**
Stockton Pk. OL4: O'ham 3F **31**
Stockton Rd. M21: Chor 5C **78**
Stockton St. M16: W Ran 1A **80**
   M27: Swin 5A **34**
Stockwood Wlk. M9: Man 5F **39**
Stokesay Cl. BL9: Bury 1B **12**

Stokesay Rd. M33: Sale 3A 88
Stokes St. M11: Man 5F 55
Stonall Av. M15: Man 5D 9
Stoneacre Ct. M27: Swin 5B 34
Stoneacre Rd. M22: Wyth 5E 109
Stonebeck Rd. M23: Wyth 1B 108
Stonechat Cl. M43: Droy 4E 57
STONECLOUGH 2D 19
Stoneclough Rd. OL1: O'ham 1A 30
Stoneclough Ri. M26: Rad 1D 19
Stoneclough Rd. BL4: Kea 2B 18
    M26: Rad .2B 18
Stonecroft OL1: O'ham 2D 117
Stonefield Dr. M8: Man 2A 52
Stonehead St. M9: Man 5B 40
Stone Hill Ind. Est. BL4: Farn 3A 18
Stone Hill Rd. BL4: Farn 3A 18
Stonehouse Wlk. M23: Wyth 4A 100
                                    (off Sandy La.)
Stonehurst Cl. M12: Man 4C 68
Stoneleigh Av. M33: Sale 3A 88
Stoneleigh Dr. M26: Rad 2D 19
Stoneleigh St. OL1: O'ham 1D 31
Stonelow Cl. M15: Man 4B 66
Stonemead Dr. M9: Man 5F 25
Stonemere Dr. M26: Rad 1E 21
Stonemill Ter. SK5: Stoc 5B 96
Stonepail Cl. SK8: Gat 1B 110
Stonepail Rd. SK8: Gat 1C 110
Stone Pale M45: White 2B 22
Stone Pl. M14: Man 2E 81
Stonesby Cl. M16: W Ran 1F 79
Stone St. M3: Man 3F 9 (2A 66)
Stoney Bank Rd. M26: Rad 2E 19
Stoneyfield Cl. M16: W Ran 3B 80
Stoneygate Wlk. M11: Man 3F 69
                                    (off Botha Cl.)
Stoneyholme Av. M8: Man 5D 39
Stoney Knoll M7: Sal 1F 51
Stoneyside Av. M28: Walk 5A 18
Stoneyside Gro. M28: Walk 5A 18
Stony Bri. La. WA15: Tim 4C 98
Stonyford Rd. M33: Sale 4F 89
Stopford St. M11: Man 3A 70
    SK3: Stoc 3F 105
Stopford Wlk. M34: Dent 2B 86
Stopley Wlk. M11: Man 2C 68
                                    (off Mill La.)
Stores Rd. M90: Man A 3C 112
Stores St. M25: Pres 5E 23
Store St. M1: Man 2F 11 (2D 67)
    M11: Man 3D 69
    OL7: A Lyme 1C 58
Storeton Cl. M22: Wyth 4A 110
Stortford Dr. M23: Wyth 1D 101
Stothard Rd. M32: Stre 4D 77
Stott Ho. OL8: O'ham 5D 117 (4A 30)
Stott La. M6: Sal 4D 49
    M24: Mid .1B 16
Stott Milne St. OL9: Chad 4D 29
Stott Rd. M27: Swin 1F 47
    OL9: Chad 1A 42
Stott's La. M40: Man 1F 55
Stott St. M35: Fail 1F 55
Stovell Av. M12: Man 3C 82
Stovell Rd. M40: Man 4C 40
Stowell St. M5: Sal 1A 64
                                    (off Dolbey St.)
Stowfield Cl. M9: Man 5D 25
Stow Gdns. M20: Man 2C 92

St Peter's Square Stop (Metro)
 .2B 10 (2B 66)
Stracey St. M40: Man 4A 54
                                    (not continuous)
Stradbroke Cl. M18: Man 5E 69
Strain Av. M9: Man 5F 25
Strand Av. M32: Stre 5E 77
STRANGEWAYS 1A 6 (3B 52)
Stranton Dr. M28: Wors 4E 33
Stratfield Av. M23: Wyth 2F 99
Stratford Av. M20: Man 3B 92
    M30: Ecc .2E 61
    OL8: O'ham 1A 44
Stratford Rd. M24: Mid 4D 27
Stratford Sq. SK8: H Grn 2E 115
Strathblane Cl. M20: Man 1D 93
Strathblane Ho. SK8: Chea 5F 103
                                    (off Ashfield Rd.)
Strathfield Dr. M11: Man 5E 55
Strathmere Av. M32: Stre 2F 77
Strathmore Av. M16: W Ran 3D 79
    M34: Dent 1B 86
Stratton Rd. M16: W Ran 3D 79
    M27: Pen .3B 34
    SK2: Stoc 3E 107
Strawberry Bank M6: Sal 4D 51
                                    (off Strawberry Rd.)
Strawberry Flds. M43: Droy 5E 57
Strawberry Hill M6: Sal 1A 4 (4D 51)
Strawberry Rd. M6: Sal 4C 50
Stray St. M11: Man 2A 70
Stream Ter. SK1: Stoc 2D 107
STREET END 4C 42
STRETFORD .4F 77
Stretford Ho. M32: Stre 4E 77
                                    (off Chapel La.)
Stretford Leisure Cen. 1B 78
Stretford Motorway Est. M32: Stre 5C 62
Stretford Rd. M15: Man 5B 10 (4A 66)
    M16: Old T 5E 65
    M41: Urm .4F 75
Stretford Station (Metro) 4F 77
Stretton Av. M20: Man 5E 93
    M32: Stre .2C 76
    M33: Sale .4A 88
Stretton Cl. M40: Man 2F 53
Stretton Way SK9: Hand 4F 115
                                    (off Sandiway Rd.)
Striding Edge Wlk.
    OL1: O'ham 1C 30
Strines St. SK14: Hyde 1F 87
Stringer St. SK1: Stoc 1C 106
Stroma Gdns. M41: Urm 5E 61
Strong St. M7: Sal 3A 52
Strontian Wlk. M11: Man 1E 69
                                    (off Edith Cavell Cl.)
Stroud Av. M30: Ecc 4D 47
Stroud Cl. M24: Mid 4C 26
Stuart Ho. M43: Droy 2C 70
Stuart Pl. M43: Droy 4F 55
Stuart Rd. M32: Stre 2F 77
    SK6: Bred .2F 97
Stuart St. M11: Man 5C 54
    OL8: O'ham 4A 30
    M24: Mid .1E 27
Stuart St. E. M11: Man 5C 54
Stuart Wlk. M24: Mid 2B 26
Stubbins Cl. M23: Wyth 2A 100
Stubbs Cl. M7: Sal 4D 37
Student Village M1: Man 4B 10

Studforth Wlk. M15: Man 5C 66
  (off Botham Cl.)
Studland Rd. M22: Wyth 3B 110
STYAL 5B 114
Styal Av. M32: Stre 2C 76
  SK5: Stoc 2B 96
Styal Country Pk. 5F 113
Styalgate SK8: Gat 3C 110
Styal Gro. SK8: Gat 3B 114
Styal Rd. M22: Wyth 1C 110
  SK8: Gat, H Grn 5C 110
  SK9: Sty 5C 114
Styal Station (Rail) 5C 114
Styhead Dr. M24: Mid 3F 15
Style St. M4: Man 2D 7 (4C 52)
Sudbury Cl. M16: Old T 5E 65
  (off Stanley Rd.)
Sudbury Dr. SK8: H Grn 1E 115
Sudell Cl. M4: Man 2F 7 (4D 53)
  (not continued)
  M40: Man 1F 7 (4E 53)
Sudell St. Ind. Est. M4: Man 2F 7
Sudgen Sports Cen. 5D 11 (3C 66)
Sue Patterson Wlk. M40: Man 2F 53
  (off Aldbourne Cl.)
Suffield Wlk. M22: Wyth 5F 109
Suffolk Av. M43: Droy 4C 56
Suffolk Dr. SK5: Stoc 2E 97
Suffolk St. M6: Sal 2C 50
  OL9: O'ham 4D 29
Sugar Mill Sq. M5: Sal 5F 49
Sugden St. OL6: A Lyme 5F 45
Sulby Av. M32: Stre 3A 78
Sulby St. M26: Rad 2D 19
  M40: Man .4C 40
Sullivan St. M12: Man 2C 82
Sulway Cl. M27: Swin 5C 34
Sumac St. M11: Man 5F 55
Sumbland Ho. M27: Clif 2D 35
Summer Av. M41: Urm 3A 76
Summercroft OL9: Chad 1D 43
Summerfield Av. M43: Droy 4A 56
Summerfield St. M21: Chor 4E 78
Summerfield Dr. M24: Mid 2C 14
  M25: Pres 3C 36
Summerfield Rd. M22: Wyth 4E 109
  M28: Wors 5C 32
Summerfield Vw. OL8: O'ham 1E 45
Summer Pl. M14: Man 3E 81
Summerseat Cl. M5: Sal 2C 64
Summers St. OL9: Chad 2E 29
Summerton Ho. M5: Sal 1C 64
  (off Buckingham St.)
Summervale Ho. OL9: O'ham 3F 29
  (off Manchester St.)
Summerville Av. M9: Man 5B 40
Summerville Rd. M6: Sal 2A 50
Sumner Rd. M6: Sal 2F 49
Sumner Way M41: Urm 3E 75
Sunbank La. WA15: Ring 4A 112
Sunbeam Wlk. M11: Man 1B 68
  (off Hopedale Cl.)
Sunbury Dr. M40: Man 3F 55
Sundance Ct. M50: Sal 2A 64
Sunderland Av. OL6: A Lyme 5E 59
Sundew Pl. M24: Mid 2F 27
Sundial Rd. SK2: Stoc 4F 107
Sunfield Rd. OL1: O'ham 1D 117 (1A 30)
Sunflower Gro. OL9: Chad 1B 28
SUN HILL 2F 31

Sunk La. M24: Mid 1C 26
Sunningdale Av. M11: Man 5D 55
  M33: Sale .5A 90
  M45: White 2E 21
Sunningdale Ct. M34: Dent 2D 85
Sunningdale Dr. M6: Sal 2C 48
  M25: Pres .4C 22
Sunningdale Ho. M33: Sale 5A 90
Sunningdale Rd. M34: Dent 4C 86
  M41: Urm .4D 75
SUNNY BANK 3C 12
Sunny Bank M26: Rad 1C 18
  OL4: Lees .4F 31
Sunnybank Av. M30: Ecc 4B 48
  M43: Droy .1B 70
  SK4: Stoc .4B 94
Sunny Bank Rd. BL9: Bury 3B 12
  M13: Man .2A 82
Sunnybank Rd. M43: Droy 1B 70
Sunny Brow Rd. M18: Man 5E 69
  M24: Mid .1A 26
Sunny Dr. M25: Pres 5B 22
Sunnyfield Rd. M25: Pres 2E 23
  SK4: Stoc .5B 94
Sunnylea Av. M19: Man 3A 94
Sunnyside M43: Droy 4B 56
  OL7: A Lyme 2B 58
Sunnyside Av. M43: Droy 3B 56
  M32: Stre .3B 78
Sunnyside Ct. M20: Man 5E 93
  M43: Droy .4B 56
Sunnyside Cres. OL6: A Lyme 5F 59
Sunnyside Gro. OL6: A Lyme 5F 59
Sunnyside Rd. M43: Droy 4B 56
Sunset Av. M22: Nor 1F 101
Sunset Bus. Pk. BL4: Kea 4E 19
Surbiton Rd. M40: Man 3D 55
Surma Cl. OL9: O'ham 2F 29
Surrey Av. M43: Droy 4B 56
Surrey Rd. M9: Man 2F 39
Surrey St. M9: Man 2F 39
  OL6: A Lyme 2F 59
  OL9: O'ham 4E 29
Surrey Way SK5: Stoc 4E 97
Surtees Rd. M23: Wyth 1C 100
Sussex Av. M20: Man 4D 93
Sussex Cl. M27: Clif 2C 34
  OL9: Chad .3D 29
Sussex Dr. M43: Droy 4C 56
Sussex Rd. SK3: Stoc 3D 105
Sussex St. M2: Man 5B 6 (1B 66)
  M7: Sal 1C 4 (3F 51)
Sutcliffe Av. M12: Man 3D 83
Sutcliffe St. M24: Mid 1E 27
  OL7: A Lyme 1B 72
  OL8: O'ham 4A 30
Sutherland Cl. OL8: O'ham 3B 44
Sutherland Rd. M16: Old T 2C 78
Sutherland St. M27: Swin 3A 34
  M30: Ecc .4D 47
Suthers St. OL9: O'ham 3E 29
Sutton Dr. M43: Droy 4A 56
Sutton Ho. M6: Sal 4B 50
Sutton Mnr. M21: Chor 4C 78
Sutton Rd. M18: Man 2E 83
  SK4: Stoc .5E 95
Sutton Way M6: Sal 4C 50
  (off Salford Shop. City)
  SK9: Hand .4F 115
  (off Sandiway Rd.)

Swailes St. OL4: O'ham 3D 31
Swaine St. SK3: Stoc 3A 118 (2A 106)
Swainsthorpe Dr. M9: Man 4A 40
Swalecliff Av. M23: Wyth 2F 99
Swallow St. M11: Man 1B 68
   M12: Man 3C 82
   OL8: O'ham 2F 43
   SK1: Stoc 5C 118 (4B 106)
Swanage Av. M23: Wyth 2F 99
   SK2: Stoc 5F 107
Swanage Rd. M30: Ecc 4D 47
Swanbourne Gdns. SK3: Stoc 5E 105
Swanhill Cl. M18: Man 4B 70
Swanley Av. M40: Man 2A 54
Swan Rd. WA15: Tim 2C 98
Swansea St. OL8: O'ham 5D 31
Swan St. M4: Man 3D 7 (5C 52)
   OL6: A Lyme 4E 59
Swan Ter. M30: Ecc 2E 61
Swanton Wlk. M8: Man 1B 52
(off Kilmington Dr.)
Swan Wlk. M22: Wyth 4F 109
(off Dakerwood Cl.)
Swarbrick Dr. M25: Pres 2B 36
Swayfield Av. M13: Man 2B 82
Swaylands Dr. M33: Sale 2D 99
Sweetnam Dr. M11: Man 5D 55
Swettenham Rd. SK9: Hand 4F 115
Swift St. OL6: A Lyme 2F 59
Swiftsure Av. M3: Sal 5C 4 (1F 65)
Swift Wlk. M40: Man 2E 55
(off Dakerwood Cl.)
Swinbourne Gro. M20: Man 1E 93
Swinburne Av. M43: Droy 4C 56
Swinburne Grn. SK5: Stoc 4F 83
Swinburne Way M34: Dent 5C 86
Swinburn St. M9: Man 3B 40
Swindells St. M11: Man 3A 70
(off Stanley St.)
   SK14: Hyde 5F 73
Swindon Cl. M18: Man 5F 69
Swinfield Av. M21: Chor 5B 78
Swinford Wlk. M40: Man 1A 40
(off Woodmere Dr.)
Swinside Cl. M24: Mid 4E 15
Swinstead Av. M40: Man 2A 54
SWINTON 4B 34
Swinton Ct. M27: Swin 5C 34
(off Park St.)
Swinton Cres. BL9: Bury 5C 12
Swinton Gro. M13: Man 5E 67
Swinton Hall Rd. M27: Pen, Swin 4B 34
Swinton Ind. Est. M27: Swin 4C 34
Swinton Leisure Cen. 4B 34
Swinton Library Art Gallery 4B 34
(off Chorley Rd.)
Swinton Lions RLFC 3A 22
SWINTON PARK 5C 34
Swinton Pk. Rd. M6: Sal 2D 49
Swinton Shop. Cen. M27: Swin 4B 34
Swinton Station (Rail) 3B 34
Swinton St. OL4: O'ham 4E 31
Swithin Rd. M22: Wyth 1A 114
Swythamley Cl. SK3: Stoc 3C 104
Swythamley Rd. SK3: Stoc 3C 104
Sycamore Av. M26: Rad 1B 20
   M34: Dent 3B 86
   OL4: O'ham 1F 31
   OL9: Chad 1B 42
Sycamore Cl. M20: Man 1E 93
   OL6: A Lyme 5F 59

Sycamore Ct. M6: Sal 4C 50
   M16: W Ran 2F 79
   M40: Man 4A 54
   SK4: Stoc 5D 95
(off Heaton Moor Rd.)
Sycamore Cres. OL6: A Lyme 2E 59
Sycamore Gro. M35: Fail 5D 43
Sycamore Pl. M45: White 3B 22
Sycamore Rd. M30: Ecc 3C 46
Sycamores, The M26: Rad 3D 19
   M33: Sale 5E 89
(off Beaufort Av.)
Sycamore St. M33: Sale 4A 90
   SK3: Stoc 3D 105
Sycamore Wlk. SK8: Chea 5A 104
Syddall Av. SK8: H Grn 1F 115
Syddall St. SK14: Hyde 4F 87
Sydenham St. OL1: O'ham 1C 30
(not continuous)
Sydney Av. M30: Ecc 5F 47
   M90: Man A 1C 112
Sydney Jones Ct. M40: Man 3E 41
Sydney St. M6: Sal 5A 50
   M27: Swin 5F 33
   M32: Stre 3F 77
   M35: Fail 5A 42
   SK2: Stoc 4E 107
Sykes Av. BL9: Bury 2D 13
Sykes Mdw. SK3: Stoc 5F 105
Sykes St. SK5: Stoc 5B 84
Sykes Wlk. SK5: Stoc 5B 84
(off Sykes St.)
Sylvan Av. M16: W Ran 2F 79
   M33: Sale 5E 89
   M35: Fail 2A 56
   M41: Urm 2F 75
   WA15: Tim 3B 98
Sylvan Cl. M24: Mid 4F 15
Sylvandale Av. M19: Man 4C 82
Sylvan St. OL9: O'ham 2E 29
Sylvester Av. SK2: Stoc 5D 107
Sylvester Way M34: Dent 5C 86
Sylvia Gro. SK5: Stoc 1A 96
Symond Rd. M9: Man 4A 26
Symons Rd. M33: Sale 3D 89
Symons St. M7: Sal 5A 38
Syndall Av. M12: Man 4F 67
Syndall St. M12: Man 4F 67

T

Tabley Av. M14: Man 3D 81
Tabley Gdns. M43: Droy 1D 71
Tabley Gro. M13: Man 3B 82
   SK5: Stoc 1A 96
   WA15: Tim 2B 98
Tabley Rd. M33: Sale 1A 100
   SK9: Hand 4F 115
Tabley St. M6: Sal 2D 51
Tabor St. M24: Mid 4B 16
Tackler Cl. M27: Swin 5B 34
Tadcaster Dr. M40: Man 1F 53
Tadcaster Wlk.
   OL1: O'ham 2E 117
Tagge La. M6: Sal 1B 50
   M27: Pen 1A 50
Tagore Cl. M13: Man 1A 82
Tahir Cl. M8: Man 5D 39
Tait M. SK4: Stoc 1B 104

Talavera St. M7: Sal 2F 51
Talbot Cl. OL4: O'ham 1E 31
Talbot Ct. M32: Stre 2A 78
Talbot Pl. M16: Old T 5D 65
Talbot Rd. M14: Man 1A 94
　　M16: Old T 2A 78
　　M32: Stre .2A 78
　　M33: Sale .4A 90
　　SK14: Hyde 5F 73
Talbot St. M24: Mid 4C 16
　　M30: Ecc 1A 62
　　OL6: A Lyme 2A 116 (4C 58)
　　SK1: Stoc 2A 118
Talford Gro. M20: Man 3C 92
Talgarth Rd. M40: Man 3E 53
Talkin Dr. M24: Mid 3A 16
Talland Wlk. M13: Man 5F 67
　　　　　　　　(off Plymouth Gro.)
Tallarn Cl. M20: Man 1E 93
Tallis St. M12: Man 2C 82
Tall Trees M7: Sal 3F 37
Tall Trees Pl. SK2: Stoc 5E 107
Tallyman Way M27: Pen 5A 36
Talmine Av. M40: Man 2A 54
Tamar Cl. BL4: Kea 4D 19
　　M45: White 1C 22
Tamar Ct. M15: Man 4F 65
Tamar Dr. M23: Wyth 2C 108
Tamarin Cl. M27: Ward 3E 33
Tamerton Dr. M8: Man 1C 52
Tameside Bus. Development Cen.
　　M34: Dent .2F 85
Tameside Ct. SK16: Duk 3D 73
Tameside Hippodrome 2B 116 (4D 59)
Tameside Leisure Pool 5C 116
Tameside Pk. Ind. Est. SK16: Duk 2D 73
Tameside Stadium 3A 58
Tameside Work Cen. OL7: A Lyme 1B 72
　　　　　　　　(off Ryecroft St.)
Tame St. M4: Man 1F 67
　　M34: Aud .3B 72
　　M34: Dent .1A 86
　　SK15: Stal .1F 73
TAME VALLEY 1F 73
Tamworth Av. M45: White 2D 23
Tamworth Cl. M15: Man 5A 66
Tamworth Ct. M15: Man 5A 66
　　OL9: O'ham 4E 29
　　　　　　　　(off Tamworth St.)
Tamworth Grn. SK1: Stoc 1D 107
Tamworth St. M15: Man 1A 80
　　OL9: O'ham 4E 29
　　SK1: Stoc .1D 107
Tandis Cl. M6: Sal 4C 48
Tandlewood M. M40: Man 2E 55
Tanfield Dr. M26: Rad 2D 19
Tanfield Rd. M20: Man 3D 103
Tangmere Cl. M40: Man 1E 41
Tangmere Dr. M16: W Ran 2F 79
Tanhill Cl. SK2: Stoc 5F 107
Tanhill La. OL8: O'ham 2C 44
Tannersfield Lodge M35: Fail 1A 56
Tanners Fold OL8: O'ham 2C 44
Tanners Grn. M6: Sal 4B 50
　　　　　　　　(off Nursery St.)
Tanners St. M18: Man 5A 70
Tanner St. SK14: Hyde 2B 87
Tannery Way M18: Man 5A 70
　　WA14: Tim .4A 98
Tanpit Wlk. M22: Wyth 4E 109

Tansey Gro. M7: Sal 5B 38
Tansley Rd. M8: Man 2D 39
Tan Yd. Brow M18: Man 1A 84
Tanyard Grn. SK5: Stoc 3B 96
Taplin Dr. M18: Man 5F 69
Taplow Wlk. M14: Man 2A 82
　　　　　　　　(off Binstead Cl.)
Tarbet Rd. SK16: Duk 3E 73
Tarbet Wlk. M8: Man 1B 52
Tariff St. M1: Man 5E 7 (1D 67)
Tarland Wlk. M11: Man 1E 69
　　　　　　　　(off Kincraig Cl.)
Tarleton Ho. M6: Sal 3E 49
　　　　　　　　(off Moss Mdw. Rd.)
Tarleton Wlk. M13: Man 4F 67
Tarnbrook Cl. M45: White 1E 23
Tarnbrook Wlk. M15: Man 5C 66
　　　　　　　　(off Wellhead Cl.)
Tarn Gro. M28: Walk 3B 32
Tarn Ho. M15: Man 5C 8
Tarns, The SK8: Gat 3D 111
Tarnside Ho. M8: Man 2A 54
Tarporley Av. M14: Man 5C 80
Tarporley Cl. SK3: Stoc 5F 105
Tarran Gro. M34: Dent 4D 87
Tarran Pl. WA14: Alt 5A 98
Tarrington Cl. M12: Man 5C 68
Tartan St. M11: Man 5D 55
Tarves Wlk. M11: Man 1D 69
　　　　　　　　(off Kincraig Cl.)
Tarvin Av. M20: Man 1C 92
　　SK4: Stoc .1F 95
Tarvin Dr. SK6: Bred 4F 97
Tarvington Cl. M40: Man 1E 53
Tarvin Way SK9: Hand 4F 115
Tasle All. M2: Man 1B 10 (1B 66)
Tatchbury Rd. M35: Fail 5C 42
Tate St. OL8: O'ham 5D 31
Tatham Cl. M13: Man 2B 82
Tatland Dr. M22: Wyth 3B 110
Tattenhall Wlk. M14: Man 5F 81
　　　　　　　　(off Ravenhall Cl.)
Tattersall St. OL9: O'ham 3F 29
Tatton Bldgs. SK8: Gat 1D 111
Tatton Ct. M14: Man 5F 81
　　SK4: Stoc .4E 95
Tatton Gro. M20: Man 2D 93
Tatton Mere Dr. M43: Droy 1D 71
Tatton Pl. M13: Man 1A 82
　　M33: Sale .3D 89
Tatton Rd. M33: Sale 3D 89
　　M34: Dent .4C 86
　　SK9: Hand 4F 115
Tatton Rd. Nth. SK4: Stoc 3E 95
Tatton Rd. Sth. SK4: Stoc 4E 95
Tatton St. M5: Sal 3A 8 (2D 65)
　　M15: Man 5C 8 (4F 65)
　　SK1: Stoc 2B 118 (2B 106)
　　SK14: Hyde 5F 87
Tatton Ter. SK16: Duk 5C 116
Tatton Vw. M20: Man 2D 93
TAUNTON 2A 58
Taunton Av. M30: Ecc 4D 47
　　M41: Urm 5D 75
　　OL7: A Lyme 1A 116 (3C 58)
Taunton Brook La.
　　OL7: A Lyme 2A 58
Taunton Grn. OL7: A Lyme 2B 58
Taunton Gro. M45: White 3C 22
Taunton Hall Cl. OL7: A Lyme 2B 58

Taunton Lawns *OL7: A Lyme* 2C 58
Taunton Pl. *OL7: A Lyme* 2B 58
Taunton Platting *OL7: A Lyme* 1B 58
(off Ney St.)
Taunton Rd. M33: Sale 4A 88
OL7: A Lyme 1A 116 (3C 58)
OL9: Chad .1C 28
Taunton St. M4: Man 1F 67
Taunton Wlk. *M34: Dent* 4C 86
(off Mancunian Dr.)
Taurus St. OL4: O'ham 1E 31
Tavern Cl. M35: Fail 5C 42
Tavern Ct. Av. M35: Fail 5C 42
Tavery Cl. M4: Man 5E 53
Tavistock Dr. OL9: Chad 1B 28
Tavistock Rd. M33: Sale 3A 88
Tavistock Sq. *M9: Man* 5F 39
(off Grangewood Dr.)
Tay Cl. OL8: O'ham 4A 30
Tayfield Rd. M22: Wyth 4E 109
Taylor Bldgs. BL4: Kea 3D 19
Taylor La. M34: Dent 1F 85
Taylor Rd. M41: Urm 3A 62
Taylor's La. M40: Man 2E 55
Taylorson St. M5: Sal 3D 65
Taylorson St. Sth. M5: Sal 4C 64
Taylor's Rd. M32: Stre 1F 77
Taylor St. M14: Man 3E 81
M18: Man 4E 69
M24: Mid .1C 26
(not continuous)
M25: Pres 5E 23
M34: Dent 1B 86
M43: Droy 1B 70
OL1: O'ham 1E 31
OL4: Lees 3F 31
OL9: Chad 2C 28
Taylor Ter. SK16: Duk 5C 116
Teak Dr. BL4: Kea 5F 19
Tealby Av. M16: Old T 1E 79
Tealby Ct. M21: Chor 4E 79
Tealby Rd. M18: Man 1D 83
Teasdale Cl. OL9: Chad 1A 42
Tebbutt St. M4: Man 2F 7 (4D 53)
Tedburn Wlk. M40: Man 2F 41
Tedder Cl. BL9: Bury 4D 13
Tedder Dr. M22: Wyth 2B 114
Teddington Rd. M40: Man 3E 41
Ted Jackson Wlk.
M11: Man 2B 68
(off Newchurch St.)
Teer St. *M40: Man* 5F 53
(off Holt Town)
Teesdale Av. M41: Urm 1C 74
Teesdale Cl. SK2: Stoc 5F 107
Teesdale Wlk. *M9: Man* 1A 40
(off Haverfield Rd.)
Tees Wlk. *OL8: O'ham* 4A 30
(off Lee St.)
Teignmouth Av. M40: Man 3E 53
Telegraphic Ho. M50: Sal 3C 64
Telegraph Rd. M17: T Pk 3C 62
Telfer Av. M13: Man 3A 82
Telfer Rd. M13: Man 3A 82
Telford Cl. M34: Aud 3A 72
Telford St. M8: Man 2E 53
Telford Wlk. M16: Old T 1F 79
Telham Wlk. M23: Wyth 1C 108
Tellison Cl. M6: Sal 1F 49
Tellison Cres. M6: Sal 1F 49

Telryn Wlk. *M8: Man* 4E 39
(off Stakeford Dr.)
Temperance St. M12: Man 2E 67
(not continuous)
Temple Dr. M27: Swin 5D 35
Temple Rd. M33: Sale 4F 89
Temple Sq. M8: Man 2D 53
Temple St. M24: Mid 5D 17
OL1: O'ham 2D 31
(off Dalton St.)
Tempus Apartments M3: Man 2A 6
Temsbury Wlk. M40: Man 2A 54
Ten Acre Ct. M45: White 2E 21
Ten Acre Dr. M45: White 2F 21
Ten Acres Astro Cen. 2C 54
Ten Acres La. M40: Man 2C 54
Tenax Circ. M17: T Pk 2D 63
Tenax Rd. M17: T Pk 3D 63
Tenbury Cl. M6: Sal 4B 50
Tenbury Dr. M24: Mid 4C 26
Tenby Av. M20: Man 2D 93
M32: Stre .1B 78
Tenby Dr. *M15: Man* 4E 65
(off Cornbrook Pk. Rd.)
Tenby Dr. M6: Sal 2F 49
Tenby Rd. OL8: O'ham 2D 43
SK3: Stoc 4D 105
Teneriffe St. M7: Sal 2F 51
Tenham Wlk. *M9: Man* 1A 40
(off Ravenswood Dr.)
Ten Ho's. OL8: O'ham 2E 45
Tennis St. M16: Old T 1D 79
Tennyson Av. BL9: Bury 1B 12
M34: Dent 5C 86
Tennyson Cl. SK4: Stoc 1D 105
Tennyson Gdns. M25: Pres 1B 36
Tennyson Rd. M24: Mid 4D 17
M27: Swin 4F 33
M43: Droy 5C 56
SK5: Stoc .4F 83
SK8: Chea 5B 104
Tennyson St. M13: Man 5E 67
OL1: O'ham 1E 31
Tenpin 10 Bowling 2F 103
Tensing Av. OL7: A Lyme 2D 59
Tensing Fold
SK16: Duk 5B 116 (1D 73)
Tensing St. OL8: O'ham 4C 44
Tentercroft OL1: O'ham 2D 117 (2A 30)
Tenterden Wlk. *M22: Wyth* 3E 109
(off Poundswick La.)
Tenth St. M17: T Pk 4F 63
Terence St. M40: Man 2F 55
Terminal Rd. E. M90: Man A 2D 113
Terminal Rd. Nth. M90: Man A 2D 113
Tern Cl. SK16: Duk 3F 73
Terrace, The M25: Pres 1D 37
Terrace St. OL4: O'ham 2D 31
Terrington Cl. M21: Chor 1A 92
Tetbury Rd. M22: Wyth 5D 109
Tetlow Gro. M30: Ecc 1E 61
Tetlow La. M7: Sal 4A 38
Tetlow St. M24: Mid 1C 26
M40: Man .2F 55
OL8: O'ham 3F 29
Tetsworth Wlk. *M40: Man* 2F 41
(off Blandford Dr.)
Teviot St. M13: Man 1A 82
Tewkesbury Av. M24: Mid 3B 16
M41: Urm .1F 75

Tewkesbury Av. M43: Droy 4C **56**
   OL6: A Lyme 5E **45**
Tewkesbury Dr. M25: Pres 2E **37**
Tewkesbury Rd. M40: Man 4F **53**
   SK3: Stoc 5D **105**
Texas St. OL6: A Lyme 5E **59**
Textile Apartments M3: Sal 4A **6**
Textile St. M12: Man 3C **68**
Textilis Ho. SK1: Stoc 3A **118**
Textilose Rd. M17: T Pk 5D **63**
Teynham Wlk. M22: Wyth 5E **109**
                     (off Selstead Rd.)

Thackeray Cl. M8: Man 1C **52**
Thackeray Gro. M43: Droy 5C **56**
Thackeray Rd. OL1: O'ham 1E **31**
Thames Cl. M11: Man 2D **69**
Thames Ct. M15: Man 4F **65**
                        (off City Rd.)
Thames Ind. Est. M12: Man 3F **67**
Thames St. OL1: O'ham 1F **117** (1C **30**)
Thanet Cl. M7: Sal 2A **52**
Thankerton Av. M34: Aud 1F **71**
Thatcher St. OL8: O'ham 5C **30**
THATCH LEACH 4B **28**
Thatch Leach OL9: Chad 4B **28**
Thatch Leach La. M45: White 2C **22**
Thaxmead Dr. M40: Man 3F **55**
Thaxted Wlk. M22: Wyth 1E **113**
The . . . .
    Names prefixed with 'The' for example
    'The Acorn Cen.' are indexed under the
    main name such as 'Acorn Cen., The'
Theatre Ho. M6: Sal 3A **50**
            (off Langworthy Rd.)
Theatre Royal 3F **87**
Theatre St. OL1: O'ham 3F **117** (2B **30**)
Thekla St. OL9: O'ham 1F **29**
Thelwall Av. M14: Man 5B **80**
Thelwall Cl. WA15: Alt 5A **98**
Thelwall Ct. M14: Man 5C **80**
Thelwall Rd. M33: Sale 5A **90**
Theta Cl. M11: Man 5D **55**
Thetford Dr. M8: Man 5D **39**
Third Av. M11: Man 4E **55**
   M17: T Pk 5F **63**
                  (not continuous)
   M27: Swin 2A **48**
   OL8: O'ham 2E **43**
Thirkhill Pl. M30: Ecc 5B **48**
Thirlby Dr. M22: Wyth 5F **109**
Thirlmere Av. M27: Swin 5C **34**
   M32: Stre 2E **77**
   OL7: A Lyme 3B **58**
Thirlmere Dr. M24: Mid 4A **16**
Thirlmere M. M24: Mid 3A **16**
Thirlmere Rd. M22: Wyth 4D **109**
   M41: Urm 2A **74**
   SK1: Stoc 4D **107**
Thirsfield Dr. M11: Man 5E **55**
Thirsk Av. OL9: Chad 1B **28**
Thirsk M. M7: Sal 1F **51**
               (off Bury New Rd.)
Thirsk St. M12: Man 3E **67**
Thistle Bank Cl. M9: Man 3E **39**
Thistledown Cl. M30: Ecc 2E **61**
Thistley Flds. SK14: Hyde 5E **87**
Thomas Cl. M34: Dent 1C **86**
Thomas Ct. M15: Man 5D **9**
Thomas Gibbon Cl. M32: Stre 4E **77**
                 (off Mitford St.)

Thomas Johnson Cl. M30: Ecc 1E **61**
                 (off Green La.)
Thomas More Cl. BL4: Kea 3B **18**
Thomas Regan Ct. M18: Man 4F **69**
                 (off Ansell Cl.)
Thomas St. BL4: Farn 1A **18**
             (Bridgewater St.)
   BL4: Farn 2A **18**
               (Old Hall St.)
   M4: Man 4D **7** (5C **52**)
   M7: Sal .4B **38**
   M8: Man 4B **38**
   M32: Stre 1F **77**
   OL4: Lees 3D **31**
   SK1: Stoc 5C **118** (4B **106**)
Thornage St. W. SK1: Stoc . . .5B **118** (4B **106**)
Thomas Telford Basin
   M1: Man 1F **11** (1E **67**)
Thompson Av. M45: White 2C **22**
Thompson Cl. M34: Dent 2E **85**
Thompson Ct. M34: Dent 2D **85**
Thompson La. OL9: Chad 5C **28**
Thompson Rd. M17: T Pk 2A **62**
   M34: Dent 2D **85**
Thompson St. M3: Man 1A **6** (4B **52**)
   M4: Man 2E **7** (5D **53**)
   M40: Man 2B **54**
   OL9: O'ham 2F **29**
                 (off Main Rd.)
Thomson Rd. M18: Man 1E **83**
Thomson St. M13: Man 4E **67**
   SK3: Stoc 5A **118** (3A **106**)
Thoralby Cl. M12: Man 5C **68**
Thoresway Rd. M13: Man 2A **82**
Thorgill Wlk. M40: Man 5C **40**
            (off Walderton Av.)
Thor Gro. M5: Sal 3B **8** (2E **65**)
Thorley Cl. OL9: Chad 2A **42**
Thorley Dr. M41: Urm 3F **75**
   WA15: Tim 5D **99**
Thorley La. M90: Man A 5B **108**
   WA15: Ring 5A **108**
   WA15: Tim 5D **99**
Thorley Rd. WA15: Tim 5E **99**
Thorley St. M35: Fail 4B **42**
Thornaby Wlk. M9: Man 1F **53**
            (off Kirklinton Dr.)
Thornage Dr. M40: Man 3E **53**
Thorn Av. M35: Fail 1A **56**
Thornbank M30: Ecc 4A **48**
Thorn Bank Lodge SK4: Stoc 4D **95**
Thornbridge Av. M21: Chor 5D **79**
Thornbury Rd. M32: Stre 1A **78**
Thornbury Way M18: Man 5E **69**
Thornby Wlk. M23: Wyth 1C **108**
Thorncliff Av. OL8: O'ham 1A **44**
Thorncliffe Av. SK16: Duk 3E **73**
Thorncliffe Gro. M19: Man 4E **83**
Thorncombe Rd. M16: W Ran 2A **80**
Thorn Ct. M6: Sal 5D **51**
Thorncross Cl. M15: Man 5B **8** (3E **65**)
Thorndale Ct. M9: Man 2E **39**
            (off Marshbrook Dr.)
   WA15: Tim 5C **98**
            (off Stockport Rd.)
Thorndale Gro. WA15: Tim 5C **98**
Thornden Rd. M40: Man 3F **53**
Thorn Dr. M22: Wyth 1C **114**
Thorndyke Gdns. M25: Pres 1D **37**
            (off Bury New Rd.)

Thorndyke Wlk. M25: Pres 1D 37
Thorne Av. M41: Urm 2C 74
Thornedge WA15: Tim 3B 98
Thorne Ho. M14: Man 3F 81
Thorneside M34: Dent 5B 72
               (not continuous)
Thorneycroft Av. M21: Chor 3D 91
Thorneycroft Cl. WA15: Tim 5D 99
Thorneycroft Rd. WA15: Tim 5D 99
Thorney Hill Cl. OL4: O'ham 3C 30
Thornfield Ct. *SK4: Stoc* 5C 94
             (off Thornfield Rd.)
Thornfield Dr. M27: Swin 5A 34
Thornfield Gro. OL6: A Lyme 4F 59
Thornfield Rd. M19: Man 3A 94
   SK4: Stoc .5C 94
Thornfield St. *M5: Sal* 1F 63
               (off Foster St.)
Thornfield Ter. OL6: A Lyme 5E 59
Thornford Wlk. *M40: Man* 2F 41
           (off Blandford Dr.)
Thorngate Rd. M8: Man 2C 52
Thorn Gro. M14: Man 5F 81
   M33: Sale .4D 89
Thorngrove Av. M23: Wyth 4F 99
Thorngrove Ho. M23: Wyth 4F 99
Thornham La. M24: Mid 1F 17
Thornham Rd. M33: Sale 1A 98
Thornhill Cl. M34: Dent 3C 84
Thornhill Dr. M28: Walk 3A 32
Thornhill Rd. M43: Droy 5D 57
   SK4: Stoc 1B 104
Thornholme Cl. M18: Man 2D 83
Thornley Brow M4: Man 4C 6 (5C 52)
Thornlea M9: Man 2C 40
   M43: Droy 1A 70
Thornlea Av. M27: Swin 1F 47
   OL8: O'ham 3E 43
Thornleigh Rd. M14: Man 4C 80
Thornley La. Nth. M34: Stoc 2B 84
Thornley La. Sth.
   M34: Dent, Stoc 3B 84
   SK5: Stoc .3B 84
Thornley Ri. M34: Aud 3F 71
Thornley Rd. M25: Pres 2E 23
Thornleys Rd. M34: Dent 1C 86
Thornley St. M24: Mid 5D 17
   SK14: Hyde 4F 87
Thornmere Cl. M27: Ward 2E 33
Thorn Rd. M27: Swin 1A 48
   OL8: O'ham 1E 45
Thorns, The M21: Chor 1D 91
Thornsett Cl. M9: Man 4A 40
Thornsgreen Rd. M22: Wyth 1F 113
Thornton Av. M34: Man 2E 71
   M41: Urm .3C 74
Thornton Cl. M16: Old T 5E 65
Thornton Cres. M25: Pres 4B 22
Thornton Dr. SK9: Hand 5F 115
Thornton Ga. SK8: Gat 5C 102
Thornton Pl. SK4: Stoc 4D 95
Thornton Rd. M14: Man 3C 80
   SK8: H Grn 5E 111
Thornton St. M40: Man 3E 53
   OL4: O'ham 5F 117 (4B 30)
Thornton St. Nth. M40: Man 3F 53
Thorntree Cl. M9: Man 5A 40
Thornway Dr. OL7: A Lyme 5B 58
Thornwood Av. M18: Man 1A 84
Thorold Gro. M33: Sale 4A 90

Thorpe Av. M26: Rad 1A 12
   M27: Swin .3A 34
Thorpebrook Rd. M40: Man 1C 54
Thorpe Cl. M34: Dent 1B 86
   WA15: Tim .4E 99
Thorpe Gro. SK4: Stoc 2F 95
Thorpe La. M34: Dent 5B 72
Thorpeness Sq. M18: Man 4F 69
Thorpe St. M16: Old T 1E 79
   M24: Mid 2E 25
Thorp Rd. M40: Man 1C 54
Thorp St. M30: Ecc 2D 61
   M45: White .4A 12
Thorsby Cl. M18: Man 5A 70
Thorsby Rd. WA15: Tim 5A 98
Thorsby Way *M34: Dent* 4C 86
              (off Tatton Rd.)
Thorverton Sq. M40: Man 4E 41
Thrapston Av. M34: Aud 1F 71
Threadmill La. M27: Swin 4F 33
Threapwood Rd. M22: Wyth 5A 110
Three Acres Dr. SK5: Stoc 3A 96
Three La. Ends M34: Dent 3B 86
Three Pits M24: Mid 1E 17
Threlkeld Cl. M24: Mid 5E 15
Threlkeld Ct. M24: Mid 5E 15
Threlkeld Rd. M24: Mid 5E 15
Thresher Cl. *M33: Sale* 5B 90
           (off Windmill Rd.)
Threshfield Dr. WA15: Tim 4D 99
Throstle Bank St. SK14: Hyde 1E 87
Throstle Hall Ct. M24: Mid 5B 16
Throstles Cl. M43: Droy 4E 57
Throstles Grn. M16: Old T 5C 64
Thruxton Cl. M16: W Ran 2A 80
Thurland Rd. OL4: O'ham 3E 31
Thurland St. OL9: Chad 1A 28
Thurlby Av. M9: Man 4A 26
Thurlby St. M13: Man 1F 81
Thurleigh Rd. M20: Man 4D 93
Thurlestone Dr. M41: Urm 2E 75
Thurloe St. M14: Man 2E 81
Thurlow St. M50: Sal 2B 64
             (not continuous)
Thurlston Cres. M8: Man 5C 38
Thurlwood Av. M20: Man 1C 92
Thursby Av. M20: Man 2C 92
Thursby Wlk. M24: Mid 4E 15
Thursfield St. M6: Sal 2D 51
Thurston Cl. BL9: Bury 4C 12
Thyme Cl. M21: Chor 4F 91
Tiber Av. OL8: O'ham 3E 43
Tib La. M2: Man 1B 10 (1B 66)
Tib St. M4: Man 5D 7 (1C 66)
   M34: Dent .3B 86
Tideswell Av. M40: Man 4F 53
Tideswell Cl. SK8: H Grn 1F 115
Tideswell Rd. M43: Droy 4A 56
Tideswell Way M34: Dent 5C 86
Tideway Cl. M7: Sal 4B 36
Tidworth Av. M4: Man 5F 53
Tiefield Wlk. *M21: Chor* 1A 92
           (off Marham Cl.)
Tilbury St. OL1: O'ham 1A 30
Tilbury Wlk. M40: Man 3F 53
Tilby Cl. M41: Urm 3A 74
Tilehurst Ct. M7: Sal 5D 37
Tilgate Wlk. *M9: Man* 1A 40
           (off Haverfield Rd.)
Tillard Av. SK3: Stoc 3D 105

Tillerman Cl. M27: Pen 4F 35
Tillhey Rd. M22: Wyth 4F 109
Tilney Av. M32: Stre 4A 78
Tilshead Wlk. *M13: Man* 4E 67
                            (off Cavanagh Cl.)
Tilson Rd. M23: Wyth 1A 100
Tilstock Wlk. M23: Wyth 3A 100
Timber Wharf
    M15: Man 4C 8 (3F 65)
Times St. M24: Mid 1D 27
Timothy Cl. M6: Sal 4D 49
TIMPERLEY 4B 98
Timperley Cl. OL8: O'ham 2C 44
Timperley Cricket, Hockey, Tennis &
    Lacrosse Club 5B 98
Timperley Fold OL6: A Lyme 1E 59
Timperley Rd. OL6: A Lyme 1D 59
Timperley Station (Metro) 3B 98
Timperley St. M11: Man 2E 69
    OL9: O'ham 2A 30
Timpson Rd. M23: Wyth 4A 100
Timson St. M35: Fail 5B 42
Tindall St. M30: Ecc 2D 61
    SK5: Stoc .2B 84
Tindle St. M28: Walk 1B 32
Tinker St. SK14: Hyde 2F 87
Tinningham Cl. M11: Man 3A 70
Tinsdale Wlk. M24: Mid 5E 15
Tinshill Cl. M12: Man 5C 68
Tinsley Cl. M40: Man 5A 54
Tintern Av. M20: Man 3B 92
    M41: Urm .5C 74
    M45: White 5B 12
Tintern Gro. SK1: Stoc 2D 107
Tintern Rd. M24: Mid 3B 16
Tintern St. M14: Man 3D 81
Tipton Dr. M23: Wyth 1D 101
Tiptree Wlk. *M9: Man* 4A 40
                          (off Batley St.)
Tirza Av. M19: Man 1B 94
Titchfield Rd. OL8: O'ham 5E 31
Tithe Barn Cl. SK4: Stoc 4B 94
Tithe Barn Rd. SK4: Stoc 4B 94
Titterington Av. M21: Chor 3D 79
Tiverton Av. M33: Sale 5B 88
Tiverton Dr. M33: Sale 5B 88
Tiverton Ho. *M6: Sal* 4C 48
                         (off Devon Cl.)
Tiverton Pl. OL7: A Lyme 2C 58
Tiverton Rd. M41: Urm 1A 76
Tiviot Dale SK1: Stoc 1B 118 (1B 106)
Tiviot Way SK5: Stoc 5B 96
Tivoli St. *M3: Man* 1A 10
                        (off Stoney St.)
Tixall Wlk. M8: Man 2A 38
Toad Pond Cl. M27: Swin 1E 47
Tobermory Cl. M11: Man 1F 69
Tobermory Rd.
    SK8: H Grn 5E 111
Todd's Pl. M8: Man 1F 53
Todd St. M3: Man 3C 6 (5C 52)
    M7: Sal 1F 51
Toft Rd. M18: Man 1E 83
Toft Way SK9: Hand 5F 115
Toledo St. M11: Man 1F 69
Tollard Av. M40: Man 2F 53
Toll Bar St. M12: Man 4A 68
    SK1: Stoc 4C 118 (3B 106)
Tollesbury Cl. M40: Man 3F 53
Toll Ga. Cl. M13: Man 1A 82

Tolworth Dr. M8: Man 5D 39
Tomcroft La. M34: Dent 3F 85
Tom Husband Leisure Complex
    . . . . .2A 4 (4D 51)
Tomlinson Cl. OL8: O'ham 4A 30
Tomlinson St. M15: Man 4A 66
    M40: Man .1E 41
Tom Lomas Wlk. *M11: Man* 5D 55
                      (off Frankland Cl.)
Tommy Browell Cl. M14: Man 2C 80
Tommy Johnson Wlk.
    M14: Man 2C 80
                   (off Up. Lloyd St.)
Tommy Taylor Cl.
    . . . . .2E 55
Tonbridge Rd. M19: Man 5D 83
    SK5: Stoc .5B 84
Tonge Cl. M45: White 5D 13
Tonge Ct. M24: Mid 1D 27
Tonge Hall Cl. M24: Mid 1D 27
Tonge Mdw. M24: Mid 1D 27
Tonge Roughs M24: Mid 1F 27
Tonge St. M12: Man 3F 67
    M24: Mid .3A 28
Tongley Wlk. *M40: Man* 2F 41
                   (off Blandford Dr.)
Tong St. BL4: Kea 4E 19
Tonman St. M3: Man 2F 9 (2A 66)
Tontin St. M5: Sal 5D 51
Tooley Ho. M3: Ecc 2F 61
Tootal Dr. M5: Sal 5E 49
    M6: Sal 4E 49
Tootal Gro. M6: Sal 5E 49
Tootal Rd. M5: Sal 5E 49
Topcliffe Rd. M9: Man 1D 41
Topcroft Cl. M22: Nor 3A 102
Topfield Rd. M22: Wyth 2E 109
Topfields Gro. M7: Sal 5F 37
Topgate Brow M27: Pen 4F 35
Topley St. M40: Man 1F 53
TOP OF HEBERS 3A 16
TOP OF MOOR 1F 31
Top o' th' Flds. M45: White 2B 22
Top o' th' Grn. OL9: Chad 5E 29
Topphome Ct. *BL4: Farn* 2A 18
                   (off Longcauseway)
Topp St. BL4: Farn 2A 18
Top Schwabe St. M24: Mid 1E 25
Topsham Wlk. *M40: Man* 2F 55
                   (off Silverwell St.)
Top St. M24: Mid 5B 16
    OL4: O'ham 1F 31
Torah St. M8: Man 3C 52
Torbay Dr. SK2: Stoc 4D 107
Torbay Rd. M21: Chor 5E 79
    M41: Urm .4A 76
Torcross Rd. M9: Man 4D 25
Torkington Av. M27: Pen 3B 34
Torkington Rd. SK8: Gat 1D 111
Torkington St. SK3: Stoc 4F 105
Torksey Wlk. M9: Man 4D 25
Torness Wlk. *M11: Man* 1D 69
                   (off Emily Beavan Cl.)
Toronto Av. M90: Man A 2D 113
Toronto Rd. SK2: Stoc 5C 106
Torpoint Wlk. M40: Man 3E 41
Torquay Cl. M13: Man 4F 67
Torrax Cl. M6: Sal 1D 49
Torre Cl. M24: Mid 3C 16
Torrens St. M6: Sal 2F 49

Torridon Wlk. M22: Wyth 1E 113
Torrington Av. M9: Man 2C 40
Torrington Rd. M27: Pen 1D 49
Torside Way M27: Pen 2B 34
Torver Dr. M24: Mid 4F 15
Torver Wlk. M22: Wyth 5D 109
Torwood Rd. OL9: Chad 1A 28
Total Fitness
    Whitefield .5B 12
Totland Cl. M12: Man 2D 83
Totnes Av. OL9: Chad 1B 28
Totnes Rd. M21: Chor 5E 79
    M33: Sale 3A 88
Tottenham Dr. M23: Wyth 4F 99
Tottington La. M25: Pres 4A 22
Tottington St. M11: Man 5E 55
Totton Rd. M35: Fail 5B 42
Touchet Hall Rd.
    M24: Mid 2F 17
Tourist Info. Cen.
    Ashton-under-Lyne 1C 116 (4D 59)
    Brinnington 3E 97
    Manchester 2B 10 (1B 66)
    Manchester Airport 1C 112
    Oldham 3E 117 (2B 30)
    Ringway 2D 113
    Salford Quays 3A 64
    Stockport, Chestergate
        . . . . .2A 118 (2A 106)
    Stockport, Market Pl.
        . . . . .1B 118 (1B 106)
Tours Av. M23: Wyth 1C 100
Towcester Cl. M4: Man 1F 67
Tower Grange M7: Sal 4F 37
Towers Bus. Pk. M20: Man 2E 103
Tower Sq. M13: Man 4E 67
                                        (off Beamish Cl.)
Towers St. OL4: O'ham 1F 31
Tower St. SK14: Hyde 4F 87
    SK16: Duk .1F 73
Towey Cl. M18: Man 4F 69
Towncliffe Wlk. M15: Man 4F 65
                                    (off Shawheath Cl.)
Towncroft M34: Dent 1C 86
Towncroft Av. M24: Mid 4B 16
TOWNFIELD 2D 31
Townfield M41: Urm 4D 75
Townfield St. OL4: O'ham 2D 31
Townfield Wlk. M15: Man 4F 65
                                    (off Shawgreen Cl.)
Towngreen Ct. M8: Man 2B 38
Town Hall La. M2: Man 5B 6
Town La. M34: Dent 3F 85
    SK16: Duk .2E 73
Town La. Ct. M34: Dent 3A 86
Townley Pk. Ind. Est.
    M24: Mid 5C 16
Townley St. M8: Man 2B 52
    M11: Man 2B 68
    M24: Mid 5C 16
Towns Cft. Lodge M33: Sale 2A 88
                                        (off Green La.)
Townsend Rd. M27: Pen 3B 34
Townsley Gro. OL6: A Lyme 2F 59
Town Sq. M33: Sale 4D 89
Town Sq. Shop. Cen.
    OL1: O'ham 4E 117 (3B 30)
Towton St. M9: Man 4A 40
Towyn Av. M5: Sal 5C 50
Toxteth St. M11: Man 3A 70

Tracey St. M8: Man 3C 38
Traders Av. M41: Urm 4A 62
Trafalgar Av. M34: Aud 3E 71
Trafalgar Bus. Pk.
    M8: Man 3A 52
Trafalgar Ct. M16: W Ran 3A 80
Trafalgar Gro. M7: Sal 2F 51
Trafalgar Ho. M34: Aud 3E 71
                                    (off Audenshaw Rd.)
    WA14: Alt .5A 98
Trafalgar Pl. M20: Man 4C 92
Trafalgar Rd. M6: Sal 5C 48
    M33: Sale .2E 89
Trafalgar Sq. M7: A Lyme 1B 72
                                        (not continuous)
Trafalgar St. M7: Sal 2A 52
    OL1: O'ham 1A 30
    OL7: A Lyme 2B 72
Trafalgar Wlk. M11: Man 2C 68
                                        (off Herne St.)
    M15: Man 5A 66
Trafford Athletics Stadium 4B 78
Trafford Av. M41: Urm 2A 76
Trafford Bank Rd. M16: Old T 5E 65
Trafford Bar Station (Metro) 5D 65
Trafford Boulevard M41: Urm 4E 61
Trafford Cen., The M41: Urm 4F 61
Trafford Ct. M15: Man 4F 65
                                        (off Stretford Rd.)
Trafford Dr. WA15: Tim 3D 99
Trafford Ecology Pk. 3E 63
Trafford Gro. BL4: Farn 1A 18
    M32: Stre .4F 77
Trafford Ho. M32: Stre 5B 64
                                        (off Chester Rd.)
Trafford Mans. M16: Old T 3D 79
TRAFFORD PARK 5E 63
Trafford Pk. Heritage Cen. 4E 63
Trafford Pk. Rd. M17: T Pk 2D 63
                                        (Moorings End.)
    M17: T Pk .5C 64
                                        (Wharf End)
Trafford Park Station (Rail) 2E 77
Trafford Pl. M15: Man 4F 65
Trafford Plaza M16: Old T 1D 79
Trafford Retail Pk. M41: Urm 5E 61
Trafford Rd. M5: Sal 4C 64
    M30: Ecc 2F 61
    M50: Sal 4C 64
Trafford St. BL4: Farn 1A 18
    M1: Man 3F 9 (2A 66)
    OL8: O'ham 5D 117 (4A 30)
Trafford Water Sports Cen. 2A 90
Trafford Way M30: Urm 3E 61
Trafford Wharf Rd. M17: T Pk 3F 63
Tragan Cl. SK2: Stoc 5F 107
Tragan Dr. SK2: Stoc 5F 107
Trail St. M6: Sal 5A 50
Trajan Ho.
    OL1: O'ham 2E 117 (2B 30)
Tramore Wlk. M22: Wyth 4F 109
Tram St. M11: Man 2E 69
Tramway Rd. OL6: A Lyme 3E 59
Tranby Cl. M22: Wyth 2B 110
Tranmere Cl. M18: Man 5D 69
Tranmere Rd. SK3: Stoc 3D 105
Transvaal St. M11: Man 1F 69
Travis Brow SK4: Stoc 2F 105
Travis St. M1: Man 3F 11 (2D 67)
    SK14: Hyde 3F 87

Traynor Cl. M24: Mid 5B 16
Tree Av. M43: Droy 4C 56
Tree Ho. Av. OL7: A Lyme 1B 58
Treelands Wlk. M5: Sal 4D 65
Tree Wlk. M32: Stre 4E 77
Tregaer Fold M24: Mid 1E 27
Tremain Wlk. *M9: Man* *5F 39*
                (off Stockwood Wlk.)
Trenam Pl. M5: Sal 5D 51
Trenant Rd. M6: Sal 2F 49
Trenchard Dr. M22: Wyth 2B 114
Trent Av. OL9: Chad 1A 28
Trent Bri. Wlk. M16: Old T 2C 78
Trent Cl. SK5: Stoc 3E 97
Trent Ct. *M15: Man* *4F 65*
                (off Johnson St.)
  SK3: Stoc .4A 106
Trentham Av. SK4: Stoc 5B 94
Trentham Gro. M40: Man 3C 40
Trentham Lawns M6: Sal 3C 50
Trentham Rd. M16: Old T 2C 78
Trentham St. M15: Man 5B 8 (3E 65)
  M27: Swin .3A 34
Trent Wlk. M43: Droy 2D 71
Trent Way BL4: Kea 4D 19
                (not continuous)
Tresco Av. M32: Stre 4A 78
Trevarrick Ct. OL4: O'ham 1E 31
Trevelyan St. M30: Ecc 5C 48
Trevor Av. M33: Sale 1B 98
Trevor Dr. M40: Man 2A 42
Trevor Gro. SK1: Stoc 3C 106
Trevor Rd. M27: Swin 1F 47
  M30: Ecc 4D 47
  M41: Urm 2B 74
Trevor St. M11: Man 3A 70
Triangle, The M4: Man 4B 6 (5B 52)
  WA15: Tim .4D 99
Trident Rd. M30: Ecc 3B 60
Trimdon Cl. M11: Man 5D 55
Trimley Av. M40: Man 2F 53
Tring Wlk. M9: Man 1D 39
Trinity Wlk. M33: Sale 4F 89
Trinity Bri. Ho. M3: Sal 4F 5
Trinity Cl. SK16: Duk 2F 73
Trinity Ct. M3: Sal 4D 5
  OL6: A Lyme 2A 116 (4C 58)
Trinity Cres. M28: Walk 2A 32
Trinity Edge M3: Sal 4E 5
Trinity Gdns. M3: Sal 3D 5 (5F 51)
Trinity Ho. OL1: O'ham 1D 117 (1A 30)
Trinity Rd. M33: Sale 4E 89
Trinity Sports Cen. 4C 66
Trinity St. M24: Mid 1B 26
  OL1: O'ham 1D 117 (1A 30)
Trinity Wlk. *M14: Man* *2D 81*
                (off Ellanby Cl.)
Trinity Way M3: Sal 5D 5 (5A 52)
Trippier Rd. M30: Ecc 2B 60
Tripps M. M20: Man 4B 92
Triscombe Way
  M16: W Ran 2A 80
Tristam Cl. M13: Man 5F 11 (4E 67)
Trojan Gdns. M7: Sal 2E 51
Trongate Wlk. *M9: Man* *5A 40*
                (off Carisbrook St.)
Troon Dr. SK8: H Grn 5E 111
Troon Rd. M23: Wyth 5B 100
Trough Ga. OL8: O'ham 2F 43
Troutbeck Av. M4: Man 5F 53

Troutbeck Rd. SK8: Gat 3D 111
Trowbridge Dr. M40: Man 3E 41
Trowbridge Rd. M34: Dent 4C 86
Trowtree Av. M12: Man 4A 68
Troydale Dr. M40: Man 2C 54
Troy Wlk. M5: Sal 3D 65
Truro Av. M32: Stre 3A 78
  OL6: A Lyme 5F 45
  SK5: Stoc 3E 97
Truro Wlk. M34: Dent 4B 86
Trust Rd. M18: Man 2E 83
Tucana Av. M7: Sal 1B 4 (4E 51)
Tudbury Way M3: Sal 3D 5 (4F 51)
Tudor Av. M9: Man 3A 40
  OL9: Chad .1F 41
Tudor Cl. SK5: Stoc 1A 96
Tudor Ct. *M16: Old T* *5E 65*
               (off Stanley Rd.)
  M25: Pres 1E 37
Tudor Gro. M24: Mid 3F 15
Tudor Ho. *M21: Chor* *5B 80*
            (off Mauldeth Rd.)
Tudor Ind. Est. SK16: Duk 4C 72
Tudor St. M24: Mid 1D 27
  OL8: O'ham 4F 29
                (not continuous)
  M40: Man 4C 66
Tuer St. M13: Man 3C 108
Tuffley Rd. M23: Wyth 3C 108
Tufton Wlk. M9: Man 5F 39
Tugford Cl. M16: W Ran 1A 80
Tuley St. M11: Man 3B 68
Tulip Av. BL4: Kea 3B 18
Tulip Cl. OL9: Chad 2A 28
Tulip Dr. WA15: Tim 5B 98
Tulip Wlk. M7: Sal 1C 4 (3F 51)
Tulketh St. Ind. Est.
  M40: Man 4B 40
Tulle Ct. M25: Pres 5C 22
Tully St. M7: Sal 5A 38
Tully St. Sth. M7: Sal 1A 52
Tulpen Sq. OL9: Chad 2D 29
Tumblewood Dr. SK8: Chea 2F 111
Tumbling Bank M9: Man 1F 39
Tunbridge Sq. M5: Sal 1C 64
Tunshill Rd. M23: Wyth 2A 100
Tuns Rd. OL8: O'ham 2D 45
Tunstall Rd. OL4: O'ham 3E 31
Tunstall St. M11: Man 3A 70
  SK4: Stoc .1A 106
Tunstead Av. M20: Man 2B 92
Tupelo St. M13: Man 5F 67
Turf La. OL9: Chad 1B 42
Turfnell Way M28: Wors 2C 46
Turley St. M8: Man 1D 53
Turnberry Rd. SK8: H Grn 5E 111
Turnberry Wlk. *M8: Man* *4E 39*
               (off Stakeford Dr.)
Turnbull Av. M25: Pres 2E 23
Turnbull Rd. M13: Man 3B 82
  M18: Man 1B 84
Turnbury Cl. M33: Sale 2D 89
Turnbury Rd. M22: Shar 1A 110
Turncroft La. SK1: Stoc 2C 106
Turner Av. M35: Fail 1A 56
Turner Dr. M41: Urm 3B 76
Turner La. OL6: A Lyme 1C 116 (3D 59)
  SK6: Bred 5B 86
Turner St. M4: Man 4D 7 (5C 52)
  M7: Sal 5A 38

Turner St. M11: Man 1E **69**
 M16: Old T 4E **65**
 M18: Man 5F **69**
 M34: Dent 5A **72**
 OL6: A Lyme 1C **116** (3D **59**)
 SK1: Stoc 1B **118** (1B **106**)
Turnfield Rd. SK8: Chea 3E **111**
Turn Moss Rd. M32: Stre 5B **78**
Turnpike Grn. M6: Sal *4B* **50**
 (off Nursery St.)
Turnpike Wlk. *M11: Man* 1B **68**
 (off Albert St.)
Turn St. OL6: A Lyme 3E **59**
Turton La. M25: Pres 4B **22**
Turton St. M11: Man 3F **69**
Turves Rd. SK8: Chea H 5F **111**
Tuscan Rd. M20: Man 3D **103**
Tuscany Vw. M7: Sal 4D **37**
Tutbury St. M4: Man 1F **67**
Tuxford Wlk. *M40: Man* *2F* **53**
 (off Palgrave Av.)
Tweedale Av. M9: Man 4E **25**
 (not continuous)
Tweedale Way OL9: Chad 2B **42**
Tweed Cl. OL8: O'ham 4A **30**
Tweedle Hill Rd. M9: Man 5D **25**
Tweedsdale Cl. M45: White 5D **13**
Tweenbrook Av. M23: Wyth 3C **108**
Twelve Yards Rd. M30: Ecc 3A **60**
 (not continuous)
Twigworth Rd. M22: Wyth 4E **109**
Twillbrook Dr. M3: Sal 2F **5** (4A **52**)
Twining Rd. M17: T Pk 2F **61**
Twirl Hill Rd. OL6: A Lyme 3F **45**
Twoacre Av. M22: Wyth 1E **109**
Two Trees La. M34: Dent 3B **86**
Twyford Cl. M20: Man 5B **92**
Tydden St. OL8: O'ham 1B **44**
Tyersall Cl. M30: Ecc 3A **48**
Tyldesley St. M14: Man 2C **80**
Tymm St. M40: Man 4E **41**
Tyndall Av. M40: Man 3C **40**
Tyndall St. OL4: O'ham 3E **31**
Tynedale Cl. SK5: Stoc 3A **96**
Tyne St. OL4: O'ham 2E **31**
Tynwald St. OL4: O'ham 2E **31**
Tynwell Wlk. *M40: Man* *2E* **53**
 (off Glendower Dr.)
Tyrol Wlk. M11: Man 2B **68**
Tyrone Cl. M23: Wyth 3F **99**
Tyro St. OL8: O'ham 1B **44**
Tyrrell Rd. SK5: Stoc 4B **84**
Tysoe Gdns. M3: Sal 3D **5** (5F **51**)
Tyson St. M8: Man 4B **38**
Tytherington Dr. M19: Man 4F **83**

U

Ukraine Rd. M7: Sal 1D **51**
Uldale Dr. M24: Mid 5A **16**
Ullock Av. M24: Mid 4F **15**
Ullswater Av. OL7: A Lyme 3C **58**
Ullswater Dr. M24: Mid 4A **16**
Ullswater Rd. M22: Wyth 4D **109**
 M41: Urm 1A **74**
 SK1: Stoc 4D **107**
 SK9: Hand 5E **115**
Ullswater Wlk. *M9: Man* 1A **40**
 (off Rockmead Dr.)

Ulverston Av. M20: Man 1C **92**
 OL9: Chad 3C **28**
Underhill Rd. OL1: O'ham 1A **30**
Underhill Wlk. M40: Man 3D **55**
Under La. OL9: Chad 1D **43**
Underwood Cl. M18: Man 4B **70**
Underwood St. SK16: Duk 2D **73**
Unicorn St. M30: Ecc 2D **61**
Union Rd. OL6: A Lyme 3E **59**
Union St. M4: Man 4D **7** (5C **52**)
 M6: Sal 3C **50**
 M12: Man 3E **67**
 M14: Man 2D **81**
 M18: Man 4A **70**
 M24: Mid 5C **16**
 M27: Pen 4C **34**
 M27: Swin 4A **34**
 OL1: O'ham 4D **117** (3B **30**)
 OL6: A Lyme 1C **116** (4D **59**)
 OL9: Chad 3D **28**
 SK1: Stoc 5B **118** (3B **106**)
 SK14: Hyde 3F **87**
Union St. W.
 OL8: O'ham 5D **117** (3A **30**)
 (not continuous)
Union Ter. *M7: Sal* *4B* **38**
 (off Bury Old Rd.)
Union Yd. OL4: O'ham 3D **31**
Unison Bus. Cen.
 M41: Urm 3A **62**
United Rd. M16: Old T 4A **64**
United Trad. Est. M16: Old T 5A **64**
Unity Dr. M7: Sal 1B **52**
Unity Way SK1: Stoc 5C **118** (3B **106**)
UNIVERSITIES 4C **66**
University of Manchester
 Beyer Building *4C* **66**
 (off Higher Cambridge St.)
 Denmark Road Building 5D **67**
 Dryden St. *4E* **67**
 (off Dryden St.)
 Ellen Wilkinson Building 5D **67**
 Granby Row 3E **11**
 Greenheys Bus. Cen. 5C **66**
 Institute of Science and Technology
 . . . . .3E **11** (2D **67**)
 John Rylands University Library
 . . . . .1A **10** (1B **66**)
 Manchester Business School East
 . . . . .5D **11** (4C **66**)
 Manchester Business School West
 . . . . .4C **66**
 McDougall Sports Cen. 5C **66**
 Sackville Street Building
 . . . . .3E **11** (2D **67**)
 Stopford Building 5D **67**
 University Place 5E **11**
 Up. Brook St. 5E **11** (4D **67**)
University of Salford
 Adelphi Building 5F **51**
 Adelphi Campus 3C **4** (5E **51**)
 Adelphi House 4B **4** (5E **51**)
 Irwell Pl. 5A **4** (1E **65**)
 Irwell Valley Campus 3D **51**
 Newton Building 3A **4** (5D **51**)
 Peel Pk. 2A **4** (5D **51**)
 Salford University Bus. Pk. 3D **51**
 Technology House 3D **51**
 (off Frederick Rd.)
University Rd. M5: Sal 1A **4** (4D **51**)

University Rd. W. M5: Sal 4A **4** (5D **51**)
UNSWORTH 3E **13**
Unsworth Way OL1: O'ham . .1D **117** (1A **30**)
Unwin Av. M18: Man 1F **83**
Unwin Ct. M6: Sal 5B **50**
(off Rosehill Cl.)
Upavon Ct. M7: Sal 1B **52**
Upavon Rd. M22: Wyth 3B **110**
Upland Rd. OL8: O'ham 5A **30**
Uplands M24: Mid 2C **26**
Uplands Rd. M41: Urm 5A **74**
Up. Brook St. M13: Man 5E **11** (4D **67**)
SK1: Stoc 3C **118** (2B **106**)
Up. Camp St. M7: Sal 2F **51**
Up. Chorlton Rd. M16: W Ran 2E **79**
Up. Conran St. M9: Man 4A **40**
Up. Cyrus St. M40: Man 5A **54**
Up. Gloucester St. M6: Sal 4C **50**
Up. Helena St. M40: Man 5A **54**
Up. Kent Rd. M14: Man 2A **82**
Up. Kirby St. M4: Man 1E **67**
Up. Lloyd St. M14: Man 2C **80**
Up. Medlock St. M15: Man 4B **66**
Uppermill Dr. M19: Man 5A **94**
Up. Monsall St. M40: Man 1A **54**
Up. Moss La. M15: Man 4A **66**
Up. Park Rd. M7: Sal 3F **37**
M14: Man 1E **81**
Up. West Gro. M13: Man 5F **67**
Up. Wharf St. M5: Sal 5B **4** (1E **65**)
Up. Wilton St. M25: Pres 5E **23**
Upton Av. SK4: Stoc 4A **94**
Upton Cl. M24: Mid 4C **26**
Upton Dr. WA14: Tim 3A **98**
Upton Wlk. OL7: A Lyme 1C **72**
(off John St. E.)
Upton Way SK9: Hand 4F **115**
(off Beeston Rd.)
Upwood Wlk. M9: Man 1A **40**
(off Sanderstead Dr.)
Urban Rd. M33: Sale 4C **88**
Urbis 3B **6** (5C **52**)
Urmson St. OL8: O'ham 1B **44**
URMSTON 3F **75**
Urmston La. M32: Stre 4C **76**
Urmston Leisure Cen. 3D **75**
Urmston Pk. M41: Urm 3A **76**
Urmston Station (Rail) 3F **75**
Usk Cl. M45: White 2E **23**
Uvedale Ho. M30: Ecc 1F **61**
(off Adelaide St.)
Uxbridge Av. M11: Man 5E **55**
Uxbridge St. OL6: A Lyme 2A **116** (4C **58**)

V

Vaal St. OL8: O'ham 1E **43**
Valance Cl. M12: Man 4C **68**
Vale Av. M26: Rad 2E **19**
M27: Pen 3C **34**
M33: Sale 3A **90**
M41: Urm 4A **74**
Vale Cl. SK4: Stoc 1B **104**
Vale Cotts. SK14: Hyde 1E **87**
(off Arnside Dr.)
Vale Ct. M24: Mid 1D **27**
Vale Dr. M25: Pres 2C **36**
OL9: O'ham 3F **29**
Vale Ho. SK4: Stoc 2A **104**

Vale La. M35: Fail 3C **56**
Valencia Rd. M7: Sal 1D **51**
Valentia Rd. M9: Man 5F **25**
Valentine St. M35: Fail 5A **42**
OL4: O'ham 3E **31**
Vale Pk. Way M8: Man 5E **39**
Valerie Wlk. M15: Man 5B **10**
Vale Rd. M43: Droy 4D **57**
SK4: Stoc 2B **104**
WA15: Tim 5C **98**
Vale St. M11: Man 5E **55**
M24: Mid 1D **27**
OL7: A Lyme 1C **58**
Vale Top Av. M9: Man 5B **40**
Valetta Cl. M14: Man 5D **81**
Valewood Av. SK4: Stoc 2C **104**
Valiant Wlk. M40: Man 3A **42**
(off Nuthurst Rd.)
Vallea Ct. M4: Man 1C **6** (4C **52**)
Valley Cl. SK8: Chea 3F **111**
Valley Ct. SK4: Stoc 2D **105**
Valley Dr. SK9: Hand 5E **115**
Valley Gro. M34: Dent 3D **87**
Valley Pk. Rd. M25: Pres 4B **22**
Valley Rd. M24: Mid 4D **17**
M41: Urm 2A **74**
SK4: Stoc 2B **104**
SK6: Bred 4F **97**
SK8: Chea 3F **111**
Valley Wlk. M11: Man 1B **68**
Vancouver Quay M50: Sal 3B **64**
Vandyke Av. M6: Sal 4D **49**
Vane St. M30: Ecc 5E **47**
Vanguard Cl. M30: Ecc 3B **60**
(off Avroe Rd.)
Varden Gro. SK3: Stoc 5F **105**
Varey St. M18: Man 5F **69**
Varley St. M40: Man 3F **53**
Varna St. M11: Man 3F **69**
Vasser Rd. M18: Man 5D **69**
Vauban Dr. M6: Sal 4D **49**
Vaudrey Dr. WA15: Tim 3C **98**
Vaudrey La. M34: Dent 3C **86**
Vaughan Av. M40: Man 4C **40**
Vaughan Ho. M13: Man 5D **67**
(off Portsmouth St.)
Vaughan Ind. Est. M12: Man 3B **68**
Vaughan Rd. M21: Chor 5F **79**
SK4: Stoc 5F **95**
Vaughan St. M12: Man 3B **68**
M30: Ecc 4D **47**
Vauxhall Av. M40: Man 3E **53**
(off Hamerton Rd.)
Vauxhall Ind. Est. SK5: Stoc 2A **96**
Vauxhall St. M40: Man 3D **53**
Vawdrey Dr. M23: Wyth 1B **100**
Vega St. M8: Man 3A **52**
Vela Wlk. M7: Sal 2B **4** (4E **51**)
Velmere Av. M9: Man 4C **24**
Velour Cl. M3: Sal 1C **4** (4F **51**)
Velvet Ct. M1: Man 3D **11**
Vendale Av. M27: Swin 1F **47**
Venesta Av. M6: Sal 4D **49**
Venetia St. M40: Man 2E **55**
Venice Ct. M1: Man 3D **11**
(off Samuel Ogden St.)
Venice St. M1: Man 3D **11** (2C **66**)
Ventnor Av. BL9: Bury 3B **12**
M19: Man 5E **83**
M33: Sale 2D **89**

Ventnor Cl. M34: Dent 5D 87
Ventnor Rd. M20: Man 5E 93
  SK4: Stoc 1C 104
Ventnor St. M6: Sal 3D 51
  M9: Man .4F 39
Ventura Cl. M14: Man 4C 80
Venture Scout Way
  M8: Man .2B 52
Venwood Ct. M25: Pres 2B 36
Venwood Rd. M25: Pres 2B 36
Verdant La. M30: Ecc 2B 60
Verdun Av. M6: Sal 4D 49
Verdun Rd. M30: Ecc 3D 47
Verdure Av. M33: Sale 2E 99
Verdure Cl. M35: Fail 5D 43
Vere St. M50: Sal 1B 64
Verity Cl. M20: Man 2D 93
Verity Wlk. M9: Man 1D 39
Verne Av. M27: Swin 4A 34
Vernon Av. M30: Ecc 5B 48
  M32: Stre 4F 77
  SK1: Stoc 1D 107
Vernon Ct. M7: Sal 3E 37
Vernon Dr. M25: Pres 2C 36
Vernon Gro. M33: Sale 4A 90
Vernon Ho. SK1: Stoc 2D 107
Vernon Mill SK1: Stoc 1C 106
Vernon Pk. WA15: Tim 4C 98
Vernon Rd. M7: Sal 3E 37
  M43: Droy 5A 56
  SK6: Bred 1F 109
Vernon St. BL4: Farn 1A 18
  M7: Sal 2F 51
  M9: Man .5A 40
  M16: Old T 5E 65
  OL6: A Lyme 3E 59
  SK1: Stoc 1B 118 (1B 106)
  SK14: Hyde 3F 87
Vernon Wlk. SK1: Stoc 2A 118
Verona Dr. M40: Mand 3E 55
Veronica Rd. M20: Man 5E 93
Verrill Av. M23: Wyth 2E 101
Verwood Wlk. M23: Wyth 1C 108
               (off Beckfield Rd.)
Vesper St. M35: Fail 4C 42
Vesta St. M4: Man 1E 67
Vestris Dr. M6: Sal 4D 49
Viaduct Rd.
  WA14: B'ath 4A 98
Viaduct St. M3: Sal 3F 5 (5A 52)
  M12: Man 1A 68
  SK3: Stoc 3A 118 (2A 106)
Vicarage Cl. M6: Sal 4D 49
Vicarage Ct. SK14: Hyde 4F 87
Vicarage Cres. OL6: A Lyme 2F 59
Vicarage Dr. SK16: Duk 2F 73
Vicarage Gdns. SK3: Stoc 3F 105
Vicarage Gro. M30: Ecc 5B 48
Vicarage La. M24: Mid 2F 27
Vicarage Rd. M27: Swin 4A 34
  M41: Urm 1D 75
  OL7: A Lyme 2D 59
  SK3: Stoc 5A 106
Vicarage St. OL8: O'ham 1E 43
Vicars Rd. M21: Chor 5C 78
Vicars St. M30: Ecc 5B 48
Viceroy Ct. M20: Man 1D 103
Vicker Cl. M27: Clif 2B 34
Vicker Gro. M20: Man 3B 92
Vickers St. M40: Man 4A 54

Victoria Av. M9: Man 4C 24
  M19: Man 5C 82
  M20: Man 5C 92
  M27: Swin 4C 34
  M30: Ecc .4B 48
  M45: White 1C 22
  WA15: Tim 4A 98
Victoria Av. E. M9: Man 5A 26
Victoria Bri. St.
  M3: Sal 4A 6 (5B 52)
Victoria Bldg., The M50: Sal 3B 64
Victoria Cl. SK3: Stoc 5A 118 (4A 106)
Victoria Ct. M11: Man 2E 69
               (off Brigham St.)
  M32: Stre 3E 77
  M45: White 2B 22
  OL7: A Lyme 1C 72
Victoria Cres. M30: Ecc 4B 48
Victoria Dr. M33: Sale 5F 89
Victoria Farm SK16: Duk 3F 73
Victoria Grange M20: Man 4C 92
            (off Barlow Moor Rd.)
Victoria Hall M14: Man 5E 81
  SK4: Stoc 3E 95
Victoria Hall M13: Man 1E 81
            (off Up. Brook St.)
  M15: Man 5C 10
            (not continuous)
Victoria Ho. M11: Man 2E 69
  M30: Sal .3C 48
Victoria La. M27: Swin 4F 33
  M45: White 2B 22
Victoria Lodge M7: Sal 2E 51
  SK16: Duk 4E 73
Victoria M. BL9: Bury 4D 13
  SK16: Duk 4E 73
Victoria Mill M43: Droy 1C 70
  SK5: Stoc 5A 84
Victoria Pde. M41: Urm 3F 75
Victoria Pk. M14: Man 1A 82
  SK1: Stoc 3D 107
Victoria Pl. M17: T Pk 4B 64
  M34: Dent 5C 86
Victoria Rd. BL4: Kea 3C 18
  M6: Sal 3C 48
  M14: Man 5D 81
  M16: W Ran 3F 79
  M19: Man 4B 82
  M22: Nor .3F 101
  M30: Ecc .4A 48
  M32: Stre 3F 77
  M33: Sale 5F 89
  M41: Urm 3D 75
  SK1: Stoc 2D 107
  SK16: Duk 4E 73
  WA15: Tim 5C 98
Victoria Sq. M4: Man 3F 7
  M45: White 2B 22
Victoria Station (Rail) 2C 6 (4C 52)
Victoria Sta. App. M3: Man . .3B 6 (5B 52)
Victoria Station Stop (Metro)
                     .4C 52
Victoria St. M3: Man 4B 6 (5B 52)
  M11: Man 2E 69
  M24: Mid .1C 26
  M34: Dent 2A 86
            (not continuous)
  M35: Fail .1F 55
  OL4: O'ham 3C 30
  OL7: A Lyme 5A 116 (1C 72)
  OL8: O'ham 4B 44

Victoria St. OL9: Chad 2D **29**
   SK16: Duk 2F **73**
Victoria St. E. OL7: A Lyme . . .5A **116** (5C **58**)
Victoria Ter. M12: Man 1B **82**
   M13: Man 1E **81**
            (off Hathersage Rd.)
Victoria Trad. Est. OL9: Chad, O'ham . .1D **43**
                      (not continuous)
Victoria Wlk. OL9: Chad 1E **29**
Victor Mann St. M11: Man 3C **70**
Victor St. M3: Sal 4D **5** (5F **51**)
   M40: Man 3E **53**
   OL8: O'ham 3D **43**
Victory Gro. M34: Aud 3E **71**
Victory Pk. Ind. Est.
   M35: Fail .5F **41**
Victory St. M14: Man 2E **81**
Vienna Rd. SK3: Stoc 5F **105**
Vienna Rd. E. SK3: Stoc 5F **105**
Viewfield Wlk. *M9: Man* 5A **40**
             (off Nethervale Dr.)
Vigo St. OL4: O'ham 4F **31**
Viking Cl. M11: Man 1B **68**
VILLAGE, THE 5B **74**
Village M17: T Pk 5F **63**
Village, The M41: Urm 4B **74**
Village Circ. M17: T Pk 4F **63**
Village Ct. M17: T Pk 4E **63**
Village St. M7: Sal 2E **51**
Village Wlk. *M11: Man* 1E **69**
            (off Bob Massey Cl.)
Village Way M4: Man 4D **7**
   M17: T Pk 4D **63**
Villa Rd. OL8: O'ham 5B **30**
Villdale Av. SK2: Stoc 4E **107**
Villemomble Sq.
   M43: Droy 1C **70**
Villiers Av. M45: White 2C **22**
Villiers Dr. OL8: O'ham 4A **30**
Villiers Ind. Est. M6: Sal 3C **50**
Villiers St. M6: Sal 3B **50**
   OL6: A Lyme 5F **59**
Vinca Gro. *M7: Sal* 1F **51**
            (off Hilton St. Nth.)
Vincent Av. M21: Chor 4C **78**
   M30: Ecc .3F **47**
   OL4: O'ham 1E **31**
Vincent St. M11: Man 2E **69**
   M24: Mid .4C **16**
Vine Av. M27: Pen 4D **35**
Vine Ct. M32: Stre 4F **77**
Vine Fold M40: Man 3B **42**
Vine Gro. SK2: Stoc 5E **107**
Vinery Gro. M34: Dent 4D **37**
Vine St. M7: Sal 3A **70**
   M11: Man .4E **23**
   M25: Pres 4E **23**
   M30: Ecc .1E **61**
   OL9: Chad 1D **43**
Vineyards, The *M7: Sal* 4E **37**
              (off Nevile Rd.)
Vineyard St. OL4: O'ham 2D **31**
Viola St. M11: Man 5F **55**
Violet Ct. M22: Wyth 3F **109**
Violet Hill Ct. OL4: O'ham 1F **31**
Violet St. M18: Man 4B **70**
   SK2: Stoc 5B **106**
Violet Way M24: Mid 2F **27**
VIP Cen., The OL1: O'ham 1E **31**
Virgil St. M15: Man 4E **65**

Virgin Active
   Castlefield 2A **10** (2B **66**)
   East Didsbury 2F **103**
   The Printworks 4C **6**
Virginia Cl. M23: Wyth 4F **99**
Viscount Dr. M90: Man A 2B **112**
   SK8: H Grn 2F **115**
Viscount St. M14: Man 2E **81**
Vivian Pl. M14: Man 1A **82**
Vixen Cl. M21: Chor 1A **92**
Voewood Ho. SK1: Stoc 3D **107**
Voltaire Av. M6: Sal 4D **49**
Vorlich Dr. OL9: Chad 1B **28**
Vue Cinema
   Bury 1D **13**
   Salford Quays 3B **64**
Vulcan Works M4: Man 1F **67**
Vyner Gro. M33: Sale 2B **88**

W

Wadcroft Wlk. *M9: Man* 4A **40**
              (off Towton St.)
Waddicor Av. OL6: A Lyme 1F **59**
Waddington St. OL9: O'ham 1E **29**
Wadebridge Av. M23: Wyth 4F **99**
Wade Cl. M30: Ecc 1F **61**
Wadeford Cl. M4: Man 4E **53**
             (not continuous)
Wade Ho. *M30: Ecc* 1F **61**
             (off Wade Cl.)
Wadesmill Wlk. M13: Man 5E **11**
Wadeson Rd. M13: Man 4F **11** (3D **67**)
Wade St. M24: Mid 3F **27**
Wade Wlk. *M11: Man* 2C **68**
Wadhurst Wlk. *M13: Man* 5E **67**
          (off Lauderdale Cres.)
Wadlow Cl. M3: Sal 2E **5** (4F **51**)
Wadsworth M. M43: Droy 1B **70**
Waggoners Ct. *M27: Swin* 5B **34**
           (off Wayfarers Way)
Wagstaff Dr. M35: Fail 5B **42**
Wagstaffe St. M24: Mid 5C **16**
Waincliffe Av. M21: Chor 4F **91**
Wain Cl. M30: Ecc 5D **47**
Wainman St. M6: Sal 2D **51**
Wainstones Grn. SK2: Stoc 5F **107**
Wainwright Av. M34: Dent 2B **84**
Wainwright Cl. SK2: Stoc 4C **106**
Wainwright St. OL8: O'ham . .5D **117** (4A **30**)
   SK16: Duk 1F **73**
Wakefield Dr. M27: Clif 5F **19**
   OL1: Chad 1E **29**
Wakefield St. M1: Man 4C **10** (3C **66**)
   OL1: Chad 1E **29**
Wakefield Wlk. *M34: Dent* 4C **86**
          (off Mancunian Way)
Wakeling Rd. M34: Dent 5A **86**
Walcott Cl. M13: Man 5F **67**
Wald Av. M14: Man 1A **94**
Waldeck Wlk. *M9: Man* 1A **40**
          (off Ravenswood Dr.)
Walden Cl. M14: Man 5C **80**
Walderton Av. M40: Man 5C **40**
Waldon Av. SK8: Chea 1F **111**
Walford St. M16: W Ran 1A **80**
Walkden Rd. M28: Walk, Wors 2A **32**
Walkden Station (Rail) 2A **32**

Walker Av. M35: Fail 1D **57**
   M45: White .3C **18**
Walker Cl. BL4: Kea 3C **18**
Walker Grn. M30: Ecc 2D **47**
Walker Ho. M5: Sal 4C **64**
   M30: Ecc *1F 61*
                  (off Barlow St.)
Walker Rd. M9: Man 5A **26**
   M30: Ecc 5C **46**
   OL9: Chad .2B **42**
Walkers Bldgs. M1: Man 1F **11**
Walkers Ct. BL4: Farn 1A **18**
Walker's Cft. M3: Man 3B **6** (5B **52**)
Walker's Rd.
   OL8: O'ham 2E **43**
Walker St. M24: Mid 2D **25**
                  (not continuous)
   M26: Rad 1E **21**
   M34: Dent .1A **86**
Walker St. *OL8: O'ham* *3F 29*
                  (off Larch St.)
   SK1: Stoc 2A **118** (2A **106**)
Wallace Av. M14: Man 2F **81**
Wallace St. OL8: O'ham 5B **30**
Wallasey Av. M14: Man 4C **80**
Wallbrook Dr. M9: Man 3E **39**
Walled Garden, The M16: W Ran 3A **80**
   M27: Swin .1F **47**
Waller Av. M14: Man 5E **81**
Wallingford Rd. M41: Urm 2A **76**
   SK9: Hand .4E **115**
Wallis St. M40: Man 2E **55**
   OL9: Chad .5C **28**
WALLNESS 3A **4** (5D **51**)
Wallness Bri. M6: Sal 3E **51**
Wallness La. M6: Sal 1A **4** (3D **51**)
Wallshaw Pl. OL1: O'ham 2C **30**
Wallshaw St. OL1: O'ham 2F **117** (2C **30**)
                  (not continuous)
Wall St. OL8: O'ham 5E **117** (4B **30**)
Wall Way M18: Man 1A **84**
Wallwork St. M11: Man 2A **70**
   SK5: Stoc .3B **84**
Wallworth Av. M18: Man 5F **69**
Wally Sq. M7: Sal 1A **52**
Walmersley Rd. M40: Man 2A **42**
Walmer St. M14: Man 2D **81**
   M18: Man .4A **70**
Walmer St. E. M14: Man 2E **81**
Walmsley Gro. M41: Urm 3F **75**
Walmsley St. SK5: Stoc 5B **96**
Walney Rd. M22: Wyth 2F **109**
Walnut Av. OL4: O'ham 1F **31**
Walnut Cl. M27: Clif 5F **19**
Walnut Gro. M33: Sale 4C **88**
Walnut Rd. M30: Ecc 3C **46**
Walnut St. M18: Man 4F **69**
Walnut Tree Rd. SK3: Stoc 3C **104**
Walnut Wlk. M32: Stre 5E **77**
Walsall St. M6: Sal 2C **50**
Walsden St. M11: Man 5E **55**
Walsh Av. M9: Man 2E **39**
Walshaw Dr. M27: Swin 5B **34**
Walsh St. OL9: Chad 3D **29**
Walsingham Av. M20: Man 4B **92**
   M24: Mid .4C **26**
Walter Greenwood Ct. *M6: Sal* *4C 50*
               (off Belvedere Rd.)
Walter Scott St. OL1: O'ham 1D **31**
Walters Dr. OL8: O'ham 1C **44**

Walter St. M9: Man 4F **39**
   M16: Old T .1E **79**
   M18: Man .4A **70**
   M25: Pres .5B **22**
   OL1: O'ham 4F **117** (3B **30**)
Waltham Rd. M16: W Ran 4A **80**
Walton Cl. OL4: O'ham 5E **31**
Walton Hall Dr. M19: Man 4F **83**
Walton Ho. M35: Fail 4B **42**
Walton Pk. Leisure Cen. 1C **98**
Walton Pk. Miniature Railway
   . . . . .1C **98**
Walton Pl. BL4: Kea 2A **18**
Walton Rd. M9: Man 4F **25**
   M33: Sale .2B **98**
Walton St. M24: Mid 4C **16**
   OL7: A Lyme 2C **58**
   SK1: Stoc .5C **118**
Walton Way M34: Dent 4A **86**
Walworth Cl. M26: Rad 2E **19**
Walwyn Cl. M32: Stre 4A **78**
Wandsworth Av. M11: Man 5F **55**
Wanley Wlk. M9: Man 1B **40**
Wansbeck Cl. M32: Stre 4A **78**
Wansbeck Lodge M32: Stre 4A **78**
Wansfell Wlk. *M4: Man* *5F 53*
                  (off Pollard St.)
Wansford St. M14: Man 2C **80**
Wanstead Av. M9: Man 1D **41**
Warbeck Cl. SK5: Stoc 3C **84**
Warbeck Rd. M40: Man 2F **41**
Warbreck Gro. M33: Sale 5F **89**
Warbrick Dr. M41: Urm 4D **75**
Warburton Cl. WA15: Haleb 3A **112**
Warburton Dr. WA15: Haleb 3A **112**
WARBURTON GREEN 2A **112**
Warburton Rd. SK9: Hand 5F **115**
Warburton St. M5: Sal 4D **65**
   M20: Man .5D **93**
   M30: Ecc 2A **62**
Warburton Way WA15: Tim 4E **99**
Warcock Rd. OL4: O'ham 2E **31**
Wardale Ct. M33: Sale 4E **89**
Warden La. M40: Man 1D **55**
Warden St. M40: Man 1D **55**
Warde St. M15: Man 4A **66**
Wardle Cl. M32: Stre 3A **78**
Wardle Rd. M33: Sale 5D **89**
Wardle St. M40: Man 4A **54**
   OL4: O'ham 3D **31**
WARDLEY 2F **33**
Wardley Av. M16: W Ran 4A **80**
Wardley Hall Ct. M27: Ward 2E **33**
Wardley Hall La. M28: Wors 4C **32**
                  (not continuous)
Wardley Hall Rd. M28: Wors 3D **33**
Wardley Ho. *M6: Sal* *3E 49*
              (off Moss Mdw. Rd.)
Wardley Ind. Est. M28: Ward 3E **33**
                  (not continuous)
Wardley Point M28: Ward 3E **33**
Wardley St. M27: Swin 4B **34**
Ward Rd. M43: Droy 1D **71**
Wardsend Wlk. *M15: Man* *4F 65*
              (off Shawgreen Cl.)
Ward St. M9: Man 2E **39**
   M20: Man .5D **93**
   M35: Fail 4A **42**
   M40: Man .4B **40**

Ward St. OL1: O'ham 1F 29
  OL9: Chad 2E 29
  SK1: Stoc 4C 106
Wareham Gro. M30: Ecc 3D 39
Wareham St. M8: Man 3D 39
Warfield Wlk. *M9: Man* *1A 40*
                (off Sanderstead Dr.)
Warford St. M24: Man 1E 7 (3D 53)
Warke, The M47: Wors 1B 46
Warley Cl. SK8: Chea 5A 104
Warley Gro. SK16: Duk 3E 73
Warley Rd. M16: Old T 2C 78
Warmington Dr. M12: Man 4A 68
Warmley Rd. M23: Wyth 3F 99
Warne Av. M43: Droy 5E 57
Warner Wlk. *M11: Man* *1B 68*
                (off Hopedale Cl.)
Warnford Cl. M40: Man 3F 55
Warren Av. SK8: Chea 1F 111
Warren Bank M9: Man 1F 39
Warren Bruce Rd.
  M17: T Pk 4F 63
Warren Cl. M24: Mid 5B 16
  M34: Dent 3F 85
Warren Dr. M27: Swin 2F 47
  WA15: Haleb 2A 112
Warrener St. M33: Sale 4F 89
Warren La. OL8: O'ham 5D 31
Warren Rd. M17: T Pk 4D 63
  M28: Walk 1A 32
  SK3: Stoc 5A 106
Warren St. M7: Sal 4B 38
  M9: Man .2E 39
  SK1: Stoc 1B 118 (1B 106)
                (not continuous)
Warre St. OL6: A Lyme . . .1B 116 (4D 59)
Warrington Rd. M9: Man 5E 25
Warrington St. OL4: Lees 3F 59
  OL6: A Lyme 1C 116 (4D 59)
Warsall Rd. M22: Shar 4A 102
Warslow Dr. M33: Sale 2A 100
Warsop Av. M22: Shar 1A 110
Warton Dr. M23: Wyth 1C 108
Warwick Av. M20: Man 4B 92
  M27: Ward 2F 33
  M34: Dent 4B 86
  M45: White 2D 23
Warwick Cl. M24: Mid 4C 26
  M45: White 2C 22
  SK4: Stoc 4F 95
  SK16: Duk 4E 73
Warwick Ct. M16: Old T 2C 78
  M24: Mid .1C 26
  M34: Dent *5C 86*
            (off Wordsworth Rd.)
  SK4: Stoc 4F 95
Warwick Dr. M33: Sale 4F 89
  M41: Urm .1D 75
Warwick Gro. M34: Aud 2E 71
Warwick Ho. *M19: Man* *3C 82*
               (off Central Av.)
  M33: Sale *4F 89*
             (off Temple Rd.)
Warwick Mall SK8: Chea 5F 103
Warwick Rd. M16: Old T 5B 64
  M21: Chor 4D 79
  M24: Mid .3D 27
  M35: Fail .2B 56
  OL6: A Lyme 2E 59
  SK4: Stoc 5E 95

Warwick Rd. Sth. M16: Old T 2C 78
Warwick St. M1: Man 4E 7 (5D 53)
  M15: Man .5B 66
  M25: Pres .5C 22
  M27: Pen .3B 34
  OL9: O'ham 5E 29
                (not continuous)
Warwick Ter. SK16: Duk 5C 116
Wasdale Av. M41: Urm 2D 75
Wasdale Dr. M24: Mid 4A 16
  SK8: Gat .3D 111
Wasdale Wlk.
  OL1: O'ham 1F 117 (1C 30)
Washbrook OL9: Chad 5D 29
Washbrook Av. OL9: Chad 5D 29
Washbrook Dr. M32: Stre 4D 77
Washford Dr. M23: Wyth 3F 99
Washington St. OL9: O'ham 2E 29
Washway Rd. M33: Sale 2A 98
Wasnidge Wlk. *M15: Man* *5B 66*
                (off Crediton Cl.)
Wastdale Av. BL9: Bury 3C 12
Wastdale Rd. M23: Wyth 2B 108
Waste St. OL1: O'ham 2C 30
Wast Water St. OL1: O'ham 1C 30
Watchgate Cl. M24: Mid 3F 15
Waterbridge M28: Wors 2B 46
Waterdale Dr. M45: White 1C 22
Waterfield Way M35: Fail 1C 56
Waterford Av. M20: Man 5F 91
Waterford Pl. SK8: H Grn 1D 115
Waterfront, The M11: Man 5C 54
Waterfront Ho. M30: Ecc 4E 47
Waterfront Quay M50: Sal 3B 64
Watergate M34: Aud 2E 71
Watergate Milne Ct. OL4: O'ham 1F 31
Waterhead OL4: O'ham 1F 31
Waterhouse Rd. M18: Man 1A 84
Waterhouse Way SK5: Stoc 1A 96
Water La. BL4: Kea 2A 18
  M43: Droy 1A 70
                (not continuous)
WATERLOO .2C 58
Waterloo Ct. *M20: Man* *3C 92*
                (off Lapwing La.)
Waterloo Gdns. OL6: A Lyme 2F 59
Waterloo Ind. Est. SK1: Stoc 2B 106
Waterloo Pl. SK1: Stoc 3C 118
Waterloo Rd. M8: Man 2B 52
  OL6: A Lyme 2D 59
  SK1: Stoc 3C 118 (2B 106)
Waterloo St. M1: Man 2C 10 (2C 66)
  M8: Man .4E 39
  M9: Man .4E 39
  OL1: O'ham 3F 117 (2B 30)
  OL4: O'ham 5F 117 (3C 30)
  OL6: A Lyme 3F 59
Watermans Cl. M9: Man 4B 40
Watermead M33: Sale 2C 98
Watermill Cl. OL7: A Lyme 2C 58
Waterpark Hall *M7: Sal* *3A 38*
                (off Montpellier M.)
Waterpark Rd. M7: Sal 4A 38
Waters Edge M28: Walk 2B 32
  OL6: A Lyme 2F 59
Waters Edge Bus. Pk. M5: Sal 4D 65
Watersheddings St. OL4: O'ham 1F 31
Watersheddings Way OL4: O'ham 1F 31
Waterside M17: T Pk 3E 63
  M33: Sale 3E 89

Waterside Arts Cen. 3D 89
Waterside Cl. M21: Chor 4F 91
   M26: Rad 2A 12
Waterside Ho. M28: Wors 2C 46
Waterside Plaza M33: Sale 3D 89
      (off Tatton Rd.)
Waterside Vw. M43: Droy 2A 70
Waterslea M30: Ecc 5E 47
Watersmeet M32: Stre 1F 77
Waterson Av. M40: Man 5C 40
Waters Reach M17: T Pk 4B 64
Water St. M3: Man 3C 8 (2F 65)
      (not continuous)
   M9: Man 4F 39
   M12: Man 2E 67
      (off Crane St.)
   M24: Mid 1B 26
      (not continuous)
   M34: Aud 3B 72
   M34: Dent 1E 85
   OL6: A Lyme 2B 116 (4D 59)
   SK1: Stoc 1B 106
   SK14: Hyde 2F 87
Waterway Ent. Pk.
   M17: T Pk 4B 64
Waterworks Rd. OL4: O'ham 1F 31
Watfield Wlk. M9: Man 5F 39
      (off Foleshill Av.)
Watford Av. M14: Man 3D 81
Watford Rd. M19: Man 2C 94
Watkin Cl. M13: Man 4E 67
Watkin St. M3: Sal 1D 5 (4A 52)
Watling Ga. WA14: Tim 2A 98
Watson Sq. SK1: Stoc 3C 118 (2B 106)
Watson St. M3: Man 3A 10 (2B 66)
   M27: Swin 3B 34
   M30: Ecc 5E 47
   M34: Dent 2D 87
   OL4: O'ham 1E 31
Watton Cl. M27: Pen 2B 34
      (off Hinchley Way)
Watts St. M19: Man 5D 83
   OL8: O'ham 2F 43
   OL9: Chad 2D 29
Waugh Av. M35: Fail 1B 56
Wavell Dr. BL9: Bury 5C 12
Wavell Rd. M22: Wyth 4F 109
Waveney Rd. M22: Wyth 2A 110
Waverley Av. BL4: Kea 3B 18
   M32: Stre 2A 78
Waverley Ct. M9: Man 4C 24
Waverley Cres. M43: Droy 4C 56
Waverley Rd. M9: Man 5B 40
   M24: Mid 3C 16
   M27: Pen 5E 35
   M33: Sale 2E 89
   SK3: Stoc 4E 105
   SK14: Hyde 5F 87
Waverley Rd. W. M9: Man 5B 40
Waverley St. OL1: O'ham 1D 31
Waverton Av. SK4: Stoc 1F 95
Waverton Rd. M14: Man 4C 80
Wavertree Rd. M9: Man 5E 25
Waybridge Ind. Est.
   M50: Sal 2F 63
Wayfarers Way M27: Swin 5A 34
Wayford Wlk. M9: Man 5E 39
      (off Hendham Va.)
Wayland Rd. M18: Man 1F 83

Wayland Rd. Sth. M18: Man 2F 83
Wayne Cl. M43: Droy 3E 57
Wayne St. M11: Man 2A 70
Wayside Gro. M28: Walk 5A 18
Weald Cl. M13: Man 5F 11 (4E 67)
Weardale Rd. M9: Man 4D 25
Wearhead Row M5: Sal 1B 64
WEASTE 5F 49
Weaste Dr. M5: Sal 4F 49
Weaste La. M5: Sal 5F 49
   M6: Sal 4E 49
Weaste Rd. M5: Sal 5F 49
Weaste Station (Metro) 1F 63
Weaste Trad. Est. M5: Sal 5F 49
Weatherall St. Nth. M7: Sal 5B 38
Weatherley Cl. OL8: O'ham 3B 44
Weaver Ct. M15: Man 4F 65
      (off Johnson St.)
Weaverham Cl. M13: Man 2B 82
Weaverham Wlk. M33: Sale 5A 90
      (off Mottram Rd.)
Weaverham Way SK9: Hand 5F 115
Weaver Ho. M7: Sal 2E 51
      (off Victoria Lodge)
Weavers Ct. M24: Mid 5B 16
Weavers Grn. BL4: Farn 2A 18
Weavers Rd. M24: Mid 5B 16
Weaver Wlk. M11: Man 3F 69
      (off Ogden La.)
Webb La. SK1: Stoc 2C 106
      (not continuous)
Webdale Dr. M40: Man 5C 40
Webster Gro. M25: Pres 2B 36
Webster St. OL8: O'ham 4B 30
Wedgewood St. M40: Man 3B 54
Wedgwood Rd. M27: Clif 2E 35
Wedhurst St. OL4: O'ham 2E 31
Weedall Av. M5: Sal 4C 64
Weir St. M15: Man 5A 42
   M35: Fail 5A 42
Welbeck Av. M41: Urm 2A 76
   OL9: Chad 1F 41
Welbeck Cl. M45: White 4B 12
Welbeck Gro. M7: Sal 5A 38
Welbeck Ho.
   OL6: A Lyme 3A 116 (5C 58)
Welbeck Rd. M28: Wors 1D 47
   M30: Ecc 3A 48
   SK5: Stoc 4B 84
Welbeck St. M18: Man 4A 70
Welbeck St. Nth.
   OL6: A Lyme 3A 116 (5C 58)
Welbeck St. Sth.
   OL6: A Lyme 3A 116 (5C 58)
      (not continuous)
   OL7: A Lyme 4A 116 (5C 58)
Welbeck Ter. OL6: A Lyme . . .3A 116 (5C 58)
Welburn Av. M22: Wyth 3A 110
Welbury Rd. M23: Wyth 2B 100
Welby St. M13: Man 1F 81
Welcomb St. M11: Man 3D 69
Welcomb Wlk. M45: White 2B 22
Welcome Pde. OL8: O'ham 1E 45
Welcroft St. SK1: Stoc 4C 118 (3B 106)
Weldon Dr. M9: Man 4F 25
Weld Rd. M20: Man 1F 93
Welfold Ho. OL4: O'ham 4D 31
Welford Grn. SK5: Stoc 3B 96
Welford Rd. M8: Man 1B 38
Welford St. M6: Sal 3D 51

Welkin Rd. SK6: Bred 5E 97
Welkin Rd. Ind. Est.
    SK6: Bred .5E 97
Welland Cl. M15: Man 4F 65
Welland Ct. M15: Man 4F 65
                                    (off Welland Cl.)
Welland St. M11: Man 2F 69
    SK5: Stoc 4B 84
Wellbank M25: Pres 1B 36
Wellbank Av. OL6: A Lyme 1F 59
Wellbank Cl. OL8: O'ham 5C 30
Wellbridge Rd. SK16: Duk 4D 73
Wellbrow Wlk. M9: Man 1A 40
                                    (off Haverfield Rd.)
Welldale M. M33: Sale 3A 90
Wellens Way M24: Mid 2E 25
Weller Av. M21: Chor 1F 91
Weller Gdns. M21: Chor 1F 91
Wellesbourne Dr. M23: Wyth 4B 100
Wellesley Av. M18: Man 4F 69
Wellfield Cl. BL9: Bury 1A 12
Wellfield Rd. M8: Man 4C 38
    M23: Wyth 4C 100
    SK2: Stoc 5E 107
Wellgate Av. M19: Man 5D 83
Wellhead Cl. M45: White 4A 12
Wellhead Cl. M15: Man 5B 66
Wellhouse Dr. M40: Man 1E 41
Welling Rd. M40: Man 4A 42
Wellington Av. M16: W Ran 3F 79
Wellington Cen. OL6: A Lyme 5F 59
Wellington Cl. M33: Sale 2E 89
Wellington Clough
    OL7: A Lyme 1B 58
Wellington Ct. OL6: A Lyme 4E 59
                                    (off Adam St.)
    OL8: O'ham 5F 29
                                    (off Frederick St.)
Wellington Cres. M16: Old T 2E 79
Wellington Gro. M15: Man 4F 65
    SK2: Stoc 4B 106
Wellington Ho. M20: Man 1E 93
                                    (off Wilmslow Rd.)
    M32: Stre 4E 77
                                    (off Sandy La.)
Wellington Mill SK3: Stoc 3A 118
Wellington Pde. SK16: Duk 5C 116
Wellington Pl. M3: Man 2E 9
Wellington Rd. M8: Man 4D 39
    M14: Man 1E 93
    M16: W Ran 3A 80
    M20: Man 1E 93
    M27: Swin 4B 34
    M30: Ecc .5A 48
    OL6: A Lyme 1A 100 (4C 58)
                                    (not continuous)
    OL8: O'ham 5E 29
    WA15: Tim 5A 98
Wellington Rd. Nth.
    SK4: Stoc 2A 118 (1D 95)
Wellington Rd. Sth.
    SK1: Stoc 3A 118 (2A 106)
    SK2: Stoc 3A 118 (2A 106)
    SK3: Stoc 3A 118 (2A 106)
Wellington St. M3: Sal 3D 5 (5F 51)
    M18: Man 5F 69
    M32: Stre 4E 77
    M34: Aud 4B 72
    M35: Fail .3C 42
    OL1: O'ham 4F 117 (3B 30)

Wellington St. OL4: O'ham 5E 117 (3B 30)
    OL6: A Lyme 3B 116 (5D 59)
    OL9: Chad 1D 29
    SK1: Stoc 3A 118 (2A 106)
    SK14: Hyde 2E 87
Wellington St. E. M7: Sal 5F 37
Wellington St. W. M7: Sal 1F 51
Wellington Ter. M5: Sal 5F 49
    SK16: Duk 5C 116
Well La. M45: White 4B 12
Well Mead SK6: Bred 5F 97
Wellmead Cl. M8: Man 2B 52
Well Mdw. SK14: Hyde 1F 87
Well Mdw. Ct. SK14: Hyde 1F 87
                                    (off Well Mdw.)
Wellpark Wlk. M40: Man 2E 55
                                    (off Langcroft Dr.)
Wells Av. M25: Pres 2E 37
    OL9: Chad 1C 28
Wells Cl. M24: Mid 2E 25
    M43: Droy 2B 70
    SK8: H Grn 2E 115
Wells Ct. SK16: Duk 4E 73
Wells Dr. SK4: Stoc 1A 104
    SK16: Duk 4E 73
Wellside Wlk. M8: Man 1C 52
                                    (off Dinnington Dr.)
Well St. M4: Man 4C 6
Wellwood Dr. M40: Man 5C 40
Wellyhole St. OL4: O'ham 3F 31
Welney Rd. M16: Old T 2D 79
Welshpool Cl. M23: Wyth 1D 101
Welshpool Way M34: Dent 4C 86
Welton Av. M20: Man 1E 103
Welwyn Cl. M41: Urm 5D 61
Welwyn Dr. M6: Sal 2C 48
Welwyn Wlk. M40: Man 5F 53
                                    (off Marcer Rd.)
Wembley Gro. M14: Man 5E 81
Wembley Rd. M18: Man 2E 83
Wembury St. M9: Man 4A 40
Wembury St. Nth. M9: Man 4A 40
Wem St. OL9: Chad 5C 28
Wemyss Av. SK5: Stoc 4B 84
Wendon Rd. M23: Wyth 1D 109
Wendover Ho. M5: Sal 1C 64
Wendover Rd. M23: Wyth 2F 99
    M41: Urm .3E 75
Wenfield Dr. M9: Man 1D 41
Wenlock Av. OL6: A Lyme 2D 59
Wenlock Cl. M12: Man 4B 68
                                    (off Wenlock Way)
Wenlock Rd. M33: Sale 1C 98
Wenlock St. M27: Swin 4F 33
Wenlock Way M12: Man 4B 68
Wenning Cl. M45: White 5E 13
Wensley Cl. M7: Sal 3C 36
                                    (off Wensley Rd.)
Wensleydale Av. SK8: Chea 5E 103
Wensleydale Cl. BL9: Bury 3C 12
    M23: Wyth 3B 108
Wensley Dr. M20: Man 3D 93
Wensley Rd. M7: Sal 4C 36
    SK5: Stoc 4B 96
    SK8: Chea 5E 103
Wentworth Av. M6: Sal 4E 49
    M18: Man 4A 70
    M41: Urm .4D 75
    M45: White 2F 21
    WA15: Tim 5C 98

Wentworth Cl. M24: Mid 1A 26
Wentworth Ct. M35: Fail 1B 56
   M45: White 1A 22
Wentworth Dr. M33: Sale 3B 88
Wentworth Rd. M27: Swin 1F 47
   M30: Ecc .3C 48
   SK5: Stoc 4B 84
WERNETH 5E 29
Werneth Av. M14: Man 3D 81
Werneth Cl. M34: Dent 3B 86
Werneth Cres. OL8: O'ham 5E 29
Werneth Hall Rd. OL8: O'ham 4F 29
Werneth St. M34: Aud 5B 72
   SK1: Stoc 1D 107
Werneth Wlk. *M34: Dent 3B 86*
               (off Werneth Cl.)
Wesley Ct. SK4: Stoc 1B 104
Wesley Dr. M28: Wors 4B 32
   OL6: A Lyme 1F 59
Wesley Mt. *SK4: Stoc 1A 106*
              (off Dodge Hill)
Wesley Sq. M41: Urm 3C 74
Wesley St. BL4: Farn 2A 18
   M11: Man 2C 68
   M27: Swin 4B 34
   M30: Ecc .5E 47
   M32: Stre 2A 78
   M35: Fail .3C 42
           (not continuous)
   SK1: Stoc 3C 118 (2B 106)
Wessenden Bank E. SK2: Stoc 5F 107
Wessenden Bank W. SK2: Stoc 5F 107
Westage Gdns. M23: Wyth 4C 100
W. Ashton St. M50: Sal 1B 64
West Av. M18: Man 5A 70
   M19: Man 1B 94
   M40: Man 4F 41
   M45: White 4A 12
   SK8: H Grn 5E 111
West Bank M11: Man 3C 70
Westbank Rd. M20: Man 3F 93
W. Bank St. M5: Sal 2A 8 (2E 65)
Westbourne Av. M27: Clif 4F 19
   M45: White 5A 12
Westbourne Dr. OL7: A Lyme 3C 58
Westbourne Gro. M9: Man 4F 39
   M20: Man 2C 92
   M33: Sale 4C 88
   SK5: Stoc 5B 84
Westbourne Pk. M41: Urm 2F 75
Westbourne Range M18: Man 1B 84
Westbourne Rd. M14: Man 5F 81
   M30: Ecc .4D 47
   M34: Dent 3A 86
   M41: Urm 3F 75
Westbourne St. OL9: O'ham 2F 29
Westbrook Ct. M18: Man 2A 84
Westbrook Rd. M17: T Pk 3E 63
   M27: Swin 5A 34
Westbrook Sq. M12: Man 4C 68
Westbrook Trad. Est. M17: T Pk 3E 63
Westbrook Wlk. M20: Man 5C 80
Westbury Rd. M8: Man 3D 39
Westbury St. OL6: A Lyme 4E 59
   SK14: Hyde 5E 73
Westbury St. Ind. Est.
   SK14: Hyde 5E 73
W. Central Dr. M27: Swin 5D 35
W. Charles St. M5: Sal 5A 4 (1D 65)
Westcott Av. M20: Man 2C 92

Westcott Ct. M15: Man 5D 9
Westcourt Rd. M33: Sale 2B 88
W. Craig Av. M40: Man 1E 41
W. Craven St. M5: Sal 3D 65
West Cres. M24: Mid 2B 26
W. Croft Ind. Est. M24: Mid 2F 25
Westcroft Rd. M19: Man 4F 93
   M20: Man 4F 93
W. Crown Av. M5: Sal 2A 8 (2D 65)
Westdale Gdns. M19: Man 3C 94
Westdean Cres. M19: Man 3B 94
W. Dean St. M5: Sal 1B 8 (1E 65)
WEST DIDSBURY 3B 92
West Dr. M6: Sal 1A 50
   M27: Swin 5D 35
   M43: Droy 1B 70
   SK8: Gat .2C 110
W. Duke St. M5: Sal 1C 8
W. Egerton St. M5: Sal 1D 65
West End Av. SK8: Gat 5C 102
West End St. OL9: O'ham 2F 29
West End Trad. Est. M27: Swin 3B 34
Westerdale OL4: O'ham 3E 31
           (not continuous)
Westerham Av. M5: Sal 1C 64
Westerhill OL6: A Lyme 4D 45
Wester Hill Rd. OL8: O'ham 3C 44
Westerling Way M16: W Ran 2A 80
Western Av. M27: Clif 2F 35
   M19: Man 2B 94
Western Circ. M19: Man 2A 64
Western Pk. M50: Sal 1A 64
Western Rd. M41: Urm 4A 74
Western St. M6: Sal 4A 50
   M18: Man 3A 84
Westfield M6: Sal 3A 50
Westfield Av. M24: Mid 2C 26
Westfield Gro. M34: Aud 5A 72
Westfield Rd. M21: Chor 4D 79
   M43: Droy 5A 56
Westfield St. M7: Sal 3F 37
   OL9: Chad 1E 29
Westford Villa SK8: Chea 1E 111
Westgate M33: Sale 4C 88
   M41: Urm 4D 75
Westgate Av. M9: Man 2E 39
Westgate Dr. M27: Swin 1B 48
Westgate Ho. *OL8: O'ham 2F 43*
           (off Hollins Rd.)
W. Gate Rd. M90: Man A 3B 112
Westgate Rd. M6: Sal 2D 49
Westgate St. OL7: A Lyme 5A 116 (1C 72)
WEST GORTON 4B 68
West Grn. M24: Mid 2D 25
West Gro. M13: Man 5F 67
   M33: Sale 5D 89
West Heaton Bowling & Tennis Club
                  . . . . .4C 94
Westhide Wlk. M9: Man 3B 40
W. High St. M5: Sal 5C 50
Westholm Av. SK4: Stoc 1D 95
Westholme Rd. M20: Man 3D 93
   M25: Pres 2E 23
W. Hope St. M5: Sal 5A 4 (1D 65)
Westhorne Fold *M8: Man 2A 38*
           (off Counthill Dr.)
WEST HULME 1A 30
Westhulme Av. OL1: O'ham 1F 29
Westhulme St. OL1: O'ham 1F 29
Westinghouse Rd. M17: T Pk 4C 62
W. King St. M3: Sal 3E 5 (5A 52)

Westland Av. SK1: Stoc 2D **107**
Westland Dr. M9: Man 5F **25**
Westlands M45: White 3B **22**
Westlands, M27: Pen 1D **49**
West Lea M34: Dent 2C **86**
Westlea Dr. M18: Man 2F **83**
Westleigh SK4: Stoc 4C **94**
Westleigh Dr. M25: Pres 1F **37**
Westleigh St. M9: Man 3A **40**
W. Marwood St. M7: Sal 1A **52**
Westmead Dr. WA15: Tim 4D **99**
West Meade M21: Chor 1C **90**
   M25: Pres 2F **37**
   M27: Swin 1C **49**
West Mdw. SK5: Stoc 4C **84**
Westmere Dr. M9: Man 1E **53**
Westminster Av. M16: W Ran 3E **79**
   M45: White 1B **22**
   OL6: A Lyme 5F **45**
   SK5: Stoc 1A **96**
Westminster Cl. M33: Sale 5A **88**
Westminster Ho. M3: Sal 3E **5**
Westminster Rd. M28: Walk 2A **32**
   M30: Ecc 4A **48**
   M35: Fail .4D **43**
   M41: Urm 1F **75**
Westminster St. M15: Man 5B **8**
   M19: Man 4D **83**
   M27: Swin 3F **33**
   OL1: O'ham 1D **31**
Westminster Way SK16: Duk 4E **73**
Westmoor Gables SK4: Stoc 4C **94**
Westmorland Av. OL7: A Lyme 3D **59**
   SK16: Duk 2F **73**
Westmorland Cl. SK5: Stoc 2E **97**
Westmorland Dr. SK5: Stoc 2D **97**
Westmorland Rd. M20: Man 1C **102**
   M30: Ecc 2C **48**
   M33: Sale 1E **99**
   M41: Urm 4E **75**
W. Mosley St. M2: Man 1C **10** (1C **66**)
Westmount Cl. M40: Man 1E **53**
Weston Av. M27: Clif 5A **20**
   M40: Man 3A **42**
   M41: Urm 4D **75**
Weston Ct. M14: Man 3F **81**
Weston Dr. M34: Dent 2C **86**
W. One Retail Pk. M30: Ecc 5C **48**
W. One Way M30: Ecc 1C **62**
Weston Gro. M22: Nor 3A **102**
   SK4: Stoc 2E **95**
Weston Hall M1: Man 3D **11** (2C **66**)
Weston St. OL8: O'ham 5E **31**
   SK5: Stoc 4A **96**
Westover Rd. M41: Urm 2E **75**
Westover St. M27: Swin 3A **34**
West Pk. Av. M34: Dent 3D **87**
West Pk. Rd. SK1: Stoc 1D **107**
West Pk. St. M5: Sal 4A **8** (3D **65**)
West Pl. M19: Man 1B **94**
West Point M16: Old T 5E **65**
                                    (off Chester Rd.)
W. Point Ent. Pk. M17: T Pk 3C **62**
W. Point Lodge M19: Man 5B **82**
                                     (off Slade La.)
Westray Cres. M5: Sal 1A **64**
Westray Rd. M13: Man 3A **82**
West Rd. M25: Pres 4B **22**
   M41: Urm 3A **62**
West Row M25: Pres 3B **36**

West St. BL4: Farn 1A **18**
   M9: Man .1C **38**
   M11: Man 5D **55**
   M24: Mid 4C **16**
   M35: Fail .5A **42**
   OL1: O'ham 3D **117** (2A **30**)
   OL4: Lees 4F **31**
   OL6: A Lyme 1B **116**
   OL9: O'ham 3F **29**
   SK3: Stoc 2F **105**
   SK14: Hyde 5F **73**
   SK16: Duk 5B **116** (1D **73**)
W. Towers St. M6: Sal 1B **64**
W. Vale Rd. WA15: Tim 5B **98**
West Vw. M34: Aud 3A **72**
West Vw. Gro. M45: White 1F **21**
West Vw. M22: Nor 3A **102**
Westville Gdns. M19: Man 3A **94**
Westway M9: Man 3D **25**
   M43: Droy 3C **70**
   OL4: Lees 4F **31**
WESTWOOD 2E **29**
Westwood Av. M7: Sal 4A **38**
   M40: Man 3A **42**
   M41: Urm 4B **76**
   WA15: Tim 4B **98**
Westwood Bus. Cen.
   OL9: O'ham 3F **29**
Westwood Cl. BL4: Farn 1A **18**
Westwood Cres. M30: Ecc 4C **46**
Westwood Dr. M27: Pen 1E **49**
   M33: Sale 1D **99**
   OL9: O'ham 2F **29**
Westwood Ho. BL4: Farn 1A **18**
                                  (off Hesketh Wlk.)
Westwood Ind. Est. OL9: O'ham 2E **29**
WESTWOOD PARK 3E **47**
Westwood Rd. M32: Stre 3D **77**
   SK8: H Grn 1D **115**
Westwood St. M14: Man 1B **80**
W. Works Rd. M17: T Pk 1E **77**
Wet Earth Colliery 4B **20**
Wet Earth Grn. M27: Pen 4F **35**
Wetherall St. M19: Man 4D **83**
Wetherby St. M11: Man 3A **70**
Wexford Wlk. M22: Wyth 4A **110**
Weybourne Av. M9: Man 2C **40**
Weybridge Rd. M4: Man 5E **53**
Weybrook Rd. M19: Man 1D **95**
Weyhill Rd. M23: Wyth 1C **108**
Weylands Gro. M6: Sal 2D **49**
Weymouth Rd. M30: Ecc 4D **47**
Whalley Av. M16: W Ran 2F **79**
   M19: Man 3D **83**
   M21: Chor 1E **91**
   M33: Sale 3E **89**
   M41: Urm 2A **76**
Whalley Cl. M45: White 5B **12**
   WA15: Tim 3B **98**
Whalley Gro. M16: W Ran 3F **79**
   OL6: A Lyme 5E **45**
WHALLEY RANGE 2F **79**
Whalley Rd. M16: W Ran 2E **79**
   M24: Mid 3B **16**
   M45: White 5B **12**
   SK2: Stoc 4E **107**
Wharf Circ. M17: T Pk 3E **63**
Wharf Cl. M1: Man 1F **11** (1D **67**)
   WA14: Alt 4A **98**
                              (off Bridgewater Rd.)

Wharfedale Av. M40: Man 3C 40
Wharfedale Rd. SK5: Stoc 5A 84
Wharf End M17: T Pk 4C 64
Wharf Rd. M33: Sale 3E 89
  WA14: Alt 4A 98
Wharfside Av. M30: Ecc 2F 61
Wharfside Bus. Cen. M17: T Pk ... 4B 64
Wharfside Way M17: T Pk 4A 64
Wharf St. OL9: Chad 1D 43
  SK4: Stoc 2F 33
  SK16: Duk 5B 116 (1D 73)
Wharton Av. M21: Chor 1F 91
Wharton Lodge M30: Ecc 4A 48
Wheat Cl. M13: Man 5E 67
Wheatcroft SK3: Stoc 5B 106
Wheater's Cres. M7: Sal 3E 51
Wheater's St. M7: Sal 3F 51
Wheater's Ter. M7: Sal 3F 51
Wheatley Rd. M27: Ward 2F 33
Wheatley Wlk. M12: Man 4C 68
              (off Woolfall Cl.)
Wheatsheaf Ind. Est. M27: Pen ... 3D 35
Wheeldale OL4: O'ham 3F 31
Wheel Forge Way M17: T Pk 3B 62
Wheler St. M11: Man 2F 69
Whernside Av. M40: Man 3C 40
  OL6: A Lyme 5E 45
Whernside Cl. SK4: Stoc 5A 96
Whewell Av. M26: Rad 1A 12
Whickham Cl. M14: Man 2D 81
Whiley St. M13: Man 1B 82
Whimberry Cl. M5: Sal 4A 8 (3D 65)
Whimberry Way M20: Man 2F 93
Whinfell Dr. M24: Mid 5E 15
Whingroves Wlk. M40: Man 1C 54
             (off Halliford Rd.)
Whinmoor Wlk. M40: Man 5D 41
            (off Bellscroft Av.)
Whinstone Way OL1: Chad 5F 17
Whirley Cl. SK4: Stoc 3F 95
Whiston Rd. M8: Man 4D 39
Whitbrook Way M24: Mid 1F 17
Whitburn Av. M13: Man 3A 82
Whitburn Rd. M23: Wyth 2C 108
Whitby Av. M6: Sal 4E 49
  M14: Man 5A 82
  M16: W Ran 2F 79
  M41: Urm 3A 76
Whitby Cl. SK8: Chea 5E 103
Whitby Rd. M14: Man 5F 81
  OL8: O'ham 1E 45
Whitby St. M24: Mid 5E 17
Whitchurch Dr. M16: Old T 5F 65
Whitchurch Rd. M20: Man 1B 92
Whiteacre Rd. OL6: A Lyme 4E 59
Whiteacres M27: Swin 5F 33
Whiteacre Wlk. M15: Man 5A 66
            (off Shearsby Cl.)
Whitebank Av. SK5: Stoc 4E 97
White Bank Rd. OL8: O'ham 3F 43
Whitebeam Cl. M6: Sal 4C 50
  WA15: Tim 1A 108
Whitebeam Ct. M6: Sal 4C 50
Whitebeck Ct. M9: Man 5C 26
Whitebrook Ct. M33: Sale 5D 89
Whitebrook Rd. M14: Man 4D 81
WHITE BROW 1B 12
White Brow BL9: Bury 1B 12
Whitecar Av. M40: Man 3A 42
Whitecarr La. WA15: Hale 3A 108

Whitechapel St. M20: Man 5D 93
White City Circ. M16: Old T 5C 64
White City Retail Pk. M16: Old T . 5C 64
White City Way M16: Old T 5C 64
Whitecliff Cl. M14: Man 2E 81
White Ct. M27: Swin 5F 33
Whitecroft Gdns. M19: Man 4A 94
Whitecroft Mdw. M24: Mid 1C 26
Whitecroft St. OL1: O'ham 1E 31
WHITEFIELD 2B 22
Whitefield Rd. M33: Sale 3B 88
  SK6: Bred 4F 97
Whitefield Station (Metro) 5B 12
White Friar Ct. M3: Sal 2E 5
Whitefriars Wlk. M22: Wyth 1F 113
WHITE GATE 1C 42
Whitegate Av. OL9: Chad 5B 28
Whitegate Bus. Cen. OL9: Chad .. 4B 28
Whitegate Cl. M40: Man 3A 42
Whitegate Dr. M5: Sal 4F 49
  M27: Clif 2D 35
WHITE GATE END 1A 42
Whitegate La. OL9: Chad 5B 28
           (not continuous)
Whitegate Pk. M41: Urm 3A 74
Whitegate Rd. OL9: Chad 1F 41
Whitegates SK8: Chea 1F 111
Whitegates Rd. M24: Mid 2E 17
  SK8: Chea 1F 111
Whitehall Rd. M20: Man 5E 93
  M33: Sale 1D 99
Whitehall St. OL1: O'ham .. 1F 117 (1B 30)
White Hart Mdw. M24: Mid 4C 16
White Hart St. SK14: Hyde 1F 87
Whitehaven Gdns. M20: Man 1C 102
Whitehaven Pl. SK14: Hyde 5E 73
Whitehead Cres. M26: Rad 2E 19
Whitehead Rd. M21: Chor 5B 78
  M27: Clif 2D 35
Whitehead St. M24: Mid 5E 17
  M34: Aud 3A 72
Whitehill Dr. M40: Man 5C 40
Whitehill Ind. Est. SK4: Stoc 2A 96
           (not continuous)
Whitehill St. SK4: Stoc 4A 96
  SK5: Stoc 4A 96
           (not continuous)
Whitehill St. W. SK4: Stoc 4F 95
Whiteholme Av. M21: Chor 4F 91
White Horse Gdns. M27: Swin ... 1E 47
           (off Worsley Rd.)
White Ho. Av. M8: Man 1A 38
Whitehouse Av. OL4: O'ham 3E 31
Whitehouse Dr. M23: Wyth 1C 108
Whitehurst Dr. M11: Man 2C 68
Whitehurst Rd. SK4: Stoc 4B 94
Whitekirk Cl.
  M13: Man 5F 11 (4D 67)
Whitelake Av. M41: Urm 3B 74
Whitelake Vw. M41: Urm 2B 74
Whitelands OL6: A Lyme 5E 59
Whitelands Ind. Est. SK15: Stal . 5F 59
Whitelands Rd. OL6: A Lyme 5E 59
Whitelands Ter. OL6: A Lyme 5E 59
Whitelea Dr. SK3: Stoc 5F 105
Whiteley Dr. M24: Mid 2E 27
Whiteley Pl. WA14: Alt 5A 98
Whiteley St. M11: Man 5D 55
  OL9: Chad 5D 29

Whitelow Rd. M21: Chor 5C 78
   SK4: Stoc 5C 94
White Mdws. M27: Swin 5B 34
White Moss Av. M21: Chor 5E 79
White Moss Gdns. M9: Man 2C 40
White Moss Rd. M9: Man 1A 40
Whiteoak Ct. M14: Man 5E 81
Whiteoak Rd. M14: Man 5E 81
Whites Cft. M27: Swin 4B 34
Whiteside Cl. M5: Sal 5F 49
Whitestone Ho. OL1: O'ham 1A 30
               (off Trafalgar St.)
White St. M6: Sal 1A 64
   M15: Man 4F 65
White Swallows Rd. M27: Swin 1C 48
White Swan Ind. Est.
   OL1: O'ham 1E 31
White Ter. SK14: Hyde 5E 87
Whitethorn Av. M16: W Ran 2F 79
   M19: Man 1B 94
Whitewater Dr. M7: Sal 5B 36
Whiteway St. M9: Man 5A 40
Whitewillow Cl. M35: Fail 1C 56
Whitfield St. M3: Man 1C 6 (3C 52)
            (off Nuneaton Dr.)
Whitford Wlk. M40: Man 4F 53
            (off Nuneaton Dr.)
Whitland Dr. OL8: O'ham 2D 43
Whit La. M6: Sal 1B 50
          (not continuous)
Whitley Gdns. WA15: Tim 4D 99
Whitley Pl. WA15: Tim 4E 99
Whitley Rd. M40: Man 3E 53
   SK4: Stoc 5D 95
Whitman St. M9: Man 4B 40
Whitmore Rd. M14: Man 4D 81
Whitnall St. M16: W Ran 1A 80
   SK14: Hyde 5F 73
Whitney Ct. OL4: O'ham 3C 30
           (off Hamilton St.)
Whitsand Rd. M23: Shar 1A 104
Whitsbury Av. M18: Man 2F 83
Whitstable Cl. OL9: Chad 3D 29
Whitstable Rd. M40: Man 3E 41
Whitswood Cl. M16: W Ran 2A 80
Whittaker Cl. M25: Pres 5E 23
Whittaker La. M25: Pres 5E 23
Whittaker St. M24: Mid 1B 26
   M40: Man 4B 40
   OL6: A Lyme 2F 59
Whittingham Gro. OL1: O'ham 1F 29
Whittington St.
   OL7: A Lyme 5A 116 (1C 72)
WHITTLE BROOK 2B 32
Whittle Brook Cl. BL9: Bury 1E 13
Whittlebrook Ho. M28: Walk 2A 32
           (off Trinity Cres.)
Whittle Gdns. M28: Walk 2A 32
           (off Whittle St.)
Whittle Gro. M28: Walk 1A 32
Whittle La. OL10: H'ood 1C 14
Whittles Av. M34: Dent 2C 86
Whittles Cft. M1: Man 1F 11
             (Ducie St.)
   M1: Man 1F 11 (1D 67)
            (Pigeon St.)
Whittle St. M4: Man 4E 7 (5D 53)
   M27: Swin 5A 34
   M28: Walk 1A 32
Whittles Wlk. M34: Dent 3C 86
Whitwell Wlk. M13: Man 1A 82

Whitwell Way M18: Man 5E 69
Whitworth Art Gallery, The 1D 81
Whitworth Cl. OL6: A Lyme 3E 59
Whitworth La. M14: Man 4F 81
Whitworth Pk. Mans.
   M14: Man 1C 80
Whitworth St. M1: Man 3C 10 (2C 66)
          (not continuous)
   M11: Man 3C 68
Whitworth St. E. M11: Man 3C 68
Whitworth St. W. M1: Man 3F 9 (2A 66)
Whixhall Av. M12: Man 4A 68
Wibbersley Pk. M41: Urm 3B 74
Wichenby Dr. M33: Sale 4C 88
Wicken St. SK2: Stoc 4E 107
Wickentree La. M35: Fail 3B 42
Wicket Gro. M27: Clif 5A 20
Wickham Ter. M24: Mid 5C 16
Wicklow Av. SK3: Stoc 4D 105
Wicklow Dr. M22: Wyth 4A 110
Wicklow Gro. OL8: O'ham 1A 44
Wickmere Wlk. M8: Man 1B 52
          (off Waterloo Rd.)
Widdop St. OL9: O'ham 2F 29
Widecombe Cl. M41: Urm 1D 75
Widgeon Cl. M14: Man 5D 81
Wiggins Teape Rd. BL9: Bury 1D 13
Wiggins Wlk. M14: Man 2E 81
         (off Bembridge Cl.)
Wighurst Wlk. M22: Wyth 5F 109
Wigley St. M12: Man 3A 68
Wigmore Rd. M8: Man 5D 39
Wigmore St. OL6: A Lyme 3F 59
Wigsby Av. M40: Man 2E 41
Wilberforce Cl. M15: Man 5A 66
Wilbraham Rd. M14: Man 4C 78
   M16: W Ran 4C 78
Wilbraham Rd. M21: Chor 4C 78
   M28: Walk 1A 32
Wilburn St. M5: Sal 2C 8 (2F 65)
          (not continuous)
Wilby St. M8: Man 1D 53
Wilcockson Ho. BL4: Farn 1A 18
         (off Hesketh Wlk.)
Wilcock St. M16: W Ran 1A 80
Wilcott Dr. M33: Sale 3A 88
Wilcott Rd. SK8: Gat 1C 110
Wildbrook Cres. OL8: O'ham 1C 44
          (not continuous)
Wildbrook Ter. OL8: O'ham 2C 44
Wildcroft Av. M40: Man 3C 40
Wilderswood Cl. M20: Man 3E 93
Wild Ho. OL8: O'ham 4B 30
Wildmoor Av. OL4: O'ham 5F 31
Wild St. M34: Dent 2B 86
   OL1: O'ham 2C 30
   OL4: Lees 3F 31
   SK2: Stoc 5C 106
   SK16: Duk 2F 73
Wildwood Cl. SK2: Stoc 5C 106
Wileman Ct. M5: Sal 5F 49
         (off Sheader Dr.)
Wilford Av. M33: Sale 1C 98
Wilford Rd. M30: Ecc 2C 60
Wilfred St. M3: Man 1F 5 (3A 52)
   M40: Man 4C 40
   OL4: O'ham 3D 31
Wilfrid St. M27: Swin 4B 34
Wilham Av. M30: Ecc 1F 61
Wilkins La. SK9: Sty 4A 114

Wilkinson Rd. SK4: Stoc 1A **118** (1A **106**)
(not continuous)
Wilkinson St. M24: Mid 1B **26**
M33: Sale 4F **89**
OL6: A Lyme 3A **116** (5C **58**)
Wilks Av. M22: Wyth 4B **110**
Willan Ent. Cen. M17: T Pk 4E **63**
Willan Ind. Est. M50: Sal 1B **64**
Willan Rd. M9: Man 5E **25**
M30: Ecc 5A **48**
Willaston Cl. M21: Chor 1C **90**
Willaston Way SK9: Hand 4F **115**
(off Sandiway Rd.)
Willdale Cl. M11: Man 5C **54**
Willdor Gro. SK3: Stoc 5D **105**
Willenhall Rd. M23: Wyth 1E **101**
Willerby Rd. M7: Sal 2A **52**
Willert St. M40: Man 2F **53**
Willesden Av. M13: Man 2A **82**
Will Griffith Wlk. M11: Man 2A **68**
(off Rylance St.)
William Chadwick Cl.
M40: Man 4E **53**
William Cl. M41: Urm 4E **75**
William Coates Av. M16: W Ran 2F **79**
William Fairburn Way
M4: Man 4D **7** (5C **52**)
William Jessop St. M1: Man 1F **11**
William Kay Cl. M16: W Ran 1A **80**
William Lister Cl. M40: Man 3F **55**
Williams Cl. M14: Man 1F **81**
(off Hope Rd.)
Williams Cres. OL9: Chad 1B **42**
Williamson La. M43: Droy 2D **71**
Williamson St. M4: Man 1E **7** (4D **53**)
OL6: A Lyme 2B **116** (4D **59**)
SK5: Stoc 1B **96**
Williamson's Yd. OL1: O'ham 2D **31**
Williams Rd. M18: Man 5E **69**
M40: Man 5D **41**
Williams St. M18: Man 5E **69**
William St. M3: Sal 4E **5** (5A **52**)
(not continuous)
M12: Man 2F **67**
M20: Man 5D **93**
M24: Mid 1D **27**
M35: Fail 3C **42**
OL7: A Lyme 5A **116** (5B **58**)
SK14: Hyde 3F **87**
Willingdon Dr. M25: Pres 4D **23**
Willis Rd. SK3: Stoc 5A **106**
Williton Wlk. M22: Wyth 3B **110**
Willock St. M7: Sal 1B **52**
Willoughby Av. M20: Man 4E **93**
Willoughby Cl. M33: Sale 3C **88**
Willow Av. M24: Mid 2E **27**
M41: Urm 3A **76**
SK5: Stoc 4B **96**
Willow Bank M9: Man 5A **40**
(off Church La.)
M14: Man 5E **81**
WA15: Tim 5C **98**
Willowbank M26: Rad 1B **20**
M27: Clif 2C **34**
Willow Bank Cl. SK2: Stoc 4F **107**
Willow Bank Ct. M20: Man 3D **103**
Willowbrook Av. M40: Man 5C **40**
Willowbrook Gdns.
M22: Wyth 2E **109**
Willow Cl. BL9: Bury 4D **13**

Willow Ct. M14: Man 5E **81**
M33: Sale 3A **90**
SK8: Gat 5C **102**
Willowdale Av. SK8: H Grn 4D **111**
Willowdene Cl. M40: Man 2E **53**
(off Dalbury Dr.)
Willow Dr. BL9: Bury 4D **13**
M33: Sale 1A **98**
SK9: Hand 5F **115**
Willow Fold M43: Droy 2D **71**
Willow Gro. M18: Man 1A **84**
M34: Dent 2A **86**
OL9: Chad 1D **29**
Willow Hill Rd. M8: Man 3C **38**
Willowmoss Cl. M28: Walk 3A **32**
Willow Pk. M14: Man 5E **81**
SK2: Stoc 4E **107**
(off Wicken St.)
Willow Rd. M25: Pres 3C **22**
M30: Ecc 3C **46**
Willows, The M21: Chor 1C **90**
SK4: Stoc 5C **94**
Willows Dr. M35: Fail 3B **56**
Willows Rd. M5: Sal 5F **49**
Willow St. M8: Man 3A **52**
M11: Man 1C **68**
M27: Swin 2F **47**
M28: Wors 5E **33**
OL1: O'ham 2C **30**
Willow Tree Ct. M30: Ecc 1E **61**
(off Aldred St.)
M33: Sale 5D **89**
Willow Tree M. SK8: H Grn 1D **115**
Willow Wlk. M43: Droy 5E **57**
Willow Way M20: Man 5E **93**
Willow Wood Cl. OL6: A Lyme 4F **59**
Wilma Av. M9: Man 5E **25**
Wilmcote Rd. M40: Man 3F **53**
Wilmington Rd. M32: Stre 3D **77**
Wilmott St. M15: Man 5B **10** (3B **66**)
(Hulme St.)
M15: Man 5C **10** (4C **66**)
(Knowles Pl.)
Wilmslow Ct. SK9: Hand 5F **115**
Wilmslow Old Rd. WA15: Ring 3B **112**
Wilmslow Rd. M14: Man 1E **81**
M20: Man 4D **93**
SK8: Chea 1F **111**
(not continuous)
SK8: Chea, H Grn 4F **111**
(not continuous)
SK9: Hand 4F **115**
(not continuous)
WA15: Ring 3B **112**
Wilmur Av. M7: Sal 1A **52**
M45: White 2C **22**
Wilpshire Av. M12: Man 2D **83**
Wilshaw Gro. OL7: A Lyme 1C **58**
Wilshaw La. OL7: A Lyme 2C **58**
Wilshaw Pl. OL7: A Lyme 2C **58**
Wilson Av. M27: Clif 2D **35**
Wilson Cres. OL6: A Lyme 3F **59**
Wilson Rd. M9: Man 3F **39**
SK4: Stoc 4D **95**
Wilsons Brow BL4: Kea 1B **18**
Wilsons Pk. M40: Man 2A **54**
Wilson St. BL4: Farn 1A **18**
M11: Man 2C **68**
M13: Man 4E **67**

Wilson St. M32: Stre 1A **78**
   M33: Sale 3D **89**
   OL8: O'ham 5A **30**
Wilson Way
   OL1: O'ham 1E **117** (1B **30**)
Wilsthorpe Cl. M19: Man 2E **95**
Wilton Av. M16: Old T 2C **78**
   M25: Pres 2F **37**
   M27: Pen 5E **35**
   SK8: H Grn 2E **115**
Wilton Ct. M25: Pres 1A **24**
   M34: Dent 1C **84**
Wilton Dr. BL9: Bury 1C **12**
Wilton Gro. M34: Dent 1C **84**
Wilton Paddock M34: Dent 1C **84**
Wilton Pl. M3: Sal 4C **4** (5F **5**)
Wilton Polygon M8: Man 3B **38**
Wilton Rd. M6: Sal 3D **49**
   M8: Man 2B **38**
   M21: Chor 5D **79**
Wilton St. M13: Man 4D **67**
   M24: Mid 2D **25**
   M25: Pres 5E **23**
   M34: Dent 1A **86**
   M45: White 2B **22**
Wilton St. OL9: Chad 1D **43**
   SK5: Stoc 3B **84**
Wiltshire Av. SK5: Stoc 4E **97**
Wiltshire Rd. M35: Fail 1C **56**
   OL9: Chad 4D **29**
Wiltshire St. M7: Sal 5A **38**
Wimbledon Dr. SK3: Stoc 4E **105**
Wimbledon Rd. M35: Fail 4D **43**
Wimbledon Ter. M40: Man 3D **55**
Wimborne Av. M41: Urm 1F **75**
   OL9: Chad 1C **28**
Wimpenny Ho.
   OL8: O'ham 5D **117**
Wimpole St. OL1: O'ham 1F **117** (1C **30**)
   OL6: A Lyme 4E **59**
                (not continuous)
Wimpory St. M11: Man 3F **69**
Wincanton Av. M23: Wyth 3F **99**
Wincanton Pk. OL4: O'ham 3F **31**
Wince Brook M24: Mid 1C **26**
Wince Brook Ct. M24: Mid 1D **27**
Wince Cl. M24: Mid 3E **27**
Wincham Cl. M15: Man 4F **65**
           (off Shawgreen Cl.)
Wincham Rd. M33: Sale 1A **98**
Winchester Av. M25: Pres 2E **37**
   M34: Dent 4B **86**
   OL6: A Lyme 4F **45**
   OL9: Chad 1B **28**
Winchester Dr. M33: Sale 4A **88**
   SK4: Stoc 1D **105**
Winchester Pk. M20: Man 5B **92**
Winchester Rd. M6: Sal 3E **49**
   M30: Ecc 3C **48**
   M32: Stre 2B **76**
   M41: Urm 2F **75**
Wincombe St. M14: Man 3D **81**
Windcroft Cl. M11: Man 2B **68**
Windermere Av. M27: Swin 5C **34**
   M33: Sale 1F **99**
   M34: Dent 3C **84**
Windermere Cl. M11: Man 2C **68**
   M25: Pres 4B **22**
   M32: Stre 2E **77**
Windermere Cres. OL7: A Lyme 3B **58**

Windermere Ho. M28: Walk 2A **32**
           (off Sandwich St.)
Windermere M. M24: Mid 3A **16**
Windermere Rd. M24: Mid 4E **15**
   M41: Urm 4E **75**
   SK1: Stoc 5D **107**
   SK9: Hand 5E **115**
   SK14: Hyde 5E **73**
   SK16: Duk 2E **73**
Windermere Wlk. OL4: O'ham 1F **31**
             (not continuous)
Winders Way M6: Sal 3D **51**
Windle Av. M8: Man 1B **38**
Windmill Av. M5: Sal 4A **8** (3D **65**)
Windmill Cl. M34: Dent 3D **85**
Windmill La. M34: Dent 3C **84**
   SK5: Stoc 4B **84**
Windmill La. Ind. Est.
   M34: Dent 2E **85**
Windmill Rd. M33: Sale 5B **90**
Windmill Trad. M34: Dent 2F **85**
Windrush Dr. M9: Man 5F **39**
Windsor Av. M27: Clif 2C **34**
   M33: Sale 2D **89**
   M35: Fail 4D **43**
   M41: Urm 3B **74**
   M45: White 2C **22**
   OL9: Chad 5C **28**
   SK4: Stoc 5C **94**
   SK8: Gat 1B **110**
Windsor Bri. M5: Sal 5D **51**
Windsor Ct. M9: Man 4C **24**
   M33: Sale *3B* **88**
           (off Wentworth Dr.)
   M34: Dent *5C* **86**
           (off Wordsworth Rd.)
Windsor Cres. M25: Pres 1A **38**
Windsor Dr. M34: Aud 1F **71**
   OL7: A Lyme 3B **58**
   SK6: Bred 5E **97**
   WA14: Tim 3B **98**
Windsor Gro. M26: Rad 2D **19**
   OL6: A Lyme 5E **45**
Windsor Ho. *M21: Chor* *5B* **80**
           (off Mauldeth Rd.)
   M34: Dent 2C **84**
Windsor Rd. M9: Man 5A **40**
   M19: Man 4C **82**
   M25: Pres 2A **38**
   M34: Dent 2C **84**
   M40: Man 3A **56**
   M43: Droy 5F **55**
   OL8: O'ham 4F **29**
             (not continuous)
   SK14: Hyde 5F **87**
Windsor St. M5: Sal 1D **65**
   M18: Man 1E **83**
   M35: Fail 4C **42**
   M40: Man 3A **56**
   SK2: Stoc 5C **106**
Windsor Ter. *SK2: Stoc* *5C* **106**
           (off Russell St.)
Windsor Wlk. SK2: Stoc 5B **106**
Windybank M9: Man 4E **25**
Winfell Dr. M40: Man 4F **53**
Winfield Av. M20: Man 2F **93**
Winfield Dr. M18: Man 4F **69**
Winford Rd. M24: Mid 3E **27**
Winford St. M9: Man 4A **40**

Wingate Dr. M20: Man 1E **103**
   M45: White 5A **12**
Wingate Rd. SK4: Stoc 4E **95**
Wingfield Dr. M27: Swin 1C **48**
Wingfield St. M32: Stre 1F **77**
Wingrave Ho. M5: Sal 5C **50**
Winifred Rd. M20: Man 5D **93**
   M40: Man 5D **41**
   M41: Urm 3E **75**
   SK2: Stoc 5C **106**
Winifred St. M30: Ecc 1D **61**
   SK14: Hyde 5F **87**
Winmarith Dr. WA15: Haleb 2A **112**
Winnall Wlk. M40: Man 1E **55**
   (off Rothman Cl.)
Winnie St. M40: Man 4C **40**
Winning Hill Cl. M18: Man 1F **83**
Winnington Grn. SK2: Stoc 5F **107**
Winnipeg Quay M50: Sal 3B **64**
Winnows, The M34: Dent 2F **85**
Winscombe Dr. M40: Man 3E **53**
Winser St. M1: Man 3C **10** (2C **66**)
Winsford Rd. M14: Man 4C **80**
Winsford Wlk. M33: Sale 5A **90**
   (off Mottram Rd.)
Winslade Cl. OL4: O'ham 1F **31**
Winsley Rd. M23: Wyth 1B **100**
Winslow Pl. M19: Man 2B **94**
Winslow St. M11: Man 2C **68**
Winstanley Cl. M6: Sal 2F **49**
Winstanley Rd. M33: Sale 3E **89**
   M40: Man 4F **53**
Winster Av. M7: Sal 1D **51**
   M20: Man 4A **92**
   M32: Stre 2C **76**
Winster Cl. M45: White 1D **23**
Winster Dr. M24: Mid 4A **16**
Winster Grn. M30: Ecc 2D **61**
Winster Gro. SK2: Stoc 5C **106**
Winster Ho. M41: Urm 2B **74**
Winster Rd. M30: Ecc 2D **61**
Winston Cl. M33: Sale 3B **88**
Winston Rd. M9: Man 4B **40**
   (not continuous)
Winswell Cl. M11: Man 5D **55**
Winterbottom St. OL9: O'ham 3F **29**
Winterburn Av. M21: Chor 4E **91**
Winterburn Grn. SK2: Stoc 5F **107**
Winterdyne St. M9: Man 5A **40**
Winterford Av. M13: Man 5F **67**
Winterford Rd. M7: Sal 5B **38**
   M8: Man 5B **38**
Winter Gdn. M4: Man 4C **6**
Wintermans Rd. M21: Chor 1A **92**
Winterslow Av. M23: Wyth 2F **99**
Winterton Rd. SK5: Stoc 4C **84**
Winthrop Av. M40: Man 2F **53**
WINTON 5D **47**
Winton Av. M34: Aud 3F **71**
   M40: Man 3F **41**
Winton Rd. M6: Sal 1F **49**
Winton St. OL6: A Lyme 1B **116** (4D **59**)
Winwood Dr. M24: Mid 4D **17**
Winwood Fold M24: Mid 2B **16**
Winwood Rd. M20: Man 3E **103**
Wirral Cl. M27: Clif 2C **34**
Wirral Cres. SK3: Stoc 3C **104**
Wisbech Dr. M23: Wyth 2B **100**
Wiseman Ter. M25: Pres 5E **23**
Wishaw Sq. M21: Chor 1A **92**

Wisley Cl. SK5: Stoc 5C **84**
Wistaria Rd. M18: Man 5F **69**
Witham Av. M22: Shar 1A **110**
Witham St. OL6: A Lyme 3F **59**
Withenfield Rd. M23: Wyth 3B **100**
Withens Grn. SK2: Stoc 5F **107**
Withies, The M30: Ecc 5D **47**
   (off Worsley Rd.)
WITHINGTON 2C **92**
Withington Grn. M24: Mid 2C **16**
Withington Leisure Cen. 2D **93**
Withington Rd. M16: W Ran 1F **79**
   M21: Chor 5F **79**
Withins Hall Rd. M35: Fail 1D **57**
Withins Rd. OL8: O'ham 2D **43**
Withnell Rd. M19: Man 5F **93**
Withycombe Pl. M6: Sal 2C **50**
Withy Gro. M4: Man 4C **6** (5C **52**)
Withypool Dr. SK2: Stoc 5D **107**
Withy Tree Gro. M34: Dent 3C **86**
Witley Dr. M33: Sale 2A **88**
Wittenbury Rd. SK4: Stoc 1D **105**
Witterage Cl. M12: Man 4B **68**
Witton Wlk. M8: Man 1B **52**
   (off Cranlington Dr.)
Woburn Dr. BL9: Bury 1B **12**
Woburn Grn. M24: Mid 4C **16**
Woburn Rd. M16: Old T 3C **78**
Woburn St. M16: W Ran 2B **80**
Woden's Av. M5: Sal 4A **8** (3E **65**)
Woden St. M5: Sal 4B **8** (3E **65**)
Wolfreton Cres. M27: Clif 1C **34**
Wollaton Wlk. M34: Dent 4A **86**
Wolseley Ho. M33: Sale 2E **89**
   (off Dargle Rd.)
Wolseley Pl. M20: Man 3D **93**
Wolseley Rd. M33: Sale 3D **89**
Wolstencvale Cl. M24: Mid 5D **17**
Wolverton Av. OL8: O'ham 1F **43**
Wolverton St. M11: Man 3B **68**
Woodacre M16: W Ran 4A **80**
Woodacre Cl. M33: Sale 1C **98**
Woodall Cl. M33: Sale 4F **89**
Woodbank Av. SK1: Stoc 3E **107**
Woodbank Cl. M41: Urm 2D **75**
Woodbank Pk. SK1: Stoc 2D **107**
Woodbank Pk. Athletic Track 2E **107**
Woodbank Works Ind. Est.
   SK1: Stoc 1D **107**
Woodbine Cres. SK2: Stoc 4B **106**
Woodbine St. M14: Man 1C **80**
Woodbourne Ct. M33: Sale 1D **99**
Woodbourne Rd. M33: Sale 1C **98**
   SK4: Stoc 2E **95**
Woodbray Av. M19: Man 3A **94**
Woodbridge Av. M34: Aud 3F **71**
Woodbridge Gro. M23: Wyth 2C **100**
Woodbridge Rd. M41: Urm 2A **74**
Woodburn Rd. M22: Nor 3F **101**
Woodbury Cres. SK16: Duk 3D **73**
Woodbury Rd. SK3: Stoc 4D **105**
Woodchurch Wlk. M33: Sale 5B **90**
   (off Mottram Rd.)
   OL9: Chad 3D **29**
Woodcliffe Lodge M25: Pres 2D **37**
Woodcock Cl. M43: Droy 4E **57**
Woodcote Rd. WA14: W Tim 2A **98**
Woodcote Wlk. M8: Man 4E **39**
   (off Nunthorpe Dr.)
Wood Cres. OL4: O'ham 1F **45**

Woodcroft SK2: Stoc 5F **107**
Woodcroft Av. M19: Man 4A **94**
WOODEND 5D **115**
Woodend Ct. SK14: Hyde 4F **87**
Woodend La. SK14: Hyde 4E **87**
Woodend Rd. M22: Wyth 2F **109**
Woodend St. OL1: O'ham 1A **30**
Woodfield M22: Wyth 3F **109**
Woodfield Av. SK14: Hyde 5F **87**
Woodfield Cl. OL8: O'ham 5E **29**
Woodfield Gro. M30: Ecc 1E **61**
  M33: Sale .2C **88**
Woodfield M. SK14: Hyde 5F **87**
Woodfield Rd. M6: Sal 3F **49**
  M8: Man 3C **38**
  M24: Mid 3A **26**
Woodfold Av. M19: Man 3C **82**
Woodford Av. M30: Ecc 5D **47**
  M34: Dent .1C **86**
Woodford Ct. M43: Droy 2D **71**
Woodford Dr. M27: Swin 2A **34**
Woodford Gdns. M20: Man 1C **102**
Woodford Rd. M35: Fail 4C **42**
Woodgarth Av. M40: Man 2F **55**
Woodgarth Dr. M27: Swin 1A **48**
Woodgarth La. M28: Wors 2B **46**
Woodgate Dr. M25: Pres 3E **23**
Woodgate Rd. M16: W Ran 4A **80**
Woodgrange Cl. M6: Sal 5A **50**
Woodgreen Dr. M26: Rad 1C **20**
Wood Gro. M34: Dent 1B **86**
  M45: White 3A **12**
Woodhall Av. M20: Man 1C **92**
  M45: White 3F **21**
Woodhall Cres. SK5: Stoc 4C **96**
Woodhall Rd. SK5: Stoc 4B **96**
Woodhall St. M35: Fail 4B **42**
Woodhalt Rd. M8: Man 4C **38**
Woodham Rd. M23: Wyth 2B **100**
Woodhead St. M16: W Ran 1A **80**
Woodhey Ct. M33: Sale 2A **98**
Wood Hey Gro. M34: Dent 3C **86**
Woodheys SK4: Stoc 5B **94**
Woodheys St. M6: Sal 5B **50**
                              (off Derg St.)
Woodhill M24: Mid 4B **16**
Wood Hill Cl. M12: Man 1D **83**
Woodhill Cl. M24: Mid 4B **16**
Woodhill Dr. M25: Pres 2D **37**
Woodhill Gro. M25: Pres 1D **37**
Woodhouse Ct. M41: Urm 1C **74**
                       (off Davyhulme Rd.)
WOODHOUSE GREEN 5E **43**
Woodhouse La. M22: Wyth 2F **109**
  M33: Sale .1A **98**
                         (not continuous)
  M90: Man A 2F **113**
Woodhouse La. E. WA15: Tim 2C **98**
Woodhouse La. Nth.
  M22: Wyth 1F **113**
WOODHOUSE PARK 5D **109**
Woodhouse Pk. Lifestyle Cen. 5D **109**
Woodhouse Rd. M22: Wyth 1F **113**
  M41: Urm .1B **74**
WOODHOUSES 1E **57**
Woodhouse St. M18: Man 5A **70**
  M40: Man .2B **54**
Woodlake Av. M21: Chor 4E **91**
Woodland Av. M18: Man 1A **84**

Woodland Cres. M25: Pres 2D **37**
Woodland Rd. M18: Man 1A **84**
  M19: Man .5C **82**
Woodlands M35: Fail 3A **56**
  M41: Urm .2E **75**
Woodlands, The M25: Pres 3B **36**
  M27: Swin .5D **35**
  M43: Droy .4A **56**
Woodlands Av. M27: Swin 1E **47**
  M30: Ecc 2C **60**
  M32: Stre .3F **77**
  M45: White 5A **12**
Woodlands Cl. M28: Wors 5A **32**
Woodlands Ct. SK2: Stoc 3F **107**
  WA15: Tim .5A **98**
                     (off Woodlands Parkway)
Woodlands Dr. M33: Sale 2E **99**
  SK2: Stoc .3E **107**
Woodlands La. WA15: Tim 5A **98**
Woodlands on Stamford, The
  OL6: A Lyme 5F **59**
                       (off Stamford St. E.)
Woodlands Pk. Rd. SK2: Stoc 3F **107**
Woodlands Parkway
  WA15: Tim .5A **98**
Woodlands Rd. M8: Man 4C **38**
  M16: W Ran 4A **80**
  M28: Wors .5A **32**
  M33: Sale .3E **89**
  OL6: A Lyme 1F **59**
  SK4: Stoc .1F **103**
  WA14: Alt .5A **98**
  WA15: Alt .5A **98**
Woodlands Road Stop (Metro) 5D **39**
Woodlands St. M8: Man 4C **38**
Woodland St. M12: Man 5D **69**
Woodlands Way M24: Mid 3B **26**
Woodland Ter. M7: Sal 2F **51**
Wood La. M24: Mid 2D **27**
  OL6: A Lyme 2D **59**
  WA15: Tim .5C **98**
Woodlark Cl. M3: Sal 5D **5**
Woodlawn Ct. M16: W Ran 2E **79**
Woodlea M28: Wors 4A **32**
  M30: Ecc 3E **47**
  OL9: Chad .2F **27**
Woodlea Av. M19: Man 2A **94**
Woodlea Chase M27: Clif 4F **19**
Woodleigh Dr. M43: Droy 3E **57**
Woodleigh St. M9: Man 3B **40**
Woodley Av. M26: Rad 1D **21**
Woodley Cl. SK2: Stoc 4F **107**
Woodliffe St. M16: Old T 5E **65**
Woodlinn Wlk. M9: Man 5F **39**
                      (off Ravelston Dr.)
Woodman St. SK1: Stoc 1A **118** (1A **106**)
Woodmere Dr. M9: Man 1A **40**
Woodnewton Cl. M18: Man 1E **83**
WOOD PARK .4F **43**
Woodpark Cl. OL8: O'ham 1C **44**
Wood Rd. M16: W Ran 2E **79**
  M33: Sale .2D **99**
  WA15: Tim .2D **99**
                         (not continuous)
Wood Rd. Nth. M16: Old T 2E **79**
Woodrow Wlk. M12: Man 4B **68**
                      (off Clowes St.)
Woods, The WA14: Alt 5A **98**
Woods Ct. M24: Mid 1E **25**
WOODS END .2A **74**

Woodsend Circ. M41: Urm 2A **74**
   (not continuous)
Woodsend Cres. Rd. M41: Urm 3A **74**
Woodsend Grn. M41: Urm 2A **74**
Woodsend Rd. M41: Urm 1A **74**
Woodsend Rd. Sth. M41: Urm 3A **74**
   (not continuous)
Woodside SK4: Stoc 2B **104**
Woodside Av. M19: Man 3B **94**
   M28: Wal .2B **32**
Woodside Cl. OL4: Lees 3F **31**
Woodside Dr. M6: Sal 4E **49**
Woodside Rd. M16: W Ran 3D **79**
Woodsmoor Rd. M27: Swin 5F **33**
Wood Sq. M43: Droy 2C **70**
Woodstock Av. SK5: Stoc 3B **96**
Woodstock Ct. SK9: Hand 4F **115**
Woodstock Dr. M27: Swin 1C **48**
   M28: Wors 2C **46**
Woodstock Grn. OL8: O'ham 1C **44**
   SK5: Stoc 2C **96**
Woodstock Rd. M16: Old T 2D **79**
   M40: Man 3E **41**
Woodstock St.
   OL4: O'ham 5F **117** (4B **30**)
Wood St. M3: Man 1F **9** (1A **66**)
   M11: Man 2D **69**
   M24: Mid 4F **15**
   M26: Rad 1A **20**
   M30: Ecc 1B **62**
   M34: Dent 1B **86**
   OL1: O'ham 1D **31**
   OL6: A Lyme 3B **116** (5D **59**)
   SK3: Stoc 3F **105**
   SK8: Chea 5F **103**
   SK16: Duk 4E **73**
Woodthorpe Ct. M25: Pres 2F **37**
Woodthorpe Grange M25: Pres 2F **37**
Woodvale M24: Mid 2C **16**
Woodvale Wlk. *M11: Man* *1B **68***
   (off Redfield Cl.)
Wood Vw. M22: Nor 2F **101**
Woodview Av. M19: Man 3B **94**
Woodville Dr. M33: Sale 3C **88**
Woodville Gro. SK5: Stoc 2B **96**
Woodville Rd. M33: Sale 3C **88**
Woodville Ter. M40: Man 3B **40**
Woodward Cl. M4: Man 5F **53**
Woodward Pl. M4: Man 5E **53**
Woodward Rd. M25: Pres 2B **36**
Woodward St. M4: Man 5E **53**
Woodwise La. M23: Wyth 2A **100**
Woolden St. M30: Ecc 4D **47**
Woolfall Cl. M12: Man 4C **68**
Woollacot St.
   OL1: O'ham 3F **117** (2B **30**)
Woollam Pl. M3: Man 2D **9** (2F **65**)
Woolley St. M8: Man 3B **52**
   OL6: A Lyme 1F **59**
Woolley Ter. *SK16: Duk* *5C **116***
   (off Queen St.)
Woolmore Av. OL1: O'ham 1A **30**
Woolpack Grn. *M6: Sal* *4B **50***
   (off Arbour Cl.)
Woolston Ho. *M6: Sal* *3E **49***
   (off Moss Mdw. Rd.)
Woolton Cl. *M40: Man* *2E **41***
   (off Pleasington Dr.)
Woolton Hall M14: Man 4F **81**
Wootton St. SK14: Hyde 1F **87**

Worcester Av. M23: Wyth 3B **100**
   M34: Dent 4C **86**
   SK5: Stoc 3E **97**
Worcester Cl. M6: Sal 3E **49**
   OL6: A Lyme 4F **45**
Worcester Rd. M6: Sal 3E **49**
   M24: Mid 4B **26**
   M27: Ward 7B **34**
   M33: Sale 5A **88**
Worcester St. OL9: O'ham 4D **29**
Wordsworth Av. BL9: Bury 1B **12**
   M8: Man 1C **52**
   M43: Droy 5C **56**
Wordsworth Cres. OL7: A Lyme 2A **58**
Wordsworth Gdns. M25: Pres 1B **36**
Wordsworth Rd. M16: Old T 2D **79**
   M24: Mid 4D **17**
   M27: Swin 3F **33**
   M34: Dent 5C **86**
   SK5: Stoc 4F **83**
Workesleigh St. M40: Man 2E **55**
World Trade Cen. M5: Sal 4C **64**
World Way M90: Man A 1D **113**
Worrall St. M5: Sal 4A **8** (3E **65**)
   M40: Man 1C **54**
   SK3: Stoc 4A **106**
   (not continuous)
Worsefold St. M40: Man 4C **40**
WORSLEY 5A **32**
Worsley Av. M40: Man 3B **40**
Worsley Brow M28: Wors 1B **46**
Worsley Ct. M14: Man 3E **81**
Worsley Cres. SK2: Stoc 4E **107**
Worsley Gro. M19: Man 4C **82**
Worsley Mill M3: Man 4D **9** (2F **65**)
Worsley Point M27: Swin 1A **48**
Worsley Rd. M27: Swin 1E **47**
   M28: Wors 2B **46**
   M30: Ecc 3C **46**
Worsley Rd. Ind. Est.
   BL4: Farn 3A **18**
Worsley St. M3: Sal 4F **5** (5A **52**)
   M15: Man 4C **8** (3F **65**)
   M27: Pen 2B **34**
   M27: Swin 5C **34**
   OL8: O'ham 4D **31**
Worthenbury Wlk. M13: Man 2A **82**
Worthing Cl. SK2: Stoc 5F **107**
Worthing St. M14: Man 3D **81**
Worthington Cl. OL7: A Lyme 2C **58**
Worthington Ct. M33: Sale 4A **90**
Worthington Dr. M7: Sal 3F **37**
Worthington Rd. M33: Sale 4A **90**
   M34: Dent 4D **87**
Worthington St. M16: Old T 1E **79**
   M40: Man 4E **41**
   OL7: A Lyme 2C **58**
Worthington Way M34: Dent 1A **86**
Worth's La. M34: Dent 5C **86**
Wortley Av. M6: Sal 4E **49**
Wortley Gro. M40: Man 2D **41**
Wray Cl. M22: Wyth 2F **109**
Wray Gdns. M19: Man 5E **83**
Wraysbury Wlk. *M40: Man* *5C **40***
   (off Hugo St.)
Wrayton Lodge M33: Sale 5D **89**
Wrekin Av. M23: Wyth 3C **108**
Wren Av. M27: Clif 1D **35**
Wrenbury Av. M20: Man 1B **92**
Wrenbury Cres. SK3: Stoc 5E **105**

Wrenbury Dr. SK8: Chea 5A **104**
Wrenbury Wlk. M33: Sale 5A **90**
(off Mottram Rd.)
Wren Cl. M34: Aud 1E **71**
Wren Gdns. M24: Mid 5B **16**
Wrengate Ho. M20: Man 5B **92**
Wren St. OL4: O'ham 3E **31**
Wren Way M11: Man 2A **68**
Wrexham Cl. OL8: O'ham 2D **43**
Wright Robinson Cl. M11: Man 2A **68**
Wright Robinson Hall
M1: Man .3E **11**
Wrights Bank Nth. SK2: Stoc 5F **107**
Wright St. M16: Old T 4E **65**
M34: Aud .2A **72**
M35: Fail .4B **42**
OL1: O'ham 3F **117** (2C **30**)
OL6: A Lyme 3F **59**
OL9: Chad 4D **29**
Wrigley Cres. M35: Fail 5B **42**
Wrigley Fold M24: Mid 3E **15**
Wrigley Head M35: Fail 4B **42**
Wrigley Head Cres.
M35: Fail .4B **42**
Wrigley's Pl. OL8: O'ham 1A **44**
Wrigley St. OL4: O'ham 2D **31**
OL6: A Lyme 3D **59**
Wroe St. M3: Sal 5C **4**
M27: Pen .1B **34**
Wroe Ter. M27: Clif 1B **34**
Wrotham Cl. M5: Sal 1C **64**
Wroxeter Wlk. M12: Man 4B **68**
(off Witterage Cl.)
Wroxham Av. M34: Dent 2C **84**
M41: Urm 2D **75**
Wroxham Rd. M9: Man 1D **39**
Wyatt Av. M5: Sal 4A **8** (3D **65**)
Wyatt St. SK4: Stoc 1A **106**
SK16: Duk 2E **73**
Wychbury St. M6: Sal 5A **50**
Wych St. OL6: A Lyme 3B **116** (5D **59**)
Wychwood Ct. M24: Mid 2D **27**
Wycliffe Ct. M41: Urm 3E **75**
(off Flixton Rd.)
Wycliffe Rd. M41: Urm 3E **75**
Wycliffe St. M30: Ecc 5E **47**
(off Watson St.)
SK4: Stoc 1F **105**
Wycombe Av. M18: Man 4A **70**
Wycombe Cl. M41: Urm 5E **61**
Wye Av. M35: Fail 5B **42**
Wye St. OL8: O'ham 4F **29**
Wykeham St. M14: Man 2C **80**
Wyke Pk. OL4: O'ham 3F **31**
Wylam Wlk. M12: Man 2D **83**
Wyndale Dr. M35: Fail 2B **56**
Wyndale Rd. OL8: O'ham 1B **44**
Wyndcliffe Dr. M41: Urm 3E **75**
(not continuous)
Wyndham Av. M27: Clif 2B **34**
Wynfield Av. M22: Wyth 2B **114**
Wynford Sq. M50: Sal 1B **64**
Wynne Av. M27: Clif 1B **34**
Wynne Cl. M11: Man 2B **68**
M34: Dent 4B **86**
Wynne Gro. M34: Dent 4B **86**
Wynne St. M6: Sal 1A **4** (4D **51**)
Wynnstay Gro. M14: Man 5E **81**
Wynnstay Rd. M33: Sale 3D **89**
Wynn St. M40: Man 3A **42**

Wynyard Cl. M33: Sale 1F **99**
Wynyard Rd. M22: Wyth 3E **109**
Wyre Cl. M45: White 5D **13**
Wyre St. M1: Man 3F **11** (2D **67**)
Wythburn Av. M8: Man 1E **53**
M41: Urm 2D **75**
Wythburn Rd. M24: Mid 3A **16**
SK1: Stoc 4D **107**
Wythburn St. M6: Sal 5A **50**
WYTHENSHAWE 3E **109**
Wythenshawe Community Farm 3C **100**
Wythenshawe Hall 3D **101**
Wythenshawe Pk. 3C **100**
Wythenshawe Rd. M23: Wyth 3A **100**
M33: Sale 4A **90**
Wythens Rd. SK8: H Grn 1D **115**
Wythop Gdns. M5: Sal 1C **64**
Wyvern Av. SK5: Stoc 3A **96**
Wyverne Rd. M21: Chor 4F **79**
Wyville Dr. M6: Sal 4B **50**
M9: Man .3D **25**
M27: Swin 1A **48**
Wyvis Cl. OL9: Chad 1C **28**

X

XQ7 Building M5: Sal 4C **64**
XS Superbowl 4E **33**

Y

Yale Rd. M18: Man 5D **69**
Yarburgh St. M16: W Ran 2A **80**
Yardley Av. M32: Stre 3C **76**
Yardley Cl. M32: Stre 3C **76**
Yarmouth Dr. M23: Wyth 2D **101**
Yarrow Wlk. M45: White 5E **13**
Yarwood Av. M23: Wyth 4B **100**
Yasmin Gdns. OL1: O'ham 1F **29**
Yates St. M24: Mid 2E **25**
OL1: O'ham 1C **30**
SK1: Stoc 5D **97**
Yattendon Av. M23: Wyth 3F **99**
Y Club, The 2E **9** (2A **66**)
Yeadon Rd. M18: Man 2F **83**
Yealand Av. SK4: Stoc 5F **95**
Yeomanry Ct. M16: W Ran 2F **79**
Yeomans Wlk. M11: Man 1B **68**
Yeovil St. M16: W Ran 2B **80**
Yewbarrow Rd.
OL1: O'ham 1F **117** (1C **30**)
Yew Cres. OL4: O'ham 1F **31**
Yewdale M27: Clif 2D **35**
Yewdale Dr. M24: Mid 5A **16**
M35: Fail .4E **43**
Yewdale Rd. SK1: Stoc 5D **107**
Yewlands Av. M9: Man 4F **25**
Yew St. M7: Sal 1E **51**
M15: Man 5A **66**
M34: Aud .5B **72**
SK4: Stoc 3D **105**
Yew Tree Av. M14: Man 3C **80**
M19: Man .4C **82**
M22: Nor .2F **101**
Yew Tree Cl. OL7: A Lyme 1C **58**
Yew Tree Cres. M14: Man 4D **81**
Yew Tree Dr. M22: Nor 2F **101**
M25: Pres 5D **23**

Yew Tree Dr. M33: Sale 4A **90**
  M41: Urm 1B **74**
  OL9: Chad 2F **27**
  SK6: Bred 5F **97**
Yew Tree Gro. SK8: H Grn 3C **110**
Yew Tree La. M23: Wyth 1D **101**
  (not continuous)
  SK16: Duk 3F **73**
Yew Tree Rd. M14: Man 2D **81**
  M20: Man 4D **81**
  M34: Dent 4A **86**
York Arc. *M1: Man* *1D **11***
  (off Parker St.)
York Av. M16: W Ran 3E **79**
  M25: Pres 2F **37**
  M27: Swin 2F **33**
  M33: Sale 3D **89**
  M41: Urm 2A **76**
  OL8: O'ham 5F **29**
York Cl. M34: Dent 1B **86**
  SK8: Chea 5C **104**
Yorkdale OL4: O'ham 2F **31**
York Dr. M90: Man A 2B **112**
York Ho. M33: Sale 3D **89**
York Pl. OL6: A Lyme 5C **58**
York Rd. M21: Chor 5D **79**
  M33: Sale 3C **88**
  M34: Dent 1A **86**
  M43: Droy 4B **56**
  OL9: Chad 1B **28**
  SK4: Stoc 3D **95**
  SK14: Hyde 5F **87**
York Rd. E. M24: Mid 4E **27**
York Rd. W. M24: Mid 4E **27**
Yorkshire St. M3: Sal 4F **5** (5A **52**)
  OL1: O'ham 3E **117** (2B **30**)

Yorkshire St. OL6: A Lyme 1B **116** (3D **59**)
  (not continuous)
York St. BL4: Farn 1A **18**
  M1: Man 3C **10** (2C **66**)
  M2: Man 5C **6** (1C **66**)
  M9: Man 4A **40**
  (not continuous)
  M13: Man 5D **11** (3C **66**)
  M19: Man 5C **82**
  M20: Man 5D **93**
  M26: Rad 1A **12**
  M34: Aud 2A **72**
  M45: White 1B **22**
  OL9: O'ham 3A **30**
  SK3: Stoc 3A **106**
York Ter. M33: Sale 2C **88**
Young St. BL4: Farn 2A **18**
  M3: Man 1F **9** (1A **66**)
Yule St. SK3: Stoc 3F **105**

Z

Zandra Ho. *M16: W Ran* 2F **79**
  (off Dudley Rd.)
Zealand St. OL4: O'ham 1E **31**
Zeta St. M9: Man 5B **40**
Zetland Rd. M21: Chor 5D **79**
Zetland St. SK16: Duk 1E **73**
Zinc Ct. *M25: Pres* *4C **22***
  (off Longfield Cen.)
Zion Arts Cen. 4A **66**
Zion Cres. *M15: Man* 4A **66**
  (off Stretford Rd.)
Zorbit M. SK14: Hyde 1F **87**
Zyburn Ct. M6: Sal 4C **48**

HOSPITALS and HOSPICES
covered by this atlas
with their map square reference

N.B. Where Hospitals and Hospices are not named on the map,
the reference given is for the road in which they are situated.

ALEXANDRA (BMI) HOSPITAL, THE
. . . . .5F **103**
Mill Lane
CHEADLE
SK8 2PX
Tel: 0161 4283656

BEECHWOOD CANCER CARE CENTRE
. . . . .5F **105**
Chelford Grove
STOCKPORT
SK3 8LS
Tel: 0161 4760384

BOLTON, SALFORD & TRAFFORD MENTAL
HEALTH NHS TRUST (PRESTWICH SITE)
. . . . .4B **22**
Bury New Road
Prestwich
MANCHESTER
M25 3BL
Tel: 0161 773 9121

BOOTH HALL CHILDREN'S HOSPITAL
. . . . .1B **40**
Charlestown Road
MANCHESTER
M9 7AA
Tel: 0161 795 7000

CASUALTY PLUS WALK-IN CENTRE
(CHEADLE) 5F **103**
The Alexandra BMI Hospital
Mill Lane
CHEADLE
SK8 2PX
Tel: 0161 4282161

CHARLES HOUSE 3B **50**
1 Charles Street
SALFORD
M6 7DU
Tel: 0161 745 7900

CHEADLE ROYAL HOSPITAL 4E **111**
100 Wilmslow Road
CHEADLE
SK8 3DG
Tel: 0161 4289511

CHERRY TREE HOSPITAL 5E **107**
Cherry Tree Lane
STOCKPORT
SK2 7PZ
Tel: 0161 4831010

CHRISTIE HOSPITAL 2D **93**
550 Wilmslow Road
MANCHESTER
M20 4BX
Tel: 0845 226 3000

FRANCIS HOUSE CHILDREN'S HOSPICE
. . . . .1E **103**
390 Parrswood Road
MANCHESTER
M20 5NA
Tel: 0161 4344118

HOPE HOSPITAL 4D **49**
Stott Lane
SALFORD
M6 8HD
Tel: 0161 7897373

MANCHESTER LIFESTYLE BMI HOSPITAL, THE
. . . . .1F **81**
108-112 Daisy Bank Road
MANCHESTER
M14 5QH
Tel: 0161 249 3000

MANCHESTER ROYAL EYE HOSPITAL . . .5D **67**
Nelson Street
MANCHESTER
M13 9WH
Tel: 0161 276 1234

MANCHESTER ROYAL INFIRMARY 5E **67**
Oxford Road
MANCHESTER
M13 9WL
Tel: 0161 276 1234

MANCHESTER SPIRE HOSPITAL 2F **79**
Russell Road, Whalley Range
MANCHESTER
M16 8AJ
Tel: 0845 6050112

MEADOWS HOSPITAL, THE 4F **107**
Owens Farm Drive
STOCKPORT
SK2 5EQ
Tel: 0161 419 6000

NEIL CLIFFE CANCER CARE CENTRE . . .2B **108**
Wythenshawe Hospital, Southmoor Road
MANCHESTER
M23 9LT
Tel: 0161 2912912

NHS WALK-IN CENTRE (BURNAGE) 2B **94**
Burnage Health Care Centre
347 Burnage Lane
MANCHESTER
M19 1EW
Tel: 0161 443 0600

NHS WALK-IN CENTRE
(CENTRAL MANCHESTER PCT) ...5E **67**
Manchester Royal Infimary
Oxford Road
MANCHESTER
M13 9WL

NHS WALK-IN CENTRE
(MANCHESTER PICCADILLY)
........................1E **11** (1D **67**)
1st Floor Gateway House
Station Approach
Piccadilly South
MANCHESTER
M1 2GH
Tel: 0161 233 2525

NHS WALK-IN CENTRE (OLDHAM) 3A **30**
Lindley House
1 John Street
OLDHAM
OL8 1DF

NHS WALK-IN CENTRE (PRESTWICH)
........................4C **22**

Fairfax Road
Prestwich
MANCHESTER
M25 1BT

NHS WALK-IN CENTRE (WITHINGTON)
........................3B **92**

Withington Community Hospital
Nell Lane
MANCHESTER
M20 2LR
Tel: 0161 217 3015

NHS WALK-IN CENTRE
(WYTHENSHAWE FORUM) 4E **109**
Health Care Centre
Forum Square
Civic Centre
Simonsway
Wythenshawe
MANCHESTER
M22 5RX
Tel: 0161 490 8082

NORTH MANCHESTER GENERAL HOSPITAL
........................3D **39**
Delaunays Road
MANCHESTER
M8 5RB
Tel: 0161 795 4567

OAKLANDS HOSPITAL 4D **49**
19 Lancaster Road
SALFORD
M6 8AQ
Tel: 0161 7877700

ROYAL MANCHESTER CHILDREN'S HOSPITAL
........................5E **35**
Hospital Road
Pendlebury
Swinton
MANCHESTER
M27 4HA
Tel: 0161 7944696

ROYAL OLDHAM HOSPITAL, THE 1F **29**
Rochdale Road
OLDHAM
OL1 2JH
Tel: 0161 624 0420

ST ANN'S HOSPICE 4E **111**
St Ann's Road North
Heald Green
CHEADLE
SK8 3SZ
Tel: 0161 4378136

ST MARY'S HOSPITAL FOR
WOMEN & CHILDREN 1E **81**
Oxford Road
MANCHESTER
M13 0JH
Tel: 0161 276 1234

STRETFORD MEMORIAL HOSPITAL
........................2D **79**
226 Seymour Grove
MANCHESTER
M16 0DU
Tel: 0161 8815353

TRAFFORD GENERAL HOSPITAL 2C **74**
Moorside Road
Urmston
MANCHESTER
M41 5SL
Tel: 0161 7484022

UNIVERSITY DENTAL HOSPITAL
OF MANCHESTER 4C **66**
Higher Cambridge Street
MANCHESTER
M15 6FH
Tel: 0161 275 6666

WITHINGTON COMMUNITY HOSPITAL
........................3B **92**
Nell Lane
MANCHESTER
M20 2LR
Tel: 0161 434 5555

WYTHENSHAWE HOSPITAL 2B **108**
Southmoor Road
Wythenshawe
MANCHESTER
M23 9LT
Tel: 0161 998 7070